P9-DEN-523

Who's Who in Russia and the CIS Republics

Who's Who in Russia and the CIS Republics

VLADIMIR MOROZOV
EDITOR

A HENRY HOLT REFERENCE BOOK
Henry Holt and Company
New York

A Henry Holt Reference Book
Henry Holt and Company, Inc.
Publishers since 1866
115 West 18th Street
New York, New York 10011

Henry Holt® is a registered
trademark of Henry Holt and Company, Inc.

Published in Canada by Fitzhenry & Whiteside Ltd.,
195 Allstate Parkway, Markham, Ontario L3R 4T8.

Library of Congress Cataloging-in-Publication Data

Who's who in Russia and the CIS Republics / [compiled by] Vladimir Morozov. — 1st ed.
p. cm. — (A Henry Holt reference book)
Includes index.
1. Former Soviet republics—Biography—Dictionaries. I. Series.
CT1203.W46 1995
920.047—dc20 94-32820
CIP

ISBN 0-8050-2691-6

Henry Holt books are available for special promotions
and premiums. For details contact:
Director, Special Markets.

First Edition—1995

Designed by Paula R. Szafranski

Printed in the United States of America
All first editions are printed on acid-free paper. ∞

1 3 5 7 9 10 8 6 4 2

Contents

Introduction

Understanding the New Russia

A new state is not constituted only by its symbols—a flag, national anthem, and so on—but by its new leaders. The fate, style, and substance of a new state can be found in the people who dominate its political, economic, and spiritual life. After the fall of the Soviet Union in 1991, Russia became a new country with new leaders shaping its present and future.

Only a couple of years ago, the closest advisers of the president of Russia would have been unknown to the general public. Newspapers never published the names of any members of the Cabinet, the most influential members of parliament, leaders of the political and public organizations, or even business leaders. Now, Russia and the other republics have embraced a western-style openness that, although still evolving, reflects Russians' and westerners' desire—and right—to know who's who: the people with influence; the people molding a new country and society.

Just since December 1991, the changes in political leaders have been dizzying. During this short period of time, in some places, like Georgia, Azerbaijan, and Tadjikistan, the leaders of different parties have managed to seize power from one another several times. This process usually is followed by deep changes in government and even in some private institutions. The present situation differs greatly from the one that existed fewer than ten years ago. At that time, the country seemed to be sound asleep. It was hardly possible to foresee any changes, even the ones concerning top political leaders. Major changes were simply announced, not anticipated. In 1964, for example, the communist party leadership suddenly denied Nikita Khruschev his powers, and he promptly sank into political oblivion.

From the bureaucracies of government agencies to the management of the Bolshoi Ballet, the names rarely changed. Promotions at the highest levels rarely came about unless someone died. In other words, people had jobs for life. The expression "to serve till you die" was, in fact, not metaphorical.

Those who followed the sluggish drama of Soviet politics could see that when the average age of the elderly leaders of the country was taken into account, there existed the risk that once change started in the country, it could accelerate at avalanche speed. The consequences would be impossible to predict.

As former British prime minister Harold Wilson said, "He who rejects change is the architect of decay." The first signs appeared in the early 1980s, when a new star appeared on the Soviet political stage. His name was Mikhail Gorbachev. It was with relief that the people saw a comparatively young (he was in his early fifties), robust leader. This optimistic and articulate fellow inspired the nation that started to believe in change again. A new slogan of *uskorenie*, a promotion of social life and economy, was proclaimed: the country declared war on the old national illness—alcoholism; all the media started cautiously unveiling what had been hidden from the public; new leaders began to appear at different levels. The necessity of change became evident and urgent. Too much decay had been built by too many old architects. Mere corrections were not enough—the whole politics had to be revamped.

The old leaders of the party, however, were neither ready nor eager for new directions. The year of 1987 became transitional; it was then that Gorbachev's *perestroika*, or "reconstruction," started, propelled by the Congress of the Central Committee of the CPSU. The party, however, still held all the reins of power.

People simply didn't want the old guard with its hidden ways to choose their leaders for them any longer. For the first time in many decades, the Soviet Union had to face strikes. Miners were first to show the initiative. Their demands were not only economic, but political. In the squares of small towns, hundreds of miners held mass meetings. Those carbon-dust- and dirt-covered workers laughed and swore at the secretaries of party committees and local leaders and forced them to resign. The heads of trade unions were next to go. The miners seized local power and created new governmental institutions that worked alongside the official ones. In the majority of cases, they never demanded that the current system be dismantled. They just wanted to make it better, to renew it. But their actions turned out to be more revolutionary: the system broke.

In 1989, with several candidates for each seat, real elections for the Supreme Soviet Parliament were held for the first time. Even though the candidates were initially chosen by the governmental institutions (with some of the deputies from the prominent families of public organizations—from CPSU to the philatelist society—inheriting the seats), the people finally acquired more freedom. Now the powers of the central government to control and regulate the parliament were restricted.

The ruling party itself never held free elections for party offices. There were one hundred candidates and exactly one hundred seats. The whole country was watching the opening ceremony of the First Congress of People's Deputies. The former unanimity for every single vote would be gone forever. In order to count the votes, the government had to install special electronic devices that were never before necessary: all previous votes had been predictable.

The First Congress started the flow of "new wave" representatives. The majority of them were Ph.D.s and professors, and all were well educated, articulate, and had experience speaking to large audiences; they differed completely from their pompous and uneducated predecessors. Among them were Gabriel Popov, an economist, who was to become a mayor of Moscow and the chairman of the Russian Movement of Democratic Reforms; Kazimira Prunskene, the first prime minister of Independent Lithuania; Anatoly Sobchak, a lawyer and mayor of Leningrad (St. Petersburg); Yury Kalmikov, minister of justice of the Russian Federation; and Sergey Stankevich, deputy chairman of the Mossovet and political adviser of the Russian president. This list of new "power stalkers," as Sobchack would describe them, is quite long.

There were people, however, who felt no necessity for power. Nuclear physicist and human rights advocate Andrei Sakharov, who had been persecuted and exiled for speaking out against Kruschev, was able to gain a unique influence over the public mind. His funeral became a great event, a manifestation of the public sorrow for a great humanitarian.

New actors appeared not only on the political stage. After the economy was freed from the web of governmental control, a new generation of the so-called "third class" was reborn. Private companies and brotherhoods, joint ventures, stock exchanges, and commercial banks seemed to pop out of the soil. The public was dazzled by successful businessmen, brokers, and financiers. Rich people appeared in the country. It was then that Artem Tarasov, a successful businessman, donated to his political party several million rubles—a prominent sum compared to the average salary of the majority of the population, which had never exceeded two hundred rubles.

With the growth of capitalism came a new economic elite: the former *nomenclatura* (bureaucrats) and government functionaries (those who used to work in ministries, trade unions, etc.); owners of small businesses, cooperatives, and farms; the bosses of the "shadow economy," (an organized crime syndicate more widespread than in the west, and with a larger impact on the economy); and the leaders of state factories and other institutions who are changing from government control to market-driven management. The representatives of this last group have created their own relatively independent organizations, such as manufacturers' associations and the Russian Union of Businessmen.

The old Soviet system, no matter how totalitarian, was unable to stop or prohibit free explorations of the mind. The national mass media, for example, had always been controlled by the ruling party, but as soon as this grip lessened, journalists began pushing the borders of *glasnost*, or "openness." Mass media became the most efficient tool to promote changes in social life. The late 1980s were marked by the flourishing of popular magazines and newspapers. The most important—and even the less significant—events of political life are now highlighted by a press that had been muzzled for so long.

The "Yeltsin phenomenon" became one of the clear examples of people's disregard and disrespect for the party. Boris Yeltsin had much experience as a party functionary and appeared at the highest levels of the CPSU during perestroika. In 1987, in a speech given on the eve of the October Revolution, he rather modestly (as it is considered now) criticized some of the party's policies. In his criticisms, he also blamed Gorbachev. Yeltsin was condemned, but was lucky to escape the political death that would have been inevitable in earlier years: he remained a member of the Central Committee of the CPSU and was promoted to minister. Despite the fact that later he admitted his behavior was a mistake and begged for a political "rehabilitation," Yeltsin's speech made him look like a guardian of the people's interest.

Yeltsin would not need to ask for forgiveness in 1989, nor in 1990. The more he condemned the system, the more chances he stood to gain votes. A number of former dissidents were elected to the Russian parliament then, and Yeltsin, faithful party member that he was, somehow became one of them. He was elected by a considerable margin, and a little later, despite all the resistance implemented by Gorbachev, was head of the Supreme Soviet of the Russian Federation.

By August 1991, the country was unstable. The new rulers were trying to strengthen their positions in politics and the economy, as well as in ideology, resulting in a division of the opinions of the party leaders, and a gain in support for the party's most active representatives. The real power, however, still belonged to the most inert leaders. Party red tape—both civil and military—was still in place to prevent change.

In order not to lose their influence completely, the conservatives made an attempt to seize power—the coup. A hurried endeavor—in mid-August the republics were to sign the new unification treaty that would make big changes among the leaders of the Soviet Union—the coup failed, and the country's stability crumbled.

The most important achievement of the August events was the simultaneous destruction of all the party institutions existing within the Soviet system. The ruling party had been the basis for the seventy-year regime. Once it was ruined, the Soviet system could exist no longer. There were feeble attempts to save it, but even those republics that did not object to the concept of a Soviet Union had no wish to feel Russia's grip again.

It is interesting to follow the careers of the leaders of the sovereign states that appeared after the destruction of the Soviet Union. These leaders had been high ranking party officials who now changed their former views and became nationalists (Kravchuk, Snegur, Gorbunov, Ruiitel, Karimov, Nijazov). Among the new leaders were pragmatists (Nazarbajev) as well as the scientists and representatives of the intelligentsia (Shushkevich, Akaev, Ter-Petrosjan, Gamsakhurdia, Landsbergis).

All the incessant transformations in the ruling elite illustrate its fluid nature. The representatives of the new wave (as well as some former party officials who, as a matter of fact, constitute this elite) have yet to find their modus vivendi. The first euphoric optimism has waned, the illusions are lost. Those who used to struggle for truth in the parliament and tried to condemn the ruling system have often turned out to be incompetent, failing to solve economic problems, as urgent as they were. Those who rose under Yelstin are often reproached for their inadequate adherence to the reforms, as well as their attempts to return to the past.

The continual conflict between the legislative and executive branches ranged from petty personal misunderstandings to honest differences of opinion. This conflict led the nation to a deadlock, resulting in the Moscow riots of October 1993. Blood was shed again. Through CNN, the world watched as Russia struggled to reinvent itself.

The muffling of the loudest opposition parties, new opportunities to control media, and a certain consolidation of the progressive ruling elite make it easier for the president and his government to take tough measures that, though necessary to bolster the economy, might bring more tension to society.

The main transitional period in Russia is all but over. The society has not yet created a list of principal values for its new life, but one thing is clear: One part of the society is no longer able to impose its views of life and further development on the other. Any attempts to do so would fail. The only way out seems to be in the historic compromise between the new on one side and the constructive parts of society on the other.

—Vladimir Morozov
Editor in Chief, *VIP Magazine*

How to Use This Book

With the breakup of the Soviet Union came tremendous changes in the leadership not only of government agencies, but of every facet of society. From uncensored newspapers to the boardrooms of joint-venture companies, new people have moved into positions of responsibility that in many cases never existed under the old Soviet system. *Who's Who in Russia* is designed to be a handy desk reference for researchers, journalists, business people, diplomats, and students—anyone who needs information quickly about the major figures in this rapidly changing part of the world. Culled from the largest data bank of its kind in the Commonwealth of Independent States, *Who's Who in Russia* is compiled by *VIP Magazine*.

In this volume, you can find leaders of the Russian Orthodox Church, presidents of commercial banks, gymnastics champions, journalists, opera singers, physicists, and even actors. All have one thing in common—they are considered leaders in their fields in the new Russia and other CIS republics.

Who's Who in Russia, then, is a book of valuable contacts. Each entry provides the person's current position, plus relevant career, education, and personal information, including addresses and phone numbers. All of the information provided has come from the biographees themselves.

If you wish to locate a contact but do not know the name of the person, the index and appendixes will be most useful. Those individuals who work independently, such as actors, writers, and directors, are listed by their professions in Appendix A. Appendix B is a listing by organization or government affiliation. For departments and ministries of the Russian government, see also Russian Federation; for example, the ambassador to France will be listed under Russian Federation as "Ambassador to France." Appendix C is a listing of entrants who have received honors or awards, and the Index of Works that follows contains books, films, plays, choregraphy, and music created by the people herein.

The Entry Categories

All of the information has been provided by the biographees, so some entries may contain more complete details than others.

Name: Last name, first name
Position: Current position or positions. The most prominent former position is also listed, such as Former Minister of Finance, if this position is a key factor for the person being included in this book.
Birthplace/Date: Unless otherwise stated, the country of birth is the Russian Federation. Some biographees provide specific information about the villages and settlements where they were born, since these places are not commonly known or may no longer exist. The specificity, too, in some cases, relates to regional or ethnic pride in the biographee's origins. Also, the names of cities and towns may have changed: St. Petersburg became Leningrad and then returned to St. Petersburg; Gorky returned to Nizhny Novgorod; Stalingrad returned to Volgograd, etc.
Nationality: Not everyone who lives in the former Soviet Union is Russian, and not everyone who lives in the Russian Federation is of Russian ethnicity. The term "nationality" can be thought of as ethnic self-identity.
Education: In addition to listing the biographees' higher education, foreign language skills are indicated.
Career: This entry traces each biographee's professional career and reflects the evolution of the Soviet Union to the Russian Federation, and in many cases, an individual's move from government work to private enterprise. The listings also reflect the numerous name changes in government agencies over the years.
Major Works: Books, articles, papers in particular areas of specialization, and artworks.
Family: Family information.
Address/Telephone: Both home and office contact information is provided, if supplied by the biographee.

About *VIP Magazine*

VIP, an international magazine of politics, public affairs, and business, is expected to reach a readership of about one hundred thousand readers. The monthly magazine addresses an intelligent reader—professionals in business, politics, academia, and the arts—and offers timely, provocative articles about, and interviews with, the most important people in the former Soviet Union and abroad in its one-hundred-plus pages per issue. *VIP* currently appears in both Russian and English, with plans underway to publish Spanish, French, and Italian language editions.

VIP's editorial board consists of thirty-five leading journalists, editors, artists, and executives. The magazine's impressive advisory board includes some of the most respected intellectuals and organizations in the CIS, and members of the Institute of Europe under the Russian Academy of Sciences regularly contribute their scholarly and political expertise to *VIP.*

Who's Who in Russia and the CIS Republics

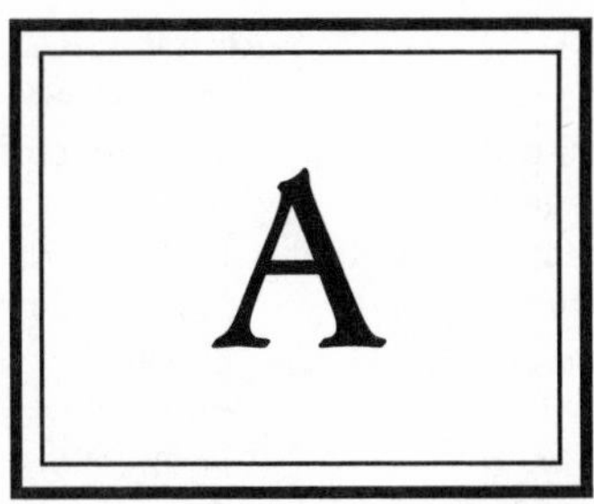

Abakumov, Igor Borisovich
POSITION: Editor in Chief of *Krestyanskiye Vedomosti (Farmers' News)* weekly
BIRTHPLACE/DATE: Kaluga, 1955
NATIONALITY: Russian
EDUCATION: Graduated from the Journalism Department at Moscow State University.
CAREER: Worked at *Leninskoye Znamya* (*Lenin's Banner*) and *Izvestia* (*News*) newspapers. From 1990, Editor in Chief of *Krestyanskiye Vedomosti.*
FAMILY: Married.
ADDRESS/TELEPHONE: 57 Gilyarovsky Street, Moscow, 125110. 284–0446 (office).

Abalkin, Leonid Ivanovich
POSITION: Director of the Institute of Economy of the Russian Academy of Sciences
CAREER: From 1952, Lecturer, then Director, of a vocational school of agriculture in Kaliningrad region. From 1961 to 1966, Junior Lecturer, Lecturer, then Senior Lecturer at the Moscow G. V. Plekhanov Institute of National Economy. From 1966, Department Head of Political Economy. From 1976, Professor, Deputy Head of the Academy of Social Sciences of the Central Committee. From 1985, Director of the Institute of Economy of the USSR Academy of Sciences. From 1988, Presidium Member of the USSR Academy of Sciences. From August 1989 to December 1990, Deputy Chairman of the Council of Ministers. Head of the State Commission for Economic Reforms. From June 1990 to December 1991, Advisor to Gorbachev. Member of the Communist Party to August 1991.
MAJOR WORKS: Articles and books on socialist political economy. 1989 to 1990: "The New Type of Economic Thinking"; "Perestroika: Ways and Difficulties"; "Soviet Society: Revolutionary Changes"; "Panorama of the Economic Perestroika"; "Difficult Turn Toward the Market."
FAMILY: Married with a daughter and a son.
ADDRESS/TELEPHONE: 27 Krasikova Street, Moscow, 117218. 129–0254 (office).

Abdrashitov, Vadim Yusupovich
POSITION: Film Director
BIRTHPLACE/DATE: Kharkov, 1945
NATIONALITY: Tatar
CAREER: From 1966 to 1967, Laboratory Assistant at the Central Laboratory of the Voykhov Chemical Plant. From 1967 to 1970, Engineer, Shop Superintendent of Moscow Electrovacuum Machinery. From 1974, Film Director of Mosfilm Studio. Member of the Confederation of Film Makers' Unions.
MAJOR WORKS: *Speech for the Defense* (1976); *Strange Woman* (1977); *The Train Has Stopped* (1982); *Parade of Planets* (1984); *Plumbum, or A Dangerous Game* (1986).
HONORS/AWARDS: Russian Federation People's Artist; Russian Federation State Prize; Komsomol Prize; Golden Plato (Italy, 1984).
FAMILY: Married with a son and a daughter.
ADDRESS/TELEPHONE: 9 Tretiaya Frunzenskaya Street, #211, Moscow, 119270. 245–6087.

Abdulatipov, Ramazan Gadzhimuradovich
POSITION: Chairman of the Russian Federation Supreme Soviet Council of Nationalities

BIRTHPLACE/DATE: Dagestan, 1946
NATIONALITY: Avar
EDUCATION: Graduated from a medical school; from the History Department at Dagestan State University; and completed postgraduate study at the Philosophy Department of Leningrad State University. In 1978, defended thesis on ethnic relations. Doctor of Philosophy, 1985.
CAREER: Head of a local dispensary in Dagestan. Served in the army. Head of the Sports Department of the Dagestan District Council Urozhai (Harvest) Sports Club. From 1978, Head of a research institute in Murmansk. From December 1989 to June 1990, Head of the Central Committee's Ethnic Relations Department. Russian Federation People's Deputy. Russian Federation Supreme Soviet member.
ADDRESS/TELEPHONE: Russian Federation Supreme Soviet Presidium, 2 Krasnopresnenskaya Naberezhnaya, Moscow, 103274. 205–6171 (office).

Abdullayev, Pulat Khabibovich
POSITION: Russian Federation Ambassador to Djibouti; Counsellor Extraordinary and Plenipotentiary, First Grade
BIRTHPLACE/DATE: Tashkent, 1942
NATIONALITY: Uzbek
EDUCATION: From 1958 to 1959, attended Tashkent Polytechnic Institute. From 1959 to 1961, attended Moscow State University. From 1961 to 1966, student at the Moscow State Institute of International Relations. Graduated from the Moscow State Institute of International Relations.
CAREER: From 1966 to 1967, Interpreter at the Soviet Embassy in Senegal; from 1967 to 1971, Attaché. From 1971 to 1972, Third Secretary of the Department of International Organizations of the USSR Ministry of Foreign Affairs; from 1971 to 1975, Second Secretary. From 1975 to 1977, First Secretary at the USSR Embassy in Belgium. From 1983 to 1986, Counsellor of the Department of International Organizations. From 1986 to 1991, Minister-Counsellor at the USSR Embassy in Belgium.
FAMILY: Married with two children.
TELEPHONE: 35–2051 (Djibouti); 244–2471 (Moscow).

Abdullin, Renat Raisovich
POSITION: Member of the Board of Directors and Director of the Political Information Department of Interfax Agency
BIRTHPLACE/DATE: Moscow, 1960
NATIONALITY: Bashkhir
CAREER: From 1982 to 1990, Junior Editor, Senior Editor, Correspondent for Moscow Radio. From 1990 to 1991, Correspondent for Interfax Agency.
FAMILY: Single.
ADDRESS/TELEPHONE: 2 Pervaya Tverskaya-Yamskaya Street, Moscow, 103006. 250–9203.

Aboimov, Ivan Pavlovich
POSITION: Russian Federation Ambassador to Hungary; Ambassador Extraordinary and Plenipotentiary
BIRTHPLACE/DATE: Zarechnoye village, Tashla district, Orenburg region, November 6, 1936
NATIONALITY: Russian
EDUCATION: Graduated in 1959 from the Latvian State Teachers' Training Institute. From 1959 to 1960, student of the training team of the Baltic Navy Air Force. From 1969 to 1972, attended the Higher Diplomatic School of the USSR Foreign Ministry. Command of Hungarian, English, German.
CAREER: In 1959, Head of the Propaganda Department of the Latvian City Komsomol Committee. From 1960 to 1963, Latvian Komsomol Functionary. From 1963 to 1969, Ideology Department Instructor, Head of the Foreign Policy Propaganda and Foreign Relations Department, Deputy Head of the Propaganda Department of the Latvian Central Committee. From 1972 to 1979, First Secretary, Counsellor at the USSR Embassy in Hungary. In 1979, Counsellor of the Fifth European Department of the USSR Foreign Ministry. From 1979 to 1983, Head of the Fifth European Department of the USSR Foreign Ministry. From 1983 to 1984, Assistant to the USSR Foreign Minister. From 1984 to 1986, Minister-Counsellor at the USSR Embassy in Hungary. In 1986, Head of the Personnel Department of the USSR Foreign Ministry. Collegium Member of the USSR Foreign Ministry. From 1986 to 1988, Chief of the Personnel and Educational Establishments Department of the USSR Foreign Ministry. From 1988 to 1990,

USSR Deputy Foreign Minister for Socialist Countries of Eastern Europe. From 1989 to 1990, Secretary-General of the Warsaw Treaty Political Consultative Committee. From 1990 to January 1992, USSR Ambassador to Hungary.
HONORS/AWARDS: Order of the Red Banner of Labor (1986); Hungarian Peace and Friendship Order (1986); Honorary Diploma of the Latvian Supreme Soviet Presidium (1967); three medals.
FAMILY: Married.
ADDRESS/TELEPHONE: Russian Federation Embassy, 1062 35 Bajza Utca, Budapest VI. 132–0911; 134–2748; 131–8985 (Embassy); Telex: 61224942 (via Trade Mission).

Abramchik, Vladimir Vasilyevich
POSITION: Director-General of the Minsk Watch Factory
BIRTHPLACE/DATE: Vitebsk, 1945
NATIONALITY: Byelorussian
CAREER: From 1968, worked from Foreman to General-Director of the Minsk Watch factory. From February 1987, Factory Director, then Director-General of the Minsk Watch Factory Industrial Complex.
FAMILY: Married with two children.
ADDRESS/TELEPHONE: 95 F. Skorina Prospekt, Minsk, 220043. 66–1930 (office).

Abramov, Sergey Aleksandrovich
POSITION: Editor in Chief of *Semya* (*Family*) newspaper
BIRTHPLACE/DATE: Moscow, April 10, 1944
EDUCATION: Graduated in 1966 from the Moscow Motor Road Institute. Speaks English.
CAREER: From 1969 to 1972, Senior Editor of the Literary Life Department of *Literaturnaya Gazeta* (*Literary Newspaper*). From 1972 to 1977, Head of the Science and Technology Department of *Smena* (*Rising Generation*) magazine. From 1977 to 1986, Special Correspondent for the Literature and Arts Department of *Pravda* (*Truth*) daily. From 1986 to 1987, Deputy Chief Editor of *Teatr* (*Theater*) magazine.
MAJOR WORKS: Author of twenty-nine books, including *The Wall*.
FAMILY: Married with a son.
ADDRESS/TELEPHONE: 3/10 Chekhov Street, Moscow 103803. 209–0651 (office); 264–1629 (home).

Abramov, Yevgeni Aleksandrovich
POSITION: Russian Federation First Deputy Minister of Internal Affairs; Lieutenant-General of the Militia (Police)
BIRTHPLACE/DATE: Moscow region, 1939
EDUCATION: Graduated from the Law Department at Moscow State University.
CAREER: From 1961, served with the agencies of internal affairs. Investigator of the Podolsk Ministry of Internal Affairs and the Investigation Department of the Moscow Regional Executive Committee's Directorate of Internal Affairs. From 1973 to 1983, held different leading positions at the Investigation Department of the Moscow Regional Executive Committee's Directorate of Internal Affairs. From 1983 to 1986, Head of the Investigation Directorate; from 1986 to 1989, Head of the Organizing and Inspection Department of the Moscow Regional Executive Committee's Directorate of Internal Affairs. From 1990 to January 1992, Russian Federation Deputy Minister of Internal Affairs, Head of the Crime Investigation Service.
ADDRESS/TELEPHONE: 16 Zhitnaya Street, Moscow, 117049. 239–5215 (office).

Adamishin, Anatoli Leonidovich
POSITION: Russian Federation First Deputy Foreign Minister; Ambassador Extraordinary and Plenipotentiary
BIRTHPLACE/DATE: Kiev, October 11, 1934
NATIONALITY: Russian
EDUCATION: Graduated from Moscow State University in 1957.
CAREER: From 1957 to 1959, Aide to the First European Department of the USSR Foreign Ministry. From 1959 to 1965, Attaché, Third Secretary, Second Secretary at the USSR Embassy in Italy. From 1965 to 1971, Second Secretary, First Secretary, Counsellor, Expert of the First European Department of the USSR Foreign Ministry. From 1971 to 1973, Senior Counsellor, Chief Counsellor of the Foreign Events Planning Department of the USSR Foreign Ministry. From 1973 to 1978, Head of the General International Problems Department of the USSR Foreign Ministry. From 1978 to 1979,

Head of the First European Department. From 1979 to 1986, Head of the First European Department; USSR Foreign Ministry Collegium Member. From 1986 to 1987, USSR Deputy Minister of Foreign Affairs. From 1987 to 1990, USSR Deputy Minister of Foreign Affairs, Chairman of the Special UNESCO Commission. From 1990 to December 1991, USSR Ambassador to Italy. From January to October 1992, Russian Federation Deputy Foreign Minister.
HONORS/AWARDS: Order of the Badge of Honor (1971); Order of the People's Friendship (1975); Order of the Red Banner of Labor (1981, 1984).
FAMILY: Married with a daughter.
ADDRESS/TELEPHONE: 32/34 Smolenskaya-Sennaya Square, Moscow. 244–9225 (office).

Adamovich, Aleksandr Mikhailovich (Ales Adamovich)
POSITION: Writer; Director of the All-Russia Research Institute of Film Making
BIRTHPLACE/DATE: Konyukhi village, Minsk region, 1927
NATIONALITY: Byelorussian
EDUCATION: Graduated from a mining and metallurgical technical school, from Minsk State University, and from the Higher Scriptwriters' Courses. Doctor of Sciences; Professor. Corresponding Member of the Byelorussian Academy of Sciences.
CAREER: During World War II, fought in guerrilla detachments in Byelorussia. From 1954, worked at the Yanka Kupala Literary Institute. Co-Founder of the April Writers' Association and of the Memorial Society. Former USSR People's Deputy.
MAJOR WORKS: Authored many well-known novels, stories, and scripts.
HONORS/AWARDS: State Prize of Byelorussia.
ADDRESS/TELEPHONE: Degtyarny Pereulok, Moscow, 103050. 299–5679; 299–6426 (office). 76-A Leninsky Prospekt, Flat #16, Minsk. 66–5864.

Afanasyev, Yuri Nikolayevich
POSITION: Rector of the Russian State Humanities University (formerly the History and Archives Institute); Russian Federation People's Deputy
BIRTHPLACE/DATE: Maina settlement, Ulyanovsk region, 1934
NATIONALITY: Russian
EDUCATION: Graduated in 1957 from Moscow State University. Doctor of History.
CAREER: From 1957 to 1964, Komsomol Official in Krasnoyarsk region. Member of the Communist Party from 1961 to 1990. From 1964 to 1968, Chair of the Central Committee's Academy of Social Sciences. In 1971, Intern at the Sorbonne, France. From 1971 to 1982, Deputy Rector of the Central Committee's Higher Komsomol School. From 1981 to 1986, Senior Researcher, Section Head, Professor at the USSR Academy of Sciences' Institute of World History. From 1983 to 1986, Editor and Editorial Board Member of *Kommunist* magazine. From December 1986, Rector of the Russian State Humanities University. From 1989, USSR People's Deputy. From July 1991, Russian Federation People's Deputy. Member of the Inter-Regional Parliamentary Faction and the Ecological Parliamentary Faction; Co-Chairman of the Memorial Society. Co-Chairman of the Coordinating Council of the Democratic Russia Movement. In January 1992, suspended membership in the Democratic Russia Movement.
FAMILY: Married with two children.
ADDRESS/TELEPHONE: 15 Nikolskaya Street, Moscow. 921–4169 (office).

Afanasyevsky, Nikolay Nikolayevich
POSITION: Russian Federation Ambassador to Belgium; Ambassador Extraordinary and Plenipotentiary
BIRTHPLACE/DATE: Moscow, October 1, 1940
NATIONALITY: Russian
EDUCATION: Graduated in 1964 from the Moscow State Institute of International Relations. Command of French and English.
CAREER: From 1962 to 1963, Aide at the USSR Embassy in France. In 1964, Aide to the Second African Department of the USSR Foreign Ministry. From 1964 to 1965, Interpreter at the USSR Embassy in Cameroon. From 1965 to 1966, Attaché at the USSR Embassy in Cameroon. Between 1966 and 1970, Attaché, Third Secretary, Second Secretary of the Translation Department of the USSR Foreign Ministry. From 1970 to 1976, Second Secretary, First Secretary, Counsellor of the First Euro-

pean Department of the USSR Foreign Ministry. From 1976 to 1977, First Secretary at the USSR Embassy in France; from 1977 to 1979, Counsellor; from 1979 to 1983, Minister-Counsellor. From 1983 to 1990, Deputy Department Head, then Department Head of the First European Department of the USSR Foreign Ministry. From 1990 to January 1992, USSR Ambassador to Belgium.
FAMILY: Married.
ADDRESS/TELEPHONE: Russian Federation Embassy, 66 Avenue de Fre, 1180 Bruxelles, Belgique. 374–6886; 374–3406; Telex: 4665272.

Agafangel (Savvin Aleksey Mikhailovich)
POSITION: Metropolitan of Odessa and Kherson
BIRTHPLACE/DATE: Burdino village, Lipetsk region, September 2, 1938
NATIONALITY: Russian
CAREER: In 1965, entered monastic life in Troitsko-Sergievaya Lavra. From 1966 to 1967, Chief Inspector Assistant of the Odessa Ecclesiastical Seminary and Office Manager of the Odessa Eparchy. In 1967, named Archimandrite. From 1967, Rector of the Odessa Ecclesiastical Seminary. From 1975, Bishop, Head of the Vinnitsa and Khmelnitsky Eparchies of the Russian Orthodox Church. From 1981, Archbishop of Vinnitsa and Bratslavsk.
HONORS/AWARDS: Order of Vladimir, Second and Third Grade.
ADDRESS/TELEPHONE: 6 Mayachy Pereulok, Odessa. 66–3185; 66–3155 (home); 66–9151 (office).

Aganbegyan, Abel Gezevich
POSITION: Rector of the Academy of National Economy; member of the Russian Academy of Sciences
BIRTHPLACE/DATE: Tbilisi, Georgia, October 8, 1932
NATIONALITY: Armenian
EDUCATION: Graduated in 1955 from the Moscow State Institute of Economics. Doctor of Economics. Professor.
CAREER: From 1955 to 1961, Economist, Sector Chief, Deputy Head of the General Economics Department of the USSR Council of Ministers' State Committee for Labor and Social Problems. Joined the Communist Party in 1956. From 1961 to 1966, Laboratory Chief at the Institute of Economics and Industrial Production Organization of the Siberian branch of the USSR Academy of Sciences. From 1964 to 1967, Scientific Chief of the Production Association of the Novosibirsk Ministry of Instrument Making, Automation Equipment and Control Systems. From 1964 to 1974, Corresponding Member of the USSR Academy of Sciences' Economics Department. From 1967 to 1985, Director of the Siberian branch of the USSR Academy of Sciences' Institute of Economics and Industrial Production Organization; Scientific Council Construction Head for the Baikal-Amur Railroad (BAM) of the USSR Academy of Sciences. From 1967 to 1985, Professor of Economics at Novosibirsk State University. From 1967 to 1988, Chief Editor of *EKO*, the journal of the Siberian branch of the USSR Academy of Sciences. From 1974, Full Member of the USSR Academy of Sciences' Economics Department. From 1987 to 1989, Academician-Secretary of the USSR Academy of Sciences' Economics Department. From 1989, Rector of the Academy of National Economy. From December 1991, member of the Russian Academy of Sciences. Founding member of the Econometric Society (1974), member of the Bulgarian Academy of Sciences (1986) and the Hungarian Academy of Sciences (1987); Corresponding Member of the British Academy of Sciences (1988).
MAJOR WORKS: Scientific works on labor productivity, wages and living standards, economic and mathematic models of long-term planning: *The Challenge: Economics of Perestroika* (1987); *Inside Perestroika: The Future of the Soviet Economy* (1989).
HONORS/AWARDS: Order of Lenin (1967); two Orders of the Red Banner of Labor (1975, 1982); medals. Honorary Doctorates from Lodz University, Poland (1975) and the University of Alicante, Spain (1989).
FAMILY: Married with two children.
ADDRESS/TELEPHONE: 82 Vernadsky Prospekt, Moscow. 434–8389 (office).

Agapov, Yuri Vasilyevich
POSITION: Director-General of the Credo-Bank; Board Chairman

Birthplace/Date: Ros, Grodno region, Byelorussia, 1958
Nationality: Russian
Education: Graduated from the Moscow Institute of Finance. Doctor of Economics.
Career: Worked as an Economist at the State Bank; Senior Researcher at a research institute.
Major Works: Authored a number of works in the field of financial and credit transactions.
Family: Married.
Address/Telephone: 15 Osipenko Street, Building 2, Moscow, 113035. 220–3435 (office).

Agayan, Aleksandr Aleksandrovich

Position: Board Chairman of the St. Petersburg Innovation Bank
Birthplace/Date: Tbilisi, Georgia, 1951
Nationality: Armenian
Education: Graduated in 1973 from Tbilisi State University, majoring in Cybernetics. From 1977 to 1980, postgraduate student at the Institute of Cybernetics. Doctor of Technology. Speaks English and Georgian.
Career: From 1973 to 1977, Junior Researcher at the Georgian Academy of Sciences' Institute of Cybernetics. Between 1981 and 1983, Senior Researcher at the Leningrad Krasnaya Zarya (Red Dawn) Scientific-Production Association. From 1983 to 1988, Computer Center Department Head of Minpromstroibank (Bank of the Ministry of Industrial Construction).
Major Works: Creator of over 50 scientific inventions.
Family: Married with two children.
Address/Telephone: 24 Tchaikovsky Street, Flat #8, St. Petersburg, 191194. 279–0004 (office).

Agayev, Tofik Ogly

Position: Acting Head of the Board of Analysis and Prognosis at the Department of International Organizations and Global Problems; Second Secretary, First Grade
Birthplace/Date: Baku, 1956
Nationality: Azerbaijanian
Education: From 1974 to 1979, student at the Moscow State Institute of International Relations. Graduated from the Moscow State Institute of International Relations. From 1979 to 1980, student of the special course for UN translators in Moscow.
Career: From 1973 to 1974, Translator at the Bureau of Scientific and Technical Information of the USSR State Bank. From 1980 to 1986, worked at the UN Secretariat in Geneva. From 1986 to 1987, Attaché of the Department of International Organizations of the USSR Foreign Ministry. From 1990 to 1991, Head of the Department of International Organizations. From 1991 to 1992, Counsellor of the USSR Foreign Ministry.
Family: Married.
Telephone: 241–0234 (office).

Aitmatov, Chingiz Torekulovich

Position: Ambassador to Luxembourg; Ambassador Extraordinary and Plenipotentiary
Birthplace/Date: Sheker village, Kirovsk region, Kirghizia (Kirgistan)
Nationality: Kirghiz
Education: From 1946 to 1948, studied at the Veterinary School in Jambul; from 1948 to 1953, studied at the Kirghiz Agricultural Institute. From 1956 to 1958, student of the Higher Writers' Courses.
Career: From 1953 to 1956, Chief Zoo Technician of the Kirghiz Research Institute of Cattlebreeding. From 1958 to 1962, Editor in Chief of *Literaturny Kazakhstan* (*Literary Kazakhstan*) magazine. From 1962 to 1970, Correspondent for *Pravda* (*Truth*) in Kirghizia. From 1970 to 1984, Chairman of the Kirghiz Union of Film Makers. From 1984 to 1989, Chairman of the Committee for Preserving Languages, Culture, National and International Traditions, and Historical Heritage of the USSR Supreme Soviet Council of Nationalities. In 1990, member of the USSR President's Council.
Honors/Awards: Hero of Socialist Labor; Order of the October Revolution; Prize of Lenin.
Family: Married with two children.
Telephone: 422–333 (Luxembourg); 244–4162 (Moscow).

Akayev, Askar

Position: President of the Kirgistan (formerly Kirghizia) Republic; Academician of the Kirghiz Academy of Sciences

BIRTHPLACE/DATE: Kyzyl-Bairak village, Keminsky region, Kirghizia
CAREER: Worked in various research institutes in Kirghizia. From 1987, Academician, then Vice President of the Kirghiz Academy of Sciences. From March 1989 to October 1990, President of the Kirghiz Academy of Sciences. People's Deputy of the USSR, member of the USSR Supreme Soviet Council of Nationalities, member of the USSR Supreme Soviet Committee for Economic Reforms. In August 1991, quit the Communist Party.
MAJOR WORKS: Author of more than 80 scientific publications on fundamental physics.
HONORS/AWARDS: Order of the Badge of Honor; Kirghiz Komsomol Prize; Order of the Grand Cross.
FAMILY: Married with four children.
ADDRESS/TELEPHONE: President's Residence, Bishkek, Kirgistan, 720003. 21–2466 (office).

Akhmedov, Khan

POSITION: Former Deputy Head of the Turkmenistan Government; Ambassador to Turkey; Ambassador Extraordinary and Plenipotentiary
BIRTHPLACE/DATE: Pakau village, Krasnovoksk region, 1936
NATIONALITY: Turkmen
CAREER: From 1959, worked for the Ashkhabad Railroad. From 1985, First Secretary of the Ashkhabad City Communist Party. From 1988, First Deputy Chairman of the Council of Ministers. From 1989, Chairman of the Turkmen Council of Ministers. From November 1990 to November 1991, Prime Minister of the Turkmen Republic, member of the Central Committee. From November 1991, Deputy Head of the Turkmen Government and Head of the Turkmen Railroad. From 1963 to 1991, member of the Communist Party.
HONORS/AWARDS: Order of the Red Banner of Labor; Order of the Badge of Honor; medals.
FAMILY: Married with four children.
ADDRESS/TELEPHONE: 24 Karl Marx Street, #24, Ashkhabad, 744014. 25–4534 (office).

Akhundova, Elmira Guseinovna

POSITION: Correspondent for *Literaturnaya Gazeta* (*Literary Newspaper*) and *Delovoy Mir* (*Business World*) in Azerbaijan; Board Secretary of the Azerbaijan Writers' Union
BIRTHPLACE/DATE: Ramenskoe, Moscow region, 1953
NATIONALITY: Azerbaijanian
EDUCATION: Doctor of Philology.
CAREER: From 1977 to 1980, Editor of Azerbaijan Television and Radio; from 1980 to 1988, Aide, Expert, and Secretary. From 1988 to 1990, Researcher, Senior Researcher at the Azerbaijan Literature Institute.
FAMILY: Married with two children.
ADDRESS/TELEPHONE: 36 Askerova Street, Baku, 370002. 93–6620 (office); 95–4047 (home).

Aksenenok, Aleksandr Georgyevich

POSITION: Russian Federation Ambassador to Algeria; Ambassador Extraordinary and Plenipotentiary
BIRTHPLACE/DATE: Chermoz, Perm region, 1942
EDUCATION: Graduated from the Moscow State Institute of International Relations in 1963. From 1964 to 1965, postgraduate student at the Moscow State Institute of International Relations. From 1990 to 1991, student of the advanced course for senior diplomats at the Diplomatic Academy.
CAREER: From 1963 to 1964, Interpreter at the USSR Embassy in Libya. From 1965 to 1966, Aide to the First African Department of the USSR Foreign Ministry. From 1968 to 1969, Attaché at the USSR Embassy in Iraq. From 1969 to 1971, Third Secretary at the USSR Embassy in Iraq. From 1971 to 1972, Third Secretary of the Middle East Department of the USSR Foreign Ministry; from 1972 to 1975, Second Secretary. From 1978 to 1981, First Secretary at the USSR Embassy in Egypt. From 1981 to 1984, Counsellor at the USSR Embassy in Yemen. From 1984 to 1988, Minister-Counsellor at the USSR Embassy in Syria. From 1988 to 1989, Chief Counsellor of the Department of Estimation of the USSR Foreign Ministry; from 1989 to 1990, Deputy Head.
MAJOR WORKS: A number of articles on Islam and the political development of Middle East countries.
FAMILY: Married with two children.
TELEPHONE: 78–0139 (Algeria); 244–4944 (Moscow).

Aksyuchits, Victor Vladimirovich

POSITION: Russian Federation People's Deputy Chairman of the Subcommittee for Liaison with Foreign and Religious Organizations of the Russian Federation Supreme Soviet Committee for Freedom of Conscience, Faith, Mercy, and Charity; Chairman of the Russian Christian-Democratic Movement Political Council; Board Chairman of the Russian People's Front

BIRTHPLACE/DATE: Vardomichi village, Western Byelorussia, 1949

NATIONALITY: Byelorussian

EDUCATION: Graduated from the Riga Navigation School and from the Moscow State University Philosophy Department in 1979. In 1979, postgraduate student of the Foreign Philosophy Department at Moscow University.

CAREER: Served in the navy. While an officer, joined the Philosophy Faculty of Moscow State University. In 1971, joined the Communist Party. In 1979, quit the Communist Party for ideological reasons and distributed samizdat literature. From 1979 to 1985, seasonal worker in Siberia and the Far East. From 1987, Co-Publisher of *Vybor* (*Choice*) religious magazine. From 1986 to 1990, worked at Perspektiva (Perspective) Cooperative and Buick Joint Venture.

FAMILY: Married with four children.

ADDRESS/TELEPHONE: 2 Krasnopresnenskaya Naberezhnaya, Moscow. 205–9086; 205–4009 (office).

Aleinikov, Boris Nikolayevich

POSITION: President of the Penza Mercantile Exchange; Vice President of the Exchange Congress

BIRTHPLACE/DATE: 1952

EDUCATION: Graduated from the Law Department at Voronezh State University.

CAREER: In 1989, received postgraduate training in Moscow. In 1989, elected Law Department Head of the Penza Regional Cooperatives Alliance, subsequently become Chairman of the Alliance.

ADDRESS/TELEPHONE: 83 Moskovskaya Street, Penza, 440600. 69–5045; 66–5630.

Aleksei II (Aleksei Mikhailovich Ridiger)

POSITION: Honorary Member of the Moscow Ecclesiastical Academy; Holy Patriarch of Moscow and All-Russia

BIRTHPLACE/DATE: Tallin, March 23, 1929

NATIONALITY: Russian

CAREER: From 1950 to 1961, Priest of the Tallin Eparchy of the Russian Orthodox Church. From 1961 to 1965, Deputy Chairman of the Foreign Relations Department of the Moscow Patriarchy and Head of the Tallin Eparchy. From 1965 to 1986, Head of the Moscow Patriarchy and the Tallin Eparchy. From 1986 to 1990, Metropolitan of Leningrad and Novgorod and Head of the Tallin Eparchy; President of the European Church Confederation; Deputy Chairman of the Soviet Peace Fund; USSR People's Deputy. In 1990, elected Patriarch of Moscow and All-Russia.

MAJOR WORKS: Author of more than 200 publications.

HONORS/AWARDS: Order of the Red Banner of Labor; Order of the People's Friendship.

ADDRESS/TELEPHONE: 57/59 Leningradskoye Chaussée, #88, Moscow. 201–2668 (home).

Alekseyev, Aleksandr Yuryevich

POSITION: Board Head of the Department of West and South Asia; Ambassador Extraordinary and Plenipotentiary, First Grade

BIRTHPLACE/DATE: Moscow, 1946

NATIONALITY: Russian

EDUCATION: Graduated from the Moscow State Institute of International Relations in 1969.

CAREER: Aide to the South Asia Department of the USSR Foreign Ministry. From 1969 to 1970, worked at the USSR Embassy in India; from 1970 to 1974, Attaché; from 1974 to 1975, Third Secretary. From 1975 to 1980, Junior Department Aide to the Central Committee. From 1980 to 1982, First Secretary at the USSR Embassy in India. From 1985 to 1987, Counsellor of the Department of South Asia of the USSR Foreign Ministry. From 1987, Division Head of the Department of South Asia; from 1987 to 1992, Deputy Head.

FAMILY: Married with a daughter.

TELEPHONE: 244–2793 (office).

Alekseyev, Sergey Pavlovich

POSITION: Director-General of the Lenexpo Foreign Economic Exhibition Association

BIRTHPLACE/DATE: Leningrad, 1947

NATIONALITY: Russian

EDUCATION: Graduated in 1973 from the Plek-

hanov Mining Institute in Leningrad. Speaks English.
CAREER: From 1973 to 1979, worked for the City Komsomol Committee. From 1979 to 1989, Foreign Exhibitions Director of the Leningrad Expocenter Association. In 1989, received managerial training in Hamburg. From 1991, President of the Union of Exhibitions and Fairs of Russia and the Independent Republics. From 1992, Vice President of the St. Petersburg Marketing Club.
FAMILY: Married with a child.
ADDRESS/TELEPHONE: 103 Bolshoi Proyezd, Vasilyevsky Ostrov, St. Petersburg, 199106. 217–2047 (office).

Alferov, Zhores Ivanovich
POSITION: Presidium Chairman of the St. Petersburg Research Center of the Russian Academy of Sciences; Director of the Ioffe Institute of Physics and Technology
BIRTHPLACE/DATE: March 15, 1930
NATIONALITY: Russian
EDUCATION: Graduated in 1952 from the Ulyanov-Lenin Electrotechnical Institute in Leningrad.
CAREER: From 1953, Engineer, Section Head, Laboratory Head, Director of the Ioffe Institute of Physics and Technology. Joined the Communist Party in 1965. From 1979, Academician of the USSR Academy of Sciences. From 1989, Presidium Chairman of the Leningrad (now St. Petersburg) Research Center of the Russian Academy of Sciences. From 1990, Vice President of the Russian Academy of Sciences. Former elected USSR People's Deputy.
MAJOR WORKS: Writings in the field of semiconductors, heterojunctions, and related instruments.
HONORS/AWARDS: Prize of Lenin (1972); USSR State Prize (1984). Member of the Franklin Institute (USA); foreign member of the German Academy of Sciences; Honorary Professor of Havana University; foreign member of the Polish Academy of Sciences; foreign member of the National Academy of Sciences (USA).
FAMILY: Married with two children.
ADDRESS/TELEPHONE: The Ioffe Institute of Physics and Technology, 26 Politekhnicheskaya Street, St. Petersburg K–21, 194021. 247–2145 (office); 552–5855 (home).

Alimpy (Aleksandr Kapitonovich Gusev)
POSITION: Head of the Russian Orthodox Staroobryadchesky (Old Belief) Church; Staroobryadchesky Metropolitan of Moscow and All-Russia
BIRTHPLACE/DATE: Gorky (now Nizhny Novgorod), July 31, 1929
NATIONALITY: Russian
CAREER: From 1946, Dockworker. From 1949 to 1950, Fireman. From 1950 to 1953, served in the army. From 1954 to 1960, worked in a fire department. From 1960 to 1963, Painter. From 1966 to 1967, Stoker at the Gorky Old Belief Church. From 1967 to 1986, Deacon of the Gorky Old Belief Church. In 1986, Archbishop of Moscow and All-Russia. In 1988, elected first Staroobryadchesky Metropolitan of Moscow and All-Russia.
ADDRESS: 29 Rogozsky Pos., Moscow.

Aliseichik, Valery Ivanovich
POSITION: President of the Soyuzvneshtrans (International Transportation) Concern
BIRTHPLACE/DATE: Khabarovsk, 1938
NATIONALITY: Russian
EDUCATION: Graduated in 1971 from the Moscow Institute of Railway Transport Engineering; in 1970, from the All-Union Foreign Trade Academy.
CAREER: From 1961 to 1963, engaged in railway transport work at different stations. From 1963 to 1967, Senior Engineer of the Chief Traffic Administration of the USSR Ministry of Railways. From 1970 to 1978, Deputy Head of the Transport Department, Deputy Head of the Main Department of International Transportation of the USSR Foreign Trade Ministry. From 1978 to 1980, Deputy Head at the Mission in Denmark. From 1989 to 1991, Director-General of Soyuzvneshtrans.
HONORS/AWARDS: Order of the Red Banner of Labor (1975); Order of the People's Friendship (1982).
FAMILY: Married with a son.
ADDRESS/TELEPHONE: 17 Gogol Boulevard, Moscow. 203–1179.

Aliyev, Geydar Aliyevich
POSITION: Deputy Chairman of the Azerbaijan Supreme Soviet; Chairman of the Nakhichevan Republic Medjalis (Parliament); former member of the Politburo

BIRTHPLACE/DATE: Nakhichevan, 1923
NATIONALITY: Azerbaijanian
CAREER: From 1941, worked at the Nakhichevan Republic Ministry of Internal Affairs. From 1943 to 1945, Head of the Nakhichevan Republic Council of People's Commissars, then returned to the Nakhichevan Internal Affairs Service. From 1950 to 1969, worked for the Azerbaijan KGB; Major-General. In 1969, First Secretary of the Azerbaijan Central Committee. From 1971 to 1989, member of the Central Committee. From 1982 to 1987, member of the Politburo. From 1983 to 1988, First Deputy Chairman of the USSR Council of Ministers. Retired in 1988. Quit the Communist Party in June 1991. People's Deputy of Azerbaijan.
HONORS/AWARDS: Twice Hero of Socialist Labor.
FAMILY: Widower with two children.
ADDRESS/TELEPHONE: 1 Narimanov Prospekt, Baku, 372001. 92–5309 (office).

Alksnis, Victor Imantovich
POSITION: Co-Chairman of the Soyuz (Union) Deputy Group; Head of the Russian Nashi (Our) Liberation; one of the leaders of the National Salvation Front
BIRTHPLACE/DATE: Tashtagol, Kemerov region, 1950
NATIONALITY: Lett
CAREER: Baltic Military Engineer of radio-electric equipment. From 1988 to present, Senior Engineer-Inspector of the Baltic Air Force. Lieutenant-Colonel. USSR People's Deputy, Latvian Supreme Soviet Deputy, member of the Soyuz Group. From 1989 to 1992, Latvian People's Deputy.
FAMILY: Married with a son and a daughter.
ADDRESS: 13703 Pribaltiysky, Riga, Latvia, 226098.

Ambartsumov, Yevgeni Arshakovich
POSITION: Chairman of the Russian Federation Supreme Soviet Committee for Foreign Affairs and International Economic Relations
BIRTHPLACE/DATE: Moscow, 1929
NATIONALITY: Armenian
EDUCATION: Graduated in 1951 from the Moscow State Institute of International Relations; postgraduate student from 1951 to 1954. Speaks English, French, German, and Italian.
CAREER: From 1954 to 1956, Editor of *Novoye Vremya* (*New Time*) magazine. From 1956 to 1959, Senior Researcher at the Institute of the World Economy and International Relations. From 1959 to 1963, Editor of the Prague-based *World Marxist Review* journal. From 1963 to 1990, Sector Head and Department Head at humanities institutes of the Academy of Sciences. From 1990, Russian Federation People's Deputy.
MAJOR WORKS: Articles and pamphlets on the history of socialism.
FAMILY: Married with a son.
ADDRESS/TELEPHONE: 2 Krasnopresnenskaya Naberezhnaya, Moscow. 205–4408 (office).

Ananyev, Anatoli Andreyevich
POSITION: Editor in Chief of *Oktyabr* (*October*) magazine
BIRTHPLACE/DATE: Aule-Ata (Jambul), Kazakhstan, July 18, 1925
EDUCATION: Graduated in 1942 from an agricultural college; in 1943, from the Kharkov Artillery School in Ferghana; in 1951, from the Kazakh Agricultural Institute; and in 1958, from the Philology Department at Kazakh State University.
CAREER: From 1940 to 1942, Apprentice Electrician at the Namangan Cotton Factory. Took part in World War II. From 1951 to 1956, Agronomist. From 1956 to 1958, Section Head at the Alma-Ata Enzyme Factory. From 1958 to 1960, Head of the Information Department, then Head of the Culture Department of *Alma-Atinskaya Pravda* (*Alma-Ata Truth*) daily. From 1960 to 1965, Deputy Editor in Chief of Jazdushi Publishers; member of the Kazakhstan Writers' Union. From 1965 to 1967, Secretary of the Kazakhstan Writers' Union. From 1967 to 1974, Board Member of the Moscow Writers' Union, Deputy Editor in Chief of *Znamya* (*Banner*) magazine. From 1974, Editor in Chief of *Oktyabr*. Former Deputy Chairman of the USSR Supreme Soviet Committee for Foreign Affairs; First Deputy Chairman of the Soviet Peace Committee. Quit the Communist Party in August 1990.
MAJOR WORKS: *Verninskiye* (short story collection, 1958); *Small Barrier* (1960); *Tanks in Diamond Formation* (1963); *Boundary-Strip* (1969);

Love Verses (1972); *Years Without War* (1984); *Memorials and Bells* (1989).
HONORS/AWARDS: Hero of Socialist Labor (1985); Medal for Labor Valor; Orders of the Great Patriotic War, First and Second Grade; Medal for the Liberation of Vienna; Order of the Badge of Honor; Order of the October Revolution; Order of Lenin.
FAMILY: Married with a daughter.
ADDRESS/TELEPHONE: *Oktyabr* Magazine Editorial Office, 11 Pravda Street, GSP, Moscow A–137, 125872. 214–6205 (office).

Anchevsky, Igor Georgyevich
POSITION: President and Co-Owner of Sagan Ltd.; President of the Korgan Center
BIRTHPLACE/DATE: Tkibuly, 1957
CAREER: From 1979, Industrial Psychologist. From 1983, Psychologist, Editor of the Kazakh Advertising Agency. From 1985, Head of the Advertising Department of the Kazakh Trade Ministry. From 1987, Editor, Host of Kazakh Television. From 1988, Head of the Advertising Department of the State Television and Radio Committee; from 1990, Director of the Marketing and Management Bureau.
FAMILY: Married with a son.
ADDRESS/TELEPHONE: 47 M. Makatayeva Street, Alma-Ata, Kazakhstan, 480002. 30–4414; 30–6156 (office)

Andreyev, Yuri Emanuilovich
POSITION: Former Moscow Government Minister
BIRTHPLACE/DATE: Moscow, 1945
CAREER: From 1960 to 1969, Fitter. From 1969 to 1989, Engineer, Senior Engineer, Group Head, then Chief Project Engineer of the Mosgidrotrans (Moscow Water Transport) Institute. From 1989 to 1990, USSR People's Deputy. From 1990 to 1991, member of the USSR Supreme Soviet Committee for Building, Budget and Finance. From 1991 to 1992, Moscow Government Deputy Prime Minister. From January to September 1992, Moscow Government Minister, Head of the Municipal Administration.
HONORS/AWARDS: Order of the Red Banner of Labor; medals.
FAMILY: Widower with two children.
ADDRESS/TELEPHONE: 13 Tverskaya Street, Moscow, 103032. 229–1124 (office).

Andreyeva, Iren Aleksandrovna
POSITION: Board Secretary of the Designers' Union; Editor in Chief of *Design for All*
BIRTHPLACE/DATE: Moscow, 1933
EDUCATION: Graduated from the History Department at Moscow State University. Speaks German and French.
CAREER: From 1964 to 1966, Art Critic at the Institute of Light Industry Assortment; from 1966 to 1979, Chief Art Critic. From 1979 to 1990, Chief Art Critic of the All-Union Fashion House. From 1978 to 1989, Lecturer at the Moscow Academic Art Theater (MKhAT) Studio-School. From 1987, Board Secretary of the Designers' Union. Member of the Democratic Russia Movement. USSR People's Deputy; Deputy Chairwoman of the Commission for Deputy's Ethics.
FAMILY: Married with a son.
ADDRESS/TELEPHONE: 10 Zhitnaya Street, Flat #92, Moscow, 117049. 238–8668 (home).

Andreyeva, Nina Aleksandrovna
POSITION: Secretary-General of the All-Union Bolshevik Party
BIRTHPLACE/DATE: Leningrad, 1938
NATIONALITY: Russian
CAREER: Researcher, Research Group Head at the Institute of Quartz Glass; Senior Lecturer of the Physical Chemistry Department at the Leningrad Technological Institute. Member of the Communist Party from 1966. From 1989, Chairwoman of the Political Executive Committee of the All-Union Yedinstvo-za Leninizm i Communisticheskiye Idealy (Unity for Leninism and Communist Ideals) Society. From November 1991, Secretary-General of the Bolshevik Party.
MAJOR WORKS: Theoretical works on multicomponent oxide systems under high temperatures. Wrote letter attacking reforms to *Sovietskaya Rossiya* (*Soviet Russia*) that appeared on March 13, 1988, under the headline "I cannot give up my principles."
FAMILY: Married with a daughter and a grandson.
ADDRESS/TELEPHONE: 37 Komintern Street, Flat

#27, Petrodvorets, St. Petersburg, 198903. 427–2469 (home).

Andrianov, Nikolay Yefimovich

POSITION: Former Gymnastics Champion; Senior Coach of the CIS National Gymnastics Team
BIRTHPLACE/DATE: Vladimir, Russian Federation, 1952
NATIONALITY: Russian
EDUCATION: Graduated from the Vladimir Institute of Physical Education.
CAREER: Many-time European and World Gymnastics Champion. Champion of the Summer Olympics of 1972 (Gold Medal), 1976 (four Gold Medals), and 1980 (two Gold Medals). From 1982 to 1992, Senior Coach of the USSR National Gymnastics Team. From 1992, Senior Coach of the CIS National Gymnastics Team.
HONORS/AWARDS: USSR Honored Master of Sports and Honored Coach; Order of Lenin; Order of the Red Banner of Labor; Order of the Badge of Honor.
FAMILY: Married with two children.
ADDRESS/TELEPHONE: 34 Frunze Street, Flat #4, Vladimir. 201–0272 (Gymnastics Federation).

Andronov, Iona Ionovich

POSITION: Deputy Chairman of the Russian Federation Supreme Soviet Commission for Foreign Affairs and International Economic Relations; Counsellor to the Russian Federation Vice President for Foreign Affairs; member of the Council of Nationalities
BIRTHPLACE/DATE: 1934
NATIONALITY: Russian
CAREER: Correspondent for *Literaturnaya Gazeta* (*Literary Newspaper*); Russian Federation People's Deputy; member of the Grazhdanskoye Obschestvo (Civic Society) Group. Member of the Communist Party to August 1991.
TELEPHONE: 205–4269 (office).

Andropov, Igor Yuryevich

POSITION: Ambassador at Large; Ambassador Extraordinary and Plenipotentiary
BIRTHPLACE/DATE: Ludgok, Karelia
NATIONALITY: Russian
EDUCATION: Graduated from the Moscow State Institute of International Relations in 1969.
CAREER: From 1960 to 1962, Junior Laboratory Assistant. From 1969, Translator at the Central Committee's Institute of Public Science. From 1970 to 1974, Junior, then Senior Researcher at the Institute of the U.S. and Canada. From 1974 to 1978, Senior Lecturer at the Diplomatic Academy of the USSR Foreign Ministry. From 1978 to 1981, Senior Counsellor of the Foreign Policy Planning Department of the USSR Foreign Ministry; from 1981 to 1986, Chief Counsellor. From 1984 to 1986, Ambassador to Greece. From 1986 to 1992, Ambassador at Large of the Russian Foreign Ministry's Group of Ambassadors at Large.
HONORS/AWARDS: Order of the Badge of Honor.
FAMILY: Married with two children.
TELEPHONE: 244–2063 (office).

Anisimov, Stanilsav Vasilyevich

POSITION: Former Russian Federation Minister of Trade and Resources
BIRTHPLACE/DATE: Suvorovo village, Nikolayev region, 1940
CAREER: From 1957 to 1960, worked at the Nikolaev Pipe Factory; from 1960 to 1962, Engineer. From 1967 to 1968, Senior Engineer of the Organizational Department; from 1968 to 1970, Sector Head for the Production of Non-Rusting Pipes. From 1970 to 1973, Department Head of the Ukrainian State Supplying Committee. From 1973 to 1978, Department Head of the USSR State Supplying Committee. From 1978 to 1982, Instructor of the Central Committee's Department of Planning and Finance. From 1982 to 1988, Instructor of the Central Committee's Economic Department. From 1988 to 1990, Deputy Chairman of the USSR State Committee of Supplies; from 1990 to 1991, First Deputy Chairman. November 1991 to September 1992, Russian Federation Minister of Trade and Resources.
FAMILY: Married with two children.
TELEPHONE: 205–0178 (office).

Anpilov, Victor Ivanovich

POSITION: Editor-Publisher of *Molniya* (*Lightning*) newspaper; Executive Committee Chairman of the Trudovaya Rossiya (Working Russia) Movement
BIRTHPLACE/DATE: Kuban, 1946

EDUCATION: Studied at a vocational school in Taganrog and studied journalism at Moscow State University.
CAREER: From 1960, worked at the Taganrog Combine Plant, served in the army, worked for a newspaper. Correspondent in Cuba. In 1985, USSR Television and Radio Correspondent in Nicaragua. Left USSR Television and Radio to begin political activity: published a newspaper, became a leader of the Communist Movement. From 1991, Secretary of the Russian Communist Labor Party.
ADDRESS/TELEPHONE: 36 Zorge Street, Moscow. 924–6218 (office).

Antonov, Guryan Vasilyevich (Gennadi)
POSITION: Head of the Old Orthodox Archdiocese; Archbishop of Novozybkov, Moscow and All Russia
BIRTHPLACE/DATE: Bokla village, Bashkiria, March 15, 1903
NATIONALITY: Russian
CAREER: From 1958 to 1979, Deacon of the Buguruslan, then the Ufa Old Believers' Community.
ADDRESS/TELEPHONE: 28 Nekrasov Street, Bryansk region, Novozybkov. 3–1910.

Arbatov, Aleksandr Arkadyevich
POSITION: Deputy Chairman of the Russian Academy of Sciences' Commission for the Study of Production Forces and Natural Resources; member of the Supreme Economic Council of the Russian Federation Supreme Soviet Presidium; Vice President of the International Academy of Environmental Reconstruction
BIRTHPLACE/DATE: Moscow, 1938
NATIONALITY: Russian
EDUCATION: Graduated in 1960 from the Gubkin Institute of Oil and Gas in Moscow; in 1966, defended a thesis; in 1980, defended thesis for doctoral degree. Doctor of Mineralogy; Doctor of Economics; Professor. Speaks English.
CAREER: From 1968 to 1970, member of the Afghanistan Union of Oil Miners. From 1962 to 1976, worked at the All-Union Oil Research Institute of the USSR Ministry of Geology. In 1976, Laboratory Head. From 1983 and 1991, member of the State Economic Commission of the USSR State Planning Committee. From 1990, International Council Member of the Global Power Engineering Studies Center.
FAMILY: Married with a son and a daughter.
ADDRESS/TELEPHONE: 26 Maronovsky Pereulok, Moscow. 238–2188 (office).

Arbatov, Georgy Arkadyevich
POSITION: Director of the Russian Academy of Sciences' Institute of the U.S. and Canada; member of the Russian President's Political Consultative Council
BIRTHPLACE/DATE: Kherson, Ukraine, May 19, 1923
NATIONALITY: Russian
EDUCATION: Graduated in 1949 from the Moscow State Institute of International Relations with a degree in International Law and International Relations. Doctor of Juridical Sciences (1955); Doctor of History (1966); Professor (1970). Academician of the Russian Academy of Sciences.
CAREER: Took part in World War II. From 1949 to 1962, contributed works on international relations issues to the magazines *Voprosy Filosofii* (*Questions of Philosophy*), *Novoye Vremya* (*New Time*), *Kommunist*, *World Marxist Review* (Prague). Joined the Communist Party in 1943. From 1962 to 1964, Ideology Section Head at the Institute of the World Economy and International Relations of the USSR Academy of Sciences. From 1964 to 1967, Central Committee Functionary. From 1967, Director of the Institute of the U.S. and Canada of the USSR (now Russian) Academy of Sciences. From 1970 to 1974, Corresponding Member of the USSR Academy of Sciences' Department of Economics. From 1970 to 1989, Editorial Board Member of *SShA: Ekonomika, Politika, Ideologiya* (*USA: Economics, Politics, Ideology*) journal. From 1971 and 1976, member of the Communist Party Central Auditing Commission. From 1974 to 1989, member of the Foreign Affairs Commission of the USSR Supreme Soviet Council of Nationalities. From 1974, Academician of the USSR Academy of Sciences' Department of Economics. Since 1988, Presidium Member of the USSR Academy of Sciences. Elected USSR People's Deputy. From 1976 to 1981, Alternate Member, and from 1981 to August 1991, Full Member of the Central Committee. From 1980 to 1988, member of the Independent Commission for

Disarmament and Security Issues (Palme Commission). From 1984 to 1989, Bureau Member of the USSR Parliamentary Group Committee. From 1985, Deputy Chairman, Chairman of the USSR UN Association. From 1988 to 1990, member of the Central Committee's Commission for International Policy. From March 1992, member of the Russian President's Political Consultative Council.
MAJOR WORKS: Authored a number of works in the field of world economy and international relations, notably on current Russian-American relations.
HONORS/AWARDS: Order of the Red Star (1943); Order of the Badge of Honor (1962); two Orders of Lenin (1975, 1983); Order of the October Revolution (1971); Orders of the Red Banner of Labor (1967, 1983); Order of the Great Patriotic War, First Grade (1985); Prize of Lenin (1975, 1983); medals.
FAMILY: Married with a son.
ADDRESS/TELEPHONE: 2/3 Khlebny Pereulok, Moscow G–69, 121814.

Arifdzhanov, Rustam Mustafayevich
POSITION: Editor in Chief of *Megapolis-Metro* newspaper
BIRTHPLACE/DATE: Samarkand, 1958
EDUCATION: Graduated in 1980 from the History Department of Azerbaijan State University. Speaks English, Turkish, and Azerbaijani.
CAREER: From 1975 to 1982, Correspondent, Deputy Managing Editor of *Molodezh Azerbaidjana* (*Youth of Azerbaijan*) newspaper. From 1981 to 1985, Special Correspondent, Head of the Culture, Science, and Education Department of the Baku newspaper. From 1985 to 1989, Tyumen Region Correspondent for *Komsomolskaya Pravda* daily. From 1989 to 1991, Editorial Board Member and Editor of *Sobesednik* (*Conversation Companion*) weekly. In 1991, History Department Head of *Megapolis* magazine.
FAMILY: Married with a child.
ADDRESS/TELEPHONE: 21 Stankevich Street, Moscow, 103032. 292–3975 (office).

Arkanov, Arkady Mikhailovich
POSITION: Writer; member of the Writers' Union
BIRTHPLACE/DATE: Kiev, 1933
EDUCATION: Graduated in 1957 from the First Moscow Sechenov Medical Institute.
CAREER: Worked for three years as a General Practitioner. Simultaneously took up literary work. From 1968, member of the Writers' Union.
MAJOR WORKS: Plays (co-authored with Gorin): *All-Europe Wedding* (1966); *The Banquet* (1969); *Small Tragedies of a Big House* (1973). Books: *A Crooked Chin* (1975); *There Are Plenty of Worlds in This World* (1984); *All* (1990).
FAMILY: Married with two children.
ADDRESS/TELEPHONE: 13 Komsomolsky Prospekt, Moscow, 119807. 241–4756 (home).

Arkayev, Leonid Yakovlevich
POSITION: Chief Coach of the CIS National Gymnastics Team
BIRTHPLACE/DATE: Moscow, 1940
NATIONALITY: Russian
EDUCATION: Graduated in 1972 from the Kuibyshev Construction Engineering Institute in Moscow; in 1982, from the Moscow Region State Institute of Physical Education.
CAREER: Coach of the gymnastic teams of Trud (Labor), Burevestnik (Stormy Petrel), and the USSR Sports Committee. To 1992, Chief of the Gymnastics Directorate of the USSR State Committee for Sports. Chief Coach of the USSR Gymnastics National Team.
HONORS/AWARDS: USSR Master of Sports (gymnastics); USSR Honored Coach; Order of Lenin; Order of the Red Banner of Labor; Order of the Badge of Honor.
FAMILY: Married with two daughters.
ADDRESS/TELEPHONE: 8 Luzhnetskaya Naberezhnaya, Moscow, 119871. 201–0272 (Gymnastics Federation).

Arkhipov, Vladimir Mikhailovich
POSITION: Retired Armed Forces General
BIRTHPLACE/DATE: Stanitsa village, Chelkar, Aktubinsk region, 1933
NATIONALITY: Russian
CAREER: From 1952, member of the Armed Forces: Division Commander, Corps Commander, Army Commander, Military District Army Commander. From 1988 to 1991, Deputy Defense Minister.
FAMILY: Married with two sons.

ADDRESS/TELEPHONE: 10 Olympysky Prospekt, Building 3, Moscow, 129090. 281–1956 (home).

Arkhipova, Irina Konstantinovna

POSITION: Opera Singer (mezzo-soprano) of the Bolshoi Theater
BIRTHPLACE/DATE: Moscow, 1925
EDUCATION: Graduated from the Moscow Conservatory.
CAREER: From 1954 to 1956, Soloist of the Sverdlovsk Opera and Ballet Theater. From 1956, Soloist of the Bolshoi Theater. Major artist of the Soviet school of vocalism. From 1986, Chairwoman of the All-Union Musical Society Board. From 1976, Teacher at the Moscow Conservatory; from 1982, Professor.
MAJOR WORKS: Parts include: Carmen; Amneris; Marfa (*Khovanshchina* by Mussorgsky); Lyubasha (*The Tsar's Bride* by Rimsky-Korsakov). First Bolshoi performer to sing numerous parts by Soviet composers: Elen (*War and Peace* by Sergei Prokofyev, 1959); Commissar (*The Optimistic Tragedy* by Kholminov, 1967).
HONORS/AWARDS: USSR People's Artist; Hero of Socialist Labor; Prize of Lenin.
FAMILY: Married with a son and a grandson.
ADDRESS/TELEPHONE: 13 Herzen Street, Moscow, 103871. 229–4307 (home).

Arnoldov, Arnold Isayevich

POSITION: Head of the Problem Group for the Theory of Culture at the Russian Academy of Sciences' Institute of Philosophy; Professor of the Department of Theory and the History of Culture at the Moscow State Institute of Culture
BIRTHPLACE/DATE: Moscow, 1915
EDUCATION: Graduated in 1940 from the Lenin Teachers' Training Institute in Moscow. Doctor of Philosophy. Speaks English.
CAREER: From 1945 to 1947, Correspondent for Soviet Informburo news agency. From 1949 to 1951, Head of the Science Department of *Literaturnaya Gazeta* (*Literary Newspaper*) weekly. From 1950 to 1970, Researcher at the USSR Academy of Sciences' Institute of Philosophy. From 1970 to 1990, Section Head for Philosophical Problems of Culture at the USSR Academy of Sciences' Institute of Philosophy. Since 1990, Head of the Problem Group for the Theory of Culture at the Russian Academy of Sciences' Institute of Philosophy. Professor of the Department of Theory and History of Culture at the Moscow State Institute of Culture. Executive Committee Member of the European Cultural Society (Hungary), Board Member of the All-Russia Philosophy Society, Editorial Board Member of *Knizhnoye Obozreniye* (*Book Review*) weekly.
MAJOR WORKS: Author of over 300 scientific papers, ten monographs, various booklets and articles. Major research directions: elaboration of theory of culture and culturology, spiritual development regularities, study of international cultural cooperation tendencies. Monographs: *Culture and Contemporaneity*; *Culture and Man*; *Mode of Life and Culture*.
HONORS/AWARDS: Russian Federation Honored Worker of Science; Order of the Great Patriotic War; twelve combat awards.
FAMILY: Married with a daughter.
ADDRESS/TELEPHONE: 4-A Chernyakhovsky Street, Flat #53, Moscow 125319. 203–5855 (office); 151–3930 (home).

Artamonov, Vyacheslav Yuryevich

POSITION: Director-General of the Elephant Broker Company
BIRTHPLACE/DATE: Moscow, 1957
EDUCATION: Graduated in 1980 from the Moscow Power Engineering Institute. Doctor of Technology. Speaks French.
CAREER: From 1980 to 1990, Lecturer of the Electromechanics Department at the Moscow Power Engineering Institute. From 1990 to September 1991, Director of the Elmeck Innovation Center.
FAMILY: Married with a daughter.
ADDRESS/TELEPHONE: 14 Energeticheskaya Street, Moscow. 362–7271 (office).

Arutyunyan, Vladimir Arutyunovich

POSITION: Director-General of the Soyuzneftexport (Oil Export) Association
BIRTHPLACE/DATE: 1938
NATIONALITY: Armenian
EDUCATION: Graduated in 1961 from the Moscow State Institute of International Relations.
CAREER: From 1965 to 1967, worked at Soyuzneftexport and the Nafta Company, Ltd. in the

United Kingdom. From 1974 to 1981, Office Director of Soyuzneftexport, Director-General of the Nafta Company, Ltd., Deputy Director-General of Soyuzneftexport.
FAMILY: Married with four children.
ADDRESS/TELEPHONE: 32/34 Smolenskaya-Sennaya Square, Moscow. 253–9498 (office).

Askerov, Eldar Aga-Yusuf Ogly
POSITION: Board Chairman of the Culture and Art Association of the Revival of Russia's Social Development Foundation
BIRTHPLACE/DATE: Baku, 1960
NATIONALITY: Azerbaijanian
EDUCATION: Graduated in 1982 from the Maurice Thorez Teachers' Training Institute of Foreign Languages in Moscow.
CAREER: From 1983 to 1985, Editor of *Za Rubezhom* (*Abroad*) weekly. From 1985 to 1988, Special Correspondent for *Sovietsky Ekran* (*Soviet Screen*) magazine. From 1988 to 1991, News Analyst of *Soviet Union* journal. Member of the Russian Federation Journalists' Union. Advocates private property, free enterprise, and the revival of Russian historical and creative traditions of culture and art.
FAMILY: Divorced with a son.
ADDRESS/TELEPHONE: 7 Profsoyuznaya Street, Flat #164, Moscow. 205–4376 (office).

Aslakhanov, Aslanbek Akhmedovich
POSITION: Chairman of the Russian Federation Supreme Soviet Committee for Legality, Law and Order, and Combatting Crime
BIRTHPLACE/DATE: Novy Atagi village, Shalinsky district, Chechen-Ingushia, March 11, 1942
NATIONALITY: Chechen
EDUCATION: Graduated in 1965 from the Grozny Teachers' Training Institute; in 1971, from the Grozny Law Institute; in 1975, from the Grozny Economics Institute; in 1981, from the Academy of the USSR Ministry of Internal Affairs. Doctor of Law.
CAREER: From 1959 to 1961, Worker, Asphalt-Layer, Team Leader. From 1962 to 1965, served in the army. From 1965 to 1967, Lecturer at the Mining Institute. From 1967 to 1975, Operational Agent, Senior Operational Agent, Economic Crime Service Chief of the Grozny Ministry of Internal Affairs. From 1975 to 1979, Deputy Chairman of the Dynamo Sports Club Regional Council, Police Department Chief, Deputy Head of the Criminal Investigation Department of the USSR Ministry of Internal Affairs Directorate at the Baikal-Amur Railway Construction. From 1981 to 1989, Senior Inspector at Large, Deputy Department Head, Department Head, Chief Inspector of the USSR Ministry of Internal Affairs. Russian Federation People's Deputy. Member of the Sovereignty and Equality Faction.
FAMILY: Married with two children.
ADDRESS/TELEPHONE: 12 Rublevskoye Chaussée, Building 1, Flat #98, Moscow (home); 2 Krasnopresnenskaya Nabereznaya, Moscow (office). 205–9448 (office); 415–9869 (home).

Astafyev, Mikhail Georgyevich
POSITION: Member of the Russian Federation Supreme Soviet Committee for Freedom of Conscience, Faith, Mercy and Charity; Chairman of the Constitutional Democrats Party; Co-Chairman of the Russian People's Front
BIRTHPLACE/DATE: Moscow, September 16, 1946
NATIONALITY: Russian
EDUCATION: Graduated in 1970 from the Physics Department at Moscow State University. Speaks English.
CAREER: From 1970 to 1972, served in the army. From 1972 to 1990, worked at the USSR Academy of Sciences' Institute of Physical Chemistry.
FAMILY: Married.
ADDRESS/TELEPHONE: 76 Prospekt Mira, Flat #34, Moscow, 129041. 204–6618 (home).

Astakhov, Yevgeni Mikhailovich
POSITION: Russian Federation Ambassador to Nicaragua; Ambassador Extraordinary and Plenipotentiary
BIRTHPLACE/DATE: Moscow, 1937
NATIONALITY: Russian
EDUCATION: Studied at the Tashkent Teachers' Training Institute from 1954 to 1959. From 1959 to 1963, studied at the Moscow State Institute of International Relations. From 1975 to 1977, student at the Diplomatic Academy of the USSR Foreign Ministry. Doctor of History.
CAREER: From 1963 to 1964, Aide on Duty at

the USSR Embassy in Brazil. In 1965, Aide-Trainee at the USSR Embassy in Brazil; from 1965 to 1968, Attaché at the USSR Embassy in Brazil; from 1968 to 1969, Third Secretary at the USSR Embassy in Brazil. From 1969 to 1971, Third Secretary of the Department of Latin America of the USSR Foreign Ministry. From 1971 to 1973, Second Secretary at the USSR Embassy in Brazil; from 1973 to 1975, First Secretary at the USSR Embassy in Brazil. From 1977 to 1978, First Secretary of the First European Department of the USSR Foreign Ministry. From 1978 to 1980, First Secretary at the USSR Embassy in Spain; from 1980 to 1985, Counsellor at the USSR Embassy in Spain. From 1985 to 1987, Division Head of the First European Department; from 1987 to 1990, Deputy Head of the First European Department.
FAMILY: Married with a daughter.
TELEPHONE: 74–153 (Managua); 244–3906 (Moscow).

Atamalyev, Farkhd Mutalib Ogly
POSITION: Editor in Chief of *Oriental Express* magazine
BIRTHPLACE/DATE: Baku, 1946
NATIONALITY: Azerbaijanian
EDUCATION: From 1969, studied at Baku University and the State Institute of Cinematography.
CAREER: From 1977 to 1978, worked for *Sovietsky Ekran* (*Soviet Screen*) magazine. From 1978 to 1987, Correspondent for *Sovietskaya Kultura* (*Soviet Culture*) newspaper. From 1987 to 1990, Department Head of *Sovietsky Muzey* (*Soviet Museum*) magazine. From January 1991, Editor in Chief of *Panorama Azerbaijana* (*Panorama of Azerbaijan*) newspaper.
FAMILY: Married with two children.
ADDRESS/TELEPHONE: 18 G. Kurina Street, #26, Moscow, 121108. 144–1592 (home); 229–0675 (office).

Avdeyev, Aleksandr Alekseyevich
POSITION: Russian Federation Ambassador to Bulgaria; Ambassador Extraordinary and Plenipotentiary
BIRTHPLACE: Kremenchug, Poltava region, 1946
NATIONALITY: Russian
EDUCATION: Graduated from the Moscow State Institute of International Relations in 1968.
CAREER: From 1968 to 1971, Senior Aide-Secretary at the USSR Consulate-General in Annabe. In 1971, Senior Aide-Secretary at the USSR Embassy in Algeria; from 1971 to 1973, Attaché. From 1973 to 1974, Attaché of the First African Department of the USSR Foreign Ministry. From 1974 to 1976, Third Secretary of the Secretariat of the Deputy Foreign Minister; from 1976 to 1977, Second Secretary. From 1977 to 1981, Second Secretary at the USSR Embassy in France; from 1981 to 1985, First Secretary. From 1985 to 1986, Counsellor of the First European Department; from 1986 to 1987, Division Head of the First European Department. From 1987 to 1990, Ambassador to Luxembourg. From 1991 to 1992, Deputy Minister of Foreign Relations. In 1991, Ambassador at Large.
FAMILY: Married with a son.
TELEPHONE: 66–8836 (Sofia); 244–2281 (Moscow).

Avdeyev, Vadim Borisovich
POSITION: General Manager of the All-Russia Real Estate Exchange
BIRTHPLACE/DATE: Moscow, 1958
NATIONALITY: Russian
EDUCATION: Graduated in 1981 from the Moscow Institute of Engineering and Physics.
CAREER: From 1981 to 1988, Engineer of the Ministry of General Mechanical Engineering. From 1988 to 1990, Section Head of the Youth Center of the City Komsomol Committee. From 1990 to 1991, Assistant Sales Manager of the All-Russia Exchange Center.
FAMILY: Married with a daughter.
ADDRESS/TELEPHONE: 8 Yaroslavskaya Street, Building 3, Moscow. 217–6009 (office).

Aven, Pyotr Olegovich
POSITION: Russian Federation Minister of Foreign Economic Relations; Deputy Chairman of the Monetary-Economic Commission of the Russian Federation Government
BIRTHPLACE/DATE: Moscow, 1955
NATIONALITY: Lett
EDUCATION: Graduated in 1977 from Moscow State University. Doctor of Economics. Good command of English and Spanish.
CAREER: From 1981 to 1988, Junior, then Se-

nior Researcher at the USSR Academy of Sciences' All-Union Systems Research Institute. From 1989 to 1991, Counsellor of the USSR Ministry of Foreign Affairs and leading researcher at the Austria-based International Institute for Applied Systems Analysis. From November 1991, Chairman of the Russian Federation Foreign Ministry's Committee for Foreign Economic Relations; Russian Federation First Deputy Minister of Foreign Affairs.
FAMILY: Married.
ADDRESS/TELEPHONE: 32/34 Smolenskaya-Sennaya Square, Moscow. 244–2450 (office).

Averbakh, Yuri Lvovich
POSITION: International Chess Grand Master; First Deputy Chairman of the Chess Federation; Editor in Chief of *Shakhmatny Vestnik* (*Chess Herald*) weekly
BIRTHPLACE/DATE: Kaluga, 1922
EDUCATION: Graduated in 1945 from the Moscow Higher Technical School. Speaks English and German.
CAREER: From 1945 to 1950, Junior Researcher at the Research Institute of the Ministry of Aviation Industry. From 1950 to 1962, Chess Coach of the Zenit Sports Society. From 1962 to present, Editor in Chief of *Shakhmatny Vestnik*. From 1962 to 1972, Deputy Chairman of the USSR Chess Federation. From 1972 to 1977, Chairman of the USSR Chess Federation. From 1977 to present, First Deputy Chairman of the Chess Federation. Russian Federation delegate to FIDE (International Chess Federation).
MAJOR WORKS: Author of over forty books on chess theory.
HONORS/AWARDS: Honored Master of Sports (chess).
FAMILY: Married with a daughter.
ADDRESS/TELEPHONE: 19-A Gogolevsky Boulevard, Building 1, Flat #45, Moscow, 121019. 245–5697 (home).

Averina (Barabash), Tatyana Borisovna
POSITION: Former Olympic Track Champion; Physical Education Instructor at Moscow State University
BIRTHPLACE/DATE: Nizhny Novgorod, 1950
NATIONALITY: Russian
EDUCATION: Graduated in 1986 from the Leningrad State Physical Education Institute; and from the Shvernik Higher School of Trade Union Movement.
CAREER: Champion of the 1976 Winter Olympics (1000- and 3000-meter races); and Finalist (1500- and 500-meter races). 1978 World Champion (1000- and 1500-meters). 1980 World Sprint Champion. From 1985 to 1987, Sports Instructor of the Burevestnik (Stormy Petrel) and Trade Union Sports Societies. From 1987, Instructor of Moscow State University's Physical Education Department.
HONORS/AWARDS: USSR Honored Master of Sports.
FAMILY: Married with two children.
ADDRESS/TELEPHONE: 6 Academician Yangel Street, Flat #71, Moscow. 201–0322 (office); 386–1010 (home).

Averintsev, Sergey Sergeyevich
POSITION: Head of the Ancient Literature Department at the Gorky Institute of World Literature of the Russian Academy of Sciences
BIRTHPLACE/DATE: Moscow, 1937
EDUCATION: Graduated in 1961 from the Philology Department, and in 1964, from the postgraduate course at Moscow University. Doctor of Philology.
CAREER: From 1965 to 1966, Editor of Mysl (Idea) Publishers. From 1966 to 1969, Researcher at the Institute of History of the Arts of the USSR Ministry of Culture. From 1969, Head of the Ancient Literature Department at the Gorky Institute of World Literature. History of World Culture Division Lecturer of the Philosophy Department at Moscow State University. From 1989, member of the UNESCO International Commission on Culture. Elected USSR People's Deputy, member of the USSR Supreme Soviet. From 1987, Corresponding Member of the USSR Academy of Sciences. Corresponding Member of the Russian Academy of Sciences from December 1991. Member of the Russian Federation Writers' Union.
MAJOR WORKS: *Plutarch and Ancient Biography: On the Place of the Classical Scholar* (1973); *Poetics of Early Byzantine Literature* (1977); *From Bosphorus to Euphrates* (1987); *An Attempt to Comment: A Talk on Culture* (1988). Authored

a number of articles in *Myths of the Peoples of the World* philosophical encyclopedia.
HONORS/AWARDS: USSR State Prize (1990).
FAMILY: Married with two children.
ADDRESS/TELEPHONE: 25-A Vorovsky Street, Moscow, 121069. 258–4564 (office).

Avraamov, Dmitri Sergeyevich
POSITION: Editor in Chief of *Zhurnalist* (*Journalist*) magazine
BIRTHPLACE/DATE: Moscow, 1932
EDUCATION: Graduated in 1955 from the Philosophy Department at Moscow State University. Doctor of Philosophy.
CAREER: From 1962 to 1963, Consultant to *Pravda* (*Truth*) newspaper. From 1963 to 1972, Editor in Chief of *Molodoy Kommunist* (*Young Communist*) magazine. From 1972 to 1989, Deputy Chief Editor of *Zhurnalist*. Professional Ethics Lecturer of the Journalism Department at Moscow State University. Chairman of the Council for Professional Ethics of the Confederation of Journalists' Unions.
MAJOR WORKS: Works in the field of professional ethics in journalism.
FAMILY: Married with a daughter and a grandson.
ADDRESS/TELEPHONE: 14 Bumazhny Proyezd, Moscow, 101453. 212–2589; 212–2058 (office).

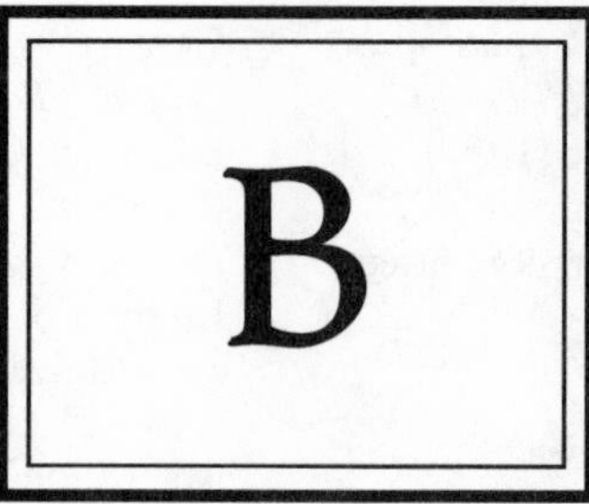

Baburin, Sergey Nikolayevich

POSITION: Russian Federation People's Deputy; member of the Russian Supreme Soviet; Leader of the Rossiya Parliamentary Faction; Board Chairman of the Russian People's Union

BIRTHPLACE/DATE: Semipalatinsk, 1959

EDUCATION: Graduated from the Law Department at Omsk State University.

CAREER: Dean of the Law Department at Omsk State University. From October 1991, Executive Secretary of the Organizational Committee of the Russian People's Union.

FAMILY: Married with three sons.

ADDRESS/TELEPHONE: 2 Krasnopresnenskaya Naberezhnaya, Moscow, 103274. 205–8180 (office).

Babynin, Igor Vladimirovich

POSITION: Director of the Informatica Research Center; Counsellor, First Grade

BIRTHPLACE/DATE: Tula, 1939

NATIONALITY: Russian

EDUCATION: Graduated from Moscow State University in 1966.

CAREER: From 1957 to 1958, Assistant Foreman at the Kirov Plant in Tula. From 1958 to 1961, served in the army. From 1966 to 1971, Junior, then Senior Researcher at the Economic Research Institute of the USSR State Planning Committee. From 1971 to 1978, Expert, Acting Department Head of the Coordinating Center of the Inter-Government Commission to Regulate the Cooperation of Socialist Countries. From 1978 to 1983, Deputy Head of the All-Union Technological Research Institute of the USSR Central Statistic Committee. From 1983 to 1986, Head of the All-Union National Mechanization of the Economy Research Institute. From 1986 to 1988, Board Head and Collegium Member of the USSR State Committee on Computation. From 1988, Director of the Informatica Research Center of the USSR (now Russian) Ministry of Foreign Affairs.

FAMILY: Married with two children.

TELEPHONE: 246–0769 (office).

Badmayev, Sanal Alekseyevich

POSITION: Russian Federation Deputy Minister of Education; member of the Supreme Soviet Committee for National Education; member of the Council of Nationalities; member of the Constitutional Committee

BIRTHPLACE/DATE: Prdjevalsk, Kirghizia (Kirgistan), 1948

NATIONALITY: Kalmyk

CAREER: From 1974 to 1976, Schoolteacher. From 1976 to 1979, School Principal. From 1979 to 1985, City Educational Committee Head. From 1985 to 1988, Instructor of the Regional Party Committee. From 1988 to 1990, Minister of National Education in Kalmykia. From 1990 to 1991, Deputy Chairman of the Russian Federation Committee for Science and National Education. From 1991, Russian Federation Deputy Minister of Education; Russian Federation People's Deputy. To August 1991, member of the Communist Party.

FAMILY: Married with two children.

ADDRESS/TELEPHONE: 2 Krasnopresnenskaya Naberezhnaya, Moscow; 6 Chistoprudny Boulevard, Moscow. 299–4960 (office).

Baidak, Valentin Ivanovich
POSITION: Trade Minister of Byelorussia
BIRTHPLACE/DATE: Minsk region, 1952
NATIONALITY: Byelorussian
CAREER: Worked from Sales Assistant to Head of the Municipal Trade Department in Minsk.
FAMILY: Single.
ADDRESS/TELEPHONE: 8 Kirov Street, #1, Minsk, 220050. 27–6121; 27–4802 (office).

Bakatin, Vadim Victorovich
POSITION: Former Chairman of the Inter-Republican Security Council
BIRTHPLACE/DATE: Kiselevsk, Kemerovo region, November 6, 1937
NATIONALITY: Russian
EDUCATION: Graduated in 1960 from the Novosibirsk Kuibyshev Civil Engineering Institute and from the Central Committee's Academy of Social Sciences.
CAREER: From 1960, Foreman, Superintendent, Section Head, Chief Engineer, and Construction Administration Head; Chief Engineer of a house-building factory in Kemerovo. From 1973, Communist Party Functionary, Second Secretary of the City Committee, Department Head, Secretary, and First Secretary of the Communist Party Regional Committee. From 1988 to 1990, USSR Minister of Internal Affairs. From 1990 to December 1991, member of the USSR President's Political Consultative Council. In 1991, member of the USSR Security Council. From August 1991 to January 1992, Chairman of the USSR KGB.
HONORS/AWARDS: Order of Lenin (1987).
FAMILY: Married.
TELEPHONE: 224–5097.

Bakirov, Ernest Aleksandrovich
POSITION: Director-General of the Moscow Mayor's Administration
BIRTHPLACE/DATE: Nizhny Novgorod (formerly Gorky), 1930
EDUCATION: Graduated in 1953 from the Geological Prospecting Department of the Moscow Gubkin Oil and Gas Institute. Doctor of Geology and Mineralogy; Professor.
CAREER: Researcher for geological expeditions; Lecturer, Deputy Dean, Dean of the Geological Department of the Gubkin Oil and Gas Institute. From 1978, Head of the Department of Oil and Gas Prospecting and Research Theory of the Gubkin Oil and Gas Institute. From 1991, Mossoviet (Moscow Council) Deputy Chairman.
MAJOR WORKS: More than 100 scientific papers, four monographs, and five textbooks.
FAMILY: Married with three sons.
ADDRESS/TELEPHONE: 13 Tverskaya Street, Moscow, 103032. 290–7391 (office).

Baklanov, Anatoli Semyonovich
POSITION: President of the Krestyanskaya Tsentralnaya Birzha (Farmers' Central Exchange) Joint-Stock Company
BIRTHPLACE/DATE: Pavlodar, Tselinograd region, 1930
NATIONALITY: Russian
EDUCATION: Graduated in 1957 from the Odessa Merchant Marine Engineering Institute; in 1979, from the Moscow Physical Engineering Institute. Doctor of Technology. Good command of English.
CAREER: From 1954, Foreman, Superintendent, Department Head of a Murmansk enterprise. From 1985, Head of the Management Division of the Moscow Physical Engineering Institute. In 1991, set up the Usluga–2 (Service–2) Research and Production Association.
FAMILY: Married with four children.
ADDRESS/TELEPHONE: 1 Pervy Institutsky Proyezd, Moscow. 188–8260 (office).

Baklanov, Grigory Yakovlevich
POSITION: Editor in Chief of *Znamya* (*Banner*) magazine
BIRTHPLACE/DATE: Voronezh, 1923
NATIONALITY: Russian
EDUCATION: Graduated in 1950 from the Gorky Literary Institute.
CAREER: Author of novels and stories about the Great Patriotic War (1941–1945), and numerous articles, essays, film scripts, and short stories. Former Board Secretary of the USSR Writers' Union. From 1986, Editor in Chief of *Znamya*. In 1991, left the Communist Party. Co-Chairman of the Writers' Union.
MAJOR WORKS: Novels: *An Inch of Land*; *The Dead Are Not Put to Shame*; *Nineteen-Year-Olds*

Forever; *July 1941*. Stories: *Friends*; *The Youngest Brother*; *One of Us*.
HONORS/AWARDS: USSR State Prize.
FAMILY: Married with two children.
ADDRESS/TELEPHONE: 8/1 25 Oktyabrya Street, Moscow, 103863. 924–1346; 291–6374.

Baklanov, Mikhail Grigoryevich
POSITION: Former Editor in Chief of *Sputnik* (*Companion*) magazine
BIRTHPLACE/DATE: Moscow, 1955
CAREER: From 1978 to 1984, Editor, then Chief Editor of Novosti Press Agency (APN). From 1984 to 1985, Correspondent in Nicaragua. From 1985 to 1989, Information Bureau Head in Panama. From 1989, Senior Editor of Novosti Press Agency in Latin America. From 1990 to December 1991, Editor in Chief of *Sputnik*; member of the USSR Journalists' Union. From December 1991, member of the Confederation of Journalists' Unions.
MAJOR WORKS: Author of books and articles about Latin American countries.
FAMILY: Married with a son.

Baklanov, Oleg Dmitrievich
POSITION: Former Deputy Chairman of the USSR Presidential Defense Council
BIRTHPLACE/DATE: Kharkov, March 17, 1932
NATIONALITY: Ukrainian
EDUCATION: Graduated in 1958 from the All-Union Power Engineering Institute (correspondence courses). Doctor of Technology.
CAREER: From 1950 to 1963, Fitter, Tuner, Master, Deputy Shop Superintendent, Shop Superintendent, Deputy Chief Engineer at a military plant in Kharkov. In 1953, joined the Communist Party. From 1963 to 1975, Chief Engineer of the Kharkov Instrument Plant. From 1975 to 1976, General Director of the USSR Ministry of General Mechanical Engineering Production. From 1976 to 1981, USSR Deputy, then USSR First Deputy Minister of General Mechanical Engineering. From April 1983 to 1988, USSR Minister of General Mechanical Engineering. From 1986, member of the Central Committee. From February 1988 to April 1990, Central Committee Secretary of the Military-Industrial Complex. From April 1991, Deputy Chairman of the USSR Presidential Defense Council. In August 1991, arrested for taking part in the attempted coup (one of the eight members of the State of Emergency Committee).
HONORS/AWARDS: Hero of Socialist Labor; Order of Lenin; Order of the October Revolution; two Orders of the Red Banner of Labor; Order of the Badge of Honor; Prize of Lenin; medals.
FAMILY: Married with a son and a granddaughter.
TELEPHONE: 229–4662 (Russian Federation Procurator's Office).

Balabanov, Yuri Sevostyanovich
POSITION: Russian Federation Ambassador to the Central African Republic; Counsellor Extraordinary and Plenipotentiary, First Grade
BIRTHPLACE/DATE: Zalesovo village, Altai, 1937
EDUCATION: Graduated from the Novosibirsk Agricultural Institute in 1960. From 1969 to 1971, student at the Higher Party School. From 1976 to 1979, student at the USSR Diplomatic Academy.
CAREER: From 1960 to 1962, Mechanic, Auditor-Mechanic, Senior Engineer of the State Farm. From 1962 to 1964, First Secretary of the District Komsomol Committee, then of the Regional Komsomol Committee; Deputy Head of the Agricultural Department of the Regional Komsomol Committee. From 1964 to 1965, Regional Communist Party Instructor in Novosibirsk. From 1965 to 1969, Second, then First Secretary of the Regional Komsomol Committee. From 1971 to 1976, First Secretary of the Koluvan District Communist Party in Novosibirsk region. From 1979 to 1981, First Secretary of the First European Department of the USSR Ministry of Foreign Affairs. From 1981 to 1982, First Secretary at the USSR Embassy in Belgium. From 1982 to 1986, Counsellor at the USSR Embassy in Belgium. From 1986 to 1987, USSR Ministry of Foreign Affairs Board Expert of Personnel and Educational Institutions. From 1987 to 1990, Department Head of Personnel and Educational Institutions.
HONORS/AWARDS: Order of the Badge of Honor; other state awards.
FAMILY: Married with a daughter.
TELEPHONE: 610–311 (Bangui); 244–4964 (Moscow).

Balala, Victor Alekseyevich

POSITION: Member of the Russian Federation Supreme Soviet Committee for Issues of the Councils of People's Deputies and the Development of Self-Government

BIRTHPLACE/DATE: Rakhya settlement, Leningrad region, 1960

NATIONALITY: Russian

EDUCATION: Graduated in 1986 from the Leningrad Institute of Mechanical Engineering. Speaks English.

CAREER: From 1977 to 1978, worked at the Research Institute of Mechanical Engineering for Transport in Leningrad. From 1978 to 1980, served in the army. From 1986 to 1990, Engineer at a chemical automation design office in Voronezh. From 1990, Russian Federation People's Deputy, member of the Supreme Soviet Committee. From 1991, Coordinating Council Member of the Russian Federation Workers' Party.

FAMILY: Married with two children.

ADDRESS/TELEPHONE: 8 Academician Korolev Street, Building 2, Flat #465, Moscow. 205–4641 (office); 216–4141 (home); 33–8829 (Voronezh home).

Balanovskaya, Nadezhda Avgustovna

POSITION: Director-General of the Tryokhgornaya Manufaktura Integrated Cotton Mill (Moscow); Board Member of the Russian Union of Industrialists and Entrepreneurs

BIRTHPLACE/DATE: Kzyl Orda, Kazakhstan, 1949

NATIONALITY: Russian

EDUCATION: Graduated in 1971 from the Kosygin Textile Institute in Moscow.

CAREER: From 1971 to 1979, worked from Forewoman to Chief Engineer of the Spinning and Weaving Factory of Serpukhov Krasny Tekstilshchik Integrated Cotton Mill. In 1977, joined the Communist Party. From 1979 to 1986, Chief Engineer, then Director of the Savino Spinning Mill. From May 1986, Director-General of Tryokhgornaya Manufaktura. Former member of the Russian Federation Central Committee.

FAMILY: Married with two sons.

ADDRESS/TELEPHONE: 15 Rodchelskaya Street, Moscow 123376. 252–2143 (office).

Barannikov, Victor Pavlovich

POSITION: Russian Federation Minister of Security; Lieutenant-General

BIRTHPLACE/DATE: Fedosyevka village, Maritime territory, 1940

NATIONALITY: Russian

EDUCATION: From 1958 to 1960, studied at Yelabuga Cultural Educational College. From 1961 to 1963, student at the Yelabuga Specialized Militia Secondary School of the USSR Ministry of Internal Affairs. In 1968, graduated from the Moscow Higher School of the USSR Ministry of Internal Affairs. Majored in Law.

CAREER: From 1957 to 1958, Turner at the Yelabuga Mechanical Works. From 1960 to 1961, Instructor of the Yelabuga District Komsomol Committee. From 1963 to 1974, worked from Inspector to Chief of the Criminal Investigation Department at the Chelyabinsk Directorate of Internal Affairs. From 1974 to 1983, worked at the Kalingrad Department of Internal Affairs. From 1983 to 1988, held leading posts at the Directorate of the USSR Ministry of Internal Affairs. From 1988 to 1989, Azerbaijan First Deputy Minister of Internal Affairs. In 1990, Russian Federation Minister of Internal Affairs. From August 1991, USSR Minister of Internal Affairs. From December 1991 to January 1992, Russian Federation Minister of Security and Internal Affairs. From January 1992, Russian Federation Director-General of the Federal Security Agency.

FAMILY: Married with two children.

ADDRESS/TELEPHONE: 2 Dzerzhinsky Street, Moscow. 924–3158 (office).

Barchuk, Vasily Vasilyevich

POSITION: Russian Federation Minister of Finance

BIRTHPLACE/DATE: Komsomolsk-on-Amur, March 11, 1941

EDUCATION: Graduated in 1966 from the All-Union Finance and Economics Institute (correspondence courses), and in 1986 from the Academy of National Economy.

CAREER: From 1958 to 1972, worked at the Financial Inspectorate. From 1972 to 1984, worked at the Russian Finance Ministry. From 1986 to April 1991, Deputy Head of the Budgetary Department, Head of the Budgetary Department of

the USSR Ministry of Finance. From April 1991, USSR Deputy Finance Minister. From November 1991 to April 1992, Russian First Deputy Finance Minister.
FAMILY: Married with a daughter.
ADDRESS/TELEPHONE: 9 Ilyinka Street, Moscow, 103097. 298–9145 (office).

Bashayev, Ibragim Yakubovich
POSITION: Board Chairman of Agrika (Agricultural) Commercial Bank
BIRTHPLACE/DATE: Chkalovo village, Pavlodar region, January 1, 1949
EDUCATION: Graduated in 1973 from the Moscow Timiryazev Academy of Agriculture, and in 1982 from the Academy's postgraduate program. Good command of English.
CAREER: From 1973 to 1977, Chief Accountant. From 1977 to 1979, Acting Director of the Bolychevo State Farm, Moscow region. From 1982 to 1986, Directorate Department Head of the Ministry of Agriculture. From 1986 to 1989, Financial Directorate Deputy Head of the Gosagroprom Agri-Industrial Committee. From 1989 to 1991, Financial Directorate Head of the State Committee for Food and Purchase.
FAMILY: Married with three children.
ADDRESS/TELEPHONE: 34 Ulyanovskaya Street, Flat #3, Moscow, 109004. 227–1041 (office).

Bashmachnikov, Vladimir Fyodorovich
POSITION: President of the Russian Peasant Farm and Agricultural Cooperatives Association
BIRTHPLACE/DATE: Ishim, Tyumen region, 1937
NATIONALITY: Russian
EDUCATION: Graduated in 1959 from Urals Gorky State University in Sverdlovsk. Doctor of Economics; Professor. Command of English and German.
CAREER: From 1960 to 1963, Deputy Chairman of the Urals Collective Farm, Economist in Sverdlovsk. From 1965 to 1972, Director of the Urals Region All-Russia Economics and Agriculture Institute. From 1972 to 1985, Department Head, Deputy Director of the All-Russia Institute of Labor Economy and Management in Kosino, Moscow region. From 1985 to 1991, Consultant to the Socio-Economic Department of the Central Committee. In 1989, Vice President of the Russian Peasant Farm and Agricultural Cooperatives Association; from January 1991, President. In 1992, member of the Russian Federation President's Entrepreneurship Council.
FAMILY: Married with three children.
ADDRESS/TELEPHONE: 1/11 Orlikov Pereulok, Room 637, Moscow. 207–8075; 975–4139; 204–4076 (office).

Bashtanyuk, Gennadi Sergeyevich
POSITION: Deputy Chairman of the Confederation of Trade Unions
BIRTHPLACE/DATE: Khamutovka village, Kursk region, 1949
NATIONALITY: Russian
CAREER: Repair Worker at the Karbalit Plant in Orekho-Zuevo. From 1972, Repair Worker, then Superintendent at the Naberezhnye Chelny Truck Production Casting Plant Industrial Complex. In 1986, Chairman of the Tatar Trade Union Regional Council. In 1989, USSR Trade Union Council Secretary. In October 1990, elected Deputy Chairman of the Confederation of Trade Unions.
FAMILY: Married with three children.
ADDRESS/TELEPHONE: 42 Leninsky Prospekt, Moscow, 117119. 938–7105; 938–8600; 938–8605.

Basilashvili, Oleg Valeryanovich
POSITION: Actor; Russian Federation People's Deputy
BIRTHPLACE/DATE: Moscow, 1934
NATIONALITY: Russian
EDUCATION: Graduated in 1956 from the Moscow Academic Art Theater (MKhAT) Studio. Good command of English.
CAREER: From 1956 to 1959, Stage Actor of the Leningrad Lenin Komsomol Theater. In 1959, transferred to the Leningrad Academic Bolshoi Drama Theater. Starred in many movies. From 1990, Russian Federation People's Deputy.
HONORS/AWARDS: USSR People's Artist.
FAMILY: Married with two daughters.
ADDRESS/TELEPHONE: 13 Borodinskaya Street, Flat #58, St. Petersburg, 196180. 113–5556 (home).

Basin, Yefim Vladimirovich

POSITION: Chairman of the Russian Federation Supreme Soviet Committee for Construction, Architecture, and Public Utilities; Russian Federation People's Deputy; member of the Council of Nationalities; member of the Left-Center Parliamentary Faction
BIRTHPLACE/DATE: Tambov region, 1940
NATIONALITY: Russian
EDUCATION: Graduated in 1962 from the Byelorussian Institute of Transport Engineers; in 1980, from the Academy of National Economy of the USSR Council of Ministers. Doctor of Economics.
CAREER: From 1962 to 1964, Senior Construction Management Foreman of SU–302 in Yaroslavl. From 1964 to 1966, Senior Superintendent. From 1966 to 1967, Chief Engineer. From 1967 to 1969, Head of SU–302. From 1969 to 1970, Deputy Manager. From 1970 to 1972, Chief Engineer of the Gortransstroi (Transport Construction) Trust in Gorky. From 1972 to 1978, Chief of the Pechorstroi Construction Directorate in Pechora. From 1980 to 1990, Deputy Head, First Deputy Head of Glavstroi (Main Construction Department), Deputy Minister of the USSR Transport Construction, Head of Glavstroi.
HONORS/AWARDS: Hero of Socialist Labor.
FAMILY: Married with two children.
ADDRESS/TELEPHONE: 14 Yaroslavskaya Street, Building 2, Flat #57, Moscow. 283–5700 (office); 205–6056 (office).

Baskin, Ilya Mikhailovich

POSITION: Former Director-General of the International Association of Entrepreneurs of Eastern Europe and Asia
BIRTHPLACE/DATE: Vitebsk region, 1956
CAREER: From 1979, Construction Management Foreman of SU–328. From 1979 to 1982, Foreman, Senior Engineer, Directorate Department Head of the Leningrad Cardboard Factory. From 1982, Supply Department Head of the Leningrad Cardboard Factory. From January to July 1983, Senior Engineer of the Communication Research Institute. From 1983 to 1988, Deputy Director of Construction at the Leningrad Sewing Factory. From 1988 to 1990, Board Chairman of the Garant Firm. From June 1990 to October 1991, Director-General of the International Association of Entrepreneurs of Eastern Europe and Asia. From January 1992, member of the Russian Federation President's Entrepeneurship Council.
FAMILY: Married with a daughter.

Basov, Nikolay Gennadyevich

POSITION: Director of the Quantum Radio-Physics Department at the Lebedev Physics Institute; Academician of the Russian Academy of Sciences; Presidium Counsellor of the Russian Academy of Sciences; Professor at the Moscow Institute of Engineering and Physics; Presidium Member of the USSR Academy of Sciences
BIRTHPLACE/DATE: Voronezh, December 14, 1922
NATIONALITY: Russian
EDUCATION: Graduated in 1950 from the Moscow Institute of Engineering and Physics.
CAREER: From 1950, worked at the Physics Institute of the USSR Academy of Sciences. In 1955, joined the Communist Party. From 1958, Deputy Director. From 1962, Laboratory Head. Founder of Quantum Electronics. Created the first quantum generator, microwave amplification by stimulated emission of radiation-maser. From 1966, Academician of the USSR Academy of Sciences.
MAJOR WORKS: In the field of semiconductor lasers, theory of strong pulse in solid-state lasers, quantum standards of frequency, and the interaction of high-power laser emission with substances.
HONORS/AWARDS: Nobel Prize (1964); Hero of Socialist Labor (1959); Prize of Lenin (1959); Order of Lenin; Honorary Member of the German Academy of Sciences in Berlin (1967).
FAMILY: Married with two children.
ADDRESS/TELEPHONE: The Lebedev Physics Institute, 53 Leninsky Prospekt, GSP–1, Moscow V–333, 117924. 135–2157 (office).

Batarchuk, Boris Aleksandrovich

POSITION: Editor in Chief of *Prolog* (*Prologue*) newspaper
BIRTHPLACE/DATE: Tyumen region, 1942
EDUCATION: Graduated from the Journalism Department at Urals Gorky State University.
CAREER: To 1974, worked at Urals regional newspapers. From 1974 to 1980, Correspondent for *Trud* (*Labor*) newspaper in the Urals. From

1980 to 1987, First Deputy Managing Editor, Managing Editor of *Trud*. From 1987 to 1990, Editor of the Prague-based *World Marxist Review* journal.
HONORS/AWARDS: Urals Journalism Award for a series of essays on America.
FAMILY: Married with a son.
ADDRESS/TELEPHONE: 42 Leninsky Prospekt, Moscow. 930–8387 (office).

Batkov, Aleksandr Mikhailovich
POSITION: Director-General of the Scientific-Research Developments and Rossoyuz Aviaprom (Aviation Industry) Programs Center; President of the Aircraft Builders' Society
BIRTHPLACE/DATE: Voronezh, 1930
NATIONALITY: Russian
EDUCATION: Graduated in 1954 from Dnepropetrovsk State University. Doctor of Technology. Speaks English.
CAREER: From 1957 to 1983, worked from Department Head to Deputy Head of the Aircraft Systems Research Institute in Moscow. From 1967 to 1983, Department Head of the Moscow Physics and Technology Institute (MFTI). From 1983, Department Head of the Moscow Aviation Institute (MAI). From 1983 to 1991, Directorate Head of the USSR Ministry of Aviation Industry.
HONORS/AWARDS: Prize of Lenin; USSR State Prize; Order of Lenin; Order of the October Revolution.
FAMILY: Married with a child.
ADDRESS/TELEPHONE: 16 Ulansky Pereulok, Moscow. 207–6917 (office).

Begalov, Yuli Vladimirovich
POSITION: Director-General of Quant International Joint Venture
BIRTHPLACE/DATE: Tbilisi, Georgia, 1962
EDUCATION: Graduated in 1988 from Moscow State University.
CAREER: From 1980 to 1981, worked at a repair-and-construction management in Tbilisi. From 1981 and 1983, served in the army. From 1988 to 1992, Director of Quant Joint-Stock Company. From 1992, Director-General of Quant International Joint Venture, specializing in oil extraction, refining, and the sale of oil products.
FAMILY: Married with two children.
ADDRESS/TELEPHONE: 36 Bolshaya Cheremushkinskaya Street, Building 3, P.O. Box 65, Moscow, 117218. 124–1444 (office).

Beisenov, Saiat Dusenbayevich
POSITION: Kazakh Labor Minister
BIRTHPLACE/DATE: Kondratievka village, Karaganda region, 1940
EDUCATION: Graduated from a vocational school in Karaganda.
CAREER: Worked as a Fitter; served in the Armed Forces; worked as a Foreman, then Engineer in Temirtau; Municipal Housing Department Head; Deputy Chairman, then Chairman of the Temirtau Municipal Executive Committee; worked at the Kazakhstan Council of Ministers.
FAMILY: Married with two daughters.
ADDRESS/TELEPHONE: 93/95 Abulay Khan Prospekt, Alma-Ata, 480091. 62–1168 (office).

Bekh, Nikolay Ivanovich
POSITION: President of the KAMAZ Joint-Stock Company; Vice President of the Russian Union of Industrialists and Entrepreneurs
BIRTHPLACE/DATE: Korosten, Zhitomir region, Ukraine, 1946
NATIONALITY: Ukrainian
EDUCATION: Graduated in 1969 from Kiev Polytechnic.
CAREER: From 1969 to 1980, worked from Engineer-Technologist to Chief Engineer of Metallurgical Works at the VAZ Production Association. From 1980 to 1984, Director of the KAMAZ Foundry Factory. From 1984 to 1986, Director-General of the KAMAZ Tractor Works Construction in Yelabuga (Tataria). In 1987, appointed Director-General of KAMAZ. Member of the USSR President's Entrepreneurship Council. Member of the Russian Supreme Economics Society.
HONORS/AWARDS: Man of the Year in Naberezhnye Chelny (1991).
FAMILY: Married with two daughters.
ADDRESS/TELEPHONE: 29 Musa Jalil Prospekt, Naberezhnye Chelny, 423408. 42–2016 (office).

Bekhtereva, Natalya Petrovna
POSITION: Supervisor of the Brain Center; Academician of the Russian Academy of Sciences
BIRTHPLACE/DATE: 1924

EDUCATION: Graduated in 1947 from the First Leningrad Medical Institute. From 1947 to 1950, postgraduate student at the Institute of the Brain, and later at the Institute of Physiology of the USSR Academy of Medical Sciences. Physiologist. Speaks English, German, and French.
CAREER: From 1950 to 1954, worked at the USSR Academy of Medical Sciences' Institute of Experimental Medicine. From 1954 to 1962, Senior Researcher, Deputy Director of the USSR Academy of Medical Sciences' Institute of Neurosurgery. Joined the Communist Party in 1960. From 1962 to 1990, Department Head, Deputy Director, Director of the Research Institute of Experimental Medicine of the USSR Academy of Medical Sciences. Former elected USSR People's Deputy.
MAJOR WORKS: In the field of physiology, psychic and bioelectric activity of the pathologic brain.
HONORS/AWARDS: Foreign member of the Austrian and Finnish Academies of Sciences; Honorary Member of a number of foreign scientific societies; USSR State Prize (1985); Order of the Red Banner of Labor.
FAMILY: Widow with a son. Granddaughter of Vladimir Bekhterev, an outstanding Russian neurologist, psychiatrist, and psychologist.
ADDRESS/TELEPHONE: The Brain Center, 9 Academician Pavlov Street, St. Petersburg, 197376. 334–1390 (office).

Beli, Mikhail Mikhailovich
POSITION: Head of the Department of Asia and the Pacific of the Ministry of Foreign Affairs; Counsellor Extraordinary and Plenipotentiary, Second Grade
BIRTHPLACE/DATE: Marganets village, Sverdlovsk region, October 20, 1945
NATIONALITY: Ukrainian
EDUCATION: Graduated from the Moscow State Institute of International Relations in 1968.
CAREER: From 1962 to 1963, Laboratory Assistant. From 1968 to 1970, Trainee at the University of Singapore. From 1970, Aide to the Southeastern Asia Department of the USSR Ministry of Foreign Affairs. From 1970 to 1971, Aide on Duty at the USSR Embassy in Singapore. From 1971 to 1972, Aide-Trainee at the USSR Embassy in Singapore. From 1973 to 1974, Attaché at the USSR Embassy in Singapore. From 1974 to 1976, Attaché of the Department of Southeastern Asia; from 1976 to 1977, Third Secretary. From 1977 to 1980, Second Secretary at the USSR Embassy in China; from 1980 to 1982, First Secretary. From 1983 to 1984, Counsellor of the Department of Southeastern Asia; from 1984 to 1985, Division Head. From 1985 to 1990, Counsellor at the USSR Mission to the UN in New York. From 1990, Board Head of the Socialist Countries of Asia Department of the USSR Ministry of Foreign Affairs. From 1990 to 1991, Department Head of the Board of Countries of the Far East and Indo-China of the USSR Ministry of Foreign Affairs; from 1991 to 1992, Deputy Head. From 1992, Deputy Department Head of Asia and the Pacific.
FAMILY: Married with two children.
TELEPHONE: 244–4446 (office).

Belonogov, Aleksandr Mikhailovich
POSITION: Russian Federation Ambassador to Canada; Ambassador Extraordinary and Plenipotentiary
BIRTHPLACE/DATE: Moscow, May 15, 1931
NATIONALITY: Russian
EDUCATION: Graduated in 1954 from the Moscow State Institute of International Relations. Doctor of Law. Good command of English and French.
CAREER: From 1954 to 1959, Aide, Senior Aide, Attaché of the Law Department of the USSR Ministry of Foreign Affairs. From 1959 to 1962, Third Secretary, Second Secretary of the International Economic Organizations Department of the USSR Ministry of Foreign Affairs. From 1962 to 1967, Second Secretary of the Second European Department of the USSR Ministry of Foreign Affairs; Third Secretary; Second Secretary; First Secretary at the USSR Embassy in the United Kingdom and Northern Ireland. From 1967 to 1984, Counsellor, Senior Counsellor, Chief Counsellor, Department Head, Deputy Head of the Foreign Policy Planning Department of the USSR Ministry of Foreign Affairs. From 1984 to 1986, USSR Ambassador to Egypt. From 1986 to 1990, USSR Ambassador to the UN and Representative of the UN Security Council. From 1990 to 1991, USSR Deputy Foreign Minister.

HONORS/AWARDS: Order of the Red Banner of Labor (1976); Order of the People's Friendship (1981); several medals.
FAMILY: Married with a daughter.
ADDRESS/TELEPHONE: The Embassy of the Russian Federation in Canada, 285 Charlotte Street, Ottawa, Ontario, KIN 8L5, Canada. 235–4341; 236–1413 (office).

Belousenko, Grigory Fyodorovich
POSITION: Board Chairman of Rosinterbank (Russian International Bank)
BIRTHPLACE/DATE: Rostov-on-Don, 1929
NATIONALITY: Russian
EDUCATION: Doctor of Economy.
CAREER: From 1954 to 1959, worked at Selkhozbank (Agricultural Bank). From 1959 to 1968, worked at the State Bank in Rostov-on-Don. From 1973 to 1986, worked at the Financial Department of the Russian Ministry of Agriculture. From 1986 to 1990, worked at the Russian Republic State Planning Committee of Agriculture.
FAMILY: Married with a child.
ADDRESS/TELEPHONE: 3 Orlikov Pereulok, Moscow, 107802. 204–4350; 204–4390 (office).

Belousov, Boris Mikhailovich
POSITION: President of the Russian Corporation of Defense Industry Joint-Stock Company
BIRTHPLACE/DATE: 1934
NATIONALITY: Russian
CAREER: Worked at machinery-building plants in Izhevsk; Department Head of the Udmurtiya Communist Party Regional Committee; Director of the Izhevsk Mechanical Plant; USSR Deputy Minister and First Deputy Minister of Defense Industry. From 1989 to October 1991, USSR Minister of Defense Industry. Former member of the Communist Party.
HONORS/AWARDS: Order of the Red Banner of Labor.
FAMILY: Married with two daughters.
ADDRESS/TELEPHONE: 12 Moroseka Street, Moscow, 129857. 206–0920.

Belov, Sergei Fadeyevich
POSITION: Board Chairman of the Russian Information Resources Exchange
BIRTHPLACE/DATE: Gorlovka, Donetsk region, 1951
NATIONALITY: Russian
EDUCATION: Graduated in 1973 from Donetsk Polytechnic; in 1984, from the Moscow Institute of Engineering and Physics; in 1990, from the Higher School of Commerce in Paris. Good command of French.
CAREER: From 1973 to 1979, Mining Engineer at a Donetsk coal mine. From 1979 to 1985, Senior Researcher, Assistant Laboratory Head of the Mining Institute. From 1991, Board Chairman of the Russian Information Resources Exchange, Director-General of a small business.
MAJOR WORKS: Scientific publications in the field of mining.
FAMILY: Married with two children.
ADDRESS/TELEPHONE: 9 Glagolev Street, Building 2, Moscow. 199–9660 (office).

Belushkin, Valery Aleksandrovich
POSITION: Director-General of the Donskaya Birzha Joint-Stock Company (Don Stock-Exchange).
BIRTHPLACE/DATE: Rostov-on-Don, 1949
EDUCATION: Graduated in 1971 from Rostov University. Speaks German and Bulgarian.
CAREER: From 1971 to 1976, Researcher at Rostov University. From 1976 to 1981, held different posts in industry. From 1981 to 1988, Chief Engineer at a plant. From 1988 to 1991, Department Head of the Rostov Region Executive Committee.
FAMILY: Married with a son.
ADDRESS/TELEPHONE: 88 Engels Street, Rostov-on-Don, 344007. 66–4579.

Belyaev, Vladimir Nikitovich
POSITION: Dean of the Moscow Institute of Engineering and Physics
BIRTHPLACE/DATE: Ilivaisk, Donetsk region, August 9, 1949
NATIONALITY: Ukrainian
EDUCATION: Doctor of Physics and Mathematics.
CAREER: From 1966 to 1967, worked for the Donetsk Railroad. From 1973 to 1974, Engineer. From 1977 to 1978, Senior Engineer. From 1978 to 1980, Laboratory Head. From 1980 to 1982,

Junior Researcher. From 1982 to 1984, Assistant. From 1985, Dean of the Moscow Institute of Engineering and Physics. From December 1990 to January 1992, USSR People's Deputy Chairman of the Supreme Soviet Committee for National Education, Presidium Member of the USSR Supreme Soviet, participated in the Spravedlivost (Justice) Deputy Group. From 1990 to 1991, USSR Supreme Soviet Deputy. Member of the Communist Party to August 1991.
MAJOR WORKS: Author of more than fifty scientific articles and publications.
HONORS/AWARDS: Lenin Komsomol Prize.
FAMILY: Married with two children.
ADDRESS/TELEPHONE: 31 Kashirskoye Chaussée, Moscow, 115409. 324–9740.

Belyanchikova, Yuliya Vasilyevna
POSITION: Editor in Chief of *Zdorovye* (*Health*) magazine
BIRTHPLACE/DATE: Saltykovka, Moscow region, 1940
EDUCATION: Graduated in 1966 from the First Medical Institute. Doctor of Medicine.
CAREER: From 1966 to 1971, Physician at the Central Hematology and Blood Transfusion Institute. From 1971 to 1989, Anchorwoman of the "Zdorovye" TV program. From 1989, Editor in Chief of *Zdorovye*. Board Member of the Russian Charity and Health Foundation, Board Member of the Russian Children's Fund.
HONORS/AWARDS: Russian Federation Honored Physician; USSR Journalists' Union Prize.
FAMILY: Married with a son.
ADDRESS/TELEPHONE: 14 Bumazhny Proyezd, Moscow, 101454. 250–5828; 212–2523 (office).

Belyayev, Albert Andreyevich
POSITION: Editor in Chief of *Kultura* (*Culture*) newspaper (formerly *Sovietskaya Kultura*)
BIRTHPLACE/DATE: Lipetsk region, 1928
EDUCATION: From 1945 to 1950, student at the Arkhangelsk Navigation School. Graduated in 1958 from the Arkhangelsk Teacher's Training College; in 1962, from the Central Committee's Academy of Social Sciences. Doctor of Philology.
CAREER: In 1943, Turner at a munitions factory. From 1950 to 1953, Navigator of the Arkhangelsk Shipping Company. From 1953 to 1959, Murmansk Region Komsomol Functionary, then First Secretary of the Komsomol Regional Committee. From 1962 to 1986, Section Head, Deputy Head of the Central Committee's Department of Culture.
FAMILY: Married with a daughter.
ADDRESS/TELEPHONE: 73 Novoslobodskaya Street, Moscow. 285–7802 (office); 214–6031 (assistant).

Belyayev, Anatoli Aleksandrovich
POSITION: Editor in Chief of *Vek XX i Mir* (*20th Century and Peace*) magazine
BIRTHPLACE/DATE: Moscow region, 1929
EDUCATION: Graduated in 1952 from the Institute of Oriental Studies, and later from the postgraduate program at Moscow State University. Doctor of Economics. Good command of English.
CAREER: From 1959 to 1962, Assistant Editor of *Pravda* newspaper. From 1962 to 1969, Editor of *Ekonomicheskaya Zhizn* (*Economic Life*) newspaper. From 1969 to 1971, Correspondent for *Socialisticheskaya Industria* (*Socialist Industry*) newspaper. From 1972 to 1976, Researcher at the International Institute of Economic Problems. From 1976 to 1981, Editor of the Prague-based *World Marxist Review* journal. Russian Federation People's Deputy.
FAMILY: Married with two children.
ADDRESS/TELEPHONE: 16/2 Tverskaya Street, Moscow. 200–3807 (office).

Berdennikov, Grigory Vitalyevich
POSITION: Russian Federation Deputy Minister of Foreign Affairs; Counsellor, First Class
BIRTHPLACE/DATE: 1950
NATIONALITY: Russian
EDUCATION: Graduated in 1973 from the Moscow State Institute of International Relations. Speaks English and French.
CAREER: From 1973 to 1978, Aide, Attaché at the Permanent USSR Mission to the UN in New York. From 1978 to 1991, Attaché, Third Secretary of the International Organizations Department of the USSR Ministry of Foreign Affairs. From 1981 to 1986, Second Secretary, First Secretary at the Permanent USSR Mission to the UN and Other International Organizations in Geneva. From 1986 to 1992, Counsellor, Department

Head, Deputy Administration Chief for Problems of Arms Limitation and Disarmament of the USSR Ministry of Foreign Affairs.
FAMILY: Married.
ADDRESS/TELEPHONE: 32/34 Smolenskaya-Sennaya Square, Moscow, 121200. 244–4056; 244–2469 (office).

Berezkin, Andrey Vladimirovich

POSITION: Director-General of the Analitik (Analyst) Joint-Stock Company; Head of the Political Geography Laboratory at Moscow State University's Geography Department; Presidium Expert of the Russian Federation Supreme Soviet
BIRTHPLACE/DATE: Moscow, 1955
NATIONALITY: Russian
EDUCATION: Graduated in 1977 from the Geography Department at Moscow State University. From 1977 to 1979, postgraduate student at Moscow State University. In 1979, studied at New York State University in the United States. Speaks English.
CAREER: From 1990 to 1991, Laboratory Head at the Moscow Institute of Political Studies. In 1991, Advisor to the USSR President, Presidium Expert of the Russian Federation Supreme Soviet.
FAMILY: Married with three children.
ADDRESS/TELEPHONE: 30 Academician Anokhin Street, Building 4, #791, Moscow. 430–2233.

Berketov, Saparbek Sultanovich

POSITION: Director-General of the Orlan Universal Stock Center
BIRTHPLACE/DATE: Alma-Ata, 1933
NATIONALITY: Kazakh
EDUCATION: Doctor of Technical Sciences.
CAREER: To 1975, worked as Technician, Senior Technician, Superintendent, Shop Head, Deputy Director of the Pavlodar Aluminum Plant. From 1975, Director of the Pavlodar Chemical Plant. From 1985, First Deputy Chairman of the Pavlodar Region Auditing Committee. From 1990, Commerce Director of the Kosmofarm Concern.
FAMILY: Married with a son.
ADDRESS/TELEPHONE: 104 Dzerzinsky Street, Pavlodar, 637000. 72–1526; 72–1023 (office).

Beskov, Konstantin Ivanovich

POSITION: Senior Coach of the Asmoral Football Team; Vice President of the USSR Football Federation
BIRTHPLACE/DATE: Moscow, 1920
NATIONALITY: Russian
EDUCATION: Graduated from the State Physical Education Institute.
CAREER: Instructor of the Metallurg Sports Club; Officer of the USSR Ministry of Internal Affairs; Senior Coach of the Central Army Sports Club Professional Football Team; Sports Information Department Head at Central Television; Senior Coach of the professional football teams of Zarya (Dawn), Lokomotiv, Spartak, the Dynamo Sports Clubs, and the USSR Olympic National Football Team.
HONORS/AWARDS: USSR Honorary Master of Sports and Honorary Coach; Order of Lenin; two Orders of the Badge of Honor; Order of the People's Friendship.
FAMILY: Married with a daughter.
ADDRESS/TELEPHONE: 4 Sadovaya-Triumfalnaya, Flat #23, Moscow, 103006. 201–0677 (office); 299–5254 (home).

Bespalov, Vladimir Vasilyevich

POSITION: Chairman of the Russian Federation Supreme Soviet Subcommittee for Industry and Energy
BIRTHPLACE/DATE: Staroye Pshenovo village, Mordva, 1953
NATIONALITY: Mordvinian
EDUCATION: Graduated in 1975 from Mordvinian State University.
CAREER: In 1975, Engineer-Technologist and Equipment Specialist. In 1976, Radio Apparatus Controller. In 1977, Senior Engineer. From 1979 to 1981, served in the army. In 1981, Technical Bureau Head. In 1985, Deputy Section Head. In 1986, Section Head. In 1990, elected Russian Federation People's Deputy.
FAMILY: Married with a daughter and a son.
ADDRESS/TELEPHONE: The Committee for Industry and Energy, 2 Krasnopresnenskaya Naberezhnaya, Moscow. 205–4004 (office); 485–5369 (home).

Bessmertnykh, Aleksandr Aleksandrovich
POSITION: Head of the Center for Political Analysis; President of the Foreign Policy Association
BIRTHPLACE/DATE: Biysk, Altai region, October 10, 1933
EDUCATION: Doctor of Law.
CAREER: From 1957, worked at the USSR Ministry of Foreign Affairs. From 1966 to 1970, Minister's Aide. From 1970 to 1983, First Secretary, Counsellor, Minister-Counsellor at the USSR Embassy in the United States. From 1983, Ministry Board Member, then Head of the U.S. Department of the USSR Ministry of Foreign Affairs. From 1986, USSR Deputy Foreign Minister. From 1988, USSR First Deputy Minister of Foreign Affairs. From May 1990, USSR Ambassador to the United States. From 1991 to August 1991, USSR Minister of Foreign Affairs. From 1990 to 1991, member of the Central Committee.
FAMILY: Married with two children.
ADDRESS/TELEPHONE: 10 Elizarova Street, Moscow. Fax: 975–2190.

Bestemyanova, Natalya Filimonovna
POSITION: Soloist of the Igor Bobrin Theater of Skating Arts
BIRTHPLACE/DATE: Moscow, 1960
NATIONALITY: Russian
EDUCATION: Graduated from the State Physical Education Institute.
CAREER: In 1967, began figure skating. From 1977, USSR National Team Member. European Figure Skating Champion in 1983. European and World Figure Skating Champion from 1985 to 1987. From 1989, Soloist of the Igor Bobrin Theater of Skating Arts.
HONORS/AWARDS: USSR Honorary Master of Sports; Winter Olympic Silver Prize (1984) and Champion (1988).
FAMILY: Married.
ADDRESS/TELEPHONE: 8 Luzhnetskaya Naberezhnaya, Moscow. 201–1231.

Bezverkhy, Sergey Fyodorovich
POSITION: Chairman of the Russian Federation State Committee for Standards (Gosstandart)
BIRTHPLACE/DATE: Zaporozhye, 1940
NATIONALITY: Ukrainian
EDUCATION: Graduated from the Zaporozhye Mechanical Engineering Institute. Doctor of Technology; Professor. Speaks German.
CAREER: From 1959 to 1962, served in the army. From 1968 to 1971, Engineer, Director of the Central Motor Proving Ground. Russian Federation People's Deputy. Member of the Industrial Union Movement.
FAMILY: Married with two children.
ADDRESS/TELEPHONE: 2 Krasnopresnenskaya Naberezhnaya, Moscow. 236–0409 (office).

Bikkenin, Nail Baryevich
POSITION: Editor in Chief of *Svobodnaya Mysl* (*Free Thought*) magazine
BIRTHPLACE/DATE: Kazan, 1931
NATIONALITY: Tatar
EDUCATION: Graduated from the Philosophy Department at Moscow State University. Doctor of Philosophy.
CAREER: Research Consultant; Deputy Department Head of *Voprosy Filosofii* (*Questions of Philosophy*) magazine; Department Consultant to *Kommunist* magazine; Central Committee Functionary; Lecturer at Moscow State University; Consulting Group Head of the Central Committee's Department for Science and Educational Institutions; Deputy Head of the Central Committee's Propaganda Department; Editorial Board Member and Editor in Chief of *Kommunist*. From August 1991, Editor in Chief of *Svobodnaya Mysl*. Former elected USSR People's Deputy. From 1987, Corresponding Member of the USSR Academy of Sciences. From December 1991, Corresponding Member of the Russian Academy of Sciences.
MAJOR WORKS: Works in the field of culture, science, ideology, and politics.
FAMILY: Married with a daughter and a son.
ADDRESS/TELEPHONE: 5 Marx-Engels Street, Moscow, 119875. 203–0365; 291–8652 (office).

Bilas, Bronislav Ivanovich
POSITION: Chairman of the Christian Evangelist Integrated Union
BIRTHPLACE/DATE: Kyklmatychi village, Lvov region, October 25, 1930
CAREER: From 1975 to 1989, Senior of the Christian Evangelist Church in Lvov region. From 1991, Chairman of the Christian Evangelist

Union. From 1992, Chairman of the Christian Evangelist Integrated Union.
FAMILY: Married with two children.
ADDRESS: 269 B. Khmelnitsky Street, Lvov.

Bilozerchev, Dmitri Vladimirovich
POSITION: Coach in Sweden
BIRTHPLACE/DATE: Moscow, 1966
NATIONALITY: Russian
EDUCATION: Graduated in 1989 from the Leningrad Military Physical Education Institute.
CAREER: Many-time European and World Gymnastics Champion; 1988 Summer Olympic Champion.
HONORS/AWARDS: Order of the People's Friendship; Order of the Badge of Honor; Medal For Labor Valor; three Olympic Gold Medals.
FAMILY: Married with a son.
ADDRESS/TELEPHONE: 5 Bolshoi Rzhevsky Pereulok, Moscow, 121069. 201–0272.

Bindar, Leonid Iosifovich
POSITION: Head of the Russian Federation Khizh Government Secretariat of the Deputy Chairman
BIRTHPLACE/DATE: Belostok, Poland, 1940
EDUCATION: Graduated in 1968 from the Leningrad Polytechnic Institute.
CAREER: From 1968 to 1991, Engineer, Section Head, Deputy Section Head, Department Head, Production Head, Deputy Chief of a scientific-production complex; Technological Department Head of the Svetlana Association; Deputy Chief Engineer of the Svetlana Association. From 1991 to May 1992, Deputy Chairman of the Committee for Economic Development of the St. Petersburg Mayor's Office. From May 1992, Head of the Russian Federation Khizh Government Secretariat of the Deputy Chairman.
HONORS/AWARDS: Medal For Labor Valor; Order of the Red Banner of Labor; USSR State Prize.
FAMILY: Married with two children.
ADDRESS/TELEPHONE: The Kremlin, Moscow. 206–3359 (office).

Biryukov, Vadim Osipovich
POSITION: Editor in Chief of *Delovye Lyudi (Business People)* magazine
BIRTHPLACE/DATE: Moscow, 1932
NATIONALITY: Russian
EDUCATION: Graduated in 1955 from the Maurice Thorez State Teachers' Training Institute of Foreign Languages.
CAREER: Staff Member of several newspapers; worked at Novosti (News) Press Agency. Worked fifteen years at TASS (Telegraph Agency of the Soviet Union): Political Analyst, Deputy Department Head, Chief of the TASS Diplomatic Service in Moscow.
FAMILY: Married with a son.
ADDRESS/TELEPHONE: 10/1 Marshal Novikov Street, Flat #11, Moscow, 123098. 333–3340 (home).

Biryulev, Sergey Vasilyevich
POSITION: Head of the Department of Regional Cooperation and Economic Problems; Counsellor Extraordinary and Plenipotentiary, First Grade
BIRTHPLACE/DATE: Moscow, June 19, 1930
NATIONALITY: Russian
EDUCATION: Graduated from the Moscow Institute of Oriental Countries in 1954.
CAREER: From 1954 to 1958, Trainee at the USSR Embassy in Pakistan. From 1958 to 1959, Attaché of the Southeastern Asia Department of the USSR Ministry of Foreign Affairs; from 1959 to 1960, Third Secretary. From 1960 to 1962, Third Secretary at the USSR Embassy in Pakistan; from 1962 to 1964, Second Secretary. From 1964 to 1965, Second Secretary of the Southern Asia Department; from 1965 to 1968, First Secretary. From 1968 to 1969, Deputy Secretary of the Party Committee of the USSR Ministry of Foreign Affairs. From 1969 to 1974, Counsellor at the USSR Mission to the UN and Other International Organizations in Geneva. From 1974 to 1977, Counsellor of the Department of International Economic Organizations of the USSR Ministry of Foreign Affairs; from 1977 to 1978, Expert; from 1978 to 1981, Division Head. From 1981 to 1987, Deputy of the USSR Permanent Representative in Geneva. From 1987 to 1990, Deputy Head of the Board for International Economic Relations of the USSR Ministry of Foreign Affairs; from 1990 to 1992, First Deputy.
HONORS/AWARDS: Order of the Badge of Honor.

FAMILY: Married with two children.
TELEPHONE: 241–2898 (office).

Bizhan, Ivan Vasilyevich
POSITION: Ukranian Deputy Minister of Defense; Colonel-General
BIRTHPLACE/DATE: Yalanets village, Vinnitsa region, November 25, 1941
NATIONALITY: Ukrainian
CAREER: Worked from Platoon Commander to Deputy Head of the General Staff Board of the USSR Air Forces. From 1991 to 1992, Ukranian First Deputy Minister of Defense. Lieutenant-General.
HONORS/AWARDS: Order of the Red Star; Order For Service to the USSR Armed Forces.
FAMILY: Married with a son.
TELEPHONE: 293–039; 293–2073 (press center).

Blokhin, Aleksandr Victorovich
POSITION: Secretary of the Russian Federation Committee for Issues of the Councils of People's Deputies and the Development of Self-Government
BIRTHPLACE/DATE: Ivanovo, 1951
NATIONALITY: Russian
EDUCATION: Graduated in 1974 from the Ivanovo Lenin Power Engineering Institute; in 1983, graduated from a postgraduate program at the Institute. Speaks English.
CAREER: From 1974 to 1977, Senior Engineer, Deputy Section Head, Section Head, Deputy Chief Power Engineering Specialist at the Lunacharsky Fizpribor Plant in Kirovsk. From 1977 to 1978, took business trip to Mongolia. From 1978 to 1980, Chief Mechanic of the Oblshveibyt Association in Ivanovo. From 1980 to 1990, Chief Power Engineering Specialist of the Shchelkovo State Biocombine. From 1989 to 1990, Assistant to USSR People's Deputy Nikolay Travkin. From 1990 to 1992, Russian Federation People's Deputy.
FAMILY: Married with a daughter.

Blokhin, Oleg Vladimirovich
POSITION: Football Player; Coach of the Olympikos Football Club (Greece)
BIRTHPLACE/DATE: Kiev, 1952
NATIONALITY: Ukrainian
EDUCATION: Graduated from the Kiev State Institute of Physical Education.
CAREER: Many-time USSR Football Champion.
HONORS/AWARDS: USSR Honorary Master of Sports; Gold Ball Prize for the best European football player (1975); European Winners' Cup (1975, 1986).
FAMILY: Married with a daughter.
ADDRESS/TELEPHONE: 5 Bolshoi Rzhevski Pereulok, Moscow, 121069. 201–0834.

Blokhin, Yuri Vitalyevich
POSITION: Supreme Economic Council Expert
BIRTHPLACE/DATE: Sukhoy Log, Sverdlovsk region, 1944
NATIONALITY: Russian
EDUCATION: Doctor of Business.
CAREER: From 1970 to 1979, Senior Laboratory Assistant, Senior Researcher at the Institute of Economy of the Moldavian Academy of Sciences. From 1979 to 1989, Laboratory Head, Department Head, Deputy Director of the Planning Research Institute of the Moldavian State Planning Committee. USSR People's Deputy. From 1989 to 1991, Deputy Chairman of the USSR Supreme Soviet Committee for Economic Reforms.
FAMILY: Married with two children.
ADDRESS/TELEPHONE: 19 Novy Arbat, Moscow. 203–6445 (office).

Bobrik, Vladimir Ilyich
POSITION: Director of the Marketing and Foreign Trade Center
BIRTHPLACE/DATE: Moscow, 1953
EDUCATION: Graduated in 1976 from the Economics and Construction Management Department at the Moscow Institute of Management. Speaks English.
CAREER: From 1976 to 1988, worked from Engineer to Researcher of the Central Research Institute of Organization, Mechanization, and Technological Construction Assistance of the USSR State Building Committee. From 1989 to 1990, Deputy Chairman of the Levsha Cooperative.
FAMILY: Married with a child.
ADDRESS/TELEPHONE: 24/35 Krzhizhanovsky Street, Building 2, Moscow. 332–7821; 332–7940 (office).

Bocharnikov, Mikhail Nikolayevich

POSITION: Russian Ambassador to Zambia; Counsellor Extraordinary and Plenipotentiary, First Grade

BIRTHPLACE/DATE: Moscow, March 6, 1948

NATIONALITY: Russian

EDUCATION: Graduated from the Moscow State Institute of International Relations in 1971.

CAREER: From 1971 to 1973, Aide-Trainee at the USSR Embassy in Ethiopia. From 1973 to 1975, Third Secretary at the USSR Embassy in Ethiopia. From 1977 to 1978, Third Secretary of the Third African Department of the USSR Ministry of Foreign Affairs; from 1978 to 1980, Second Secretary; from 1980 to 1982, First Secretary. From 1982 to 1985, First Secretary at the USSR Embassy of Ethiopia. From 1985 to 1988, Counsellor at the USSR Embassy in Ethiopia. From 1988, Head of the African Department. From 1988 to 1990, Department Head of the African Board of the USSR Ministry of Foreign Affairs. From 1990 to 1992, Minister-Counsellor at the USSR Embassy in Zimbabwe.

HONORS/AWARDS: Medal For Labor Valor.

FAMILY: Married with a daughter.

TELEPHONE: 25–2183 (Lusaca); 244–2471 (Moscow).

Bocharov, Mikhail Aleksandrovich

POSITION: President of the Butek and Rusbaltvest Joint-Stock Companies

BIRTHPLACE/DATE: Aleksandrovsk, Sakhalin region, 1941

NATIONALITY: Russian

EDUCATION: Graduated from the Law Department at Krasnoyarsk State University.

CAREER: Worked from Engineer to Deputy Director-General of the Norilskgazprom (Norilsk Gas Industry) Association. Deputy Director of the All-Union Research Institute of Natural Gas. From 1981, Director of the Butovo Construction Materials Integrated Works. From 1989, President of the Butek Concern. In July 1990, left the Communist Party. Elected USSR People's Deputy; Secretary of the USSR Supreme Soviet Committee for Building and Architecture; Russian Federation People's Deputy. From July 1990 to September 1991, Chairman of the Russian Federation Supreme Economic Council.

FAMILY: Married with a son.

ADDRESS/TELEPHONE: 30 Yartsevskaya Street, Moscow. 149–0429 (office).

Bogdanov, Feliks Petrovich

POSITION: Russian Federation Ambassador to Romania; Ambassador Extraordinary and Plenipotentiary

BIRTHPLACE/DATE: Moscow, December 11, 1934

NATIONALITY: Russian

EDUCATION: Graduated in 1958 from the Moscow State Institute of International Relations, and in 1972 from the Higher Diplomatic School of the USSR Ministry of Foreign Affairs. Good command of French, Hungarian, and English.

CAREER: From 1958 to 1963, Practical Student, Secretary of the Consulate Department; Interpreter; Attaché at the USSR Embassy to Hungary. From 1963 to 1967, Attaché, Third Secretary, Second Secretary of the Fifth European Department of the USSR Ministry of Foreign Affairs. From 1967 to 1970, First Secretary at the USSR Embassy in Upper Volta. From 1972 to 1973, Counsellor, then Minister-Counsellor at the USSR Embassy in Hungary. From 1979 to 1985, Deputy Head of the Fifth European Department. From 1985 to 1987, USSR Ambassador to Burkina Faso. From 1987 to 1990, USSR Ambassador to Belgium. From 1990 to 1991, USSR Ambassador to Romania.

FAMILY: Married.

ADDRESS/TELEPHONE: Embasada Russian Federation in Romania, Bucuresti sos Kiseleff 6, Romania. 17–0120; 17–1309 (Consulate Department); Telex: 6511317 (Consulate Department via TASS).

Bogomolov, Oleg Timofeyevich

POSITION: Director of the Russian Academy of Sciences' Institute of World Economic and Political Research; Academician of the Russian Academy of Sciences; member of the President's Political Consultative Council

BIRTHPLACE/DATE: Moscow, August 20, 1927

NATIONALITY: Russian

EDUCATION: Graduated in 1949 from the Moscow Institute of Foreign Trade. Doctor of Econom-

ics (1967); Professor (1969). Speaks English, German, and French.
CAREER: From 1949 to 1951, Consultant to the USSR Ministry of Foreign Trade. In 1950, joined the Communist Party. From 1951 to 1954, Lecturer at the Institute of Foreign Trade. From 1954 to 1956, Senior Advisor to the Secretariat of the Council for Mutual Economic Assistance. From 1956 to 1962, Senior Researcher, then Sector Chief at the Economic Studies Research Institute of the USSR State Planning Committee. From 1962 to 1969, Consultant, then Consulting Group Chief at the Central Committee's Liaison Department for Communist and Workers' Parties of Socialist Countries. From 1967 to 1978, Division Head at Moscow University; Professor. From 1962 and 1969, member of the Central Committee. From 1969, Director of the Institute of the Socialist World Economy of the USSR (now Russian) Academy of Sciences. From 1970 to 1986, Commission Member of the Comecon (Council for Mutual Economic Assistance) of the USSR Council of Ministers Presidium. From 1972 to 1981, Corresponding Member of the USSR Academy of Sciences' Department of Economics. From 1980, Professor at the Central Committee's Academy of Social Sciences. From 1981, Academician of the USSR Academy of Sciences' Department of Economics. Former elected USSR People's Deputy. From 1989, member of the Committee for Economic Reforms of the USSR Council of Ministers. From 1990, Executive Committee Consultant of the International Economic Association. From 1991, member of the Consultative Council of the Russian Federation Supreme Soviet Chairman; Chairman of the Russian Federation Association of Economists; member of the Council for Foreign Policy of the Russian Federation Ministry of Foreign Affairs.
MAJOR WORKS: More than 300 publications on international economy and post-communist economic problems.
HONORS/AWARDS: Order of the October Revolution (1975); two Orders of the Red Banner of Labor (1971, 1987).
FAMILY: Married with children.
ADDRESS/TELEPHONE: Novocheryomushkinskaya Street, Moscow, 117418. 120–8200.

Bokan, Yuri Ivanovich
POSITION: President of the Social Ecology of Man Via Mass Creativity Public Organization (Dark-Blue Movement); Chairman of the Republican Humanitarian Party
BIRTHPLACE/DATE: Dobromil, Ukraine, 1945
NATIONALITY: Russian
EDUCATION: Graduated from the Tbilisi Conservatory (piano) and from the All-Union Finance and Economics Institute. Doctor of Philosophy.
CAREER: Music Teacher in Tbilisi; First Secretary of the Khabarovsk City Komsomol Committee; Culture Department Head of the Komsomol Central Committee; Consultant to the Central Committee's Department for Contacts with Socio-Political Organizations.
MAJOR WORKS: Scientific works on public creativity problems.
FAMILY: Married.
ADDRESS/TELEPHONE: 15 Varvarka Street, Moscow, 103012. 206–3134 (office).

Bokov, Stanislav Nikolayevich
POSITION: Chairman of the All-Russia Foreign Trade Tekhnopromexport (Technical and Industrial Equipment Export) Association
BIRTHPLACE/DATE: Chelyabinsk, 1937
NATIONALITY: Russian
EDUCATION: Graduated in 1961 from the Moscow Power Engineering Institute.
CAREER: To 1976, Assembly Worker of the Mosenergomontazh (Moscow Energy Equipment) Trust at the Cherepetskaya State Regional Electric Power Station in Tula region. From 1976 to 1981, Chief Engineer of the Iran Construction Management. From 1981 to 1990, Deputy Chairman of Tekhnopromexport.
HONORS/AWARDS: Order of the Badge of Honor.
FAMILY: Married with two sons.
ADDRESS/TELEPHONE: 18/1 Ovchinnikovskaya Naberezhnaya, Moscow. 220–1523; 231–0122.

Boldin, Valery Ivanovich
POSITION: Former USSR Presidential Chief of Staff and member of the USSR Presidential Council
BIRTHPLACE/DATE: July 9, 1935
NATIONALITY: Russian

EDUCATION: Graduated in 1961 from the Economics Department at the Moscow Timiryazev Academy of Agriculture and from the Central Committee's Academy of Social Sciences. Doctor of Economics.
CAREER: From 1953 to 1960, Radio Mechanic of the Moscow-Ryazan Railway Administration. In 1960, Staff Member of *Pravda* (*Truth*) daily. From 1961 to 1965, Central Committee Functionary. From 1969, Economics Analyst, Agricultural Editor and Editorial Board Member of *Pravda*, and Lecturer at the Higher Economics Courses of the USSR State Planning Committee. From 1981, Central Committee Assistant Secretary. From 1985 to 1987, Agriculture Assistant to the Central Committee General Secretary. From 1985 to 1989, Deputy of the USSR Supreme Soviet Council of the Union. From 1987, General Department Head of the Central Committee. From 1986 to 1988, Alternate Member of the Central Committee. From 1988, Full Member of the Central Committee. From 1990 to August 1991, Head of the USSR President's Cabinet; USSR People's Deputy; member of the Presidential Council. In August 1991, arrested on charges related to the attempted coup. On December 18, 1991, released for health reasons.
FAMILY: Married with a daughter.
TELEPHONE: 229–4662 (Russian Federation Procurator's Office).

Boldyrev, Yuri Yuryevich
POSITION: Russian Federation Chief State Inspector; Control Department Head of the Russian President's Administration
BIRTHPLACE/DATE: Leningrad, 1960
NATIONALITY: Russian
EDUCATION: Graduated in 1983 from the Leningrad Electrical Engineering Institute and in 1989 from the Leningrad Philosophy and Economics Institute. Majored in Labor Sociology.
CAREER: Senior Engineer at the Leningrad Central Research Institute of Ship Electronics, Electrical Engineering, and Technology. From 1989 to December 1991, USSR People's Deputy; member of the USSR Supreme Soviet Committee for Issues of the Councils of People's Deputies and the Development of Self-Government; member of the USSR Supreme Soviet Committee for State Construction; member of the USSR Supreme Soviet Inter-Regional Parliamentary Faction. From 1990 to February 1992, member of the Supreme Consultative Coordination Council of the Russian Supreme Soviet Chairman.
FAMILY: Married.
ADDRESS/TELEPHONE: 2 Krasnopresnenskaya Naberezhnaya, Moscow. 205–5016; 205–9229 (office).

Bolgarin, Gennadi Romanovich
POSITION: Vice President of the Social Ecology of Man Via Mass Creativity Public Organization (Dark-Blue Movement); Political Council Member of the Republican Humanitarian Party
BIRTHPLACE/DATE: Tbilisi, 1946
EDUCATION: Graduated in 1971 from the Tbilisi Conservatory (piano). Speaks English.
CAREER: From 1970 to 1974, Teacher at a secondary music school, music college, and conservatory. Participated in republican TV music programs. From 1974 to 1976, Lecturer at the Moscow State Culture Institute. From 1976, Music Editor, Film Making Manager, Head of the International Department's Advertising and Information Service of the USSR Goskino (State Committee for Cinematography). In the late 1980s, Co-Founder of the Social Ecology of Man Organization.
MAJOR WORKS: Author of many TV and radio productions, publications in Soviet and foreign press, and *Our Holidays*.
FAMILY: Married with two children.
ADDRESS/TELEPHONE: 15 Varvarka Street, Moscow, 103012. 206–3134; 206–4587; Fax: 200–3262.

Boltyansky, Andrey Vladimirovich
POSITION: PetroSoviet (St. Petersburg Council) Deputy; Russian Federation People's Deputy
BIRTHPLACE/DATE: Moscow, 1955
NATIONALITY: Russian
EDUCATION: Graduated in 1977 from the Mathematics and Mechanics Department of Leningrad State University, and in 1980 from the postgraduate course. In 1981, defended Doctor's thesis.
CAREER: Assistant Professor of the Higher Mathematics Division at the Leningrad Technological Institute for the Pulp-and-Paper Industry. In

1989, left the Institute to take up politics. In 1988, following the First Social-Democratic Conference, founded the Social-Democratic Club (Renaissance). Co-Chairman of the Leningrad Bloc of Democratic Organizations Elections–90. Russian Federation People's Deputy.
ADDRESS/TELEPHONE: PetroSoviet, 3 Isaakiyevskaya Square, St. Petersburg. 319–9818.

Bondarchuk, Anatoli Pavlovich
POSITION: Professor of the Department of Track and Field at the Kiev State Institute of Physical Education; Coach of the CIS Track and Field National Hammer-Throwing Team
BIRTHPLACE/DATE: Starokonstantinovo, Khmelnitsk region, May 31, 1940
NATIONALITY: Ukrainian
EDUCATION: Doctor of Education; Professor.
CAREER: Hammer-Throwing Champion. From 1977, Professor of the Track and Field Department at the Kiev State Institute of Physical Education.
HONORS/AWARDS: USSR Honorary Master of Sports; USSR Honorary Coach. European Hammer-Throwing Champion (1969); European Cup (1970, 1973); European Championship Bronze Medal (1971); Summer Olympic Champion (1972); Summer Olympic Bronze Medal (1976).
FAMILY: Married with two children.
ADDRESS/TELEPHONE: The Department of Track and Field, 1 Fizkultura Street, Kiev–5, 232650. 227–5452 (office).

Bondarenko, Aleksandr Pavlovich
POSITION: Ambassador at Large; Ambassador Extraordinary and Plenipotentiary
BIRTHPLACE/DATE: Aktyubensk, June 10, 1922
NATIONALITY: Russian
EDUCATION: Graduated from the Moscow State Institute of International Relations in 1949.
CAREER: From 1940 to 1942, Military Unit Komsomol Bureau Secretary in the Far East. From 1942, Commissar of the Stalingrad Chemical Platoon. From 1942 to 1943, hospitalized for medical treatment. From 1943, Instructor of the Aktyubinsk Municipal Military Committee. From 1943 to 1944, Public School Military Instructor. From 1949 to 1950, Trainee of the Third European Department of the USSR Ministry of Foreign Affairs. From 1950 to 1953, Aide, Senior Aide at the USSR Auditing Mission in Germany. From 1953 to 1954, Expert at the USSR Supreme Commissar Administration in Germany. From 1954 to 1955, Expert at the USSR Embassy in the German Democratic Republic and the USSR Supreme Commissar in Germany. From 1955 to 1957, Second Secretary of the Third European Department; from 1957 to 1961, First Secretary; from 1961 to 1962, Counsellor. From 1962 to 1967, Minister-Counsellor at the USSR Embassy in the Federal Republic of Germany. From 1971 to 1990, Acting Head, Head, and Board Member of the Third European Department.
HONORS/AWARDS: Order of the Great Patriotic War; Order of the Red Banner of Labor; Order of the People's Friendship.
FAMILY: Single.
TELEPHONE: 241–5354 (office).

Bondarev, Grigory Semyonovich
POSITION: Russian Federation People's Deputy; member of the Russian Federation Supreme Soviet Committee for Foreign Affairs and International Economic Relations Assistant Professor at Moscow N.E. Bauman Technical University; Engineer; Researcher; Political Council Member of Russia's Republican Party; Coordinator of the Republican and Social-Democratic Parliamentary Faction; Organizing Committee Member of the Parliamentary Reform Coalition
BIRTHPLACE/DATE: Drogobych, Lvov region, 1946
EDUCATION: Graduated in 1970 from the Bauman Higher Technical School.
CAREER: From 1970 to 1972, served in the army. From 1972 to 1977, Plant Engineer.
MAJOR WORKS: Development of the Russian Federation Law on Russian Federation Citizenship.
FAMILY: Married with two children.
ADDRESS/TELEPHONE: 2 Krasnopresnenskaya Naberezhnaya, Moscow. 205–5120; 205–8414 (office).

Bondarev, Yuri Vasilyevich
POSITION: Writer; Board Member of the Confederation of Writers' Unions

BIRTHPLACE/DATE: Orsk, Orenburg region, 1924
EDUCATION: Graduated in 1951 from the Gorky Literary Institute in Moscow.
CAREER: In 1949, wrote first publications. Board Chairman of the Russian Federation Writers' Union. Board Secretary of the USSR Writers' Union. From 1987, member of the USSR Academy of Sciences' Academic Council for Problems of Russian Culture.
MAJOR WORKS: *Commanders' Youth* (1956); *The Last Salvoes* (1959); *Relatives* (1969); *The Silence* (1962); *The Two* (1964); *The Burning Snow* (1969); *The Shore* (1975); *The Choice* (1980); *Temptation* (1990). Film scripts.
HONORS/AWARDS: USSR State Prizes; Russian Federation State Prize; Prize of Lenin; Hero of Socialist Labor.
FAMILY: Married with two children.
ADDRESS/TELEPHONE: 19 Lomonosov Prospekt, Flat #148, Moscow, 117311. 246–2703 (office).

Borisenkov, Yevgeni Panteleymonovich
POSITION: Director of the Voyenkov Main Geophysical Observatory; Editor in Chief of *Chelovek i Stikhiya* (*Man and the Elements*) collection; Chief Editor of the *Atlas of Hydrometeorological Data of the World's Continents*; member of the International Commission for Dynamical Meteorology; Corresponding Member and Vice President of the Petrovskaya Academy of Arts and Sciences
BIRTHPLACE/DATE: Vyazma, 1924
NATIONALITY: Russian
EDUCATION: Graduated in 1952 from the Leningrad Institute of Hydrometeorology. From 1955 to 1957, advanced student at the Meteorology Department of the Mozhaisky Military Academy. In 1957, defended thesis for a degree of Doctor; in 1964, for a degree of Postdoctor. Doctor of Physics and Mathematics; Professor. Speaks English.
CAREER: From 1952 to 1955, served in the army. From 1963 to 1972, Deputy Director of the Research Institute of the Arctic and Antarctic. From 1972, Director of the Voyenkov Main Geophysics Observatory. From 1956 to 1982, Professor of the Physics of Atmosphere Division at Leningrad University. From 1982, Professor at the Leningrad Institute of Hydrometeorology. From 1971 to 1979, Chairman of the International Commission for Polar Meteorology. From 1985 to 1991, Editorial Board Member of *Radioaktivnost v Okruzhayushchei Srede* (*Environmental Radioactivity*) magazine.
MAJOR WORKS: *Circulation of Carbon and the Climate* (1989); *Atmospheric Energy Issues* (1962); *Millennial Chronicle of Outstanding Natural Phenomena* (1989); *The Climate and Human Activity* (1976); *Numerical Methods of Weather Forecasts*.
HONORS/AWARDS: Russian Federation Honored Worker of Science and Technology.
FAMILY: Married with two children.
ADDRESS/TELEPHONE: 7 Karbyshev Street, St. Petersburg, 194018. 247–4390 (office).

Borisov, Oleg (Albert) Ivanovich
POSITION: Head of the Oleg Borisov Private Theatrical Company
BIRTHPLACE/DATE: Privolzhsk, Ivanovo region, 1929
EDUCATION: Graduated in 1961 from the Moscow Academic Art Theater (MKhAT) Studio School.
CAREER: From 1951 to 1964, Actor of the Kiev Lesya Ukrainka Theater. From 1964 to 1983, Actor of the Leningrad Bolshoi Drama Theater. From 1983 to 1989, Actor of the Moscow Academic Art Theater. From May 1991, Founder and Head of the Oleg Borisov Private Theatrical Company; Board Member of the Russian Union of Theater Workers; member of the Russian Union of Film Makers.
MAJOR WORKS: Performed in stage productions: *Summer Residents* (Maxim Gorky); *And Quiet Flows the Don* (Mikhail Sholokhov); *Uncle Vanya* (Anton Chekhov); *A Gentle Creature* (Fyodor Dostoevski). Performed in films: *The Train Has Stopped*; *Rafferti*; *The Only Witness*; *Servant*.
HONORS/AWARDS: USSR People's Artist; two USSR State Prizes; Gold Cup (Venice, 1990); Nika Prize; Russian Federation State Prize (1991).
FAMILY: Married with a son.
ADDRESS/TELEPHONE: 39 Bolshaya Gruzinskaya Street, Flat #202, Moscow, 123056. 253–8253 (home).

Borkovsky, Gennadi Alekseyevich

POSITION: Rector of the Russian State Herzen Teachers' Training Institute; Academician of the Russian Academy of Sciences

BIRTHPLACE/DATE: Altai region, 1941

NATIONALITY: Russian

EDUCATION: From 1963 to 1965, postgraduate student at the Leningrad State Teachers' Training Institute. In 1968, received the Doctor degree; in 1986, received the Postdoctor degree. Doctor of Physics and Mathematics; Professor.

CAREER: From 1968, Senior Researcher at the Leningrad State Teachers' Training Institute. From 1987, Professor; Rector of the State Military University; member of the Creative Teaching Association; member of the Teacher's Association. Kuibyshev District Council Deputy.

MAJOR WORKS: Author of more than 150 publications.

FAMILY: Married with a child.

ADDRESS/TELEPHONE: 48 Moika Street, St. Petersburg, 191186. 312–1195.

Borodin, Yuri Ivanovich

POSITION: Director of the Clinical and Experimental Lymphology Research Institute of the Russian Academy of Sciences, Siberian branch; member of the Academy of Medical Sciences

BIRTHPLACE/DATE: Blagoveshchensk, Amur region, 1929

NATIONALITY: Russian

EDUCATION: Graduated in 1953 from the Novosibirsk Medical Institute. Doctor of Medicine; Professor. Speaks German.

CAREER: From 1962 to 1964, Director of the Experimental Biology and Medicine Institute of the USSR Academy of Medical Sciences, Siberian branch. From 1964 to 1971, Anatomy Division Head, then Rector of the Novosibirsk Medical Institute. From 1980 and 1989, Presidium Chairman and Vice President of the USSR Academy of Medical Sciences; elected USSR People's Deputy. From 1989 to 1991, USSR Supreme Soviet Presidium Member, Chairman of the USSR Supreme Soviet Committee for Public Health, member of the Communist Parliamentary Faction, member of Siberia and the Far East Parliamentary Faction, and member of Medical Workers for the Protection of Public Health Parliamentary Faction. Presidium Academician of the USSR Academy of Medical Sciences and the USSR (now Russian) Academy of Sciences.

FAMILY: Married with a son and a daughter.

ADDRESS/TELEPHONE: 2 Academician Simakov Street, Novosibirsk, 630117. 32–4552 (office).

Borovik, Artyom Genrikhovich

POSITION: Editor in Chief of *Sovershenno Sekretno* (*Top Secret*) newspaper; Director-General of the International Detective and Political Novel Association, Moscow Headquarters; Editor in Chief of *Detektiv i Politika* (*Detective and Politics*) magazine; Editor in Chief of "Sovershenno Sekretno" (Top Secret) TV program

BIRTHPLACE/DATE: Moscow, 1960

EDUCATION: Graduated in 1982 from the International Journalism Department at the Moscow State Institute of International Relations. Good command of English and Spanish.

CAREER: From 1982 to 1987, Correspondent-Intern, Correspondent, Senior Correspondent for *Sovietskaya Rossiya* (*Soviet Russia*) daily. From 1987 to 1990, Commentator, International Department Head of *Ogonyek* magazine. From 1990, Deputy Editor in Chief of *Sovershenno Sekretno* newspaper and Deputy Director-General of the International Detective and Political Novel Association, Moscow Headquarters. From 1990 to 1991, Acting Editor in Chief of *Sovershenno Sekretno*. Former member of the USSR Writers' Union.

HONORS/AWARDS: USSR Journalists' Union Prize; International Prize of the Armed Forces International Journal.

FAMILY: Married with a son.

ADDRESS/TELEPHONE: 40 Kalinin Prospekt, Flat #104, Moscow. 291–9581; 291–9862.

Borovik, Genrikh Avyezerovich

POSITION: Chairman of the Peace and Accord World Federation; Political Analyst at Ostankino TV and Radio Broadcasting Company

BIRTHPLACE/DATE: Pyatigorsk, 1927

NATIONALITY: Russian

EDUCATION: Graduated from the International Journalism Department at the Moscow State Institute of International Relations.

CAREER: From 1982 to 1987, Editor in Chief of

Teatr (*Theater*) magazine. USSR People's Deputy of the Movement for Peace Organization; member of the USSR Supreme Soviet's Committee for Foreign Affairs; member of the International Prizes of Lenin Committee. In 1987, elected Chairman of the Soviet Peace Committee (now the Peace and Accord World Federation).
MAJOR WORKS: Books: *One Murder History*; *A Story-Chronicle* (1980); *One Year of Restless Sun* (1971). Plays: *Three Minutes of Martin Grow* (1971); *Interview in Buenos Aires* (1976); *Agent 00* (staged in 1982). Novel-essay: "Prologue" (1984). Screenplays, essays.
HONORS/AWARDS: USSR State Prize (1977); Lenin and State Prizes.
FAMILY: Married with children.

Borovoy, Konstantin Natanovich
POSITION: President of the Russian Mercantile Exchange (RME); Board Member of the Russian Union of Industrialists and Entrepreneurs; Leader of the Ekonomicheskaya Svoboda (Economic Freedom) Party
BIRTHPLACE/DATE: Moscow, 1948
EDUCATION: Graduated in 1970 from the Moscow Institute of Railway Engineers and in 1974 from the Mechanics and Mathematics Department at Moscow State University. Doctor of Technology.
CAREER: Computer Engineer and Research Fellow at a number of research institutes. Worked at the Computer Engineering Division of the Moscow Institute of Railway Engineers, and at the Moscow Institute of Land Management Engineers. Assistant Professor. From 1987, engaged in business. Publisher of *My i Kompyuter* (*The Computer and Us*) magazine. Board Chairman of the Business Cooperation and Social Development Association of the USSR Charity and Health Foundation. From 1990 to 1992, General Manager of the Russian Mercantile Exchange; Co-Founder of the Military-Industrial Investment and Rinaco (Russian Investment Joint-Stock Companies). In May 1992, founded the Economic Freedom Party.
FAMILY: Married with two children.
ADDRESS/TELEPHONE: The Russian Mercantile Exchange, 3/4 Novaya Ploshchad, Entrance 2, Moscow. 924–7862 (office).

Borshchevsky, Eduard Iosifovich
POSITION: Head of the Department of Regional Cooperation and Economic Problems; Counsellor Extraordinary and Plenipotentiary, First Grade
BIRTHPLACE/DATE: Borisov, Minsk region, July 16, 1934
NATIONALITY: Byelorussian
EDUCATION: Studied at Byelorussian State University. Graduated from the Moscow State Institute of International Relations in 1959.
CAREER: From 1950 to 1952, School Library Head. From 1952, Regional Komsomol Committee Department Head. From 1959 to 1963, Aide to the Byelorussian Foreign Minister. From 1963 to 1965, Second Secretary of the European Department at the USSR Permanent Mission to the UN in Geneva. From 1965 to 1968, First Secretary at the USSR Permanent Mission in Geneva. From 1968 to 1970, Department Head of the Byelorussian Ministry of Foreign Affairs. From 1970 to 1973, Deputy Manager of the Byelorussian Council of Ministers. From 1973 to 1979, Deputy Permanent Representative of the USSR in Geneva. From 1979 to 1987, Deputy Head of the Ministry of Naval Fleet. From 1987 to 1988, Expert of the Department of International Economic Relations of the USSR Ministry of Foreign Affairs; from 1988, Deputy Head. From 1988 to 1990, General Secretary of the Special Personnel Commission Secretariat. From 1990 to 1992, Deputy Head of the Department of International Economic Relations.
HONORS/AWARDS: Order of the Red Banner of Labor.
FAMILY: Married with two children.
TELEPHONE: 241–7997.

Borzov, Valery Filippovich
POSITION: Chairman of the Ukrainian National Olympics Committee; Minister
BIRTHPLACE/DATE: October 20, 1949
NATIONALITY: Ukrainian
CAREER: 1969, 1971, and 1974 European Champion (short distance races). In 1972, Champion of the Summer Olympics (100- and 200-meter races). Secretary of the Ukranian Central Komsomol Committee; Chairman of the State Sports Committee.
HONORS/AWARDS: USSR Honored Master of Sports; European Cup (1975); Summer Olympic

Silver Medal (4 x 100-meter relay race, 1976); Summer Olympic Bronze Medals (100-meter race and 4 x 100-meter relay race, 1976).
FAMILY: Married with a daughter.
ADDRESS/TELEPHONE: The Sports and Youth Ministry, 42 Esplanadnaya Street, Kiev 23. 220–0944; 220–0200 (office).

Bosenko, Nikolay Vasilyevich
POSITION: Former USSR People's Deputy; former USSR Supreme Soviet Presidium Member; former USSR Supreme Soviet Chairman of the Committee of Veterans and Invalids
BIRTHPLACE/DATE: Pyatigorsk, Stavropol region, 1918
NATIONALITY: Russian
EDUCATION: Graduated from the Artillery Academy in 1945.
CAREER: From 1945 to 1953, Dispatcher, Foreman, Technical Department Head of a repair factory. From 1957 to 1959, State Farm Director. From 1957 to 1961, held leading positions on the Stavropol Region Agriculture Board. From 1961 to 1973, District Party Committee Secretary, Secretary, then Head of the Stavropol Communist Party Regional Committee. From 1973 to 1985, Chairman of the Russian Agricultural Industry Equipment Supply Committee. From May 1989, USSR People's Deputy, USSR Supreme Soviet Presidium Member, Chairman of the USSR Supreme Soviet Committee of Veterans and Invalids. Former member of the Communist Deputy Group.
FAMILY: Married with a son.
ADDRESS/TELEPHONE: 27 Kalinin Prospekt, Moscow. 203–5207 (office).

Bossert, Victor Davidovich
POSITION: Former Board Chairman and President of PI-fond (Investment and Progress)
BIRTHPLACE/DATE: Omsk region, 1948
NATIONALITY: Russian
EDUCATION: Graduated from the Business School at George Washington University.
CAREER: Engineer, Shop Head, Factory Director of the Omsk Motor-Building Industrial Complex. In 1987, elected Director-General of RAF Plant (the first democratic elections of Director-General in the Soviet Union).
FAMILY: Married with three children.
ADDRESS/TELEPHONE: 18 Aviatsiyas Street, Elgava, Latvia. 2–0243 (office).

Bostorin, Oleg Vladimirovich
POSITION: Russian Ambassador to Thailand; Secretariat Representative of the UN Economic and Social Commission for Asia and the Pacific
BIRTHPLACE/DATE: Rybinsk, Yaroslav region, October 1, 1931
NATIONALITY: Russian
EDUCATION: Graduated from the Moscow State Institute of International Relations in 1954.
CAREER: From 1954 to 1956, Trainee at the USSR Mission in Thailand. From 1958 to 1959, Attaché of the Secretariat of the USSR Deputy Foreign Minister. From 1960 to 1962, Second Secretary of the Secretariat of the USSR Deputy Foreign Minister. From 1962 to 1964, Second Secretary at the USSR Embassy in Thailand. From 1964 to 1966, First Secretary of the Secretariat of the USSR Deputy Foreign Minister. From 1966 to 1969, Aide to the USSR Deputy Foreign Minister. From 1969 to 1972, Counsellor at the USSR Embassy in Singapore. From 1972, Expert of the Department of Southeastern Asia of the USSR Ministry of Foreign Affairs; from 1972 to 1978, Deputy Head. From 1978 to 1979, Minister-Counsellor at the USSR Embassy in the Philippines. From 1979 to 1985, USSR Ambassador to Cambodia. From 1985 to 1986, Chief Counsellor of the Foreign Policy Planning Board of the USSR Ministry of Foreign Affairs. From 1986 to 1988, Deputy Department Head of the Foreign Policy Planning Board. From 1989 to 1991, Department Head of Southern Asia.
HONORS/AWARDS: Order of the People's Friendship.
FAMILY: Married with two children.
TELEPHONE: 234–9824 (Bangkok).

Botvinnik, Mikhail Moiseyevich
POSITION: International Chess Grand Master
BIRTHPLACE/DATE: Repino village, Leningrad region, 1911
EDUCATION: Graduated from the Electromechanical Department at Leningrad Polytechnic. From 1932 to 1937, postgraduate student. Doctor of Technology; Professor.
CAREER: From 1932 to 1944, Engineer and Lab-

oratory Assistant at Leningrad Polytechnic. During World War II, Head of the Perm High-Voltage Insulation Service. From 1944 to 1954, Senior Engineer of the Technical Directorate of the Ministry of Electric Power. From 1954, worked at the All-Union Electric Power Engineering Research Institute; from 1974, Sector Head of the Institute. In 1948, won the World Chess Tournament. In 1951, finished in a draw versus Bronshtein. In 1954, finished in a draw versus Smyslov. In 1958, won the World Chess Return Match versus Smyslov. In 1961, won the World Chess Return Match versus Tahl. In 1963, lost the World Chess Tournament versus Petrosyan.
MAJOR WORKS: A four-volume edition *Analytical and Critical Works*. Four monographs on cybernetics, three monographs on electrical engineering.
HONORS/AWARDS: USSR Honored Master of Sports; Russian Federation Honored Cultural Worker; Honorary Doctor of Mathematics at Serrare University, Italy (1991); Russian Federation Honored Worker of Science and Technology; two Orders of the Badge of Honor; Order of Lenin; Order of the Red Banner of Labor; Order of the October Revolution. Seven-time Chess Champion of the USSR (1931 to 1952).
FAMILY: Widower with a daughter.
ADDRESS/TELEPHONE: 7 Third Frunzenskaya Street, Flat #154, Moscow, 119270. 291–8717 (office); 242–1586 (home).

Bovin, Aleksandr Yevgenyevich
POSITION: Russian Ambassador to Israel; Ambassador Extraordinary and Plenipotentiary
BIRTHPLACE/DATE: Leningrad, August 9, 1930
NATIONALITY: Russian
CAREER: From 1953 to 1954, Krasnodar Region People's Judge. From 1954 to 1955, Propaganda Department Head of the Neftegorsk District Communist Party. From 1955 to 1956, People's Judge, Scientific Consultant to the Philosophy Department of *Kommunist* magazine. From 1963 to 1968, Consultant to the Central Committee. From 1968 to 1972, Consultant Group Head of the Central Committee. From 1972, Political Correspondent for *Izvestia* (*News*) daily. From 1991, USSR Ambassador to Israel. Russian Supreme Soviet Deputy. To August 1991, member of the Communist Party.
MAJOR WORKS: Numerous articles in magazines and newspapers.
HONORS/AWARDS: USSR State Prize; Order of Lenin; Order of the October Revolution; Order of the Red Banner of Labor.
FAMILY: Married with a daughter.
ADDRESS/TELEPHONE: 32/34 Smolenskaya-Sennaya, Moscow, 121200. 510–5172 (Tel Aviv); 244–4013 (Moscow).

Boyko, Vitaly Ivanovich
POSITION: Chairman of the All-Russia Tekhnopromimport (Technical and Industrial Equipment Import) Foreign Trade Association
BIRTHPLACE/DATE: 1937
NATIONALITY: Ukrainian
EDUCATION: Graduated in 1960 from the Odessa Institute of Naval Engineering and in 1975 from the All-Union Foreign Trade Academy.
CAREER: From 1966 to 1971, worked for the All-Union Sudimport Association at the USSR Trade Mission in Greece. From 1979 to 1984, Senior Engineer, Deputy Director, Section Director of Tekhnomashexport (Machinery Export) Foreign Trade Association; USSR Deputy Trade Representative in Indonesia; Deputy Director-General, then Director-General of Tekhnomashexport.
FAMILY: Married with a son.
ADDRESS/TELEPHONE: 18/1 Ovchinnikovskaya Naberezhnaya, Moscow. 220–1257; 233–9243; 220–1831 (office).

Bragin, Nikolay Yevgenyevich
POSITION: Director-General of the Sokolniki Railway-Carriage Repair Works (SVARZ)
BIRTHPLACE/DATE: Kaliningrad, 1948
NATIONALITY: Russian
EDUCATION: Graduated in 1975 from the Moscow Metallurgical Institute and in 1985 from the Central Committee's Higher Party School.
CAREER: From 1965 to 1967, Turner at the Moscow Serp i Molot (Sickle and Hammer) Metallurgical Works. From 1967 to 1969, Mechanic at the Moscow Automechanical Institute. From 1969 to 1979, Superintendent of the SVARZ shop. From 1979 to 1988, Functionary of the Sokolniki District Communist Party Committee in Moscow.

FAMILY: Married with a son.
ADDRESS/TELEPHONE: 15/17 Matrosskaya Tishina Street, Moscow, 107014. 268–0066 (office).

Braginsky, Aleksandr Pavlovich
POSITION: Moscow Government Minister
BIRTHPLACE/DATE: Moscow, 1948
EDUCATION: Graduated in 1972 from the Moscow Institute of Radio Engineering, Electronics, and Automation. Doctor of Physics and Mathematics; Professor.
CAREER: From 1968 to 1981, Laboratory Assistant-Electrician of the All-Union Electrotechnical Institute; held various posts, from Engineer to Researcher. From 1981 to 1990, Researcher, Assistant Professor, Professor at the Moscow Institute of Railway Engineers. From 1990 to 1991, Chairman of the Mossoviet (Moscow Council) Standing Commission. From 1991 to 1992, Deputy Director-General of the Moscow Mayor's Department.
FAMILY: Married with a child.
ADDRESS/TELEPHONE: 56 Novoarbatsky Prospekt, Moscow. 290–8876 (office).

Bratishchev, Igor Mikhailovich
POSITION: Head of the Economic Theory Division of the Rostov-on-Don Institute of Railway Engineers; member of the Russian Federation Supreme Soviet Committee for Inter-Republican Relations and Regional Policies; Co-Chairman of the Russian Communists Group
BIRTHPLACE/DATE: Orel, 1938
NATIONALITY: Russian
EDUCATION: Graduated in 1965 from Rostov State University; from 1965 to 1968, postgraduate student. Doctor of Economics; Professor.
CAREER: From 1956 to 1957, Metallurgist in Novorossiysk. From 1957 to 1960, served in the army. From 1969 to 1978, Assistant Professor of the Political Economy Department at the Nedelin Higher Military Command School in Rostov. From 1978 to 1986, Assistant Professor. From 1986, Russian Federation People's Deputy; Coordinator of the Russian Unity Opposition Bloc; member of the Russian Communist Workers Party.
FAMILY: Married with a daughter.
ADDRESS/TELEPHONE: 145 Taganrogskaya Street, Flat #51, Rostov-on-Don, 344069. 31–9399 (home).

Brezhnev, Vladimir Arkadyevich
POSITION: President of the Transstroi (Transport Construction) State Corporation
BIRTHPLACE/DATE: Dneprodzerzhinsk, 1931
NATIONALITY: Russian
EDUCATION: Graduated from the Odessa Hydrotechnical Institute.
CAREER: From 1959, held different posts, including Manager of the Yugozaptransstroi (Southwest Transport Construction) Trust of the Povolzhye and South Glavzheldorstroi (Main Railway Construction) of the USSR Transport Construction Ministry. From 1975, USSR Deputy, then First Deputy Minister of Transport Construction. From 1985 to September 1991, USSR Minister of Transport Construction.
FAMILY: Married with two children and two grandchildren.
ADDRESS/TELEPHONE: 21 Sadovo-Spasskaya Street, Moscow, 107217. 262–2570 (secretary).

Brumel, Valery Nikolayevich
POSITION: Journalist; Writer
BIRTHPLACE/DATE: Tobuzino village, Chita region, Siberia, 1942
NATIONALITY: Russian
EDUCATION: Graduated from the Lvov State Institute of Physical Education.
CAREER: In 1960, High Jump Silver Medalist. In 1964, Summer Olympic Champion. In 1962, European Champion. Set six World High Jump Records.
MAJOR WORKS: Novels, stories, plays, and screenplays.
HONORS/AWARDS: USSR Honored Master of Sports; Sportsman of the Year (1961, 1962, 1963).
FAMILY: Divorced with a son and a grandson.
ADDRESS/TELEPHONE: 5 Rzhevski Pereulok, Moscow, 121069. 241–8676 (home).

Brutents, Karen Nersesovich
POSITION: Counsellor to the President of the International Foundation for Socio-Economic and Political Studies (The Gorbachev Foundation)
BIRTHPLACE/DATE: Baku, 1924
NATIONALITY: Armenian

EDUCATION: Graduated from the Baku Medical Institute and from Azerbaijan State University. From 1954 to 1958, postgraduate student at the Central Committee's Academy of Social Sciences in Moscow. Doctor of Philosophy; Doctor of History. Good command of English and French.
CAREER: From 1945 to 1951, Physician. From 1959 to 1960, Consulting Editor of the Prague-based *World Marxist Review* journal. From 1961 to 1991, Aide, Consultant, Deputy Head, and First Deputy Head of the Central Committee's International Department. From May to December 1991, Deputy Aide to the USSR President.
FAMILY: Married with two children.
ADDRESS/TELEPHONE: 49 Leningradsky Prospekt, Moscow, 125468. 290–5802 (home); 943–9976 (office).

Bryachikhin, Aleksey Mikheyevich
POSITION: Prefect of the Western Prefecture of Moscow
BIRTHPLACE/DATE: Elektrostal, Moscow region, 1942
NATIONALITY: Russian
EDUCATION: Graduated from the All-Union Extramural Construction Engineering Institute and from the Central Committee's Academy of Social Sciences. Doctor of Economics.
CAREER: From 1960, worked at the Elektrostal Works in Moscow region. From 1963 to 1965, served in the army and held different leading posts in the Komsomol. From 1970 to 1974, Deputy Head of the Moscow Region Directorate, then of a Production Association of the Meat Industry. From 1974, First Deputy Chairman of the Zagorsk City Executive Committee. From 1979, Instructor of the Moscow Region Communist Party; Chairman of the Solntsevo District Council of People's Deputies in Moscow. In 1987, elected First Secretary of the Sevastopol District Communist Party. From 1990 to July 1991, Chairman of the Sevastopol District Council of People's Deputies in Moscow. To August 1991, member of the Politburo.
FAMILY: Married with a daughter.
ADDRESS/TELEPHONE: 12 Ivan Franko Street, Moscow, 121355. 443–4335 (office).

Bubka, Sergey Nazarovich
POSITION: Board President of the Bubka Sports Club
BIRTHPLACE/DATE: Voroshilovgrad, December 4, 1963
CAREER: In 1985, winner of the European Cup and World Cup for Pole-Vaulting. In 1985 and 1986, European Champion. In 1988, winner at the Summer Olympics. In 1991, World Champion. Set twenty-eight World Records.
HONORS/AWARDS: Honored Master of Sports.
FAMILY: Married with two sons.
TELEPHONE: 99–2042 (Donetsk home).

Bukin, Andrey Anatolyevich
POSITION: Soloist of the Igor Bobrin Theater of the Skating Arts; former Figure Skating Champion
BIRTHPLACE/DATE: Moscow, 1957
NATIONALITY: Russian
EDUCATION: Graduated from the State Institute of Physical Education.
CAREER: In 1965, began figure skating. From 1977, member of the USSR National Team. In 1982, 1983, and 1987, USSR Champion. In 1983, European Champion. From 1985 to 1987, European and World Figure Skating Champion. In 1988, Winter Olympic Champion. Serviceman of the Central Army Sports Club. From 1988 to 1990, Staff Member of the Figure Skating Federation.
HONORS/AWARDS: Winter Olympic Silver Medal (1984).
FAMILY: Married.
ADDRESS/TELEPHONE: 8 Luzhnetskaya Naberezhnaya, Moscow. 201–1231.

Bulay, Igor Borisovich
POSITION: Russian Ambassador to Argentina; Counsellor, First Grade
BIRTHPLACE/DATE: Moscow, May 17, 1947
NATIONALITY: Russian
EDUCATION: From 1965 to 1970, student at the Moscow State Institute of International Relations; then postgraduate student. Doctor of History.
CAREER: From 1975 to 1976, Trainee at the USSR Mission to the UN in New York. From 1978 to 1979, Junior Researcher. From 1979 to 1985, Instructor of the International Information Department of the Central Committee. From 1985 to 1991, Counsellor at the USSR Embassy in the United States. From 1991 to 1992, Expert of the Information Department of the USSR Ministry of

Foreign Affairs. From 1992 to 1993, Board Head of the Information and Press Department.
FAMILY: Married with two children.
TELEPHONE: 201–2536 (office).

Bulgak, Vladimir Borisovich
POSITION: Russian Federation Minister of Communications
BIRTHPLACE/DATE: Moscow, 1941
NATIONALITY: Russian
EDUCATION: Graduated in 1963 from the Moscow Telecommunications Institute and in 1972 from the Moscow G.V. Plekhanov Institute of National Economy. Doctor of Technology.
CAREER: In 1963, Mechanic of the Radio Systems and Radio Instruments Division at the Moscow Electrotechnical Communications Institute; Instructor of the Moscow City Komsomol Committee. From 1963 to 1968, held leading posts on different Komsomol committees. From 1968 to 1983, held engineering and administrative posts at the Moscow Municipal Radio Broadcasting Network. From 1983 to 1988, Head of the Main Planning and Finance Directorate. From 1988 to 1989, Head of the Main Economics Directorate. In 1990, Head of the Main Directorate for Communications Maintenance of the USSR Ministry of Communications. From 1990 to 1991, Russian Federation Minister of Communication, Information Science, and Space Research.
FAMILY: Married with a daughter.
ADDRESS/TELEPHONE: 5 Delegatskaya Street, Moscow, 103091. 973–3046 (office); 973–1464 (assistant).

Bulygin, Victor Vasilyevich
POSITION: Member of the Russian Federation Supreme Soviet; member of the Committee for Construction, Architecture, and Municipal Housing Economy
BIRTHPLACE/DATE: Tumenka village, Valuiki district, Belgorod region, 1932
EDUCATION: Graduated in 1964 from the Central Committee's Higher Party School and in 1965 from the Kursk Agricultural Institute.
CAREER: From 1947 to 1951, worked at the Michurin Collective Farm in Valuiki. From 1951 to 1956, worked at the Black Sea Fleet. From 1956 to 1959, involved in electoral activities for the Michurin Collective Farm Komsomol. From 1964 to 1972, Chairman of the Krasny Putilovets Collective Farm in Valuiki. From 1972 to 1973, Chairman of the Valuiki District Executive Committee. From 1973 to 1982, Second Secretary of the Valuiki City Communist Party. From 1982 to 1991, First Deputy Chairman, then Chairman of the Belgorod Region Agricultural and Industrial Union.
FAMILY: Married with a son and a daughter.
ADDRESS/TELEPHONE: 2 Krasnopresnenskaya Naberezhnaya, Moscow. 205–5095 (office).

Bunich, Pavel Grigoryevich
POSITION: Vice Rector of the Russian Government's Academy of National Economy; President of the International Leaseholders' and Entrepreneurs' Union; Vice President of the Russian Union of Industrialists and Entrepreneurs; member of the President's Political Consultative Council; Russian Supreme Soviet Presidium Member of the Scientific Council; Corresponding Member of the Russian Academy of Sciences
BIRTHPLACE/DATE: Moscow, October 25, 1929
NATIONALITY: Russian
EDUCATION: Graduated in 1952 from the Economics Department at Moscow State University and in 1955 from the postgraduate program. Doctor of Economics.
CAREER: From 1955 to 1966, worked from Senior Research Fellow to Deputy Director of the Research Institute of the USSR Ministry of Finance. From 1966 to 1971, Laboratory Head at the Central Economics and Mathematics Institute of the USSR Academy of Sciences. From 1971 to 1975, Presidium Member of the Far Eastern Research Center (FERC) of the USSR Academy of Sciences; Director of the Khabarovsk Research Institute of the FERC. From 1976 to 1990, Department Head at the Sergo Ordzhonikidze Institute of Management in Moscow; elected USSR People's Deputy. From July 1990 to August 1991, member of the Central Committee. From 1990 to December 1991, President of the USSR Leaseholders' and Entrepreneurs' Union. In 1991, member of the USSR President's Entrepreneurship Council; Vice President of the USSR Scientific and Industrial Union. From 1991, Vice Rector of the Academy of

National Economy of the USSR Council of Ministers.
MAJOR WORKS: Author of 600 scientific papers on economics.
HONORS/AWARDS: Order of the Red Banner of Labor; Order of the Badge of Honor; Order of the Eagle (1992); medals.
FAMILY: Married with a son.
ADDRESS/TELEPHONE: 82 Vernadsky Prospekt, Moscow, 117571. 434–0109 (office); 243–3322 (home).

Buravlev, Konstantin Eduardovich
POSITION: First Deputy Prime Minister of the Moscow Government (Economic Reforms Department)
BIRTHPLACE/DATE: Monshan settlement, Penza region, 1957
EDUCATION: Graduated in 1985 from the All-Union Civil Engineering Institute (by correspondence).
CAREER: From 1974 to 1989, Technician of the Construction and Technological Bureau of Glavmospromstroimaterialy (Moscow Department of Industrial Construction Materials); held various engineering and technological, as well as leading posts. From 1989 to 1990, Industrial Cooperative Chairman. From 1990 to 1991, Chairman of the Mossoviet (Moscow Council) Standing Commission. From 1991 to 1992, Deputy Chairman of the Moscow Construction Committee (Mosstoikomitet).
FAMILY: Single.
ADDRESS/TELEPHONE: 13 Tverskaya Street, Moscow. 229–2451 (office)

Burbulis, Gennadi Eduardovich
POSITION: Russian Federation Secretary of State to the President; Vice President of the President's Consultative State Council
BIRTHPLACE/DATE: Sverdlovsk (now Yekaterinburg) region, 1945
NATIONALITY: Russian
EDUCATION: Graduated in 1974 from Urals Gorky State University; from 1975 to 1978, postgraduate student at Urals Polytechnic. Doctor of Philosophy; Assistant Professor. Good command of German.
CAREER: From 1974 to 1975, and from 1978 to 1981, Assistant; from 1981 to 1982, Senior Lecturer; from 1982 to 1983, Assistant Professor of the Philosophy Division at Urals Polytechnic. From 1983 to 1986, Social Sciences Department Head. From 1986 to 1989, Deputy Director of Research at the All-Union Institute of Advanced Personnel Training of the USSR Ministry of Non-Ferrous Metallurgy in Sverdlovsk. In 1989, elected USSR People's Deputy. From 1989 to 1990, Subcommittee Chairman of the USSR Supreme Soviet's Committee for Issues of the Councils of People's Deputies and the Development of Self-Government. From 1990, Plenipotentiary Chairman of the Russian Federation Supreme Soviet, and Working Group Head of the Consultative Coordination Council. From 1991, Russian Federation Secretary of State and Secretary of the President's State Council; from 1991, Russian Federation First Deputy Chairman of the Government; on April 14, 1992, relieved of post at personal request.
FAMILY: Married with a son.
ADDRESS/TELEPHONE: The Kremlin, Moscow, 103132. 224–0735; 206–2629 (office).

Burkov, Valery Anatolyevich
POSITION: Russian Federation Chairman of the President's Coordinating Committee for the Affairs of Invalids; Counsellor to the Russian Federation President
BIRTHPLACE/DATE: Shadrinsk, Kurghan region, April 26, 1957
NATIONALITY: Russian
EDUCATION: Graduated in 1978 from the Chelyabinsk Higher School of Military Aviation Navigators and in 1988 from the Gagarin Higher Air Force Academy. Speaks German.
CAREER: Served in Afghanistan. In 1984, ranked Major; and in 1991, Colonel. In 1988, elected Central Board Presidium Member of the All-Russian Society of Invalids; Chairman of the Preparatory Committee to set up the Coordinating Committee for the Affairs of Invalids.
HONORS/AWARDS: Hero of the USSR (October 17, 1991); Order of the Red Banner of Combat; Order of Lenin.
FAMILY: Married with a son.
ADDRESS/TELEPHONE: 2 Krasnopresnenskaya Naberezhnaya, Moscow. 205–9518 (office).

Burlak, Vadim Nikolayevich

POSITION: Board Chairman of the World and Nature Public Center; President of the Global Problems of Survival Research Center
BIRTHPLACE/DATE: Moscow, 1943
NATIONALITY: Ukrainian
EDUCATION: Graduated in 1975 from the Moscow Law Institute. Speaks English.
CAREER: From 1975 to 1980, Senior Editor, Department Head of Yuridicheskaya Literatura (Legal Literature) Publishers. From 1980 to 1987, member of the Literary Workers' Trade Union Committee. From 1987 to 1992, President of the Travels in Defense of Peace and Nature Club.
MAJOR WORKS: *The Life-Long Choice* (1981); *The Usual Sunday*; *The Taiga Silhouettes* (1985); *Looking for the White Jay* (1989); *Ask Grass and Stars* (1990); *My America* (1991).
FAMILY: Married with a child.
ADDRESS/TELEPHONE: 10 1905 Goda Ulitsa, Moscow. 291–8182.

Burlakov, Matvey Prokopyevich

POSITION: Russian Federation Representative of the Western Military Troops; Colonel-General
BIRTHPLACE/DATE: Ulan-Ude, Mongolia, August 19, 1935
NATIONALITY: Russian
CAREER: From 1957, Armed Forces Platoon Commander, Company Commander. From 1968 to 1969, Regiment Deputy Commander. From 1969 to 1973, Regiment Commander. From 1973 to 1977, Division Commander. From 1977 to 1979, Army Corps Commander. From 1979 to 1983, Army Commander. From 1983 to 1988, Chief of Staff and First Deputy Commander of the Zabaikalsk Military District Troops. From 1988 to 1990, Chief Commander of the Southern Military Troops. From 1990 to 1992, Chief Commander of the Western Military Troops.
FAMILY: Married with a son and a daughter.
TELEPHONE: 293–1413 (office).

Burlakova, Yelena Borisovna

POSITION: Department Head of Chemical Physics; Editor of *Radiobiology* magazine
BIRTHPLACE/DATE: Moscow, 1934
NATIONALITY: Russian
EDUCATION: From 1956 to 1960, postgraduate student at Moscow State University. Doctor degree (1962); Postdoctor degree (1970).
CAREER: From 1960 to present, Junior Researcher, Senior Researcher, Laboratory Head, Department Head at the Institute of Chemical Physics. From 1970 to 1980, Expert of SEV (European Cooperation Council of Biophysics). From 1987, Chairwoman of the Scientific Council of Radiobiology of the USSR (now Russian) Academy of Sciences. In 1989, member of international committees in radiobiology and radioecology. From 1990, Expert Coordinator of the Chernobyl Commission.
MAJOR WORKS: Author of more than 300 publications.
HONORS/AWARDS: State Prize in Science.
FAMILY: Married with two children.
ADDRESS/TELEPHONE: 4 Kosygin Street, Moscow, 117334. 137–6420.

Burlatsky, Fyodor Mikhailovich

POSITION: Publicist; Leading Researcher at the Institute of the U.S. and Canada of the Russian Academy of Sciences
BIRTHPLACE/DATE: Kiev, 1927
NATIONALITY: Russian
EDUCATION: Graduated in 1947 from the Tashkent Law Institute. Doctor of Philosophy; Professor. Speaks English.
CAREER: To 1965, Consultative Group Member of the Central Committee Liaison Department for Communist and Workers' Parties of Socialist Countries. To 1983, engaged in research work. From 1983, Political Analyst of *Literaturnaya Gazeta* (*Literary Newspaper*). From 1991, Editor in Chief of *Literaturnaya Gazeta*; in August 1991, relieved of post. Elected USSR People's Deputy; member of the USSR Supreme Soviet Committee for International Affairs; member of the USSR Writers' Union. In 1991, introduced the Social-Democratic Movement as an alternative to the Communist Party. Member of the Russian Writers' Union; member of the PEN Club; President of the International Political Research Center of Federal and Constitutional Rights.
MAJOR WORKS: *A Legend of Machiavelli* (Gold Medal, Italian Senate, 1988); *New Thinking*; *Leaders and Advisors*; *Khrushchev*; *Sociology,*

Politics, International Relations; *The Burden of Decision-Making* (a play about JFK).
HONORS/AWARDS: USSR Journalists' Union International Prize of Vorovsky (1987); Order of the Red Banner of Labor (1966).
FAMILY: Married with two sons and a daughter.
ADDRESS/TELEPHONE: 2/3 Khlebny Pereulok, Moscow. 140–6944 (home); 205–2841 (office).

Burlay, Yan Anastasyevich
POSITION: Foreign Ministry, Director of the Department of Central and South America; Ambassador Extraordinary and Plenipotentiary
BIRTHPLACE/DATE: Moscow, 1947
NATIONALITY: Ukrainian
EDUCATION: Graduated from the Moscow State Institute of International Relations in 1970.
CAREER: From 1970 to 1972, Aide on Duty at the USSR Embassy in Uruguay. From 1972 to 1974, Attaché at the USSR Embassy in Uruguay. From 1974 to 1975, Attaché of the Department of Latin America; from 1975 to 1977, Third Secretary; from 1977 to 1978, Second Secretary. From 1978 to 1981, Second Secretary at the USSR Embassy in Venezuela. From 1981 to 1985, First Secretary at the USSR Embassy in Venezuela. From 1985 to 1986, Counsellor of the First Latin America Department; from 1986 to 1987, Acting Sector Head; from 1987, Sector Head; from 1987 to 1989, Deputy Head. From 1989 to 1992, Deputy Head, then Head of the Department of Latin America.
FAMILY: Married with two children.
TELEPHONE: 244–3295 (office).

Burlayev, Konstantin Eduardovich
POSITION: First Deputy to the Moscow Mayor
BIRTHPLACE/DATE: Monshan village, Penza region, 1957
CAREER: From 1974 to 1989, held technical and engineering positions. From 1989 to 1990, Chairman of an industrial cooperative. From 1990 to 1991, Chairman of the Mossoviet (Moscow Council) Commission. From 1991 to 1992, Deputy Chairman of the Moscow Construction Committee.
FAMILY: Single.
ADDRESS/TELEPHONE: 13 Tverskaya Street, Moscow. 229–2451 (office).

Burmistrov, Vladimir Nikolayevich
POSITION: Russian Trade Representative in Italy
BIRTHPLACE/DATE: 1929
CAREER: From 1965 to 1967, Representative of Aviaexport at the USSR Trade Mission in Syria. From 1967 to 1970, Office Director of Aviaexport. From 1970 to 1974, USSR Trade Representative in the People's Democratic Republic of Yemen. From 1974 to 1978, Deputy Chairman of Aviaexport. From 1978 to 1982, USSR Trade Representative in the Republic of Cuba, Director-General of Tractorexport, USSR Deputy Minister of Foreign Trade, then USSR Deputy Minister of Foreign Economic Relations.
ADDRESS/TELEPHONE: 32 Smolenskaya-Sennaya Square, Moscow, 1212000. 244–2450.

Burokiavicius, Mikolas Martinovich
POSITION: Former First Secretary of the Lithuanian Central Committee
BIRTHPLACE/DATE: Alitus, 1927
NATIONALITY: Lithuanian
EDUCATION: Degree in History; Professor.
CAREER: In 1942, worked at a factory in Udmurtiya. From 1944, held various positions in the Komsomol and Communist Party. From 1946, member of the Communist Party. From 1963, Senior Researcher at the Party History Institute of the Lithuanian Central Committee, Department Head of the Civil Engineering Institute, Professor at the Teachers' Training Institute. From 1989, Secretary, and from 1990, First Secretary of the Provisional Lithuanian Central Committee. In April 1990, elected First Secretary of the Lithuanian Central Committee. USSR Politburo member.
FAMILY: Married with a daughter.
TELEPHONE: 291–2653 (Moscow).

Bykov, Andrey Valeryanovich
POSITION: Board Chairman of the Power and Mechanical Engineering Joint-Stock Bank (St. Petersburg); member of the Russian Bank Association
BIRTHPLACE/DATE: Cherepovets, 1962
NATIONALITY: Russian
EDUCATION: Graduated in 1985 from the Leningrad Institute (now St. Petersburg University) of Finance and Economics. Speaks English.
CAREER: From 1985 to 1986, Cash Transactions

Inspector of the Leningrad Region State Bank. From 1986 to 1987, Senior Economist of the Leningrad Region Department of Industry Credits. From 1988 to 1989, Economist of Agroprombank (Bank of Agriculture and Industry). From 1989, worked at the Power and Mechanical Engineering Bank.
FAMILY: Married.
ADDRESS/TELEPHONE: 8 Gogol Street, St. Petersburg, 191065. 311–9502 (office).

Bykov, Dmitri Vasilyevich
POSITION: Ambassador at Large; Ambassador Extraordinary and Plenipotentiary
BIRTHPLACE/DATE: Vanovye village, Tambovsk region, October 10, 1925
NATIONALITY: Russian
EDUCATION: Graduated in 1954 from the Moscow State Institute of International Relations.
CAREER: From 1942 to 1943, worked at the Moscow Likhachev Plant. From 1943 to 1948, served in combat. From 1948 to 1949, Turner at the Moscow Likhachev Plant. From 1954 to 1956, Aide to the Treaty and Law Department of the USSR Ministry of Foreign Affairs; from 1956 to 1958, Attaché; from 1958 to 1960, Third Secretary; from 1960 to 1961, Second Secretary; from 1967 to 1968, First Secretary; from 1968 to 1971, Counsellor; from 1971 to 1973, Sector Head. From 1973 to 1978, Counsellor at the USSR Permanent Mission to the UN in New York; from 1978 to 1980, Senior Counsellor. From 1980 to 1987, Deputy Head of the Treaty and Law Department of the USSR Ministry of Foreign Affairs. From 1987 to 1991, Deputy Head at the USSR Permanent Mission to the UN. From 1992, Senior Counsellor of the Commonwealth of Independent States (CIS) Department of the Russian Ministry of Foreign Affairs.
HONORS/AWARDS: Order of the Patriotic War; Order of the Red Star; war medals.
FAMILY: Married.
TELEPHONE: 244–103 (office).

Bykov, Rolan Anatolyevich
POSITION: President of the Film and TV Center for Children and Youth; Actor; Film Director
BIRTHPLACE/DATE: Kiev, 1929
NATIONALITY: Ukrainian
EDUCATION: Graduated in 1951 from the Shchukin Theater School.
CAREER: From 1951 to 1959, Actor of the Moscow Theater for Young Spectators. From 1955, Film Actor. From 1958 to 1960, Chief Stage Director of the Lenin Komsomol Theater in Leningrad. From 1960 to 1990, Actor and Film Director of Mosfilm (Moscow Film) Studio. From 1986 to 1989, Art Director of the Yunost (Youth) Association at Mosfilm Studio. From 1989, President of the Film and TV Center for Children and Youth. Elected USSR People's Deputy. Member of the USSR Supreme Soviet Committee for Science, Culture and Education. Board Secretary of the USSR Union of Film Makers. Presidium Member of the Russian Children's Fund. From 1990, Art Director of Studio 12-A, Art Director of the Higher Film Directors' Courses. From December 1991, Children's Section Head of the Russian Union of Film Makers.
MAJOR WORKS: Film parts: *Strolling Around Moscow* (1964); *The Greatcoat* (1960); *Andrei Rublev* (1977); *The Commissar*; and others. Productions include: *Seven Nurses* (1962); *Attention, Tortoise!* (1970); *The Telegram* (1972); *Scare-Crow* (1984).
HONORS/AWARDS: Grand Prix of the International Film Festival in Spain (1972); USSR State Prize; Grand Prix in France and Canada; Golden Nika Prize for Best Male Role in *The Commissar*; Russian Federation State Prize for *Letters of the Dead Man*.
FAMILY: Married with a son.
ADDRESS/TELEPHONE: 12-A Chistoprudny Boulevard, Moscow, 101000. 227–9300; 227–9317 (office).

Byshovets, Anatoli Fyodorovich
POSITION: Senior Coach of the CIS (formerly USSR) National Football Team
BIRTHPLACE/DATE: Kiev, 1946
NATIONALITY: Ukrainian
EDUCATION: Graduated in 1970 from the Kiev State Institute of Physical Education.
CAREER: Coach of the Moscow Dynamo team; Coach of the Soviet Olympic Football Team; winner of the 1988 Seoul Olympics.
FAMILY: Married with two sons.

Address/Telephone: 8 Luzhnetskaya Naberezhnaya, Moscow. 201–1706 (office).

Bystrov, Yevgeni Ivanovich

Position: Former Editor in Chief of *Megapolis* international magazine
Birthplace/Date: Moscow, 1941
Nationality: Russian
Career: From late 1950s to 1986, held leading positions at Glavmosstroi (Main Moscow Construction Bureau). From 1986 to 1990, Chairman of the Moscow Planning Committee; First Deputy Chairman of the Moscow City Council. From 1990 to 1991, Chief Office Manager of the USSR President; Chairman of the Moscow Economic Council; member of the Moscow Executive Council.
Family: Married with two children.
Address/Telephone: 13 Tverskaya Street, Moscow, 103032. 199–8151.

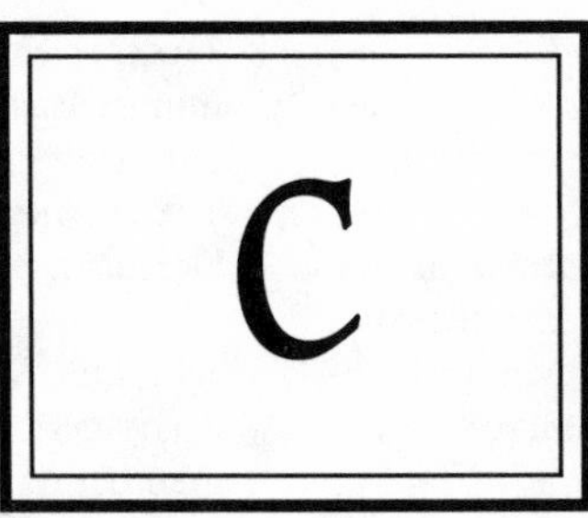

Chakhkiyev, Bashir Akhmedovich

POSITION: Assistant Professor at Chechen (formerly Chechen-Ingush) University; Chairman of Ingushia State Radio and Television

BIRTHPLACE/DATE: Chechen-Ingushia, 1938

NATIONALITY: Ingush

EDUCATION: Graduated from the Alma-Ata Industrial Secondary School in 1956. From 1954 to 1960, student, then postgraduate student at Baku State University. Defended Doctor's thesis at Tbilisi State University. Doctor of History.

CAREER: From 1960, worked in the television industry. From 1966 to 1971, Senior Lecturer at Chechen-Ingush University. From 1971 to 1973, Special Correspondent for Chechen-Ingush Central Television. From 1973 to 1975, Safety Engineer of the North-Caucasian Directorate of Warm Waters in Grozny. In 1975, Editor of Central Television. From 1989, Acting Assistant Professor at Chechen-Ingush University. From January 1991, Board Member of the All-Union Association of Victims of Unlawful Repressions. In 1991, participated in Congresses of the North Caucasus Peoples. Member of the Communist Party to 1973.

FAMILY: Married with five children.

ADDRESS/TELEPHONE: 18 Pobedy Pr., Flat #18, Grozny, 364051. 22–2533 (office).

Chaplin, Boris Nikolayevich

POSITION: Russian Federation Deputy Foreign Minister

BIRTHPLACE/DATE: Moscow, 1931

EDUCATION: Graduated from the Moscow Mining Institute; from 1959 to 1962, postgraduate student. Science Degree in Technology. Speaks German.

CAREER: From 1955 to 1958, Miner, then Section Chief at a Kemerovo region mine; Staff Member of a mining research institute. To 1962, Assistant Professor at the Moscow Mining Institute. From 1962, Deputy Secretary, then Secretary of the Moscow Mining Institute Party Committee; Second Secretary of the Moscow Oktyabrsky District Party Committee; First Secretary of the Moscow Cheryomushki District Party Committee. From 1974 to 1986, Ambassador to Vietnam; Alternate Member of the Central Committee; Delegate to the Twenty-fourth, Twenty-fifth, Twenty-sixth, and Twenty-seventh Communist Party Congresses. From 1986 to December 1991, USSR Deputy Foreign Minister.

HONORS/AWARDS: Order of the October Revolution (1981); Order of the Red Banner of Labor (1971, 1974); Order of the People's Friendship (1977); Order of the Badge of Honor (1969); Ho Chi Minh Order (1986); USSR State Prize (1967); medals.

FAMILY: Married.

ADDRESS/TELEPHONE: 32/34 Smolenskaya-Sennaya Square, Moscow, 121200. 244–1606; 244–2469; 244–4662.

Chazov, Yevgeni Ivanovich

POSITION: Academician of the Russian Academy of Sciences; Academician of the Russian Academy of Medical Sciences; Director-General of the Cardiology Research Center

BIRTHPLACE/DATE: Gorky (now Nizhny Novgorod), June 10, 1929

Nationality: Russian
Education: Graduated in 1953 from the Kiev Medical Institute. Speaks English, German, Spanish, and Czech.
Career: From 1953 to 1965, worked at the Moscow First Medical Institute and the Institute of Therapy of the USSR Academy of Medical Sciences. From 1967, Professor and Director of the Institute of Therapy. From 1967 to 1987, Chief of the Main (Fourth) Department (in service to USSR government and Party leaders) of the USSR Health Ministry and, concurrently, Deputy Minister of the USSR Health Ministry and Chief of the First Aid Department at the Myasnikov Cardiology Institute. From 1971, Academician of the USSR Academy of Medical Sciences. From 1973, Editor of *Terapevtichesky Arkhiv* (*Therapeutic Archives*) magazine. From 1975 to 1987, Director-General of the Cardiology Research Center. From 1979, Academician of the USSR Academy of Sciences. From 1987 to 1990, USSR Health Minister. From 1990, Director-General of the Cardiology Research Center.
Major Works: *Myocardial Infarction* (1971); *Cardiac Rhythm Disorders* (1972); *Anti-Coagulants and Fibrinolytics* (1977); other monographs. More than 300 articles in the field of cardiology.
Honors/Awards: Hero of Socialist Labor; Prize of Lenin (1982); State Prizes (1969, 1976); Russian Honored Worker of Science; Honorary Member of the American Heart Association and the Swedish Medical Society.
Family: Married with three children.
Address/Telephone: 15-A Third Cherepkovskaya Street, Moscow, 121552. 415–0025 (secretary).

Chechevatov, Victor Stepanovich
Position: Colonel-General; Commander of the Far East Military District; former Commander of the Kiev Military District.
Birthplace/Date: Mordovo-Bely Klyuch village, Korsunski, 1945
Nationality: Russian
Career: From 1963, Armed Forces Division Commander, Army Commander, First Deputy Military District Commander. From 1991, Commander of the Kiev Military District. In February 1992, released from duties. Member of the Communist Party to 1991.
Family: Married with a son.
Telephone: 293–2938; 293–1413 (Ministry of Defense).

Chelnokov, Mikhail Borisovich
Position: Russian Federation People's Deputy; member of the Russian Federation Supreme Soviet Committee for Science and Education
Birthplace/Date: Moscow, 1938
Nationality: Russian
Education: Graduated in 1961 from the Moscow Aviation Institute (MAI); from 1961 to 1965, postgraduate student. Doctor of Technology; Assistant Professor. Speaks English.
Career: In 1961, worked at a design bureau. From 1969, Lecturer of the Physics Division at the Moscow N.E. Bauman State Technical Institute. Nominated himself as a candidate for the post of Russian Federation Supreme Soviet Chairman at the Fifth Congress.
Family: Married.
Address/Telephone: 2 Krasnopresnenskaya Naberezhnaya, Moscow. 205–4435 (office).

Chelyshev, Yevgeni Petrovich
Position: Academician-Secretary of the Russian Academy of Sciences; Academician-Secretary of the Literature and Language Division of the Russian Academy of Sciences; President of the Russia-India Society
Birthplace/Date: Moscow, October 10, 1921
Nationality: Russian
Education: Graduated in 1949 from the Military Institute of Foreign Languages; then postgraduate student.
Career: From 1949, Lecturer, Deputy Chief, Division Chief at the Military Institute of Foreign Languages. From 1955 to 1988, Researcher, Sector Head and Department Head at the Institute of Oriental Studies of the USSR Academy of Sciences. From 1987, Academician of the USSR Academy of Sciences.
Major Works: Indian literature.
Honors/Awards: International Nehru Prize (1967); Vivecanada Prize (1987); two Orders of the Red Star; Order of the Great Patriotic War; Medal For Merit in Combat.

FAMILY: Married with two children and two grandsons.
ADDRESS/TELEPHONE: 32-A Leninsky Prospekt, Moscow, 117334. 938–5432; 938–1936 (office).

Cherkizov, Andrey Aleksandrovich
POSITION: Director-General of the Russian Intellectual Property Agency (RAIS)
BIRTHPLACE/DATE: Moscow, 1954
NATIONALITY: Russian
CAREER: From 1977 to 1989, Freelancer. From 1989 to 1991, First Deputy Director-General of Inter-Verso Joint Venture Publishing House. From 1991, Political Analyst of *Moscow Echo*. From 1992, Political Advisor to the President of the RAIS, Board Member of the Russia-Germany Society.
MAJOR WORKS: Numerous publications in periodicals.
FAMILY: Married with a son.
ADDRESS/TELEPHONE: 6-A B. Bronnaya Street, Moscow, 103670. 203–3377 (office).

Chernavin, Vladimir Nikolayevich
POSITION: Admiral; CIS Commander in Chief of the Navy
BIRTHPLACE/DATE: Nikolayev, 1928
NATIONALITY: Russian
EDUCATION: Graduated from the Naval Academy and from the General Staff Military Academy.
CAREER: From 1947, served in the Armed Forces. Division Commander, Flotilla Commander, Fleet Commander, Head of the Main Staff of the Naval Fleet. From 1985, Commander in Chief of the Naval Fleet and USSR Deputy Defense Minister. Former USSR People's Deputy.
HONORS/AWARDS: Hero of the USSR.
FAMILY: Married with a daughter.
ADDRESS/TELEPHONE: 12 Frunze Street, Moscow. 293–2869; 293–1413 (office).

Chernenko, Andrey Grigoryevich
POSITION: Head of the Russian Public Relations Center of the Russian Federation Security Ministry; Colonel
BIRTHPLACE/DATE: Khabarovsk, 1953
EDUCATION: Graduated in 1980 from the Journalism Department at Moscow State University. Speaks English.
CAREER: Trainee, Department Head of *Kommunar* youth newspaper in Tula region; Correspondent for *Sovietskaya Rossia* (*Soviet Russia*); Analyst of *Sovietskaya Kultura* (*Soviet Culture*) newspapers. Special Correspondent, then Assistant Editor of *Pravda* (*Truth*). From 1989 to 1991, Editor in Chief and Editorial Board Member of *Shchit i Mech* (*Shield and Sword*) and *Sovietskaya Militsia* (*Soviet Militia*) magazines. Former Chief of the Public Relations Center of the USSR Ministry of Internal Affairs.
FAMILY: Married with two children.
ADDRESS/TELEPHONE: 22 Kuznetsky Most, Moscow, 101000. 224–5217 (office).

Chernichenko, Yuri Dmitryevich
POSITION: Writer; Co-Chairman of the April Writers' Association; Chairman of the Peasants' Party of Russia; First Secretary of the Confederation of Writers' Unions
BIRTHPLACE/DATE: Graivoron, Kursk region, 1929
EDUCATION: Graduated in 1953 from the Philology Department at Kishinev State University.
CAREER: In 1959, wrote first publications. In 1963, published first book of essays *Anthey and Boboshko*. From 1960 to 1970, published articles in *Novy Mir* (*New World*), *Yunost* (*Youth*), *Zvezda* (*Star*), *Nash Sovremennik* (*Our Contemporary*) magazines, and *Pravda* (*Truth*) and *Literaturnaya Gazeta* (*Literary Newspaper*) newspapers. From mid–1970s, Propaganda Department Television Commentator and Agriculture Department Television Analyst. From 1986, Board Secretary of the USSR Writers' Union. In 1989, elected Co-Chairman of the April Writers' Association. From 1990 to 1991, USSR People's Deputy. From April 1991, Chairman of the Farmers' Party. From August 1991, First Secretary of the Moscow Writers' Organization. From September 1991, Co-Chairman of the Secretariat of the USSR Writers' Union. From December 1991, Board Secretary of the Russian Writers' Union.
MAJOR WORKS: Collections of essays: *To Be the Master?; Round the Combine*; *Long-Distance Trip*.
HONORS/AWARDS: Order of the Badge of Honor.
FAMILY: Married with a son.

ADDRESS/TELEPHONE: 5 Kosygin Street, Flat #221, Moscow, 117334. 137–4877 (home).

Chernikov, Nikolay Vikulovich

POSITION: Board Chairman of Vostokstroi (Construction in the Eastern USSR) Commercial Bank
BIRTHPLACE/DATE: Krasny Yar village, Altai, 1931
NATIONALITY: Russian
EDUCATION: Graduated from the Khabarovsk Institute of Railway Engineers. In 1990, graduated from the Diplomatic Academy of the USSR Foreign Ministry's Institute of International Relations.
CAREER: In 1950, joined the Communist Party. Accountant, then Chief Accountant of Vostokstroi Ministry; from 1987 to 1990, Finance Administration Head.
HONORS/AWARDS: Russian Federation Honored Economist; medals.
FAMILY: Married with a son.
ADDRESS/TELEPHONE: 41 Vernadsky Prospekt, Moscow, 117947. 434–8377 (office).

Chernomyrdin, Victor Stepanovich

POSITION: Chairman of the Russian Federation Council of Ministers
BIRTHPLACE/DATE: Cherny Otrog, Orenburg region, 1938
NATIONALITY: Russian
EDUCATION: Doctor of Technical Sciences.
CAREER: 1957, Metalworker at the Orsk Refinery; from 1960 to 1962, Machinist, Operator; from 1966 to 1967, Technological Unit Head. From 1967 to 1969, Instructor of the Orsk City Communist Party. From 1969 to 1973, Deputy Head, then Head of the Industry and Transportation Department of the Orsk Region Communist Party. From 1973, Deputy Chief Engineer of the Orenburg Gas Refinery; from 1973 to 1978, Director. From 1978 to 1982, Instructor of the Heavy Industry Department of the Central Committee. From 1982 to 1985, USSR Deputy Minister of the Gas Industry. From 1983, Head of the All-Union Tyumengazprom (Tyumen Gas Industry) Association. From 1985 to 1989, USSR Minister of the Gas Industry. From 1989 to 1992, Board Chairman of the Gazprom Consortium. From May 1992, Russian Federation Deputy Chairman of Power Industry. USSR Supreme Soviet Deputy. From 1961 to 1991, member of the Communist Party and the Central Committee.
HONORS/AWARDS: Order of the October Revolution; Order of the Red Banner of Labor; Order of the Badge of Honor.
FAMILY: Married with two sons.
ADDRESS/TELEPHONE: The Kremlin, Moscow. 206–4598 (reception).

Chernyayev, Anatoli Sergeyevich

POSITION: Research Group Head of the International Foundation for Socio-Economic and Political Studies (The Gorbachev Foundation)
BIRTHPLACE/DATE: Moscow, May 25, 1921
NATIONALITY: Russian
EDUCATION: Graduated in 1947 from Moscow State University. Doctor of History.
CAREER: World War II veteran. From 1950 to 1958, Senior Lecturer, then Acting Division Head at Moscow State University. From 1953 to 1958, Instructor of the Central Committee. From 1958 to 1961, Consulting Editor and Deputy Department Head of the Prague-based *World Marxist Review* journal. From 1961 to 1970, Expert, Deputy Department Head, then Head Consultant of the Central Committee's International Department. From 1970 to 1986, Deputy Head of the Central Committee's International Department. From 1976 to 1981, member of the Communist Party Central Auditing Commission. From 1981 to 1986, Alternate Member of the Central Committee. In 1986, Full Member of the Central Committee. From February 1986, Aide to the Central Committee's General Secretary. Former elected USSR People's Deputy. In 1991, Aide to the USSR President.
FAMILY: Married with a daughter.
ADDRESS/TELEPHONE: 49 Leningradsky Prospekt, Moscow, 125468. 158–9444.

Chervyakov, Aleksander Alekseyevich

POSITION: Editor in Chief of *Svobodny Mir* (*Free World*) newspaper
BIRTHPLACE/DATE: Tula, 1957
CAREER: From 1982 to 1985, Operative Officer, District Officer of the District Militia Office, Senior Legal Consultant to MPO Polimer. From 1985 to 1990, Legal Department Head of Geopri-

bortsvetmet (Geology Equipment and Non-Ferrous Metals). From 1990 to 1992, Editor of the independent publication *Solidarnost, Put k Pravde (Solidarity, A Way to Truth)*. From March 1992, Editor in Chief of *Svobodny Mir*. Political Council Member of the Confederation of Free Liberals.
FAMILY: Divorced.
ADDRESS/TELEPHONE: 3 Banny Pereulok, Flat #17, Moscow, 1129110. 971–6838 (office).

Cheshinsky, Leonid Stepanovich
POSITION: Chairman of the Committee for Grain Products of the Russian Federation Ministry of Trade and Material Resources; Russian Federation President's Representative
BIRTHPLACE/DATE: Voronezh region, 1945
NATIONALITY: Russian
EDUCATION: Graduated in 1967 from the Voronezh Technological Institute. In 1983, studied at the Academy of National Economy. Speaks French.
CAREER: From 1967 to 1968, Elevator Mechanical Engineer in Rossosh, Voronezh region. From 1968 to 1975, Chief Engineer, then Chief of a grain depot in Voronezh region. From 1975 to 1977, Director of the Voronezh Mixed Feed Factory. From 1977 to 1983, Deputy Head, then Head of the Voronezh Regional Production Directorate of Grain Products. From 1983 to 1985, Russian Federation Deputy Minister of Procurement. From 1986 to 1990, Russian Federation Deputy Minister of Grain Products. From 1990 to 1991, Russian Federation Minister of Grain Products. In 1991, Russian Federation Minister of Procurement.
FAMILY: Married with two children.
ADDRESS/TELEPHONE: 6 Krzhyzhanovsky Street, Moscow, 117292. 129–6436 (office).

Chesnokov, Andrey Eduardovich
POSITION: Tennis Player
BIRTHPLACE/DATE: Moscow, February 2, 1966
NATIONALITY: Russian
EDUCATION: Graduated in 1988 from the Central State Institute of Physical Education. Speaks English.
HONORS/AWARDS: USSR Master of Sports, International Class; winner of numerous tennis tournaments, including Canada (1991), Monte Carlo (1990), Tel-Aviv (1990), Orlando (1988), Florence (1987).
FAMILY: Married with a child.
ADDRESS/TELEPHONE: 10 Academician Chalomei Street, Flat #352, Moscow. 143–4253 (home); 201–1249 (office).

Chiburdanidze, Maya Grigoryevna
POSITION: Professional Chess Player
BIRTHPLACE/DATE: Kutaisi, 1961
NATIONALITY: Georgian
CAREER: International Chess Grand Master. Winner of the World Championship in 1978, versus N. Gaprindashvili; in 1984, versus I. Livitina; in 1986, versus E. Akhmylovskaya; in 1988, versus N. Ioseliani; in 1981, tie versus N. Alexandria. USSR Honored Master of Sports (chess).
FAMILY: Single.
ADDRESS/TELEPHONE: The Department of Physical Training and Sports, 49-A Chavchavadze Pr., Tbilisi, 380062. 23–0203; 22–5375 (office)

Chikin, Valentin Vasilyevich
POSITION: Editor in Chief of *Sovietskaya Rossia (Soviet Russia)* newspaper; Russian Federation People's Deputy
BIRTHPLACE/DATE: Moscow, 1932
NATIONALITY: Russian
EDUCATION: Graduated from Moscow State University.
CAREER: From 1951, Assistant Editor of *Moskovsky Komsomolets (Moscow Komsomol Member)* newspaper. Assistant Editor, Deputy Editor in Chief of *Komsomolskaya Pravda (Komsomol Truth)*. From 1971, Deputy; First Deputy Editor in Chief of *Sovietskaya Rossiya (Soviet Russia)*. From 1984 to 1986, First Deputy Chairman of the USSR State Committee for Publishing, Printing, and the Book Trade. Member of the Russian Central Committee.
FAMILY: Married with two sons.
ADDRESS/TELEPHONE: 24 Ulitsa Pravdy, Moscow 125868. 257–2772; 257–2217 (office).

Chilingarov, Artur Nikolayevich
POSITION: Co-Chairman of the Russian Fund for International Humanitarian Aid and Cooperation; Counsellor to the Russian Federation Supreme Soviet Chairman

BIRTHPLACE/DATE: Leningrad, 1939
NATIONALITY: Armenian
EDUCATION: Graduated in 1963 from the Makarov Higher Naval Engineering School. Doctor of Geography. Speaks English.
CAREER: From 1957 to 1958, Fitter at the Ordzhonikidze Baltic Shipbuilding Plant in Leningrad. From 1963 to 1965, Engineer-Hydrologist at the Arctic Research Observatory of the Yakutia Arctic and Antarctic Research Institute. From 1965 to 1969, First Secretary of the Bulun District Komsomol Committee in Tikhy. In 1969, Junior Researcher at the Leningrad Arctic and Antarctic Research Institute. From 1969 to 1971, Chief of the North Pole–19 Drifting Research Station at the Arctic and Antarctic Research Institute. From 1971 to 1973, Chief of the Bellinghausen Antarctic Station (the seventeenth Soviet Antarctic research expedition of the Leningrad Arctic and Antarctic Research Institute). From 1973 to 1974, Assistant Chief of the North–25 and North–26 High-Latitude Expeditions. From 1974 to 1979, Chief of the Amderma Hydrometeorological Service of the USSR State Committee for Hydrometeorology. From 1979 to 1986, Collegium Member and Head of the Department of Personnel and Educational Establishments. From 1986 to 1991, Deputy Chairman of the USSR State Committee for Hydrometeorology and Environmental Control.
HONORS/AWARDS: Hero of the USSR; Order of Lenin; Gold Star; USSR State Prize.
FAMILY: Married with two children.
ADDRESS/TELEPHONE: 19 Novy Arbat Street, Moscow. 203–8517; 203–1856 (office).

Chizhov, Lyudvig Aleksandrovich
POSITION: Russian Federation Ambassador to Japan
BIRTHPLACE/DATE: Radomyshl, Zhitomir region, 1936
NATIONALITY: Russian
EDUCATION: Graduated from the Moscow State Institute of International Relations of the USSR Foreign Ministry and from postgraduate study at the USSR Foreign Ministry's Diplomatic Academy. Speaks Japanese and English.
CAREER: From 1960 to 1962, Aide at the USSR Embassy to Japan. From 1962 to 1965, Interpreter, Attaché at the USSR Embassy in Japan. From 1965 to 1968, Attaché, then Third Secretary of the USSR Foreign Ministry's Far East Department; from 1968 to 1971, Second, then First Secretary. From 1971 to 1976, First Secretary at the USSR Embassy in Japan. From 1976 to 1977, Counsellor at the USSR Embassy in Japan. From 1977, Counsellor of the USSR Foreign Ministry's Second Far East Department; from 1978 to 1980, Deputy Department Head. From 1980 to 1986, Minister-Counsellor at the USSR Embassy in Japan. From 1986 to 1987, Pacific Countries Department Head of the USSR Foreign Ministry. From 1987 to 1990, Head of the Pacific and Southeast Asia Department of the USSR Foreign Ministry. From 1990 to December 1991, USSR Ambassador to Japan.
HONORS/AWARDS: Order of the Badge of Honor; Labor Valor Jubilee Medal; Honorary Diploma of the Russian Federation Supreme Soviet Presidium.
FAMILY: Married.
ADDRESS/TELEPHONE: Russian Federation Embassy in Japan, 1–1 Azabudai, 2-chome, Minato-ku, Tokyo 106, Japan. 583–4224; 583–5982; 583–4297; 583–4445 (Consulate Department); Telex: 7224231 SOVPOSOL J (Consulate Department).

Chubais, Anatoli Borisovich
POSITION: Deputy Chairman of the Russian Federation Government; Chairman of the Russian Federation State Committee for Managing State Property; Russian Federation Minister
BIRTHPLACE/DATE: Borisiv, 1955
NATIONALITY: Russian
EDUCATION: Graduated in 1977 from the Leningrad (now St. Petersburg) Institute of Economics and Engineering. Doctor of Economics. Speaks English.
CAREER: From 1977 to 1982, Engineer, Assistant Lecturer at the Leningrad Institute of Economics and Engineering; from 1982 to 1990, Assistant Professor. In 1990, Deputy Chairman of the Leningrad City Executive Committee. In 1991, Chief Economic Advisor to the Mayor of St. Petersburg.
FAMILY: Married with two children.
ADDRESS/TELEPHONE: 9 Proyezd Vladimirova, Moscow, 103685. 298–7545 (office); 291–5512 (press secretary).

Chudnovsky, Grigory Aleksandrovich

POSITION: Board Chairman of Optimum Commercial Bank; Chairman of the Moscow Banking Union's Auditing Commission
BIRTHPLACE/DATE: Moscow, 1951
EDUCATION: Graduated in 1974 from the Moscow Institute of Finance. Doctor of Economics. Good command of English.
CAREER: From 1974 to 1976, served in the Armed Forces. From 1981 to 1987, Department Head of the Russian USSR State Bank. From 1988 to 1989, Deputy Directorate Head of USSR Zhilsotsbank (Bank for Housing and Social Activities). From July 1989, Board Chairman of Optimum Commercial Bank; Board Chairman of Amak and Reksons Joint Ventures; Board Member of Tsentr–100 (Center–100) Joint Venture.
FAMILY: Married with a son.
ADDRESS/TELEPHONE: 9 Krymsky Val, Moscow. 238–0066; 238–0000 (office).

Chupakhin, Vladimir Leonidovich

POSITION: Editor in Chief of *Krasnaya Zvezda* (*Red Star*) newspaper
BIRTHPLACE/DATE: Berznyaki, Perm region, 1941
NATIONALITY: Russian
CAREER: 1969, First Rank Captain. From 1973 to 1979, Correspondent, Department Head of *Flag Rodiny* (*Flag of the Motherland)* newspaper. From 1979 to 1987, Senior Writer for *Krasnaya Zvezda* newspaper; from 1987 to 1992, Deputy Editor in Chief. From 1992, Editor in Chief of *Krasnaya Zvezda*.
HONORS/AWARDS: Medal For Merit in Combat; USSR Journalists' Union Prize (1979).
FAMILY: Married with two children.
ADDRESS/TELEPHONE: 38 Khoroshevskoye Chaussée, Moscow. 941–2158 (office).

Churkin, Vitaly Ivanovich

POSITION: Russian Federation Deputy Foreign Minister; Ambassador Extraordinary and Plenipotentiary
BIRTHPLACE/DATE: Moscow, February 21, 1952
NATIONALITY: Russian
EDUCATION: Graduated in 1974 from the Moscow State Institute of International Relations of the USSR Foreign Ministry. Doctor of History. Speaks English, French, and Mongolian.
CAREER: From 1974 to 1979, held various posts in the Translation Department of the USSR Foreign Ministry. In 1979, appointed Third Secretary of the U.S. Department of the USSR Foreign Ministry. In 1982, Second, then First Secretary at the USSR Embassy in the United States. From 1987, Official of the Central Committee's International Department. From 1989, Advisor of the USSR Foreign Ministry; Press Secretary for Foreign Minister Eduard Shevardnadze. From 1990 to 1991, Information Directorate Head of the USSR Foreign Ministry; Board Member of the USSR Foreign Ministry. From 1991 to April 1992, Information Directorate Head of the Russian Federation Foreign Ministry.
FAMILY: Married.
ADDRESS/TELEPHONE: 32/34 Smolenskaya-Sennaya Square, Moscow, 121200. 244–3059 (office).

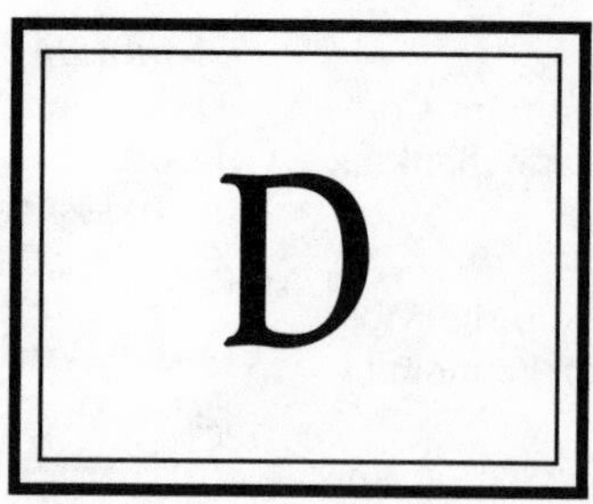

Dagayev, Leonid Sergeyevich
POSITION: Deputy Chairman of the Kazakh KGB
BIRTHPLACE/DATE: Tashkent, 1941
CAREER: From 1966, Driver; Security Service Engineer; served in the Counter-Espionage Unit.
FAMILY: Married with two children.
ADDRESS/TELEPHONE: 108 N. Batyra Street, Alma-Ata. 8–3272; 69–3596; 62–8766 (office).

Danilov, Victor Petrovich
POSITION: Chief Researcher at the Russian History Institute of the Russian Academy of Sciences; Editorial Staff Member of *Voprosy Istorii* (*Questions of History*) magazine
BIRTHPLACE/DATE: Orsk, Orenburg region, 1925
NATIONALITY: Russian
EDUCATION: From 1950 to 1953, postgraduate student at the History Institute of the USSR Academy of Sciences. Doctor of History; Professor.
CAREER: From 1954 to 1958, Junior Researcher, Senior Researcher. From 1958 to 1960, Consultant to *Kommunist* magazine. From 1960, Chief Researcher at the Russian History Institute of the USSR Academy of Sciences. From 1960 to 1991, Editorial Staff Member of *Istoricheskiye Zapiski* (*Historical Notes*) magazine.
MAJOR WORKS: More than 200 publications.
FAMILY: Married with two children.
ADDRESS/TELEPHONE: 19 D. Ulyanov Street, Moscow, 117036. 126–9431.

Danilov-Danilyants, Victor Ivanovich
POSITION: Russian Federation Minister of Ecology and Natural Resources
BIRTHPLACE/DATE: Moscow, 1938
NATIONALITY: Russian
EDUCATION: Graduated in 1960 from Moscow State University. Doctor of Economics; Professor. Good command of English.
CAREER: From 1960 to 1964, Junior Researcher, Engineer at Moscow State University's Computer Center. From 1964 to 1976, Junior Researcher, Leading Engineer, Laboratory Head at the USSR Academy of Sciences' Central Economics and Mathematics Institute. From 1976 to 1980, Laboratory Head at the All-Union Systems Analysis Research Institute. From 1980 to 1991, Laboratory Head, Department Head at the USSR Council of Ministers' Academy of National Economy. From 1991, USSR Deputy Minister of Ecology and Natural Resources.
FAMILY: Married with three sons.
ADDRESS/TELEPHONE: 6 Bolshaya Gruzinskaya, Moscow. 229–8313 (office).

Dasayev, Rinat Faizrakhmovich
POSITION: Goalkeeper of the USSR National Football Team; playing under contract with the Spanish Seville Football Club
BIRTHPLACE/DATE: Astrakhan, 1957
EDUCATION: Graduated from the Moscow Regional Institute of Physical Education.
HONORS/AWARDS: USSR Honored Master of Sports.
FAMILY: Married with two children.
ADDRESS/TELEPHONE: 5 Bolshoi Rzhevski Per-

eulok, Moscow, 121069. 202–9624 (Sovintersport).

Davydov, Vitaly Semyoenovich
POSITION: Senior Coach; Head of the Moscow Dynamo Hockey Team
BIRTHPLACE/DATE: Moscow, 1939
NATIONALITY: Russian
CAREER: From 1963 to 1970, European Ice Hockey Champion. From 1963 to 1971, World Champion. In 1964, 1968, and 1972, winner at the Winter Olympics. From 1978 to 1980, Senior Coach of the USSR National Youth Team. From 1981 to 1984, Senior Coach of the Hungarian National Team.
HONORS/AWARDS: USSR Honored Master of Sports; USSR and Russian Federation Honored Coach; Order of the Red Banner of Labor; Honor For Labor Achievements from the Komsomol Central Committee.
FAMILY: Married with two children.
ADDRESS/TELEPHONE: 3–66 N. Bashilova Street, Moscow, 125083. 213–4665.

Delyagin, Mikhail Gennadyevich
POSITION: Chief Professional of the Russian President's Group of Experts
BIRTHPLACE/DATE: Moscow, 1968
NATIONALITY: Russian
CAREER: From 1990 to 1991, Expert of the Russian Supreme Soviet.
MAJOR WORKS: "What For and How Do Ministries Fight?" (1990); "About Different Approaches to Estimating the Financial Balance of Consumer Markets."
HONORS/AWARDS: USSR Academy of Sciences Prize; Prize of Mena Bank.
FAMILY: Single.
ADDRESS/TELEPHONE: The Kremlin, Moscow. 224–0349 (office).

Dementey, Nikolay Ivanovich
POSITION: Deputy of the Byelorussian Supreme Soviet
BIRTHPLACE/DATE: Kholtino village, Vitebsk region, 1931
CAREER: Worked as a Teacher at an agriculture school, Agronomist, and Director of an automobile and tractor store. From 1957, member of the Communist Party. From 1958, District Committee Instructor Secretary, then Department Head of the Regional Communist Party. From 1970, Inspector of the Byelorussian Central Committee. From 1977, Agriculture Department Head of the Byelorussian Central Committee. In 1979, elected Secretary of the Byelorussian Central Committee. In 1989, elected Chairman of the Byelorussian Supreme Soviet. In August 1991, resigned. From September 1991, Chairman of the Byelorussian Supreme Soviet Commission for Citizenship.
FAMILY: Married with a son.
ADDRESS/TELEPHONE: House of Government, Minsk, 220010. 8–0172; 29–6004 (office).

Dementyev, Andrey Dmitryevich
POSITION: Editor in Chief of *Yunost* (*Youth*) monthly magazine; Co-Chairman of the Executive Committee of the Russian Writers' Union
BIRTHPLACE/DATE: Tver, 1928
EDUCATION: Graduated in 1952 from the Moscow Gorky Literary Institute. Good command of French.
CAREER: From 1952, worked for Tver regional newspapers; radio and publishing houses.
MAJOR WORKS: First collection of poems (1955). About 20 books.
HONORS/AWARDS: USSR State Prize; Lenin Komsomol Prize.
FAMILY: Married with two daughters and a son.
ADDRESS/TELEPHONE: 2/1 Tverskaya Street, Moscow. 251–3122 (office).

Demin, Mikhail Timofeyevich
POSITION: Prefect of the Northern Prefecture of Moscow
BIRTHPLACE/DATE: Moscow, October 31, 1938
NATIONALITY: Russian
EDUCATION: Graduated in 1966 from the Moscow Power Engineering Institute.
CAREER: From 1956 to 1957, Pattern Maker at a defense plant. From 1957 to 1960, served in the Armed Forces. From 1960 to 1961, Pattern Maker, and from 1961 to 1964, Mechanic at a defense plant. From 1964 to 1970, Engineer, then Senior Engineer; from 1970 to 1976, Leading Engineer; from 1976 to 1979, Sector Head; from 1979 to 1984, Secretary of the Communist Party Committee at the Electrotechnical Research Institute. From

1984 to 1987, Deputy Director-General of the Delta Research and Production Association and Director of Plastik Plant. From 1987 to 1991, Chairman of the Moscow Timiryazev District Executive Committee. Deputy of the Timiryazev District Council.
FAMILY: Married with a daughter.
ADDRESS/TELEPHONE: 27 Timiryazevskaya Street, Moscow. 976–1008 (office).

Denisenko, Bella Anatolyevna
POSITION: Russian Federation First Deputy Minister of Health; member of the Radical Democrats Faction; member of the Democratic Russia Movement; member of the Committee for Health Protection
BIRTHPLACE/DATE: Kansk, Krasnoyarsk region, 1941
NATIONALITY: Russian
EDUCATION: Graduated in 1965 from the Krasnoyarsk Medical Institute. From 1966 to 1968, undertook clinical studies at the Cardiology Division of the Novokuznetsk State Institute for Auxiliary Advanced Studies of Physicians (GIDUV). From 1968 to 1970, postgraduate student. Doctor of Medicine; Professor.
CAREER: From 1965 to 1966, Physician at the Krasnoyarsk Grain Factory. From 1970 to 1977, Assistant; from 1977 to 1985, Assistant Professor of the GIDUV Cardiology Division. From 1985 to 1990, Head of the GIDUV Therapy Division. From 1990, Subcommittee Chairman of the Russian Federation Supreme Soviet Committee for Health Protection; Russian Federation People's Deputy. From November 1990, Russian Federation Deputy Minister of Health.
MAJOR WORKS: Author of 130 scientific papers; *Myocardial Infarction of the Right and Left Ventricles* monograph; two inventions.
FAMILY: Married with two sons.
ADDRESS/TELEPHONE: 13 Plotnikov Pereulok, Flat #18, Moscow. 241–9702 (home); 292–3433 (office).

Derbisov, Erkeshbay Zaylaubayevich
POSITION: Kazakh Finance Minister; Head of the Kazakh State Tax Inspection
BIRTHPLACE/DATE: Koyiankus village, Alma-Ata region, 1941
CAREER: Accountant, Department Head, Board Head, Deputy, then First Deputy of the Kazakh Finance Ministry. From 1990 to 1991, Chairman of the Price State Commission.
FAMILY: Married with three children.
ADDRESS/TELEPHONE: 97 Abylatkhana Prospekt, Alma-Ata, 480091. 8–3272; 62–4075 (office).

Derkovsky, Oleg Mikhailovich
POSITION: Ambassador to the United Arab Emirates; Ambassador Extraordinary and Plenipotentiary
BIRTHPLACE/DATE: Kharkov, August 2, 1939
NATIONALITY: Ukrainian
EDUCATION: Graduated from the Moscow State Institute of International Relations in 1963. From 1974 to 1976, postgraduate student at the Diplomatic Academy of the USSR Foreign Ministry.
CAREER: From 1961 to 1963, Trainee at the USSR Embassy in Iraq. In 1964, Aide to the Middle East Department, Senior Aide-Secretary at the USSR Consulate in Batzra, Iraq. From 1964 to 1966, Translator at the USSR Embassy in Iraq. From 1967 to 1969, Attaché of the Middle East Department. From 1969 to 1971, Third Secretary at the USSR Embassy in Yemen; from 1973 to 1974, First Secretary. In 1976, First Secretary of the Middle East Department. From 1976 to 1977, First Secretary at the USSR Embassy in Egypt. From 1977 to 1981, Counsellor. From 1981 to 1983, Counsellor of the Middle East Department; from 1983 to 1985, Division Head. From 1985 to 1990, Counsellor at the USSR Embassy in the United States. From 1990 to 1992, Deputy Head of the Middle East and Northern Africa Department of the USSR Foreign Ministry.
FAMILY: Married.
TELEPHONE: 244–4013.

Deryabin, Yuri Stepanovich
POSITION: Ambassador to Finland; Ambassador Extraordinary and Plenipotentiary
BIRTHPLACE/DATE: 1932
NATIONALITY: Russian
EDUCATION: Graduated in 1954 from the Moscow State Institute of International Relations. Speaks Finnish, Norwegian, English, and German.
CAREER: From 1954, worked in the Foreign

Ministry. From 1980 to 1983, Counsellor-Envoy at the USSR Embassy in Finland. From 1983 to 1986, Deputy Head of the USSR Foreign Ministry's Department of Scandinavian Countries. From 1986 to 1987, Deputy Head of the Second European Department. From 1987 to 1991, Department Head; Directorate Head for European Security and Cooperation. From 1991 to 1992, USSR Deputy Foreign Minister.
ADDRESS/TELEPHONE: Suurlahetysto, Tehtaankatu 1 B, 00140, Helsinki 14, Suomi. 66–1876; 66–1877; 60–7050.

Dezhkin, Vadim Vasilyevich
POSITION: Head of the Department of Nature Preserves and Rare Animals at Glavokhota's (Main Hunting Administration) Central Research Forestry Institute (CRFI)
BIRTHPLACE/DATE: Tambov, 1930
NATIONALITY: Russian
EDUCATION: Graduated in 1953 from the Moscow Fur Trade Institute. Doctor of Biology. Speaks English.
CAREER: From 1953 to 1962, Senior Researcher at a nature preserve in Voronezh. From 1962 to 1968, Chief Hunting Expert of Centrosoyuz and Glavokhota. From 1968 to 1969, Staff Member of a nature laboratory of the USSR Ministry of Agriculture. From 1969, Staff Member, Head of the Department of Nature Preserves and Rare Animals of Glavokhota's CRFI. From 1982, member of the Russian Academy of Sciences' Commission for Nature Preserves; member of the Higher Ecological Council, member of the Russian Federation Supreme Soviet Committee for Ecology.
MAJOR WORKS: Author of more than 200 publications and books.
FAMILY: Married with two children.
ADDRESS/TELEPHONE: 18 Teterinsky Pereulok, Moscow. 297–9909 (office).

Diligensky, German Germanovich
POSITION: Editor in Chief of *World Economy and International Relations* magazine
BIRTHPLACE/DATE: Moscow, 1930
NATIONALITY: Russian
EDUCATION: Graduated in 1952 from the History Department of Moscow State University. Doctor of History; Professor.
CAREER: Researcher at the History Institute; Senior Researcher at the Institute of the World Economy and International Relations of the USSR Academy of Sciences; Department Head of the Institute of the International Labor Movement of the USSR Academy of Sciences.
MAJOR WORKS: In the fields of socio-political problems of Western society, the social psychology of mass conscience, and socio-political problems of modern Soviet society.
HONORS/AWARDS: State Prize.
FAMILY: Married with a son.
ADDRESS/TELEPHONE: 23 Profsoyuznaya Street, Moscow. 128–4709 (office).

Dmitryev, Andrey Victorovch
POSITION: Board Chief Executive of the Central and South America Department of the Russian Foreign Ministry; Counsellor Extraordinary and Plenipotentiary, First Grade
BIRTHPLACE/DATE: Moscow, April 10, 1941
NATIONALITY: Russian
EDUCATION: Graduated from the First Maurice Thorez Teachers' Training Institute in 1966. From 1968 to 1969, postgraduate student at the UN Translation School in Moscow. From 1976 to 1978, postgraduate student at the Diplomatic Academy of the USSR Foreign Ministry. From 1986 to 1987, postgraduate student of the advanced course for senior diplomats at the Diplomatic Academy.
CAREER: From 1966 to 1968, Translator. From 1969 to 1976, worked at the UN Secretariat. From 1978 to 1980, Second Secretary at the USSR Embassy in Brazil; from 1980 to 1984, First Secretary. From 1984 to 1985, First Secretary of the Second Latin America Department; from 1985 to 1986, Counsellor. From 1987 to 1989, Minister-Counsellor at the USSR Embassy in Peru. From 1989 to 1992, Minister-Counsellor at the USSR Embassy in Nicaragua.
FAMILY: Married with two children.
TELEPHONE: 244–3906.

Dmitryev, Dmitri Ivanovich
POSITION: Board Chairman of Tekhnokhimbank (Technology and Chemistry) Joint-Stock Bank
BIRTHPLACE/DATE: Leningrad, 1947

EDUCATION: Graduated in 1969 from the Leningrad (now St. Petersburg) Institute of Finance and Economics. Speaks Croatian.
CAREER: From 1969 to 1976, Economist, Senior Economist, Head of the Operational Department of the Leningrad USSR State Bank. From 1976 to 1988, Department Manager of the Kalinisky USSR State Bank, Department Manager of Promstroibank (Industrial Construction Bank).
FAMILY: Married with two children.
ADDRESS/TELEPHONE: 10 Naberezhnaya Krasnogo Flota, St. Petersburg, 190000. 311–6994 (office).

Dmitryev, Mikhail Yegorovich
POSITION: Deputy Chairman of the Russian Federation Supreme Soviet Committee for Inter-Republican Relations, Regional Policies, and Cooperation Issues
BIRTHPLACE/DATE: Leningrad, February 24, 1961
NATIONALITY: Russian
EDUCATION: Graduated in 1983 from the Voznesensky Leningrad (now St. Petersburg) Finance and Economics Institute (LFEI). In 1989, defended thesis for the Doctor degree. Speaks English and French.
CAREER: From 1983 to 1990, worked at the LFEI Research Department. In 1990, elected Russian Federation People's Deputy.
FAMILY: Married.
ADDRESS/TELEPHONE: 30-B Dubninskaya Street, Flat #227, Moscow, 127591. 485–5460.

Dneprov, Eduard Dmitryevich
POSITION: Former Russian Federation Minister of Education
BIRTHPLACE/DATE: Moscow, 1936
NATIONALITY: Russian
EDUCATION: From 1948 to 1954, student at the Nakhimov Navy School. Graduated in 1958 from the Frunze Higher Navy School and in 1961 from Leningrad State University. Doctor of History.
CAREER: From 1958 to 1971, Officer of the Northern and Baltic Fleet. From 1971 to 1974, Senior Researcher at the General Pedagogics Research Institute. From 1974 to 1975, Editorial Research Group Head of Pedagogika Publishers. From 1975 to 1976, Editor in Chief of Pedagogika Publishers. From 1976 to 1978, Department Head of Scientific and Pedagogical Information. From 1978 to 1988, Head of the Laboratory for the History of Education and Pedagogics in Pre-Revolutionary Russia at the General Pedagogics Research Institute. From 1988 to 1990, Director of the Pedagogical Innovation Center of the USSR Academy of Pedagogical Sciences. From November 1991 to December 1992, Russian Federation Minister of Education.
FAMILY: Married with a child.
ADDRESS/TELEPHONE: 6 Chistoprudny Boulevard, Moscow, 101856. 924–8468; 932–1246 (office).

Dodolev, Yevgeni Yuryevich
POSITION: Editor in Chief of *Novy Vzglyad* (*New Outlook*) newspaper; Vice President of the Novy Vzglyad Joint-Stock Company
BIRTHPLACE/DATE: Moscow, 1957
EDUCATION: Graduated in 1981 from the Lenin State Teachers' Training Institute in Moscow. Speaks English and Polish.
CAREER: From 1981 to 1985, Engineer-Programmer of the USSR Goskomizdat (State Committee for Publishing). From 1985 to 1987, Youth Department Editor of *Moskovsky Komsomolets* (*Moscow Komsomol Member*) daily. From 1987 to 1989, News Analyst of *Smena* (*Rising Generation*) magazine. From January 1992, Editor in Chief of *Novy Vzglyad* newspaper. From August 1992, Popular News Editor of *Moskovsky Komsomolets*.
MAJOR WORKS: *The Pyramid–1* (co-authored with Gdlyan); *The Red Mafia* (published in Britain in 1989); *The Kremlin Secrets* (published in the United States in 1991); *The Lawless Times Mafia* (1991); *Corruption, Soviet-Style* (published in France in 1991); *The Brezhnevs Family Chronicle* (published in the United States in 1991); *Behind the Kremlin Scenes* (published in France in 1992).
HONORS/AWARDS: Two Prizes of the Russian Journalists' Union.
FAMILY: Married with a child.
ADDRESS/TELEPHONE: 6 Varvarka Street, Moscow. 298–0979 (office).

Dokukin, Aleksandr Nikolayevich (Gedeon)
POSITION: Metropolitan of Stavropol and Baku

Birthplace/Date: Novopokrovskaya village, Krasnodar territory, December 18, 1929
Nationality: Russian
Education: Graduated in 1960 from the Moscow Theological Academy.
Career: From 1953 to 1965, Priest in Kislovodsk. From 1965 to 1967, Priest in Petrozavodsk (Karelia). From 1967 to 1972, Bishop, Administrator of the Smolensk Diocese of the Russian Orthodox Church. From 1972 to 1989, Archbishop of Novosibirsk and Barnaul.
Address/Telephone: 155 Dzerzhinsky Street, Stavropol. 235–0454; 230–2118; 230–2431.

Doletsky, Stanislav Yakovlevich
Position: Corresponding Member of the Russian Academy of Medical Sciences
Birthplace/Date: Moscow, November 10, 1919
Nationality: Russian
Education: Graduated in 1947 from the First Moscow Medical Institute. Speaks English and Polish.
Career: From 1943 to 1945, Chief Army Surgeon of a front-line hospital. From 1945 to 1959, worked at the Second Moscow Medical Institute. From 1959 to 1960, Department Head of the Leningrad Pediatrics Medical Institute. From 1960, Department Head of the Central Institute for the Advanced Studies of Physicians of the USSR Health Ministry. From 1975, Corresponding Member of the USSR Academy of Medical Sciences; member of the International Society of Surgeons; member of the British Association of Pediatric Surgeons.
Major Works: More than twenty books, textbooks, and monographs.
Honors/Awards: Two USSR State Prizes.
Family: Married with two children.
Address/Telephone: 7 Sadovaya-Kudrinskaya Street, Flat #67, Moscow, 123242. 254–0082 (home); 268–4354 (office).

Dolgov, Vyacheslav Ivanovich
Position: Ambassador to Austria; Ambassador Extraordinary and Plenipotentiary
Birthplace/Date: Bryansk, July 31, 1937
Nationality: Russian
Education: Graduated from the Moscow State Institute of International Relations in 1961.
Career: From 1961 to 1963, Interpreter at the USSR Embassy in Great Britain. From 1963 to 1965, Attaché. From 1965 to 1968, Third Secretary of the Second European Department. From 1968 to 1972, Second Secretary at the USSR Embassy in Canada; from 1972 to 1973, First Secretary. From 1973 to 1974, First Secretary of the First European Department; from 1974 to 1977, Sector Head. From 1977 to 1982, Counsellor at the USSR Embassy in Great Britain. From 1984 to 1986, Deputy Head of the First European Department. From 1986 to 1990, Deputy Head of the Pacific and Southeastern Asia Department. From 1990, Ambassador to Fiji, Nauru, Vanuatu, and Austria.
Honors/Awards: Order of the Badge of Honor.
Family: Married with two children.
Telephone: 241–7821.

Dolmatov, Vladimir Petrovich
Position: Editor in Chief of the Russian Federation Supreme Soviet's *Rodina* (*Motherland*) journal
Birthplace/Date: Chuvashevo village, Sverdlovsk region, 1948
Nationality: Russian
Education: Graduated in 1976 from the Journalism Department at Gorky State University. Speaks German.
Career: From 1968 to 1969, Photographer for a district newspaper. From 1976 to 1982, Special Correspondent for the Urals regional workers' newspaper. Correspondent for *Sovietskaya Rossiya* (*Soviet Russia*) newspaper for the Kemerovo and Tomsk regions. From 1985 to 1987, Editor of *Sovietskaya Rossiya*. From 1988 to 1990, Deputy Editor in Chief of *Rodina*.
Family: Married with a daughter.
Address/Telephone: 26 Volgogradsky Prospekt, Moscow, 125865. 270–0960 (office); 970–5254 (home).

Dorofeyev, Vitaly Vadimovich
Position: Director-General of Avtopromimport (Importer of Automobile Industry Products) Foreign Economic Association

BIRTHPLACE/DATE: Moscow, 1935
EDUCATION: Graduated in 1959 from the Bauman Higher Technical School in Moscow and in 1969 from the All-Union Academy of Foreign Trade.
CAREER: From 1961 to 1967, Senior Engineer of the Mashinoimport (Import of Machinery) All-Union Association. From 1967 to 1989, Deputy Director of Avtopromimport.
HONORS/AWARDS: Order of the Red Banner of Labor; Medal For Labor Valor; Veteran of Labor Medal.
FAMILY: Married with a daughter and granddaughter.
ADDRESS/TELEPHONE: Avtopromimport, 50/2 Pyatnitskaya Street, Moscow. 231–8126.

Drach, Ivan Fyodorovich
POSITION: Kiev Board Chairman of the Ukrainian Writers' Union; Chairman of the Ukrainian Poet and Scriptwriter Organization
BIRTHPLACE/DATE: Telizentsy village, Kiev region, 1936
CAREER: Russian Language and Literature Teacher; Instructor of the District Komsomol Committee; Editorial Staff Member of *Literaturnaya Ukraine* (*Literary Ukraine*) newspaper and *Vitchyzna* (*Fatherland*). In 1962, joined the Ukrainian Writers' Union. Co-Founder and Leader of the Ukranian Rukh Movement; from 1989, Chairman; from March 1992, Co-Chairman.
MAJOR WORKS: Author of numerous poems and scripts.
HONORS/AWARDS: Ukrainian State Shevchenko Prize; USSR State Prize.
FAMILY: Married with two children.
ADDRESS/TELEPHONE: 6 Zlotovratskaya Street, Kiev–34, 252034. 224–8081 (office); 27–2401 (home).

Dronov, Vitaly Yakovlevich
POSITION: Board Chairman of the Moscow Commercial Bank for Social Development (Glavmosstroibank)
BIRTHPLACE/DATE: Tambov, 1937
NATIONALITY: Russian
EDUCATION: Graduated from the Moscow Finance and Economics Institute.
CAREER: Department Manager, City Department Head of the Tambov USSR State Bank. Department Head, Deputy Head of the Russian USSR State Bank. Deputy Department Head of the USSR State Bank Board and of USSR Zhilbank (Housing Bank).
FAMILY: Married with a daughter.
ADDRESS/TELEPHONE: 20 Tverskoi Boulevard, Moscow, 103009. 229–9648 (office).

Drozdov, Aleksandr Alekseyevich
POSITION: Editor in Chief of *Rossiya* (*Russia*)
BIRTHPLACE/DATE: Moscow, 1952
EDUCATION: Graduated in 1974 from the International Law Department at the Moscow Institute of International Relations and in 1975 from the Foreign Intelligence School. Good command of English and Japanese.
CAREER: From 1975 to 1979, worked at the Foreign Intelligence Center. From 1979, Trainee, Correspondent for *Komsomolskaya Pravda* (*Komsomol Truth*) daily. From 1981 to 1987, *Komsomolskaya Pravda* Correspondent in Japan. From 1987 to 1988, Editor of the International Affairs Department; Editorial Board Member of *Komsomolskaya Pravda*. From 1988 to 1990, Managing Editor of *Komsomolskaya Pravda*. From August to October 1990, Assistant to the First Deputy Chairman of the Russian Federation Supreme Soviet. In October and November 1990, Executive Director of *Rossiya*. In November 1990, quit the secret service.
FAMILY: Married with two children.
ADDRESS/TELEPHONE: 24 Pravdy Street, GSP, Moscow, 125865. 257–2491 (office).

Druk, Mircha George
POSITION: Chairman of the National Christian-Democratic Front (formerly the National Front) of Moldavia
BIRTHPLACE/DATE: Pochumbeuts village, Moldavia, 1941
NATIONALITY: Moldavian and Romanian dual citizenship
CAREER: Worked in the Economics Department at Moscow State University; Teacher at Chernovitsy University. In 1989, Director of the Moldavian National Center for Economic Cooperation with Foreign Countries. In 1990, elected Moldavian People's Deputy. From May 1990 to 1991, Chair-

man of the Moldavian Council of Ministers. From October 1990 to 1991, member of the Moldavian Presidential Council. In December 1991, Chairman of the Moldavian National Council for Unification with Romania. In February 1992, nominated for the Presidency of Romania. In 1992, relieved of post as People's Deputy.
MAJOR WORKS: Author of scientific publications in the field of industrial management and management psychology.
FAMILY: Married with two daughters.

Drukov, Anatoli Matveyevich
POSITION: Ambassador to India; Ambassador Extraordinary and Plenipotentiary
BIRTHPLACE/DATE: Voronezh, September 4, 1936
NATIONALITY: Russian
EDUCATION: From 1954 to 1960, student at the Moscow State Institute of International Relations. Graduated from the Moscow State Institute of International Relations.
CAREER: From 1960 to 1961, Aide on Duty, Trainee at the USSR Embassy in Pakistan. From 1962 to 1964, Attaché of the Southern Asia Department. In 1966, Third Secretary. From 1966 to 1967, Third Secretary of the Secretariat of the Deputy Foreign Minister. From 1967 to 1969, Second Secretary. From 1969 to 1973, First Secretary at the USSR Embassy in Zambia. From 1973 to 1978, Aide to the Deputy Minister. From 1978 to 1979, Expert of the Southeastern Asia Department; from 1979 to 1983, Deputy Head; in 1983, Acting Head; in 1983 and 1986, Deputy Head. From 1986 to 1987, Deputy Head of the Socialist Countries of Asia Department. From 1987 to 1990, Ambassador to Singapore. From 1990 to 1991, Personnel Head and Collegium Member of the USSR Foreign Ministry.
FAMILY: Married with two children.
TELEPHONE: 244–2793.

Dubenitsky, Yakov Nikolayevich
POSITION: Board Chairman of Promstroibank Joint-Stock Industrial Construction Bank
BIRTHPLACE/DATE: Brest region, 1938
NATIONALITY: Byelorussian
EDUCATION: Graduated from the Minsk Finance and Credit Technical Institute. Graduated in 1959 from the Economics Department at Moscow State University.
CAREER: From 1959 to 1960, Building Administration Department Head in Krasnoyarsk. From 1960 to 1963, Planning and Finance Department Head at the Directorate of Tashkent Gas Mains. From 1963 to 1965, Planning Chief of the Economic and Financial Department of the Bukhara-Urals Gas Main Construction Directorate. From 1965 to 1972, worked at the Planning and Economic Administration of the USSR Ministry of Gas Industry; from 1972 to 1977, Deputy Administration Head. From 1977 to 1985, Head of the Finance and Credit Directorate for Chemical, Oil, and Gas Industries of the USSR Promstroibank. From 1985 to 1987, Deputy Board Chairman; from 1987 to 1990, First Deputy Board Chairman; from 1990 to 1991, Board Chairman of the USSR Promstroibank.
FAMILY: Married with a son.
ADDRESS/TELEPHONE: 13 Tverskoi Boulevard, Moscow. 203–7522 (office).

Dubinin, Yuri Vladimirovich
POSITION: Ambassador at Large; Ambassador Extraordinary and Plenipotentiary
BIRTHPLACE/DATE: Nalchik, Kabardino-Balkaria, October 7, 1930
NATIONALITY: Russian
EDUCATION: Graduated in 1954 from the Moscow State Institute of International Relations. Doctor of History (1978). Good command of English, Spanish, and French.
CAREER: From 1954 to 1956, Trainee at the USSR Embassy in France. From 1956 to 1959, Staff Member of the UNESCO Secretariat in Paris. From 1959 to 1963, Third Secretary; Second Secretary; Aide to the Head of the First European Department (Benelux States, France, Italy, Portugal, Spain, Switzerland) of the USSR Foreign Ministry. From 1963 to 1968, First Secretary, then Minister-Counsellor at the USSR Embassy in France. From 1968 to 1978, Deputy Head, then Head of the First European Department of the USSR Foreign Ministry. From 1978 to 1986, USSR Ambassador to Spain. In 1986, USSR Ambassador to the UN. From 1986 to 1990, member of the Communist Party Central Auditing Commission. From 1986 to 1990, USSR Ambassador to the United States.

From 1990 to September 1991, USSR Ambassador to France.
HONORS/AWARDS: Order of the Red Banner of Labor; Order of the People's Friendship; Order of the Badge of Honor; Jubilee Labor Valor Medal.
FAMILY: Married with three daughters.
ADDRESS/TELEPHONE: 3 Yuzhinsky Pereulok, Flat #34, Moscow, 103104. 203–2749 (home); 244–1696 (office).

Dudayev, Dzhokhar Museyevich
POSITION: President of the Chechen Republic; Chairman of the Chechen Cabinet of Ministers; Chief Commander of the Chechen Armed Forces
BIRTHPLACE/DATE: Chechen, 1944
CAREER: From 1957, Commander of the Strategic Air Forces Division in Tartu (Estonia); Garrison Commander. Resigned after Division withdrew from Estonia and relocated to Grozny. From 1990, Head of the Executive Committee of the Chechen National Congress.
FAMILY: Married with two sons and a daughter.
ADDRESS/TELEPHONE: 29 Pobeda Pr., Grozny, 364051. 22–0902; 22–8573; 22–6401.

Dudenkov, Anatoli Petrovich
POSITION: Director of the Tver Progresspromb ank (Industrial Progress) Joint-Stock Bank
BIRTHPLACE/DATE: Rzhavchik, Oryol region, 1938
NATIONALITY: Russian
EDUCATION: Graduated in 1964 from the Moscow Institute of Finance and Economics. Good command of German.
CAREER: From 1959 to 1962, Economist of the Kalinin (now Tver) Region Gosbank (USSR State Bank). From 1962 to 1965, Inspector; from 1965 to 1971, Senior Economist; from 1971 to 1974, City Administration Deputy Head; from 1974 to 1977, Deputy Manager of the Kalinin Gosbank. From 1977 to 1987, Manager of the Kalinin Stroibank (Construction Bank). From 1987 to 1991, Administration Manager of the Tver USSR Promstroibank (Industrial Construction Bank).
FAMILY: Married with two children.
ADDRESS/TELEPHONE: 35 Sovietskaya Street, Tver, 170000. 3–2563.

Dudenkov, Ivan Grigoryevich
POSITION: Board Chairman of Bytbank Commercial Bank of Consumer Services Development
BIRTHPLACE/DATE: Baika village, Serdobsky district, Penza region, 1929
EDUCATION: Graduated in 1951 from the Astrakhan Technical Institute of Fish Industry. Speaks English.
CAREER: From 1951 to 1956, Engineer, Chief Engineer, Director of the Fish Industry Mechanical Engineering Enterprise of Astrakhan Region. From 1957 to 1969, First Secretary of the Ikryansky District Communist Party; Second Secretary of the Astrakhan Regional Communist Party. From 1969 to 1974, Chairman of the Astrakhan Regional Executive Committee. From 1974 to 1990, Russian Federation Minister of Consumer Services for the Population.
FAMILY: Married with two children.
ADDRESS/TELEPHONE: 7 Stanislavsky Street, Moscow. 290–1774 (office).

Dunayev, Andrey Fyodorovich
POSITION: Russian Federation First Deputy Minister of Internal Affairs
BIRTHPLACE/DATE: Ulyanovsk region, 1939
NATIONALITY: Mordvinian
EDUCATION: From 1957 to 1959, student at the Alma-Ata Specialized Secondary Police School of the USSR Ministry of Internal Affairs. Graduated in 1963 from the Higher School of the USSR Ministry of Internal Affairs; and in 1990, from the Academy of the USSR Ministry of Internal Affairs.
CAREER: From 1959 to 1962, Senior Officer of the Investigation Department. From 1962 to 1965, Senior Economic Crime Department Officer of the Kustanai Regional Executive Committee's Internal Affairs Directorate. From 1965 to 1967, Deputy Head of the Internal Affairs Directorate of the Jetygarinsky City Executive Committee. From 1967 to 1970, Head of the Internal Affairs Directorate of the Teryingul District Executive Committee. From 1970 to 1973, Head of the Ulyanovsk Internal Affairs Directorate. From 1973 to 1978, Head of the Criminal Investigation Department of the Chechen-Ingush Ministry of Internal Affairs. From 1979 to 1980, Dagestan Deputy Minister of Internal Affairs. From 1980 to 1985, Head of the Internal Affairs Directorate of the Vologda Regional

Executive Committee. From 1985 to 1986, worked at the USSR Ministry of Internal Affairs. From 1986 to 1990, Head of the Kaliningrad Specialized Secondary Police School. In 1990, Deputy Head of the Law Correspondence School of the Ministry of Internal Affairs. From 1990 to 1991, Russian Federation Deputy Minister of Internal Affairs. From November 1991 to January 1992, Russian Federation Minister of Internal Affairs.
FAMILY: Married with two children.
ADDRESS/TELEPHONE: 16 Zhitnaya Street, Moscow, 117049. 239–6335 (office).

Dushenkin, Vladimir Nikolayevich
POSITION: Editor in Chief of *Vneshnyaya Torgovlya* (*Foreign Trade*) magazine
BIRTHPLACE/DATE: Moscow, 1930
NATIONALITY: Russian
EDUCATION: Graduated in 1952 from the Moscow Institute of Foreign Trade. Command of English and French.
CAREER: Economist; Deputy Head of a USSR foreign trade firm. Head of the Economic Information Department at the Telegraph Agency of the Soviet Union (TASS) office in London; Head of the TASS Economic Information Department; Head of the TASS office in Singapore; Head of the TASS United Economic Information Department.
HONORS/AWARDS: Government awards; journalism prizes.
FAMILY: Married with a child.
ADDRESS/TELEPHONE: 11 Minskaya Street, Moscow, 121108. 145–6894 (phone/fax).

Dzasokhov, Aleksandr Sergeyevich
POSITION: Co-Chairman of the International Association For Dialogue and Cooperation with the Countries of Asia and the Pacific; Russian Federation People's Deputy; member of the Russian Federation Supreme Soviet; Council Member of the Russian Afro-Asian Solidarity and Cooperation Society
BIRTHPLACE/DATE: Ordzhonikidze (now Vladikavkaz), North Ossetia, April 3, 1934
NATIONALITY: Ossetian
EDUCATION: Graduated from the North Caucasian Mining and Metallurgical Institute in Ordzhonikidze and from the postgraduate program at the Central Committee's Academy of Social Sciences. Doctor of History.
CAREER: In 1957, joined the Communist Party. From 1957 to 1961, First Secretary of the Ordzhonikidze City Komsomol Committee; Coordinator of the Komsomol Central Committee. From 1961 to 1965, Executive Secretary of the USSR Committee of Youth Organizations (CYO); Head of a group of young Soviet experts in Cuba. From 1965 to 1967, Executive Secretary; First Deputy Chairman of the USSR CYO. From 1967 to 1975, Executive Secretary. From 1976 to 1977, Deputy Chairman; from 1977 to 1986, First Deputy Chairman of the USSR Afro-Asian Solidarity Committee. From 1986 to 1988, USSR Ambassador to Syria. From 1988 to 1990, First Secretary of the North-Ossetian Communist Party. From 1990 to 1991, member of the Politburo; Secretary of the Central Committee.
HONORS/AWARDS: Order of the October Revolution; Order of the People's Friendship; Order of the Red Banner of Labor; medals.
FAMILY: Married with two sons and a granddaughter.
ADDRESS/TELEPHONE: Krasnopresnenskaya Naberezhnaya, Moscow. 202–2314; 202–4156; 205–3417 (office).

Dzhaganova, Altynshash Kairdzhanovna
POSITION: Editor in Chief of *Kazakhstan Aelderi* magazine; Chairwoman of the Supreme Soviet Committee for Women's Rights
BIRTHPLACE/DATE: Astrakhanka village, Tselinograd region, 1943
NATIONALITY: Kazakh
CAREER: From 1988, Editor at Zazushy and Kazakhstan publishing houses; Chairwoman of the Committee for Women, Family, Motherhood, and Childhood Issues; Kazakh Presidium Member; Kazakh Supreme Soviet People's Deputy.
MAJOR WORKS: Author of novels, short stories, plays, and film scripts.
FAMILY: Married with two sons and a daughter.
ADDRESS/TELEPHONE: 50 Z. Zula Street, Alma-Ata, 480044. 33–2952; 69–5714 (office); 69–5998 (home).

Dzhikovich, Vladimir Veliykovich
POSITION: Board Chairman of the St. Petersburg

Timber Industry Bank; Chairman of the Russian Banks Auditing Association
BIRTHPLACE/DATE: Leningrad, 1951
CAREER: Worked from Engineer to Chief Accountant. From 1987 to 1989, Chief Accountant of the Mongolenergostroi (Mongolian Power Industry) Trust.
FAMILY: Married with a child.
ADDRESS/TELEPHONE: 5 Krapivny Pereulok, St. Petersburg, 191065. 541–8217 (office).

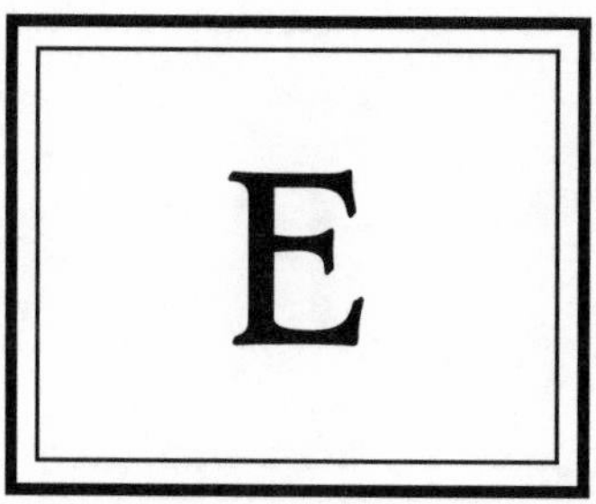

Eisen, Artur Arturovich

POSITION: Bass Singer of the Bolshoi Theater
BIRTHPLACE/DATE: Moscow, 1929
EDUCATION: Graduated in 1948 from the Shchukin Drama School and in 1956 from the Moscow Conservatory. Professor.
CAREER: From 1949, Soloist of the Aleksandrov Folk Song and Dance Company. From 1956, Soloist of the Bolshoi Theater. From 1975, Teacher at the Gnesiny Musical Teachers' Training Institute.
MAJOR WORKS: Parts in *Ivan Khovanskiy*; *Vaskov*; *Mephistopheles*.
HONORS/AWARDS: USSR People's Artist.
FAMILY: Married with a daughter and a grandson.
ADDRESS/TELEPHONE: 8/2 Okhotny Ryad, Moscow. 249–3087 (home).

Eksler, Aleksey Andreyevich

POSITION: Inter-Party Liaison Coordinator of the Free Labor Party
BIRTHPLACE/DATE: Smolensk, 1935
EDUCATION: Graduated in 1960 from the Moscow Power Engineering Institute.
CAREER: From 1960 to 1963, Engineer, Senior Engineer, Junior Researcher at the Defense Ministry's Research Institute. From 1964 to 1965, Leading Engineer; from 1965 to 1974, Sector Head; from 1974 to 1980, Leading Designer at the Research Institute of the Ministry of Electronics Industry. From 1980 to 1986, Laboratory Head of the Communications Industry Ministry. From 1986 to January 1991, Leading Designer at the All-Union Standards Research Institute. In November 1990, joined the Free Labor Party. In February 1991, elected Inter-Party Liaison Coordinator of the Free Labor Party.
FAMILY: Married with a daughter and a grandson.
ADDRESS/TELEPHONE: 18 P. Romanov Street, Building 2, Flat #8, Moscow, 109193. 277–6702; 279–5731 (office); 189–3435 (home).

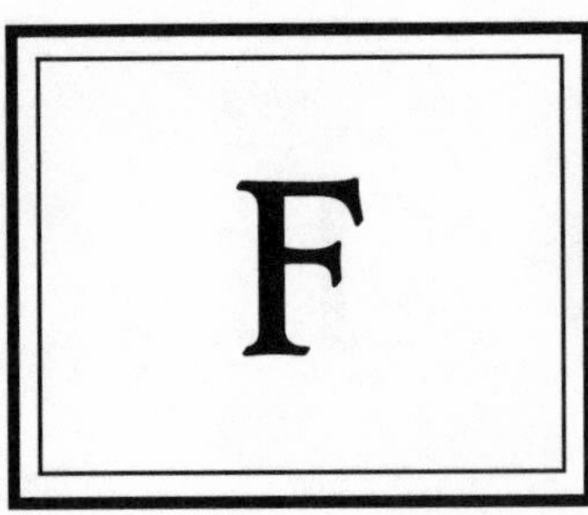

Fadeyev, Gennadi Matveyevich

POSITION: Russian Federation Minister of Railways

BIRTHPLACE/DATE: Shimanovsk, Amur region, April 10, 1937

EDUCATION: Graduated in 1961 from the Khabarovsk Institute of Railway Engineers.

CAREER: Head, Shunting Dispatcher, Duty Official, Senior Chief Assistant of Taishet Station Railways of the East-Siberian Railway. From 1963, Chief Station Engineer, Deputy Head, then Head of the Railway Traffic Department. Headed the Nizhnyudinsk, Taishet, and Krasnoyarsk branches of the East-Siberian Railway. From 1977, First Deputy Head. From 1979 to 1984, Head of Krasnoyarsk Railway. From 1984 to 1987, Head of Oktyabrskaya Railway. From 1987, Deputy Minister-Head of the Main Transportation Directorate of the Ministry of Railways; from 1988, First Deputy Minister. Russian Federation People's Deputy, Russian Federation Supreme Soviet Member.

ADDRESS/TELEPHONE: 2 Novaya Basmannaya Street, Moscow, 107174. 262–9901.

Fadeyev, Nikolay Sergeyevich (Serapion)

POSITION: Metropolitan of Tula and Belev

BIRTHPLACE/DATE: Moscow, May 27, 1933

NATIONALITY: Russian

EDUCATION: Graduated in 1966 from the Moscow Ecclesiastical Academy; from 1966 to 1969, postgraduate student at the Moscow Ecclesiastical Academy.

CAREER: From 1969 to 1971, Expert of the Foreign Church Relations Department of the Moscow Patriarchy. From 1971 to 1974, Russian Orthodox Church (ROCh) Representative at the Antioch Patriarchy (Syria). From 1975 to 1982, Bishop, Administrator of the Irkutsk ROCh Diocese. From 1982 to 1987, Archbishop, Administrator of the Vladimir ROCh Diocese. From 1990, Metropolitan, Administrator of the Tula ROCh Diocese.

ADDRESS/TELEPHONE: 61 Zhukovsky Street, Tula. 235–0454; 230–2118; 230–2431 (Moscow).

Fedosov, Pyotr Anatolyevich

POSITION: Board Advisor of Svobodnaya Rossiya (Free Russia) People's Party (SRPP)

BIRTHPLACE/DATE: 1951

NATIONALITY: Russian

EDUCATION: Graduated in 1973 from the Moscow State Teachers' Training Institute Department of Foreign Languages. From 1987 to 1989, studied in Dortmund, Germany. Doctor of History. Speaks German, Danish, English.

CAREER: From 1973 to 1976, Interpreter. To 1986, Lecturer. From 1990, engaged in political activity for the Communist Party and SRPP. From January 1992, Counsellor of SRPP.

FAMILY: Married with two sons.

ADDRESS/TELEPHONE: 9 Kolpachny Pereulok, Moscow. 175–4970; 297–0301.

Fedulova, Alevtina Vasilyevna

POSITION: Chairwoman of the Russian Union of Women

BIRTHPLACE/DATE: Elektrostal, Moscow region, 1940

NATIONALITY: Russian

EDUCATION: Graduated from the Chemistry and Biology Department of the Krupskaya Regional

Teachers' Training Institute in Moscow. Graduated from the Central Committee's Academy of Social Sciences.
CAREER: To 1968, Secondary School Teacher. From 1968, First Secretary of the Elektrostal City Komsomol Committee, then Secretary of the Moscow District Komsomol Committee. From 1971, Central Council Chairwoman of the All-Union Lenin Pioneer Organization. From 1977 to 1984, Secretary of the All-Union Komsomol Central Committee. From 1984, Executive Secretary of the Soviet Peace Committee. Former member of the Central Committee. From 1987 to 1991, First Deputy Chairwoman of the Soviet Women's Committee. From 1991 to 1992, Chairwoman of the Soviet Women's Committee.
FAMILY: Married with a son, a grandson, and a granddaughter.
ADDRESS/TELEPHONE: 6 Nemirovich-Danchenko Street, Moscow, 103832. 229–3223.

Fesunenko, Igor Sergeyevich
POSITION: Bureau Chief of the Ostankino State Television and Radio Company
BIRTHPLACE/DATE: 1933
NATIONALITY: Russian
CAREER: Worked at the Central Archives Directorate. From 1957, Journalist. From 1963 to 1966, worked at the Department of Foreign Broadcasting of the State Television and Radio Committee. From 1966 to 1978, Television and Radio Correspondent in Cuba, Brazil, Portugal. From 1978 to 1991, Political Analyst of Central Television. From November 1991, Office Head of the Ostankino State Television and Radio Company in Rome.
MAJOR WORKS: A number of books on Brazilian football.
FAMILY: Married with a daughter.
ADDRESS: 59 Vernadsky Prospekt, Building 415, Flat #19, Moscow, 117415. 233–7798.

Filaret (Vakhromeyev Kirill Varfolomeyevich)
POSITION: Metropolitan of Minsk and Slutsk; Permanent Member of the Holy Synod of the Russian Orthodox Church; Patriarch's Exarch of Byelorussia
BIRTHPLACE/DATE: Moscow, March 21, 1935
NATIONALITY: Russian
EDUCATION: Doctor of Theology.
CAREER: From 1961 to 1963, Lecturer at the Moscow Ecclesiastical Academy; from 1963 to 1965, Inspector; from 1966 to 1975, Rector. In 1975, took the orders of Metropolitan. From 1975 to 1978, Metropolitan of Minsk and Byelorussia, Patriarch's Exarch of Central Europe (Berlin). From 1978 to 1984, Patriarch's Exarch of Western Europe. From 1984 to 1990, Chairman of the Foreign Affairs Department of the Moscow Patriarchy. From 1989 to 1992, USSR People's Deputy.
HONORS/AWARDS: Order of the People's Friendship.
ADDRESS/TELEPHONE: 10 Osvobozhdeniya Street, Minsk, 220004. Moscow: 230–2118; 230–2431; 954–0454.

Filatov, Leonid Alekseyevich
POSITION: Actor and Producer
BIRTHPLACE/DATE: Kazan, 1946
NATIONALITY: Russian
EDUCATION: Graduated in 1969 from the Shchukin Drama School at the Yevgeni Vakhtangov Theater in Moscow.
CAREER: From 1969, Actor of the Taganka Drama and Comedy Theater in Moscow. Now, one of the leading actors of this theater. Starred in many popular feature films. In 1991, made debut as Film Director and Scriptwriter of *Sukiny Deti* (*Sons of a Bitch*). Member of the USSR Union of Film Makers; from December 1991, Board Member.
MAJOR WORKS: Performed in plays: *Hamlet*; *Master and Margarita*; *The Dead and the Alive*; *The House on the Embankment*. Starred in films: *The Loop*; *A Forgotten Tune for the Flute*; *The Chosen Ones*; *The Contender*. Produced: *Sons of a Bitch*.
HONORS/AWARDS: Russian Federation Honored Artist.
FAMILY: Married with a child.
ADDRESS/TELEPHONE: 12 Rogozhsky Val, Flat #106, Moscow, 109147. 278–4232; 278–8812 (home).

Filatov, Sergey Aleksandrovich
POSITION: Head of the Russian Federation President's Staff
BIRTHPLACE/DATE: Moscow, 1936

NATIONALITY: Russian
EDUCATION: Graduated in 1964 from the Moscow Power Engineering Institute. Doctor of Technology. Speaks English.
CAREER: From 1955 to 1969, Researcher, Komsomol Committee Secretary of the Serp i Molot (Sickle and Hammer) Metallurgical Plant. From 1969 to 1990, Head of the Department of Metallurgy Automation at the All-Union Research Institute of Metal Mechanical Engineering. From 1990, Russian Federation People's Deputy, Russian Federation Supreme Soviet Member, member of the Committee for Economic Reforms. From January 1991, Presidium Secretary, and from November 1991, First Deputy Chairman of the Russian Federation Supreme Soviet; member of the Democratic Russia Faction. From 1993, Head of the Russian Federation President's Staff.
HONORS/AWARDS: USSR State Prize.
FAMILY: Married with two children and three grandchildren.
ADDRESS/TELEPHONE: 2 Krasnopresnenskaya Naberezhnaya, Moscow. 205–5767.

Filippov, Andrey Nikolayevich
POSITION: Board Chairman of the Siberian Commercial Bank (Sibbank) in Krasnoyarsk
BIRTHPLACE/DATE: Moscow, 1957
NATIONALITY: Russian
EDUCATION: Graduated in 1979 from the International Economic Relations Department at the Moscow Institute of Finance. Speaks French and English.
CAREER: From 1979 to 1983, French Credits Specialist of the Foreign Banking Credits Board of the USSR Vneshtorgbank (Foreign Trade Bank). From 1983 to 1988, Assistant to the Deputy Board Chairman of the USSR Vneshtorgbank. From 1989 to 1990, Monetary and Economic Board Expert of the International Economic Cooperation Bank.
FAMILY: Married with a daughter.
ADDRESS/TELEPHONE: 144-A Bograd Street, Krasnoyarsk, 660021. 21–3050 (office).

Filippov, Pyotr Sergeyevich
POSITION: Head of the Russian Federation President's Analytical Center of Socio-Economic Policy
BIRTHPLACE/DATE: Odessa, 1945
NATIONALITY: Russian
EDUCATION: In 1967, graduated from LIAP. From 1971 to 1974, postgraduate student.
CAREER: From 1967, Engineer at Lenelectronmash. In 1969, Laboratory Head at the Kirov Works. From 1974 to 1976, Director of the Children's Mountain Skiing School. From 1977 to 1978, Head of the Computing Center at the Kirov Plant. From 1978 to 1986, Mechanic at a motor park. From 1986 to 1987, Leading Specialist of the Electro All-Union Industrial and Technical Institute. From 1987 to 1990, Department Head of *Echo* magazine. From 1990, Chairman of the Russian Federation Supreme Soviet Subcommittee for Privatization. Member of the Demokraticheskaya Rossiya (Democratic Russia) Party, member of the Committee for Economic Reforms and Private Property. Russian Federation People's Deputy, PetroSoviet (St. Petersburg Council) People's Deputy.
FAMILY: Married.
ADDRESS/TELEPHONE: 30-B Dubininskaya Street, Flat #250, Moscow; Novaya Ploschad, Entrance 10, Room 509, Moscow. 485–5448 (home); 205–4528 (office); 355–2962 (St.Petersburg).

Filshin, Gennadi Innokentyevich
POSITION: Russian Government Trade Representative in Austria
BIRTHPLACE/DATE: 1931
NATIONALITY: Russian
EDUCATION: Graduated in 1954 from the Economics Department at Moscow State University. Doctor of Economics. Speaks English.
CAREER: For a number of years, Economics Lecturer at various educational establishments; held leading posts at state bodies and economic organizations. Former Department Head of the Institute of Industrial Production Economics of the USSR Academy of Sciences' Siberian branch. From July 1990 to February 1991, Deputy Chairman of the Russian Federation Council of Ministers. Former USSR People's Deputy. Member of the USSR Supreme Soviet Planning and Budget Commission. From May 1991, Russian Federation Deputy Minister of Foreign Economic Relations.
FAMILY: Married with two children.
ADDRESS/TELEPHONE: 32/34, Smolenskaya-

Sennaya, Moscow, 121200. 244–2450 (Ministry of Foreign Economic Relations).

Finko, Oleg Aleksandrovich

POSITION: Editor in Chief of *Yuridicheskaya Gazeta* (*Legal Newspaper*)
BIRTHPLACE/DATE: Moscow, 1941
EDUCATION: Graduated in 1966 from the Far Eastern University; from 1966 to 1969, postgraduate student at the Far Eastern University. Doctor of History; Assistant Professor. Speaks German and Chinese.
CAREER: From 1961 to 1966, Concrete Worker, then Foreman in the Far East. Until 1975, Journalist at regional newspapers in the Russian Far East. From 1976 to 1980, Assistant Professor of the Journalism Department at Moscow State University. From 1980 to 1982, Senior Correspondent, Special Correspondent for *Komsomolskaya Pravda* (*Komsomol Truth*) daily. From 1982 to 1990, worked from Department Head to Deputy Chief Editor of Sovremennik (Contemporary), Khudozhestvennaya Literatura, and Iskusstvo Publishers. Member of the Russian Union of Lawyers; member of the Russian Writers' Union.
MAJOR WORKS: *Unceasing Memory*; *Retribution for Silence*; *Forgotten Love*.
FAMILY: Widower with a daughter.
ADDRESS/TELEPHONE: 11 Kolpachny Pereulok, Building 2, Moscow, 101000. 923–3537 (office).

Firsov, Andrey Petrovich

POSITION: President of the Aziatskaya Birzha Joint-Stock Company.
BIRTHPLACE/DATE: Anzherosudzhensk, Kemerovo region, 1957
NATIONALITY: Russian
EDUCATION: Doctor of Geology and Mineralogy.
CAREER: From 1978 to 1987, Senior Laboratory Assistant, Junior Researcher at the Institute of Geology of the USSR Academy of Sciences' Siberian branch. From 1988, Deputy Chairman of the Youth Housing Complex. From 1989 to 1990, Researcher at the Geological Institute. From January 1991, President of Aziatskaya Birzha.
FAMILY: Married with two children.
ADDRESS/TELEPHONE: 23 Sovietskaya Street, Ulan-Ude, 670031. 22–681; 22–881.

Fokin, Vitold Pavlovich

POSITION: Deputy Chairman of the Ukraine State Council
BIRTHPLACE/DATE: Novonikolayevka village, Zaporozhsk region, October 25, 1932
NATIONALITY: Russian
EDUCATION: Doctor of Technical Sciences.
CAREER: From 1954 to 1972, Assistant Section Head, Section Head at Lugansk region mines, Manager of the Pervomayskugol (Pervomaysk Coal) Trust, Chief Engineer of the Voroshilovgradugol (Voroshilovgradugol Coal) Group of Enterprises, Head of the Sverdlovantratsit Group of Enterprises. From 1971 to 1987, Deputy, then First Deputy Chairman of the Ukraine State Planning Committee. From 1987, Chairman of the Ukraine State Planning Committee and Deputy Chairman of the Ukraine Council of Ministers. From August 1990, Chairman of the Ukraine State Committee for Economics. From November 1990 to September 1992, Chairman of the Ukraine Council of Ministers, Ukraine Prime Minister. From February 1992, Deputy Chairman of the Ukraine State Council. Supreme Soviet Deputy of the Eleventh Convocation. USSR People's Deputy. Member of the Communist Party from 1954 to 1991. Member of the Central Committee from 1990 to 1991.
HONORS/AWARDS: Two Orders of the Red Banner of Labor; Order of the Badge of Honor.

Fomenko, Aleksander Vladimirovich

POSITION: Editor in Chief of *Politika* (*Politics*) newspaper
BIRTHPLACE/DATE: Sevastopol, 1961
EDUCATION: Graduated in 1984 from the Philology Department at Moscow State University. Speaks English, German, French, Italian, Spanish, Serbo-Croatian, modern Greek, Portuguese.
CAREER: From 1984 to 1986, served in the army. From 1986 to 1988, Editorial Staff Member of *Nash Sovremennik* (*Our Contemporary*) magazine, Senior Editor of Sovremennik (Contemporary) Publishers. In 1988 and 1989, Editorial Board Member, Head of the Criticism and Art Department of *Molodaya Gvardia* (*Young Guard*) magazine. From 1989 to 1990, Editorial Board Member, Political Science Department Head of *Literaturnaya Rossiya* (*Literary Russia*) newspaper.

From 1991, Editor in Chief of *Obozrevatel* (*Observer*). Member of the Russian Writers' Union.
MAJOR WORKS: Social and political journalism, critical articles on literature, art, theater, and books.
FAMILY: Married with two daughters.
ADDRESS/TELEPHONE: 7/2 Tverskoi Boulevard, Moscow. 202–8903 (office).

Fonotov, Andrey Georgyevich
POSITION: Russian Federation First Deputy Minister of Science, Higher Education and Technical Policy
BIRTHPLACE/DATE: Leningrad, 1947
EDUCATION: Graduated in 1970 from the Economics and Cybernetics Department at Moscow State University. Postgraduate student at the Central Institute of Economics and Mathematics. Doctor of Economics. Speaks English.
CAREER: From 1972 to 1986, Junior, then Senior Researcher at the Central Institute of Economics and Mathematics of the USSR Academy of Sciences. From 1986 to 1990, Deputy Director of Science at the USSR Academy of Sciences' Institute of Economics and Forecasts of Scientific and Technical Progress.
MAJOR WORKS: Over 100 works on planning and forecasting theory of scientific and technical progress.
FAMILY: Married with two children.
ADDRESS/TELEPHONE: 11 Tverskaya Street, Moscow, 103905. 229–7872 (office).

Frantskevich, Mikhail Ivanovich
POSITION: Board Chairman of Aviabank
BIRTHPLACE/DATE: Brest region, 1943
NATIONALITY: Byelorussian
EDUCATION: Graduated from the Saratov Institute of Economics and from the Moscow Finance and Economics Institute.
CAREER: Worked at the Chelyabinsk Bank Administration. Chief Board Expert of the State Bank; Director of Donats Bank (Vienna, Austria); Deputy Administration Head of the USSR State Bank Board.
FAMILY: Married with two children.
ADDRESS/TELEPHONE: 16 Ulansky Pereulok, Moscow, 101849. 207–5856 (office).

Freidkin, Lev Grigoryevich
POSITION: Director-General and President of the Chelyabinsk Investment and Mercantile Exchange.
BIRTHPLACE/DATE: Chelyabinsk, 1955
EDUCATION: Graduated in 1977 from the Chelyabinsk Polytechnical Institute. Graduated in 1988 from the USSR Internal Affairs Ministry's Higher School. From 1991, student at the Academy of National Economy.
CAREER: From 1977 to 1979, Army Officer. From 1979 to 1981, Engineer. From 1981 to 1991, Chief of the Construction and Assembly Department of the Chelyabinsk Regional Executive Committee Board of Internal Affairs. From 1991, President of the Chelyabinsk Investment and Mercantile Exchange, Vice President of the Congress of Bourses. From October 18, 1991, Vice President of the Russian Investment Exchange.
FAMILY: Married with two children.
ADDRESS/TELEPHONE: 5 Elkin Street, Chelyabinsk, 454000. 33–9825 (office).

Frolov, Konstantin Vasilyevich
POSITION: Vice President of the Russian Academy of Sciences; Director of the State Research Institute of Mechanical Engineering Science
BIRTHPLACE/DATE: Kaluga region, July 22, 1932
NATIONALITY: Russian
EDUCATION: Graduated in 1956 from the Bryansk Transport Engineering Institute.
CAREER: Joined the Communist Party in 1956. From 1956, worked at the Blagonravov State Theoretical Engineering Research Institute; from 1975, Director. From 1984, Academician of the USSR Academy of Sciences. From 1985, Academician of the All-Union Lenin Agricultural Academy. From 1985, Vice President of the USSR Academy of Sciences. Former elected USSR People's Deputy. USSR Supreme Soviet Member.
MAJOR WORKS: Founded a new research field: operator's biomechanics under the influence of machine vibration; elaborated theoretical principles of vibration-proof systems taking into account an operator's condition.
HONORS/AWARDS: USSR State Prize.
FAMILY: Married with a child.
ADDRESS/TELEPHONE: The Blagonravov Theoretical Engineering Institute, 4 Griboyedov Street,

Moscow, GSP, 101830. 228–8730; 237–2731 (office).

Fronin, Vladislav Aleksandrovich

POSITION: Editor in Chief of *Komsomolskaya Pravda* (*Komsomol Truth*) newspaper
BIRTHPLACE/DATE: Andreyevka village, Ulyanovsk region, 1952
EDUCATION: Graduated from Kazan State University.
CAREER: Practical Student of the Working Youth Department of *Komsomolskaya Pravda*; Correspondent, Editorial Board Member, Managing Editor of *Komsomolskaya Pravda*; Propaganda Department Head of the All-Union Komsomol Central Committee.
FAMILY: Married with a daughter.
ADDRESS/TELEPHONE: 24 Pravda Street, Moscow, 125850. 257–2728 (office).

Furmanov, Boris Aleksandrovich

POSITION: Deputy Chairman of the Russian Federation President's Council of Experts
BIRTHPLACE/DATE: Severodonetsk, Voroshilovgrad region, 1936
CAREER: From 1959 to 1961, Foreman. From 1961 to 1963, Estimate Group Project Head. From 1963 to 1966, Technical Department Head. From 1966 to 1969, Chief Engineer of the Construction Directorate. From 1969 to 1970, Deputy Head of the Technical Directorate of Glavk. From 1970 to 1971, Trust Manager. From 1971 to 1974, Technical Directorate Head of Glavk. From 1974 to 1978, Chief Engineer of a group of enterprises. From 1978 to 1982, Deputy Head of Glavk. From 1982 to 1986, Construction Department Head of the Regional Party Committee. From 1986 to 1990, Deputy USSR Minister of Heavy Industry. From October 1990 to Novenber 1991, Chairman of the Russian Federation State Committee for Architecture and Construction. From November 1991, Minister of Architecture, Construction and Municipal Economy. Member of the Communist Party from 1969 to 1991.
HONORS/AWARDS: USSR Council of Ministers Prize.
FAMILY: Married with a daughter and a son.
ADDRESS/TELEPHONE: 2 Georgyevski Pereulok, Moscow, 103828. 206–3038; 206–2948.

Fuzhenko, Ivan Vasilyevich

POSITION: Rear Commanding Officer of the Commonwealth of Independent States Joint Armed Forces; Colonel-General
BIRTHPLACE/DATE: Subbotsy village, Znamenka district, Kirovograd region, June 5, 1937
NATIONALITY: Ukrainian
EDUCATION: Graduated in 1957 from the Odessa Military School; in 1970, from the Mikhail Frunze Military Academy; and in 1978, from the General Staff Military Academy.
CAREER: From 1954, served in the Armed Forces. Division Commander, Army Commander, First Deputy Army Group Commander, First Deputy Commander of a military district. From 1989, Commander of the Turkistan Military District. Former elected USSR People's Deputy.
FAMILY: Married with two children.
TELEPHONE: 293–28679; 293–1413 (office).

Fyodorov, Andrey Vladimirovich

POSITION: Advisor to the Russian Federation Vice President
BIRTHPLACE/DATE: Moscow, 1955
NATIONALITY: Russian
EDUCATION: Graduated in 1977 from the Philosophy Department at Moscow State University. Speaks English, Finnish, Swedish, Czech, and Norwegian.
CAREER: From 1977 to 1989, Aide, Head of the International Organizations Section of the USSR Committee of Youth Organizations, Secretary of the Preparatory Committee of the Moscow Youth and Students Festival, Official of the Democratic Youth World Federation, Vice President of the International Students' Union. From 1989 to 1990, Aide to the Central Committee's International Department. From July to November 1990, member of the Innovation Council of the Russian Federation Council of Ministers' Chairman. From October to November of 1991, Russian Federation Deputy Foreign Minister.
MAJOR WORKS: Articles on international affairs and issues of Russian domestic policy.
HONORS/AWARDS: Order of the People's Friendship.
FAMILY: Married with two children.

ADDRESS/TELEPHONE: The Kremlin, Moscow. 224–0677 (office).

Fyodorov, Boris Grigoryevich

POSITION: Former Finance Minister; Former Vice Chairman of the Russian Federation Council of Ministers
BIRTHPLACE/DATE: Moscow, 1958
NATIONALITY: Russian
EDUCATION: Graduated in 1980 from the Moscow Institute of Finance. Doctor of Economics. Speaks English.
CAREER: From 1980 to 1987, Economist, then Senior Economist of the Main Monetary-Economic Directorate of the USSR State Bank. From 1987 to 1989, worked at the USSR Academy of Sciences' Institute of the World Economy and International Relations. From 1989 to 1990, Consultant to the Socio-Economic Department of the Central Committee. From 1990 to 1991, Russian Federation Finance Minister, Head of Soviet Operations at the European Bank of Reconstruction and Development. From 1991 to January 1994, Financial Policy Counsellor of the Russian Federation Government; Finance Minister.
FAMILY: Married with two children.
ADDRESS/TELEPHONE: 4 Staraya Ploshchad, Moscow. 206–4630 (office).

Fyodorov, Nikolay Vasilyevich

POSITION: Russian Federation Minister of Justice
BIRTHPLACE/DATE: 1958
NATIONALITY: Chuvash
EDUCATION: Graduated from Kazan State University and from the postgraduate program at the State and Law Institute of the USSR Academy of Sciences. Doctor of Law.
CAREER: Lecturer and Legal Advisor at Chuvash State University. Senior Lecturer of the Scientific Communism Division at Chuvash State University. Former USSR People's Deputy, member of the USSR Supreme Soviet Committee for Legislation, Law, and Order.
FAMILY: Married with two children.
ADDRESS/TELEPHONE: 10-A Yermolova Street, Moscow. 209–6055; 209–7895 (office).

Fyodorov, Svyatoslav Nikolayevich

POSITION: Director-General of the Mikrokhirurgiya Glaza (Eye Microsurgery Institute) Scientific and Technological Complex; Co-Chairman of the Economic Freedom Party
BIRTHPLACE/DATE: Proskurov (Ukraine), 1927
NATIONALITY: Russian
EDUCATION: Graduated in 1952 from the Rostov-on-Don Medical Institute. In 1955, began clinical studies, graduating in 1957. Doctor of Medicine. Professor.
CAREER: Doctor in Veshenskaya village, Rostov region, then in Lysva, Sverdlovsk region. In 1958, Clinical Department Head of a Cheboksary hospital. In 1960, implanted the first artificial crystalline lens. Later, Ophthalmology Division Head at the Arkhangelsk Medical Institute. In 1967, by decision of the USSR Health Ministry, transferred to Moscow as Laboratory Head for Artificial Crystalline Lens Implantation. In 1969, engaged in artificial cornea implantation. In 1973, developed the world's first surgical procedure for glaucoma treatment in early stages. In 1974, performed the first operations for the treatment and correction of short-sightedness. In 1980, Founder and Director-General of Mikrokhrirurgiya Glaza. From 1983, Director-General of the Mikrokhirurgiya Glaza Complex. From 1989 to 1991, USSR People's Deputy, member of the USSR Supreme Soviet Committee for Economic Reforms. Former Chairman of the USSR Health and Charity Foundation. Corresponding Member of the Russian Academy of Sciences. From June 1992, Co-Chairman of the Economic Freedom Party (PEF), Political Council Chairman of the PEF. From 1957, member of the Communist Party. Former member of the Demokraticheskaya Rossiya (Democratic Russia) Movement.
HONORS/AWARDS: Hero of Socialist Labor.
FAMILY: Married with two daughters.
ADDRESS/TELEPHONE: 59-A Beskudnikovsky Boulevard, Moscow, 127486. 905–4045.

Gabrielyants, Grigory Arkadyevich
POSITION: President of Geoservice, a scientific technical consulting firm
BIRTHPLACE/DATE: Baku, 1934
NATIONALITY: Armenian
CAREER: From 1965 to 1968, Chief Geologist, Expedition Head, Deputy Director of the Turkmenia Gas Research Institute. From 1968 to 1972, Lecturer at the Moscow Gubkin Institute of Oil and Gas. From 1973 to 1979, Head of the Oil Prospecting Department; from 1979 to 1987, Deputy Director-General of the Oil and Geophysics Research Institute; from 1987 to 1989, Director. From 1989 to 1991, USSR Geology Minister. Member of the Communist Party to 1991.
MAJOR WORKS: Books about methods of oil prospecting; textbook, *Geology of Oil Field.*
HONORS/AWARDS: USSR State Prize.
FAMILY: Married with two sons.
ADDRESS: 8 Kedrov Street, Moscow.

Gabuzov, Oleg Semyonovich
POSITION: Director of the Glavokhota Hunting Preserves Administration
BIRTHPLACE/DATE: Baku, 1933
NATIONALITY: Armenian
EDUCATION: Doctor of Biology; postdoctoral degree.
CAREER: From 1956 to 1960, Deputy Director of a hunting farm in Moscow region. From 1960 to 1961, Fauna Engineer of the Moscow Municipal Forest and Park Department. From 1961 to 1967, Engineer and Hunting Specialist of Soyuzgipromskhoz (Soviet Union Water Industry). From 1967 to 1970, Deputy Head of the All-Union Military-Hunting Society. From 1971, Deputy Head of Glavokhota. Member of the Ornithology Society.
MAJOR WORKS: Author of 193 publications.
FAMILY: Married with a child.
ADDRESS/TELEPHONE: Losinoostrovskaya, Lesnaya Dacha, Block 18, Moscow, 129347. 582–1308 (office).

Gadziev, Fuad Nazim Ogly
POSITION: Press Attaché at the Azerbaijan Plenipotentiary Mission in Moscow
BIRTHPLACE/DATE: Baku, 1957
NATIONALITY: Azerbaijanian
CAREER: From 1980 to 1983, Interpreter for the USSR Youth Organizations Committee. From 1983 to 1992, worked in the USSR Central Komsomol Committee.
FAMILY: Married.
ADDRESS/TELEPHONE: 16 Stanislavsky Street, Moscow, 103009. 202–5072; 229–3206 (office).

Gaidar, Yegor Timurovich
POSITION: Head of Russia's Choice Party; Former Deputy Prime Minister
BIRTHPLACE/DATE: Moscow, March 19, 1956
NATIONALITY: Russian
EDUCATION: From 1978 to 1980, postgraduate student at Moscow State University. Doctor of Economics.
CAREER: From 1980 to 1986, Acting Junior Researcher, then Senior Researcher at the Institute of Systems Analysis. From 1986 to 1987, Senior Researcher, then Chief Researcher at the Institute of Economics and Forecasts of Scientific and Technical Progress. From 1987 to 1990, Deputy Head of

the Economy Department of *Kommunist* magazine. From 1990, Head of the Economy Department of *Pravda* (*Truth*) daily. From 1990 to 1991, Director of the Economic Policy Institute of the USSR Academy of National Economy. From November 1991, Russian Federation Government Deputy Chairman, Russian Federation Economics and Finance Minister. From December 1991, Head of the Russian Federation Monetary-Economic Council. From February 1992 to April 1992, Russian Federation Finance Minister. From March 1992, Russian Federation Government First Deputy Chairman for Economic Reforms; Scientific Council Member of the Research Center for International Economic Reforms. In June 1992, appointed Official Representative of the Russian Federation President, while the Russian Federation Supreme Soviet considered the draft of "About the Council of Ministers—Russian Federation Government." From June 1992 to January 1994, Acting Chairman of the Russian Federation Government; Deputy Prime Minister.
FAMILY: Married with a son.
ADDRESS/TELEPHONE: 5 Ogarev Street, Moscow, 103918. 203–88169 (office).

Galayev, Victor Ilyich
POSITION: Director-General of the Sovintersport (International Sports Council) All-Russian Foreign Trade Organization
BIRTHPLACE/DATE: Kemerovo region, February 13, 1944
CAREER: To 1965, Sports Instructor in Omsk. From 1965 to 1971, Propaganda Instructor, Head of the Physical and Military Education Department of the Kemerovo Regional Komsomol Committee. From 1971 to 1980, Komsomol Leader of the Sports Federation, Deputy Head of the Physical and Military Education Department of the Komsomol Central Committee. From 1980 to 1983, Winter Sports Department Head of the USSR Sports Committee. From 1983 to 1988, Communist Party Secretary of the USSR Sports Committee. From June 1988 to December 1991, Director-General of USSR Sovintersport.
HONORS/AWARDS: Medal For Labor Valor.
FAMILY: Married with a son.
ADDRESS/TELEPHONE: 5 Rzhevsky Pereulok, Moscow, 121069. 291–9149 (office).

Galazov, Akhsarbek Khadzimurzayevich
POSITION: North Ossetian Supreme Soviet Chairman
BIRTHPLACE/DATE: Khumalag village, North Ossetia, October 15, 1929
NATIONALITY: Ossetian
EDUCATION: Doctor of Education.
CAREER: From 1952 to 1958, Teacher of Russian language and literature at a Khumalag public school. From 1958 to 1959, School Inspector of the North Ossetian Ministry of Education. From 1959 to 1960, Director of the Ossetia Postgraduate Teacher's Training Institute. From 1960 to 1961, School and College Instructor of the North Ossetian Regional Communist Party. From 1961 to 1975, North Ossetian Minister of Education. From 1975 to 1976, Deputy Chairman of the North Ossetian Council of Ministers. From 1976 to 1990, Rector at North Ossetian State University. From 1990 to November 1990, First Secretary of the North Ossetian District Communist Party and Supreme Soviet Chairman. Member of the Communist Party from 1959 to 1991. Russian Federation People's Deputy.
FAMILY: Married with three children.
ADDRESS/TELEPHONE: Svoboda Square, Vladikavkaz, 362019. 3–3524; 3–3516.

Gamsakhurdia, Zviad Konstantinovich
POSITION: Georgian Politician and Writer; former President of Georgia
BIRTHPLACE/DATE: Born in 1939
NATIONALITY: Georgian
EDUCATION: Honored Doctor of Philology.
CAREER: Worked as a Senior Researcher at the Rustavelli Georgian Literature Institute. Oppositional political activist. Publisher and Editor of the first samizdat (underground dissident literature) publications in Georgia. Founder and Chairman of the Georgian Helsinki Union. In 1989, elected Chairman of the nationalist St. Iliya Society. Repeatedly arrested and imprisoned in Tbilisi and Moscow for political activities. In November 1990, after the Round Table Free Georgia Party won the first multi-party elections in Georgia, elected Chairman of the Georgian Supreme Soviet. From April 1991 to January 1992, President of Georgia. Dismissed from post on January 6, 1992,

during the military riots; lawsuit was filed against him.
MAJOR WORKS: Many monographs and scientific publications in the field of Georgian culture, theology, anthropology and foreign literature; poetry and songs.
FAMILY: Married with three sons.
TELEPHONE: 291–1359.

Ganin, Vladimir Aleksandrovich
POSITION: Director-General of the Public Relations Joint-Stock Company
BIRTHPLACE/DATE: Moscow, 1955
NATIONALITY: Russian
CAREER: From 1976 to 1980, Radio Program Editor of the Podolsk Mechanical Engineering Plant. From 1980 to 1984, Editor of *Sputnik* magazine of the APN Publishing House. From 1984 to 1988, Senior Scientific Editor of *Argumenty i Facty* (*Arguments and Facts*) weekly newspaper. From 1988 to 1990, Editor-Consultant of *Problemy Mira i Socializma* (*Problems of Peace and Socialism*) international magazine, based in Prague. From 1990 to 1991, Correspondent for *Delovoy Mir* (*Business World*) magazine. From 1991 to 1992, Correspondent for *VIP* magazine.
FAMILY: Married with a son and a daughter.
ADDRESS/TELEPHONE: 27/3 First Kolobovsky Pereulok, Moscow, 103051. 257–2738.

Gaprindashvili, Nonna Terentyevna
POSITION: President of the Georgian National Olympics Committee
BIRTHPLACE/DATE: Zugdidi village, Georgia, 1941
CAREER: Chess Champion in 1962, World Champion versus Bykova; World Champion in 1965, 1969, and 1972, versus A. Kushnir; World Champion in 1975, versus A. Aleksandriay. Ten-time winner of the World Chess Olympics; member of the USSR Team. International Grand Master.
HONORS/AWARDS: USSR Honored Master of Sports.
FAMILY: Married with a son.
ADDRESS/TELEPHONE: 49-A Chavchavadze Street, Tbilisi, 380062. 23–0203.

Gasanov, Gasan Aziz Ogly
POSITION: Prime Minister of Azerbaijan Republic
BIRTHPLACE/DATE: Tbilisi, October 20, 1940
NATIONALITY: Azerbaijanian
CAREER: Instructor of the Baku City Komsomol Committee. Secretary of the Oktyabr Region Komsomol Committee. Sector Head of the Azerbaijan Central Komsomol Committee. From 1967, Instructor, Sector Head, Deputy Department Head of the Azerbaijan Central Committee. USSR People's Deputy. Azerbaijan People's Deputy. From 1963 to 1991, member of the Communist Party.
FAMILY: Married with two children.
ADDRESS/TELEPHONE: 68 Lermontov Street, Baku, 370066. 92–7232 (office).

Gasinsky, Grigory Yakovlevich
POSITION: President of Parfumflakon (Perfume Bottle) Joint-Stock Company
BIRTHPLACE/DATE: Kiev, 1947
CAREER: From 1963 to 1965, Designer at the Kiev Bolshevi Mechanical Engineering Plant. Engineer-Technologist, then Chief Engineer of a glass factory. From 1983, worked at the Moscow Crystal Plant. From 1984, Director of the Moscow Crystal Plant.
FAMILY: Married with a son.
ADDRESS/TELEPHONE: 36/4 B. Novodmitrovskaya Street, Moscow, 125015. 185–6738 (office).

Gavrilov, Igor Trofimovich
POSITION: USSR Trade Representative in Australia
BIRTHPLACE/DATE: Moscow, 1930
NATIONALITY: Russian
EDUCATION: Doctor of Geography; Doctor of Geology and Mineralogy.
CAREER: From 1961 to 1968, worked at institutes of the USSR Geology Ministry. From 1969 to 1990, Deputy Head of the Department for the Rational Consuming of Natural Resources at Moscow State University. From 1990 to 1991, Russian Federation Council of Ministers Deputy Chairman. From 1991 to 1992, Deputy Chairman of the Inter-State Economic Committee. From 1992, Counsellor to the Russian Federation Vice President.
MAJOR WORKS: More than seventy publications

on geophysics, ecology and the rational consuming of natural resources.
HONORS/AWARDS: Veteran of Labor Medal.
FAMILY: Married with a daughter.

Gazabayev, Chahit
POSITION: Former Moslem Clergy Administration Chairman of the Chechen-Ingush Republic; Mufti
BIRTHPLACE/DATE: Shubar-Kuduk village, Aktyubensk region (Kazakhstan)
NATIONALITY: Chechen
CAREER: From 1983 to 1985, Imam-Khatib of the Prigorodskoe village mosque in Chechen-Ingush. From 1985 to 1990, North Caucasus Representative of the Moslem Clergy Administration in Chechen-Ingush. From 1990 to 1991, Moslem Clergy Administration Chairman of the Chechen-Ingush Republic.
FAMILY: Married with three children.
ADDRESS: 29 Figurnaya Street, Grozny.

Gdlyan, Telman Khorenovich
POSITION: President of the All-Russian Fund for Progress, Human Rights, and Charity; Leader of the People's Party of Russia
BIRTHPLACE/DATE: Akhalkalaksky region, Georgia, 1940
EDUCATION: Graduated from the Saratov Kursky Law Institute in 1968.
CAREER: From 1968 to 1970, Investigator of the Baryshevsk Region Prosecutor's Office in Ulyanovsk. From 1970 to 1973, Investigator of the Zavolzhsky Region Prosecutor's Office in Ulyanovsk. From 1973 to 1983, Senior Investigator of the Ulyanovsk Region Prosecutor's Office. From 1982 to 1989, Senior Investigator for the USSR General Prosecutor. From 1983 to 1989, USSR Prosecutor's Office Investigation Group Head of the Uzbeksko-Kremlevsky (Uzbek-Kremlin) Case Investigation. USSR People's Deputy and Armenian People's Deputy. Coordinating Council Member of the Democraticheskaya Rossiya (Democratic Russia) Movement. Leader of the People's Party of Russia. From 1962 to 1990, member of the Communist Party.
MAJOR WORKS: *Piramida* (*Pyramid*) with B. Dodolin; *Mafia of Lawlessness Time*.
FAMILY: Married with a son and a daughter.
ADDRESS/TELEPHONE: 15 Novy Arbat, Moscow, 121801. 202–0109; 202–0643 (secretary).

Gerashchenko, Victor Vladimirovich
POSITION: Chairman of the Central Bank of Russia
BIRTHPLACE/DATE: Leningrad, December 21, 1937
NATIONALITY: Russian
EDUCATION: Graduated from the Moscow Institute of Finance in 1960.
CAREER: From 1960, Accountant of the USSR State Bank. From 1961 to 1965, Accountant, Inspector, Expert, Department Head of the USSR Vneshtorgbank (Foreign Trade Bank). From 1965 to 1967, Director of the Moscow Narodny (People's) Bank in London. From 1967 to 1972, Deputy Department Manager, then Manager of the Moscow Narodny Bank in Lebanon. From 1972 to 1974, Deputy Directorate Head of the USSR Vneshtorgbank. From 1974 to 1977, Board Chairman of the Sovietsky (Soviet) Bank in the Federal Republic of Germany. From 1977 to 1982, Manager of the Moscow Narodny Bank in Singapore. From 1982 to 1989, Directorate Head, Deputy Board Chairman of the USSR Vnesheconombank. From 1989 to 1991, Board Chairman of the USSR State Bank. From July 1990 to 1991, member of the Central Committee. In 1991 to 1992, Head of the Credits and Monetary Policies Department of the Reforma International Foundation for Economic and Social Reforms. From October 1993, Chairman of the Central Bank of Russia
HONORS/AWARDS: Two Orders of the Red Banner of Labor; medals.
FAMILY: Married with a daughter and a son.
ADDRESS/TELEPHONE: 12 Neglinnaya Street, Moscow. 925–2919 (office).

Gerasimov, Gennadi Ivanovich
POSITION: Former Russian Ambassador to Portugal; Ambassador Extraordinary and Plenipotentiary
BIRTHPLACE/DATE: Kazan, 1930
NATIONALITY: Russian
CAREER: From 1953 to 1955, Senior Researcher at Moscow State University. From 1955 to 1959,

Journalist, Editor, Deputy Chief Secretary of *Novoye Vremya* (*New Time*) magazine. From 1959 to 1961, Editorial Department Correspondent for *Trud* (*Labor*) daily. From 1961 to 1964, Editor, Editor-Consultant of *Problemy Mira i Socializma* (*Problems of Peace and Socialism*) magazine, based in Prague. From 1964 to 1967, Aide to the Central Committee. From 1967 to 1972, Political Correspondent for Novosti (News) Press Agency (APN); from 1972 to 1978, Head of APN in the United States. From 1978 to 1983, APN Political Correspondent. From 1983 to 1986, APN Deputy Board Chairman, Editor in Chief of *Moscow News* newspaper. From 1986 to 1990, Information Department Head of the USSR Foreign Ministry. USSR Foreign Ministry Collegium Member.
HONORS/AWARDS: Medal For Victory in the War with Japan; Medal on the 30th Anniversary of Victory in the Patriotic War; Medal on the 40th Anniversary of Victory in the Patriotic War.

Gerasimov, Valery Ivanovich
POSITION: Deputy Chairman of the Russian Federation Supreme Soviet Committee for Health Care, Social Services and Physical Education; Russian Council Member
BIRTHPLACE/DATE: Oktyabrsky village, Ryazan region, 1953
CAREER: From 1976, Surgeon. From 1977 to 1981, Surgery Department Head of Central Regional Hospital. From 1981 to 1983, Intern, Hospital Surgery Chairman. From 1983 to 1986, Deputy Chief Doctor. From 1986 to 1988, Military Surgeon in Afghanistan. From 1988 to 1990, Hospital Head. Russian Federation People's Deputy, member of the Russian Republic Council; member of the Left-Center Faction; member of the Medical Staff Group; member of the Reform Coalition.
FAMILY: Married with two children.
ADDRESS/TELEPHONE: 2 Krasnopresnenskaya Naberezhnaya, Moscow, 103274. 205–6245 (office); 216–4150 (home).

Gerasimov, Vladimir Nikolayevich
POSITION: Board Chairman of the Centrocredit Furniture Industry Crediting and Development Commercial Bank
BIRTHPLACE/DATE: Moscow, 1949
NATIONALITY: Russian
CAREER: Accountant, then Senior Accountant of the Kirov State Bank. Deputy Head of Berezkov State Bank. Deputy Head of the USSR State Bank. Deputy Board Chairman of the AMBI Joint-Stock Commercial Bank.
FAMILY: Married with a daughter.
ADDRESS/TELEPHONE: 9/2 Kolbovsky Pr., Moscow, 103051. 299–6090; 299–5562.

Gidaspov, Boris Veniaminovich
POSITION: Corresponding Member of the Russian Academy of Sciences; former First Secretary of the Leningrad District Communist Party
BIRTHPLACE/DATE: Kuibyshev, April 16, 1933
NATIONALITY: Russian
EDUCATION: Doctor of Chemisty; Professor.
CAREER: From 1955, Assistant at the Kuibyshev Industrial Institute; from 1959, Assistant, Laboratory Engineer, Junior Researcher, Senior Lecturer, Acting Docent, Docent; from 1965, Dean and Professor. From 1969, Division Head of the Leningrad (now St. Petersburg) Institute of Technology. From 1971, Special Design Chief Designer of the Technolog Technological Bureau. From 1977, Director of the State Institute of Applied Chemistry. From 1985, Director-General of the Scientific Industrial Complex. From 1988, Board Chairman of Tekhnokhim in Leningrad. From 1989, First Secretary of the Leningrad District Communist Party. In 1990, elected Secretary of the Central Committee. To August 1991, member of the Communist Party. USSR People's Deputy.
HONORS/AWARDS: Prize of Lenin; USSR State Prize; Order of Lenin; Order of the October Revolution; Order of the Red Banner of Labor.
FAMILY: Married with a child.
ADDRESS/TELEPHONE: 4 Staraya Square, Moscow, 103132. 206–2511.

Gik, Yevgeni Yakovlevich
POSITION: Deputy Editor in Chief of *Poisk* (*Search*) newspaper; International Chess Master
BIRTHPLACE/DATE: Baku, 1943
EDUCATION: From 1970 to 1973, postgraduate student at the Steel and Alloy Institute.
CAREER: From 1966 to 1969, Researcher at the Institute of Problems Management of the USSR Academy of Sciences. From 1973 to 1990, Senior

Researcher, Laboratory Head at the Institute of Management Mechanization in Non-Industrial Spheres. Member of the Moskva (Moscow) Literary Professionals Association; member of the Confederation of Journalists' Unions. Member of the Russian Chess Union.
MAJOR WORKS: Publications on chess theory, also works in the field of applied mathematics and cybernetics.
ADDRESS/TELEPHONE: 18 Lomonosov Proyezd, Moscow, 117296. 939–0716 (home).

Glazychev, Vyacheslav Leonidovich
POSITION: President of the Academy of Urban Environment
BIRTHPLACE/DATE: Moscow, 1940
NATIONALITY: Russian
EDUCATION: Doctor of Philosophy.
CAREER: Architect at the State Institute of Communications. Department Head at the Institute of Architectural Theory and History. Sector Head at the Institute of Culture. Secretary in Chief of the Soviet-American Culture Initiative Fund. Professor at the Institute of Architecture.
FAMILY: Married with a son and a granddaughter.
ADDRESS/TELEPHONE: 8 Krymsky Val, Moscow, 107078. 250–0302 (office).

Glinsky (Vasilyev), Dmitri Yuryevich
POSITION: Board Chairman of the Molodaya Rossiya (Young Russia) Union; Council Member of the Novaya Rossiya (New Russia) Party
BIRTHPLACE/DATE: Moscow, 1970
NATIONALITY: Russian
CAREER: In 1988, participated in organizing the Demokraticheskaya Soyuz (Democratic Union) Party. In 1989, Founding Member of the Union of Constitutional Democrats; worked for *Grazhdanskoye Dostoinstvo* (*Civil Dignity*) newspaper. From 1990, Chairman of the Molodaya Rossiya Union; Founding Member of the Liberal Forum. From 1991, member of the Demokraticheskaya Rossiya (Democratic Russia) Coordinating Council, member of the Demokraticheskaya Rossiya Council for Inter-Republican Relations.
MAJOR WORKS: Works on history, sociology, politics.
FAMILY: Single.
ADDRESS/TELEPHONE: 5–76 Astrakhansky Pereulok, Moscow, 129010. 280–0816 (home); 202–1645 (office).

Glukhov, Aleksey Iliych
POSITION: European Department Director of the Russian Foreign Ministry; Ambassador Extraordinary and Plenipotentiary
BIRTHPLACE/DATE: Moscow, May 16, 1935
NATIONALITY: Russian
EDUCATION: Graduated from the Moscow State Institute of International Relations in 1959.
CAREER: From 1959 to 1960, Senior Aide of the Translation Bureau of the USSR Foreign Ministry; from 1960 to 1962, Attaché; from 1962 to 1965, Third First Secretary; from 1965 to 1967, Second Secretary of the First European Department. From 1967 to 1970, First Secretary; from 1970 to 1971, Counsellor; from 1971 to 1977, Sector Head; from 1977 to 1983, Deputy Head; from 1983 to 1987, Minister-Counsellor at the USSR Embassy in France. From 1987 to 1989, First Deputy Head of the Humanitarian and Cultural Relations Department of the USSR Foreign Ministry; from 1989 to 1990, Head of the Cultural Relations Department; from 1990 to 1992, Head of the First European Department. Collegium Member.
HONORS/AWARDS: Order of the Red Banner of Labor; Order of the People's Friendship; Order of the Badge of Honor.
FAMILY: Married with three children.
TELEPHONE: 244–4162 (office).

Gnedovsky, Yuri Pertovich
POSITION: Board Chairman of the Russian Federation Union of Architects
BIRTHPLACE/DATE: 1930
EDUCATION: In 1962, received degree in Architecture for thesis "New Types of Spacious Movie Theaters."
CAREER: Deputy Director of the Mezentsev Experimental Projects Institute. Participated in an architectural contest for the best spacious movie theater model. Co-Architect of the Taganka Theater. Former Board Secretary of the USSR Union of Architects. Coordinating Committee Member of the International Architects' Union.

HONORS/AWARDS: International Biennale of Architecture Prize in Sofia; USSR State Prize.

Godmanis, Ivars Teodorovich

POSITION: Chairman of the Latvian Council of Ministers
BIRTHPLACE/DATE: Riga, 1951
NATIONALITY: Lett
EDUCATION: Degree in Physics and Mathematics.
CAREER: Senior Lecturer at the University of Latvia. From 1974, engaged in research; spent a year in the United States on a Soviet-American exchange program for young scientists. From 1988, Lecturer of the Latvian People's Front Political Committee; in October 1989, elected Deputy Chairman. In March 1990, elected Latvian People's Deputy; Chairman of the Supreme Soviet Latvian People's Front Faction.
FAMILY: Married with two children.
ADDRESS/TELEPHONE: 36 Svoboda Boulevard, Riga, LVI520. 33–2232.

Godunov, Andrey Vladimirovich

POSITION: Board Chairman of the Fund for the Social and Economic Rehabilitation of Invalids; Director-General of Petrovod International Joint-Venture, Ltd.
BIRTHPLACE/DATE: Sevastopol, 1952
NATIONALITY: Russian
EDUCATION: From 1984 to 1986, student at the Navy Academy.
CAREER: From 1974 to 1984, served on the North Navy Fleet Nuclear Submarines. From 1986 to 1991, Senior Researcher at the International Relations Research Institute of the USSR Defense Ministry. From 1990 to 1991, Co-Chairman of the Democratic Platform of the Leningrad Communist Party. In November 1991, discharged from the Armed Forces with the rank of Captain. From 1991, member of the Russian Federation Republican Party Collegium. Board Member of the International Movement for Democratic Reforms. From November 1991, Director-General of Pushkinskaya–10 Joint-Stock Company. From 1991, Deputy Director-General of J-J-Soviet Soviet-Australian Joint-Venture.
FAMILY: Married with two children.
TELEPHONE: 259–9652; 259–9643 (office).

Goldansky, Vitaly Iosifovich

POSITION: Academician of the Russian Academy of Sciences; Director of the Institute of Chemical Physics
BIRTHPLACE/DATE: Vitebsk, July 18, 1923
CAREER: From 1942 to 1952, worked at the Institute of Chemical Physics. From 1952 to 1961, worked at the Physics Institute of the USSR Academy of Sciences. From 1951, Lecturer at the Moscow Engineering Physics Institute; from 1961, Professor. From 1961, worked at the Chemical Physics Institute; from 1987, Director. Academician of the USSR Academy of Sciences. From 1992, Academician of the Russian Academy of Sciences. To 1991, member of the Communist Party.
MAJOR WORKS: In the field of nuclear and radiation chemistry: experimentally proved for the first time proton electrical polarization; provided theoretical grounding for the existence of bi-proton radiation of an atomic nucleus.
HONORS/AWARDS: Prize of Lenin; Order of the Red Banner of Labor; Mendeleyev Medal; Karpinsky Prize (East Germany).
FAMILY: Married with two children.
ADDRESS/TELEPHONE: 4 Kosygin Street, Moscow, B–334, GSP–1, 117977. 137–3232.

Golembiovsky, Igor Nestorovich

POSITION: Editor in Chief of *Izvestia* (*News*) daily
BIRTHPLACE/DATE: Samtredia, Georgia, September 7, 1935
NATIONALITY: Russian
EDUCATION: Graduated from the Philology Department at Tbilisi State University. Good command of Spanish.
CAREER: From 1966, Editorial Assistant, Special Correspondent, First Deputy Managing Editor, Mexican Correspondent, Acting Managing Editor, Managing Editor of *Izvestia*. From 1988, Deputy Editor in Chief.
FAMILY: Married with a son.
ADDRESS/TELEPHONE: 5 Pushkin Square, Moscow, 103791. 209–9100 (office).

Golenkolsky, Tankred Grigoryevich

POSITION: Editor in Chief of *Yevreyskaya Gazeta* (*Jewish Newspaper*)
BIRTHPLACE/DATE: Kharbin, China, 1931

EDUCATION: Degree in Philology.
CAREER: To 1960, Language and Literature Lecturer at a number of institutes. From 1960 to 1971, Department Head at Novosibirsk State University. From 1971 to 1974, Laboratory Head, Department Head at the Far East Scientific Center of the USSR Academy of Sciences. From 1974 to 1980, Freelancer at Radio-Moscow. From 1980 to 1988, Director of International Exhibitions and Fairs, Consultant to the USSR State Publishing House. From 1988 to 1990, Director-General of a Soviet-American enterprise.
MAJOR WORKS: Seven books on American literature and culture. Translated ten American novels into Russian.
FAMILY: Divorced with two children.
TELEPHONE: 125–6784 (office).

Golovin, Yuri Victorovich
POSITION: Board Chairman of Petrovsky Commercial Bank
BIRTHPLACE/DATE: Sevastopol, 1961
EDUCATION: Graduated in 1983 from the Leningrad Institute of Finance and Economics (now St. Petersburg University of Finance and Economics). Speaks English.
CAREER: From 1983 to 1985, served in the army. From 1985 to 1987, Senior Economist of Stroibank (Construction Bank). From 1987 to 1990, Chief Accountant of Spetsstroi (Special Construction) Trust.
FAMILY: Married with two children.
ADDRESS/TELEPHONE: 14 Kalyayev Street, St. Petersburg, 191028. 275–7622 (office).

Gonchar, Nikolay Nikolayevich
POSITION: Chairman of the Moscow City Council of People's Deputies
BIRTHPLACE/DATE: Murmansk, 1946
EDUCATION: Doctor of Economics.
CAREER: From 1972 to 1973, Engineer of the Moscow Power Engineering Institute. From 1973 to 1975, Department Head of the Moscow City Council for Scientific Research. From 1976 to 1982, Department Head at the Research Institute for the Complex Development of National Economy. From 1982 to 1987, Deputy Chairman, First Deputy Chairman of the Bauman District Council of People's Deputies Executive Committee. From 1987 to 1990, Secretary of the Bauman Region Communist Party. From 1989, Chairman of the Bauman District Council of People's Deputies Executive Committee; from 1990, Chairman. In June 1991, elected Chairman of the Moscow City Council of People's Deputies. Engaged in scientific research on the management of municipal structures. From 1972 to 1991, member of the Communist Party.
HONORS/AWARDS: Medal For Labor Valor; Medal For Labor Distinction.
FAMILY: Married with a daughter.
ADDRESS/TELEPHONE: 13 Tverskaya Street, Moscow, 103032. 229–5570 (office).

Goncharov, Andrey Aleksandrovich
POSITION: Art Director of the Mayakovsky Theater in Moscow; Art Council Chairman of the Russian Federation Ministry of Culture
BIRTHPLACE/DATE: Moscow, 1918
CAREER: From 1942 to 1943, Director of the First Front Theater (for soldiers during the war). From 1944 to 1951, Producer of the Moscow Satire Theater. From 1951 to 1966, Producer of the Yermolova Theater in Moscow. From 1958 to 1966, Chief Producer of the Spartakovsky Drama Theater. From 1967, Chief Producer of the Mayakovsky Theater. From 1951, Lecturer at the State Institute of Dramatic Art. From 1981, Production Department Head. Secretary of the USSR (now Russian) Union of Theater Workers.
MAJOR WORKS: Theatrical productions at the Satire Theater: *Belugin's Marriage* after Ostrovsky; *Rivals* after Shchedrin. At the Yermolova Theater: *European Chronicle* after Arbuzov. At the Spartakovsky Drama Theater: *View from the Bridge* by Miller; *Zimovka Law* by Gorbatov. At the Mayakovsky Theater: *Lady Macbeth from Mtsensky District* by Leskov; *Bankrupt* by Ostrovsky; *Vanyushin Children* by Naidenov; *Sunset* by Babel. Books, articles, and theatrical essays.
HONORS/AWARDS: Hero of Socialist Labor; Russian Federation State Prize; Order of the Patriotic War; Order of the Red Star; Order of the Red Banner of Labor.
FAMILY: Married with a child.
ADDRESS: 19 Herzen Street, Moscow, 103009 (office).

Gorbachev, Mikhail Sergeyevich

POSITION: President of the International Foundation for Socio-Economic and Political Studies (The Gorbachev Foundation)

BIRTHPLACE/DATE: Privolnoye village, Stavropol region, March 2, 1931

EDUCATION: Graduated from Moscow State University's Department of Law.

CAREER: After graduation, became a Lawyer in Stavropol. In March 1962, elected Party Leader of the Stavropol Industrial Collective and State Farm Administration. From December 1962, Head of the Stavropol Region Communist Party. From August 1968, Second Secretary; from April 1970, First Secretary; from 1978, Secretary of the Central Committee. From 1979, Alternate Member of the Politburo; from October 1980, Full Member. From March 1985, General Secretary of the Central Committee; on July 10, 1990, re-elected General Secretary; held this position to August 1991. From October 1988, Presidium Chairman of the USSR Supreme Soviet. In March 1990, elected USSR President; resigned on December 25, 1991. Former USSR Supreme Soviet Deputy, Russian Federation Supreme Soviet Deputy. From 1952 to 1991, member of the Communist Party.

HONORS/AWARDS: Albert Schweitzer Prize; Honored Doctor of Philosophy of Bar-Ilan University (June 1992).

FAMILY: Married with a daughter and two granddaughters.

ADDRESS/TELEPHONE: The Gorbachev Foundation, Leningradsky Prospekt 49, Moscow, 125468. 943–9879/29 (office); Fax: 943–9426.

Gorbunov, Anatoli Valeryanovich

POSITION: Chairman of the Latvian Supreme Soviet; Head of the Latvian Government Security Council

BIRTHPLACE/DATE: Ludzensky district, Latvia, 1942

NATIONALITY: Lett

CAREER: From 1959, Foreman-Builder at the Nikratse State Farm in Latvia; Senior Technician at the Latgidrokhimstroi (Latvian Chemical Construction Administration) Institute; Chief Mechanic, Komsomol Committee Secretary at the Riga Polytechnical Institute. First Secretary of the Kirov Region Komsomol Committee. From 1974, Head of the Industrial Transport Department; First Secretary of the Kirov Region Communist Party; Secretary of the Riga City Communist Party. From 1984, Head of the Administration Department of the Latvian Central Committee. From 1985, Secretary of the Latvian Central Committee. From 1989, Chairman of the Latvian Supreme Soviet. In September 1990, quit the Latvian Communist Party.

FAMILY: Married with a son.

ADDRESS/TELEPHONE: 11 Yakaba Street, Riga, 226811. 32–2938.

Gordeyev, Vyacheslav Mikhailovich

POSITION: Art Director of the Moscow Russian Ballet State Theater

BIRTHPLACE/DATE: Moscow, 1948

CAREER: Began career at the Bolshoi Theater in 1968; in 1970, became a leading dancer of the Bolshoi; in 1984, Head of the Classical Ballet Group; in 1988, the group became known as the Russian Ballet Theater.

MAJOR WORKS: Staged approximately thirty choreographic compositions, three ballet performances, including *Memory* (B. Petrov); *Unexpected Maneuvers or Wedding to a General* (Rossini); *Lively Pictures* (Mozart, Handel, Bach).

HONORS/AWARDS: Artists of the Russian Ballet Theater became Honored Citizens of Atlanta and New Orleans (United States, 1987); two Gold Medals (1988).

FAMILY: Married.

TELEPHONE: 229–1336 (home).

Gorelik, Aleksandr Semyonovich

POSITION: Director of the Foreign Ministry's Department of International Organizations; Counsellor, First Grade

BIRTHPLACE/DATE: Moscow, September 24, 1952

NATIONALITY: Russian

EDUCATION: Graduated from the Moscow State Institute of International Relations in 1974.

CAREER: From 1974 to 1975, Aide at the USSR Embassy in Guinea; from 1975 to 1977, Interpreter; from 1977, Attaché. From 1977 to 1980, Attaché of the Second African Department of the Foreign Ministry. From 1980 to 1983, Third Secretary; from 1983 to 1986, Second Secretary at the

USSR Embassy in Guinea. From 1986 to 1988, First Secretary; from 1988, First Secretary, Acting Department Head of the First African Department. From 1988 to 1990, First Secretary of the African Countries Department of the USSR Foreign Ministry. From 1990, Counsellor. From 1990 to 1991, Head of the Department of International Organizations; from 1991 to 1992, Deputy Board Head; from 1992 to 1993, Deputy Head.
FAMILY: Married with a daughter.
TELEPHONE: 244–4211 (office).

Gorlov, Aleksandr Georgyevich
POSITION: Editor in Chief of the United Editorial Board of *Militsia* magazine and *Shchit i Mech* (*Shield and Sword*) newspaper
BIRTHPLACE/DATE: Stavropol region, 1940
EDUCATION: Graduated in 1967 from the Journalism Department at Rostov State University. Doctor of History. Speaks German.
CAREER: From 1960 to 1987, Correspondent for *Kavkazskaya Zdravnitsa* (*Caucasus Sanitorium*) newspaper, served in the interior troops, worked for a number of army newspapers and journals, including *Na Boyevom Postu* (*On Guard*) magazine, Head of the Interior Troops Press Department. From 1987 to 1992, Editor in Chief of *Na Boyevom Postu*. Member of the Confederation of Journalists' Unions.
MAJOR WORKS: Author of over ten books, including *The White Favorites*; *Fiery, Fiery Horse*.
FAMILY: Married with two children.
ADDRESS/TELEPHONE: 24 Ivanovskaya Street, Moscow, 127434. 211–0854; 211–1853 (office).

Gorodinsky, Mikhail Lvovich
POSITION: Director-General of Soyuzpatent (Patent Experts Organization); Vice President of the Moscow Trade and Industry Department; President of the Russian IPP (International Organization for the Protection of Industrial Property) Group
BIRTHPLACE/DATE: Khmelnitsky, 1927
NATIONALITY: Russian
EDUCATION: Doctor of Law (1979).
CAREER: From 1950 to 1963, worked at the USSR Foreign Trade Ministry. In 1963, Founder of Soyuzpatent. Expert of the Russian Federation Supreme Soviet Committee for Science.
HONORS/AWARDS: Honored Lawyer of Russia.
FAMILY: Married with a child.
ADDRESS/TELEPHONE: 5/2 Ilyinka, Moscow, 103735. 925–1661 (office).

Gorokhova, Galina Yevgenyevna
POSITION: Chairman of the Russian Union of Athletes
BIRTHPLACE/DATE: Moscow, 1938
NATIONALITY: Russian
CAREER: Fencing Champion of the Summer Olympics in 1960, 1968, and 1972. Sports Instructor of the Dynamo Sports Club in Moscow. Coach, Leading Fencing Coach of the USSR State Committee for Sports. Chief Expert of the Summer Sports Main Administration of the USSR State Committee for Sports. Chairman of the USSR Union of Athletes. From 1991, State Fencing Coach. World Champion nine times; USSR Champion six times.
HONORS/AWARDS: Order of the Red Banner of Labor; Medal For Labor Valor; two Medals For Labor Distinction; USSR Honored Master of Sports.
FAMILY: Single with a daughter.
ADDRESS/TELEPHONE: 8 Luzhnetskaya Naberezhnaya, Moscow. 201–1329; 201–1911 (office).

Gorshkov, Aleksandr Georgyevich
POSITION: Head of the CIS National Figure Skating Team; Deputy Chairman of the Figure Skating Federation
BIRTHPLACE/DATE: Moscow, 1946
NATIONALITY: Russian
CAREER: From 1967 to 1976, member of the USSR National Figure Skating Team. In 1976, Olympic Champion; World Champion, 1970 to 1974; European Champion, 1970, 1971, 1973 to 1976. From 1977, worked at the USSR State Committee for Sports. From 1984, member of the Committee of Ice Dancing Technique.
HONORS/AWARDS: USSR Honored Master of Sports.
FAMILY: Married with a daughter.
ADDRESS/TELEPHONE: 60 Novocheremushinskaya Street, #342, Moscow.

Goryacheva, Svetlana Petrovna

POSITION: Deputy General Prosecutor of Vladivostok; member of the Russian Federation Supreme Soviet Committee for Ecology and the Rational Consuming of Natural Resources
BIRTHPLACE/DATE: Risovy village, Primorsky region, June 3, 1946
CAREER: From 1974, Consultant to the Justice Department of the Primorsky Region Executive Committee in Vladivostok. From 1976 to 1986, Prosecutor of the General Control Department of the Primorsky Region Prosecutor's Office. From 1986 to 1990, Prosecutor of the Vladivostok Nature Protection Prosecutor's Office. From 1990 to 1991, Russian Federation Supreme Soviet Deputy Chairman in Moscow. From 1992, Vladivostok Deputy General Prosecutor. Russian Federation People's Deputy. Member of the Rossiya Faction. Member of the Communist Party to 1991.
FAMILY: Married with a son.
ADDRESS/TELEPHONE: Prosecutor's Office, Vladivostok. 22–7252 (office).

Govorukhin, Stanislav Sergeyevich

POSITION: Film Producer; Publicist
BIRTHPLACE/DATE: Bereznyaki village, Perm region, 1936
CAREER: From 1959 to 1961, worked for Kazan TV Studio. From 1966 to 1986, Producer for Odessa Film Studio. From 1987, Producer for Mosfilm Studio. Member of the USSR Union of Film Makers. From 1991, member of the Confederation of Film Makers' Unions.
MAJOR WORKS: Producer of: *Vertical*; *Angel's Day*; *Meeting Place Should Not Be Changed*; *Adventures of Tom Sawyer*. Scriptwriter of: *Pirates of the 20th Century*. Appeared in *Assa*; *Among Grey Stones*; *Sons of a Bitch*. Creator of documentary films: *It Is Impossible to Leave Like That*; *Invasion*; *Russian*.
FAMILY: Married with a son.
TELEPHONE: 134–6815 (home).

Grachev, Andrey Serafimovich

POSITION: Politician; Publicist; International Department Correspondent for *Moscow News*
BIRTHPLACE/DATE: Moscow, 1941
NATIONALITY: Russian
EDUCATION: Graduated from the Moscow State Institute of International Relations in 1964. Doctor of History.
CAREER: From 1964 to 1972, Soviet Representative of the Democratic Youth International Federation. From 1973 to 1977, worked at the International Department of the Central Committee. From 1977 to 1985, worked at the International Information Department of the Central Committee. From 1966 to 1991, Sector Head, Deputy Head of the Ideological and International Department of the Central Committee. From September 1991 to December 1991, USSR President's Aide, Head of the USSR President's Press Service.
FAMILY: Married with a son.
ADDRESS/TELEPHONE: 16/2 Tverskaya Street, Moscow, 103829. 921–9112 (home).

Grachev, Pavel Sergeyevich

POSITION: Russian Federation Minister of Defense; General of the Army
BIRTHPLACE/DATE: Rvy village, Lenin district, Tula region, January 1, 1948
NATIONALITY: Russian
EDUCATION: Graduated in 1969 from the Ryazan Higher Airborne Paratroopers School. Graduated in 1981 from the Mikhail Frunze Military Academy. Graduated in 1990 from the General Staff Military Academy.
CAREER HISTORY: From 1965, served in the Armed Forces. From 1981 to 1982, Deputy Commander; from 1982 to 1983, USSR Paratroops Regiment Commander in Afghanistan. From 1983 to 1985, Deputy Commander of the Airborne Paratroops Division in USSR territory. From 1985 to 1988, USSR Airborne Paratroops Division Commander in Afghanistan. From 1990, First Deputy Commander in Chief; from September 1991, Commander in Chief of the Airborne Forces. From August to December 1991, Chairman of the Russian Federation State Committee for Defense and Security, USSR First Deputy Defense Minister. From December 1991, First Deputy Commander in Chief of the CIS United Armed Forces, Chairman of the Russian Federation State Committee for Defense Issues. From April 3, 1992, Russian Federation First Deputy Defense Minister. From May 7, 1992, Russian Federation Acting Defense Minister. On May 7, 1992, conferred the rank of General of the Army.

HONORS/AWARDS: Hero of the Soviet Union; Order of Lenin; Order of the Red Banner of Labor; Order of the Red Star; Order for Service to the Fatherland in the Armed Forces; Afghani Order of the Red Banner.
FAMILY: Married with two sons.
ADDRESS/TELEPHONE: 37 Myasnitskaya Street, Moscow. 293–2869; 293–1413; 293–8969 (office).

Granberg, Aleksandr Grigoryevich
POSITION: Counsellor to the Russian Federation President on CIS Economic and Social Issues; Chairman of the Committee for Inter-Republican Relations, Regional Policies, and Cooperation Issues; Chairman of the Russian National Committee for Pacific Economic Cooperation
BIRTHPLACE/DATE: Moscow, 1936
CAREER: From 1960, Accountant of the USSR State Planning Committee. In 1984, elected Corresponding Member of the USSR Academy of Sciences. From 1989, Academician, Director of the Institute of Economics and Industrial Production Organization of the Siberian branch of the USSR Academy of Sciences. From 1991, Chairman of the Russian Federation Supreme Soviet Committee for Inter-Republican Relations, Regional Policies, and Cooperation Issues.
FAMILY: Married.
ADDRESS/TELEPHONE: 7 Vavilov Street, Moscow, 117822. 135–4529 (office); 224–0624 (aide).

Granik, Irina Vadimovna
POSITION: Parliament Correspondent for Pal Inform Business News Agency
BIRTHPLACE/DATE: Moscow, 1961
CAREER: From 1983 to 1990, Programmer. From 1990 to 1991, Journalist for the Postfactum Agency and *Economic Bulletin*. Journalist for *Moscow News* and *Rossiya* (*Russia*) newspapers.
FAMILY: Single.
ADDRESS/TELEPHONE: 35 Leningrad Chaussée, #24, Moscow, 125212. 281–5430 (home).

Granin, Daniil Aleksandrovich
POSITION: Writer; Publicist
BIRTHPLACE/DATE: Volyn, Kursk region, 1919
NATIONWIDE: Ukrainian
CAREER: Fought in World War II. Chief Engineer of the Kirov Plant in Leningrad. From 1949 to 1950, worked at a research institute. Published first works in 1949. From 1986 to 1991, Board Secretary of the USSR Writers' Union. Member of the President's Consultative Council. Member of the Higher Consultative Coordination Council of the Russian Federation Supreme Soviet Chairman. Corresponding Member of the Berlin Art Academy. Founder of the All-Union Charity Movement. From April 1992, member of the President's Consultative Council. Former USSR People's Deputy.
MAJOR WORKS: *I Go into the Storm*; *Klavdiya Vilor*; *Siege Boo*; *Dear Roman Avdeyevich*; several scripts.
HONORS/AWARDS: Heine Prize; Hero of Socialist Labor; USSR State Prize.
FAMILY: Married with a daughter and a grandson.
ADDRESS/TELEPHONE: 8 Malaya Posadskaya, #14, St. Petersburg. 232–8553 (home).

Grazhdankin, Nikolay Ivanovich
POSITIONS: Chairman of the Novgorod Region Council of People's Deputies
BIRTHPLACE/DATE: Kandaurovka village, Orenburg region, 1948
NATIONALITY: Russian
CAREER: From 1971 to 1977, Engineer. From 1977 to 1983, Chairman of the Starorussky Region Executive Committee. From 1983 to 1985, First Secretary of the Voloshin District Communist Party. From 1985 to 1990, First Secretary of the Mozhaisk District Communist Party, Novgorod region. From 1990 to 1991, Chairman of the Regional Executive Committee, Chairman of the District Council of People's Deputies.
FAMILY: Married with two children.
ADDRESS/TELEPHONE: Sofiyskaya Square, Dom Sovetov, Novgorod, 1743005. 7–5460.

Grebnev, Aleksandr Danilovich
POSITION: Board Chairman of the Moscow Innovation Joint-Stock Bank
BIRTHPLACE/DATE: Kirovsk, Murmansk region, 1944
CAREER: Design Bureau Engineer at a research institute. From 1982, Chief Engineer of the USSR Construction Bank. From 1988, Deputy Director

of the Moscow Experimental Center. Member of the Communist Party to 1985.
FAMILY: Married with two children.
ADDRESS/TELEPHONE: 2 Rybny Pereulok, Moscow, 103012. 298–3601 (office); Fax: 298–3648.

Grib, Victor Ivanovich
POSITION: Chairman of the Tekhnomashimport (Technical Equipment Inmport) Foreign Trade Complex
BIRTHPLACE/DATE: Lyublino, Moscow region, 1933
EDUCATION: From 1962 to 1965, student at the Foreign Trade Academy.
CAREER: From 1957 to 1962, Chief Engineer, Engineer-Designer at the Rubber Industry Research Institute of the USSR Ministry of Oil and Chemical Industry. From 1965 to 1974, Office Director of the Neftechimpromexport (Oil and Chemical Products Export) Chemical Industry Enterprise; from 1974 to 1979, Deputy Chairman. From 1979 to 1981, Counsellor in Ethiopia. From 1981 to 1985, Deputy Chairman; from 1986 to 1988, Chairman of Neftechimproexport.
FAMILY: Married with three sons.
ADDRESS/TELEPHONE: 19 Trubnikovsky Pereulok, Moscow, 121819. 248–8300 (office).

Grigorovich, Yuri Nikolayevich
POSITION: Art Director and Director of the State Academic Ballet at the Bolshoi Theater
BIRTHPLACE/DATE: Leningrad, 1927
CAREER: In 1946, Ballet Dancer of the Kirov Opera and Ballet Theater: danced in *Bakhchisaraysky Fountain*; *The Nutcracker*; and *Swan Lake*. In 1947, staged first ballet performances for children: *Little Stork* by Klebanov and *Seven Brothers* by Varlamov. In 1957, staged first ballet at the Kirov Theater. From 1963, Dancer, Producer, Chief Producer, President of the Dance Section of the International Dance Theater at the Bolshoi Theater. President of the Choreographers Association of the USSR Music Society. Permanent Chairman of the International Ballet Contests. In October 1990, organized a new ballet company, the Bolshoi Theater Grigorovich Studio.
MAJOR WORKS: *Stone Flower* by Prokofyev; *Legend about Love* by Melikov; *The Nutcracker* by Tchaikovsky; and *Spartak* by Khachaturyan.
HONORS/AWARDS: USSR Honored Artist; Prize of Lenin; State Prize; Hero of Socialist Labor.
FAMILY: Married.
ADDRESS/TELEPHONE: 8/2 Okhotny Ryad, Moscow. 292–0595 (home).

Grigoryanets, Sergey Ivanovich
POSITION: Chairman of the Glasnost Public Foundation; Editor in Chief of *Daily Glasnost* newspaper; Director-General of Sign K-CP Publishing House
BIRTHPLACE/DATE: Kiev, 1941
NATIONALITY: Russian
CAREER: Former Literary Critic of *Yunost* (*Youth*) magazine; worked for *Novy Mir* (*New World*) and Moscow Radio. In 1975, arrested and sentenced to Chistopol Jail for five years for circulating anti-Soviet literature. From 1981, participated in publishing *V*, an information bulletin; from 1982, Editor in Chief. In February 1983 arrested again and sentenced to seven years in jail and five years in exile; released in July 1987. Former Co-Chairman of the Movement for Freedom and Democracy. From 1988, Board Chairman of the Journalists' Independent Trade Union.
MAJOR WORKS: Social and political articles.
HONORS/AWARDS: Golden Pen Prize (International Publishing Association, Washington, D.C.)
FAMILY: Married with two children.
ADDRESS/TELEPHONE: 11 Povarskaya Street, Moscow, 121069. 474–4590; 202–8519 (office).

Grigoryev, Ivan Glebovich
POSITION: President of the Nizhny-Volzhskaya Mercantile and Raw Material Exchange Joint-Stock Company; Director-General of the ITEX Joint-Stock Company
BIRTHPLACE/DATE: Volgograd, 1957
NATIONALITY: Russian
CAREER: From 1980 to 1988, Journalist for *Molodoy Leninets* (*Young Lenin*) and *Vecherny Volgograd* (*Evening Volgograd*) newspapers. From 1988, Director-General of the Information Technology, Electronics and Computer Systems Joint-Stock Company. Board Member of the Russian Stock Exchange Union.
FAMILY: Married with a son.
ADDRESS/TELEPHONE: 65 Chuikov Street, Vol-

gograd, 400005. 34–7419; 34–7429; Fax: 34–7419.

Griko, Nikolay Petrovich

POSITION: Board Chairman of Neva-Credit-Bank
BIRTHPLACE/DATE: Leningrad, 1957
EDUCATION: Graduated in 1984 from the Leningrad Finance and Economics Institute (LFEI); from 1984 to 1987, postgraduate student at the Leningrad Finance and Economics Institute. Doctor of Economics.
CAREER: From 1987 to 1990, Lecturer of the Money Circulation and Credit Division at LFEI.
FAMILY: Married with a child.
ADDRESS/TELEPHONE: 21 Sadovaya Street, St. Petersburg, 191029. 310–3191 (office).

Grinevsky, Oleg Alekseyevich

POSITION: Ambassador to Sweden; Ambassador Extraordinary and Plenipotentiary
BIRTHPLACE/DATE: Moscow, June 3, 1930
NATIONALITY: Russian
EDUCATION: Graduated from the Moscow State Institute of International Relations in 1954; from 1954 to 1957, postgraduate student.
CAREER: From 1957 to 1958, Attaché of the International Organizations Department of the USSR Foreign Ministry; from 1958 to 1960, Third Secretary; from 1960 to 1964; Second Secretary; from 1964 to 1964, Counsellor; from 1965 to 1974, Deputy Head. From 1974 to 1978, Deputy Head of the Middle East Department. From 1978 to 1983, Department Head and Collegium Member. From 1983 to 1991, Head of the USSR Delegation of the USSR Foreign Ministry at the Stockholm Conference. From 1989 to 1991, USSR Delegation Head at the Vienna Conferences.
HONORS/AWARDS: Order of the Badge of Honor; Order of the People's Friendship;
Professor of South Hampton University.
FAMILY: Married with three children.
TELEPHONE: 618–5345 (Stockholm); 244–2863 (Moscow).

Grishenko, Boris Sergeevich

POSITION: Vice President and Political Analysis Department Director of the Interfax Agency
BIRTHPLACE/DATE: Chita, 1937
CAREER: From 1960 to 1967, worked at *Leningradskaya Pravda* (*Leningrad Truth*). From 1967 to 1970, Leningrad Correspondent for TASS (Telegraph Agency of the Soviet Union). From 1970 to 1991, Correspondent, Editorial Head, Political Correspondent, Deputy Editor in Chief of the USSR Service at the TASS Central Office. From 1991, Editor of *Presidentsky Vestnik* (*President's Bulletin*).
HONORS/AWARDS: USSR Journalists' Union Prize.
FAMILY: Married with a son.
ADDRESS/TELEPHONE: 2 Pervaya Tverskaya-Yamskaya Street, Moscow, 103006. 250–9203 (office).

Gritsenko, Nikolay Nikolayevich

POSITION: Economist; Rector of the Academy of Labor and Social Relations; Special Committee Member of the Russian Management Academy
BIRTHPLACE/DATE: Voronezh village, Sumy region, July 11, 1929
EDUCATION: Doctor of Economics; Professor.
CAREER: From 1949 to 1950, Foreman of the Zhdanov Metal Plant. From 1950 to 1952, served in the army. From 1952 to 1958, Foreman, then Komsomol leader at a plant in Chelyabinsk. From 1960 to 1986, Deputy Chairman, First Deputy Chairman of the All-Union Board of Scientific and Technical Societies. From 1986 to 1990, Rector of the Higher School of the Trade Union Movement. From 1989 to 1992, USSR People's Deputy. USSR Supreme Soviet Deputy. USSR Supreme Soviet Presidium Member. Former member of the Communist Party.
FAMILY: Married with two children.
ADDRESS/TELEPHONE: 90 Lobachevsky Street, Moscow, 117454. 432–3378 (office).

Gromov, Boris Vsevolodovich

POSITION: Deputy Defense Minister of the Russian Federation; Colonel-General
BIRTHPLACE/DATE: Saratov, November 7, 1943
NATIONALITY: Russian
EDUCATION: Graduated in 1962 from the Kalinin (now Tver) Suvorov Military School; in 1965, from the Sergey Kirov Combined Command Higher Military School in Leningrad; in 1972, from the Mikhail Frunze Military Academy; in

1984, with gold medal from the Voroshilov Military Academy of the General Staff.
CAREER: From 1962, served in the Baltic Military District Army. From 1967 to 1969, Platoon Leader. From 1972 to 1974, Battalion Commander. From 1974 to 1975, Regiment Chief of Staff; from 1975 to 1978, Regiment Commander; in 1975, Major; in 1977, Lieutenant-Colonel. From 1978 to 1980, Division Chief of Staff of the North-Caucasian Military District. Joined the Communist Party in 1966. From January 1980 to July 1983, Chief of Staff and Army Unit Commander of the Limited Contingent of USSR Troops in Afghanistan (Fortieth Army). In 1982, Major-General. After service in the Carpathian Military District, returned to Afghanistan as Commander of the Fortieth Army (Lieutenant-General), which withdrew in 1989. In 1989, Kiev Military District Commander; Colonel-General. Former USSR People's Deputy. Member of the USSR Supreme Soviet Committee for the Affairs of Soldiers-Internationalists (Afghan Veterans). From December 1990 to September 1991, First Deputy Minister of Internal Affairs of the USSR. During the 1991 Russian Federation Presidential Elections, ran for Vice President with Presidential candidate Nikolay Ryzhkov. From early 1992 to June 1992, First Deputy Commander of the General Purpose Armed Forces. On June 24, 1992, appointed Russian Federation Deputy Defense Minister.
HONORS/AWARDS: Order For Service in the USSR Armed Forces, Third Class; Order of the Red Star; two Orders of the Red Banner; Order of Lenin; Gold Star of the Hero of the USSR; medals.
FAMILY: Married with two sons.
ADDRESS/TELEPHONE: 12 Frunze Street, Moscow. 293–2869; 296–8900 (office).

Gromov, Feliks Nikolayevich

POSITION: Chief Commander of the Russian Federation Navy Fleet; Admiral
BIRTHPLACE/DATE: Vladivostok, 1937
NATIONALITY: Russian
CAREER: From 1960 to 1979, worked from Group Commander to Cruiser Commander. From 1979 to 1982, Staff Division Chief of the Leningrad Military Submarine Base. From 1982 to 1988, Strategic Squadron Commander of the Pacific Navy Fleet. From 1984 to 1988, First Deputy Commander of the Northern Navy Fleet; from 1988 to 1992, Commander. From February to August 1992, First Deputy Commander of the Russian Federation Navy Fleet.
HONORS/AWARDS: Order of the October Revolution; Order For Service in the USSR Armed Forces; ten medals.
FAMILY: Married with a son and a daughter.
ADDRESS/TELEPHONE: 6 Kozlovsky Pereulok, Moscow, 103175. 204–2016 (Navy); 204–2276 (office).

Gromov, Vasily Petrovich

POSITION: Ambassador to Chile; Ambassador Extraordinary and Plenipotentiary
BIRTHPLACE/DATE: Navesnoye village, Orlov region, October 1, 1936
NATIONALITY: Russian
EDUCATION: Graduated from the Moscow Agricultural Academy in 1960. From 1968 to 1971, postgraduate student at the Foreign Trade Academy.
CAREER: From 1960 to 1961, Department Head of the Vnukovsky State Farm, Moscow region. From 1961 to 1964, Senior Accountant of the Committee of the National Institute of Agricultural Reform and State Planning in Cuba. From 1965 to 1968, Senior Accountant of the Economic Counsellor's Office at the USSR Embassy in Cuba. From 1971 to 1973, Second Secretary at the USSR Embassy in Chile. From 1973 to 1974, Second Secretary of the Latin America Department. From 1974 to 1978, First Secretary at the USSR Embassy in Mexico. From 1978 to 1991, Counsellor; from 1981, Expert of the First Latin America Department. From 1981, Expert of the Personnel Department of the USSR Foreign Ministry. From 1981 to 1984, Sector Head of the First Latin America Department. From 1984 to 1987, Minister-Counsellor at the USSR Embassy in Ecuador. From 1987 to 1990, Minister-Counsellor at the USSR Embassy in Nicaragua. From 1990 to 1991, Deputy Head of the Latin America Board. From 1991 to 1992, First Deputy Head; from 1992, Board Head of the Central and South America Department.
FAMILY: Married with two children.
TELEPHONE: 244–3295.

Gromyko, Anatoli Andreyevich

POSITION: Corresponding Member of the Russian Academy of Sciences

BIRTHPLACE/DATE: Moscow, April 15, 1932

NATIONALITY: Russian

CAREER: From 1961 to 1965, First Secretary at the USSR Embassy in London. From 1966 to 1968, Sector Head of the Institute of Africa of the USSR Academy of Sciences. From 1968 to 1973, Sector Head of the Institute of the U.S. and Canada. From 1973 to 1974, Ambassador at Large in Washington. From 1974 to 1976, Ambassador at Large at the USSR Embassy in Berlin. From 1976, Director of the Institute of Africa of the Russian Academy of Sciences.

MAJOR WORKS: Publications in the field of social, economic, political, and international problems in African countries, and on U.S. foreign and domestic policies.

HONORS/AWARDS: USSR State Prize.

FAMILY: Married with three children.

ADDRESS/TELEPHONE: 30/1 Aleksey Tolstoy Street, Moscow, 103001. 203–4960 (home).

Grushin, Boris Andreyevich

POSITION: President of Vox Populi Poll Service

BIRTHPLACE/DATE: Moscow, 1929

NATIONALITY: Russian

EDUCATION: From 1952 to 1955, postgraduate student at Moscow State University. Doctor of Philosophy; Professor.

CAREER: From 1956 to 1962, employee, then Editor of *Komsomolskaya Pravda* (*Komsomol Truth*) daily. From 1960 to 1967, organized the Poll Institute of *Komsomolskaya Pravda*. From 1962 to 1965, Department Editor of *Problemy Mira i Socializma* (*Problems of Peace and Socialism*) magazine. From 1966 to 1967, Sector Head at the Institute of Philosophy of the USSR Academy of Sciences. From 1967 to 1974, Project Head at the Institute of Social Research (now the Institute of Sociology). In 1974, fired from the Institute. From 1974 to 1987, worked at the Central Economics and Mathematics Institute, *Problemy Mira i Socializma*, then Sector Head at the Institute of Philosophy. From 1987 to 1989, Deputy Director of the All-Union Poll Center. From 1990, Director-General of the Poll Service. Corresponding Member of the National Academy of Education.

FAMILY: Married with three children.

ADDRESS/TELEPHONE: 76 Vernadsky Prospekt, Moscow, 117454. 433–7066 (office).

Gubenko, Nikolay Nikolayevich

POSITION: Committee Chairman of the Russian Center of Artists; President of the International Culture Association

BIRTHPLACE/DATE: Odessa, August 17, 1941

NATIONALITY: Ukrainian

CAREER: From 1964, Actor of the Taganka Drama and Comedy Theater; Producer for Mosfilm Studio. From 1987 to 1989, Chief Producer for the Moscow Drama and Comedy Theater. From 1989 to December 1991, USSR Minister of Culture. To August 1991, member of the Communist Party.

MAJOR WORKS: Theater roles: *I Am Twenty*; *The Last Crook*; *First Messenger*; *Boris Godunov*. Movie roles: *Director*; *I Want to Speak*; *They Fought for the Motherland*. Produced films: *Podranki*; *And Life, and Tears, and Love . . .*; *Forbidden Zone*.

HONORS/AWARDS: Russian State Prize; Komsomol Prize; Russian Federation People's Artist.

ADDRESS/TELEPHONE: 35 Arbat, Moscow, 121835. 248–2591 (office).

Gubin, Dmitri Markovich

POSITION: Coordinator of the Kharkov Region New United Ukraine Organization; Deputy Chairman of the Kharkov Region Democratic Revival of Ukraine Movement

BIRTHPLACE/DATE: Kharkov, 1966

NATIONALITY: Ukrainian

CAREER: From 1982 to 1986, active member of literary groups. In 1988, involved in the Chance Group in Kharkov. From 1989, Deputy Chairman of the Anti-Fascist Center. From 1989 to 1990, member of the Constitutional Democrats Union. From October 1990, Representative Council Member of the Demokraticheskaya Rossiya (Democratic Russia) Movement; from July 1991, Deputy Chairman of the Representative Council. From February 1992, Coordinating Council Member of the Moscow Demokraticheskaya Rossiya. Co-Author of the alternative Russian Federation Con-

stitution. Member of the Constitutional Democrats, member of the Democratic Revival of Ukraine Movement.
FAMILY: Single.
ADDRESS/TELEPHONE: 27 Lenin Prospekt, Kharkov, Ukraine, 310086. 32–0634 (home).

Gudev, Vladimir Victorovich
POSITION: Ambassador to Iran; Ambassador Extraordinary and Plenipotentiary
BIRTHPLACE/DATE: Moscow, September 17, 1940
NATIONALITY: Russian
EDUCATION: From 1960 to 1961, student at Cairo University in Egypt; from 1961 to 1963, student at the Moscow State Institute of International Relations; graduated from the Moscow State Institute of International Relations. From 1973 to 1975, postgraduate student at the Diplomatic Academy of the USSR Foreign Ministry.
CAREER: From 1963 to 1965, Translator at the USSR Embassy in Egypt; from 1965 to 1967, Attaché. From 1967 to 1968, Attaché of the Middle East Department. From 1968 to 1970, Third Secretary at the USSR Embassy in Syria; from 1970 to 1973, Second Secretary. From 1975, First Secretary of the Middle East Department. From 1975 to 1979, First Secretary at the USSR Embassy in Iraq. From 1979 to 1982, Counsellor of the Middle East Department. From 1982 to 1984, Sector Head; from 1984 to 1986, Deputy Head; from 1986 to 1987, Head of the Middle East and Northern Africa Department.
FAMILY: Married with a daughter.
TELEPHONE: 244–4416.

Gudushkin, Stanislav Markovich
POSITION: Deputy Minister of Justice; State Advisor of Justice, Second class
BIRTHPLACE/DATE: Moscow, 1939
EDUCATION: From 1956 to 1959, student at the Moscow Institute of Electronic Technology. From 1962 to 1964, student at Moscow State University. Doctor of Law.
CAREER: To 1959, Laboratory Assistant at the Moscow Institute of Chemistry and Technology. From 1964 to 1973, Detective, then Senior Detective of the Zhdanov District Public Prosecutor's Office in Moscow. From 1973 to 1974, Kirov District Deputy Prosecutor, Consultant to the Department of Legislature of the Russian Federation Ministry of Justice. From 1974 to 1979, Russian Federation Deputy Minister of Justice. From 1979 to 1992, Head of the Department of the Constitution of the Russian Federation Ministry of Justice. From February 1992, Russian Federation Deputy Minister of Justice.
MAJOR WORKS: Articles on justice and legislature.
FAMILY: Married with a daughter.
ADDRESS/TELEPHONE: 10-A Yermolova Street, K–51, GSP, Moscow, 101434. 209–6057.

Gulyayev, Nikolay Alekseyevich
POSITION: Speed Skater
BIRTHPLACE/DATE: Vologda, 1966
NATIONALITY: Russian
CAREER: In 1987, European and World Champion. In 1988, Olympic Champion (1000-meters). From 1989, Officer of the USSR Army Athletics Team. Currently works in Holland.
HONORS/AWARDS: USSR Honored Master of Sports; Medal For Labor Valor.
FAMILY: Married with a child.
ADDRESS/TELEPHONE: 2 Vtoroy Polevoy Pereulok, #146, Moscow. 201–0322 (office); 268–5634 (home).

Gumenyuk, Gennadi Vladimirovich
POSITION: Ambassador to Chad; Counsellor Extraordinary and Plenipotentiary, Second Grade
BIRTHPLACE/DATE: Moscow, December 23, 1939
NATIONALITY: Russian
EDUCATION: Graduated from the Moscow State Institute of International Relations in 1967. From 1978 to 1980, postgraduate student at the Diplomatic Academy of the USSR Foreign Ministry.
CAREER: From 1957 to 1962, Assembler, Senior Technician in Moscow. From 1967 to 1968, Secretary of the Consulate Department at the USSR Embassy in Poland. From 1968 to 1970, Attaché. From 1970 to 1971, Third Secretary of the Fourth European Department; from 1971 to 1973, Second Secretary. From 1973 to 1975, Second Secretary at the USSR Embassy in Ethiopia; from 1975 to 1978, First Secretary. From 1980, Counsellor at the USSR Embassy in Mauritius. From 1981 to

1983, Counsellor of the Third African Department. From 1983 to 1987, Counsellor at the USSR Embassy in Rwanda. From 1987 to 1988, Sector Head of the Third African Department. From 1988 to 1991, Minister-Counsellor at the USSR Embassy in the Congo.
FAMILY: Married with a daughter.
TELEPHONE: 244–2211.

Gunayev, Benjamin Avtolumovich
POSITION: Director-General of the Bezopasnost (Security) Research and Industrial Center; President of the Prometey International Charity Association
BIRTHPLACE/DATE: Derbent, Tataria, 1934
EDUCATION: Doctor of Technology.
CAREER: From 1956 to 1979, USSR Army Officer. From 1979 to 1991, Department Head of the USSR Gosstroi (State Construction Administration). From 1991, Director-General of Bezopasnost. From 1992, President of Prometey.
FAMILY: Married with two children.
ADDRESS/TELEPHONE: 4 Volkov Pereulok, Moscow. 252–1963 (office).

Gurzinov, Vladimir Vladimirovich
POSITION: Chief Coach of the Moscow Dynamo Hockey Team; Coach of the Combined Hockey Team of the Commonwealth of Independent States
BIRTHPLACE/DATE: Moscow, 1940
NATIONALITY: Russian
CAREER: From 1963 to 1969, World and European Hockey Champion. Sports Instructor of the Moscow State Stadium. From 1974 to 1979, Chief Coach of the Moscow Dynamo. From 1979 to 1989, Chief Coach of the Riga Dynamo Hockey Team, Coach of the Combined Hockey Team. World Champion seven times, Olympic Champion three times. Currently employed in Turko, Finland.
HONOR/AWARDS: Order of the Red Banner; two Orders of the Badge of Honor; USSR Honored Master of Sports (hockey); USSR and Latvian Honored Coach.
FAMILY: Married with a son and a daughter.
ADDRESS/TELEPHONE: The Dynamo Club, 36 Leningradsky Prospekt, Moscow. 212–8111; 571–6537 (office).

Gusarov, Yevgeni Petrovich
POSITION: Ambassador to the Republic of South Africa; Ambassador Extraordinary and Plenipotentiary
BIRTHPLACE/DATE: Moscow, July 30, 1950
NATIONALITY: Russian
EDUCATION: Graduated from the Moscow State Institute of International Relations in 1972.
CAREER: From 1972, Aide to the Second European Department. From 1972 to 1975, Aide on Duty, Aide-Trainee at the USSR Consulate-General in Montreal; from 1975 to 1977, Senior Aide-Trainee; from 1977 to 1978, Attaché of the Second European Department; from 1978 to 1979, Second Secretary. From 1981 to 1983, Second Secretary at the USSR Embassy in Canada; from 1983 to 1985, First Secretary. From 1986, Sector Head of the Second European Department; from 1986 to 1988, Deputy Head. From 1988 to 1989, Deputy Head of the Department of the United States and Canada. From 1990 to 1991, Deputy Head of the European Security and Cooperation Department of the USSR Foreign Ministry; from 1991 to 1992, Head. From 1992, Head of the European Department.
FAMILY: Married with a son.
TELEPHONE: 244–2211.

Guseinov, Rafael Gzhagidovich
POSITION: Azerbaijan First Deputy Plenipotentiary Representative to Moscow
BIRTHPLACE/DATE: Baku, 1949
NATIONALITY: Azerbaijanian
CAREER: From 1974 to 1979, Editor of *Molodezh Azerbaijana* (*Azerbaijan Youth*) newspaper. From 1985 to 1989, Editorial Board Member of *Komsomolskaya Pravda* (*Komsomol Truth*) daily. From 1989 to 1991, Consultant to the International Department of the Central Committee. Azerbaijan Supreme Soviet Deputy. Former member of the Communist Party.
FAMILY: Married with two children.
ADDRESS/TELEPHONE: 16 Stanislavsky Street, Moscow. 229–1649; 202–4551 (office).

Gusenov, Georgy Georgyevich
POSITION: Chief Secretary of the Political Council of the All-Union Civic Accord Public Organiza-

tion; member of the Russian People's Front Executive Committee
BIRTHPLACE/DATE: Moscow, 1939
NATIONALITY: Russian
CAREER: From 1961 to 1989, worked for industrial enterprises. From 1990 to 1991, worked at Moscow district newspaper *Preobrazhenka*. From 1989 to 1990, Commercial Director of the Baikal Experimental Complex. In 1991, organized political and ecological programs of the Grazhdanin (Citizen) Association. In 1987, Organizer and elected Chairman of the People's Action Coordinating Committee; in 1988, this organization merged with the Moscow People's Front. On June 11, 1988, convicted for organizing meetings in Moscow. Co-Founder of the Democratic Platform of the Communist Party and the Democratic Communist Movement. Former member of the Communist Party.
HONORS/AWARDS: Veteran of Labor Medal.
FAMILY: Married with a son and a daughter.
ADDRESS/TELEPHONE: 26 Vtoraya Vladimirovskaya, Building 1, #45, Moscow, 111401. 306–2990 (home); 205–6911 (office).

Gusenkov, Vitaly Semyonovich
POSITION: Consultant of the Group of Advisors, Consultants, and Aides of the International Foundation for Socio-Economic and Political Studies (The Gorbachev Foundation)
BIRTHPLACE/DATE: Moscow, 1935
NATIONALITY: Russian
CAREER: To 1992, worked at the USSR Foreign Ministry in the Central Committee's International Department. USSR President's Aide.
FAMILY: Married with a son.

Gusev, Pavel Nikolayevich
POSITION: Editor in Chief of *Moskovsky Komsomolets* (*Moscow Komsomol Member*) newspaper; Moscow Government Counsellor for Mass-Media Issues
BIRTHPLACE/DATE: Moscow, April 4, 1949
EDUCATION: Graduated in 1971 from the Moscow Geological Prospecting Institute; in 1986, from the Gorky Literary Institute (by correspondence). In 1975, completed the postgraduate course at the Moscow Geological Prospecting Institute.
CAREER: Joined the Communist Party in 1970. From 1971 to 1975, Junior Research Fellow at the Moscow Geological Prospecting Institute. From 1975 to 1976, Second Secretary; and from 1976 to 1980, First Secretary of the Krasnopresnensky District Komsomol Committee. From 1980 to 1983, Executive Organizer of the International Department of the Komsomol Central Committee. From January to October 1992, Minister of the Moscow Government; Head of the Information and Propaganda Department. Mossoviet (Moscow Council) People's Deputy. Chairman of the Moscow Journalists' Union.
FAMILY: Divorced with two children.
ADDRESS/TELEPHONE: 7 Ulitsa 1905 Goda Street, Moscow. 292–1708 (office); 259–5036 (editorial office).

Gushin, Lev Nikitovich
POSITION: Editor in Chief of *Ogonyek* (*Beacon*) weekly
BIRTHPLACE/DATE: Moscow, 1944
CAREER: From 1967 to 1973, Chief Engineer at a research institute. From 1973 to 1983, First Secretary of the Kuntsevo District Komsomol Committee, Editor of *Moskovsky Komsomolets* (*Moscow Komsomol Member*) newspaper. From 1983, Editor of *Sovietskaya Rossiya* (*Soviet Russia*). From 1984, Deputy Editor in Chief of *Komsomolskaya Pravda* (*Komsomol Truth*). From 1987 to September 1991, First Deputy Editor in Chief of *Ogonyek*.
FAMILY: Married with three children.
ADDRESS/TELEPHONE: 14 Bumazhny Pereulok, Moscow, 1011456. 285–7964 (office).

Guvenaly, Pojarkov Vladimir Kirillovich
POSITION: Metropolitan of Krutitsi and Kolomna; member of the Holy Synod of the Russian Orthodox Church
BIRTHPLACE/DATE: Yaroslavl, 1935
NATIONALITY: Russian
EDUCATION: Doctor of Theology.
CAREER: From 1961 to 1962, member of the Department of Foreign Church Affairs of the Moscow Patriarchy. From 1962 to 1963, Editor of the magazine of the European Division of the Russian Orthodox Church. From 1963 to 1965, Head of the Russian Spiritual Mission in Jerusalem, Israel.

From 1965 to 1969, Bishop of Zaraisk, Deputy Chairman of the Department of Foreign Church Affairs of the Moscow Patriarchy. From 1972, Metropolitan, member of the Holy Synod. From 1977, Metropolitan of Krutitsi and Kolomna. To 1981, Chairman of the Department of Foreign Church Affairs of the Moscow Patriarchy. Deputy Board Chairman of the USSR-Cyprus Friendship Society.
HONORS/AWARDS: Order of the People's Friendship; Gold Medal for the Struggle for Peace.
ADDRESS/TELEPHONE: 113 Vernadsky Prospekt, Flat #246, Moscow; 1/Moscow Church Department, Novodevichy Prospekt, Moscow. 235–0454; 230–2118; 230–2431.

Gvishiani, Dzherman Mikhailovich
POSITION: Honored Rector of the Systems Analysis Institute of the Russian Academy of Sciences
BIRTHPLACE/DATE: Akaltsikhe, Georgia
NATIONALITY: Georgian
EDUCATION: Doctor of Philosophy; Professor; Academician.
CAREER: From 1951 to 1953, served in the navy. From 1953 to 1955, Lecturer-Consultant. From 1955 to 1957, Chairman of the State Committee for New Technology. From 1957 to 1962, Head of the International Relations Department of the State Committee for Research Coordination. From 1962 to 1976, Deputy Chairman of the State Committee for Science and Technology. From 1976, Director of the Systems Analysis Institute of the USSR (now Russian) Academy of Sciences. From 1979 to 1989, member of the International Energy Club. Professor at the Prague Foreign Economy School. Member of the Swedish Royal Academy of Engineering, the Finnish Academy of Technical Sciences, the American International Academy, and the Rome Club. Chairman of the International Cooperation Support Committee of the Russian Union of Industrialists and Entrepreneurs. President of the Perspective Research Fund.
MAJOR WORKS: More than 400 publications, including *Main Principles of Theory Management*; *Business Sociology*; *The Social Role of Science*.
FAMILY: Widower with two children.
ADDRESS/TELEPHONE: 9 60-Letiya Octyabrya Prospekt, Moscow, 117312. 135–7575 (office).

Ignatenko, Aleksandr Stepanovich

POSITION: Former Deputy Defense Minister of Ukraine; Personnel Head of the Ukrainian Defense Ministry; Major-General

BIRTHPLACE/DATE: Usak village, Sumskay region, 1945

NATIONALITY: Ukrainian

CAREER: Held leading positions in the Army; Military Expert for the Head of the East German Tank Formation. From 1990, Deputy Army Commander in Zabaikalsky Military District.

FAMILY: Married with three children.

ADDRESS/TELEPHONE: Ukraine Defense Ministry, Kiev–168. 293–0319; 293–2073 (press center).

Ignatenko, Vitaly Nikitovich

POSITION: Director-General of ITAR-TASS (Information Agency)

BIRTHPLACE/DATE: Sochi, 1941

CAREER: From 1963 to 1975, Trainee to the First Deputy Editor in Chief of *Komsomolskaya Pravda* (*Komsomol Truth*) daily. From 1975 to 1978, Deputy Director-General of TASS. From 1978 to 1986, Department Head of the Central Committee. From 1986 to 1990, Editor in Chief of *Novoye Vremya* (*New Time*) magazine. From 1990 to August 1991, Aide to the USSR President; Head of the Press Center. From August 1991 to January 1992, Director-General of TASS.

HONORS/AWARDS: Order of the People's Friendship; Prize of Lenin.

FAMILY: Married with a son.

ADDRESS: 10 Tverskoi Boulevard, Moscow, 103009.

Ignatyev, Kirill Borisovich

POSITION: Coordinating Committee Member of the Democraticheskaya Rossiya (Democratic Russia) Movement; Moscow Chairman of the Russian Deputy Corps Academy; Chairmen's Board Head of Ostankino TV and Radio Broadcasting Company

BIRTHPLACE/DATE: Moscow, 1966

NATIONALITY: Russian

CAREER: Inspector of the Russian Foreign Policy Archives. From 1989 to 1990, Engineer for Informelectro Research Institute. From January to October 1990, Aide to the Rector of the Russian Deputy Corps Academy. To May 1991, Editorial Commission Member of Democratic Russia. Moscow Member of the Democratic Russia Movement.

FAMILY: Single.

ADDRESS/TELEPHONE: 12 Academician Korolev Street, Moscow. 217–9410; 215–8368 (office); 271–3804 (home).

Iliya II (Shiolashvili, Irakly Georgyevich)

POSITION: Catholic Patriarch of All-Georgia

BIRTHPLACE/DATE: Vladikavkaz, December 4, 1933

NATIONALITY: Georgian

CAREER: From 1960 to 1963, Priest of Batumi Cathedral. From 1967 to 1969, Episcopate; Head of the Batumi Eparchy of the Georgian Orthodox Church. From 1969 to 1978, Metropolitan; Head of the Abkhaz Eparchy.

ADDRESS/TELEPHONE: 4 Sionskaya Street, Tbilisi. 72–5059.

Ilyichev, Gennadi Victorovich
POSITION: Ambassador to Lebanon; Ambassador Extraordinary and Plenipotentiary
BIRTHPLACE/DATE: Tverstianka village, Kalinin region, February 20, 1938
NATIONALITY: Russian
EDUCATION: Graduated from the Suvorov Military School in Kalinin in 1957 and from the Moscow State Institute of International Relations in 1963.
CAREER: From 1961 to 1962, Aide on Duty and Interpreter at the USSR Embassy in Iraq. From 1963 to 1966, Aide on Duty and Trainee at the USSR Embassy in Kuwait. From 1966 to 1968, Attaché of the Middle East Department. In 1968, Attaché at the USSR Embassy in Syria. From 1968 to 1970, Third Secretary at the USSR Embassy in Syria; from 1970 to 1972, Second Secretary. From 1972 to 1974, Second Secretary of the Middle East Department. From 1974 to 1978, First Secretary at the USSR Embassy in Yemen. From 1978 to 1980, Counsellor of the Middle East Department; from 1980 to 1982, Sector Head. From 1982 to 1988, Minister-Counsellor at the USSR Embassy in Yemen. From 1988 to 1989, Deputy Head of the Department of the Middle East and Northern Africa; from 1989 to 1990, Senior Counsellor.
FAMILY: Married with two children.
TELEPHONE: 244–3250.

Ilyichev, Victor Ivanovich
POSITION: Academician of the Russian Academy of Sciences; Director of the Pacific Oceanology Institute
BIRTHPLACE/DATE: August 25, 1932
NATIONALITY: Russian
CAREER: From 1956 to 1961, Researcher at the Sukhumi Acoustics Institute of the USSR Academy of Sciences; from 1961 to 1978, Director. From 1978, Director of the Pacific Oceanology Institute. From 1986 to 1991, Presidium Chairman of the Far Eastern Scientific Center of the USSR Academy of Sciences. From 1989 to 1991, Vice President of the USSR Academy of Sciences; Chairman of the Pacific branch of the USSR Academy of Sciences.
MAJOR WORKS: In the field of hydroacoustics and bioacoustics.
FAMILY: Married with two children.
ADDRESS/TELEPHONE: 7 Radio Street, Vladivostok, 690032. 135–3501; 137–3761 (Vladivostok); 243–2656.

Ilyin-Adaev, Kirill Olegovich
POSITION: Director of IMA-Press Agency
BIRTHPLACE/DATE: Moscow, 1967
NATIONALITY: Russian
EDUCATION: Graduated from the Journalism Department at Moscow State University in 1989.
CAREER: From 1989 to 1990, Junior Editor at APN (Novosti Press Agency); Editor at IMA-Press Agency.
FAMILY: Married.
ADDRESS/TELEPHONE: 11 Second Kazachiy Pereulok, Moscow, 109180. 283–0346 (office).

Ilyinsky, Igor Pavlovich
POSITION: Head of the State Law Department at the Moscow State Institute of International Relations
BIRTHPLACE/DATE: Varnavino village, Nizhegorodsky region, 1927
NATIONALITY: Russian
EDUCATION: Doctor of Philosophy.
CAREER: In 1968, Professor at the Moscow State Institute of International Relations; Senior Researcher at the State Law Institute of the USSR Academy of Sciences. From 1970 to 1973, Department Head of *Problemy Mira i Socializma* (*Problems of Peace and Socialism*) in Prague. From 1973 to 1974, Deputy Department Head at the Academy of Social Sciences of the Central Committee. From 1974 to 1977, Head of the State Law Department at the Moscow State Institute of International Relations; from 1977 to 1982, Dean of the International Law Department.
MAJOR WORKS: *Socialist Self-Government* (1987); *Democratization of Soviet Society* (1989).
HONORS/AWARDS: Order of the Red Banner of Labor; Order of the Badge of Honor.
FAMILY: Married with two children.
ADDRESS/TELEPHONE: 76 Vernadsky Prospekt, Moscow. 249–3843 (home); 434–9449 (secretary).

Ioann Snychev, Ivan Matveyevich
POSITION: Metropolitan of St. Petersburg and Ladoga; Permanent Member of the Holy Synod of the Russian Orthodox Church

BIRTHPLACE/DATE: Maychka village, Kherson region, October 9, 1927
NATIONALITY: Russian
CAREER: From 1956 to 1957, Lecturer at the Minsk Ecclesiastical Seminary. From 1957 to 1959, Priest of the Presentation at the Blessed Virgin Cathedral in Cheboksary. From 1959 to 1960, Lecturer at the Saratov Ecclesiastical Seminary. From 1960 to 1965, Priest at the Intercession Cathedral in Kuibyshev. From 1965 to 1990, Bishop; Head of the Kuibyshev Russian Orthodox Church Diocese.
ADDRESS/TELEPHONE: 18 First Berezovaya Al, St. Petersburg, 197022. 234–9305; 234–5424 (secretary).

Ionaytis, Vladislav Vladislavovich
POSITION: Ambassador to Zaire; Counsellor Extraordinary and Plenipotentiary, First Grade
BIRTHPLACE/DATE: Panevezis, Lithuania, July 15, 1935
NATIONALITY: Lithuanian
EDUCATION: Graduated from a Teachers' Training Institute in 1954 and from the Moscow State Institute of International Relations in 1963. From 1978 to 1979, postgraduate student of the advanced course for senior diplomats at the Diplomatic Academy.
CAREER: From 1960 to 1962, Interpreter in Guinea. From 1963 to 1964, Aide-Trainee at the USSR Embassy in Vietnam. From 1964 to 1965, Senior Aide. From 1965 to 1966, Attaché. From 1966 to 1967, Third Secretary. From 1967 to 1968, Third Secretary of the Southeastern Asia Department. From 1968 to 1970, Second Secretary. From 1970 to 1974, First Secretary at the USSR Embassy in Cameroon. From 1976 to 1977, Counsellor of the Second African Department. From 1977 to 1978, Sector Head. From 1979 to 1983, Counsellor at the USSR Embassy in Rwanda. From 1983 to 1985, Expert of the USSR Foreign Ministry Personnel Department. From 1985 to 1988, USSR Consul-General in Khoshemin.
FAMILY: Married.

Isakov, Victor Fyodorovich
POSITION: Russian Federation Ambassador to India; Ambassador Extraordinary and Plenipotentiary
BIRTHPLACE/DATE: Leningrad, December 12, 1932
NATIONALITY: Russian
EDUCATION: Graduated in 1956 from the Moscow State Institute of International Relations. Doctor of History. Speaks English and Spanish.
CAREER: From 1956 to 1966, Aide to the American Countries Department of the USSR Foreign Ministry. From 1956 to 1961, Aide-Intern, Senior Aide-Intern, Attaché at the USSR Embassy in the United States. In 1961, Attaché of the American Countries Department of the USSR Foreign Ministry. In 1962, joined the Communist Party. From 1963 to 1967, Third Secretary, Second Secretary at the USSR Embassy in the United States. From 1967 to 1971, Second Secretary, First Secretary, Counsellor of the U.S. Department of the USSR Foreign Ministry. From 1971 to 1977, Counsellor at the USSR Embassy in the United States. From 1977 to 1978, Sector Head of the U.S. Department of the USSR Foreign Ministry. From 1978 to 1983, Deputy Head of the U.S. Department of the USSR Foreign Ministry. From 1983 to 1986, Minister-Counsellor at the USSR Embassy in the United States. From 1986 to 1988, USSR Ambassador to Brazil (from September 1986 to October 1986, worked in the USSR Foreign Ministry Central Administration). From 1988 to January 1992, USSR Ambassador to India.
FAMILY: Married.
ADDRESS/TELEPHONE: The Russian Embassy in India, Shantipath Chanakyapuri, New Delhi, India, 110021. 60–6026; 60–6137; 60–5875.

Isakov, Vladimir Borisovich
POSITION: Member of the Russian Federation Supreme Soviet Committee for Industry and Power Engineering
BIRTHPLACE/DATE: 1950
NATIONALITY: Russian
EDUCATION: Graduated from the Rudenko Law Institute in Sverdlovsk (now Yekaterinburg). Doctor of Law.
CAREER: To 1990, State Law Division Head of the Sverdlovsk Law Institute. In 1990, elected Chairman of the Council of the Republic. Russian Federation People's Deputy. Member of the Russian Federation Supreme Soviet.
FAMILY: Married with three children.

ADDRESS/TELEPHONE: 2 Krasnopresnenskaya Naberezhnaya, Moscow, 103274. 205–9065; 205–5398; 205–4604 (office).

Isayev, Aleksandr Sergeyevich
POSITION: Director of the International Forestry Institute of the Russian Academy of Sciences
BIRTHPLACE/DATE: Moscow, 1931
NATIONALITY: Russian
EDUCATION: Academician; Doctor of Biology.
CAREER: From 1954 to 1960, Engineer. From 1960, Researcher; from 1972, Deputy Director; from 1977, Director of the Sukachev Timber and Wood Institute of the USSR Academy of Sciences. From 1982 to 1988, Chairman of the Krasnoyarsk Presidium of the Siberian branch of the USSR Academy of Sciences. From 1988 to December 1991, Chairman of the USSR State Committee for Forestry. In 1984, Academician of the USSR Academy of Sciences. From September 1991, Director of the International Forestry Institute. From December 1991, Director of the Ecology and Forestry Productivity Center.
HONORS/AWARDS: Honorary Member of the Bulgarian Academy of Sciences; Gold Medal of International Forestry and Research Organizations.
FAMILY: Married with two children.
ADDRESS/TELEPHONE: 69 Novocheremushenskaya Street, Moscow, 117418. 332–8652 (office).

Isayev, Aleksandr Sergeyevich
POSITION: Director-General of the Research Institute of Economics, Planning, and Management of the Aviation Industry
BIRTHPLACE/DATE: Moscow, 1933
NATIONALITY: Russian
EDUCATION: Doctor of Technical Science; Professor.
CAREER: From 1957 to 1983, worked at the Institute of Automatic Systems. From 1970 to 1983, Head of the Division of Planning and Efficiency of Aviation Complexes. From 1983, Director of Economics, Planning, and Management of the Aviation Industry; member of the Moscow Ecological Council.
MAJOR WORKS: Author of more than 200 publications.
HONORS/AWARDS: USSR State Prize; Honored Mayor of Oklahoma.
FAMILY: Married with a child.
ADDRESS/TELEPHONE: 26 Ulansky Pereulok, Moscow, 103045. 207–7619 (office); 208–2621.

Isayev, Boris Mikhailovich
POSITION: Socio-Economic Development Department Head of the Russian Federation Supreme Soviet; member of the Russian Federation Supreme Soviet
BIRTHPLACE/DATE: Ryazan region, 1935
NATIONALITY: Russian
CAREER: Teacher at a school of agriculture; Engineer in Tataria; member of the Communist Party; Deputy Chairman of the Tatar Council of Ministers; Deputy Minister of the Russian Ministry of Bakery Products. From April 1990, Chairman of the Chelyabinsk Council of People's Deputies Executive Committee; Russian Federation People's Deputy.
FAMILY: Married with three children.
ADDRESS/TELEPHONE: 2 Krasnopresnenskaya Naberezhnaya, Moscow, 103274. 205–6965 (office).

Ishchuk, Aleksey Alekseyevich
POSITION: Prefect of the Zelenograd Prefecture of Moscow
BIRTHPLACE/DATE: Moscow, September 28, 1941
NATIONALITY: Ukrainian
EDUCATION: Graduated in 1969 from the Moscow Aviation Institute (MAI).
CAREER: From 1969 to 1970, Laboratory Head, then Senior Engineer of MAI. From 1970 to 1974, Planning Department Instructor of the Zelenograd District Communist Party. From 1975, Zelenograd City Council Deputy. From 1981 to 1982, Vice Rector of Management and Administration at the Moscow Institute of Electronic Technology. From 1982 to 1988, First Deputy Chairman, and from 1988 to 1991, Chairman of the Zelenograd City Executive Committee.
FAMILY: Married with two children.
ADDRESS/TELEPHONE: 1 Tsentralny Prospekt, Zelenograd, Moscow, 103482. 535–6220.

Iskander, Fazil Abdulovich
POSITION: Writer
BIRTHPLACE/DATE: Sukhumi, 1929

EDUCATION: Graduated in 1954 from the Gorky Literary Institute.
CAREER: From 1955 to 1957, Assistant Editor for newspapers in Bryansk and Kursk; Editor at a publishing house in Sukhumi. Elected USSR People's Deputy from the Sukhumi City District. Vice President of Mir Kultury (World of Culture) Intellectuals' Association. Member of the USSR Writers' Union. Member of the PEN Club. Member of the April Writers' Association. Member of the Russian Writers' Union.
MAJOR WORKS: *Sozvezdiye Kozlotura* (*The Constellation of Kozlotur*); *Sandro iz Chegema* (*Sandro from Chegem*).
HONORS/AWARDS: Sakharov Prize (May 1991); USSR State Prize.
FAMILY: Married with two children.
ADDRESS/TELEPHONE: 23 Krasnoarmeyskaya Street, Flat #104, Moscow, 125319. 151–5285.

Iskenderov, Akhmed Akhmedovich
POSITION: Editor in Chief of *Voprosy Istorii* (*Questions of History*) magazine
BIRTHPLACE/DATE: Baku, 1927
NATIONALITY: Azerbaijanian
EDUCATION: Graduated in 1950 from the Institute of Military Interpreters; in 1955, from the Philosophy Department at Moscow State University; in 1957, from the postgraduate program at the USSR Academy of Sciences' Institute of Oriental Studies. Doctor of History; Professor.
CAREER: From 1958 to 1965, worked at the Prague-based *World Marxist Review* journal. From 1965 to 1968, Consultant to the Central Committee's Information Department. In 1969, held positions at the USSR Academy of Sciences: Deputy Director of the Institute of the International Labor Movement; Deputy Director of the Institute of World History. From 1979, Corresponding Member of the USSR Academy of Sciences. Deputy Chairman of the Soviet Afro-Asian Solidarity Committee; Vice President of the USSR-Japan Society; Bureau Member of the History Department of the USSR Academy of Sciences. From December 1991, Corresponding Member of the Russian Academy of Sciences. Expert on Japanese history and culture, the national liberation movement of Asian and African peoples, and the methodology of historical analysis. Vice President of the Russia-Japan Society; Bureau Member of the History Department of the Russian Academy of Sciences.
MAJOR WORKS: *Sixteenth-Century Feudal Japanese Settlement; National-Liberation Movement: Problems, Regularities, Prospects; Africa: Politics, Economics, Ideology.*
HONORS/AWARDS: Order of the Badge of Honor.
FAMILY: Married with two children.
ADDRESS/TELEPHONE: 1/2 Maly Putinkovsky Pereulok, Moscow, 103781. 209–7908 (office).

Ispravnikov, Vladimir Olegovich
POSITION: Chairman of the Russian Federation Higher Economic Council; Deputy Chairman of the Russian Supreme Soviet; People's Deputy
BIRTHPLACE/DATE: Omsk, 1948
NATIONALITY: Russian
EDUCATION: From 1975 to 1979, postgraduate student of the Economics Department at Moscow State University. Doctor of Economics.
CAREER: From 1972 to 1974, Technician, then Engineer at a machine-building plant. From 1974 to 1975, Lecturer. From 1980 to 1990, Lecturer. From 1983 to 1990, Laboratory Head engaged in research on industrial enterprises and local governments.
FAMILY: Married with a daughter.
ADDRESS/TELEPHONE: 2 Krasnopresnenskaya Naberezhnaya, Moscow, 103274. 205–4156.

Ivanenko, Victor Valentinovich
POSITION: Russian Federation Security Minister; Major-General
BIRTHPLACE/DATE: Tyumen region, 1947
NATIONALITY: Russian
EDUCATION: Graduated from the Tyumen Industrial Institute. Graduated in 1970 from the KGB courses.
CAREER: From 1974 to 1979, member of the Samatlor Oilfields Commission for the Prevention of Emergencies. In 1986, Deputy Head of the Tyumen Region KGB Directorate; Senior Inspector of the USSR KGB Inspectorate; then Department Head in charge of inspection of Russian Territorial Government Bodies; Deputy Directorate Head. In May 1991, appointed Acting Chairman of the Russian KGB. From August 1991, Chairman of the

Russian KGB. From November 1991 to November 1992, Director-General of the Russian Federal Security Agency, Russian Federation Minister.
FAMILY: Married with three daughters.
ADDRESS/TELEPHONE: 12 Lubyanka, Moscow. 224–5097 (office).

Ivanilov, Yuri Pavlovich
POSITION: Member of the Russian Federation Supreme Soviet Committee for Economic Reforms and the Committee for the Management of State Property; Russian Federation People's Deputy; member of the Industrial Union Faction; member of the Reform Coalition
BIRTHPLACE/DATE: Kiev, 1931
NATIONALITY: Russian
EDUCATION: From 1957 to 1960, postgraduate student at the Central Institute of Economics and Mathematics of the USSR Academy of Sciences. Doctor of Physics and Mathematics.
CAREER: From 1954 to 1957, Assistant at the Azerbaijan Industrial Institute. From 1960 to 1971, Assistant, Docent, Deputy Dean of the Moscow Physics and Technology Institute. From 1971 to 1976, Deputy Director of the Scientific Information Center. From 1976 to 1982, Professor, then Dean of the Moscow Physics and Technology Institute. From 1982 to 1991, Department Head of the USSR Academy of Sciences' Calculation Center.
FAMILY: Married with three children.
ADDRESS/TELEPHONE: 46 Pervomayskaya Street, Dolgoprudnoye, Moscow Region. 216–4149 (home).

Ivanov, Aleksandr Nikolayevich
POSITION: Director of the Salanf Firm
BIRTHPLACE/DATE: Tambov, 1953
NATIONALITY: Russian
CAREER: Engineer; Researcher. From 1991, Board Member of the Russian Union of Young Entrepreneurs.
MAJOR WORKS: Author of scientific publications on the rational consuming of natural resources.
FAMILY: Married with two daughters.
ADDRESS/TELEPHONE: P.O. Box 325, Moscow, 107078. 265–9849; Fax: 261–3482.

Ivanov, Igor Sergeyevich
POSITION: Ambassador to Spain; Ambassador Extraordinary and Plenipotentiary
BIRTHPLACE/DATE: Moscow
NATIONALITY: Russian
EDUCATION: Graduated from the Moscow State Teachers' Training Institute of Foreign Languages in 1969.
CAREER: In 1969, Trainee at the Institute of the International Labor Movement of the USSR Academy of Sciences. From 1969 to 1973, Junior Researcher at the Institute of the World Economy and International Relations of the USSR Academy of Sciences. In 1973, Second Secretary of the First European Department of the USSR Foreign Ministry. From 1973 to 1977, Senior Engineer at the USSR Trade Mission in Madrid. From 1977 to 1978, First Secretary at the USSR Embassy in Spain. From 1978 to 1980, Counsellor at the USSR Embassy in Spain. From 1980 to 1983, Minister-Counsellor at the USSR Embassy in Spain. From 1983 to 1984, Expert of the First European Department. From 1984 to 1985, Counsellor of the USSR Foreign Ministry. From 1985 to 1986, Minister Aide. From 1986 to 1987, Deputy Department Head of the USSR Foreign Ministry General Secretariat; from 1987 to 1989, First Deputy Head. From 1989 to 1991, Head of the General Secretariat and Collegium Member.
HONORS/AWARDS: Order of the Badge of Honor.
FAMILY: Married with a daughter.
TELEPHONE: 411–0706.

Ivanov, Sergey Nikolayevich
POSITION: Subcommittee Chairman of the Russian Federation Supreme Soviet Committee for Defense and Security; member of the Left-Center Faction
BIRTHPLACE/DATE: Baa village, Chita region, July 21, 1951
NATIONALITY: Russian
EDUCATION: Doctor of Law.
CAREER: From 1981 to 1990, Lecturer; Senior Lecturer; Docent. From 1990, Russian Federation People's Deputy.
FAMILY: Married with two children.
ADDRESS/TELEPHONE: 8 Academician Korolev Street, Moscow, 129515. 216–4120.

Ivanov, Vitaly Pavlovich
POSITION: Admiral-Commander in Chief of the Navy; Head of the Kuznetsov Naval Academy
BIRTHPLACE/DATE: Poltava, 1935
NATIONALITY: Russian
CAREER: From 1953, held positions in the USSR Navy: Division Commander; Deputy Flotilla Commander; Head of the Naval Fleet's Main Staff. From 1985, Baltic Fleet Commander.
FAMILY: Married with two daughters.
ADDRESS/TELEPHONE: St. Petersburg. 293–6122; 293–5303; 204–2082.

Ivanov, Vyacheslav Vsevolodovich
POSITION: Director of the Russian State Library of Foreign Literature
BIRTHPLACE/DATE: Moscow, August 21, 1929
NATIONALITY: Russian
EDUCATION: Doctor of Philology; Professor.
CAREER: From 1954 to 1959, Assistant, then Acting Docent at Moscow State University; Acting Deputy Editor in Chief of *Problemy Lingvistiki* (*Linguistics Problems*) magazine. From 1959 to 1961, Translation Group Head, then Researcher of mathematical linguistics at the Institute of Precise Mechanics and Calculation Equipment of the USSR Academy of Sciences. From 1963, Senior Researcher, then Sector Head at the Institute of Slavic Languages. In 1968, Honorary Member of the British Academy of Sciences. From 1979, member of the USSR Writers' Union; USSR People's Deputy. From 1989, Director of the State Library of Foreign Literature. From 1990, Division Head of the Theory and History of World Culture at Moscow State University; Vice President of the Soviet Culture Association; member of the USSR Supreme Soviet Council of Nationalities Committee for Preserving Languages, Culture, National and International Traditions, and Historical Heritage.
HONORS/AWARDS: Prize of Lenin.
FAMILY: Married with a son.
ADDRESS/TELEPHONE: 1 Ulyanovskaya Street, Moscow, 109189. 297–2839; Fax: 227–2039.

Ivashchenko, Igor Georgyevich
POSITION: Ambassador to the Yemen Republic; Counsellor Extraordinary and Plenipotentiary, First Grade
BIRTHPLACE/DATE: Moscow, August 5, 1938
NATIONALITY: Russian
EDUCATION: Graduated from the Moscow State Institute of International Relations in 1962. From 1970 to 1972, student at the Higher Diplomatic School of the USSR Foreign Ministry; from 1978 to 1979, took the postgraduate course for senior diplomats.
CAREER: In 1961, Interpreter at the USSR Embassy in Lebanon. From 1962 to 1965, Secretary at the USSR Consulate in Aleppo. From 1965 to 1967, Senior Aide to the Middle East Department of the USSR Foreign Ministry. From 1967 to 1968, Attaché at the USSR Embassy in Yemen Republic; from 1968 to 1969, Third Secretary; from 1969 to 1970, Second Secretary. From 1972 to 1976, First Secretary at the USSR Embassy in Iraq. From 1976 to 1978, First Secretary of the Middle East Department. From 1979 to 1983, Counsellor at the USSR Embassy in Jordan. From 1983 to 1984, Counsellor of the Middle East Department; from 1984 to 1986, Sector Head. From 1986 to 1987, Deputy Head of the Middle East and Northern Africa Department. From 1987 to 1991, Minister-Counsellor at the USSR Embassy in Lebanon.
FAMILY: Married with two children.
TELEPHONE: 244–4013.

Ivashko, Vladimir Antonovich
POSITION: Former Deputy Secretary-General of the Central Committee; former member of the Politburo
BIRTHPLACE/DATE: 1932
NATIONALITY: Ukrainian
CAREER: From 1957, Lecturer at various institutes in Kharkov. In 1973, began career in the Communist Party. In 1978, Secretary of the Kharkov Regional Party Committee. From 1986 to 1990, Secretary of the Ukrainian Central Committee; First Secretary of the Dnepropetrovsky District Party Committee; First Secretary of the Ukrainian Central Committee. From June to July 1990, Ukraine Supreme Soviet Chairman.
FAMILY: Married with a son.
ADDRESS/TELEPHONE: 4 Staraya Square, Moscow, 103132. 206–2511.

Izvekov, Nikolay Yakovlevich
POSITION: Director-General of the Serp i Molot (Sickle and Hammer) Metallurgical Plant

BIRTHPLACE/DATE: Zhdanov, 1935
NATIONALITY: Russian
CAREER: From 1959 to 1979, worked at a metallurgical plant in Asha, Sverdlovsk region. From 1979 to 1986, worked at a regional management office of the Ferrous Metallurgy Ministry.
FAMILY: Married with two children.
ADDRESS/TELEPHONE: 11 Zolotorozhsky Val, Moscow, 109033. 278–4500.

Izyumov, Yuri Petrovich

POSITION: Editor in Chief of *Glasnost* (*Free Speech*) newspaper
BIRTHPLACE/DATE: Moscow, 1932
EDUCATION: Graduated in 1950 from the Journalism Department at Moscow State University. Speaks English.
CAREER: From 1951 to 1980, Deputy Chief Editor of the newspapers *Moskovsky Komsomolets* (*Moscow Komsomol Member*), *Pionerskaya Pravda* (*Young Pioneer Truth*), *Vechernyaya Moskva* (*Evening Moscow*). From 1980 to 1990, First Deputy Editor in Chief of *Literaturnaya Gazeta* (*Literary Newspaper*). Mossoviet (Moscow Council) People's Deputy.
MAJOR WORKS: *The Rising America; Unofficial Tours; Lenin in Moscow* story collection.
HONORS/AWARDS: Order of the People's Friendship; Order of the Badge of Honor; Order of the Red Banner of Labor; Russian Federation Supreme Soviet Presidium Honorary Certificate; Russian Federation Honored Cultural Worker.
FAMILY: Married with two daughters.
ADDRESS/TELEPHONE: 14 Novaya Ploshchad, Moscow. 206–4037 (office).

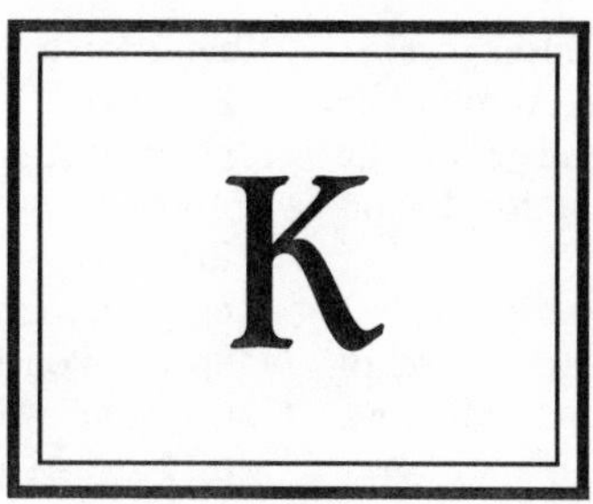

Kachanov, Aleksandr Ivanovich

POSITION: Russian Federation Trade Representative in China

BIRTHPLACE/DATE: 1928

EDUCATION: Graduated in 1952 from the Krasnodar Institute of the Food Industry. Doctor of Economics. Speaks English.

CAREER: From 1969 to 1974, Counsellor for Economic Issues at the USSR Embassy in Mongolia. From 1974 to 1978, Head of the Department of Economic and Technical Cooperation with the Mongolian People's Republic of the USSR State Committee for Economic Relations. From 1978 to 1983, Counsellor for Economic Issues at the USSR Embassy in Cuba. From 1983, First Deputy Chairman of the USSR State Committee for Foreign Economic Relations, then USSR First Deputy Minister of Foreign Economic Relations.

ADDRESS/TELEPHONE: 32/34 Smolenskaya-Sennaya Square, Moscow, 121200. 244–2450; 244–1606 (office).

Kadagishvili, Amiran

POSITION: President of the Caucasus Stock Exchange

BIRTHPLACE/DATE: 1949

CAREER: Worked in an academic institute for ten years; then ten years at the Calculation Equipment Management Office. From 1986, Head of a stockholding firm of the Russian Commodity Exchange. Founded regional Stock Exchange.

FAMILY: Married with two sons.

ADDRESS/TELEPHONE: 71 K. Tsambeuli Prospekt, Tbilisi, 380020. 98–6266; 74–3549; 74–6266.

Kadakin, Aleksander Mikhailovich

POSITION: Ambassador to Nepal; Ambassador Extraordinary and Plenipotentiary, First Grade

BIRTHPLACE/DATE: Kishenev, July 22, 1949

NATIONALITY: Russian

EDUCATION: Graduated from the Moscow State Institute of International Relations in 1972.

CAREER: From 1966 to 1967, Technician-Translator of the Special Design Bureau at the Kishenev Vibropribor Plant. In 1972, Trainee at the USSR Embassy in India; from 1972 to 1975, Attaché. From 1975 to 1978, Third Secretary; from 1978 to 1980, Second Secretary of the Secretariat of the USSR First Deputy Foreign Minister; from 1980 to 1983, First Secretary; from 1983 to 1986, Assistant to the First Deputy Foreign Minister; from 1988 to 1989, Assistant to the Deputy Foreign Minister; from 1989 to 1991, Minister-Counsellor at the USSR Embassy to India. From 1991, First Deputy Board Head of the General Secretariat of the USSR Foreign Ministry; from 1991 to 1992, Minister-Counsellor at the USSR (now Russian) Embassy in India.

FAMILY: Single.

TELEPHONE: 244–2793.

Kadannikov, Vladimir Vasilyevich

POSITION: Director-General of the AvtoVAZ (Volga Automobile Plant) Production Association

BIRTHPLACE/DATE: Gorky (now Nizhny Novgorod), 1941

NATIONALITY: Russian

EDUCATION: Graduated in 1967 from Gorky Polytechnic.

CAREER: Worked at the Gorky Automobile

Plant. From 1967, worked from Engineer to First Deputy Director-General of VAZ Automobile Plant. USSR People's Deputy. Member of the Council of the Union's Commission for Labor, Prices, and Social Policy.
FAMILY: Married with two children.
ADDRESS/TELEPHONE: Moscow Directorate of AvtoVAZ, 3 Gorokhovsky Pereulok, Moscow, 103064. 263–2222 (office).

Kafarova, Elmira Mikail Kyzy
POSITION: Former Chairman of the Azerbaijan Supreme Soviet
BIRTHPLACE/DATE: Baku, 1934
NATIONALITY: Azerbaijanian
EDUCATION: Completed postgraduate studies at Azerbaijan University. Doctor of Philology.
CAREER: From 1955, Deputy Secretary of the Komsomol Committee. From 1961, Party Functionary. From 1966, First Secretary of the Azerbaijan Komsomol Central Committee. From 1970, worked for the Azerbaijan Central Committee. From 1971, Secretary of the Baku City Party Committee. From 1980, Azerbaijan Minister of Education. From 1983, Azerbaijan Foreign Minister. From 1987, Deputy Chairman of the Azerbaijan Council of Ministers. From 1989, Presidium Chairman of the Azerbaijan Supreme Soviet, Deputy Chairman of the USSR Supreme Soviet. From May 1990, Chairman of the Azerbaijan Supreme Soviet; USSR People's Deputy; Azerbaijan Supreme Soviet Deputy.
FAMILY: Married.

Kagalovsky, Konstantin Grigoryevich
POSITION: Economic Counsellor of the Russian Federation Government; Counsellor for Mutual Relations with International Financial Organizations
BIRTHPLACE/DATE: 1957
EDUCATION: Graduated from the Moscow Institute of Finance. Doctor of Economics.
CAREER: Former Director of the Economic Reforms International Research Center.
ADDRESS/TELEPHONE: 4 Staraya Square, Moscow 103132. 206–2171; 206–4669 (office).

Kainarskaya, Irina Yakovlevna
POSITION: Editor in Chief of TV-Progress Independent Agency
BIRTHPLACE/DATE: Moscow, 1945
EDUCATION: Graduated in 1970 from the Philology Department at Moscow State University. Speaks Polish and English.
CAREER: From 1971 to 1974, Editor-Consultant of Novosti (News) Press Agency. From 1974 to 1991, Control Editor, then Department Head of Progress Publishers. International Programs Coordinator. From 1984, Board Member of the Russian-Polish Friendship Society.
FAMILY: Married.
ADDRESS/TELEPHONE: 17 Zubovsky Boulevard, Moscow. 246–1441 (office).

Kalinin, Arnold Ivanovich
POSITION: Ambassador to Cuba; Ambassador Extraordinary and Plenipotentiary
BIRTHPLACE/DATE: Allaysky region, September 7, 1929
NATIONALITY: Russian
EDUCATION: Graduated from the Moscow State Institute of International Relations in 1951. From 1951 to 1954, postgraduate student. Doctor of Law.
CAREER: From 1954 to 1957, Lecturer. From 1957 to 1960, Researcher at the Institute of the World Economy and International Relations. From 1960 to 1969, Aide, then Sector Head of the International Department of the Central Committee. From 1969 to 1974, Minister-Counsellor at the USSR Embassy in Cuba. From 1974 to 1982, Ambassador to Portugal. From 1982 to 1983, Expert of the First European Department. From 1983 to 1987, Ambassador to Angola. From 1987 to 1989, Department Head of the USSR Foreign Ministry; from 1989 to 1991, Board Head.
MAJOR WORKS: More than thirty publications, including *The Political System of Mexico*; *The Political System of Ecuador.*
HONORS/AWARDS: Order of the Red Banner of Labor; Order of the People's Friendship.
FAMILY: Married with a daughter.
TELEPHONE: 244–3295.

Kalinin, Nikolay Vasilyevich
POSITION: Head of the Armed Forces Academy

BIRTHPLACE/DATE: Malye Kurashki village, Rabotki district, Gorky region, 1937
NATIONALITY: Russian
EDUCATION: Graduated from the Mikhail Frunze Military Academy and from the Academy of General Staff. Colonel-General.
CAREER: Joined the Communist Party in 1958. From 1958 to 1965, Platoon Commander, Company Commander, Battalion Commander, Army Unit Chief of Staff, Airborne Infantry Regiment Commander, Army Corps Commander, Army Commander, First Deputy Commander of the Soviet Army Group in Germany, Commander of the Siberian Military District. From 1987 to 1989, Airborne Infantry Troops Commander. From 1989, Moscow Military District Commander. On August 29, 1991, following the attempted coup, relieved of his command by presidential decree. On December 19, 1991, appointed Chief of Staff and First Deputy Area Commander in Chief.
FAMILY: Married with two children.
ADDRESS/TELEPHONE: 3/5 Krasnokazarmennaya Street, Moscow. 293–2869; 261–3838; 293–1413 (office).

Kalinin, Yuri Ivanovich
POSITION: Central Administration Head of Correction Institutions of the Russian Federation Ministry of Internal Affairs; Major-General of the Militia
BIRTHPLACE/DATE: Saratov region, 1946
CAREER: From 1971, worked in the Internal Affairs Service; Foreman, Inspector, Deputy Head, Head of Correction Institutions. From 1982 to 1988, Saratov Region Communist Party Department Head of Correction Institutions. From 1988 to 1991, Department Head of Correction Institutions of the USSR Ministry of Internal Affairs. From 1991 to January 1992, Deputy Head of the Correction Complex of the Russian Federation Ministry of Internal Affairs.
ADDRESS/TELEPHONE: The Russian Ministry of Internal Affairs, 23 B. Bronnaya, Moscow, 103104. 239–7500.

Kalinina, Lidiya Georgyevna
POSITION: Editor in Chief of *Domostroi* (*Housebuilder*) weekly
BIRTHPLACE/DATE: Rostov region, 1956
NATIONALITY: Russian
EDUCATION: Graduated in 1982 from the Journalism Department at Moscow State University.
CAREER: Began working in 1974 as a Merchandise Expert; contributed to various periodicals. Worked at *Studenchesky Meridian* (*Student Meridian*) magazine and *Moskovsky Stroitel* (*Moscow Construction*) newspaper.
FAMILY: Single.
ADDRESS/TELEPHONE: 19 Novy Arbat, Building 1, Moscow, 121019. 291–0872 (office).

Kalmyk, Valerya Nikolayevna
POSITION: Ambassador to Costa Rica; Counsellor Extraordinary and Plenipotentiary, First Grade
BIRTHPLACE/DATE: Bogorodsk, Tula region
NATIONALITY: Russian
EDUCATION: Graduated from Moscow State University in 1962, then postgraduate student.
CAREER: To 1971, Lecturer at Moscow State University. From 1971 to 1975, Komsomol Secretary of Moscow University. From 1975 to 1978, Senior Lecturer. From 1978 to 1986, Permanent Representative of the Soviet Women's Committee at the International Democratic Women's Federation in East Germany. From 1986 to 1987, Foreign Relations Secretary of the Soviet Women's Committee; from 1987 to 1991, Deputy Head.
HONORS/AWARDS: Order of the Badge of Honor.
FAMILY: Married with a daughter.
TELEPHONE: 244–3295.

Kalnins, Kharalds
POSITION: Head of the German Lutheran Church; Archbishop
BIRTHPLACE/DATE: Leningrad, July 22, 1911
NATIONALITY: Lett
CAREER: From 1946 to 1974, Priest in Latvia.
FAMILY: Married.
ADDRESS/TELEPHONE: 8 Remines Street, Riga.

Kalvanas, Ionas
POSITION: Chairman of the Consistory of the Evangelical Lutheran Church of Lithuania; Bishop
BIRTHPLACE/DATE: Ruobezu village, Lithuania, April 24, 1914
NATIONALITY: Lithuanian
CAREER: From 1940 to 1955, Priest of the Taur-

agsky Lutheran Church. From 1955 to 1970, Consistory Member of the Lithuanian Evangelical Lutheran Church.
FAMILY: Married with six children.
ADDRESS: 68 Gagarin Street, Taurage.

Kapinos, Vladimir Aleksandrovich
POSITION: Board Chairman of the Morbank Merchant Marine Joint-Stock Bank
BIRTHPLACE/DATE: Tomsk region, 1940
EDUCATION: Graduated from the Credit and Economics Department at the Moscow Finance Institute.
CAREER: From 1957 to 1966, worked at several banks, then at the Far Eastern Shipping Company. Deputy Head of the Main Economics Department of the USSR Ministry of Merchant Marines.
FAMILY: Married with two children.
ADDRESS/TELEPHONE: 1/4 Rozhdestvenka Street, Moscow, 103759. 926–1165 (office).

Kapitonov, Victor Arsenyevich
POSITION: Coach of the Rus Professional Cycling Team
BIRTHPLACE/DATE: Tver, 1933
NATIONALITY: Russian
EDUCATION: Graduated in 1968 from the State Lesgaft Physical Education Institute in Leningrad.
CAREER: 1960 Summer Olympic Champion (180-km cycling race). Former Coach of the USSR National Cycle-Racing Team. Coach of the USSR National Team.
HONORS/AWARDS: USSR Honored Master of Sports; USSR Honored Coach; Order of the Badge of Honor; Order of Lenin; Order of the People's Friendship.
FAMILY: Married with two children.
ADDRESS/TELEPHONE: 8 Luzhnetskaya Naberezhnaya, Moscow. 201–1741 (office); 213–2132 (home).

Kapitsa, Mikhail Stepanovich
POSITION: Director of the Russian Academy of Sciences' Institute of Oriental Studies; Editor in Chief of *Asia and Africa Today* magazine
BIRTHPLACE/DATE: Khmelnitsky region, November 5, 1921
NATIONALITY: Ukrainian
EDUCATION: Graduated in 1941 from the Central Committee's School of Interpreters; in 1943, from the USSR Army Military Institute of Foreign Languages.
CAREER: From 1943 to 1960, engaged in diplomatic work at the USSR Embassy in China and the USSR Foreign Ministry. Joined the Communist Party in 1947. From 1960 to 1962, USSR Ambassador to Pakistan. From 1962 to 1982, worked at the USSR Foreign Ministry. From 1982 to 1987, Deputy USSR Foreign Minister. From 1987, Chairman of the Soviet Afro-Asian Solidarity Committee. From 1987, Director of the Academy of Sciences' Institute of Oriental Studies. From 1987, Corresponding Member of the USSR Academy of Sciences. From December 1991, Corresponding Member of the Russian Academy of Sciences. USSR People's Deputy.
MAJOR WORKS: Publications on the modern history of China and international relations in the Far East and Asia.
HONORS/AWARDS: USSR State Prize (1982).
FAMILY: Married with three children.
ADDRESS/TELEPHONE: The Institute of Oriental Studies, 12 Rozhdestvenka Street, GSP, Moscow, 103777. 921–1884 (office); 331–0235 (home).

Kapralov, Yuri Semyonovich
POSITION: Ambassador to Angola; Ambassador Extraordinary and Plenipotentiary
BIRTHPLACE/DATE: Moscow, November 8, 1943
NATIONALITY: Russian
EDUCATION: Graduated from the Moscow State Institute of International Relations.
CAREER: From 1967 to 1969, Interpreter at the USSR Embassy in Egypt; from 1969 to 1971, Attaché; from 1971 to 1972, Third Secretary; from 1972 to 1973, Second Secretary. From 1973 to 1975, Second Secretary of the U.S. Department of the USSR Foreign Ministry; from 1975 to 1978, First Secretary. From 1978 to 1980, First Secretary at the USSR Embassy in the United States. From 1980 to 1983, Counsellor. From 1983 to 1984, Sector Head of the U.S. Department. From 1984 to 1988, Assistant to the Department Head, Consultant to the Central Committee. From 1988 to 1990, Ambassador to Lesotho.
FAMILY: Married with a daughter.
TELEPHONE: 244–2211.

Karachurin, Rif Allayarovich

POSITION: Director-General of the Russian Automobile Industry Department of the Russian Federation Ministry of Industry; Russian Federation People's Deputy; member of the Russian Federation Supreme Soviet Committee for Foreign Affairs and International Economic Relations

BIRTHPLACE/DATE: Karnashevo village, Gilminsky district, Bashkiria, January 30, 1941

NATIONALITY: Tatar

EDUCATION: Graduated in 1970 from the Chelyabinsk Institute of Agricultural Mechanization and Electrification.

CAREER: From 1960 to 1965, worked in agriculture: Mechanic, Workshop Chief. From 1965 to 1968, Junior, then Senior Researcher. From 1968 to 1978, Foreman, Senior Foreman, Deputy Workshop Chief, Workshop Chief, Deputy Chief Technologist, Deputy Chief Engineer, then Deputy Director of the Chelyabinsk Machine-Building Factory. From 1978 to 1982, Director of the Tyumen Tractor-Motor Electrical Equipment Factory. From 1982 to 1986, Director, Director-General of the Oktyabrsky Avtopribor (Automobile Equipment) Factory in Bashkiria. From 1986 to 1988, Head of the Main Department for Electrical Equipment Production and Electronics of the Ministry of Automobile Industry. From 1989 to 1990, Deputy Minister, Director-General of the Yelabuga Motor Works (under construction).

FAMILY: Married with two daughters.

ADDRESS/TELEPHONE: 10/36 Astrakhansky Pereulok, #90, Moscow. 280–6758 (home); 921–6211 (office).

Karaganov, Sergey Aleksandrovich

POSITION: Deputy Director of the Russian Academy of Sciences' Institute of European Studies

BIRTHPLACE/DATE: Moscow, 1952

NATIONALITY: Russian

EDUCATION: Graduated from the Economics Department at Moscow University. Doctor of History.

CAREER: Junior Researcher, Senior Researcher, Sector Head of the Institute of the U.S. and Canada; Department Head of the Institute of European Studies.

MAJOR WORKS: In the field of foreign policy, economics, disarmament, and European security.

FAMILY: Married with a daughter.

ADDRESS/TELEPHONE: 18 Okhotny Ryad, Building 3, Moscow 103873. 203–6834.

Karamanov, Uzakbay Karamanovich

POSITION: Kazakh State Counsellor

BIRTHPLACE/DATE: Uialy village, Kzyl-Ordynsk region, 1937

NATIONALITY: Kazakh

CAREER: In 1959, Construction Industry Foreman in Aktyubensk. From 1967 to 1980, worked in construction management, and for the Kazakh Construction Ministry. From April 1987, Chairman of the Kazakh State Committee for Technical Equipment. From November 1990 to October 1991, Chairman of the Kazakh Council of Ministers; Kazakh Republic People's Deputy.

FAMILY: Married with three children.

ADDRESS/TELEPHONE: The Republican Cabinet of Ministers, Republic Square, Alma-Ata. 62–3097 (office).

Karasev, Valentin Ivanovich

POSITION: Politician; former USSR President's Counsellor for Relations with Political and Public Organizations

BIRTHPLACE/DATE: 1952

NATIONALITY: Russian

CAREER: Former Head of the Division of Socio-Political History of Twentieth Century Political Science at the Kramatorsk Industrial Institute.

FAMILY: Married with two daughters.

Karasin, Grigory Borisovich

POSITION: Head of the Department of Africa and the Middle East of the Russian Foreign Ministry; Counsellor Extraordinary and Plenipotentiary

BIRTHPLACE/DATE: Moscow, August 23, 1949

NATIONALITY: Russian

CAREER: From 1972 to 1974, Interpreter at the USSR Embassy in Senegal; from 1974 to 1976, Attaché. From 1976 to 1977, Attaché of the First African Department of the USSR Foreign Ministry. From 1977 to 1978, Third Secretary of the Secretariat of the Deputy Foreign Minister. From 1979 to 1981, Second Secretary at the USSR Embassy in Australia. From 1981 to 1985, Second Secretary;

from 1985 to 1987, First Secretary of the Second European Department; from 1987 to 1988, Counsellor. From 1988 to 1992, Counsellor at the USSR Embassy in Great Britain.
FAMILY: Married with two children.
TELEPHONE: 244–2211

Karaulov, Andrey Victorovich
POSITION: Host of the "Moment of Truth" TV show
BIRTHPLACE: Kaliningrad, Moscow region
CAREER: From 1983 to 1986, Correspondent for *Teatralnaya Zhizn* (*Theatrical Life*). From 1986 to 1988, Editor of the Literature Department of *Ogonyek* (*Beacon*) weekly magazine. From 1988 to 1990, Columnist for *Nashe Nasledie* (*Our Legacy*) magazine. In 1990, Head of the Literature and Art Department of *Nezavissimaya Gazeta* (*Independent Newspaper*).
MAJOR WORKS: "Theater in the 80s"; "Around the Kremlin."
FAMILY: Married with two children.
ADDRESS/TELEPHONE: 5th Yamskoye Pole, Moscow, 125124. 251–4050 (Russian TV).

Karavdin, Victor Semyonovich
POSITION: Board Chairman of Aeroflot Bank
BIRTHPLACE/DATE: Chelyabinsk, 1948
NATIONALITY: Russian
EDUCATION: Graduated from Odessa State University. Majored in Economics.
CAREER: Economist, Senior Economist, Department Head of the Ministry of Civil Aviation.
FAMILY: Married with two children.
ADDRESS/TELEPHONE: 37 Leningradsky Prospekt, Moscow, 125836. 292–0759; Fax: 155–5951.

Karimov, Islam Abguganievich
POSITION: President of the Uzbek Republic; Honored Representative of the Friendship Fund Between the Peoples of Central Asia and Kazakhstan
BIRTHPLACE/DATE: Samarkand, January 30, 1938
NATIONALITY: Uzbek
EDUCATION: Doctor of Economics.
CAREER: From 1960, Assistant Foreman, Foreman, Technologist of the Tekhselmash (Agricultural Machinery) Plant. From 1961, Engineer, Chief Engineer of the Tashkent Aviation Industry Complex. From 1964, member of the Communist Party. From 1966, Department Head, Assistant to the Chairman, Sector Head, Management Director, First Deputy Chairman of the Uzbek State Planning Committee. From 1983, Uzbek Minister of Finance. From 1986, Deputy Chairman, then Chairman of the Uzbek Council of Ministers. From December 1986, First Secretary of the Kashkadarsk Region Party Committee. From 1989, First Secretary of the Uzbekh Communist Party. From 1990 to 1991, member of the Central Committee and Politburo; People's Deputy. In October 1991, joined the Uzbek People's Democratic Party.
HONORS/AWARDS: Order of the Red Banner of Labor; Order of the People's Friendship
FAMILY: Married with two daughters.
ADDRESS/TELEPHONE: 43 Uzbekhestanskaya Street, Tashkent, 170163. 395–456; 395–300 (office).

Karlov, Yuri Yevgenyevich
POSITION: Russian Representative to the Vatican; Ambassador Extraordinary and Plenipotentiary
BIRTHPLACE/DATE: Pepel, Vitebsk region, January 3, 1937
NATIONALITY: Byelorussian
EDUCATION: Graduated from the Moscow State Institute of International Relations.
CAREER: From 1961 to 1963, Secretary of the Consulate Department at the USSR Embassy in Romania. From 1963 to 1965, Attaché of the First European Department; from 1965 to 1967, Third Secretary. From 1967 to 1968, Third Secretary at the USSR Embassy in Italy; from 1968 to 1972, Second Secretary; from 1972 to 1975, First Secretary of the First European Department; from 1975 to 1978, Counsellor. From 1978 to 1980, Counsellor at the USSR Embassy in Italy and Consulate-General in San Marino. From 1980 to 1984, Minister-Counsellor at the USSR Embassy in Italy. In 1984, Expert of the First European Department; from 1984 to 1986, Deputy Department Head. From 1986 to 1989, Secretary of the USSR UNESCO Commission. From 1989 to 1990, Expert of the First European Department.

Honors/Awards: Order of the Badge of Honor.
Family: Married with two children.
Telephone: 244–0862.

Karpets, Igor Ivanovich
Position: Director of the Research Institute for Strengthening Law and Legal Regulations of the Russian Federation Procurator's Office
Birthplace/Date: Leningrad, 1921
Career: From 1952 to 1963, Leningrad Homicide Directorate Head; Deputy Head of the Internal Affairs Directorate. From 1963 to 1969, Director of the Research Institute for Studying Causes and Prevention of Criminality. From 1969 to 1970, Head of the USSR Homicide Directorate; Lieutenant-General of the Militia. From 1979 to 1984, Research Institute Head of the Ministry of Internal Affairs. From 1985, State Justice Counsellor, Second Grade; Vice President of the International Homicide Association; member of the International Criminal Law Directorate in Italy.
Major Works: More than 200 publications in the field of international criminal law and criminology.
Honors/Awards: Order of Lenin; Order of the Badge of Honor; Order of the Patriotic War; USSR State Prize; Vavilov Prize.
Family: Married with a son.
Address/Telephone: 15 Second Zvenigorodskaya Street, Moscow, 123022. 256–0114 (office); 202–2560.

Karpinsky, Len Vyacheslavovich
Position: Editor in Chief of *Moscow News* weekly
Birthplace/Date: Moscow, November 26, 1929
Education: Graduated in 1951 from Moscow State University. Good command of English.
Career: From 1952 to 1955, Lecturer at the Gorky (now Nizhny Novgorod) Teachers' Training Institute of Foreign Languages. From 1955 to 1957, Secretary of the Gorky Regional Komsomol Committee. From 1957 to 1958, First Secretary of the Gorky City Komsomol Committee. From 1958 to 1959, Propaganda Department Head of the Komsomol Central Committee and Editor in Chief of *Molodoy Kommunist* (*Young Communist*) magazine. From 1959 to 1962, Secretary of the Komsomol Central Committee. From 1962 to 1967, Editorial Board Member of *Pravda* (*Truth*) daily. From 1967 to 1969, *Izvestia* (*News*) Correspondent. From 1969 to 1973, Senior Researcher at the Institute of Specific Social Research. From 1973 to 1975, Fiction Department Head of Progress Publishers. From 1975 to 1976, Department Chief Bibliographer of the All-Union Book Chamber. From 1976 to 1979, Freelancer. From 1989, *Izvestia* Columnist. From 1991, Editor in Chief of *Moscow News*. From June 1992, member of the Foreign Policy Council of the Russian Federation Foreign Ministry.
Family: Married with four children.
Address/Telephone: 16/2 Tverskaya Street, Moscow, 103829. 209–1984 (office).

Karpov, Anatoli Yevgenyevich
Position: Chess Player; International Grand Master; President of the International Peace Fund Association
Birthplace/Date: Zlatoustye, Chelyabinsk region, 1951
Nationality: Russian
Education: Graduated in 1978 from the Economics Department at Leningrad State University.
Career: In 1966, Chess Master. From 1970, International Grand Master. In 1976 and 1983, USSR Chess Champion. In 1985, lost the World Chess Championship title to Garry Kasparov. To 1990, President of the International Association of Grand Masters. Until 1991, Editor in Chief of *64 Chess Review* magazine. Former USSR People's Deputy. To 1991, Board Chairman of the Soviet Peace Fund. Council of Trustees Chairman of Chernobyl-Assistance, an international nongovernmental humanitarian organization. Council of Trustees Chairman of the New Names Charity Program.
Major Works: Books on chess theory.
Honors/Awards: USSR Honored Master of Sports (1974); World Chess Champion (1975, 1978, 1981); Oscar Chess Prize (nine times); Order of Lenin (1981); Order of the Red Banner of Labor. Winner of international chess tournaments: Moscow (1971), Hastings (1971, 1972), San Antonio (1972), Madrid (1973), Amsterdam (1985), Brussels (1986), Tilburg (1988).

FAMILY: Married with a son.
ADDRESS/TELEPHONE: 10 Prechistenka Street, Moscow, 119889. 202–4171 (assistant).

Karpov, Victor Pavlovich

POSITION: Diplomat; Ambassador Extraordinary and Plenipotentiary
BIRTHPLACE/DATE: Penza, October 9, 1928
NATIONALITY: Russian
EDUCATION: Graduated from the Moscow State Institute of International Relations of the USSR Foreign Ministry. Doctor of History. Good command of French and English.
CAREER: From 1954 to 1968, Senior Aide, Assistant, Senior Assistant, Department Head of the Information Committee of the USSR Foreign Ministry. From 1958 to 1962, First Secretary of the Foreign Policy Information Board of the USSR Foreign Ministry. From 1962 to 1966, First Secretary, Counsellor at the USSR Embassy in the United States. From 1966 to 1979, Senior Counsellor, Chief Counsellor of the Directorate for Foreign Policy Planning of the USSR Foreign Ministry. From 1979 to 1986, Ambassador at Large of the USSR Foreign Ministry. In 1986, Head of the Directorate for General International Problems; USSR Foreign Ministry Collegium Member. From 1986 to 1988, Head of the Directorate for Arms Limitation and Disarmament Problems of the USSR Foreign Ministry. From 1988 to 1991, Deputy USSR Foreign Minister. Russian Federation Foreign Ministry Reserve.
HONORS/AWARDS: Order of the Red Banner of Labor (1981, 1988); Order of the Badge of Honor (1966); medals.
FAMILY: Married.
ADDRESS/TELEPHONE: 32/34 Smolenskaya-Sennaya Square, Moscow, 121200. 244–1606; 244–2469; 244–4662.

Karyakin, Yuri Fyodorovich

POSITION: Journalist; Senior Researcher at the Russian Academy of Sciences; member of the Consultative Council of the Russian Federation Minister of Culture and Tourism
BIRTHPLACE/DATE: Perm, 1930
NATIONALITY: Russian
EDUCATION: Graduated in 1952 from the Philosophy Department at Moscow State University.
CAREER: From 1956 to 1961, Staff Member of *History of the USSR* journal. From 1961 to 1965, Staff Member of the Prague-based *World Marxist Review*. From 1965 to 1966, *Pravda* (*Truth*) Special Correspondent. From 1967 to 1991, Senior Researcher at the USSR Academy of Sciences' Institute of the International Labor Movement. From 1978, Board Secretary of the USSR Writers' Union. USSR People's Deputy. President of the Russian Federation President's Consultative Council. From December 1991, Board Secretary of the Russian Writers' Union.
MAJOR WORKS: *Raskolnikov's Self-Deception*; *A Banned Book Is Set Free* (about Aleksandr Radishchev, co-authored with Y. Plimak); *Chernyshevsky or Nechayev?* (co-authored with A. Volodin and Y. Plimak). Contributor to the book *No Other Way*, to collections and monographs, as well as to political journals.
FAMILY: Married with children.
ADDRESS/TELEPHONE: 3 Ivan Babushkin Street, Flat #366, Moscow, 117292. 124–1677 (home).

Kasatonov, Igor Vladimirovich

POSITION: First Deputy Commander of the Russian Navy
BIRTHPLACE/DATE: Vladivostok, 1939
CAREER: From 1960 to 1972, Anti-Aircraft Battery Commander on the Gnevny (The Angry) torpedo-boat destroyer. Senior Commander, Commander of the Provorny (The Swift) submarine destroyer of the Black Sea Fleet. From 1972 to 1975, Commander of the Ochakov submarine destroyer of the Black Sea Fleet. From 1975 to 1979, Submarine Destroyers Division Chief of Staff. From 1979 to 1982, Division Commander of the Black Sea Fleet. From 1982 to 1988, Kolsky Flotilla Commander of the Northern Fleet; from 1988 to 1991, First Deputy Commander of the Northern Fleet. From September 1991, Commander of the Black Sea Fleet.
HONORS/AWARDS: Order of the Red Star; nine medals.
FAMILY: Married with a daughter and two sons.
TELEPHONE: 204–2116.

Kashin, Vladimir Ivanovich

POSITION: Party and Political Leader; former Russian Politburo member

BIRTHPLACE/DATE: Nazaryevo village, Ryazansky region, in 1948
NATIONALITY: Russian
CAREER: From 1971, Agronomist at a collective farm in Piazanskay region. Worked as Agronomist, Senior Researcher, Laboratory Head, Chief Agronomist in Krasnay Poyma (Experimental Agricultural Complex) in Moscow region. From 1980, Director of a selection farm in Moscow region. From 1985, First Secretary of the Serebriano-Prudny Party Committee. From 1990, Regional Council of People's Deputies Chairman; Secretary of the Russian Central Committee.
FAMILY: Married with a son.

Kashirin, Yuri Alekseyevich
POSITION: Former Olympic Champion; Road Racing Coach in Egypt
BIRTHPLACE/DATE: Pervoye Storozhevoye village, Voronezh region, January 20, 1959
NATIONALITY: Russian
EDUCATION: Graduated in 1984 from the Rostov-on-Don Institute of Railway Engineering. Good command of English.
CAREER: 1980 Olympic and 1983 World Champion. Silver Prize winner of the 1977 Age-Group Competitions and the 1981 World Championship. Winner of the Milk Race (United Kingdom) in 1979 and 1982; the Tour Breton (France) in 1983; and the Settimana Bergamaska Race (Italy) in 1985. From 1988 to 1992, Coach of the USSR Road Racing National Team.
HONORS/AWARDS: Russian Federation Honored Master of Sports.
FAMILY: Married with two children.
ADDRESS/TELEPHONE: 8 Luzhnetskaya Naberezhnaya, Moscow, 119871. 201–1791.

Kashlev, Yuri Borisovich
POSITION: Russian Federation Ambassador to Poland; Ambassador Extraordinary and Plenipotentiary
BIRTHPLACE/DATE: Tedzene village, Turkmen Republic, 1934
NATIONALITY: Russian
EDUCATION: From 1951 to 1954, student at the Moscow Institute of Oriental Studies. Graduated from the Moscow State Institute of International Relations in 1957. Doctor of History. Good command of English, German, and Chinese.
CAREER: In 1957, Trainee at the USSR Embassy in China. From 1957 to 1961, Interpreter at the Secretariat of the International Agency of Nuclear Energy in Vienna; from 1961 to 1965, Section Head, Department Head of the USSR Committee of Youth Organizations. From 1965 to 1968, Department Instructor of the Central Committee. From 1968 to 1970, Counsellor of the USSR Foreign Ministry Information Department. From 1970 to 1971, Counsellor at the USSR Embassy in Great Britain. From 1971 to 1972, Information Department Counsellor. From 1972 to 1974, Sector Head; from 1974 to 1977, Deputy Department Head; from 1977 to 1978, First Deputy Department Head; from 1978 to 1982, Chief Secretary at the USSR UNESCO Commission. From 1982 to 1986, Information Department Head. From 1986 to 1989, Administration Office Head for Humanitarian and Cultural Relations of the USSR Foreign Ministry. Collegium Member. From 1989 to 1990, Ambassador at Large.
HONORS/AWARDS: Order of the Red Banner of Labor; Order of the People's Friendship; Order of the Badge of Honor.
FAMILY: Married with two children.
ADDRESS/TELEPHONE: Ambasada ZSRR, RP 00–761 Warszawa, Ul. Belwederska, 49. 21–3453; 21–5575; 21–5954; 49–4085 (consulate department); Telex: 63813530 Warszawa.

Kasim-Zade, Elbay Enver Ogly
POSITION: Chief Architect of Baku
BIRTHPLACE/DATE: Baku, 1948
NATIONALITY: Azerbaijanian
CAREER: From 1975, worked in design organizations in Baku. In 1977, became member of the USSR Architects' Union. From 1990, Secretary of the Azerbaijan Architects' Union.
FAMILY: Married with two children.
ADDRESS: 8 Bolshaya Morskaya Street, #45, Baku, 370014.

Kasrashvili, Makvala Filimonovna
POSITION: Opera Singer (lyric/dramatic soprano) of the Bolshoi Academic Theater
BIRTHPLACE/DATE: Kutaisi, 1942
NATIONALITY: Georgian

EDUCATION: Graduated in 1966 from the Tbilisi State Conservatory.
CAREER: From 1966, Soloist of the Bolshoi Academic Theater. Performed at the Metropolitan Opera House, Covent Garden, La Scala, Arena de Verona, and the Chicago and Munich Opera Houses.
MAJOR WORKS: Parts include: Tatiana in *Eugene Onegin*; Natasha Rostova in *War and Peace*; Desdemona in *Othello*; Jeanne D'Arc in *The Maiden of Orlean*; Tosca, Lubka in *Semyon Kotko*; romances by Tchaikovsky, Rachmaninoff, M. de Fali.
HONORS/AWARDS: USSR People's Artist; Second Prize at the Montreal International Vocalists Contest (1973); Georgian State Prize (1983).
ADDRESS/TELEPHONE: The Bolshoi Academic Theater, 1 Teatralnaya Square, Moscow, 103009; 8/2 Okhotny Ryad, Moscow. 292–6690 (office); 292–0304.

Kasyanenko, Vasily Ignatyevich
POSITION: Corresponding Member of the Russian Academy of Sciences
BIRTHPLACE/DATE: Kazakhstan, January 1, 1924
EDUCATION: Graduated in 1955 from the Krasnodar Teachers' Training Institute; in 1960, from the Academy of Social Sciences. Good command of German.
CAREER: From 1948 to 1949, Komsomol Functionary. From 1949 to 1956, Editor in Chief of *Adygeiskaya Pravda* daily. From 1960 to 1962, Department Head, Academic Secretary of the All-Union Znaniye (Knowledge) Society Board. From 1962 to 1982, Staff Member of the Institute of Marxism-Leninism. From 1982 to 1991, Editor in Chief of *Voprosy Istorii KPSS* (*Communist Party Questions of History*) magazine. From 1987, Corresponding Member of the USSR Academy of Sciences. From 1992, Staff Member of the World History Institute of the Russian Academy of Sciences.
MAJOR WORKS: Monographs: *Russian-American Business Relations*; *Gaining USSR Economic Independence*; *Soviet Mode of Life*; *History and Contemporaneity*; *New Economic Policy and Shareholding Entrepreneurship in the USSR*.
FAMILY: Married with two daughters.
ADDRESS/TELEPHONE: 32-A Leninsky Prospekt, Moscow, 117334. 938–1009; 938–1911.

Katushev, Konstantin Fyodorovich
POSITION: Advisor to the Moscow Vice Mayor
BIRTHPLACE/DATE: Bolshoi Boldino, Gorky (now Nizhny Novgorod) region, October 1, 1927
NATIONALITY: Russian
EDUCATION: Graduated in 1951 from Gorky Polytechnic with a degree in Mechanical Engineering Design.
CAREER: From 1951 to 1957, Designer, Senior Designer, then Deputy Chief Designer of the Experimental Designing Department at the Gorky Automobile Plant. Held senior posts in Communist Party organizations. Secretary of the USSR Central Committee, Deputy Chairman of the USSR Council of Ministers, USSR Permanent Representative to the Council for Mutual Economic Assistance (CMEA), USSR Ambassador to the Republic of Cuba, and Chairman of the State Committee for Foreign Economic Relations. From 1988 to 1991, USSR Minister of Foreign Economic Relations.
HONORS/AWARDS: Three Orders of Lenin; two Orders of the October Revolution; three Orders of the Red Banner of Labor; Order of the Badge of Honor; medals.
FAMILY: Married with a daughter.
ADDRESS/TELEPHONE: 4 Skatertny Pereulok, Moscow. 290–2647 (office).

Kebich, Vyacheslav Frantsevich
POSITION: Chairman of the Byelorussian (Belorus) Council of Ministers
BIRTHPLACE/DATE: Byelorussia, 1936
CAREER: From 1958, Engineer-Technologist at the Minsk Plant of Automatic Lines. Director-General of the Minsk Industrial Complex. From 1980, Party Functionary; Second Secretary of the Byelorussian City Communist Party in Minsk; Head of the Department of Heavy Industry of the Byelorussian Central Committee. From 1985, Deputy Chairman of the Byelorussian Council of Ministers; Chairman of the Republican State Planning Committee.
FAMILY: Married with two children
ADDRESS/TELEPHONE: Dom Pravitelstva (House

of Government), Minsk, 10. 29–0010; 29–6007 (office).

Kenyaykin, Valery Fyodorovich

POSITION: Russian Foreign Ministry Head of Personnel; Counsellor Extraordinary and Plenipotentiary, Second Grade
BIRTHPLACE/DATE: Kalinin, February 26, 1946
NATIONALITY: Mordovian
EDUCATION: Graduated from the Institute of Oriental Languages in 1970. From 1982 to 1984, postgraduate student at the Diplomatic Academy.
CAREER: From 1970 to 1972, Aide on Duty at the USSR Embassy in Mali; from 1972 to 1974, Attaché. From 1974 to 1976, Third Secretary of the First African Department; from 1976 to 1977, Second Secretary. From 1977 to 1979, Second Secretary at the USSR Embassy in Belgium; from 1979 to 1982, First Secretary. From 1984 to 1988, First Secretary at the USSR Embassy in Italy; from 1988 to 1989, Counsellor; from 1989 to 1990, Minister-Counsellor at the USSR Embassy in Italy and the Consulate-General in the Republic of San Marino. From 1990 to 1991, Deputy Head of the First European Department. From 1991 to 1992, Acting Head of Personnel and Educational Institutions of the USSR Foreign Ministry.
FAMILY: Married with a son.
TELEPHONE: 244–2680.

Kerestedzhiyants, Leonid Vladimirovich

POSITION: Russian Federation Ambassador to Croatia; Ambassador Extraordinary and Plenipotentiary
BIRTHPLACE/DATE: Melitopol, Zaporozhye region, Ukraine, July 11, 1931
NATIONALITY: Armenian
EDUCATION: Graduated in 1955 from the Leningrad Marine Technical Institute. Good command of Serbo-Croatian and Bulgarian.
CAREER: From 1955 to 1956, Engineer at a Leningrad plant. From 1956 to 1963, Komsomol Official in Leningrad, then Moscow. From 1963 to 1969, Chairman of the Sputnik International Youth Tourism Agency in Moscow. From 1970 to 1973, First Secretary at the USSR Embassy in Yugoslavia; from 1973 to 1975, Counsellor for Cultural Issues. From 1975 to 1978, Section Head of the USSR Foreign Ministry Department for Cultural Ties with Foreign Countries. From 1978 to 1986, Counsellor for Cultural Issues, Attaché for Cultural Issues. Counsellor, Minister-Counsellor at the USSR Embassy in Bulgaria. In 1986, Deputy Head of the USSR Foreign Ministry Personnel Department. From 1986 to 1987, First Deputy Department Head of the USSR Foreign Ministry Main Administration for Personnel and Educational Establishments. From 1987 to 1989, Deputy Chairman of the USSR State Committee for Foreign Tourism in Moscow. From 1989 to 1992, Chairman of the Main Production and Commerce Administration for Services.
FAMILY: Married.
ADDRESS/TELEPHONE: 32/34 Smolenskaya-Sennaya Square, Moscow, 121200. 244–1606; 244–4278.

Kezbers, Ivars Yanovich

POSITION: Former Chairman of the Latvian Democratic Labor Party
BIRTHPLACE/DATE: Valok, 1944
NATIONALITY: Latvian
EDUCATION: Doctor of History.
CAREER: Chief Secretary of the Latvian Youth Organizations Committee; Deputy Department Head of the Latvian Komsomol Central Committee; Instructor of the Latvian Central Committee. From 1973, Attaché, Third Secretary at the USSR Embassy to Sweden. From 1978, Presidium Chairman of the Latvian Committee for Cultural Relations with Compatriots Living Abroad; Chairman of the Latvian State Television and Radio Broadcasting Committee. From 1988, Chairman of the Latvian State Committee for Culture; Secretary of the Latvian Central Committee. After the Latvian Communist Party divided in 1990, elected Central Committee First Secretary of the Latvian Independent Communist Party, which became the Latvian Democratic Labor Party. Director-General of Dansklat Soviet-Danish Joint Venture.
FAMILY: Married with two children.
ADDRESS/TELEPHONE: 33 Duboltu Prospekt, #4, Yurmala, 2015. 76–0016 (home).

Khabitsov, Boris Batrbekovich

POSITION: Director-General of Soyuzforinvest Joint-Venture
BIRTHPLACE/DATE: Vladikavkaz, 1945

EDUCATION: Graduated in 1967 from the Economics Department at Moscow State University. From 1969 to 1970, postgraduate student at Moscow State University. Doctor of Economics. Good command of French.
CAREER: From 1968 to 1969, worked in Algeria. From 1971 to 1980, Science Department Head of the All-Union Technological Information Research Institute. From 1980 to 1987, Directorate Head of the Russian Federation Ministry of Timber Industry. Deputy Board Chairman of the Association of Joint Ventures, International Amalgamations, and Organizations.
FAMILY: Married with two sons.
ADDRESS/TELEPHONE: 4/6 Trety Monetchikovsky Pereulok, Moscow. 233–8787 (office).

Khalitov, Akhmet Kharisovich
POSITION: Member of the Supreme Soviet Council; Secretary-General of the Central Committee of the Liberal-Democratic Party; Editor in Chief of *Liberal* magazine
BIRTHPLACE/DATE: Yelabuga, 1929
NATIONALITY: Tatar
EDUCATION: Graduated from the Moscow Timiryazev Academy of Agriculture, and from the Academy's postgraduate course. Specialized in Agrochemistry.
CAREER: Senior Agronomist, then Chairman of a Moscow region collective farm. Joined the Communist Party in 1954. Laboratory Head at the Soil Institute, then at the USSR Ministry of Agriculture. From 1977, Laboratory Head at the Central Institute of Agrochemical Maintenance of Agriculture. In 1981, expelled from the Communist Party.
MAJOR WORKS: More than a hundred theoretical papers and other publications; holds five patents.
ADDRESS/TELEPHONE: 3 Rybnikov Pereulok, Third Floor, Moscow. 923–6370 (office).

Khaliulin, Vakhit Khadiyevich
POSITION: Deputy Chairman of Roskomagentstvo
BIRTHPLACE/DATE: Moscow, 1946
NATIONALITY: Tatar
EDUCATION: Graduated in 1971 from the Moscow Power Engineering Institute; in 1979, from the Academy of Foreign Trade. Speaks German and Hungarian.
CAREER: From 1973 to 1976, Senior Controller at a specialized design office of gas chromatographs. From 1979 to 1981, Senior Engineer at Licensintorg Foreign Trade Association. From 1981 to 1986, worked at the Soviet Trade Mission in Hungary. From 1986 to 1991, Senior Expert, Deputy Director of the Licensintorg Company.
FAMILY: Married with three children.
ADDRESS/TELEPHONE: 5 Yaroslavskoye Chaussée, Moscow, 129348. 182–2117; 182–3329 (office).

Kharichev, Igor Aleksandrovich
POSITION: Coordinating Council Member of the Democratic Russia Movement; member of the Democratic Congress Consultative Council
BIRTHPLACE/DATE: Samara, 1947
NATIONALITY: Russian
EDUCATION: Graduated in 1971 from Latvian State University; in 1975, completed the postgraduate program at the Astronomy Council of the USSR Academy of Sciences in Moscow. Speaks English and Lettish.
CAREER: From 1975 to 1989, worked at the Construction Materials Research Institute. From 1989, engaged in scientific and journalistic work, wrote articles on culture and science in *Literaturnaya Gazeta* (*Literary Newspaper*), *Nedelya* (*Week*) newspapers, and other publications. Involved in politics from February 1989. Agent and Coordinator of Sergey Stankevich's Election Campaign. From May 1989 to 1990, member of the Moscow People's Front, organized the Cheryomyshki District Electors' Club; from August 1989 to 1990, Coordinating Council Member of the Moscow Electors' Association. From April 1990, organized trips for Russian political activists to Baltic countries and the Ukraine on behalf of the Sodruzhestvo (Commonwealth) Fund. From June 1990 to November 1991, Organizing Department Head of the Sodruzhestvo Fund.
FAMILY: Married with three children.
ADDRESS/TELEPHONE: 26 Litovsky Boulevard, Flat #244, Moscow, 117588. 425–5397 (home); 206–4327 (office).

Kharlanov, Iven Ivenovich
POSITION: Specialist-Expert of the Russian Federation President's Council of Experts
BIRTHPLACE/DATE: Omsk, 1959
NATIONALITY: Russian
EDUCATION: Graduated in 1980 from the Economics Department at Moscow State University. Speaks English and French.
CAREER: From 1980 to 1990, Junior Researcher at the Institute of Scientific Information on Social Sciences of the USSR Academy of Sciences. From 1990 to 1991, Expert of the Russian Federation Supreme Soviet Chairman's Council of Experts. From 1990, Sverdlovsk District Deputy in Moscow.
FAMILY: Married with a son.
ADDRESS/TELEPHONE: The Kremlin, Moscow. 925–0728 (office).

Khazanov, Gennadi Victorovich
POSITION: Artistic Director of the Mono Variety Show Company
BIRTHPLACE/DATE: Moscow, 1945
EDUCATION: Graduated in 1969 from the Moscow State Variety Circus School.
CAREER: From 1961 to 1964, Adjuster at the Moscow Radio-Assembly Plant. From 1969 to 1973, Comedian of the Roskontsert (Russian Concert Association). From 1979 to 1987, Actor of the Moskontsert (Moscow Concert Association). Member of the Russian Union of Theater Workers.
MAJOR WORKS: Variety performances: "The Selected"; "Little Tragedies"; "Yesterday, Today, Tomorrow . . . ." Regularly participates in TV entertainment programs: "Around Things Laughable"; "Full House." Starred in the film *Ha-Ha-Khazanov.* Involved in *Players–21* theatrical performance.
FAMILY: Married with a daughter.
ADDRESS/TELEPHONE: 15 Kalanchevskaya Street, Moscow. 204–8406 (office)

Khazanov, Valery Gershevich
POSITION: Executive Secretary of the Russian Center of the International Theater Institute
BIRTHPLACE/DATE: Lvov, 1948
EDUCATION: Graduated in 1972 from the Moscow Institute of Foreign Languages; in 1986, completed postgraduate study at the Art Criticism Research Institute. Speaks French, English, Polish, Italian, and Spanish.
CAREER: From 1972 to 1986, Senior Consultant to the Soviet Center of the International Theater Institute. From 1986 and 1992, Foreign Commission Chairman of the USSR Union of Theater Workers. From 1986, Executive Secretary of the Soviet Center of the International Theater Institute. From 1987, Board Member of the American-Soviet Theatrical Initiative (ASTI).
FAMILY: Single.
ADDRESS/TELEPHONE: 10 Strastnoi Boulevard, Moscow, 103031. 250–9298 (office); Fax: 230–2258.

Khizha, Georgy Stepanovich
POSITION: Russian Federation Government Deputy Chairman of the Russian Federation Commission for Exports Control
BIRTHPLACE/DATE: Ashkhabad, May 2, 1938
NATIONALITY: Russian
EDUCATION: Graduated in 1961 from the Leningrad Polytechnical Institute; trained as Engineer-Mechanic. Doctor of Technology. Speaks English.
CAREER: Former Director-General of the Svetlana Association. Nominated USSR People's Deputy, but withdrew candidacy. Chairman of the St. Petersburg Association of Industrial Enterprises. To 1992, Deputy Mayor-Chairman of the St. Petersburg Collegium.
HONORS/AWARDS: USSR State Prize.
FAMILY: Married with two daughters.
ADDRESS/TELEPHONE: 4 Staraya Square, Moscow. 206–2744 (office).

Khlystun, Victor Nikolayevich
POSITION: Russian Federation Minister of Agriculture; Chairman of the Russian Government Commission for Social Development of the Countryside
BIRTHPLACE/DATE: Kokchetav region, Kazakhstan, 1946
NATIONALITY: Russian
EDUCATION: Graduated in 1970 from the Moscow Civil Engineering Institute. Doctor of Economics.
CAREER: From 1970 to 1971, Assistant Lecturer of the Land Use Division at the Moscow Institute

of Land Tenure Engineering. From 1977 to 1980, Communist Party Bureau Secretary. From 1980 to 1990, Pro-Rector for Scientific Work at the Moscow Civil Engineering Institute. From 1990 to 1991, Chairman of the Russian Federation Committee for Land Reform. In 1991, Chairman of the Russian Federation State Committee for Land Reform and Support of Peasant Farms.
FAMILY: Married with two children.
ADDRESS/TELEPHONE: 1 Orlikov Pereulok, Moscow. 207–4243; 207–8936 (office).

Khodorkovsky, Mikhail Borisovich
POSITION: Board of Directors Chairman of the Association of Credit and Financial Enterprises (MENATEP)
BIRTHPLACE/DATE: Moscow, 1963
NATIONALITY: Russian
EDUCATION: Graduated in 1986 from the Moscow Mendeleyev Institute of Chemical Technology (MKhTI). Speaks English.
CAREER: From 1986 to 1987, Deputy Secretary of the MkhTI Komsomol Committee. From 1987 to 1989, Director of the Youth Center for Scientific and Technological Activity, and the Youth Initiative Foundation. From 1989 to 1990, Board Chairman of the Commercial Innovation Bank for Scientific and Technological Progress. From 1990 to 1991, Director-General of MENATEP.
FAMILY: Married with two children.
ADDRESS/TELEPHONE: 20 Shchipok Street, Moscow, 113054. 235–7752 (office).

Khomsky, Pavel Osipovich
POSITION: Chief Stage Director of the Mossoviet Theater
BIRTHPLACE/DATE: Moscow, 1925
EDUCATION: For four years studied at the State Institute of Dramatic Art, then transferred to and graduated from the Opera and Drama Studio at the Stanislavsky and Nemirovich-Danchenko Musical Theater; during World War II, studied at an artillery school.
CAREER: From 1943, performed at an army theater at the front. During the 1950s and 1960s, Stage Director of the Riga Theater of Russian Drama, the Lenin Komsomol Theater for Young Spectators in Riga, the Lenin Komsomol Theater in Leningrad, and the Moscow Theater for Young Spectators. From 1973, Stage Director; from 1985, Chief Stage Director of the Mossoviet Theater. Professor at the Lunacharsky State Dramatic Art Institute. From December 1991, Professor at the Russian Dramatic Art Academy.
MAJOR WORKS: Productions include: *The Brothers Karamazov*; *Maxim at the End of the Millennium*; *Jesus Christ Superstar*; *Halfway to the Top*.
HONORS/AWARDS: Russian Federation Honored Worker of Art; Russian Federation People's Artist.
FAMILY: Married with three children.
ADDRESS/TELEPHONE: 16 Bolshaya Sadovaya Street, Moscow. 299–4437.

Khozin, Grigory Sergeyevich
POSITION: Member of the Higher Ecological Council of Russia
BIRTHPLACE/DATE: Novosibirsk, 1933
NATIONALITY: Russian
EDUCATION: Graduated in 1956 from the Moscow Institute of Foreign Languages. In 1970, defended thesis for doctoral degree; in 1985, for postdoctoral degree. Doctor of History; Professor. Speaks English, German, and French.
CAREER: From 1956 to 1962, Officer-Instructor of the Minsk Suvorov College. From 1962 to 1968, Staff Member of *Aviation and Astronautics* magazine. From 1968 to 1985, Senior Researcher, Section Head at the Institute of the U.S. and Canada. From 1985, Philosophy Professor at Moscow University. From 1991, UN Expert on the transfer of resources from military activities to environmental protection. Member of the Astronautics Committee of Russia. Member of the Tsiolkovsky Academy of Astronautics. Member of the Journalists' Union.
FAMILY: Married with two children.
ADDRESS/TELEPHONE: Moscow State University, Leninsky Gory, Moscow, 117513. 939–2745 (office).

Khrennikov, Tikhon Nikolayevich
POSITION: Coordinating Council Co-Chairman of the International Association of Composers' Organizations; Composer
BIRTHPLACE/DATE: Yelets, 1913
NATIONALITY: Russian

EDUCATION: Graduated from the Moscow State Conservatory. Professor.
CAREER: From 1941 to 1954, Music Director of the Central Soviet Army Theater in Moscow. From 1948, Secretary-General of the USSR Composers' Union. From 1966, Professor at the Moscow Conservatory. USSR People's Deputy. Member of the Council of Nationalities' Foreign Affairs Commission.
MAJOR WORKS: Operas include: *In the Storm*; *Frol Skobelev*; *The Mother*. Also composed concertos for the violin, piano and orchestra, symphonies.
HONORS/AWARDS: Hero of Socialist Labor; Lenin and State Prizes (1942, 1946, 1952, 1967); Russian Federation State Prize (1979); USSR People's Artist.
FAMILY: Married with a child.
ADDRESS/TELEPHONE: 8/10 Nezhdanova Street, Moscow, 103009. 229–5444; 229–3521 (office).

Khshtoyan, Vilen Vartanovich
POSITION: Director-General of the United Prodex Company; Board Chairman of the Sodruzhestvo (Commonwealth) Trading House
BIRTHPLACE/DATE: Moscow, 1932
NATIONALITY: Armenian
EDUCATION: Graduated in 1956 from the Moscow Institute of Finance; in 1967, from the All-Union Foreign Trade Academy.
CAREER: From 1956 to 1958, Senior Economist of the USSR State Bank. From 1958 to 1962, Department Director of the Russian-Iranian Bank. From 1962, Administration Head, Deputy Main Administration Head of the Vneshtorg (Foreign Trade) All-Union Association. From 1971 to 1974, Deputy USSR Trade Representative to Egypt. From 1982 to 1987, Deputy USSR Trade Representative to Malaysia. From 1988 to January 1992, Vneshposyltorg (Foreign Trade) Director-General. From 1990 to January 1992, Board Chairman of the Torgovy Dom (House of Trade) All-Union Association.
HONORS/AWARDS: Order of the Badge of Honor.
FAMILY: Married with a daughter and a grandson.
ADDRESS/TELEPHONE: 2 Tryokhgorny Val, Moscow. 205–6252; 255–0101 (office).

Khudonazarov, Dovlatnazar
POSITION: Chairman of the Confederation of Film Makers' Unions
BIRTHPLACE/DATE: Khorog, Tajikistan, 1944
NATIONALITY: Tajik
EDUCATION: Graduated in 1965 from the USSR State Institute of Cinematography.
CAREER: From 1958 to 1960, Assistant Cameraman at Tajikfilm Studio; from 1965, Cameraman, Chief Cameraman, Film Director. First Secretary of the Tajik Film Makers' Union. USSR People's Deputy.
HONORS/AWARDS: Tajikistan Honored Worker of Arts; Rudaki State Prize of Tajikistan; government awards.
FAMILY: Married with a son and a daughter.
ADDRESS/TELEPHONE: 13 Vasilyevskaya Street, Moscow, 123825. 250–4114; 251–5370; 251–1440.

Khvatov, Gennadi Aleksandrovich
POSITION: Commander of the Soviet Pacific Fleet; Admiral
BIRTHPLACE/DATE: Myshkino village, Yaroslavl region, 1934
NATIONALITY: Russian
EDUCATION: Graduated from the Naval Academy and the General Staff Academy.
CAREER: From 1952, served in the USSR Armed Forces. Division Commander, Flotilla Commander, Chief of Staff, First Deputy Fleet Commander.
FAMILY: Married with two sons.
ADDRESS/TELEPHONE: 12 Frunze Street, Moscow. 293–2869; 293–1413 (office).

Khvorostovsky, Dmitri Aleksandrovich
POSITION: Opera Singer
BIRTHPLACE/DATE: Krasnoyarsk, 1962
EDUCATION: Graduated in 1987 from the Krasnoyarsk State Arts Institute.
CAREER: From 1985, performed at the Krasnoyarsk Opera and Ballet Theater. In 1991, Soloist of the Moscow Opera Center for Art (MOZART).
HONORS/AWARDS: First Prize at the Glinka All-Union Vocalists Contest (1987); First Prize at the International Vocalists Contest (Toulouse, France, 1988); First Prize (and the title World's Best Baritone) at the BBC Vocalists Contest in Cardiff

(Great Britain); Russian Federation Honored Artist.
FAMILY: Married.
ADDRESS/TELEPHONE: 15 Shmidtovsky Proyezd, P.O. Box 202, Moscow, 123100. 944–5913 (office).

Kireyev, Genrikh Vasilyevich
POSITION: Ambassador at Large; Ambassador Extraordinary and Plenipotentiary
BIRTHPLACE/DATE: Vashutino village, Moscow region, April 13, 1929
EDUCATION: Graduated from the Moscow State Institute of International Relations in 1952. From 1952 to 1954, studied at the USSR Embassy Trainee's School in China. From 1954 to 1956, studied at the Diplomatic Institute in Peking.
CAREER: From 1956 to 1959, Secretary at the USSR Consulate-General in Shanghai. From 1959 to 1960, Attaché of the Far East Department. From 1960 to 1963, Third Secretary at the USSR Embassy in China; from 1963 to 1965, Consulate Department Head at the USSR Embassy in China; from 1965 to 1966, First Secretary. From 1966 to 1969, First Secretary of the Far East Department; from 1969 to 1970, Counsellor. From 1970 to 1975, Sector Head of the First Far East Department. From 1975 to 1979, Deputy Department Head. From 1979 to 1984, Minister-Counsellor at the USSR Embassy in China. From 1984 to 1986, Deputy Department Head of the First Far East Department. From 1986 to 1987, Deputy Head of the Socialist Countries of Asia Department. From 1987 to 1989, Department Head. From 1989, USSR Delegation Head at the neogtiations with China for arms limitation and strengthening border relations. From 1992, Ambassador at Large, Russian Delegation Head of the Joint Russian-Chinese Frontier Committee.
HONORS/AWARDS: Order of the Badge of Honor.
FAMILY: Married with two children.
TELEPHONE: 244–4262.

Kirichenko, Vadim Nikitovich
POSITION: Deputy Chairman of the Russian Federation State Committee for Economic Cooperation with CIS Member-States
BIRTHPLACE/DATE: Ramenskoye village, Moscow region, 1931
NATIONALITY: Russian.
EDUCATION: Graduated in 1953 from Moscow State University. Doctor of Economics; Professor.
CAREER: From 1957 to 1961, Lecturer at Moscow University. From 1961, worked from Researcher to Director of the Economics Research Institute of the USSR State Planning Committee. From 1986 to 1987, Director of the Institute of Economic Research and Head of the Economics and Social Development Prospects Department of the USSR State Planning Committee. From 1987, Economics Department Head of the USSR Council of Ministers' Business Administration. From 1989 to 1991, Chairman of the USSR State Committee for Statistics. From 1991, Deputy Chairman of the Russian Federation State Committee for Economic Cooperation with CIS Member-States.
FAMILY: Married with a son and a daughter.
ADDRESS/TELEPHONE: 7 Varvarka Street, Moscow, 103012. 206–7022 (office); 290–2482 (home).

Kirill (Gundyayev, Vladimir Mikhailovich)
POSITION: Metropolitan of Smolensk and Kaliningrad; Permanent Member of the Holy Synod of the Russian Orthodox Church; Chairman of the Foreign Relations Department of the Moscow Patriarchy
BIRTHPLACE/DATE: Leningrad, 1946
NATIONALITY: Russian
CAREER: From 1970 to 1971, Assistant Inspector at the Leningrad Ecclesiastical Academy. From 1971 to 1974, Russian Orthodox Church Representative to the World Council of Churches in Geneva. From 1974 to 1985, Rector of the Leningrad Ecclesiastical Academy, Bishop, then Archbishop of Vyborg. From 1985, Archbishop of Smolensk and Vyazma. From 1990, Chairman of the Foreign Relations Department of the Moscow Patriarchy, Metropolitan of Smolensk and Kaliningrad. From 1991, Archbishop of Smolensk and Kaliningrad.
ADDRESS/TELEPHONE: The Foreign Relations Department of the Moscow Patriarchy, 2 Danilovsky Val, Moscow, 113191. 954–0454 (secretary); 230–2118; 230–2431.

Kirpichnikov, Yuri Aleksandrovich
POSITION: Editor in Chief of *Delovoy Mir* (*Business World*) newspaper
BIRTHPLACE/DATE: Barnaul, 1939
EDUCATION: Graduated in 1973 from the Journalism Department at Moscow State University. Command of French.
CAREER: From 1956 to 1963, Mine Worker at the Aktashsky Ore Factory. From 1968 to 1971, Interpreter in Guinea and Congo. From 1973 to 1980, Editor of *Za Rubezhom* (*Abroad*) weekly. From 1980 to 1982, International Department Head of *Gudok* (*Factory Bell*) newspaper. From 1982 to 1986, Editor-Consultant of the Prague-based *World Marxist Review* journal. In 1986, Editor-Consultant of *Kommunist* magazine. In 1987, Collegium Member and International Department Editor of *Socialisticheskaya Industria* (*Socialist Industry*) daily. Member of the International Congress of Industrialists and Entrepreneurs. Member of the Economic and Social Reforms Foundation. Member of the Foreign Investments in Russia Foundation.
FAMILY: Married with two children.
ADDRESS/TELEPHONE: 39 Kutuzovsky Prospekt, Moscow, 121170. 249–9864 (office).

Kiselev, Sergey Borisovich
POSITION: Ambassador to Seychelles; Counsellor Extraordinary and Plenipotentiary, Second Grade
BIRTHPLACE/DATE: Moscow, October 16, 1947
NATIONALITY: Russian
EDUCATION: Graduated from the Moscow State Institute of International Relations in 1971. From 1990 to 1991, student of the advanced course for senior diplomats at the Diplomatic Academy of the USSR Foreign Ministry.
CAREER: From 1971 to 1972, Trainee at the USSR Embassy in Burma; from 1972 to 1974, Senior Aide-Trainee; from 1974 to 1975, Attaché. From 1975 to 1978, Attaché of the Southern Asia Department. From 1979 to 1980, Third Secretary of the Southeast Asia Department. From 1980 to 1982, Second Secretary. From 1982 to 1983, First Secretary of the Secretariat of the USSR Deputy Foreign Minister. From 1983 to 1986, First Secretary of the Secretariat of the First USSR Deputy Foreign Minister. From 1986 to 1987, Counsellor. From 1987 to 1988, Department Head of the USSR Foreign Ministry's General Secretariat.
FAMILY: Married.
TELEPHONE: 244–4944 (Moscow).

Kiselev, Vladimir Ivanovich
POSITION: Ambassador to Bolivia; Counsellor Extraordinary and Plenipotentiary, First Grade
BIRTHPLACE/DATE: Slavyansk, Donetsk region, January 16, 1935
NATIONALITY: Ukrainian
EDUCATION: Graduated from Moscow State University in 1957. From 1967 to 1969, postgraduate student at Donetsk State University. From 1974 to 1977, postgraduate student at the Diplomatic Academy of the USSR Foreign Ministry. Doctor of History.
CAREER: From 1957 to 1958, Department Head of the Gorlovka City Komsomol Committee. From 1958 to 1960, Instructor, Deputy Department Head of the Donetsk Region Komsomol Committee; from 1960 to 1963, Secretary; from 1963 to 1965, Secretary of the Industrial Komsomol Committee. From 1965 to 1967, and from 1969 to 1970, Senior Lecturer at Donetsk State University. From 1970 to 1972, Secretary of the Donetsk State University Party Committee. From 1972 to 1973, Docent. From 1973 to 1974, First Secretary of the Voroshilovgrad District Party Committee in Donetsk. In 1977, First Secretary of the Latin America Department. From 1977 to 1980, First Secretary at the USSR Embassy in Cuba. From 1980 to 1984, Attaché. From 1984 to 1985, Counsellor of the First Latin America Department. From 1985 to 1987, Acting Sector Head. From 1987 to 1991, Minister-Counsellor at the USSR Embassy in Cuba.
FAMILY: Married with three children.
TELEPHONE: 244–3263.

Kiselev, Yevgeni Alekseyevich
POSITION: Host of the "Itogi" (Results) political program of the Russian Ostankino TV and Radio Broadcasting Company
BIRTHPLACE/DATE: Moscow, 1956
CAREER: From 1979 to 1981, Interpreter for Soviet Military Counsellors in Afghanistan. From 1981 to 1984, Language Teacher at the KGB Higher School. From 1984 to 1987, involved in

broadcasting for countries in the Middle and Central East. From 1987 to 1990, Editor in Chief of the TV Information Department; Correspondent; Commentator; Host of the "Vremya" (Time) and "Utro" (Morning) programs. In 1991, Host of "Vesti" (News) TV program.
FAMILY: Married with a son.
ADDRESS/TELEPHONE: 19 Academician Korolev Street, Moscow, 127000. 215–8246; 217–9216 (office); 181–4446 ("Itogi").

Kisin, Victor Ivanovich
POSITION: Russian Federation Trade Representative to Portugal; Vice President of the Russian Union of Industrialists and Entrepreneurs
BIRTHPLACE/DATE: Moscow, March 9, 1941
NATIONALITY: Russian
EDUCATION: Graduated in 1969 from the Moscow Gubkin Institute of Oil and Gas. Doctor of Technology.
CAREER: From 1966 to 1990, worked from Fitter to Head of the Modern Technology Department. USSR People's Deputy. Coordinating Secretary of the Scientific and Industrial Group of the USSR People's Deputies. From July 1990 to 1991, Russian Federation Minister of Industry. Vice President of the USSR Scientific and Industrial Union. From August to November 1991, member of the Committee for the Efficient Management of the USSR National Economy. Corresponding Member of the Academy of Engineering.
FAMILY: Married with two children.
ADDRESS/TELEPHONE: 64 Leninsky Prospekt, Flat #435, Moscow, 117296. 206–7016 (office); 930–0678 (home).

Kisin, Yevgeni Vladimirovich
POSITION: Pianist
BIRTHPLACE/DATE: Moscow, 1971
EDUCATION: Graduated from the Gnesiny Specialized Secondary Music School in Moscow. Studied with A.P. Kantor at the Moscow Gnesiny State Musical Institute.
CAREER: At 11, performed first solo concert. At 12, debuted at the Grand Hall of the Moscow Conservatory; played two Chopin concertos with orchestra conducted by Dmitri Kitayenko. Toured Britain, Germany, Japan, United States, France, the Netherlands, Spain, and other countries. Performed a concert of Tchaikovsky works with the Berlin Philharmonic Society under the baton of Herbert von Karajan. Performances are widely recorded both in Russia and abroad.
HONORS/AWARDS: Golden Diapason Prize (France); Edison Prize (the Netherlands); Crystal Prize (Osaka, Japan); International Prize of the Italian Music Academy (1991).
FAMILY: Single.
ADDRESS/TELEPHONE: 14/2 Herzen Street, Moscow. 269–8657 (home); 923–9732 (Goskotcert).

Kislov, Aleksandr Konstantinovich
POSITION: Director of the Russian Academy of Sciences' Institute of Peace; Deputy Director of the Russian Academy of Sciences' Institute of the World Economy and International Relations
BIRTHPLACE/DATE: Moscow, September 11, 1929
NATIONALITY: Russian
EDUCATION: Graduated in 1952 from the Moscow State Institute of International Relations of the USSR Foreign Ministry. Doctor of Law; Doctor of History (1985); Professor (1989).
CAREER: Joined the Communist Party in 1954. From 1955 to 1971, worked at TASS (Telegraph Agency of the Soviet Union). From 1971 to 1986, worked at the Institute of the U.S. and Canada.
MAJOR WORKS: Scientific works on U.S. foreign policy and the situation in the Middle East.
FAMILY: Married with three children.
ADDRESS/TELEPHONE: 23 Profsoyuznaya Street, GSP–7, Moscow, 117571. 128–9389 (office); 438–6159 (home).

Kislyak, Sergey Ivanovich
POSITION: Board Head of the International Scientific and Technical Cooperation; Counsellor, First Grade
BIRTHPLACE/DATE: Moscow, September 1950
NATIONALITY: Ukrainian
EDUCATION: Graduated from the Moscow Institute of Engineering Physics. From 1974 to 1977, postgraduate student at the All-Union Foreign Trade Academy.
CAREER: From 1973 to 1974, Engineer-Physicist at the Kurchatov Atomic Energy Institute. From 1977 to 1980, Third Secretary of the International Organizations Department of the USSR Foreign

Ministry; from 1980 to 1981, Second Secretary. From 1981 to 1985, Second Secretary at the USSR Permanent Mission to the UN. From 1985 to 1988, First Secretary at the USSR Embassy in the United States. From 1988 to 1991, Deputy Head of the International Organizations Department.
HONORS/AWARDS: Medal For Labor Valor.
FAMILY: Married with a daughter.
TELEPHONE: 244–2694.

Kivelidi, Ivan Kharlampyevich
POSITION: Director-General of the Vneshekonomkooperatsiya (Foreign Economic Cooperation) Association; Vice President of the Russian League of Entrepreneurs and Cooperative Societies
BIRTHPLACE/DATE: Sukhumi, Abkhasia, 1949
NATIONALITY: Greek
EDUCATION: Graduated in 1966 from the Moscow Gubkin Institute of Oil and Gas. Command of English.
CAREER: From 1989 to 1990, Director-General of the Interagro Association. In 1991, member of the USSR President's Entrepreneurship Council.
FAMILY: Divorced with two children.
ADDRESS/TELEPHONE: 14 Pereulok Tokmakova, Moscow. 267–8548 (office); 261–2276 (League).

Klimov, Fyodor Matveyevich
POSITION: Board Chairman of the Orbita Commercial Bank
BIRTHPLACE/DATE: Mogilev region, Byelorussia, 1935
NATIONALITY: Russian
EDUCATION: Graduated from the Byelorussia State Institute of National Economy, majoring in Administration and Economics.
CAREER: Bookkeeper at a clothing factory in Kaluga, Chief Accountant at the Kalugapribor (Kaluga Equipment) Plant, Finance Board Head of the USSR Ministry of Communciation.
FAMILY: Married with a son and a grandson.
ADDRESS/TELEPHONE: 6 Vtoroy Spasonalivkovsky Pereulok, Moscow. 238–8720 (office).

Klimov, Oleg Aleksandrovich
POSITION: President of the Exportkhleb (Bread Export) Foreign Economic Joint-Stock Company
BIRTHPLACE/DATE: Moscow, 1936
NATIONALITY: Russian
EDUCATION: Graduated in 1958 from the Institute of Foreign Trade.
CAREER: From 1964 to 1967, worked at the All-Union Exportkhleb Association; Staff Member of the Trade Mission to Kuwait. From 1974 to 1978, Deputy Department Head, then Department Head of the USSR Foreign Trade Ministry's Main Administration. Staff Member of the Trade Mission in Sweden. Director of the Soyuzpromexport (Industrial Export Union) Firm. Deputy Director-General of Exportkhleb; from July 1987, Director-General.
FAMILY: Married with three children.
ADDRESS/TELEPHONE: 32/34 Smolenskaya-Sennaya Square, Moscow. 244–4701 (office).

Klimov, Yelem Germanovich
POSITION: Film Director; member of the Consultative Council of the Russian Federation Minister of Culture and Tourism
BIRTHPLACE/DATE: Volgograd, 1933
EDUCATION: Graduated in 1957 from the Moscow Aviation Institute; in 1964, from the State Film Institute.
CAREER: Engineer at the Mikhail Mil Experimental Designers Office. Worked at Mosfilm (Moscow Film) Studio. In 1960, Director of the film *Fiancé*; in 1964, Director of *Welcome, or Unauthorized Persons Not Admitted.* From 1986 to 1990, First Secretary of the Board of the USSR Union of Film Makers. From 1991, member of the European Cinematography Academy.
MAJOR WORKS: *Sport, Sport, Sport, And Still I Believe . . .*; *The Agony*; *Parting*; and *Go and See.*
HONORS/AWARDS: Honorary Member of the American and British Academies of Cinematography; Fipressi Prize at the Venice Film Festival (1982); Gold Prize of the Fourteenth Moscow Film Festival; Russian Federation Honored Artist.
FAMILY: Widower with a son.
ADDRESS/TELEPHONE: 13 Vasilyevskaya Street, Moscow, 123825. 242–4247 (home).

Klimova, Marina Vladimirovna
POSITION: Figure Skater
BIRTHPLACE/DATE: Sverdlovsk, 1966
EDUCATION: Graduated from the State Institute of Physical Education.
CAREER: From 1973, Figure Skater. From 1981,

member of the USSR National Team. Bronze Medalist at the 1984 Winter Olympics. Finalist at the 1988 Winter Olympics and at the 1985 through 1987 European and World Championships. 1992 Olympic Champion.
HONORS/AWARDS: USSR Honored Master of Sports.
FAMILY: Married.
ADDRESS/TELEPHONE: 8 Luzhnetskaya Naberezhnaya, Moscow. 201–1231 (Figure Skating Federation).

Klyuchnikov, Igor Konstantinovich
POSITION: Board Chairman of the St. Petersburg Stock Exchange; Professor at St. Petersburg (formerly Leningrad) State University
BIRTHPLACE/DATE: Chernovtsy, Ukraine, 1949
NATIONALITY: Russian
EDUCATION: Graduated in 1970 from the Leningrad Institute of Finance and Economics. Doctor of Economics. Command of English.
CAREER: From 1970 to 1977, Economist, Senior Economist, Department Head of the Leningrad USSR State Bank. From 1977 to 1981, Lecturer, Assistant Professor at the Leningrad Marine Technical Institute. From 1981 to 1983, Assistant Professor at the Leningrad Engineering and Economics Institute. From 1983 to 1986, Academic Secretary of the Economics Department of the Leningrad USSR Academy of Sciences. From 1986, Management Division Professor at St. Petersburg State University.
FAMILY: Married with a child.
ADDRESS/TELEPHONE: 36 Plekhanov Street, St. Petersburg, 190107. 312–7993 (office).

Klyuyev, Vladimir Vladimirovich
POSITION: Director-General of the Moscow Spectr (Spectrum) Research Industrial Association; Doctor of Technical Science; Professor
BIRTHPLACE/DATE: Moscow, 1937
NATIONALITY: Russian
CAREER: From 1960 to 1964, Junior Researcher at the Moscow Bauman State Technical Institute. From 1964 to 1970, Senior Researcher, Department Head of the Moscow Research Institute of Introscopy; from 1970 to 1976, Director. From 1976 to 1986, Director-General of Spectr. From 1986 to 1988, First Secretary of the Leningrad District Communist Party. From 1987, member of the USSR Academy of Sciences. Chairman of the International Standardization Committee.
HONORS/AWARDS: USSR Council of Ministers Prize.
MAJOR WORKS: More than 200 scientific publications in the field of technical diagnostics.
FAMILY: Married with two sons.
ADDRESS/TELEPHONE: 135 Usachev Street, Moscow, 119048. 245–5657 (secretary).

Kobets, Konstantin Ivanovich
POSITION: Russian Federation State Counsellor for Defense; Chief Military Inspector of the Russian Federation Armed Forces; Army General
BIRTHPLACE/DATE: Kiev, July 16, 1939
NATIONALITY: Russian
EDUCATION: Graduated in 1959 from the Kiev Institute of Communications; in 1967, from the Military Academy of Communications; in 1978, from the General Staff Academy. Doctor of Military Science; Professor.
CAREER: From 1978 to 1986, Signals District Commanding Officer, Signals Troops Commanding Officer, Deputy Chief of Staff of the Far Eastern Forces. From 1987, Signals Commander of the USSR Armed Forces, Deputy Chief of the General Staff. From August 19 to August 21, 1991, Russian Federation Defense Minister. From September 1991, Chairman of the Russian Federation State Committee for Defense and Security, Russian Federation State Counsellor for Defense, Chairman of the Committee for the Preparation and Realization of Army Reforms. Russian Federation People's Deputy.
HONORS/AWARDS: Numerous government awards.
FAMILY: Married with a son.
ADDRESS/TELEPHONE: 2 Krasnopresnenskaya Naberezhnaya, Moscow. 205–6505 (office).

Koksanov, Igor Vladimirovich
POSITION: Vice President of the Sudprom Russian Shipbuilding Corporation
BIRTHPLACE/DATE: Perm, 1928
NATIONALITY: Russian
EDUCATION: Graduated in 1955 from the Leningrad Marine Technical Institute.
CAREER: Mathematics Teacher at a night school,

Military Representative at a shipbuilding works. From 1961 to 1965, worked at the Leningrad Rubin Design and Assembly Office. From 1965 to 1973, Chief Administrative Deputy Head of the USSR Shipbuilding Industry Ministry. From 1973 to 1985, Shipbuilding Industry Section Head of the Central Committee's Defense Industry Department. From 1985, First Deputy Minister. From 1988 to November 1991, USSR Minister of Shipbuilding Industry.
HONORS/AWARDS: Order of the October Revolution.
FAMILY: Married.
ADDRESS/TELEPHONE: 11 Sadovo-Kudrinskaya, Moscow, 123231. 252–1447; 252–7407 (both office).

Kokshirov, Boris Nikolayevich
POSITION: Director of the Waterproof Fabrics Industrial Complex; member of the Russian Federation Supreme Soviet Committee for Industry and Power Engineering; Russian Federation People's Deputy
BIRTHPLACE/DATE: Pavlovsky Posad, Moscow region, March 14, 1933
EDUCATION: Graduated in 1967 from the Moscow Textile Institute.
FAMILY: Married with three children.
ADDRESS/TELEPHONE: 20 Entuziastov Street, Flat #14, Balashov, Saratov Region. 3–0978 (office); 9–2154 (home).

Kokunko, Georgy Valentinovich
POSITION: Acting Ataman of the Moscow Cossacks Society; Deputy Chief of Staff of the Union of Russian Cossack Troops, Staff Member of the Propaganda and Social Initiatives Center of the All-Russia Society for the Protection of Historical and Cultural Monuments (ARSPHCM)
BIRTHPLACE/DATE: Moscow, 1961
NATIONALITY: Cossack
EDUCATION: Graduated in 1983 from the Moscow Geological Institute.
CAREER: In the early 1980s, worked at the Moscow ARSPHCM. From 1985 to 1987, worked at the Preobrazhentsky Historical Restoration Club at the Preobrazhentsky Old Belief Complex in Moscow. From 1987 to 1989, Restoration Chairman of the Monuments Patronage Department of the Moscow ARSPHCM.
FAMILY: Married.
ADDRESS/TELEPHONE: 8-B Varvarka Street, Moscow. 298–5602 (office).

Kolesnikov, Mikhail Petrovich
POSITION: First Deputy Chief of General Staff of the Russian Federation Armed Forces; Colonel-General
BIRTHPLACE/DATE: Eisk, Krasnodar region, June 30, 1939
EDUCATION: Studied at the Armed Forces Academy.
CAREER: From 1959, Maintenance Platoon Commander of the Motorized Infantry Regiment of the Far East Military District. From 1960 to 1961, Senior Armoured Vehicles Engineer of the Tank Training Regiment of the Motorized Infantry Training Division of the Far East Military District; from 1961 to 1963, Foreman of the Combat Vehicles Maintenance Shop of the Tank Training Regiment of the Motorized Infantry Training Division. From 1963 to 1966, Senior Armoured Vehicles Engineer. From 1966 to 1967, Deputy Commander of the Training Company of the Tank Training Regiment of the Motorized Infantry Division. From 1975 to 1977, USSR Army Tank Regiment Commander in Germany.
FAMILY: Married with a son.
TELEPHONE: 293–2869; 293–1413 (office).

Kolesov, Anatoli Ivanovich
POSITION: Deputy Head of the CIS Sports Council Secretariat
BIRTHPLACE/DATE: Litvinskoye village, Osakarovsky district, Karaghanda region, Kazakhstan, 1938
NATIONALITY: Russian
EDUCATION: Graduated in 1958 from the Kazakh State Institute of Physical Education (KSIPC); in 1984, from the Academy of Social Sciences of the Central Committee (by correspondence).
CAREER: Coach of the Kazakh Republican Council of the Burevestnik (Stormy Petrel) Voluntary Sports Society. Weight Lifting Instructor at KSIPC. Chief and Senior Coach of the Greco-Roman Wrestling Team of the Central Army

Sports Club. Senior Coach of the USSR Greco-Roman Wrestling National Team. From 1961 to 1991, Deputy Chairman of the USSR Committee for Physical Education and Sports.
HONORS/AWARDS: USSR Honored Master of Sports; World Champion; European Champion; 1964 Summer Olympic Wrestling Champion; Order of the People's Friendship; two Orders of the Badge of Honor; Order of the Red Banner of Labor.
FAMILY: Married with two sons.
ADDRESS/TELEPHONE: 8 Luzhnetskaya Naberezhnaya, Moscow. 201–1298.

Kolokolov, Boris Leonidovich
POSITION: Russian Federation Deputy Foreign Minister; Ambassador Extraordinary and Plenipotentiary
BIRTHPLACE/DATE: 1924
NATIONALITY: Russian
EDUCATION: Graduated in 1956 from the Moscow State Institute of International Relations. Speaks English and French.
CAREER: From 1942 to 1950, served in the army; participated in World War II. From 1956 to 1962, worked at the UN European Department's Secretariat in Geneva. From 1962 to 1969, worked at the USSR Foreign Ministry's Department of Protocol. From 1973 and 1981, USSR Ambassador to Tunisia.
ADDRESS/TELEPHONE: 32/34 Smolenskaya-Sennaya Street, Moscow 121200. 244–1606; 244–9230 (office).

Kolosovsky, Andrey Igorevich
POSITION: Special Plenipotentiary Representative of Russia to the United States
BIRTHPLACE/DATE: Moscow, 1956
NATIONALITY: Russian
CAREER: From 1978 to 1980, Staff Member of the USSR Embassy in Cuba. From 1980 to 1986, Diplomatic Staff Member, Attaché, Third Secretary of the International Organizations Directorate of the USSR Ministry of Foreign Affairs. From 1986 to 1990, Assistant to the USSR Deputy Foreign Minister. From 1990, Department Head of the International Organizations Directorate of the USSR Ministry of Foreign Affairs. From 1990 to 1991, Political Department Head of the USSR Ministry of Foreign Affairs. In 1991, Russian Federation Deputy Foreign Minister.
FAMILY: Married with a son.
ADDRESS/TELEPHONE: The Russian Federation Embassy, 1125 16th Street NW, Washington, D.C., 20036. (202) 628–6412; (202) 628–7551 (office).

Komendant, Grigory Ivanovich
POSITION: Chairman of the Evangelical Christian-Baptist Union
BIRTHPLACE/DATE: Stavishche village, Dunayevtsy district, Khmelnitsky region, Ukraine, January 8, 1946
NATIONALITY: Ukrainian
EDUCATION: Graduated in 1975 from the Theological Seminary in Hamburg.
CAREER: From 1975 to 1978, Presbyter of the Dunayevtsy Community of Evangelical Christian-Baptists. From 1979 to 1990, Senior Presbyter of Kiev region. From 1981, Deputy Senior Presbyter of the Ukraine.
FAMILY: Married with two children.
ADDRESS/TELEPHONE: 3 Maly Vuzovsky Pereulok, Moscow. 297–3363; 297–8164; 297–6700; 227–8947.

Komplektov, Victor Georgyevich
POSITION: Special Representative of the Foreign Minister at the Pridnestrovye (Dniester River) Region Peace Negotiations; Ambassador at Large; Ambassador Extraordinary and Plenipotentiary
BIRTHPLACE/DATE: Moscow, January 3, 1932
NATIONALITY: Russian
EDUCATION: Studied at the Moscow State Institute of International Relations.
CAREER: From 1955 to 1956, Staff Member of the Department of American Countries of the USSR Foreign Ministry. From 1956 to 1959, worked at the USSR Embassy in the United States. From 1959 to 1962, Attaché, Third Secretary of the Department of American Countries of the USSR Foreign Ministry. From 1962 to 1963, Second Secretary of the Department of the United States of the USSR Foreign Ministry. From 1963 to 1968, Second Secretary, First Secretary, Counsellor at the USSR Embassy in the United States. From 1968 to 1978, Counsellor, Deputy Head of the Department of the United States of the USSR Foreign Ministry. From 1978 to 1982, Head of the Depart-

ment of the United States; USSR Foreign Ministry Collegium Member. From 1982 to 1991, USSR Deputy Foreign Minister. From 1991 to March 1992, USSR Ambassador to the United States.
HONORS/AWARDS: Order of the Badge of Honor; Order of the October Revolution; Order of the Red Banner of Labor; medals.
FAMILY: Married.
ADDRESS/TELEPHONE: 32/34 Smolenskaya-Sennaya, Moscow, 121200. 244–1606; 244–2469 (office).

Kon, Igor Semyonovich

POSITION: Chief Researcher at the Russian Academy of Sciences' Institute of Ethnology and Anthropology; Sexologist; Academician of the Russian Academy of Pedagogical Sciences
BIRTHPLACE/DATE: Leningrad, 1928
EDUCATION: Graduated from the History Department at the Herzen Teachers' Training Institute in Leningrad. Doctor of Philosophy; Professor. Command of English.
CAREER: From 1950 to 1952, Senior Teacher of the World History Division at the Vologda Teachers' Training Institute. From 1953 to 1956, Assistant to the Marxism-Leninism Department, Acting Assistant Professor at the Leningrad Chemical Pharmaceutical Institute. From 1956 to 1961, Assistant Professor of the Dialectical and Historical Materialism Division at Leningrad State University. From 1961 to 1967, Philosophy Department Professor at Leningrad State University. From 1967 to 1968, Acting Department Head of the Institute of Philosophy. From 1968 to 1970, Sector Head, and from 1970 to 1972, Department Head, Senior Researcher at the USSR Academy of Sciences' Institute of Socio-Political Research. From 1972 to 1974, Philosophy Department Professor at the Institute of Social Sciences. From 1974 to 1975, Acting Senior Researcher at the Institute of Philosophy. From 1975 to 1985, Acting Senior Researcher, Senior Researcher at the Leningrad Ethnography Institute. From 1985, Senior Researcher, Leading Researcher, then Chief Researcher at the Institute of Ethnology and Anthropology. From 1988, Academician of the USSR Academy of Pedagogical Sciences. Full Member of the International Academy of Sexology and the Polish Sexological Academy.
MAJOR WORKS: Scientific papers on sociology, sexology, philosophy, psychology.
HONORS/AWARDS: Honorary Professor of Cornell University (United States); Medal For Labor Valor; Veteran of Labor Medal.
FAMILY: Single.
ADDRESS/TELEPHONE: 48 Vavilov Street, Flat #372, Moscow, 117333. 137–5576 (home).

Kondrashov, Stanislav Nikolayevich

POSITION: Political Analyst of *Izvestia (News)* daily
BIRTHPLACE/DATE: Kulebaki, Nizhny Novgorod region, 1928
NATIONALITY: Russian
EDUCATION: Graduated in 1951 from the Moscow State Institute of International Relations.
CAREER: From 1951 to 1957, Foreign Department Staff Member of *Izvestia*. From 1957 to 1961, *Izvestia* Correspondent in Egypt; from 1961 and 1968, Correspondent in the United States. From 1968 to 1971, International Commentator, Editor-Commentator of the Foreign Department of *Izvestia*. From 1971 to 1976, *Izvestia* Correspondent in the United States. From 1976 to 1977, Editorial Board Member, Deputy Editor in Chief of *Izvestia*.
FAMILY: Married with three children.
ADDRESS/TELEPHONE: 5 Pushkinskaya Square, Moscow, GSP, 103791. 209–9100 (office).

Kondratyev, Georgy Grigoryevich

POSITION: Russian Federation Deputy Defense Minister; Turkistan Military District Commander
BIRTHPLACE/DATE: Klintsy, Bryansk region, November 17, 1922
NATIONALITY: Russian
EDUCATION: Graduated with distinction in 1965 from the Malinovsky Military Academy. In 1985, graduated with distinction and gold medal from the USSR Supreme Soviet General Staff Academy.
CAREER: Served in the army as a Tank Platoon Commander, then Tank Company Commander. From 1973, Regiment Chief of Staff. From 1974, Regiment Commander. From 1978, Deputy Division Commander, Division Commander. In 1985 appointed First Deputy Army Commander of the Turkistan Military District. From 1987, Army

Commander, from 1989, First Deputy Commander of the Turkistan Military District Troops.
HONORS/AWARDS: Order of the Red Banner; Order of the Red Star; Order For Service to the Motherland and the USSR Armed Forces, Second and Third Class.
FAMILY: Married with two children.
ADDRESS/TELEPHONE: 12 Frunze Street, Moscow. 293–2869; 293–1413 (office).

Konovalov, Aleksandr Nikolayevich
POSITION: Director of the Burdenko Institute of Neurosurgery
BIRTHPLACE/DATE: Moscow, 1933
NATIONALITY: Russian
EDUCATION: Graduated in 1957 from the First Moscow Medical Institute. Professor. Good command of English and German.
CAREER: From 1957, Junior Research Fellow, Senior Researcher, Deputy Director of the Burdenko Institute of Neurosurgery. From 1982, Academician of the USSR Academy of Medical Sciences. From 1992, Academician of the Russian Academy of Medical Sciences.
MAJOR WORKS: Scientific works on vascular neurosurgery, neurooncology, neurotraumatology.
FAMILY: Married with a son.
ADDRESS/TELEPHONE: 5 Fadeyev Street, Moscow, 125047. 251–6526 (office); 258–7618 (home).

Konovalov, Vitaly Fyodorovich
POSITION: Russian Federation First Deputy Minister of Nuclear Energy
BIRTHPLACE/DATE: Sverdlovsk (now Yekaterinburg), 1932
NATIONALITY: Russian
EDUCATION: Graduated from Kirov Urals Polytechnic, majoring in Mechanical Engineering. Doctor of Technology.
CAREER: Foreman, Senior Foreman, Shop Head of a metallurgical works; Director of mechanical and machinery construction plants. From 1986, Head of the Main Board of the USSR Ministry of Medium-Size Machine-Building. From 1988, Deputy Minister of Medium-Size Machine-Building. From 1989 to 1991, USSR Minister of Nuclear Energy and Industry.
FAMILY: Married with a daughter.
ADDRESS/TELEPHONE: 24/26 Bolshaya Ordynka Street, Moscow. 239–4430 (office).

Koptyug, Valentin Afanasyevich
POSITION: Vice President of the Russian Academy of Sciences; Chairman of the Siberian Branch of the Russian Academy of Sciences
BIRTHPLACE/DATE: Kaluga region, June 9, 1931
NATIONALITY: Russian
EDUCATION: Graduated in 1954 from the Moscow Mendeleeyev Institute of Chemical Technology.
CAREER: From 1960 to 1966, Laboratory Head at the Novosibirsk Organic Chemistry Institute of the Siberian branch of the USSR Academy of Sciences. Joined the Communist Party in 1961. From 1966 to 1980, worked at the Division of Organic Chemistry of Novosibirsk University. From 1979, Academician of the USSR Academy of Sciences. From 1980, Vice President of the USSR Academy of Sciences, Chairman of the Siberian branch of the USSR Academy of Sciences. From December 1991, Vice President of the Russian Academy of Sciences, Chairman of the Siberian branch of the Russian Academy of Sciences.
MAJOR WORKS: General scientific studies on the mechanisms of aromatic compounds and molecular regroupings of carbonating ions; *Isometrization of Aromatic Compounds* monograph.
HONORS/AWARDS: Hero of Socialist Labor.
FAMILY: Married with two children.
ADDRESS/TELEPHONE: 14 Leninsky Prospekt, Moscow V–71, GSP–1, 117901; 17 Akademik Lavrentyev Prospekt, Novosibirsk 90, 630090. 234–2549 (Moscow office); 35–0567 (Novosibirsk office).

Kopylov, Sergey Vladimirovich
POSITION: Cyclist; Instructor at the Tula Higher Athletic Mastership School
BIRTHPLACE/DATE: Tula, July 29, 1960
EDUCATION: Graduated from the Tula Physical Education Institute.
CAREER: In 1981, World Cycling Champion (sprint). In 1983, World Champion (1000-meter time trial). In 1980, Olympic Bronze Medal.
HONORS/AWARDS: USSR Honored Master of Sports.
FAMILY: Married with two children.

ADDRESS/TELEPHONE: The Regional Sports Committee, Tula. 25–2028.

Korepanov, Sergey Ivanovich

POSITION: Editor in Chief of *Business and Banks* newspaper

BIRTHPLACE/DATE: Miass, Chelyabinsk region, 1949

EDUCATION: Graduated in 1977 from the Journalism Department at Moscow State University. Speaks English.

CAREER: From 1977 to 1979, Correspondent for *Izvestia* daily. From 1979 and 1986, TASS (Telegraph Agency of the Soviet Union) Correspondent, Editor. From 1986 to 1988, Special Correspondent for *Socialisticheskaya Industria* (*Socialist Industry*) newspaper. From 1987 to 1991, Director-General of the Informbank Informational and Commercial Agency.

MAJOR WORKS: Over 200 scientific and critical articles.

HONORS/AWARDS: Moscow Journalists' Prize.

FAMILY: Married with a daughter.

ADDRESS/TELEPHONE: 10/1 Dekabristov Street, Flat #71, Moscow, 127567. 907–8210 (home).

Korobchenko, Victor Alekseyevich

POSITION: First Deputy Premier of the Moscow Government

BIRTHPLACE/DATE: Strunino, Vladimir region, 1947

EDUCATION: Graduated in 1971 from the Moscow Bauman State Technical Institute.

CAREER: From 1971 to 1989, Engineer; worked at the Baumansky District Komsomol Committee and the District Communist Party Committee; Secretary and Chairman of the Baumansky District Council of People's Deputies. From 1989 to 1990, First Deputy Chairman of the Moscow City Executive Committee Planning Commission. From 1990 to 1992, First Deputy Chairman of the Mossoviet (Moscow Council) Executive Committee, Head of the Department of Public Policy and Daily Services to the Population. From 1991 to 1992, Deputy Premier of the Moscow Government, Head of the Municipal Social Policies Complex.

HONORS/AWARDS: Order of the People's Friendship; two medals.

FAMILY: Married with two children.

ADDRESS/TELEPHONE: 13 Tverskaya Street, Moscow. 292–1727 (office).

Korolev, Vladimir Mikhailovich

POSITION: Director-General of the Second Watch-Making Factory Production Association

BIRTHPLACE/DATE: Uglich, 1947

NATIONALITY: Russian

EDUCATION: Graduated in 1970 from the Ryazan Institute of Radio Engineering.

CAREER: From 1972 to 1985, worked from Engineer-Technician to Deputy Director of the Uglich Watch-Making Factory. From 1985 to 1987, Chief Engineer of the USSR Ministry of Machinery and Construction.

MAJOR WORKS: Numerous inventions.

FAMILY: Married with two children.

ADDRESS/TELEPHONE: 8 Leningradsky Prospekt, Moscow, 125040. 251–2937 (office).

Korostelev, Yuri Victorovich

POSITION: Moscow Government Minister

BIRTHPLACE/DATE: Omsk, 1945

EDUCATION: Graduated in 1972 from the Patrice Lumumba Friendship University; from 1972 to 1977, postgraduate student.

CAREER: From 1963 to 1972, Fitter at the Shchekinskaya Regional Power Station. From 1977 to 1989, Communist Party and Council Functionary, Executive Council Chairman of the Cheryomushki District Council. From 1989 to 1990, Deputy Chairman of the Moscow City Executive Committee Planning Commission. From 1990 to 1992, Head of the Main Finance Administration.

HONORS/AWARDS: Medal For Labor Valor; Veteran of Labor Medal.

FAMILY: Married with two children.

ADDRESS/TELEPHONE: 2/2 Miusskaya Street, Moscow. 251–3526 (office).

Korotich, Vitaly Alekseyevich

POSITION: Writer; U.S. Correspondent for *Vzglyad i Drugiye* (*Glance and Others*) newspaper

BIRTHPLACE/DATE: Kiev, 1936

NATIONALITY: Ukrainian

EDUCATION: Graduated in 1959 from the Kiev Medical Institute. In the 1960s, defended doctoral dissertation in Medicine.

Career: Worked as a Physician in Kiev. First publications appeared in 1954. In 1961, joined the USSR Writers' Union. Joined the Communist Party of the Soviet Union in 1967. To 1978, engaged in creative work and lectured in the United States at the invitation of a number of universities. From 1966 to 1969, Board Secretary of the Ukrainian Writers' Union. From 1978, Editor of *Inostrannaya Literatura* (*Foreign Literature*) magazine. From 1981 to 1991, Board Secretary of the USSR Writers' Union. From 1986, Editor in Chief of *Ogonyek* (*Beacon*) magazine and Co-Chairman of the April Writers' Association. From December 1991, member of the Russian Writers' Union.
Major Works: Collections of poems: *Gold Hands*; *Odor of the Heavens*; *Cornflower Street*; *Diary.* Short stories and essays: "Oh, Canada!"; "Stars and Stripes"; "Man at Home"; "Perpendicular Spoon" (co-authored with Imant Ziedonis); "Cubic Capacity"; "Reflections on a Visit to America." Story: "Evil Memory." Novel: *The Tenth of May.*
Honors/Awards: Nikolay Ostrovsky Prize of the Ukrainian Komsomol for a collection of poems, *Possibility.*
Family: Married with two sons.
Address/Telephone: 7 Ulitsa 1905 Goda, Moscow. 298–0979 (office).

Korzun, Sergey Lvovich
Position: Editor in Chief of Moscow's Ekho Moskvy (Moscow Echo) Radio Station
Birthplace/Date: 1956, Moscow
Nationality: Russian
Career: From 1978 to 1990, Newscaster, Host of the International Moscow Radio Programs in French.
Family: Married with a son.
Address/Telephone: 7 Nikolskaya Street, Moscow, 103012. 297–8058 (office).

Kostikov, Vyacheslav Vasilyevich
Position: Press Secretary of the Russian Federation President
Birthplace/Date: Moscow, 1940
Nationality: Russian
Education: Graduated in 1966 from the Journalism Department at Moscow State University and the Academy of Foreign Trade. Completed journalism courses at Sheffield University (Britain) in 1968. Speaks English.
Career: From 1966 to 1967, Correspondent for Novosti (News) Press Agency in India. From 1967 to 1972, and from 1978 to 1982, and from 1988 to 1992, Editor, Political Analyst of Novosti Press Agency. From 1972 to 1978, and from 1982 to 1988, Information Department Staff Member at the UNESCO Secretariat in France. Contributor to *Izvestia* newspaper and *Ogonyek* magazine. Has published in the Western press. Former Leading Columnist for the major Indian newspaper the *Times.*
Major Works: Author of stories and novels: *Heir*; *Mistral*; *Opening-Day* and others; and an analytical study of the destinies of Russian emigrants.
Family: Married with a daughter.
Address/Telephone: The Kremlin, Moscow. 224–0542 (office).

Kotelnikov, Vladimir Aleksandrovich
Position: Chairman of the Council for International Cooperation in the Exploration and Use of Outer Space (Intercosmos); Academician of the Russian Academy of Sciences
Birthplace/Date: Kazan, August 24, 1908
Nationality: Russian
Education: Graduated in 1931 from the Moscow Power Engineering Institute.
Career: From 1931 to 1954, Lecturer at the Moscow Power Engineering Institute; from 1947, Professor. Joined the Communist Party in 1948. From 1953, Academician of the USSR Academy of Sciences. From 1954 to 1970, Director of the Institute of Radio Engineering and Electronics of the USSR Academy of Sciences. From 1970, Vice President of the USSR Academy of Sciences. From 1973 to 1980, Russian Federation Supreme Soviet Chairman.
Major Works: Scientific works on the development of radio reception methods, radio interference resistance, potential interference-proof theory, and the radio location of Mars, Venus, and Mercury.
Honors/Awards: Twice Hero of Socialist Labor; USSR State Prize; Prize of Lenin; six Orders of Lenin; Popov Gold Medal; Keldysh Gold Medal; Lomonosov Gold Medal of the USSR Academy of

Sciences; Honorary Member of the American Institute of Electronics and Radio Electronics; foreign member of the Czechoslovak Academy of Sciences; Honorary Doctor of technology of the Prague Higher Technical School; foreign member of the Polish Academy of Sciences; foreign member of the Mongolian Academy of Sciences; foreign member of the Bulgarian Academy of Sciences.
FAMILY: Married with a child.
ADDRESS/TELEPHONE: 14 Leninsky Prospekt, Moscow 117901. 954–3006 (office).

Kovalchenko, Ivan Dmitryevich
POSITION: Academician; Secretary of the History Department of the Russian Academy of Sciences
BIRTHPLACE/DATE: Bryansk region, November 26, 1923
NATIONALITY: Russian
EDUCATION: Graduated in 1952 from Moscow State University.
CAREER: From 1955, Lecturer at Moscow State University. From 1966, Head of the Division of Source Study of the History of the USSR; from 1967, Professor. From 1969, Editor in Chief of *Istoria SSSR* (*History of the USSR*) magazine. From 1987, Academician of the USSR Academy of Sciences.
MAJOR WORKS: Scientific papers on agrarian history and the history of Russia's economic development in the nineteenth and early twentieth centuries. Works on historiography and source study.
HONORS/AWARDS: State Prize; Grekov Prize of the USSR Academy of Sciences.
FAMILY: Married with two children.
ADDRESS/TELEPHONE: MGU, Leninsky Gory, Moscow V–234, GSP–3, 119899. 939–3597 (office); 938–0679 (home).

Kovalev, Anatoli Gavrilovich
POSITION: Former Russian Federation Deputy Foreign Minister; Ambassador Extraordinary and Plenipotentiary
BIRTHPLACE/DATE: May 18, 1923
NATIONALITY: Russian
EDUCATION: Graduated in 1948 from the Moscow State Institute of International Relations of the USSR Foreign Ministry.
CAREER: From 1941 to 1943, Head of Lighting Effects at the USSR Bolshoi Theater. During 1948 and 1949, Staff Member of the Third European Department of the USSR Foreign Ministry. From 1949 to 1951, Aide, Senior Assistant at the Soviet Military Administration in Germany. From 1951 to 1953, Section Head of the Political Counsellor's Department at the Soviet Control Commission in Germany. From 1953 to 1954, Assistant to the Supreme Commissar at the USSR Supreme Commissar Office in Germany. From 1954 to 1955, Deputy Department Head at the USSR Embassy in the German Democratic Republic (East Germany) and the USSR Supreme Commissar Office in Germany. From 1955 to 1958, First Secretary, Counsellor of the Third European Department of the USSR Foreign Ministry. From 1958 to 1959, Assistant to the USSR Foreign Minister. From 1959 to 1965, Head of the Group of Consultants to the USSR Foreign Minister. From 1965 and 1971, Department Head of the First European Department (Benelux Nations, France, Italy, Portugal, Spain, Switzerland) of the USSR Foreign Ministry. From 1971 to 1986, USSR Deputy Foreign Minister of Western Europe. From 1971 to 1985, Head of the Directorate for Foreign Policy Planning of the USSR Foreign Ministry. From 1986 to 1990, member of the Communist Party Central Auditing Commission. From 1986 to 1991, USSR First Deputy Foreign Minister. From 1992, Russian Federation First Deputy Foreign Minister.
MAJOR WORKS: Editor of the *Diplomatic Encyclopaedia*.
HONORS/AWARDS: Order of Lenin; two Orders of the October Revolution; three Orders of the Red Banner of Labor; State Prize.
FAMILY: Married.
ADDRESS/TELEPHONE: 32/34 Smolenskaya-Sennaya Square, Moscow, 121200. 244–1606; 244–2464; 244–4662.

Kovalev, Feliks Nikolayevich
POSITION: Ambassador at Large; Ambassador Extraordinary and Plenipotentiary
BIRTHPLACE/DATE: Kondorovo village, August 18, 1927
NATIONALITY: Russian
EDUCATION: Graduated from the Moscow State Institute of International Relations in 1950. Doctor of History.

Career: From 1953 to 1955, Department Head Assistant to the Information Committee of the USSR Foreign Ministry; from 1955 to 1958, Senior Department Head Assistant. From 1958 to 1959, Department Aide to the Soviet Union Central Committee. From 1959 to 1961, First Secretary of the International Information Board. From 1961 to 1963, First Secretary of the Agreement and Law Department of the USSR Foreign Ministry. From 1963 to 1966, First Secretary at the USSR Embassy in Argentina. From 1966 to 1967, Counsellor. From 1967 to 1971, Expert of the Agreement and Law Department. From 1971 to 1980, Deputy Department Head. From 1980 to 1986, Ambassador to Ecuador. From 1986 to 1992, Head of the Diplomatic History Department. From 1992, Russian Federation Delegation Head at the Georgia Negotiations.
Honors/Awards: Order of the People's Friendship; Order of the Badge of Honor.
Family: Married with two children.
Telephone: 244–2998.

Kovalev, Yevgeni Yevgenyevich
Position: Director of the Scientific Research Testing Center for Radiation Safety of Space Objects
Birthplace/Date: Tekhvin, 1929
Nationality: Russian
Education: Graduated in 1952 from the Moscow Engineering Physics Institute (MIFI). Doctor of Technology (1955); Professor of Nuclear Physics. Speaks English.
Career: From 1956, Senior Researcher at the Institute of Biophysics. From 1964, Department Head at the Institute of Medical and Biological Problems. From 1975, Sector Head for Radiation Safety of Space Flights. From 1978, Corresponding Member of the Astronautics International Academy. From 1978 to 1986, member of the International Commission for Radiation Protection. Member of the Astronautics International Academy and the Astronautics International Federation.
Honors/Awards: USSR State Prize.
Family: Married with two children.
Address/Telephone: 40 Schukinskaya Street, Moscow, 123182. 190–5131.

Kovalev, Yuri Nikolayevich
Position: Board Chairman of Lenregionbank, the Leningrad Regional Commercial Bank of Economic Stabilization
Birthplace/Date: Leningrad, 1952
Career: From 1974 to 1991, Worker, Department Head, Secretary of the Severny Press Plant Party Committee. From 1991 to 1992, worked in commercial offices; Bank Founder.
Family: Married with a child.
Address/Telephone: 1–3 Dumskaya Street, St. Petersburg, 191011. 110–4432 (office).

Kovylov, Aleksey Ivanovich
Position: President of the International Committee of Youth Organizations
Birthplace/Date: Moscow, 1954
Nationality: Russian
Education: Graduated in 1976 from the History Department at Moscow State University. Doctor of History.
Career: In 1976, Junior Aide to the Committee of Youth Organizations (CYO). From 1987 to 1989, President of the World Federation of Democratic Youth. From September 1989 to 1990, CYO First Deputy Chairman. From 1990, Editorial Board Member of *Yunost* (*Youth*) magazine. From 1990 to 1991, CYO Chairman.
Major Works: Scientific works on problems of the international youth movement and the history of Italy.
Honors/Awards: Medal For Labor Distinction.
Family: Married with a daughter.
Address/Telephone: 7/8 Moroseika Street, Moscow. 206–8909.

Kozak, Roman Yefimovich
Position: Producer of the Konstantin Stanislavsky Drama Theater in Moscow
Birthplace/Date: Vinnitsa, Ukraine, 1957
Education: Graduated in 1982 from the Moscow Art Theater Studios.
Career: In the 1980s, Actor of the Maxim Gorky Academic Art Theater in Moscow. To 1989, Producer of the Chelovek (Man) Theater-Studio. Art Director of the Fifth Studio at the Moscow Art Theater. From 1991, Art Director of the Stanislavsky Drama Theater.

MAJOR WORKS: Productions: *Cinzano*; *Masquerade* by Lyudmila Petrushevskaya and others.
FAMILY: Married with a daughter.
ADDRESS/TELEPHONE: 23 Tverskaya Street, Moscow. 299–4436; 299–5684 (office).

Kozayev, Valery Kuzmich
POSITION: First Deputy North Ossetian Prosecutor; North Ossetian People's Deputy
BIRTHPLACE/DATE: Sdiza village, North Ossetia, 1949
CAREER: From 1968, worked at a ship repair plant in Saratov. From 1974, Senior Investigator of the Procurator's office in Alma-Ata. Russian Federation Supreme Soviet Legislation Committee Member.
FAMILY: Married with two sons.
ADDRESS/TELEPHONE: 8 Pushkin Street, Vladikavkaz. 34–604.

Kozemyakin, Nikolay Aleksandrovich
POSITION: Chief Manager of the Yuzhnaya Universalnaya Birzha (Southern Universal Stock Exchange) Joint-Stock Company
BIRTHPLACE/DATE: Gorlovka, Donetsk region, 1947
NATIONALITY: Russian
CAREER: From 1969, Metalworker at the Chernomorsk Ship-Building Plant; from 1973, Deputy Secretary of the Plant Komsomol Committee. From 1976, Chief Engineer. From 1977, Inspector of the Nikolayevsk City Communist Party. From 1980, Industrial Transport Department Instructor of the City Party Committee. From 1983, Chief Engineer of the Soyuzprommekhanizatsia (Industrial Mechanization) Institute.
FAMILY: Married with two children.
ADDRESS/TELEPHONE: 23 Rabochaya Street, Nikolaev, 327020. 37–2100 (home); 39–2199 (office).

Kozevnikov, Igor Nikolayevich
POSITION: Russian Federation Deputy Minister of Internal Affairs; Investigating Committee Head; Lieutenant-General
BIRTHPLACE/DATE: Leningrad, 1940
CAREER: From 1963, worked for the Internal Affairs Service: Operational Agent, Investigator, Senior Investigator, Senior Investigator at Large, Deputy Department Head, Department Head, Chief of Staff. From 1985 to 1991, Deputy, then First Deputy Head of the Central Investigating Committee of the USSR Ministry of Internal Affairs. From September 1991 to January 1992, Deputy USSR Minister of Internal Affairs.
ADDRESS/TELEPHONE: 6 Ogareva Street, Moscow, 117049. 222–6134 (office).

Kozlov, Victor Vasilyevich
POSITION: Chairman of the Atomenergoexport (Nuclear Energy Export) Foreign Trade Association
BIRTHPLACE/DATE: Moscow, 1944
NATIONALITY: Russian
EDUCATION: Graduated in 1966 from the Moscow Institute of Chemical Engineering; in 1977, from the All-Union Academy of Foreign Trade.
CAREER: From 1966 to 1970, Engineer, Senior Engineer at the Soyuzmashproyekt (Soviet Union Machinery Projects) Institute. From 1970 to 1973, Senior Engineer of the Heavy Power and Transport Engineering Ministry. From 1974 and 1979, Senior Engineer, Expert, Deputy Head of the Computerization Department of Atomenergoexport. From 1979 to 1983, Expert, Head of the Atomenergoexport Mission to Finland. From 1984 to 1987, Acting Director, Director of the State-of-the-Art Technology Office, Deputy Chairman of Atomenergoexport. From 1987 and 1988, Deputy Head of the Main Personnel Department of the USSR State Committee for Foreign Economic Relations. From 1988 to 1990, Deputy Communist Party Secretary of the USSR Ministry of Foreign Relations.
HONORS/AWARDS: Medal for Labor Distinction; Ten Years of Afghan Revolution Medal.
FAMILY: Married with a daughter.
ADDRESS/TELEPHONE: 18/1 Ovchinnikovskaya Naberezhnaya, Moscow. 220–1436; 231–8014 (office).

Kozlovsky, Pavel Pavlovich
POSITION: Defense Minister of Byelorussia (Belorus)
BIRTHPLACE/DATE: Volkovnia village, Brest region, March 9, 1940
CAREER: Served in the Sredneaziatsky, Zakavkazsky, Severo-Kavkazsky (Middle Asia, South

Caucasus, North Caucasus) military districts; Regiment Commander, Chief of Staff and Division Commander. From 1989, Army Commander in Byelorussia. From 1991 to 1992, Chief of Staff, First Deputy Commander of the Byelorussian Military District.
FAMILY: Married with three children.
ADDRESS/TELEPHONE: 1 Kommunisticheskaya Street, Minsk, 220003. 33–0352

Kozyrev, Andrey Vladimirovich
POSITION: Russian Federation Foreign Minister; Ambassador Extraordinary and Plenipotentiary
BIRTHPLACE/DATE: Brussels, 1951
NATIONALITY: Russian
EDUCATION: Graduated in 1974 from the Moscow State Institute of International Relations. In 1977, defended thesis on détente problems. Speaks English, Spanish, and Portuguese.
CAREER: Began working at the Moscow Kommunar Factory. From 1974 to 1988, Aide, Senior Aide, Attaché, Third, Second, First Secretary, Counsellor, Department Head of the International Organizations Directorate of the USSR Foreign Ministry. From 1988 to 1989, Deputy Head, and from 1989 to 1990, Head of the International Organizations Directorate.
MAJOR WORKS: Numerous articles and monographs, including *The World and Us as Mirrored by the UN.*
FAMILY: Married with a daughter.
ADDRESS/TELEPHONE: 32/34 Smolenskaya-Sennaya Square, Moscow. 244–4021 (office).

Kozyrev, Nikolay Ivanovich
POSITION: Russian Federation Ambassador to Ireland; Ambassador Extraordinary and Plenipotentiary
BIRTHPLACE/DATE: 1934
NATIONALITY: Russian
EDUCATION: Graduated in 1958 from the Moscow State Institute of International Relations; in 1970, from the Higher Diplomatic School of the USSR Foreign Ministry.
CAREER: From 1958, Interpreter, Attaché, Third, Second, First Secretary at the USSR Embassy to Iran. From 1976 to 1979, Counsellor, Sector Head of the Department of Middle East Countries of the USSR Foreign Ministry. From 1979 to 1983, Counsellor at the USSR Embassy to Iran. From 1984 to 1987, Minister-Counsellor at the USSR Embassy in Afghanistan. From 1987 to 1991, USSR Foreign Ministry Ambassador at Large.
FAMILY: Married with a daughter.
ADDRESS/TELEPHONE: 32/34 Smolenskaya-Sennaya Street, Moscow 121200. 244–1606.

Kozyreva, Aleksandra Mikhailovna
POSITION: Board Chairwoman of Tveruniversalbank (Universal Bank of Tver)
BIRTHPLACE/DATE: Tver (formerly Kalinin) region, 1948
NATIONALITY: Russian
EDUCATION: Graduated in 1971 from the Kalinin Polytechnical Institute.
CAREER: From August 1971 to November 1977, Engineer, Senior Engineer of the USSR Regional Stroibank (Construction Bank). From November 1977 to December 1987, Deputy Head, Technological Department Head, Deputy Manager of the USSR Regional Stroibank. From December 1987 to January 1991, Regional Board Head of the USSR Zhilsotsbank (Housing and Social Life Bank).
FAMILY: Divorced with two daughters.
ADDRESS/TELEPHONE: 13 Sovietskaya Street, Tver. 3–1243 (office).

Krainev, Vladimir Vsevolodovich
POSITION: Pianist; Teacher at the Moscow Conservatory
BIRTHPLACE/DATE: Krasnoyarsk, April 1, 1944
EDUCATION: Graduated from the Moscow Conservatory. Student of Henrich Neihaus.
CAREER: From 1966, Soloist of the Moscow Philharmonic Society. One of the leading Soviet pianists. Modern music is widely represented in repertoire.
HONORS/AWARDS: First Prize at the International Pianists Contests: Viana da Mota Contest (Lisbon, 1964); Tchaikovsky Contest (Moscow, 1970); Second Prize at the International Pianists Contest (Britain, 1963); USSR State Prize; Lenin Komsomol Prize; Order of the Badge of Honor; USSR People's Artist.
FAMILY: Married.
ADDRESS/TELEPHONE: 31 Tverskaya Street,

Moscow, 103050. 158–2456 (home); 299–4861 (office).

Krasavin, Igor Nikolayevich

POSITION: Russian Federation Ambassador to Iceland; Ambassador Extraordinary and Plenipotentiary
BIRTHPLACE/DATE: Piryatin, Poltava region, Ukraine, May 3, 1930
NATIONALITY: Russian
EDUCATION: Graduated in 1953 from the Moscow State Institute of International Relations of the USSR Foreign Ministry. Good command of French, English, Finnish, and Italian.
CAREER: From 1953 to 1956, Interpreter at the USSR Mission in Finland. From 1956 to 1957, Attaché at the USSR Embassy in Finland. From 1957 to 1958, worked in the Scandinavian Countries Department Reserve of the USSR Foreign Ministry. From 1958 to 1965, Attaché, Third Secretary, Second Secretary of the Scandinavian Countries Department of the USSR Foreign Ministry. From 1965 to 1972, First Secretary at the USSR Embassy in Finland. From 1972 and 1975, Counsellor, Section Head of the Scandinavian Countries Department of the USSR Foreign Ministry. From 1975 to 1980, Counsellor, Minister-Counsellor at the USSR Embassy in Finland. From 1980 to 1986, Deputy Head of the Scandinavian Countries Department of the USSR Foreign Ministry. In 1986, Deputy Head of the Second European Department of the USSR Foreign Ministry. From 1986 to 1991, USSR Ambassador to the Republic of Iceland.
FAMILY: Married.
ADDRESS/TELEPHONE: The Embassy of Russia in Iceland, 33 Gardastracti, Reykjavik, Iceland. 1–5156; 2–8564.

Krasikov, Aleksandr Aleksandrovich

POSITION: President of the Business Commercial Tourism Company
BIRTHPLACE/DATE: Moscow, 1953
NATIONALITY: Russian
EDUCATION: Graduated in 1980 from the Moscow Regional Teachers' Training Institute (by correspondence).
CAREER: Served in the army, then Factory Superintendent. From 1985, Head of the Main Department of the Committee for Vocational Training, then Planning and Financial Department Chief of the Committee for Public Education of the Moscow City Executive Committee. From 1989, Directorate Chief for Tourist Centers and Hotels of the USSR Sputnik Agency for International Youth Tourism.
HONORS/AWARDS: Master of Sports (cycling).
FAMILY: Married with a daughter.
ADDRESS/TELEPHONE: TGO Izmailovo, 71 Izmailovskoye Chaussée, Building D, Moscow. 166–5661; Fax: 166–5221; Telex: 412226.

Krasikov, Anatoli Andreyevich

POSITION: Head of the Russian Federation President's Press Service
BIRTHPLACE/DATE: Moscow, 1931
EDUCATION: Graduated in 1954 from the Moscow State Institute of International Relations. Doctor of History. Speaks French, Italian, Spanish, and English.
CAREER: From 1954 to 1989, worked at TASS (Telegraph Agency of the Soviet Union): Editor-Trainee, Executive Editor, Head of the TASS Offices in Italy and France, Deputy Chief Editor of Foreign Information; from 1972 to 1992, Collegium Member, Editor of the Analytical and Planning Department, Chief Editor of the Department of Information for Abroad; from 1978, Deputy Director-General. From April 1992, worked at *Nezavissimaya Gazeta* (*Independent Newspaper*): headed the International Affairs Department, Editorial Board Member. From 1981 to 1991, USSR Representative at the UNESCO International Program for Communications Development; member of the USSR Commission for UNESCO Affairs. Member of the Scientific Committee for Global Security. President-Coordinator of the Association of Business and Cultural Ties with Italy.
MAJOR WORKS: Books about the Vatican and how the Spanish experienced the transition from dictatorship to democracy.
HONORS/AWARDS: Two Orders of the Red Banner of Labor; Order of the People's Friendship; Badge of Honor; Russian Federation Honored Worker of Culture.
FAMILY: Married with a daughter.
ADDRESS/TELEPHONE: The Kremlin, Moscow. 224–0343 (office).

Kravchenko, Leonid Petrovich

POSITION: Former Chairman of the All-Union State Television and Radio Company; Political Analyst of *Yuridicheskaya Gazeta* (*Legal Newspaper*)
BIRTHPLACE/DATE: Tureyevka village, Bryansk region, May 10, 1938
NATIONALITY: Russian
CAREER: From 1961 to 1967, Staff Writer, Deputy Department Head of *Stroitelnaya Gazeta* (*Construction Newspaper*) daily. From 1967 to 1971, Deputy Editor of the Moscow and Moscow Region Broadcasting Department, Deputy Executive Director of Central Television Broadcasting of the USSR State Radio and Television Committee. From 1971, worked in the Propaganda Department of the Central Committee. From 1975, Editor in Chief of *Stroitelnaya Gazeta*. From 1980, Editor in Chief of *Trud* (*Labor*) newspaper. From 1985, First Deputy Chairman of the USSR State Radio and Television Committee. From 1988, Director-General of TASS. From 1990, Chairman of the USSR State Television and Radio Committee. From February 1991 to August 1991, Chairman of the All-Union State Television and Radio Company. Member of the USSR Supreme Soviet Committee for Foreign Affairs. Chairman of the USSR Hockey Federation. USSR People's Deputy. Member of the Communist Party to August 1991.
MAJOR WORKS: A number of publications, documentaries, scripts, and books, including *Competition and Press* and *Blue Genre Secrets*.
HONORS/AWARDS: Two Orders of the Red Banner of Labor.
FAMILY: Married with two children.

Kravchuk, Leonid Makarovich

POSITION: President of the Ukraine
BIRTHPLACE/DATE: Rovno region, 1934
NATIONALITY: Ukrainian
CAREER: Teacher; from 1960, Communist Party Functionary: Consultant, Lecturer, Department Head of the Chernovtsy Region Party Committee. From 1970, Functionary of the Ukraine Central Committee: Section Head, Inspector, Assistant to the Central Committee Secretary, First Deputy Department Head. From 1980, Propaganda and Agitation Department Head. From 1988, Ideology Department Head of the Central Committee. From 1989, Secretary of the Ukraine Central Committee, Alternate Member of the Ukraine Politburo. From June 1990, Second Secretary of the Central Committee, member of the Politburo. From July 1990, Ukraine Supreme Soviet Chairman. From 1991, President of the Ukraine. From February 1992, Chairman of the newly founded Ukrainian State Duma (Council). Ukranian People's Deputy. Former member of the Communist Party.
FAMILY: Married with a son.
ADDRESS/TELEPHONE: 11 Bankovskaya Street, Kiev, 252220. 291–5278 (office).

Krazman, Denis Leonidovich

POSITION: Chairman of the Moscow Democratic Russia Movement's Commission on Problems of Liaison with Servicemen and Law-Enforcement Bodies; Deputy Chairman of the Moscow Anti-Fascist Center
BIRTHPLACE/DATE: July 6, 1969
NATIONALITY: Russian
EDUCATION: Studied at a specialized secondary school. Graduated in 1987 from Vocational Training School #166.
CAREER: From 1987, worked at the Voskhod (Dawn) Research and Production Association in Moscow. From November 1987 to December 1990, served in the army. From February 1990, worked at a Moscow mill. In April 1991, elected Deputy Chairman of the Moscow Anti-Fascist Center; and Group Coordinator for Maintaining Order. From March 1991, Administrative Committee Member of the Moscow Democratic Russia Movement. From June 20, 1991, Chairman of the Democratic Russia Movement's Commission on Problems of Liaison with Servicemen and Law-Enforcement Bodies.
FAMILY: Single.
ADDRESS/TELEPHONE: 7 Kapotnya Microdistrict, Block 4, Flat #42, Moscow, 109429. 355–2139 (home).

Krivenko, Aleksandr Konstantinovich

POSITION: Chairman of the Prodintorg Foreign Trade Association
BIRTHPLACE/DATE: Kirovograd region, 1939
NATIONALITY: Ukrainian
EDUCATION: Graduated in 1965 from Moscow

State University; in 1972, from the All-Union Academy of Foreign Trade.
CAREER: From 1972 and 1977, worked at the All-Union Raznoexport (Various Export) Association, the Amtorg (American Trade) Association in the United States; Office Head, then Company Director of the All-Union Soyuzplodimport (Fruit Import) Association.
FAMILY: Married with two sons.
ADDRESS/TELEPHONE: 32/34 Smolenskaya-Sennaya Square, Moscow. 244–2629; 244–2252 (office).

Krivonogov, Sergey Olegovich
POSITION: Vice President of the Public Relations Agency Consortium
BIRTHPLACE/DATE: Moscow, 1966
EDUCATION: Graduated in 1988 from the Moscow State Institute of International Relations. Speaks French, Portuguese.
CAREER: From 1988 to 1990, Editor of the Main Western Europe Editorial Office of Novosti (News) Press Agency. From 1990 to 1991, Moscow Representative of the French advertising firm Carat. From 1991 to 1992, Public Relations Director of the Europe Plus USSR Joint-Venture.
FAMILY: Single.
ADDRESS/TELEPHONE: 27/3, First Kolobovsky Pereulok, Moscow. 923–4046 (office).

Krivonosov, Konstantin Andreyevich
POSITION: Chairman of the Russian Liberal Party
BIRTHPLACE/DATE: Moscow, 1949
EDUCATION: Graduated cum laude in 1970 from the Mechanical Engineering Department at the Moscow Engineering and Economics Institute. Majored in Engineering and Economy. Good command of English and Italian.
CAREER: From 1971 to 1985, Staff Member of the Foreign Trade Ministry. From 1987, Head of the Eterna-Primavera Foreign Economic Relations Consultancy Company. Joined the Democratic Movement in 1984. Moscow People's Front Activist.
FAMILY: Married.
ADDRESS/TELEPHONE: M.B. 42, Moscow, 117311. 131–7026 (office).

Krivov, Victor Dmitryevich
POSITION: Deputy Head of the Russian Federation President's Council of Experts
BIRTHPLACE/DATE: Tashkent, 1962
EDUCATION: Graduated in 1986 from the Moscow Institute of Economics and Statistics; in 1989, from postgraduate courses at Moscow University. Speaks English and Uzbek.
CAREER: From 1990 to 1991, Expert of the Russian Federation Supreme Soviet Chairman's Council of Experts.
FAMILY: Married with a daughter.
ADDRESS/TELEPHONE: The Kremlin, Moscow. 224–1510 (office).

Krupin, Vladimir Nikolayevich
POSITION: Editor in Chief of *Moskva* (*Moscow*) magazine; Secretary of the Russian Writers' Union
BIRTHPLACE/DATE: Kirovsk region, 1941
EDUCATION: Graduated in 1967 from the Teachers' Training Institute.
CAREER: From 1967 to 1970, Editor of the Literature and Drama Department of Central Television. From 1971 to 1975, Senior Editor of Sovremennik (Contemporary) Publishers. From 1976 to 1991, engaged in creative work, Secretary of the USSR Writers' Union.
FAMILY: Married with two children.
ADDRESS/TELEPHONE: 20 Arbat Street, GSP–2, Moscow. 291–7110.

Krylov, Vasily Ivanovich
POSITION: Editor in Chief of *Business Week*
BIRTHPLACE/DATE: Moscow, 1926
NATIONALITY: Russian
EDUCATION: Graduated in 1951 from the Moscow Automobile and Highway Engineering Institute. Speaks English.
CAREER: From 1951 to 1957, Censor at Glavlit (Print Literature Administration). From 1957 to 1963, Staff Member of the All-Union Academy of Foreign Trade. From 1963 to 1967, Head of the TASS (Telegraph Agency of the Soviet Union) Commercial Department in London. From 1967 to 1971, Deputy Chief Editor of the Foreign Commercial Information Bulletin. From 1971 to 1976, Head of the TASS Commercial Department in New York. From 1976 to 1984, Deputy Editor in Chief and Department Head at the All-Union Re-

search Institute of Marketing of the Foreign Trade Ministry. From 1984 to 1987, Head of the TASS Commercial Department in New York. From 1987 to 1990, Department Head of the Research Institute of Foreign Economic Relations of the USSR Council of Ministers.
ADDRESS/TELEPHONE: 22 Tverskaya-Yamskaya Street, Moscow. 251–0701 (office).

Kryuchkov, Vladimir Aleksandrovich
POSITION: Former Chairman of the State Security Committee (KGB); former USSR Security Council Member; General of the Army
BIRTHPLACE/DATE: Volgograd, February 29, 1924
NATIONALITY: Russian
EDUCATION: Graduated in 1949 from the All-Union Law Institute (by correspondence); and in 1954, from the Higher Diplomatic School of the USSR Foreign Ministry.
CAREER: From 1944 to 1945, First Secretary of the Barrikady Komsomol District Committee in Stalingrad region. In 1946, Second Secretary of the Stalingrad City Komsomol Committee. From 1946 to 1947, Investigator of the Procurator's Office in the Traktorozavodsky district of Stalingrad region. From 1947 to 1950, Investigation Department Procurator of the Stalingrad Regional Procurator's Office. From 1950 to 1951, Kirov District Procurator in Stalingrad. From 1954 to 1955, Third Secretary of the Fourth European Department (Czechoslovakia, Poland) of the USSR Foreign Ministry. From 1955 to 1959, Third Secretary at the USSR Embassy to Hungary. From 1959 to 1965, Advisor, Sector Head at the Central Committee's Liaison Department for Communist and Workers' Parties of Socialist Countries. From 1965, Assistant to the Secretary of the Central Committee (Yuri Andropov). From 1967 to 1971, Chief of the Secretariat of the USSR KGB. From 1971 and 1974, First Deputy Chief, Acting Chief of the USSR KGB's First Main Administration. From 1974 to 1988, Chief of the USSR KGB's First Main Administration. From 1974, USSR KGB Collegium Member. From 1978, Deputy Chairman; and from 1988, Chairman of the KGB. From 1991, USSR Security Council Member. In August 1991, during the attempted coup, member of the State Emergency Committee. From August 1991, under arrest.
HONORS/AWARDS: Two Orders of Lenin; Order of the October Revolution; Order of the Red Banner; two Orders of the Red Banner of Labor; Order of the Badge of Honor; medals.
FAMILY: Married with two children and grandchildren.
ADDRESS/TELEPHONE: Russian Federation Procurator's Office, Moscow. 229–4662.

Kucher, Valery Nikolayevich
POSITION: Editor in Chief of *Rossiyskiye Vesti* (*Russian News*) newspaper
BIRTHPLACE/DATE: Kiev, 1941
NATIONALITY: Ukrainian
EDUCATION: Graduated in 1969 from the Magnitogorsk State Teachers' Training Institute. Speaks French and English.
CAREER: From 1969 to 1970, Schoolteacher. From 1970, Staff Member of a factory newspaper, Deputy Editor at the Magnitogorsk Metallurgical Plant, Correspondent for *Chelyabinsky Rabochy* (*Chelyabinsk Worker*) newspaper. From 1983 to 1990, Editor of *Magnitogorsky Rabochy* (*Magnitogorsk Worker*) newspaper. USSR People's Deputy. From 1990 to January 1992, member of the USSR Supreme Soviet Committee for Legislation.
FAMILY: Married with a daughter and a grandson.
ADDRESS/TELEPHONE: 26 Volgogradsky Prospekt, Eighth Floor, Moscow. 270–0741.

Kucherenko, Igor Mikhailovich
POSITION: Member of the Russian Federation Supreme Soviet Committee for Legality, Law and Order, and Combatting Crime
BIRTHPLACE/DATE: Chechen-Ingushia, 1947
NATIONALITY: Russian
EDUCATION: Graduated in 1982 from the Academy of the USSR Ministry of Internal Affairs.
CAREER: From 1965 to 1966, worked for the North-Crimean Channel Construction. From 1966 to 1969, served in the navy. From 1970 to 1975, worked at the Leningrad Admiralty Association. From 1975 to 1990, served in the militia, from Divisional Inspector to Deputy Head of the Internal Affairs Department. From 1989, Russian Federation People's Deputy. From 1990 to 1991,

Deputy Chairman of the LenSoviet (Leningrad Council). Member of the Democratic Russia Movement and the Radical Democrats Faction.
FAMILY: Married with a son and a daughter.
ADDRESS/TELEPHONE: 2 Krasnopresnenskaya Naberezhnaya, Moscow. 290–9267 (home); 205–4293 (office).

Kudinov, Oleg Petrovich

POSITION: Director-General of the Rosbumaga (Russian Paper) Investment Company; Acting Director of the Rosbumaga Exchange
BIRTHPLACE/DATE: Minsk, 1952
NATIONALITY: Russian
EDUCATION: Graduated in 1974 from the Riga Institute of Civil Aviation. In 1986, defended thesis for doctoral degree. Doctor of Economics. Speaks English and Lettish.
CAREER: From 1974 to 1978, Engineer of the Latvian Board of Civil Aviation, Department Head. From 1978 to 1980, Junior Researcher at the Latvian Academy of Sciences' Institute of Philosophy of Law. From 1980 to 1986, Junior, then Senior Researcher at the All-Union Institute of Systems Analysis Research of the USSR Academy of Sciences. From 1986, Commercial Director of the Business-Intellect Enterprise.
FAMILY: Married with two children.
ADDRESS/TELEPHONE: 12 Kachalov Street, Moscow. 290–4635.

Kudryavtsev, Aleksandr Petrovich

POSITION: Rector of the Moscow Architectural Institute
BIRTHPLACE/DATE: Moscow, 1937
CAREER: From 1960 to 1987, Architect at the Central Research Institute of Entertainment and Sport Complexes. From 1977 to 1982, Assistant Professor at the Moscow Architecture Institute. From 1982 to 1985, Editor in Chief of *USSR Architecture* magazine. From 1985 to 1987, Vice President of the USSR Union of Architects. Honorary Member of the American Institute of Architects, Board Member of the International Union of Architects, Vice President of the European Society of Culture, Board Member of the Moscow Union of Architects. USSR People's Deputy.
MAJOR WORKS: More than fifty publications, including: *Universal History of Architecture*; *The Development of Socialist Arts in Central and South-Eastern Europe*; *Traditions in Russian and Soviet Architecture.*
HONORS/AWARDS: USSR Council of Ministers Prize.
FAMILY: Married with two children.
ADDRESS/TELEPHONE: 11 Rozhdestvenka Street, Moscow. 924–7990 (office).

Kudryavtsev, Gennadi Georgyevich

POSITION: Chairman of the Board of Directors of the Intertelecom (International Telecommunications) Joint-Stock Society
BIRTHPLACE/DATE: Slavinka village, Primorye region, 1941
NATIONALITY: Russian
EDUCATION: Graduated in 1974 from the All-Union Electrical Engineering Institute.
CAREER: From 1958 to 1959, Diesel-Operator at an urban power station. From 1959 to 1969, Electrician, served in the army. From 1969 to 1970, Senior Engineer; from 1970 and 1974, Department Head; from 1974 to 1980, Deputy Head of the Main Department of Linear-Cable and Radio-Relay Communication Facilities of the USSR Ministry of Communications. From 1980 to 1991, USSR First Deputy Minister of Communications. In 1991, USSR Minister of Communications.
HONORS/AWARDS: Order of the October Revolution; Order of the Badge of Honor.
FAMILY: Married with two children.
ADDRESS/TELEPHONE: 7 Tverskaya Street, Moscow, 103 GSP. 292–5691 (office).

Kudryavtsev, Valery Georgyevich

POSITION: Editor in Chief of *Sovietsky Sport* (*Soviet Sport*) newspaper and *Sovietsky Sport + 8* weekly
BIRTHPLACE/DATE: Petrozavodsk, 1938
EDUCATION: Graduated from the Journalism Department at Moscow State University; and from the Academy of Social Sciences. Good command of German.
CAREER: From 1961, Editor at Iskusstvo (Art) Publishers; then *Sportivnaya Zhizn Rossii* (*Russian Sports Life*) magazine. From 1968, worked from Assistant Editor to Editor in Chief of *Sovietsky Sport*. From 1979 to 1983, worked at the

Sports Department and the Newspaper Department of the Central Committee.
FAMILY: Married with a daughter.
ADDRESS/TELEPHONE: 8 Arkhipov Street, Moscow. 923–8956.

Kudryavtsev, Vladimir Nikolayevich
POSITION: President of the Russian Afro-Asian Solidarity and Cooperation Society
BIRTHPLACE/DATE: Moscow, April 10, 1923
NATIONALITY: Russian
EDUCATION: Graduated in 1949 from the Military Law Academy of the USSR Armed Forces.
CAREER: Took part in World War II. Joined the Communist Party in 1945. From 1949 to 1952, Adjunct at the Military Law Academy. From 1952 to 1956, Lecturer at the Military Law Academy. From 1956 to 1960, Lecturer at the Lenin Military Political Academy. From 1960 to 1963, worked at the USSR Supreme Soviet Military Judicial Board. From 1963 to 1973, Deputy Director, Director of the All-Union Institute for the Investigation and Prevention of Crime. From 1973 to 1988, Director, and from 1988, Honorary Director of the State and Law Institute of the USSR Academy of Sciences. From 1984, Academician of the USSR Academy of Sciences. From 1988, Vice President of the USSR Academy of Sciences. USSR People's Deputy.
HONORS/AWARDS: USSR State Prize.
FAMILY: Married with two sons.
ADDRESS/TELEPHONE: 10 Prechistenka Street, Moscow. 202–2314 (office).

Kugultinov, David Nikitovich
POSITION: Poet; Board Member of the Confederation of Writers' Unions
BIRTHPLACE/DATE: Abganer-Kakhankiny village, Western Ulus, Kalmykia, 1922
NATIONALITY: Kalmyk
EDUCATION: Completed the Higher Literary Courses in 1940.
CAREER: From 1940 to 1944, took part in World War II. From 1944, Lecturer at a school in Biysk, Altai region. In 1945, subjected to illegal reprisals; stayed in Norilsk, Krasnoyarsk region for over ten years. From 1957, Executive Secretary; from 1961 to 1964, and from 1972 to 1989, Board Chairman of the Kalmykian Writers' Union. From 1981, Board Member of the USSR Writers' Union. From 1989 to 1991, member of the USSR Supreme Soviet Presidium.
HONORS/AWARDS: USSR and Russian Federation State Prizes; two Orders of the Red Banner of Labor; Order of the People's Friendship; Hero of Socialist Labor; Kalmykia People's Poet.
FAMILY: Married.
ADDRESS/TELEPHONE: 20 Klykov Street, Flat #3, Elista, 358000. 6–2587 (home).

Kukhtenkov, Aleksey Semyonovich
POSITION: Chairman of the Vostokintorg (Eastern International Trade) Foreign Trade Association
BIRTHPLACE/DATE: Moscow, 1946
NATIONALITY: Russian
EDUCATION: Graduated in 1970 from the Foreign Trade and Economics Department at the Moscow State Institute of International Relations.
CAREER: From 1970 to 1989, Engineer, Senior Engineer, Deputy Director, Director, Deputy Director-General, First Deputy Director-General of Raznoexport (Various Export) Association. From 1977 and 1981, Russion Federation Trade Representative in the United States. From 1989 to 1990, Chief of the Economic Relations Board of the USSR Trade Ministry. From 1990, Executive Secretary of the Soviet-American Commission of the USSR Ministry of Foreign Economic Relations.
FAMILY: Married with a daughter.
ADDRESS/TELEPHONE: 32/34 Smolenskaya-Sennaya Square, Moscow. 205–6055 (office).

Kulakov, Mikhail Petrovich
POSITION: Chairman of the CIS Seventh-Day Adventists Church Council; President of the European-Asian Department of the Seventh-Day Adventists Church General Confederation
BIRTHPLACE/DATE: Leningrad, March 29, 1927
NATIONALITY: Russian
EDUCATION: Doctor of Theology (United States).
CAREER: From 1962 to 1976, Presbyter of the Seventh-Day Adventists (SDA) Communities in Alma Ata and Chimkent (Kazakhstan). From 1976 to 1990, Senior Preacher of the Russian Federation SDA Communities. From 1990, Chairman of the SDA Church Council. From 1991, Chairman of the All-Union SDA Church Council.
FAMILY: Married with six children.

ADDRESS/TELEPHONE: 26 Furmanov Street, Tula. 476–5348 (home); 25–4966 (Tula).

Kulakova, Galina Alekseyevna

POSITION: Former Olympic Skiing Champion of the National Ski-Racing Team; Coach of the Udmurtian State Sports Committee
BIRTHPLACE/DATE: Logachi village, Votkinsk District, Udmurtia, 1942
NATIONALITY: Russian
EDUCATION: Graduated from the Prokopyevsk Physical Education Institute in Kemerovo region.
CAREER: In 1972, Winter Olympic Skiing Champion. In 1968, Silver Medalist (5-km). In 1976, Bronze Medalist (10-km). Silver Medal (5-km) in 1968; in 1978 (20-km); and in 1980 (20-km). Bronze Medal in 1970 (10-km), and in 1976 (10-km). Worked at the Votkinsk Machinery Construction Plant. Skiing Coach of the Prokopyevsk Municipal Trud (Labor) Council.
HONORS/AWARDS: USSR Honored Master of Sports.
ADDRESS/TELEPHONE: 4 Votkinskoye Chaussée, Flat #35, Izhevsk. 24–0613.

Kulesha, Vadim Anatolyevich

POSITION: Director-General of the Beloretsk Metallurgical Complex; Russian Federation People's Deputy
BIRTHPLACE/DATE: Beloretsk, Bashkiria, 1932
NATIONALITY: Russian
EDUCATION: Graduated in 1956 from the Urals Polytechnical Institute. Doctor of Technology. Speaks English.
CAREER: From 1956 to 1959, Foreman of the Technological Workshop of Cold Rolled Stock at the Beloretsk Metallurgical Complex. From 1959 to 1961, Deputy Workshop Head. From 1961 to 1971, Head of the Cold Rolled Stock Workshop. From 1971 to 1979, Deputy Chief Engineer, Deputy Director of the Beloretsk Metallurgical Complex. Member of the Committee for Industry and the Committee for Economic Reforms. Member of the Industrial Union Faction.
FAMILY: Married with a son and a daughter.
ADDRESS/TELEPHONE: The Beloretsk Metallurgical Combine, Blyukher Street, Beloretsk. 4–0504 (home); 3–0438; 4–4500 (office).

Kulikov, Aleksandr Nikolayevich

POSITION: Russian Federation Deputy Minister of Internal Affairs; Lieutenant-General of the Militia
BIRTHPLACE/DATE: Bendery, Moldavia, 1941
CAREER: Served in the militia from 1965. Militia Batallion Deputy Commander in Yoshkar-Ola; Deputy Head of the City Militia Office; Head of the Leninsky District Militia Office of Yoshkar-Ola. From 1975 to 1981, held different positions in the Baikal-Amur Railroad Construction Militia. From 1983 to 1987, Deputy Head of the Kuzbass Militia. From 1987 to 1990, Head of the Mary Region Militia in Turkmenistan. From 1990 to 1991, Head of the Transport Militia, Deputy Head of the Public Security Service, Head of the Transport Militia Control Center of the Russian Federation Ministry of Internal Affairs. From September 1991 to January 1992, USSR Deputy Minister of Internal Affairs.
ADDRESS/TELEPHONE: 16 Zhitnaya Street, Moscow, 117049. 239–6311 (office).

Kulikov, Valeryan Nikolayevich

POSITION: Board Chairman of the Moscow Izdat-Bank Commercial Publishing Bank
BIRTHPLACE/DATE: Moscow, April 24, 1937
NATIONALITY: Russian
EDUCATION: Graduated in 1958 from the Moscow Institute of Finance; in 1974, completed the postgraduate program. Doctor of Economics.
CAREER: From 1958 to 1959, Inspector, Senior Inspector of the Moscow USSR Promstroibank (Industrial Construction Bank). From 1959 to 1964, Chief Inspector of the Control and Auditing Department of the USSR Stroibank (Construction Bank). From 1964 to 1965, Head of the Department of Construction Financing of USSR Stroibank's Planning Department. From 1965 to 1977, Head of the Control and Auditing Department of the USSR Stroibank. From 1977 to 1984, Head of the Department for Financing and Crediting Contracting Organizations of the USSR Stroibank. From 1984 to 1987, Deputy Board Chairman of the USSR Stroibank. From 1987 to 1988, Deputy Board Chairman of the USSR Promstroibank, Head of the Department for Crediting and Financing the Fuel and Energy Complex. From 1988 to 1989, First Deputy Board Chairman of the USSR

State Bank. From 1989 to 1991, Deputy Chairman of the USSR State Control Committee. From 1991 to 1992, First Deputy Chairman of the USSR State Bank.
HONORS/AWARDS: Order of the Red Banner of Labor; Order of the Badge of Honor; Medal For Labor Valor; Veteran of Labor Medal.
FAMILY: Married with a son.
ADDRESS/TELEPHONE: 26 Petrovka Street, Moscow, 101401. 200–6869 (office).

Kunadze, Georgy Fridrikhovich
POSITION: Russian Federation Deputy Foreign Minister
BIRTHPLACE/DATE: 1948
NATIONALITY: Russian
EDUCATION: Graduated in 1971 from the Institute of Oriental Languages at Moscow State University. Doctor of History. Speaks English and Japanese.
CAREER: From 1971 to 1983, Senior Researcher-Technologist, Junior Researcher, Senior Researcher at the USSR Academy of Sciences' Institute of Oriental Studies. From 1983 to 1987, Science Attaché at the USSR Embassy in Japan. From 1987 to 1991, Sector Head, Department Head of the Institute of the World Economy and International Relations of the USSR Academy of Sciences.
ADDRESS/TELEPHONE: 32/34 Smolenskaya-Sennaya Street, Moscow 121200. 244–1606; 244–9221 (office).

Kunyayev, Stanislav Yuryevich
POSITION: Editor in Chief of *Nash Sovremennik* (*Our Contemporary*) magazine
BIRTHPLACE/DATE: Kaluga, 1932
EDUCATION: Graduated in 1957 from the Philology Department at Moscow State University.
CAREER: From 1957 to 1959, Staff Member of *Zavety Ilyicha* (*Lenin's Legacy*) newspaper in Irkutsk region. From 1960 to 1963, Poetry Department Head of *Znamya* (*Banner*) magazine. From 1963, engaged in creative work. From 1976 to 1980, Secretary of the Moscow Writers' Organization. Champion of the national revival of Russia. Board Secretary of the Russian Writers' Union.
FAMILY: Married with a son.
ADDRESS/TELEPHONE: 30 Tsvetnoi Boulevard, Moscow. 200–2424.

Kupriyanova, Anastasiya Victorovna
POSITION: Editor in Chief of *Krestyanka* (*Country Woman*) magazine
BIRTHPLACE/DATE: Nadvornoye, Ivano-Frankovsk region, 1948
NATIONALITY: Russian
EDUCATION: Graduated from the Gorky Literary Institute.
CAREER: Correspondent for district newspapers. Literature Teacher at a rural school. Correspondent on a contract basis. Executive Secretary of *Moskovsky Komsomolets* (*Moscow Komsomol Member*) newspaper. Special Correspondent for *Sovietskaya Rossiya* (*Soviet Russia*) and *Socialisticheskaya Industria* (*Socialist Industry*) newspapers.
FAMILY: Married with a daughter.
ADDRESS/TELEPHONE: 14 Bumazhny Proyezd, Moscow, 101460. 212–2063.

Kurkova, Bella Alekseyevna
POSITION: Administration Director of the St. Petersburg All-Russia State TV and Radio Broadcasting Company
BIRTHPLACE/DATE: Bryansk, 1935
NATIONALITY: Russian
EDUCATION: Graduated from the Journalism Department at Leningrad State University.
CAREER: Correspondent for *Sovietskaya Chukotka* (*Soviet Chukot*) newspaper. Correspondent for *Leninsky Iskry* (*Lenin's Sparks*) children's newspaper. In 1969, began working for the Leningrad Television and Radio Broadcasting Committee: Editor, Deputy Editor in Chief of the Information Department, Editor in Chief of the Youth Department, Editor in Chief of the Art Department. Co-Founder of the socio-political TV program "Pyatoye Koleso" (The Fifth Wheel). From June 1991, Administration Director of the St. Petersburg All-Russia State TV and Radio Broadcasting Company. Member of the USSR Journalists' Union. Russian Federation People's Deputy. PetroSoviet (St. Petersburg Council) People's Deputy. From December 1991, member of the Confederation of Journalists' Unions.
HONORS/AWARDS: USSR Writers' Union Prize.

FAMILY: Married.
ADDRESS/TELEPHONE: 6 Chapygina Street, St. Petersburg. 104–1450 (office).

Kurtashin, Vladimir Yegorovich
POSITION: President of Kriogenika Concern
BIRTHPLACE/DATE: Kremlevo village, Skopin district, Ryazan region, 1932
EDUCATION: Graduated in 1955 from Tula Polytechnic. Doctor of Technology; Professor. Academician of the Engineering Academy.
CAREER: From 1955 to 1959, Foreman, Shop Superintendent in Chelyabinsk. From 1959 to 1963, Assistant Shop Superintendent, Chief of Press-Tools Production at the Uzlovoye Machinery Construction Complex. From 1963 to 1980, Assistant Shop Superintendent, Shop Superintendent, Chief Engineer, Deputy Production Director, Director of the Kriogenmash Association in Balashikha, Moscow region. From 1980 to 1986, Directorate Head; from 1986, Director-General of Soyuzkriogenmash Association. Board Chairman of the Kriogenika Inter-Republican Association. USSR People's Deputy. From May 1989 to 1991, member of the USSR Supreme Soviet Presidium, Chairman of the Committee for Industry and Power Engineering, member of the Workers' Parliamentary Faction, the Research-and-Production Parliamentary Faction, and the Otechestvo (Fatherland) Parliamentary Faction.
HONORS/AWARDS: Hero of Socialist Labor; USSR Honored Inventor; USSR State Prize; Order of the Red Banner of Labor; Medal For Labor Valor; Veteran of Labor Medal.
FAMILY: Married with a daughter and two grandchildren.
ADDRESS/TELEPHONE: 67 Lenin Prospekt, Balashikha, Moscow Region. 521–1774; 203–5665 (office).

Kuzmenok, Vladimir Vladimirovich
POSITION: Vice Chairman of the General Trade Union Confederation
BIRTHPLACE/DATE: Kryuki village, Gomel region, Byelorussia, 1950
NATIONALITY: Byelorussian
EDUCATION: Graduated from the Kaliningrad Higher School of Naval Engineering.
CAREER: From 1970, Sailor, Third, Second, and Senior Assistant to the Captain at the Kaliningrad Expeditionary Fleet Base. From 1980, Managing Captain at the Kaliningrad Fishing Fleet Base. From 1987, Captain of an Angolan ship. From 1988, Communist Party Functionary. In July 1989, elected Central Committee Chairman of the Trade Union of Fishery Workers. In October 1990, elected Vice Chairman of the USSR General Trade Union Confederation.
FAMILY: Married with two sons.
ADDRESS/TELEPHONE: 42 Leninsky Prospekt, Moscow. 938–8242 (office).

Kuzmin, Fyodor Mikhailovich
POSITION: Head of the Frunze Military Academy; Colonel-General
BIRTHPLACE/DATE: Kopanovka village, Enotaevsk district, Volgograd region, 1937
NATIONALITY: Russian
CAREER: From 1956, served in the USSR Armed Forces: Division Commander, Corps Commander, Army Commander, First Deputy Military District Commander. From 1989 to 1992, Pribaltiysky (Baltics) Military District Commander.
FAMILY: Married with two sons.
TELEPHONE: 293–2869; 293–1413 (office).

Kuznetsov, Anatoli Mikhailovich
POSITION: Russian President's Representative in Novgorod region; Russian Federation People's Deputy
BIRTHPLACE/DATE: Kostroma, August 29, 1938
NATIONALITY: Russian
EDUCATION: From 1961 to 1963, student at the Kaunas Specialized Secondary Militia School in Lithuania. Graduated in 1970 from the Law Department at the All-Union Law Institute (by correspondence).
CAREER: From 1953 to 1955, worked at a regional zagotzerno (grain procuring) office in Kostroma. From 1955 to 1961, worked at the Oktyabr (October) Footwear Factory in Kostroma. From 1963 to 1983, Divisional Militia Inspector, Senior Operative Divisional Inspector of the Department for Combatting the Embezzlement of Socialist Property (OBKhSS); OBKhSS Department Head; Deputy Chief of the Militia District Department; Chief of the District Militia Department; Deputy OBKhSS Chief of the Magadan Region Internal

Affairs Administration; OBKhSS Chief of the Magadan Region Internal Affairs Administration. From 1983 to 1985, Senior Counsellor of the Tsarandoi Command in Farvet and the Gerosit Provinces in Afghanistan. From 1986 to 1992, OBKhSS Chief; Chief of the Department for Combatting Economic Crime, Deputy Head of the Criminal Militia Service in Novgorod region. Russian Federation People's Deputy, member of the Russian Federation Supreme Soviet Constitutional Commission.

FAMILY: Married with four children.

ADDRESS/TELEPHONE: 13 Rakhmaninov Street, Building 1, Flat #45, Novgorod. 3–0259 (home); 7–4046 (office).

Kuznetsov, German Serapionovich

POSITION: Kirgistan (formerly Kirghizia) Republic First Vice Premier

BIRTHPLACE/DATE: Ivanovo, 1948

NATIONALITY: Russian

EDUCATION: Doctor of Economics.

CAREER: Served in the army, worked as an Electrician, Engineer, Deputy Department Head of the Krasnoyarsk TV Factory. From 1972, Komsomol and Communist Party Functionary: Deputy Secretary of the Factory Party Committee, Instructor of the Regional Party Committee, Party Committee Secretary of the Krasnoyarsk Industrial Complex, First Secretary of the Divnogorsk City Party Committee. From August 1987, Secretary of the Frunze City Party Committee. In November 1990, member of the Presidential Council of Kirghizia. From January 1991 to March 1992, Vice President of the Kirgistan Republic. People's Deputy of Kirghizia.

FAMILY: Married with two children.

ADDRESS/TELEPHONE: House of Government, Bishkek, 720003. 21–8935 (office).

Kvitsinsky, Yuli Aleksandrovich

POSITION: Vice President of the Foreign Policy Association; Ambassador Extraordinary and Plenipotentiary

BIRTHPLACE/DATE: Rzhev, Tver region, September 28, 1936

NATIONALITY: Russian

EDUCATION: Graduated in 1959 from the Moscow State Institute of International Relations of the USSR Foreign Ministry. Doctor of Law (1968). Good command of German, Norwegian, French, English, and Spanish.

CAREER: From 1959 to 1960, Interpreter at the USSR Embassy in the German Democratic Republic (East Germany). From 1960 to 1965, Attaché; from 1965 to 1969, Second Secretary; and from 1969 to 1978, Deputy Head of the Third European Department (Austria, East Germany, West Germany) of the USSR Foreign Ministry. From 1978 to 1981, Minister-Counsellor at the USSR Embassy in the Federal Republic of Germany (West Germany). From 1981 to 1986, Ambassador at Large of the USSR Foreign Ministry. From 1985 to 1986, Soviet Delegation Head at the Nuclear and Space Arms Negotiations in Geneva. From 1986 to 1990, USSR Ambassador to West Germany. From 1986 to 1989, Alternate Member of the Central Committee. From 1989 to 1990, Full Member of the Central Committee. From 1990 to August 1991, USSR Deputy Foreign Minister.

HONORS/AWARDS: Order of the October Revolution; Order of the Red Banner of Labor; Order of the People's Friendship.

FAMILY: Married.

ADDRESS/TELEPHONE: 32/34 Smolenskaya-Sennaya Square, Moscow, 121200. 244–1606; 244–2469; 244–4662.

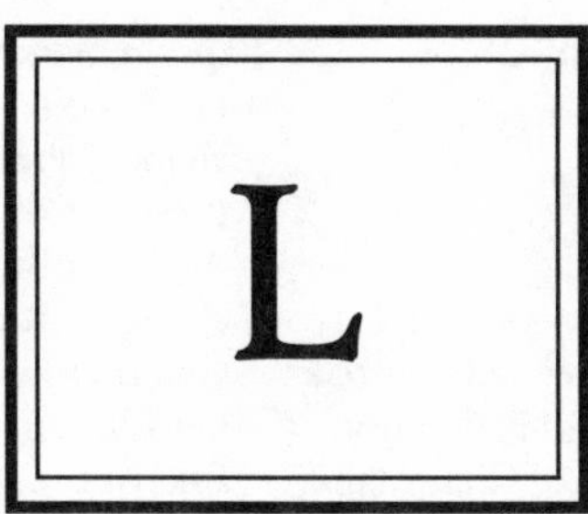

Lagovsky, Igor Konstantinovich

Position: Editor in Chief of *Nauka i Zhizn* (*Science and Life*) magazine
Birthplace/Date: Kineshma, Ivanovo region, 1922
Nationality: Russian
Education: Graduated in 1951 from the Moscow N.E. Bauman State Technical Institute.
Career: From 1941 to 1945, fought in World War II. From 1951 to 1956, Editor of *Yuny Tekhnik* (*Young Technician*) magazine; from 1957, Deputy Editor in Chief. In 1957, joined the Communist Party. From 1960, Managing Editor of *Nauka i Zhizn*; from 1961, Deputy Editor in Chief. Board Member of the Znaniye (Knowledge) Society.
Honors/Awards: Russian Federation Honored Cultural Worker; Order of the Red Banner of Labor; Order of the Badge of Honor.
Family: Married with a child and grandchildren.
Address/Telephone: 24 Myasnitskaya Street, Moscow, 101877. 923–2122 (office).

Lagutin, Boris Nikolayevich

Position: Board Chairman of the All-Union Health Improvement and Sports Foundation
Birthplace/Date: Moscow, 1938
Nationality: Russian
Education: Graduated in 1971 from Moscow State University.
Career: In 1964 and 1968, Summer Olympic Boxing Champion; World and European Champion. Executive Manager of the Komsomol Central Committee Sports Department; Deputy Chairman of the Russian Council of the Spartak Voluntary Sports Society.
Honors/Awards: Russion Federation Honored Master of Sports.
Family: Married with two sons.
Address/Telephone: 14/2 Solyanka Street, Moscow. 921–1046; 227–5656 (office); 283–8551 (home).

Lakhova, Yekaterina Filippovna

Position: Russian Federation People's Deputy
Birthplace/Date: Sverdlovsk (now Yekaterinburg), 1948
Nationallity: Russian
Education: Graduated in 1972 from the Yekaterinburg Medical Institute. From 1976 to 1978, clinical student at the Medical Institute.
Career: From 1972 to 1976, Physician at a children's clinic. From 1978 to 1981, Department Head of a children's clinic. From 1981 to 1987, Deputy Head of a Sverdlovsk City Health Care Department. From 1987 to 1990, Deputy Head of the Main Public Health Administration; Committee Chairwoman of the Russian Federation Supreme Soviet. From 1991, Russian Federation State Counsellor; Chairwoman of the Coordinating Council for Women, Family, Motherhood, and Childhood Issues; Russian Federation People's Deputy. From September 1992 to 1993, Counsellor to the Russian Federation President for Women, Family, Motherhood, and Childhood Issues.
Family: Married with a son.
Address/Telephone: 8/2 Korolev Street, Flat

#575, Moscow. 206–4439 (office); 286–2722 (home).

Lakshin, Vladimir Yakovlevich

POSITION: Editor in Chief of *Inostrannaya Literatura* (*Foreign Literature*) magazine; member of the Consultative Council of the Russian Federation Minister of Culture and Tourism; Board Chairman of the Roerich Foundation; Chairman of the Chekhov Commission of the Russian Academy of Sciences; member of the Russian PEN Center Executive Committee
BIRTHPLACE/DATE: Moscow, 1933
EDUCATION: Graduated in 1955 from Moscow State University's Philology Department. Doctor of Philology.
CAREER: From 1958, Lecturer at Moscow State University. From 1961 and 1962, Head of the Criticism Department of *Literaturnaya Gazeta* (*Literary Newspaper*). From 1962 to 1970, Deputy Editor in Chief of *Novy Mir* magazine. From 1970 and 1986, Consultant to *Inostrannaya Literatura*. From 1987 to 1989, First Deputy Editor in Chief of *Znamya* (*Banner*) magazine.
MAJOR WORKS: *Tolstoy and Chekhov*; *Open Door*; *Five Great Names*.
ADDRESS/TELEPHONE: 41 Pyatnitskaya Street, Moscow. 233–5147 (office).

Landsbergis, Vitautas

POSITION: Member of the Lithuanian Seim (Parliament); Leader of the Opposition
BIRTHPLACE/DATE: Kaunas, 1932
NATIONALITY: Lithuanian
CAREER: From 1953 to 1963, Professor at the Lithuanian Conservatory. From 1957 to 1974, Professor at the Vilnius Teachers' Training Institute. In 1975, returned to the Lithuanian Conservatory. One of the founders of the Sayudis Movement; in 1988, elected Chairman. In February 1989, elected Chairman of the Lithuanian Republic Supreme Soviet.
MAJOR WORKS: Author of books on Lithuanian composers M. Churlyunis and C. Sasnauskas.
FAMILY: Married with three children.
ADDRESS/TELEPHONE: 53 Gedimino Street, Vilnius, 2026, Lithuania. 22–4475 (office).

Lapshin, Mikhail Ivanovich

POSITION: President of the Transnational Exchange; President of the Moscow Brokers Guild; President of the House of Brokers; President of the Agrarian Branch of the Russian Commodities Exchange; Russian Federation People's Deputy; Chairman of the Russian People's Deputies Agrarian Faction
BIRTHPLACE/DATE: Ussuriysk, Primorsky region, 1945
CAREER: From 1970 to 1989, Engineer, Laboratory Head, Department Head of the Moscow Atominform Central Research Institute. From 1989 to 1990, worked at the All-Union Research Institute for Information and Feasibility in Production Management. From 1990 to 1991, Director of the Kobos Cooperative Information Center. To August 1991, member of the Communist Party. From 1991, Co-Chairman of the Socialist Workers' Party.
FAMILY: Married with a daughter.
ADDRESS/TELEPHONE: 35 Myasnitskaya, Moscow. 207–6867 (office).

Lashch, Vera Grigoryevna

POSITION: Chairwoman of the Russian Union of Work Collectives
BIRTHPLACE/DATE: Moscow, July 27, 1947
NATIONALITY: Russian
EDUCATION: Graduated in 1976 from the Power Engineering Department at the All-Union Polytechnical Institute (by correspondence).
CAREER: From 1963 to 1976, Controller, Instrument Tester, Engineer-Designer at the Second Moscow Instrument-Making Factory. From 1976 to 1977, worked in Mongolia. From 1977 to 1978, Senior Engineer of the Rubber Industry Research Institute. From 1973 to 1990, member of the Communist Party. From 1978 to 1991, Chief Metrologist, member, and Deputy Secretary of the Kauchuk Production Association Communist Party. In 1989, elected member of the Council of Work Collectives (CWC); in 1990, elected CWC Chairwoman. In October 1990, elected member of the Coordinating Council of the Moscow Union of Work Collectives. In December 1990, elected Co-Chairwoman of the Union of Work Collectives. From 1991 to 1992, Chief Specialist of the Supreme Economic Council Secretariat of the Rus-

sian Federation Supreme Soviet. In March 1992, elected to the Constituent Congress.
FAMILY: Single with a daughter.
ADDRESS/TELEPHONE: 3/5 Pugovishnikov Pereulok, Flat #29, Moscow, 119021. 246–9661 (home); 291–5547 (office).

Latsis, Otto Rudolfovich
POSITION: Political Analyst of *Izvestia* (*News*) daily
BIRTHPLACE/DATE: Moscow, June 22, 1934
NATIONALITY: Lett
EDUCATION: Graduated in 1956 from Moscow State University's Journalism Department. Doctor of Economics.
CAREER: From 1956 to 1960, Staff Member of *Sovietsky Sakhalin* regional newspaper. In 1959, joined the Communist Party. From 1960 to 1964, Consultant to *Ekonomicheskaya Gazeta* (*Economic Newspaper*). From 1964 to 1971, Special Correspondent; Economic Analyst of the Industrial Department of *Izvestia*. From 1971 to 1975, Editor-Consultant, then Head of the Socialist Countries Department of the Prague-based *World Marxist Review* journal. From 1975 to 1986, Senior Researcher, Department Head at the USSR Academy of Sciences' Institute of the Socialist World Economy. From 1986, Political Analyst. From 1987, First Deputy Editor in Chief of *Kommunist* (*Communist*) magazine. From 1990 to 1991, member of the Central Committee. In 1991, Board Member of the Socio-Political Studies Foundation.
MAJOR WORKS: Monographs: "Associations in Council for Mutual Economic Aid (CMEA) Countries" (1978); "Economic Centralization and Management Centralism." Books: *Interconnection* (1987); *The Art of Adding Up* (1984); *Beyond the Square* (1989); *The Turning Point* (1990).
FAMILY: Married with two children.
ADDRESS/TELEPHONE: 5 Pushkin Square, Moscow. 209–1594 (office); 331–3454 (home).

Latynina, Larisa Semyonovna
POSITION: Deputy Director of the Russian Fizkultura i Sport (Physical Education and Sports) Charity Foundation
BIRTHPLACE/DATE: Kherson, 1927
EDUCATION: Speaks French.
CAREER: In 1956, 1960, and 1964 Summer Olympic Gymnastics Champion. Many-time World and European Champion. From 1967 to 1977, Senior Coach of the USSR National Gymnastics Team. From 1977 to 1980, Senior Expert of the Olympics–80 Coordinating Committee. From 1981 to 1990, Coach of the USSR National Gymnastics Teams of the Moscow Committee on Sports. In 1990, Deputy Chairwoman of the All-Union Zdorovye (Health) Foundation.
HONORS/AWARDS: USSR Honored Master of Sports; USSR Honored Coach; Order of Lenin; three Orders of the Badge of Honor; Order of the People's Friendship.
FAMILY: Married with a daughter.
ADDRESS/TELEPHONE: 4 Tolmachevsky Pereulok, Moscow. 238–6210; 261–8527 (office); 235–0540 (home).

Laverov, Nikolay Pavlovich
POSITION: Vice President of the Russian Academy of Sciences; Acting Director of the Institute of Geology, Mineralogy, and Geochemistry
BIRTHPLACE/DATE: Pozharishche village, Konosha district, Arkhangelsk region, January 12, 1930
NATIONALITY: Russian
EDUCATION: Graduated in 1954 from the Moscow Kalinin Institute of Non-Ferrous Metals and Gold. From 1955 to 1958, postgraduate student at the Moscow Institute of Non-Ferrous Metals. Doctor of Geology and Mineralogy; Professor. Speaks Spanish, Italian, and English.
CAREER: From 1958 to 1966, Academic Secretary of Expedition No. 1 of the Institute of Geology, Mineralogy, and Geochemistry. In 1959, joined the Communist Party. From 1966 to 1983, Deputy Head of the Research Organizations Administration; Head of the All-Union Geological Foundation. From 1972, Collegium Member of the USSR Ministry of Geology. From 1983 to 1987, Vice Rector, First Vice Rector of the Academy of National Economy of the USSR Council of Ministers. From 1987, Academician of the USSR Academy of Sciences. From 1987 to 1989, President of the Kirgistan Academy of Sciences. From 1988, Vice President of the USSR (now Russian) Academy of Sciences. From 1989, Deputy Chairman of the USSR Council of Ministers; Chairman

of the USSR State Committee for Science and Technology. Member of the Central Committee.
HONORS/AWARDS: Order of the Red Banner of Labor; Order of the Badge of Honor.
FAMILY: Married with two children.
ADDRESS/TELEPHONE: 14 Leninsky Prospekt, Moscow. 954–2968; 231–7270 (office).

Lavrinovich, Mikhail Fyodorovich
POSITION: Director-General of the BelavtoMAZ (Byelorussian Automobile Complex) Industrial Association; President of the Minsk State Enterprises Association
BIRTHPLACE/DATE: Telusha village, Mogilev region, 1929
NATIONALITY: Byelorussian
CAREER: Worked from Adjuster to Deputy Director of the Minsk Automobile Plant.
HONORS/AWARDS: Two Orders of the Red Banner of Labor; Order of the Badge of Honor; Byelorussian State Prize.
FAMILY: Married with two children.
ADDRESS/TELEPHONE: 2 Socialisticheskaya Street, Minsk, 220831. 469–600 (office).

Lavrov, Kirill Yuryevich
POSITION: President of the International Confederation of Theater Unions; Art Director of the Leningrad Gorky Academic Drama Theater; member of the Consultative Council of the Russian Federation Minister of Culture and Tourism
BIRTHPLACE/DATE: Leningrad (now St. Petersburg), 1925
NATIONALITY: Russian
EDUCATION: Graduated in 1945 from the Aviation Engineering Institute.
CAREER: From 1943, served in the Armed Forces; worked at the Lesya Ukrainka Theater in Kiev. In 1955, joined the Gorky Academic Drama Theater Company in Leningrad; starred in many films. From May 1987 to 1991, Board Chairman of the USSR Union of Theater Workers. From July 1989, Art Director of the Leningrad Gorky Drama Theater. From 1990 to 1991, member of the International Prizes of Lenin Committee; member of the Council of Nationalities Committee for Preserving Languages, Culture, National and International Traditions, and Historical Heritage. USSR People's Deputy.
HONORS/AWARDS: USSR People's Artist; Hero of Socialist Labor; USSR State and Lenin Prizes; Order of Lenin; Hammer and Sickle Gold Medal.
FAMILY: Married with children.
ADDRESS/TELEPHONE: 12 Tverskaya Street, Building 7, Flat #228, Moscow, 103009. 209–2436; 209–0372 (office).

Lavrov, Sergey Victorovich
POSITION: Russian Federation Deputy Foreign Minister; Envoy Extraordinary and Plenipotentiary, First Class
BIRTHPLACE/DATE: 1950
NATIONALITY: Russian
EDUCATION: Graduated in 1972 from the Moscow State Institute of International Relations. Speaks English, French, and Sinhalese.
CAREER: From 1972 to 1976, Trainee, Attaché at the USSR Embassy to Sri Lanka Republic. From 1976 to 1981, Third, then Second Secretary of the International Economic Relations Directorate of the USSR Foreign Ministry. From 1981 to 1988, First Secretary, Counsellor, Senior Counsellor at the USSR Permanent Mission to the UN in New York. From 1988 to 1992, Deputy, then First Deputy Chief of the International Organizations Department of the USSR Foreign Ministry. In 1992, appointed Director of the International Organizations and Global Problems Department of the Russian Federation Foreign Ministry.
FAMILY: Married.
ADDRESS/TELEPHONE: 32/34 Smolenskaya-Sennaya Street, Moscow, 121200. 244–1606 (office).

Lazarev, Aleksandr Nikolayevich
POSITION: Chief Conductor of the Bolshoi State Academic Theater
BIRTHPLACE/DATE: Moscow, 1945
EDUCATION: Graduated in 1972 from the Moscow Conservatory and in 1974 from the postgraduate course at the Moscow Conservatory.
CAREER: From 1973, Conductor of the Bolshoi State Academic Theater.
HONORS/AWARDS: Lenin Komsomol Prize; Glinka Prize.
FAMILY: Married with a daughter.
ADDRESS/TELEPHONE: 8/2 Okhotny Ryad, Moscow. 292–0658 (office); 292–0593 (secretary).

Lebed, Aleksandr Ivanovich
POSITION: Commander of the Fourteenth Army in Transdnyestria (Dniester River Region); Major-General
BIRTHPLACE/DATE: Novocherkassk, Rostov region, 1950
EDUCATION: Graduated in 1973 from the Ryazan Higher Aviation School and in 1985 from the Frunze Military Academy.
CAREER: In 1985, Deputy Airborne Regiment Commander; Regiment Commander; Deputy Airborne Division Commander. From 1988 to 1991, Commander of the Kaunas, then Tula Airborne Divisions. In 1991, Airborne Forces Deputy Commander of Combat Training and Military Educational Establishments. During the August 1991 attempted coup, Head of the White House (Russian Parliament Headquarters) Defense as Commander of the Tula Airborne Troops. To June 1992, worked for the Russian Defense Committee.
ADDRESS/TELEPHONE: 12 Frunze Street, Moscow. 293–2869; 293–1413 (office).

Lebedev, Platon Leonidovich
POSITION: President, Board Chairman, and Finance Director of the MENATEP Commercial Innovation Bank
BIRTHPLACE/DATE: Moscow, 1956
NATIONALITY: Russian
EDUCATION: Graduated in 1981 from the Moscow G.V. Plekhanov Institute of National Economy. Speaks English.
CAREER: From 1981 to 1989, Economist, Directorate Head of the Zarubezhgeologiya (Foreign Geology) Joint-Stock Company.
FAMILY: Married with two children.
ADDRESS/TELEPHONE: 20 Shchepok Street, Moscow. 924–4868 (office).

Leksin, Vladimir Nikolayevich
POSITION: Member of the Russian Federation Supreme Economic Council; Department Head of the Russian Academy of Sciences' Institute of Systems Analysis; Professor at the Academy of National Economy of the Russian Federation Government
BIRTHPLACE/DATE: Noginsk, Moscow region, 1934
EDUCATION: Graduated in 1958 from the Moscow Institute of Non-Ferrous Metals and Gold. Doctor of Economics; Professor. Speaks German.
CAREER: From 1958 to 1964, Junior Researcher, Academic Secretary of the USSR Academy of Sciences. From 1964 to 1970, Chief Metallurgist of the USSR Ministry of Non-Ferrous Metallurgy. From 1970 to 1977, Economics Department Head of a research institute. From 1977 to 1979, Department Head of the USSR State Planning Committee's Council for the Study of Production Forces. From 1979 to 1987, Department Head of the Institute of Development. From 1974 to 1977, Professor at the Institute of Steel and Alloys.
MAJOR WORKS: More than 200 publications on the efficient use of natural resources, environment, and socio-economic problems of regional development.
FAMILY: Married with three children.
ADDRESS/TELEPHONE: 9 60-Letiya Oktyabrya Prospekt, Moscow, 117312. 135–4488; 203–8640 (office).

Leleko, Valery Vladimirovich
POSITION: President of the Medasko Medical Insurance Company
BIRTHPLACE/DATE: Alma-Ata, 1954
EDUCATION: Graduated in 1979 from the Second Medical Institute.
CAREER: From 1980 to 1990, Cardiologist at the Institute of Cardiology; Physician for the Moscow Ambulance Service.
FAMILY: Married with a son.
ADDRESS/TELEPHONE: 3 Krylatskiye Kholmy, Moscow, 121609. 413–9485; 413–9545 (office).

Lemeshev, Mikhail Yakovlevich
POSITION: Chief Resercher of the Russian Academy of Sciences Commission on Production Forces and Natural Resources
BIRTHPLACE/DATE: Tomilichi village, Bryansk region, 1927
NATIONALITY: Russian
EDUCATION: Doctor of Economics; Professor; Academician.
CAREER: From 1956 to 1961, Junior Researcher at the Research Institute of Economics of the USSR State Planning Committee. From 1961 to 1972, Senior Researcher, Head of various branches of the Industrial Relations Section. From 1972 to 1977,

Head of the Systems Analysis Section of the Siberian branch of the USSR Academy of Sciences. From 1977 to 1985, Department Head of the Central Institute of Economics and Mathematics of the USSR Academy of Sciences. From 1986, Head of the Laboratory of Ecological and Economic Problems, Head of the Commission on Production Forces. From 1974, United Nations Environmental Expert, President of the Russian Anti-Nuclear Society, Board Member of the Ecology and Peace Association. Member of the Revival of Russia Movement.
HONORS/AWARDS: Estonian Academy of Sciences and Tartu University Karl Ber Prize.
FAMILY: Married with children.
ADDRESS/TELEPHONE: 26 Maronovsky Pereulok, Moscow, 117994. 238–2123 (office).

Leonov, Vladimir Afanasyevich
POSITION: Board Chairman of the Uralcredit (Urals Region Credit) Commercial Bank; District Council Chairman
BIRTHPLACE/DATE: Altai region, 1953
NATIONALITY: Russian
EDUCATION: Graduated in 1983 from the Barnaul Finance and Economics Institute.
CAREER: From 1977 to 1983, Engineer, then Senior Inspector of the Altai Stroibank (Construction Bank); from 1983 to 1986, Head of the Baikal-Amur Finance Department. From 1986, Manager of the Uralcredit Commercial Bank.
FAMILY: Married.
ADDRESS/TELEPHONE: 10 Blyukher Street, Chegdomysh, Khabarovsk Region, 682080. 9–1961 (office).

Leonov, Yuri Yuryevich
POSITION: Editor in Chief of *Rabochy* (*Worker*) newspaper; Executive Committee Chairman of the Zashchita (Protection) United Trade Unions of Independent Workers
BIRTHPLACE/DATE: Moscow, 1963
CAREER: From 1985, Secondary School Teacher of social sciences, Russian language, and literature. In 1987, Editor in Chief of the Moscow Kalinin Construction Factory newspaper. In 1989, Organizing Committee Head of the Workers' Party Foundation (established in March 1990). Editorial Board Member of *Rabochaya Gazeta* (*Workers' Newspaper*); proletarian newspapers; a Marxist magazine.
MAJOR WORKS: Publications on political economy.
FAMILY: Single.
ADDRESS/TELEPHONE: P.O. Box 48, Moscow, 115380. 252–4415 (office); 255–0695.

Lerner, Edvin Yuryevich
POSITION: President of the Konsolidatsiya All-Union Confederation of Trade Unions (formerly Trade Unions of Cooperatives and Other Forms of Free Enterprise); Vice President of the Ukraine Cooperative Alliance; President of the Center for the Economics of Legal Protection Association; President of Vybor–89 (Choice–89) Diversified Production Firm; Chairman of the Board of Directors of the Artel Joint-Stock Company
BIRTHPLACE/DATE: Kharkov, Ukraine, 1934
EDUCATION: Graduated in 1969 from the Kharkov Higher Engineering Military School.
CAREER: Served in the Armed Forces for thirty years. From 1987, Chairman of the Informator Information and Mediator Cooperative. From 1988, Chairman of the Kharkov Region Cooperative Alliance.
FAMILY: Married with two children.
ADDRESS/TELEPHONE: 42 Leninsky Prospekt, Building 6-A, Moscow, 117119. 938–8023 (office).

Ligachev, Yegor Kuzmich
POSITION: Former USSR Chief Ideologist; former member of the Politburo
BIRTHPLACE/DATE: Dubinkino village, Novosibirsk region, 1920
NATIONALITY: Russian
CAREER: From 1943 to 1944, worked at the Novosibirsk Chkalov Aircraft Plant. From 1944, member of the Communist Party. From 1944 to 1949, Komsomol Functionary in Novosibirsk, First Secretary of the District Committee, Secretary, then First Secretary of the Novosibirsk Komsomol Regional Committee. From 1949 to 1965, Communist Party and Soviet Functionary-Lecturer, Department Head of the City Party Committee, Department Head of the Regional Party Committee, Head of the Regional Directorate for Culture, Deputy Chairman of the Regional Execu-

tive Committee, First Secretary of the District Party Committee, Secretary of the Novosibirsk Party Regional Committee, Section Head, Deputy Department Head of the Central Committee. From 1965, First Secretary of the Tomsk Region Party Committee. From 1983, Secretary of the Central Committee. From 1985 to 1990, member of the Politburo. From 1976 to 1990, member of the Central Committee. From 1985 to 1988, USSR Chief Ideologist. From 1988 to 1990, Chairman of the Central Committee Commission for Agriculture. Merit Pension Recipient.

MAJOR WORKS: *Enigma of Gorbachev*; *Memoirs of the Kremlin and Old Square*.

HONORS/AWARDS: Two Orders of Lenin; Order of the October Revolution; two Orders of the Red Banner of Labor; Order of the Badge of Honor.

FAMILY: Married with children.

Likhachev, Dmitri Sergeyevich

POSITION: Board Chairman of the Russian International Culture Foundation (formerly the Soviet Cultural Foundation); Academician of the Russian Academy of Sciences; member of the Consultative Council of the Russian Federation Minister of Culture and Tourism Ministry of Culture and Tourism

BIRTHPLACE/DATE: St. Petersburg, November 28, 1906

NATIONALITY: Russian

EDUCATION: Graduated in 1923 from the Soviet Workers' School in Petrograd; in 1928, from the Linguistics and Literature Department of Leningrad State University. Doctor of Philology (1941); Postdoctor of Philology (1947); Professor (1951).

CAREER: From 1928 to 1932, prisoner at the Solovetsky Concentration Camp; participated in the Belomorkanal (White Sea Channel) construction. From 1932 to 1933, Literary Editor at the Socio-Economic Literature Publishers in Leningrad. From 1933 to 1934, Foreign Languages Proofreader at the Komintern (Community International) Print Shop in Leningrad. From 1934 to 1938, Scientific Proofreader, Literary Editor, Editor at the USSR Academy of Sciences' Publishing House (Leningrad branch). From 1938 to 1941, Junior Researcher; from 1941 to 1954, Senior Researcher at the Institute of Russian Literature (Pushkin House) of the USSR Academy of Sciences. From 1946 to 1951, Assistant Professor of the History Department at Leningrad State University. From 1948, member of the Learned Council of the USSR Academy of Sciences' Institute of Russian Literature. From 1951 to 1953, Professor of the History Department at Leningrad University. From 1953 to 1970, Corresponding Member of the USSR Academy of Sciences' Literature, and Language Department. From 1954, Section Head of Old Russian Literature at the Institute of Russian Literature. From 1955, Board Member of the Literature and Language Department of the USSR Academy of Sciences. From 1956, member of the USSR Writers' Union. From 1960, member of the State Russian Museum; member of the Soviet Slavists Committee. From 1961 to 1962, Deputy of the Leningrad City Council. From 1970, Full Member of the USSR Academy of Sciences' Literature, and Language Department and History Department. From 1974, Board Member of the USSR Academy of Sciences' Archeographical Commission, From 1975, Board Member of the Leningrad Section of the USSR Academy of Sciences' Archeographical Commission. From 1982, Presidium Member of the Central Council of the All-Russian Society for the Preservation of Historical and Cultural Monuments. From 1983, Pushkin Commission Chairman of the Soviet Cultural Foundation. USSR People's Deputy.

MAJOR WORKS: *National Self-Awareness in Ancient Russia* (1945*); The Origin of Russian Literature* (1952); *Poetics of Ancient Russian Literature* (1979*); Notes About Russians* (1981).

HONORS/AWARDS: Hero of Socialist Labor (1986); Order of Lenin (1986); Order of the Red Banner of Labor (1966); State Prize (1952, 1969); Prize of the Presidium of the USSR Academy of Sciences (1954, 1985); Medal For Labor Valor (1954); Veteran of Labor Medal (1986); Medal For the Defense of Leningrad (1942); For Labor Valor in the Great Patriotic War 1941–1945 (1946). Foreign medals, awards, and honors: Georgi Dimitrov Order (Bulgaria, 1986); two Bulgarian Orders of Cyril and Methodius, First Class (1963, 1977). Honorary Doctorates from foreign universities: Bordeaux (1982); Budapest (1985); Edinburgh (1971); Oxford (1967); Sofia (1988); Zurich (1983). Member of the Austrian, Bulgar-

ian, Hungarian, and Serbian Academies of Sciences; Corresponding Member of the Göttingen (Germany) and British Academies of Sciences.
FAMILY: Married with a daughter.
ADDRESS/TELEPHONE: 4 Makarov Naberezhnaya, St. Petersburg, V–164, 199164. 218–1274 (St. Petersburg); 202–6984 (Moscow).

Likhanov, Albert Anatolyevich
POSITION: Writer; Chairman of the Russian Children's Foundation; President of the International Association of Children's Foundations; Corresponding Member of the Academy of Pedagogical Sciences
BIRTHPLACE/DATE: Kirov, 1935
NATIONALITY: Russian
EDUCATION: Graduated from the Journalism Department of Urals State University in Sverdlovsk (now Yekaterinburg). Corresponding Member of the Academy of Pedagogical Sciences.
CAREER: In 1962 joined the Communist Party. From 1975, Editor in Chief of *Smena* (*Rising Generation*) magazine. In 1979, elected Chairman of the All-Union Council of Creative Youth. From 1982, President of the Komsomol Central Committee's Association of Writers and Artists for Children and Youth. From 1988, Head of the Soviet Children's Foundation; elected USSR People's Deputy; member of the USSR Supreme Soviet's Committee for Science, Education, and Culture. From December 1991, Chairman of the Russian Children's Foundation.
MAJOR WORKS: *Stars in September* (1967); *Steep Slopes* (1971); *Supreme Penalty* (1982); *Kikimora* (1983); *Dramatic Pedagogy* (1987, International Janusz Korczak Prize); *Family Circumstances* trilogy [*Labyrinth* (1970); *Clean Pebbles* (1967); *Fraud* (1973)].
HONORS/AWARDS: Lenin Komsomol Prize (1976).
FAMILY: Married with a son and a grandson.
ADDRESS/TELEPHONE: The Russian Children's Foundation, 11/2 Armyansky Pereulok, Moscow, 101963. 925–8200 (office); 925–2678 (secretary).

Lipitsky, Vasily Semyonovich
POSITION: Board Chairman of the Svobodnaya Rossiya (Free Russia) People's Party; Deputy Director of the Analytical Center at the Institute for Socio-Political Studies; member of the Mossoviet (Moscow Council); Co-Chairman of the Democratic Movement of Russia; Board Member of the All-Russia Grazhdanskoye Soglasiye (Civic Accord) Movement
BIRTHPLACE/DATE: Moscow, 1947
NATIONALITY: Ukrainian
EDUCATION: Graduated in 1970 from the History Department of Moscow State University. Speaks French.
CAREER: From 1970 to 1973, Central Staff Instructor of Student Construction Teams. From 1973 to 1983, Senior Researcher, Department Head, Deputy Laboratory Head at Moscow State University. From 1983 to 1991, Senior Researcher, Section Head of the Marxism-Leninism Institute of the Central Committee. From 1991, Deputy Director of the Analytical Center at the Institute for Socio-Political Studies. From 1990 to 1991, Coordinator of the Democratic Movement of Communists; member of the Russian Federation Central Committee. In August 1991, removed from the Central Committee and expelled from the Communist Party.
FAMILY: Married with two children.
ADDRESS/TELEPHONE: 9-A Kolpachny Pereulok, Moscow. 292–9131.

Lisin, Aleksandr Ivanovich
POSITION: Editor in Chief of *Vechernyaya Moskva* (*Evening Moscow*) newspaper
BIRTHPLACE/DATE: Khorol, Poltava region, July 12, 1941
NATIONALITY: Russian
EDUCATION: Graduated in 1965 from Moscow State University's Journalism Department and in 1976 from postgraduate studies at the Central Committee's Academy of Social Sciences. Doctor of Philosophy.
CAREER: Editorial Assistant, Correspondent, Department Head, Deputy Editor of *Pravda Severa* (*Truth of the North*) newspaper.
HONORS/AWARDS: Order for Distinguished Service.
FAMILY: Married.
ADDRESS/TELEPHONE: 3 Kutuzov Prospekt, Building 1, Flat #63, Moscow. 259–0526.

Litvinchuk, Victor Ivanovich

POSITION: Editor in Chief of *Sputnik* (*Companion*) magazine of the Russian Novosti Information Agency
BIRTHPLACE/DATE: Moscow, 1948
EDUCATION: Graduated in 1971 from the Moscow Institute of Foreign Languages and in 1985 from the Central Committee's Academy of Social Sciences. Speaks French and German.
CAREER: From 1973 to 1985, Aide, Chief Editor of the Western Europe Department, Editor-Consultant of Novosti Press Agency (APN). From 1985 to 1990, Head of the APN in Cambodia. From 1990 and 1991, Department Head, Commercial Director of *Sputnik* magazine.
FAMILY: Married with two children.
ADDRESS/TELEPHONE: 4 Zubovsky Boulevard, Moscow. 201–2919 (office).

Lobov, Vladimir Nikolayevich

POSITION: Former USSR Deputy Defense Minister and Chief of the General Staff of the USSR Armed Forces; General of the Army; President of Zashchitnik Otechestva (Defender of the Fatherland) Inter-Republican Foundation for Humanitarian Assistance to Servicemen
BIRTHPLACE/DATE: Bashkiria, July 22, 1935
NATIONALITY: Russian
EDUCATION: Graduated from the Ryazan Artillery School and from the Frunze and General Staff Academies. Doctor of History; Doctor of Military Science; Professor.
CAREER: From 1954 to 1981, Soldier, Sergeant, Platoon Company, Battalion Commander, Regiment Commander, Division Commander. In 1980, held military post in the Byelorussian Military District. From 1981 to 1984, First Deputy Commander of the Leningrad Military District. From 1984 to 1987, Commander of the Central Asian Military District. From 1987, First Deputy Chief of the General Staff, Chief of Staff of the Warsaw Treaty Forces. Head of the Frunze Military Academy. From 1989, Army General. From September to December 1991, Chief of the General Staff of the USSR Armed Forces.
HONORS/AWARDS: Order of the Red Banner (1985); Order of Kutuzov, Second Class; Order of the Red Star; two Orders for Service to the Fatherland in the Soviet Armed Forces, Second and Third Classes.
FAMILY: Married.
ADDRESS/TELEPHONE: 12 Frunze Street, Moscow. 293–2869; 293–1413 (office).

Logunov, Anatoli Alekseyevich

POSITION: Supervisor of Studies at the Institute of High Energy Physics of the Russian Federation Ministry of Nuclear Energy; Advisor to the President of the Russian Academy of Sciences; Head of the Department of Quantum Theory and High Energy Physics
BIRTHPLACE/DATE: Obsharovka village, Kuibyshev region, December 30, 1926
NATIONALITY: Russian
EDUCATION: Doctor of Physics and Mathematics.
CAREER: From 1951, worked at Moscow State University. From 1956 to 1963, Deputy Director of the Theoretical Physics Laboratory at the Joint Institute for Nuclear Research in Dubna. From 1963 to 1977, Director of the Institute of High Energy Physics in Serpukhov. From 1977, Rector of Moscow State University; elected USSR People's Deputy. From 1972, Academician. From 1974, Vice President of the USSR (now Russian) Academy of Sciences. Deputy of the USSR Supreme Soviet of the Ninth, Tenth, and Eleventh Convocations. From 1960 to 1991, member of the Communist Party. From 1986 to 1990, member of the Central Committee.
MAJOR WORKS: Works on quantum field theory and elementary particle physics: developed dispersion correlation method and physical processes at high energies (inclusive processes).
HONORS/AWARDS: Prize of Lenin (1970); State Prize (1973, 1984); Hero of Socialist Labor.
FAMILY: Married with three sons and six grandchildren.
ADDRESS/TELEPHONE: The Russian Academy of Sciences Presidium, 14 Leninsky Prospekt, Moscow–71, GSP–1, 117901. 146–9538 (home); 939–1647 (office); 952–5801 (Presidium).

Logunov, Valentin Andreyevich

POSITION: Editor in Chief of *Rossiyskaya Gazeta* (*Russian Newspaper*)

BIRTHPLACE/DATE: Vladimirovka village, Tambov region, July 27, 1938
NATIONALITY: Russian
CAREER: From 1963 to 1966, Writer, Department Head of *Komsomolets Zabaikaliya* (*Komsomol Member of Transbaikal Region*) newspaper. From 1966 to 1968, Editor in Chief of *Selsky Stroitel* (*Rural Builder*) newspaper. From 1968 to 1970, Editor in Chief of *Zabaikalskaya Magistral* (*Transbaikal Highway*) newspaper. From 1970 to 1971, Film Editor of the Chita Region Television and Radio Committee. From 1971 to 1979, Department Head of *Zabaikalsky Rabochiy* (*Transbaikal Worker*) newspaper. From 1979 to 1987, Staff Correspondent, Deputy Editor in Chief of *Gudok* (*Factory Bell*) newspaper. From 1987 to 1989, Deputy Editor in Chief of *Moskovskaya Pravda* (*Moscow Truth*) newspaper. From April to November 1990, Russian Federation Deputy Minister of Press and Mass Media. From November 1990, Editor in Chief of *Rossiyskaya Gazeta*. From 1989 to 1991, USSR People's Deputy.
FAMILY: Married with two sons.
ADDRESS/TELEPHONE: 24 Pravdy Street, Moscow. 257–2252 (office).

Lomeiko, Vladimir Borisovich
POSITION: Russian Federation Permanent Representative to UNESCO (Paris); Ambassador Extraordinary and Plenipotentiary
BIRTHPLACE/DATE: Novorossiysk, November 27, 1935
NATIONALITY: Byelorussian
EDUCATION: From 1954 to 1960, student at the Moscow State Institute of International Relations. Doctor of History.
CAREER: From 1954 to 1960, worked at the USSR Foreign Ministry. From 1960 to 1962, Interpreter, Attaché at the USSR Embassy in the German Democratic Republic (GDR). From 1962 to 1966, Senior Aide, Deputy Chairman of the USSR Committee for Youth Organizations. From 1966 to 1968, Department Instructor of the Central Committee. From 1968 to 1970, Deputy Editor in Chief of Novosti (News) Press Agency (APN). From 1970 to 1972, Bureau Chief of APN in Cologne, Germany. From 1972 to 1976, Editor in Chief; Board Member of APN. From 1976 to 1978, Political Analyst of APN. From 1978 to 1984, Foreign Affairs Analyst of *Literaturnaya Gazeta* (*Literary Newspaper*). From 1984 to 1986, Head of the Press Department; Board Member of the USSR Foreign Ministry. From 1986 to 1988, Ambassador at Large of the USSR Foreign Ministry.
HONORS/AWARDS: Order of the Badge of Honor.
FAMILY: Married.
ADDRESS/TELEPHONE: Representation Permanente de l'Russie aupres de l'UNESCO, 40–50 Boulevard Lannes, Paris. 45–04–37–52.

Lopatin, Mikhail Alekseyevich
POSITION: Air Defense Commander of the Ukraine Air Forces
BIRTHPLACE/DATE: Svoboda village, Mogilev region, 1940
NATIONALITY: Byelorussian
CAREER: From 1962 to 1965, worked on governmental assignment in Cuba. From 1971 to 1973, Battery Commander. From 1978 to 1983, Head of the Anti-Aircraft Forces Directorate. From 1984 to 1986, Ukraine Air Defense Division Commander. Air Defense Detached Army Commander in Kiev.
HONORS/AWARDS: Order for Service to the Motherland, Second and Third Degree.
FAMILY: Married with two sons.
ADDRESS/TELEPHONE: Ukraine Defense Ministry, 168, Kiev. 293–0319; 293–2073 (press service).

Lopukhin, Vladimir Mikhailovich
POSITION: Temporary Staff Advisor to the Russian Federation Chairman of the Government
BIRTHPLACE/DATE: Moscow, 1952
NATIONALITY: Russian
CAREER: From 1975 to 1977, Aide at the Institute of the World Economy and International Relations of the USSR Academy of Sciences. From 1977 to 1983, Junior Researcher at the All-Union Research Institute of System Studies, USSR Academy of Sciences. From 1983 to 1991, Senior Researcher, Laboratory Head at the Institute of National Economic Forecast of the USSR Academy of Sciences. In 1991, Russian Federation Deputy Minister of Economics. From November 1991 to

May 1992, Russian Federation Minister of Fuel and Power Engineering. From December 1991, Deputy Chairman of the Russian Federation Government Commission for the Efficient Regulation of Resources Provision.

Lopukhin, Yuri Mikhailovich

POSITION: Director of the Physical and Chemical Medicine Research Institute of the Russian Federation Ministry of Health; Academician of the USSR Academy of Medical Sciences; Academician of the Russian Academy of Sciences
BIRTHPLACE/DATE: Kazakhstan, 1924
NATIONALITY: Russian
CAREER: From 1945 to 1964, engaged in scientific work at the Second Moscow Medical Institute. From 1964 to 1984, Rector of the Second Moscow Medical Institute.
MAJOR WORKS: On atherosclerosis, detoxication, absorption therapy.
HONORS/AWARDS: USSR State Prize (1971, 1979); Russian Federation State Prize.
FAMILY: Married with two children.
ADDRESS/TELEPHONE: 1-A Malaya Pirogovskaya Street, Moscow, 119435. 246–4401 (office); 249–4401 (home).

Loskutov, Andrey Iosifovich

POSITION: Editor in Chief of IMA-Press News Agency
BIRTHPLACE/DATE: Volgograd, 1958
NATIONALITY: Russian
EDUCATION: Graduated in 1981 from the Journalism Department at Moscow State University. Speaks German and French.
CAREER: From 1981, Junior Editor, Editor, Senior Editor, Editor in Chief of Novosti (News) Press Agency's Youth Department.
FAMILY: Married with two daughters.
ADDRESS/TELEPHONE: 11 Second Kazachy Pereulok, Building 2, Moscow, 109180. 238–6574 (office).

Lubenchenko, Konstantin Dmitryevich

POSITION: Director-General of the Russian Supreme Soviet Parliamentary Center; Advisor to the Chairman of the Russian Constitutional Court
BIRTHPLACE/DATE: Mozhaisk, Moscow region, 1945
NATIONALITY: Russian
EDUCATION: Graduated in 1973 from the Law Department at Moscow State University. Doctor of Law. Speaks German.
CAREER: From 1976 to 1981, Assistant to the Theory of State and Law Department at Moscow University. From 1981 to 1989, Assistant Professor at Moscow University. From 1989 to 1991, USSR People's Deputy; USSR Supreme Soviet Member; Vice Chairman of the Committee for Legislation, Law and Order. From October 1991, Chairman of the USSR Supreme Soviet Council of the Union (left post when the USSR Supreme Soviet dissolved). In 1991, Board Member of the Socio-Political Research Foundation.
FAMILY: Married with a son.
ADDRESS/TELEPHONE: 2 Tsvetnoi Boulevard, Moscow. 208–0940; 206–1659 (assistant); 208–3862 (office).

Luchinsky, Pyotr Kirillovich

POSITION: Chairman of the Moldova Republic Parliament; Ambassador Extraordinary and Plenipotentiary
BIRTHPLACE/DATE: Starye Gadulyany village, Floreshty region, Moldavia (Moldova), January 27, 1940
NATIONALITY: Moldovian
EDUCATION: Doctor of Philosophy.
CAREER: In 1960, Instructor of the Moldavian Komsomol Central Committee. In 1962, Department Head of the Kishinev City Komsomol Committee. From 1963 to 1964, Instructor of the Moldavian Komsomol Central Committee. From 1964 to 1965, First Secretary of the Beltsk City Komsomol Committee. From 1964 to 1991, member of the Communist Party. From 1966 to 1976, Second Secretary, First Secretary of the Moldavian Komsomol Central Committee; Secretary of the Moldavian Central Committee. From 1976 to 1978, First Secretary of the Kishinev City Party Committee. From 1978 to 1986, Deputy Head of the Propaganda Department of the Central Committee. From 1986 to 1989, Second Secretary of the Tajik Central Committee. From 1989 to 1990, First Secretary of the Moldavian Central Committee. From 1989 to 1992, USSR People's Deputy. From 1992, USSR Supreme Soviet Deputy of the Eleventh Convocation.

HONORS/AWARDS: Two Orders of the Red Banner of Labor; Order of the People's Friendship.
FAMILY: Married with two sons.

Lukasik, Yulian Stanislavovich
POSITION: Editor in Chief of *Megapolis-Continent* newspaper
BIRTHPLACE/DATE: Yekimtsevo village, Kostroma region, 1943
CAREER: Correspondent for *Pravda Severa* (*Truth of the North*) newspaper in Arkhangelsk; Staff Correspondent, Department Head of *Vodny Transport* (*Water Transport*) newspaper; Deputy Department Head of *Trud* (*Labor*) newspaper; Deputy Editor in Chief of *Megapolis-Continent*.
FAMILY: Married with children.
ADDRESS/TELEPHONE: 12/27 M. Gnezdikovsky Pereulok, Building 3, Moscow, 103009. 229–8459 (secretary).

Lukin, Vladimir Petrovich
POSITION: Russian Federation Ambassador to the United States
BIRTHPLACE/DATE: Omsk, July 13, 1937
NATIONALITY: Russian
EDUCATION: Graduated in 1959 from the History Department at the Moscow Lenin State Teachers' Training Institute. From 1961 to 1964, postgraduate student at the Institute of the World Economy and International Relations. Doctor of History; Professor; Honorary Doctor of Simon Bolivar University (Colombia). Speaks English, Spanish, and French.
CAREER: From 1959 to 1961, Researcher at the History Museum. From 1965 to 1968, Editor at the Prague-based *World Marxist Review* journal. In August 1968, expelled from Czechoslovakia for protest against the Soviet troops' invasion. From 1968 to 1987, Head of the Far Eastern Policy Sector at the Institute of the U.S. and Canada. From 1987 to 1989, Deputy Directorate Head of the USSR Foreign Ministry; Head of the Department of the Pacific and Southeast Asia, Deputy Head of the Assessment and Planning Directorate of the USSR Foreign Ministry. From 1989 to 1990, Head of the Analysis and Forecast Group of the USSR Supreme Soviet's Secretariat; Russian Federation People's Deputy. From 1990 to 1992, member of the Russian Federation Supreme Soviet; Chairman of the Committee for International Affairs and Foreign Trade Relations.
FAMILY: Married with two children.
ADDRESS/TELEPHONE: The Embassy of Russia, 1125 16th Street N.W., Washington, DC, 20036. (202) 628–7551; Telex: 232248400.

Lukinsky, Vladimir Ivanovich
POSITION: Deputy Chairman of the Roscomagentstvo Russian Commercial Agency; Director of the Prominter Firm (International Industry)
BIRTHPLACE/DATE: Skopin, Ryazan region, 1947
CAREER: From 1971 to 1981, Department Head of the All-Union Litsenzintorg (Licensed International Trade) Association. From 1981 to 1985, Acting Director-General of the Tekhnikol Joint-Stock Company in Italy.
FAMILY: Married with two children.
ADDRESS/TELEPHONE: 5 Yaroslavskoye Chaussée, Moscow, 129348. 182–2117 (office).

Lukyanenko, Levko Grigoryevich
POSITION: Deputy of the Ukraine Supreme Soviet; Chairman of the Krainsk (Ukranian) Republican Party
BIRTHPLACE/DATE: Khripovka village, Chernigov region, 1927
NATIONALITY: Ukrainian
EDUCATION: Graduated from Moscow State University.
CAREER: From 1953 to August 1961, member of the Communist Party. In 1959, founded the underground Ukranian Workers and Peasants Union. In 1961, sentenced to death (a fifteen-year imprisonment was substituted for execution). In 1976, released; Co-Founder of the Ukranian Helsinki Treaty Group. In 1978, voted to be a recidivist and sentenced to ten years imprisonment and five years in exile. In 1989, returned to Western Ukraine. In 1988, the Helsinki Group renewed activity as the Ukranian Helsinki Union; in April 1990, at its First Congress, became the Ukranian Republican Party, headed by Lukyanenko.
HONORS/AWARDS: Ukranian President's Honorary Distinction.
ADDRESS/TELEPHONE: The Embassy of Russia in Canada, 285 Charlotte Street, Ottawa, Ontario, KIN 8L5, Canada. 235–4341; 236–1413.

Lukyanov, Anatoli Ivanovich

POSITION: Under arrest from August 30, 1991
BIRTHPLACE/DATE: Smolensk, May 7, 1930
NATIONALITY: Russian
EDUCATION: Graduated from Moscow State University in 1953.
CAREER: From 1955 to August 1991, member of the Communist Party. From 1956 to 1961, Senior Consultant to the USSR Council of Ministers Juridicial Commission. From 1961 to 1976, Senior Aide, Deputy Head of the Department for Activities of the USSR Supreme Soviet Presidium Councils. From 1976 to 1977, Consultant to the Central Committee's Department for Party Organization Work. From 1977 to 1983, Head of the Secretariat of the USSR Supreme Soviet Presidium. From 1983, First Deputy Head, and from 1985, General Department Head of the Central Committee. From 1985 to 1987, Secretary of the Central Committee and Head of the Central Committee's Department for Administrative Bodies. From 1988 to 1989, First Deputy Chairman of the USSR Supreme Soviet Presidium. From 1989 to 1990, First Deputy Chairman of the USSR Supreme Soviet. From 1990 to 1991, Chairman of the USSR Supreme Soviet. In September 1991, released from duties at the Extraordinary Congress of People's Deputies. Former USSR Supreme Soviet Deputy; former Chairman of the USSR Supreme Soviet.
MAJOR WORKS: A monograph on state law; collected poems; more than 150 scientific publications.
HONORS/AWARDS: Order of the October Revolution; Order of the Red Banner of Labor; medals.
FAMILY: Married with a daughter.
TELEPHONE: 229–4662 (Russian Federation Office of the Public Prosecutor).

Luntovsky, Georgy Ivanovich

POSITION: Board Chairman of the Voronezhkreditprombank Commercial Bank (Voronezh Credit Industrial Bank); Director-General of the Voronezh Joint-Stock Bank
BIRTHPLACE/DATE: Kursk, 1950
NATIONALITY: Russian
CAREER: From 1969 to 1971, served in the army. From 1971 to 1973, Engineer of the Kursk Region Stroibank (Construction Bank). From 1973 to 1974, Technical Supervision Head of the Kursk Region Consumer Services Directorate. From 1974 to 1979, Credit Inspector; Senior Credit Inspector; Deputy Department Head; Department Head of the Kursk Region Stroibank. From 1979 to 1981, Deputy Department Head of the Baikal-Amur Stroibank in Tynda city. From 1981 to 1985, Office Manager of the Gara Stroibank in Chita region. From 1985 to 1986, Deputy Head of Construction at Voronezhvodstroi (Voronezh Marine Engineering). From 1986 to 1988, Manager of the Kominternovski State Bank in Voronezh. From 1988 to 1990, Deputy Directorate Head of the Voronezh Region State Bank. From 1990 to 1991, Voronezh Region Directorate Head of the USSR Promstroibank (Industrial Construction Bank).
FAMILY: Married with two children.
ADDRESS/TELEPHONE: 25 Ordzhonikidze Street, Voronezh, 394000. 55–5374 (office).

Lushchikov, Sergey Gennadyevich

POSITION: Lawyer
BIRTHPLACE/DATE: Buisk village, Sumy district, Kirov region, March 10, 1951
NATIONALITY: Russian
CAREER: From 1972, worked in the Komi Republic Office of the Public Prosecutor. From 1974 to 1975, Assistant Prosecutor of Pechora city. From 1975 to 1981, Prosecutor of the Komi Republic Office of the Public Prosecutor. From 1981 to 1983, Senior Assistant Prosecutor of the Komi Republic Office of the Public Prosecutor. From 1986 to 1990, Deputy Komi Republic Minister of Justice. From 1990 to 1991, USSR Minister of Justice. From 1991 to 1992, Deputy Chairman of the USSR Supreme Soviet Committee on Legislation; elected USSR Supreme Soviet Deputy. To August 1991, member of the Communist Party.
FAMILY: Married with two daughters.
TELEPHONE: 206–0058 (office).

Luzhkov, Yuri Mikhailovich

POSITION: Mayor of Moscow
BIRTHPLACE/DATE: Moscow, 1936
EDUCATION: Graduated in 1958 from the Moscow Gubkin Institute of Oil and Gas.
CAREER: In 1968, joined the Communist Party. In 1975, elected Deputy of the Babushkinsky District Council. From 1977 to 1990, Deputy of the Mossoviet (Moscow Council). From 1987 to

1990, Deputy of the Russian Federation Supreme Soviet. From 1987 to 1990, First Deputy Chairman of the Moscow City Executive Committee. From 1990 to June 1991, Chairman of the Mossoviet Executive Committee. From June 1991 to June 1992, Vice Mayor of Moscow. From August to October 1991, Deputy Head of the Committee for the Efficient Management of the National Economy.
MAJOR WORKS: *72 Hours of Agony: August 1991, The Start and Finish of the Communist Putsch in Russia* (Magisterium Publishers, 1992).
HONORS/AWARDS: USSR State Prize; USSR Honored Worker of Chemical Industry; Russian Federation Honored Worker of Chemical Industry; Order of Lenin; Order of the Red Banner of Labor; medals.
FAMILY: Married with two sons and a daughter.
ADDRESS/TELEPHONE: 13 Tverskaya Street, Moscow. 925–4605 (secretary).

Lvov, Yuri Ivanovich
POSITION: President of the Saint Petersburg Bank Joint-Stock Company
BIRTHPLACE/DATE: Leningrad, 1945
CAREER: In 1973, Engineer of the Research Institute of Chemical Machinery. From 1974 to 1979, Credit Inspector; Department Head of the Leningrad Region Stroibank (Construction Bank). From 1979 to 1987, City Directorate Head of the Leningrad Stroibank. From 1987 to 1990, Leningrad Region Directorate Head of the Zhilsotsbank (Housing and Social Services Bank).
FAMILY: Married.
ADDRESS/TELEPHONE: 70–72 Fontanka Street, St. Petersburg, 191038. 315–8327; 219–8529 (office).

Lysenko, Anatoli Grigoryevich
POSITION: Director-General of the Russian State TV and Radio Broadcasting Company
BIRTHPLACE/DATE: 1937
EDUCATION: Graduated from the Moscow Railway Engineering Institute.
CAREER: Contributer, Staff Member, and Deputy Chief Editor of the Central Television Youth Department. Founder and Producer of "Vzglyad" (Glance), a popular youth TV program.
FAMILY: Married with a daughter.
ADDRESS/TELEPHONE: 19/21 Pyataya Ulitsa Yamskogo Polya Street, Moscow, 125124. 214–4817 (office).

Lysenko, Vladimir Nikolayevich
POSITION: Member of the Russian Supreme Soviet Committee for Mass Media and Relations with Public Organizations
BIRTHPLACE/DATE: Odessa, January 4, 1956
NATIONALITY: Russian
CAREER: From 1982 to 1990, Political Science Professor at the Moscow Aviation Institute. From 1985, Chairman of the Orbita (Orbit) political student club at the Moscow Aviation Institute. In 1987, Co-Founder of the Memorial Society. In 1989, Co-Founder of the Democratic Platform (Democratic faction of the Communist Party). Delegate to the Twenty-Eighth Congress of the Communist Party; left the Communist Party. From 1990, Co-Chairman of the Republican Party of Russia. In January 1991, founded the Democratic Congress of the Former USSR. In December 1991, Co-Founder of the Congress of Democratic Forces of the Russian Federation Republics. From September 1991, member of the Russian Federation Supreme Soviet Committee for Mass Media. From 1990, Russian Federation People's Deputy. From 1984 to 1990, member of the Communist Party.
MAJOR WORKS: *Comprehension; From Totalitarianism To Democracy; The October Revolution: New Approaches.* Articles in foreign publications.
FAMILY: Married with two children.
ADDRESS/TELEPHONE: 2 Krasnopresnenskaya Naberezhnaya, Moscow, 103274. 205–5916 (office).

Lysov, Pavel Aleksandrovich
POSITION: Chairman of the Political Relations Subcommittee of the Russian Federation Supreme Soviet Committee for Inter-Republican Relations; Coordinator of the Smena-Novaya Politika (Rising Generation-New Politics) Faction
BIRTHPLACE/DATE: Magadan region, 1959
NATIONALITY: Russian
CAREER: From 1983, Professor, Senior Sports Instructor at the Magadan Voluntary Society of Assistance to the Army, Air Force, and Navy. From 1985, Department Head, Executive Secretary of

Magadansky Komsomolets (*Magadan Komsomol Member*) newspaper. From 1990, Russia People's Deputy; member of the Committee for Mass Media.
FAMILY: Married with two daughters.
ADDRESS/TELEPHONE: 8/2 Koroleva Street, Flat #556, Moscow; 2 Krasnopresnenskaya Naberezhnaya, Moscow, 103274. 216–7809 (home); 205–5074; 205–9497 (office).

Lyubimov, Aleksandr Mikhailovich
POSITION: Director of the M Studio (International Programs and Video-Exchange) of Ostankino Television; Director-General of the Vzglyad iz Podpollya (Glance from the Underground) Joint-Stock Company
BIRTHPLACE/DATE: Moscow, 1962
NATIONALITY: Russian
CAREER: From 1985 to 1987, Staff Member of the European Foreign Broadcasts Department of the State Television and Radio Committee. From 1987, Staff Member of the Department of Youth Programs; Commentator. From February 1992, Director of the M Studio of International Programs and Video-Exchange of Ostankino Television. Member of the Smena-Novaya Politika Faction. Russian Federation People's Deputy.
FAMILY: Single.
ADDRESS/TELEPHONE: 19 Koroleva Street, Moscow, 127427. 215–4338 (office); 263–0527 (home).

Lyubimov, Yuri Petrovich
POSITION: Art Director of the Moscow Taganka Theater of Drama and Comedy
BIRTHPLACE/DATE: Moscow, September 30, 1917
NATIONALITY: Russian
EDUCATION: Graduated in 1940 from the Vakhtangov Theater-Studio.
CAREER: From 1940 to 1946, served in the army. From 1947 to 1984, member of the Communist Party. From 1946 to 1964, Actor and Director at the Vakhtangov Theater. From 1964 to 1984, Director of the Moscow Taganka Theater of Drama and Comedy. In 1984, deprived of Soviet citizenship by decree of the USSR Supreme Soviet. From 1984 to 1988, lived in Haifa, Israel. In 1989, Soviet citizenship was restored; reelected Art Director of the Taganka Theater. Restored productions of *Boris Godunov* by Pushkin (banned in 1983) and *The Alive* by Boris Mozhayev; staged new productions, including *The Suicide* by Fyodor Dostoevski and *The Feast During the Plague* by Aleksandr Pushkin.
MAJOR WORKS: Roles: Oleg Koshevoi in *The Young Guard* by Aleksandr Fadeyev; Chris in *All My Sons* by Arthur Miller; Benedict in *Much Ado About Nothing* by William Shakespeare; Mozart in *The Little Tragedies* by Aleksandr Pushkin. Productions: *The Good Woman of Szechwan* (1963); *Ten Days that Shook the World* by John Reed (1965); *Mother* by Maxim Gorky (1969); *Hamlet* (1972); *Crime and Punishment* and *The Possessed* by Dostoevski (1985, London Covent Garden Theater); *Master and Margarita* by Mikhail Bulgakov (The Swedish Royal Theater); *Lulu* by Alban Berg (The Chicago Opera House).
HONORS/AWARDS: Russian Federation Honored Artist; USSR State Prize (1952); Order of the Red Banner of Labor.
FAMILY: Married with a son.
ADDRESS/TELEPHONE: 76 Chkalov Street, Moscow. 271–0027; 271–2826 (office).

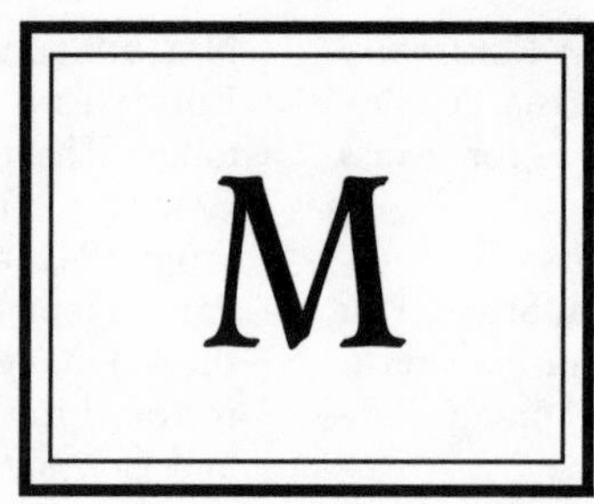

Magomadov, Vakha Denisovich
POSITION: Board Chairman of the Privatbank in Grozny
BIRTHPLACE/DATE: Gankino village, North Kazakh region, 1953
NATIONALITY: Chechen
EDUCATION: Graduated in 1985 from the Novosibirsk Institute of National Economy and in 1986 from the Grozny Oil Institute.
CAREER: From 1976 to 1979, Chief of the Repair and Mechanical Works in Karshi, Uzbekistan. From 1979 to 1984, Head of the Repair and Mechanical Works at an Assembly Plant in Urengoy, Tyumen region. From 1985 to 1989, Novosibirsk Region Department Manager of Agroprombank (Agriculture and Industry Bank).
FAMILY: Married with four children.
ADDRESS/TELEPHONE: 27 Pervomayskaya Street, Grozny. 22–7512 (office).

Makarov, Igor Mikhailovich
POSITION: Chief Scientific Secretary of the Russian Academy of Sciences; Academician of the Russian Academy of Sciences
BIRTHPLACE/DATE: Saratov, October 22, 1927
NATIONALITY: Russian
CAREER: From 1950 to 1962, worked at the Institute for Automation and Telemechanics (now the Institute for Management Problems) of the USSR Academy of Sciences. From 1953, member of the Communist Party. From 1962 to 1975, worked for the Central Committee; Deputy Head of the Central Committee's Science Department. From 1975 to 1988, USSR Deputy Minister of Higher Education.
MAJOR WORKS: More than 140 scientific works and eleven monographs on the theory of automated control systems and principles of calculation and construction of automation.
HONORS/AWARDS: Order of the Red Banner of Labor; Order of the October Revolution; State Prize (1984).
FAMILY: Married with a son.
ADDRESS/TELEPHONE: 14 Leninsky Prospekt, GSP–1 Moscow–71, 117901. 954–4485 (office).

Makashov, Albert Mikhailovich
POSITION: Colonel-General; Central Committee Member of the Working Communist Party of Russia
BIRTHPLACE/DATE: Levaya Rossosh village, Voronezh region, July 12, 1938
CAREER: From 1950 to September 1991, served in the army. Reconnaissance Platoon, Group, Company Commander of the USSR Army in Germany. Reconnaissance Company, Tank Regiment Reconnaissance Head, Motorized Infantry Battalion Commander in the Caucasus Military District. First Deputy Common-to-All-Arms Army Commander; Twentieth Common-to-All-Arms Army Commander of the USSR Army in Germany. First Deputy Commander of the Trans-Caucasus Military District. From 1988 to 1989, Special Yerevan District Commander. From 1989 to 1991, Commander of the Privolzhsko-Uralsky Military District. Former Commander of the Privolzhsko-Uralsky Military District. From 1989, involved in politics; Leader of the Communist Initiative Movement. In October 1991, dismissed from the Armed Forces; organized a new Communist Party based

on the Communist Initiative Movement. From 1991, member of the Russian Central Committee and Organization Bureau. From February 1992, Coordinating Committee Member of the Otchizna (Fatherland) Movement. From March 1992, Coordinating Committee Member of the Trudovaya Rossiya (Working Russia) Movement; member of the Political Council of Combined Opposition. From 1989 to 1992, USSR People's Deputy. To August 1991, member of the Communist Party.
HONORS/AWARDS: Medal for the Defense of Moscow.
FAMILY: Married with three children and five grandchildren.
TELEPHONE: 203–9023.

Makeyev, Yevgeni Nikolayevich
POSITION: Russian Federation Permanent Representative to the United Nations and Other International Organizations in Geneva
BIRTHPLACE/DATE: Pishnur village, Arbazh district, Kirov region, April 28, 1928
NATIONALITY: Russian
CAREER: From 1950 to 1951, Aide at the USSR Embassy in the People's Republic of China. From 1951 to 1953, Secretary at the USSR Consulate-General in Tianjun, China. From 1953 to 1954, Senior Aide to the Treaties and Legal Department of the USSR Foreign Ministry. From 1954 to 1956, Third Secretary of the International Organizations Department. From 1956 to 1957, Third Secretary, Second Secretary of the International Economic Organizations Department of the USSR Foreign Ministry. From 1957 to 1960, Assistant, Secretary to the Head of the International Economic Organizations Department of the USSR Foreign Ministry. From 1960 to 1961, First Secretary; from 1961 to 1964, Counsellor; from 1964 to 1967, Deputy Permanent Representative of the USSR to the UN (New York). From 1967 to 1968, Deputy Head; from 1968 to 1971, Head of the Second European Department of the USSR Foreign Ministry. From 1971 to 1980, Deputy Permanent Representative of the USSR to the UN (New York). From 1980 to 1986, Head of the International Economic Organizations Department of the USSR Foreign Ministry.
HONORS/AWARDS: Order of the Red Banner of Labor; Order of the People's Friendship; Order of the Badge of Honor.
FAMILY: Married with two children.
ADDRESS/TELEPHONE: Representation Permanente de la Russie aupres de la office des Nations Unies. 810–4122; 733–18170; 734–4044; 734–4756.

Makharadze, Vakhtang Vakhtangovich
POSITION: Board Chairman of the Interferma and Alfakor Enterprises; member of the Board of Directors of the American-Russian Business Council
BIRTHPLACE/DATE: Georgian Republic, 1954
NATIONALITY: Georgian
CAREER: From 1979 to 1985, Engineer. From 1985 to 1987, Department Head of the Institute of Oceanology of the USSR Academy of Sciences. In 1987, Chairman of the Ferma Cooperative Society. From 1989, Board Chairman of the Interferma and Alfakor Joint Venture Enterprises.
FAMILY: Married with three children.
ADDRESS/TELEPHONE: P.O. Box 553, Moscow, 119021. 203–5088 (office).

Makhkamov, Kakhar
POSITION: Former President of the Tajik Supreme Soviet Council; First Secretary of the Tajik Communist Party
BIRTHPLACE/DATE: Moscow, 1932
EDUCATION: Studied at the Leningrad Mining Institute.
CAREER: From 1961 to 1965, Chairman of the Leningrad City Executive Committee. From 1982 to 1985, Chair of the Tajik Supreme Soviet Planning Administration. From 1989 to 1991, USSR People's Deputy. In 1991, President of the Tajik Supreme Soviet.

Maksimov, Yuri Pavlovich
POSITION: Former Commander of the Strategic Forces of the Commonwealth of Independent States (CIS) Unified Armed Forces; General of the Army
BIRTHPLACE/DATE: Kryukovka village, Michurin district, Tambov region, June 30, 1924
NATIONALITY: Russian
CAREER: From 1942, served in the army. From 1943 to 1950, Machine-Gun Platoon Company Commander. From 1959 to 1965, General Staff Operator-Officer of the USSR Armed Forces; Bat-

talion Commander; Regiment Staff Head; Regiment Commander; Division Staff Head. From 1965 to 1973, Motorized Infantry Division Commander; First Deputy of the Army Commander. From 1973 to 1979, First Deputy Commander. From 1979 to 1984, Commander of the Turkistan Military District. In 1984, held crucial position in the USSR Ministry of Defense. From 1985 to 1991, Commander in Chief of the Strategic Missile Forces; USSR Deputy Minister of Defense. From 1991 to March 1992, Commander in Chief of the Strategic Deterioration Forces. From March to October 1992, Commander of the Strategic Forces of the CIS Unified Armed Forces; elected to the USSR Supreme Soviet of the Tenth and Eleventh Convocations. From 1989 to 1992, USSR People's Deputy. From 1943 to 1991, member of the Communist Party.
HONORS/AWARDS: Hero of the Soviet Union; two Orders of Lenin; three Orders of the Red Banner; Order of the October Revolution; two Orders of the Patriotic War, First Class.
FAMILY: Married with two sons.
TELEPHONE: 598–7922; 598–7557 (office).

Maksimova, Yekaterina Sergeyevna

POSITION: Ballet Dancer of the Bolshoi State Academic Theater; Academician; Assistant Professor of Choreography at the State Institute of Dramatic Art (GITIS); Full Member of the Academy of Arts
BIRTHPLACE/DATE: Moscow, 1939
CAREER: From 1957, danced in the Bolshoi Theater Troupe. Performs in foreign theaters in France, Great Britain, and other countries.
MAJOR WORKS: Giselle; Maria in *Bakhchisarai Fountain;* Katerina in *Stone Flower;* Zolushka (Cinderella); Odetta-Odylia in *Swan Lake*; Juliet in *Romeo and Juliet*. From 1977 to 1978, acted in comic ballet films *Galateya* and *Old Tango*. In 1980, played Nathalie in the ballet film *Nathalie*.
HONORS/AWARDS: USSR People's Artist; First Prize of the Moscow Ballet Dancers Contest (1954); Prize of the International Ballet Dancers Contest in Vienna (1959).
FAMILY: Married.
ADDRESS/TELEPHONE: 5/13 Smolenskaya Naberezhnaya, Flat #62, Moscow, 121099. 244–0227 (home).

Malashenko, Igor Yevgenyevich

POSITION: Former Political Director; First Deputy Chairman of the Ostankino Television and Radio Company; Director-General of Ostankino TV
BIRTHPLACE/DATE: Leninabad, Tajik Republic, 1932
NATIONALITY: Tajik
EDUCATION: Doctor of Philosophy.
CAREER: From 1961, Chairman of the Leninabad City Executive Committee; Head of the Tajik Republic State Planning Committee. From 1965, Deputy Chairman of the Tajik Republic Council of Ministers. From 1982, Chairman of the Tajik Republic Council of Ministers; Chairman of the Tajik Republic Supreme Soviet. From 1985, First Secretary of the Tajik Republic Central Committee. From November 1990, President of Tajikistan. In September 1991, resigned from post by demand of a majority of the Supreme Soviet Deputies and the people. From 1989 to 1992, USSR People's Deputy. From 1957 to 1991, member of the Central Committee; member of the Politburo.
HONORS/AWARDS: A number of awards.
FAMILY: Married.
ADDRESS/TELEPHONE: 42 Prospekt Lenina, Dushanbe, 734051. 232–343; 223–821 (office).

Malei, Mikhail Dmitryevich

POSITION: Advisor to the Russian Federation President on Economic Conversion Problems; Full Member of the Russian Academy of Sciences
BIRTHPLACE/DATE: Volyntsy village, Verkhnedvinsk district, Vitebsk region, October 9, 1941
EDUCATION: From 1964 to 1969, student at the Leningrad Technology Institute. Doctor of Technical Sciences.
CAREER: From 1961 to 1964, served in the USSR Army in the German Democratic Republic (GDR). From 1969 to 1983, Engineer, Laboratory Head, Department Head of the All-Union Research Institute. From 1983 to 1986, Chief Engineer of the All-Union Potentsial (Potential) Scientific and Industrial Association. From 1986 to 1988, Deputy Science Head of the Glavelektroistochnik (Main Electricity Source) of the USSR Ministry of Electrotechnical Industry. From 1988 to 1990, Director of the All-Union Research Institute of Information and Technical and Economic Studies in Electrical Engineering. From 1990 to 1991,

Chairman of the Russian Federation State Committee for State Property Management; Deputy Chairman of the Russian Federation Council of Ministers. From 1989 to 1992, Russian Federation People's Deputy. From 1963 to 1991, member of the Communist Party.
MAJOR WORKS: More than 100 inventions in different fields of engineering; more than 100 publications on materials science, chemistry, and electrical engineering.
HONORS/AWARDS: Order of the People's Friendship; medals.
FAMILY: Married with a daughter.
ADDRESS/TELEPHONE: 10 Ilyinka Street, Moscow, 103132. 206–5483 (office).

Malgin, Andrey Victorovich
POSITION: Editor in Chief of *Stolitsa* (*Capital City*) magazine; Deputy of the Moscow Council
BIRTHPLACE/DATE: Sevastopol, 1958
CAREER: From 1982 to 1986, Correspondent, Senior Correspondent for *Literaturnaya Gazeta* (*Literary Newspaper*). From 1986 to 1990, Columnist; Head of the Literature and Arts Department of *Nedelya* (*Week*) newspaper. Member of the Russian Writers' Union; member of the Journalists' Union.
MAJOR WORKS: *Robert Rozhdestvensky* (1990).
FAMILY: Married with a child.
ADDRESS/TELEPHONE: 22 Petrovka Street, Moscow, 101425. 921–6745; 928–2349 (office).

Malinov, Aleksandr Vasilyevich
POSITION: Editor in Chief of *Nauka i Biznes* (*Science and Business*) weekly; President of the TOO Ekorad Advertising Firm
BIRTHPLACE/DATE: Moscow, June 9, 1937
EDUCATION: Doctor of Technical Sciences.
CAREER: From 1970, Journalist for *Nedelya* (*Week*) newspaper; *Sovietskaya Rossiya* (*Soviet Russia*) newspaper. Editor in Chief of *NTR* and the *Znaniye* (*Knowledge*) society newsletter. From October 1990, Editor in Chief of *Radical;* member of the Scientific Magazines Section of the Moscow Administration of the Confederation of Journalists' Unions.
FAMILY: Married with a son.
ADDRESS/TELEPHONE: 5 Sredny Karetny Pereulok, K–51, Moscow, 103051. 923–7694; Fax: 923–6731.

Malkevich, Vladislav Leonidovich
POSITION: Former Presidium Chairman of the Chamber of Commerce
BIRTHPLACE/DATE: 1936
NATIONALITY: Russian
EDUCATION: Doctor of Technical Sciences; Doctor of Economics.
CAREER: From 1959, Radio Engineer; held executive economic and scientific positions at the USSR Ministry of Radio Industry. From 1971, held positions at the USSR Foreign Trade Ministry. From 1983, Deputy, then USSR First Deputy Foreign Trade Minister. From February 1988 to August 1991, Presidium Chairman of the Chamber of Commerce.
HONORS/AWARDS: Order of Lenin; Order of the Red Banner of Labor; Order of the People's Friendship.
FAMILY: Married with two children.
TELEPHONE: 206–7775 (Chamber of Commerce).

Malyshev, Nikolay Grigoryevich
POSITION: Advisor to the Russian Federation President on Science and Higher Education; Head of the Analytical Center for Presidential Social Programs; Corresponding Member of the Russian Academy of Sciences
BIRTHPLACE/DATE: Moscow, July 3, 1945
NATIONALITY: Russian
EDUCATION: Doctor of Technical Sciences; Professor.
CAREER: From 1969 to 1970, Engineer. Worked at the Taganrog Institute of Radio Engineering: From 1970 to 1972, Assistant; from 1972 to 1973; Senior Lecturer; from 1973 to 1976, Assistant Professor; from 1976 to 1979, Head of Automation and Telemechanics; from 1979 to 1986, Pro-Rector for Scientific Work; from 1986 to 1990, Rector. From 1990 to 1991, Deputy Chairman of the Russian Federation Council of Ministers; Chairman of the Russian Federation State Committee for Science and Higher Education. From November 1991, Russian Federation State Advisor on Science and Higher Education. From 1967 to 1991, member of the Communist Party.

FAMILY: Married with two children.
ADDRESS/TELEPHONE: 4 Staraya Square, Moscow, 103302. 206–4748.

Mamatov, Victor Fyodorovich
POSITION: Athlete
BIRTHPLACE/DATE: Belovo, Kemerovo region, 1937
NATIONALITY: Russian
EDUCATION: Doctor of Pedagogics.
CAREER: From 1956 to 1966, Technician for the Survey Department of Sibgidrotrans (Siberian Water Transport). From 1966 to 1973, Instructor of the Novosibirsk Region Sports Committee. From 1973 to 1976, Coach of the USSR Youth National Team. From 1976 to 1981, Director of the Novosibirsk Physical Training Technical Secondary School. From 1981 to 1985, Senior Coach of the USSR National Biathlon Team. From 1985 to 1987, Skiing Directorate Head of the USSR State Physical Training and SportsCommittee.
HONORS/AWARDS: Four-time World Champion; Winter Olympic Biathlon Champion (1968, 1972); two Orders of the Red Banner of Labor; USSR Honored Master of Sports; medals.
FAMILY: Married with two sons.
ADDRESS/TELEPHONE: 4 Severnoye Chertanovo, Flat #11, Moscow. 319–3701 (home).

Mamedov, Georgy Enverovich
POSITION: Russian Federation Deputy Foreign Minister; Envoy Extraordinary and Plenipotentiary, First Class
BIRTHPLACE/DATE: September 9, 1947
NATIONALITY: Russian
EDUCATION: Graduated in 1970 from the Moscow State Institute of International Relations. Doctor of History. Speaks English and Swedish.
CAREER: From 1970 to 1977, worked at the Institute of the U.S. and Canada of the USSR Academy of Sciences. From 1977 to 1981, Staff Member of the USSR Embassy to the United States. From 1981 and 1989, Second Secretary, First Secretary, Counsellor, Deputy Department Head, First Deputy Chief of the USSR Foreign Ministry Directorate of the U.S. and Canada.
ADDRESS/TELEPHONE: 32/34 Smolenskaya-Sennaya Square, Moscow, 121200. 244–9255 (office).

Manukovsky, Andrey Borisovich
POSITION: Director-General of the International Business School at the Moscow State Institute of International Relations; Vice President of the Russian Association of Business Schools; Board Member of the European Foundation for Management Development (Brussels); Editorial Board Member of *Ekonomicheskiye Nauki* (*Economic Sciences*) magazine
BIRTHPLACE/DATE: Moscow, 1960
NATIONALITY: Russian
EDUCATION: Graduated in 1981 from the International Economic Relations Department at the Moscow State Institute of International Relations (MGIMO). In 1991, studied at the University of Virginia in the United States. Assistant Professor; Doctor of Economics. Speaks English and French.
CAREER: From 1981 to 1984, Lecturer at the Moscow State Institute of International Relations. From 1984 to 1989, Deputy Dean, Senior Lecturer at the Moscow State Institute of International Relations.
FAMILY: Married with two children.
ADDRESS/TELEPHONE: 76 Vernadsky Prospekt, Moscow, 117454. 434–9196 (office).

Manukyan, Vazgen Mikaelovich
POSITION: Defense Minister of the Armenian Republic; Armenia Supreme Soviet Deputy
BIRTHPLACE/DATE: Leninakan (now Kumairi), February 13, 1946
NATIONALITY: Armenian
EDUCATION: Doctor of Physics and Mathematics.
CAREER: From 1969, Junior Researcher at the Armenian Academy of Sciences' Computer Center. From 1972, Lecturer, Assistant Professor, Senior Researcher at Yerevan State University. From 1988, member of the Karabakh Committee. From November 1989, Board Member of the Armenian National Movement. On December 10, 1988, arrested as one of the Karabakh Committee Leaders. On May 31, 1989, discharged. From 1990, Chairman of the Armenian Council of Ministers. From September to October 1992, Armenian Republic State Minister of Defense. From September 1992, member of the National Security Council of the Armenian Republic President.

MAJOR WORKS: Scientific works on functions theory.
FAMILY: Married with three children.
ADDRESS/TELEPHONE: The House of Government, Ploshchad Respubliki, Yerevan, 375010. 520–360.

Marchuk, Guri Ivanovich
POSITION: Director of the Computing Mathematics Institute of the Russian Academy of Sciences; Presidium Member of the Russian Academy of Sciences
BIRTHPLACE/DATE: Orenburg region, June 8, 1925
NATIONALITY: Russian
EDUCATION: Doctor of Physics and Mathematics; Professor; Academician of the USSR Academy of Sciences.
CAREER: From 1953 to 1962, Department Head at the Institute of Physics and Energy in Obninsk. From 1962 to 1963, Deputy Director of Research at the Institute of Mathematics of the Siberian branch of the USSR Academy of Sciences. In 1963, Scientific Secretary of the Science Committee of the USSR Council of Ministers. From 1963 to 1980, Director of the Computer Center of the Siberian branch of the USSR Academy of Sciences. From 1969 to 1975, Deputy Presidium Chairman of the Siberian branch of the USSR Academy of Sciences. From 1975 to 1980, Vice President of the USSR Academy of Sciences; Chairman of the Siberian branch of the USSR Academy of Sciences. From 1980 to 1986, Deputy Chairman of the USSR Council of Ministers; Chairman of the USSR State Committee for Science and Technology. From 1985 to 1988, Chairman of the COMECON (Council for Mutual Economic Assistance) Committee for Scientific and Technical Cooperation. From 1986 to 1991, President of the USSR Academy of Sciences. From 1991, Head of the Council of Presidents of the Academies of Sciences of the Independent States. Foreign member of the Academies of Sciences of Czechoslovakia, Bulgaria, and the German Democratic Republic (GDR); Honorary Academician of the Finnish Academy. USSR Supreme Soviet Deputy of the Ninth, Tenth, and Eleventh Convocations. From 1989 to 1992, USSR People's Deputy. From 1947 to 1991, member of the Communist Party.
MAJOR WORKS: Computing and applied mathematics; created algorithms of numerical solution of neutrons transfer equations that were used as a basis for calculating the critical parameters of nuclear reactors; studies on methods of short-term weather forecasts, atmosphere, and ocean dynamics; developed numerical methods of automated sytems control.
HONORS/AWARDS: Hero of Socialist Labor; four Orders of Lenin; Prize of Lenin; USSR State Prize.
FAMILY: Married with three children.
ADDRESS/TELEPHONE: 32-A Leninsky Prospekt, Moscow, 117334. 954–3506 (secretary); 938–6859.

Martynov, Andrey Vladimirovich
POSITION: Vice President of the Interfax Joint-Stock Company
BIRTHPLACE/DATE: Moscow, 1964
NATIONALITY: Russian
CAREER: From 1986 to 1988, North European Department Correspondent for the USSR State Television and Radio Committee. From 1988 to 1990, Commentator for the USSR State Television and Radio Committee. From 1990 to 1991, Director of the Economic Information Department of the Interfax News Agency.
FAMILY: Divorced.
ADDRESS/TELEPHONE: 2 Pervaya Tverskaya-Yamskaya Street, Moscow, 103006. 250–9637 (office).

Mashits, Vladimir Mikhailovich
POSITION: Chairman of the Russian Federation State Committee for Cooperation with the Member-States of the Commonwealth
BIRTHPLACE/DATE: Moscow, April 17, 1953
NATIONALITY: Russian
EDUCATION: Doctor of Economics.
CAREER: From 1973 to 1980, Engineer, Senior Economist, Junior Researcher at the Research Institute of the USSR Central Statistics Board. From 1980 to 1990, Senior Engineer, Junior Researcher, Senior Researcher, Laboratory Head at the Central Economics and Mathematics Institute of the USSR Academy of Sciences. From 1990 to 1991, Laboratory Head at the Institute for Market Problems. In 1991, Deputy Director of Science at the Institute of Economic Policy of the Academy of National

Economy. From November 1991, Russian Federation Government Plenipotentiary Representative for the Economic Community.
FAMILY: Married with two daughters.
ADDRESS/TELEPHONE: 7 Varvarka Street, Moscow, 103073. 206–7055 (office).

Mashkov, Vitaly Vladimirovich
POSITION: Sverdlovsk Region Representative of the Russian Federation President; member of the Russian Federation Supreme Soviet Committee for Industry, Power Engineering, and Power Conversion; member of the Demokraticheskaya Rossiya (Democratic Russia) Movement and the Left-Center Faction
BIRTHPLACE/DATE: Borovichi, May 25, 1944
NATIONALITY: Russian
EDUCATION: Doctor of Technical Science.
CAREER: From 1962 to 1968, Laboratory Assistant. From 1968 to 1976, Engineer. From 1976 to 1987, Senior Engineer. From 1987 to 1991, Head of the Special Scientific and Technical Bureau. Russian Federation People's Deputy.
FAMILY: Married with two children.
ADDRESS/TELEPHONE: 107 Bolshakova Street, Flat #47, Yekaterinburg, 620031; 1 Oktyabrskaya Place, Yekaterinburg. 7–0034 (Sverdlov region home); 51–2161 (office).

Maslakov, Arkady Dmitryevich
POSITION: Director-General of the Stroimaterialy (Construction Materials) Scientific and Industrial Association; Board Member of the Byelorussian Union of Entrepreneurs; Vice President of the Minsk Union of Small Enterprises and Entrepreneurs
BIRTHPLACE/DATE: Izhenka village, Slavgorod district, Mogilev region, 1930
EDUCATION: Doctor of Science.
CAREER: Assistant to the Architecture Department at the Byelorussian Polytechnical Institute. Worked at the Trust # 5 Ferro-Concrete Structures and Parts Plant: Shop Superintendent; Chief Engineer; Director. Regional Soviet People's Deputy.
MAJOR WORKS: Nine inventions; more than 150 scientific publications.
HONORS/AWARDS: Byelorussian Republic Honored Inventor.
FAMILY: Married with a daughter.
ADDRESS/TELEPHONE: 22 Pervomayskaya Street, Building 2, Flat #26–27, Minsk, 220088. 36–8095.

Maslennikov, Arkady Afrikanovich
POSITION: Editor in Chief of *Birzhevye Vedomosti* (*Stock Exchange News*) newspaper; Vice President of the Society for Friendship Between the People of Russia and Finland; Observation Council Chairman of the All-Russia Exchange Bank; member of the Confederation of Journalists' Unions
BIRTHPLACE/DATE: Kostroma region, 1931
CAREER: From 1954 to 1965, Senior Researcher at the Institute of the World Economy. From 1965 to 1989, Correspondent in India, Pakistan, and Great Britain; Department Editor; Editorial Board Member of *Pravda* (Truth) newspaper. From 1989 to 1991, Press Service Head of the USSR Supreme Soviet newspaper.
HONORS/AWARDS: Honored Worker of Culture.
FAMILY: Married with a daughter and three grandsons.
ADDRESS/TELEPHONE: 7 Bolshaya Ordynka, Flat #5, Moscow, 113035. 188–2053; 233–3863 (office).

Maslyukov, Yuri Dmitryevich
POSITION: Politician
BIRTHPLACE/DATE: Leningrad, September 30, 1937
NATIONALITY: Russian
CAREER: Engineer at a research institute; Deputy Department Head; First Deputy Director; Chief Engineer. From 1970, Chief Engineer of a branch of the Izhevsk Construction Plant. From 1974 to 1979, Head of the Central Technical Directorate; Board Member. From 1979 to 1982, USSR Deputy Minister of the Defense Industry. From 1982 to 1985, First Deputy Chairman of the USSR State Planning Committee. From 1985 to 1988, Deputy Chairman of the USSR Council of Ministers. From 1988 to 1991, First Deputy Chairman of the USSR Council of Ministers; Chairman of the USSR State Planning Committee. From 1991 to 1992, USSR Deputy Prime Minister; Deputy of the USSR Supreme Soviet of the Eleventh Convocation. From 1990 to 1991, member of the USSR Presidential Council. From 1966 to 1991, member of the Com-

munist Party. From 1988, Alternate Member, and from 1989, Full Member of the Politburo.
Honors/Awards: Order of Lenin; Order of the October Revolution; Order of the Red Banner of Labor; Order of the Badge of Honor.
Family: Married with a child.
Address/Telephone: 13 Marx Prospekt, Moscow, 103009. 292–4476.

Matrosov, Aleksandr Sergeyevich
Position: Minister of Moscow Government; Head of the Moscow City Department of Engineering Provision
Birthplace/Date: Kirsanovsky state collective farm, Tambov region, February 15, 1935
Career: From 1958 to 1974, Work Superintendent, Senior Work Superintendent, Construction Directorate Head of Glavmosstroi (Main Moscow Construction Administration) and Glavmosinzstroi (Main Moscow Construction Administration). From 1974 to 1987, Head of the Moscow City Executive Committee's Department of Water-Supply and Sewer Systems. From 1987 to 1988, Deputy Chairman of the Moscow City Executive Committee. From 1988 to 1991, Head of the Central Directorate of Housing Services and Engineering Provision of the Moscow City Executive Committee. From 1991 to 1992, Deputy Premier of Moscow Government.
Honors/Awards: Order of the Badge of Honor; two Orders of the Red Banner of Labor; Order of the People's Friendship; Order of the October Revolution; State Prize; three medals.
Family: Married with three daughters.
Address/Telephone: 4 Maly Komsomolsky Pereulok, Moscow, 101000. 292–1795 (office).

Mau, Vladimir Aleksandrovich
Position: Board of Directors Member of the Institute for Economic Problems of the Transitional Period; Laboratory Head
Birthplace/Date: Moscow, December 29, 1959
Nationality: Armenian
Career: From 1981 to 1991, Aide-Researcher, Junior Researcher, Senior Researcher at the USSR Academy of Sciences' Institute of Economics. From 1991, Laboratory Head at the Institute of Economic Policy of the Academy of National Economy and the Russian Academy of Sciences. From 1992, Assistant to the Acting Chairman of the Russian Government.
Major Works: *In Search of Systematic Character* (1991).
Family: Married with a son.
Address/Telephone: 2/5 Orekhovo-Zavodsky Pereulok, Flat #101, Moscow, 199110. 280–2165 (home); 202–4598 (office).

Mazayev, Ivan Sergeyevich
Position: President of the Chemical Industry Commercial Bank (Khimbank); Assistant Professor at the Moscow Institute of Chemical Industry
Birthplace/Date: Klepovka village, Voronezh region, 1933
Nationality: Russian
Career: Financial Department Head of the Kursk Khimvolokno (Chemical Fiber) Industrial Association. Deputy Director of Economics of the Khimvolokno Association in Klinsk city. Deputy Directorate Head of the Ministry of Chemical Industry. Financial Directorate Head of the Ministry of Medical Industry.
Major Works: Scientific works on finance and money circulation.
Family: Married with two children and three grandchildren.
Address/Telephone: 20 Myasnitskaya (formerly Kirova) Street, Moscow, 101851. 928–4978 (office).

Mazayev, Vladimir Aleksandrovich
Position: Board Chairman of Prio-Vneshtorgbank (Foreign Trade Bank)
Birthplace/Date: Ryazan, 1961
Nationality: Russian
Education: Graduated in 1983 from the Moscow Institute of Management.
Career: From 1983 to 1989, Engineer, Laboratory Head, Chief of the Financial Department at the Ryazan Machinery Factory. From 1989 to 1990, Board Chairman of Prio-Bank. From 1990 to 1991, Board Chairman of Agroprombank (Bank of Agriculture and Industry).
Family: Married.
Address/Telephone: 24/5 Griboyedov Street, Ryazan, 390006. 459–7549 (Moscow); 44–4720 (office).

Medved, Aleksandr Vasilyevich

POSITION: President of the Byelorussia Federation of Free-Style Wrestling; Vice President of the Byelorussia International Olympics Committee
BIRTHPLACE/DATE: Belaya Tserkov, Kiev region, 1937
NATIONALITY: Russian
CAREER: In 1964, 1968, and 1972, Summer Olympic Champion; seven-time World and European Free-Style Wrestling Champion. From 1972, Instructor, Senior Instructor, Head of the Physical Training Department at the Minsk Center.

Medvedev, Sergey Konstantinovich

POSITION: Political Correspondent for the Television News Agency of the Ostankino TV and Radio Company
BIRTHPLACE/DATE: Kaliningrad, June 2, 1958
NATIONALITY: Russian
CAREER: From 1981, Correspondent, Commentator for All-Union Radio. From 1987, Special Correspondent, Commentator for Central Television. From 1990, Political Correspondent, Program Host, Reporter from the Congresses.
FAMILY: Married with a son.
ADDRESS/TELEPHONE: 19 Koroleva Street, Moscow. 930–1525 (home).

Mefody (Nemtsov, Nikolay Fyodorovich)

POSITION: Metropolitan of Voronezh and Lipetsk; Chairman of the Russian Children's Foundation
BIRTHPLACE/DATE: Rovenki, Voroshilovgrad region, February 16, 1949
NATIONALITY: Ukrainian
CAREER: From 1976 to 1979, Aide, Deputy Chairman of the Foreign Affairs of the Church Department of the Moscow Patriarchy. From 1979 to 1980, Priest of the Placement of the Vestment Temple of the Donskoi Monastery in Moscow. From 1980 to 1982, Bishop; Administrator of the Irkutsk and Chita Russian Orthodox Church Dioceses. In 1985, Archbishop. From 1985 to 1988, Archbishop of Voronezh and Lipetsk.
ADDRESS/TELEPHONE: 6 Osvobozhdeniya Truda Street, Voronezh. 55–3435 (office).

Melikyan, Gennadi Georgyevich

POSITION: Russian Federation Minister of Labor
BIRTHPLACE/DATE: Kropotkin, Krasnodarsky region, 1947
NATIONALITY: Russian
EDUCATION: Graduated in 1979 from Moscow State University. Doctor of Economics. Speaks English.
CAREER: From 1977 to 1986, Leading Economist, Section Head, Deputy Head of the Labor Organization Department of the USSR State Labor Committee. From 1986 to 1991, Assistant to the Management Head of the USSR Council of Ministers; Department Head of the USSR Council of Ministers' State Commission for Economic Reforms; Deputy Chairman of the State Council for Economic Reforms. From 1991, Vice President of the International Foundation for Economic and Social Reforms.
FAMILY: Married with a son and a daughter.
ADDRESS/TELEPHONE: 1 Birzhevaya Square, Moscow. 928–0683 (office).

Melnichenko, Vladimir Yefimovich

POSITION: Director of the Central Lenin Museum
BIRTHPLACE/DATE: Khashuri village, Georgian Republic, 1946
EDUCATION: Doctor of History.
CAREER: From 1971 to 1976, Junior Researcher at a research institute. From 1976 to 1987, Instructor, Consultant, Head of the Science and Educational Institutions Section of the Ukranian Central Committee. From 1987 to 1989, Deputy Director of a research institute. From 1989 to 1991, Section Head of the Ideology Department of the Central Committee.
MAJOR WORKS: Monographs and scientific and feature publications on history problems and Lenin studies.
FAMILY: Married with two sons.
ADDRESS/TELEPHONE: 2 Revolutsii Place, Moscow, 103012. 924–4529 (office).

Melnik, Sergey Grigoryevich

POSITION: Chairman of the Soyuztranzit (Union Transit) Firm
BIRTHPLACE/DATE: Alma-Ata, 1939

NATIONALITY: Ukrainian
CAREER: From 1963 to 1965, worked at the Research Institute of the USSR State Planning Committee. From 1965 to 1969, Senior Commodity Expert of the All-Union Soyuzpromeksport (Industrial Export) Association. From 1969 to 1972, worked at the All-Union Almazyuvelireksport (Diamond and Jewelry Export) Association. From 1972 to 1973, worked at the Foreign Trade Ministry. From 1973 to 1980, worked at the All-Union Soyuzvneshtrans (International Transport) Association. From 1984 to 1987, worked at the Saima Laims Joint-Stock Association (Finland).
FAMILY: Married with a son.
ADDRESS/TELEPHONE: 32/34 Smolenskaya-Sennaya, Moscow, 121200. 244–3951 (office).

Melnikov, Aleksandr Grigoryevich
POSITION: Former member of the Russian Federation Politburo; Secretary of the Russian Federation Central Committee
BIRTHPLACE/DATE: Orekhovo-Zuyevo, Moscow region, 1930
NATIONALITY: Russian
CAREER: Capital Construction Directorate Engineer at an enterprise in Tomsk. Served in the army. From 1956, Komsomol, Soviet, and Communist Party Functionary; Head of the Seversk City Komsomol Committee, Tomsk region; Instructor, Department Head of the City Party Committee; Chairman of the Seversk City Executive Committee. First Secretary of the Seversk City Communist Party. Deputy Construction Department Head of the Tomsk Region Party Committee. From 1973, Secretary, Second Secretary, First Secretary of the Tomsk Region Party Committee. From 1986 to 1988, Construction Department Head of the Central Committee. From 1988, First Secretary of the Kemerovo Region Communist Party. From 1986 to 1990, member of the Central Committee. From 1990 to August 1991, Secretary of the Russian Federation Central Committee.
HONORS/AWARDS: A number of awards.
FAMILY: Married with two daughters.

Melnikov, Igor Ivanovich
POSITION: Director of the Omega Company
BIRTHPLACE/DATE: Arkhangelsk, 1949
EDUCATION: Graduated in 1971 from the Moscow Mining Institute. Speaks English.
CAREER: From 1971 to 1981, Engineer, Laboratory Head at the All-Union Research Institute; developed radioelectronic software. From 1981 to 1990, Head of the Computerization Laboratory of the USSR Academy of Sciences' Institute of Socio-Economic Problems.
FAMILY: Married with a son.
ADDRESS/TELEPHONE: 19 Vlasov Street, Building 2, Flat #29, Moscow, 117335; P.O. Box 104, Moscow. 936–4237; 237–3880 (office); 128–4349 (home).

Mesyats, Gennadi Andreyevich
POSITION: Vice President of the Russian Academy of Sciences; Chairman of the Urals branch of the Russian Academy of Sciences; Director of the Institute of Electrophysics of the Urals branch of the Russian Academy of Sciences; President of the Demidov Foundation
BIRTHPLACE/DATE: Kemerovo, February 28, 1936
NATIONALITY: Russian
CAREER: From 1958 to 1969, worked at Tomsk Polytechnic. From 1969 to 1977, Deputy Director of the Institute of Atmosphere Optics of the Siberian branch of the USSR Academy of Sciences. From 1977 to 1986, Director of the Institute of High-Current Electronics of the USSR Academy of Sciences. From 1984, Academician of the USSR Academy of Sciences. From 1986 to 1987, Presidium Chairman of the Urals Scientific Center of the USSR Academy of Sciences.
MAJOR WORKS: More than 400 publications on high-current emission electronics, gas electronics, high-current accelerators, and high-capacity pulse equipment. Twenty-five inventions; two discoveries.
HONORS/AWARDS: Order of Lenin; Order of the Red Banner of Labor; Order of the Badge of Honor; State Prize; Council of Ministers Prize.
FAMILY: Married with a son.
ADDRESS/TELEPHONE: The Urals Branch of the Russian Academy of Sciences, 91 Pervomayskaya, GSP–169 Sverdlovsk, 620219. 938–1856 (Moscow); 44–0223 (office).

Mikhailov, Nikolay Vasilyevich
POSITION: President of the Vympel (Pennant) Inter-Governmental Joint-Stock Corporation; Chairman of the Moscow City Union of State Scientific-Industrial Enterprises
BIRTHPLACE/DATE: Sevsk, Bryansk region, 1937
CAREER: From 1961 to 1969, worked at the Podolsk City Electro-Mechanical Plant. From 1969, Chief Engineer of the Gomel Radio Engineering Plant. From 1975, Chief Engineer of the Vympel Central Scientific-Industrial Association. From 1979 to 1987, Director of the Radio Engineering Plant Research Institute. From 1987, Director-General of Vympel.
HONORS/AWARDS: State Prize.
FAMILY: Married with a son.
ADDRESS/TELEPHONE: P.O. Box 83, Moscow, 101000. 152–9595.

Mikhailov, Victor Nikitovich
POSITION: Russian Federation Minister of Nuclear Energy
BIRTHPLACE/DATE: Moscow region, February 12, 1934
NATIONALITY: Russian
EDUCATION: Doctor of Technical Sciences; Professor.
CAREER: From 1958 to 1969, Engineer; Department Head at the Institute of Experimental Physics. From 1969 to 1988, Deputy Director, Director, Chief Constructor of the Research Institute of Pulse Equipment. From 1988 to 1990, Deputy USSR Minister of Medium Engineering Industry. From 1990 to 1991, Deputy USSR Minister for Nuclear Energy and Industry. USSR People's Deputy.
MAJOR WORKS: More than 260 scientific works on nuclear physics and nuclear energy.
HONORS/AWARDS: Order of the Red Banner of Labor; Order of the Badge of Honor; State and Lenin Prizes.
FAMILY: Married with a son.
ADDRESS/TELEPHONE: 24/26 B. Ordynka, Moscow, 101000. 233–3751 (office).

Mikhalchenko, Aleksandr Ivanovich
POSITION: President of the Montazhspetsstroi (Specialized Construction) Joint-Stock Corporation
BIRTHPLACE/DATE: Abramovka village, Kiev region, 1935
NATIONALITY: Ukrainian
CAREER: From 1958 to 1973, Foreman, Work Superintendent.

Mikhalchuk, Oleg Nikolayevich
POSITION: Editor in Chief of *Narodnaya Gazeta* (*People's Newspaper*)
BIRTHPLACE/DATE: Khanty-Mansiisk, Tyumen region, 1957
EDUCATION: Graduated in 1981 from Moscow State University. Speaks German.
CAREER: From 1981 to 1985, Department Head, Deputy Editor of district newspapers in Shchelkovo, Moscow region. From 1985 and 1991, Deputy Department Head, Department Head, News Analyst of *Narodnaya Gazeta*.
FAMILY: Married with two daughters.
ADDRESS/TELEPHONE: 7 Ulitsa 1905 Goda, GSP, D–22, Moscow, 123847. 259–4897 (office).

Mikhalkov, Nikita Sergeyevich
POSITION: Actor; Film Producer; Advisor to the Russian Vice President on Culture and Cultural Relations with Foreign Countries; Russian Federation People's Artist
BIRTHPLACE/DATE: Moscow, 1945
NATIONALITY: Russian
CAREER: From 1961, Board Member of the Soviet Culture Foundation. From January 1992, Presidium Member of the Russian International Culture Foundation; Chairman of the Russian Federation Tennis Federation.
MAJOR WORKS: First film part in *Clouds Over Borsk*. Parts in: *I'm Walking Through Moscow* (1963); *Red Tent; The Nest of Gentlefolk* by Turgenev (1969); *An Unfinished Piece for Mechanical Piano* (1977); *Sibiriada* (1979). Films produced: *A Quiet Day at the End of War* (1971); *Bondwoman of Love* (1976); *An Unfinished Piece for Mechanical Piano* (1977); *Five Evenings* (1979); *Several Days in the Life of Oblomov; Kinfolk* (1982); *Without Witness*. In 1988, staged *Mechanical Piano* based on Chekhov's stories in the Di Roma Theater (Italy). Co-produced films (with Italian companies): *Black Eyes* (1988); *Hitchhiker* (1990).
HONORS/AWARDS: Fipressi Prize at the Moscow

International Film Festival for *Without Witnesses*; Golden Lion Prize for *Urga* (1991).
FAMILY: Married with three children.
ADDRESS: 6 Gogolevski Boulevard, Moscow, 121019; 4 Maly Kozikhinski Pereulok, Moscow, 103001.

Mironov, Valery Ivanovich
POSITION: Russian Federation Deputy Defense Minister; Colonel-General
BIRTHPLACE/DATE: Moscow, December 19, 1943
CAREER: Platoon, then Company Commander. From 1973 to 1975, Staff Head; Deputy Regiment Commander. From 1975 to 1977, Commander of the Motorized Infantry Regiment. From 1977 to 1979, Deputy Division Commander. From 1979, Division Commander. From 1979 to 1982, participated in combat operations in Afghanistan. From 1984, First Deputy Army Commander. From 1989, First Deputy Commander of the Leningrad Military District. From 1991, Commander of the Pribaltiysky Military District (Baltic). From 1991 to 1992, Commander of the Northwestern Armed Forces.
FAMILY: Married with a daughter.
TELEPHONE: 293–8921 (office).

Mironov, Vladimir Nikolayevich
POSITION: President of the Inter-Bank Financial Firm; member of the Svobodnaya Rossiya (Free Russia) People's Party
BIRTHPLACE/DATE: Moscow, 1954
CAREER: From 1977 to 1980, Attaché at the USSR Embassy in Belgium. From 1980 to 1987, Staff Member of the General International Problems Directorate. From 1987 to 1989, Researcher at the Institute of Social Sciences of the Central Committee. From 1989 to 1990, Department Editor of *Kommunist* (*Communist*) magazine. From 1991 to 1992, Deputy Director-General of the Vozrozhdeniye (Revival) Social Development of Russia Foundation of the Russian Federation Supreme Soviet.
MAJOR WORKS: Articles and monographs on international affairs and the reconstruction of Russia.
FAMILY: Single.
ADDRESS/TELEPHONE: 10 Lunacharsky Street, Flat #15, Moscow, 109383. 241–8907 (office).

Mironov, Vyacheslav Petrovich
POSITION: Head of the Russian Federation Armed Forces; Colonel-General
BIRTHPLACE/DATE: Moscow, 1938
NATIONALITY: Russian
CAREER: From 1959, served in the Armed Forces. Directorate Head of the Defense Ministry; First Deputy Head of Arms of the USSR Defense Ministry. From 1990, USSR Deputy Defense Minister of Arms, USSR Defense Ministry Head of Arms.
FAMILY: Married with a daughter.
ADDRESS/TELEPHONE: 9-A Moskvoretskaya Naberezhnaya, K–160, Moscow, 103160. 293–2869; 293–1413; 293–2235 (office).

Miroshnichenko, Irina Petrovna
POSITION: Actress of the Moscow Pushkin Theater; Deputy Minister of Culture
BIRTHPLACE/DATE: Barnaul, Altai region, 1947
CAREER: From 1967, Actress of the Moscow Chekhov Academic Arts Theater; Presidium Member of the City Committee of the Cultural Workers' Union; Board Member of the USSR Federation of Cultural Workers' Unions; Elected member of the Central Electoral Commission for the Election of USSR People's Deputies to the Supreme Soviet. Member of the Cultural Workers' Union of the Russian Culture Foundation.
MAJOR WORKS: Parts in plays: Masha in *The Seagull* by Chekhov; Masha and Olga in *Three Sisters* by Chekhov; Sarra in *Ivanov;* Arkadina in *The Seagull* by Chekhov; Ranevskaya in *The Cherry Orchard* by Chekhov; Tatiana in *Jubilee*; Mrs. Cheevley in *Ideal Husband* by Oscar Wilde; Zhenia in *Valentin i Valentina* by M. Roshin. Parts in films: Maria Magdalena in *Andrei Rublev*; Elena Andreyevna in *Uncle Vanya*; parts in *This Sweet Word Freedom*; *Red Haired Honest Man in Love*; *World in Other Dimension*; *Unmatched Characters*.
HONORS/AWARDS: Order of the Badge of Honor; Medal For the Development of Tselina (Virgin Land); Russian Federation People's Artist.
ADDRESS/TELEPHONE: 23 Tverskoi Boulevard, Moscow. 203–8582 (office); 250–1720 (home).

Mirsaidov, Shukurulla Rakhmatovich
POSITION: Representative of the Uzbekistan International Foundation for the Facilitation of Privatization and Foreign Investment
BIRTHPLACE/DATE: Leningrad, February 14, 1939
NATIONALITY: Uzbek
EDUCATION: Doctor of Economics.
CAREER: From 1959 to 1963, Economist, Senior Economist, Section Head of the Tashkent Region Planning Committee. From 1963 to 1964, Chair Assistant at the Tashkent Institute of National Economy. From 1964 to 1971, Deputy Chairman of the Region Planning Committee; Directorate Head of the Tashkent Region Executive Committee. From 1971 to 1981, Chairman of the City Planning Committee, Deputy Chairman of the Tashkent City Executive Committee. From 1981 to 1984, Deputy Chairman, First Deputy Chairman of the Uzbekistan State Planning Committee. From 1984 to 1985, Head of the Uzbekistan Central Statistics Board. From 1985 to 1988, Chairman of the Tashkent City Executive Committee. From 1988 to 1989, Department Head of the Uzbekistan Central Committee. From 1989 to 1990, Chairman of the Uzbekistan State Planning Committee; Deputy Chairman of the Uzbek Republic Council of Ministers. In 1990, Chairman of the Uzbek Republic Council of Ministers. From 1990 to January 1992, Vice President of the Uzbek Republic. In 1992, State Secretary of the Uzbekistan President. Uzbek Republic People's Deputy. From 1962 to 1991, member of the Communist Party. From 1990 to 1991, member of the Central Committee.
HONORS/AWARDS: Order of the Red Banner of Labor; two Orders of the Badge of Honor; Order of the People's Friendship.
FAMILY: Married with two children.
ADDRESS/TELEPHONE: 3 Solyanka Street, Building 3, Moscow, 109028. 34–9627; 34–8537 (Uzbekistan office).

Mishcharin, Aleksandr Nikolayevich
POSITION: Editor in Chief of *Novaya Rossiya* (*New Russia*) magazine
BIRTHPLACE/DATE: Moscow, 1939
EDUCATION: Graduated in 1960 from the Drama Department of the Shchepkin Drama School and in 1962 from the Higher Screenwriting Courses of the USSR Union of Film Makers.
CAREER: From March 1991, Editor in Chief of *Voskreseniye* (*Resurrection*) magazine. From 1992, Editor in Chief of *Novaya Rossiya* magazine. President of the Moskvina 8 Joint-Stock Company; President of the Editorial Board of *Voskreseniye* Joint-Stock Company. Member of the Writers' Union; member of the Confederation of Film Makers' Unions.
MAJOR WORKS: Plays: *Equal to Four Frances; Silver Wedding; The Princesses*; *Fair Lady* (a collection of plays). Novel: *Career* (1989). Films: *The Mirror; Sardor; Moustached Male Nurse.* Radio performance: "Five Dialogues with Son."
HONORS/AWARDS: Russian Federation State Prize.
FAMILY: Married with a son.
ADDRESS/TELEPHONE: 8 Moskvin Street, Moscow. 229–2201; 229–1419 (office).

Mishenkov, Pyotr Grigoryevich
POSITION: Deputy Russian Federation Minister of Internal Affairs; Lieutenant-General
BIRTHPLACE/DATE: Tver region, 1937
CAREER: From 1959 to 1962, Instructor; Assistant to the Head of the Political Department of the Ozerny Reformatory Institution in Irkutsk region. From 1965 to 1971, Assistant to the Head of the Political Department of Places of Confinement; Deputy Head of the Political Department of the Reformatory Institutions Directorate (UITU); worked at the Directorate of Internal Affairs (UVD) of the Arkhangelsk Region Executive Committee. From 1971 to 1975, Deputy Head of the UVD UITU of the Arkhangelsk Region Executive Committee for Routine and Operational Work. From 1977 to 1981, Deputy Head of the Arkhangelsk Region UVD. From 1981 to 1991, worked at the USSR Ministry of Internal Affairs: First Deputy Head of the Central Reformatory Institutions Directorate (GUITU); Deputy, First Deputy Head of the Personnel Directorate; Deputy Head of the Academy; Head of GUITU, First Deputy Head of the Central Reformatory Affairs Directorate. From September 1991 to January 1992, Deputy Minister of Reformatory Affairs and the Social Rehabilitation Service of the Russian Federation Ministry of Internal Affairs. From January 1992, Russian

Federation Deputy Minister of Internal Affairs (supervises the Central Execution of Punishments Directorate, Central Forest Reformatory Institutions Directorate, Fire-Prevention and Emergency Rescue Works Service).
ADDRESS/TELEPHONE: 6 Ogareva Street, Moscow, 103109. 222–4780 (office).

Mishustina, Larisa Pavlovna
POSITION: Chairwoman of the Glasnost Commission of the Sverdlovsk Region Council; member of the Russian Federation Supreme Soviet Committee for Mass Media; member of the Left-Center Faction
BIRTHPLACE/DATE: Kursk region, 1949
NATIONALITY: Russian
CAREER: From 1973 to 1990, worked at the Urals Polytechnic newspaper. Russian Federation People's Deputy.
FAMILY: Married with two children.
ADDRESS/TELEPHONE: The Regional Council of People's Deputies, 1 Oktyabrskaya Place, Sverdlovsk. 51–5660 (office).

Mitta, Aleksandr Naumovich
POSITION: Producer at Mosfilm Studio
BIRTHPLACE/DATE: Moscow, March 28, 1933
CAREER: Member of the USSR Union of Film Makers. From 1992, member of the Confederation of Film Makers' Unions.
MAJOR WORKS: Films: *My Friend Kolka* (1961); *Without Fear and Reproach* (1963); *The Bell's Ringing, Open the Door* (1966); *Sparkle, Sparkle, My Star* (1969); *Point, Point, Comma . . .* (1973); *Moscow, My Love* (1974); *Tale of How Tsar Peter Married Off His Moor* (1976); *Crew* (1981); *Tale of Wandering* (1982); *Safety Limit* (1988); *Step* (1988); *Lost In Siberia* (1991).
HONORS/AWARDS: USSR Honored Worker of Art; Order of the Badge of Honor; Moscow and Lenin Komsomol Prize.
FAMILY: Married with a son.
ADDRESS: 28 M. Gruzinskaya, Flat #105, Moscow, 123557.

Mityayev, Ivan Ivanovich
POSITION: Director-General of the Moscow Investment Fund Joint-Stock Company
BIRTHPLACE/DATE: Lyubertsy, Moscow region, 1965
CAREER: From 1987 to 1988, Commodity Expert of the Raznoexport (Various Export) Foreign Trade Association. From 1988 to 1989, Assistant to the Director of the Institute of Socio-Economic Problems of Population of the USSR Academy of Sciences. From 1989 to 1991, Section Head at the Central Institute of Public Opinion. From 1991 to 1992, Chief Manager of the VPM-Center.
FAMILY: Single.
ADDRESS/TELEPHONE: 20 Bakhrushina Street, Moscow, 113054. 235–8254 (office).

Mityukov, Mikhail Alekseyevich
POSITION: Chairman of the Russian Federation Supreme Soviet Legislative Committee; Presidium Member of the Russian Federation Supreme Soviet
BIRTHPLACE/DATE: Ust-Uda village, Irkutsk region, January 7, 1942
NATIONALITY: Russian
EDUCATION: Graduated in 1968 from Irkutsk State University. Doctor of Law.
CAREER: From 1968 to 1977, Regional Court Member. From 1968 to 1987, Deputy Chairman of the Khakass Regional Court in Abakan city. From 1987 to 1990, Lecturer; Head of the National History, Law, and State Department at the Abakan Teachers' Training Institute. From July to November 1991, Deputy Chairman of the Russian Federation Supreme Soviet Committee for Legislation. Member of the Svobodnaya Rossiya (Free Russia) People's Party. From 1990, Russian Federation People's Deputy.
FAMILY: Married with three children.
ADDRESS/TELEPHONE: 2 Krasnopresnenskaya Naberezhnaya, Moscow. 205–7777 (office).

Moiseyev, Nikita Nikolayevich
POSITION: Chairman of the Russian Government Council for Emergencies, Analyses, and Governmental Decisions; Advisor to the Computer Center of the Russian Academy of Sciences; Chairman of the Scientific Council for Ecological and Political Education Development
BIRTHPLACE/DATE: Moscow, August 23, 1917
NATIONALITY: Russian
EDUCATION: Doctor of Physics and Mathemat-

ics; Professor; Academician of the Russian Academy of Sciences.
CAREER: From 1941 to 1948, Officer of the army. From 1948 to 1954, Assistant Professor at Rostov State University. From 1954, Deputy Director, Advisor to the USSR (now Russian) Academy of Sciences' Computer Center. From 1968, member of the International Academy of Astronautics; from 1966, Board Member of the International Institute of Life.
MAJOR WORKS: More than 300 publications and twenty books. *Human-Being, Environment, Society.*
HONORS/AWARDS: Order of Lenin; Order of the Red Banner of Labor; USSR State Prize.
FAMILY: Married with two children.
ADDRESS: 61/1 Leninsky Prospekt, Flat #172, Moscow, 117333.

Molchanov, Vladimir Kirillovich
POSITION: Art Director of the "Before and After Midnight" program of Progress Independent TV
BIRTHPLACE/DATE: 1950
NATIONALITY: Russian
CAREER: From 1973, worked at Novosti Press Agency (APN); APN Correspondent in the Netherlands. From 1987, worked at Central Television: Anchorman of the "Vremya" (Time) news program; Author and Host of the "Before and After Midnight" program. To 1991, Political Analyst of Central Television.
MAJOR WORKS: *Retribution Must Take Place.*
HONORS/AWARDS: Komsomol Central Committee; USSR Union of Writers Prize and the Central Trade Unions Council Prize for *Retribution Must Take Place.*
FAMILY: Married with a daughter.
ADDRESS/TELEPHONE: 17 Zubovsky Boulevard, Moscow, 119847. 245–3558 (office).

Morozov, Aleksey Mikhailovich
POSITION: Deputy Head of the Secretariat of the Vice Premier; Executive Secretary of the Group for Negotiations with the Big Seven
BIRTHPLACE/DATE: Leningrad, 1955
EDUCATION: From 1973 to 1978, student at Leningrad State University.
CAREER: From 1978 to 1980, Lecturer at Khartum University (Sudan). From 1980 to 1981, Economist of the Central Technical and Economic Information Bureau of the USSR Tsentrosoyuz (Central Union). From 1981 to 1989, worked at youth organizations. From 1990 to 1991, Researcher at the Institute of Economic Policy of the USSR Academy of Sciences and the Academy of National Economy. From October 1991, Assistant to the Russian Federation Government First Deputy Prime Minister.
ADDRESS/TELEPHONE: Staraya Place, Moscow. 206–4630 (office).

Morozov, Sergey Nikolayevich
POSITION: Editor in Chief of *Za Rubezhom* (*Abroad*) newspaper
BIRTHPLACE/DATE: Moscow, 1934
NATIONALITY: Russian
EDUCATION: Doctor of History.
CAREER: From 1957 to 1989, worked at the Novosti (News) Press Agency Publishing House; the Institute of the Peoples of Asia; the Institute of the International Working-Class Movement of the USSR Academy of Sciences; and the Central Committee's Propaganda and International Information Departments.
FAMILY: Married with a son.
ADDRESS/TELEPHONE: 24 Pravdy Street, Moscow, 125867. 257–2894 (office).

Morozov, Yuri Valentinovich
POSITION: Chairman of the Auditing Commission of the Russian Union of Proprietors; Chairman of the Cooperative Society; Co-Chairman of the Anti-Monopoly Exchanges Conference; member of the Licensing Commission for the Right to Exercise Exchange Operations of the State Committee for Anti-Monopoly Policy
BIRTHPLACE/DATE: Moscow, 1955
CAREER: In 1980, Accountant.
FAMILY: Married with two children.
ADDRESS/TELEPHONE: 66 Sushevsky Val, Moscow. 971–6722 (office).

Moshanu, Aleksandr Konstantinovich
POSITION: Chairman of the Moldavian Republic Supreme Soviet; former Parliament Speaker of Moldavia (Moldova) Republic
BIRTHPLACE/DATE: Branishte village, Ryshkan region, 1932

NATIONALITY: Moldavian
EDUCATION: Doctor of History; Professor.
CAREER: From 1957, worked at the Institute of History of the Moldavian Republic Academy of Sciences. From 1976, Lecturer, Department Head, Dean of the History Department at Moldavia University. Chairman of the Association of Moldavian Historians. In February 1990, elected Moldavian Republic People's Deputy.
MAJOR WORKS: About 100 works on the current history of foreign countries and on the history of Moldova.
FAMILY: Married with two sons.
ADDRESS/TELEPHONE: The Parliament of Moldova, Shtefan Chel Mare Boulevard, Kishinev, 233404.

Mukhammad, Sodyk Muhammad Yusuf
POSITION: Chairman of the Ecclesiastical Directorate of the Central Asia Moslems (SADUM); Mufti
BIRTHPLACE/DATE: Bulak-Pashi village, Hojiabad district, Andizhan region, Uzbekistan, April 13, 1952
NATIONALITY: Uzbek
CAREER: From 1980 to 1982, Aide to the International Relations Department of SADUM. From 1982 to 1989, Pro-Rector of the Tashkent Islamic Institute. Elected USSR People's Deputy.
FAMILY: Married with three children.
ADDRESS/TELEPHONE: 103 Zarkainar Street, Tashkent. 44–2460 (office).

Muladzhanov, Shud Saidovich
POSITION: Editor in Chief of *Moskovskaya Pravda* (*Moscow Truth*) newspaper; President of the Moskovskaya Pravda Joint-Stock Company; member of the Confederation of Journalists' Unions
BIRTHPLACE/DATE: Dushanbe, 1953
CAREER: From 1975 to 1991, Correspondent, Department Head, Executive Secretary, Political Analyst.
FAMILY: Married with two children.
ADDRESS/TELEPHONE: 7 Ulitsa 1905 Goda, Moscow, 123846. 259–1404 (office).

Muranov, Anatoli Ivanovich
POSITION: Russian Federation Deputy Minister of Justice
BIRTHPLACE/DATE: Saltykovo village, Ryazan region, 1942
EDUCATION: Graduated in 1963 from the Moscow Higher Military Command School and in 1970 from the Military-Political Academy. Graduated from the Law Department at Moscow State University.
CAREER: From 1970 to 1972, Military Tribunal Member of the Omsk Military District Garrison. From 1972 to 1974, Military Tribunal Member in Chita. From 1974 to 1980, Inspector, Senior Inspector of the Military Tribunal Directorate of the USSR Justice Ministry. From 1980 and 1983, Deputy Chairman of the Moscow Military District Court Martial. From 1983 to 1988, Instructor of the Central Committee's Administrative Agencies Department. From 1988 to 1991, Chief of the Military Tribunal Directorate of the USSR Ministry of Justice. From 1991 to 1992, USSR Deputy Minister of Justice and Chief of the Military Tribunal Directorate of the Russian Federation Justice Ministry. From 1992, Russian Federation Deputy Minister of Justice; Chief of the Military Tribunal Directorate of the Russian Federation Justice Ministry. State Legal Advisor, Second Class. Lieutenant-General.
MAJOR WORKS: Articles on military justice issues.
FAMILY: Married with two children.
ADDRESS/TELEPHONE: 10-A Yermolova Street, Moscow. 222–0298.

Murashev, Arkady Nikolayevich
POSITION: Head of the Moscow Main Internal Affairs Directorate (City Police). Co-Chairman of the Demokraticheskaya Rossiya (Democratic Russia) Movement
BIRTHPLACE/DATE: Zagan, Poland, 1957
NATIONALITY: Russian
EDUCATION: Graduated in 1980 from the Moscow Bauman State Technical Institute.
CAREER: Researcher at the USSR Academy of Sciences' Institute of High Temperatures. From 1987, Mossoviet (Moscow Council) Deputy. From 1989 to 1991, USSR People's Deputy; Coordinating Committee Chairman of the Democratic Rus-

sia Movement's Liberal Union. From August 1991, Deputy Chairman of the Municipal Assembly. From September 1991, Head of the Moscow Main Internal Affairs Directorate; Co-Chairman of the Democratic Russia Movement. From April 1992, President of the Russian Chess Federation.
FAMILY: Married.
ADDRESS/TELEPHONE: 38 Petrovka Street, Moscow, 103836. 200–8510 (office); 203–4539.

Muravsky, Valery Tudor
POSITION: Former Moldavian Republic Prime Minister
BIRTHPLACE/DATE: Sprota village, 1949
NATIONALITY: Moldavian
CAREER: From 1971 to 1979, worked at the Republican Committee for Prices and Price Formation. From 1976 to 1984, Department Head; from 1988, Economic Directorate Head of the Moldavian Republic Ministry of Construction Materials Industry. From June 1990, Moldavian Republic Finance Minister. From March 1991, Deputy Prime Minister. From May 1991, Moldavian Republic Prime Minister. In June 1992, the government of the Moldavian Republic resigned.
FAMILY: Married.
ADDRESS/TELEPHONE: Kishenev. 23–3572.

Muravyev, Igor Vladislavovich
POSITION: Deputy Chairman of the Russian Federation Supreme Soviet Committee for Issues of the Councils of People's Deputies and the Development of Self-Government; member of the Democratic Party of the Smena-Novaya Politika (Rising Generation-New Politics) Faction; Russian Federation People's Deputy
BIRTHPLACE/DATE: Voronezh, 1960
NATIONALITY: Russian
EDUCATION: Completed postgraduate studies at the Voronezh Polytechnical Institute (VPI).
CAREER: From 1982 to 1983, Engineer at the Voronezh Polytechnical Institute. From 1983 to 1985, Platoon Commander of the USSR Army Troops in Germany. From 1985 to 1990, Senior Engineer, Junior Researcher, Researcher at VPI.
FAMILY: Married with two children.
ADDRESS/TELEPHONE: 8 Academician Korolev Street, Building 2, Flat #524, Moscow. 205–9089 (office); 216–4068 (home).

Musaelyan, Gennadi Samvelovich
POSITION: Editor in Chief of *Moscow* magazine; Director-General of the Russian Press House
BIRTHPLACE/DATE: Yerevan, 1936
EDUCATION: Graduated from Moscow State University.
CAREER: Head of the Foreign Department of *Gudok* (Factory Bell) newspaper; Head of the Current Politics Department of *Mezhdunarodnaya Zhizn* (*International Life)* magazine; Literary Analyst of *Sovietskaya Rossiya* (*Soviet Russia*) newspaper; Head of the Foreign Department of the USSR Journalists' Union; member of the Confederation of Journalists' Unions.
HONORS/AWARDS: Moscow Journalists' Union Prize.
FAMILY: Married with a daughter.
ADDRESS/TELEPHONE: 8-A Suvorovsky Boulevard, Moscow. 928–7083 (office).

Muzykantsky, Aleksandr Ilyich
POSITION: Prefect of the Central Administrative District; Deputy Premier of the Moscow Government; Coordinating Council Member of the Demokraticheskaya Rossiya (Democratic Russia) Movement
BIRTHPLACE/DATE: Moscow, February 4, 1941
NATIONALITY: Ukrainian
EDUCATION: From 1958 to 1963, student at the Moscow Institute of Railway Transport Engineers.
CAREER: From 1957 to 1958, Metalworker for the USSR Ministry of Communications' Design Bureau. From 1963 to 1987, Engineer; Group Head; Senior Researcher; Department Head; from 1987 to 1990, Deputy Chief Engineer of the Central Proyektstalkonstruktsiya (Design of Steel Structures) Research Institute of the USSR State Construction Committee. From 1990 to 1991, Acting Deputy Chairman of the Moscow City Executive Committee, Head of the Department for Relations with Soviets, Mass Media, Public Organizations, and City Populations. In 1991, Deputy Chairman of the Moscow Council Executive Committee.
FAMILY: Married with two children.
ADDRESS/TELEPHONE: 13 Tverskaya Street, Moscow, 103032. 292–6580 (office).

Nadvikov, Aleksey Matveyevich

POSITION: Director of the Kalibr Instrument Factory

BIRTHPLACE/DATE: Smolensk region, 1937

NATIONALITY: Russian

CAREER: From 1959, worked at the Machine-Building Plant of the Smolensk Ministry of Aviation Industry. From 1963 to 1972, worked at the Smolensk Radio Parts Factory. From 1973 to 1976, Deputy Director-General of the Feniks Scientific and Industrial Association; Head of the Smolensk Central Design and Technology Bureau of the Ministry of Electronic Industry. From 1976 to 1986, worked at the Moscow Ministry of Electronic Industry. From 1986, Director-General of the Kalibr Industrial Association.

MAJOR WORKS: Fourteen inventions; scientific and technical publications.

FAMILY: Married with two sons.

ADDRESS/TELEPHONE: 9 Godovikova Street, Moscow, 129085. 287–2469; 287–3881 (office).

Nagibin, Yuri Markovich

POSITION: Writer

BIRTHPLACE/DATE: Moscow, 1920

CAREER: From 1943 to 1953, Journalist. From 1943, Military Correspondent for *Trud* (*Labor*) newspaper; member of the USSR Writers' Union. From 1984, Film Maker. From 1991, Moscow Secretary of the Russian Writers' Union.

MAJOR WORKS: Screenplays: *Chairman; Night Guest; Dersu Uzala*. Fiction and nonfiction books: *Island of Love; Patience; Stand Up and Go; Urgent Business Trip, or Dear Margaret Thatcher* (1990); *Big Heart; Not Somebody Else's Profession.*

HONORS/AWARDS: Oscar for *Dersu Uzala*; Europe's Best Writer Prize.

FAMILY: Married.

ADDRESS/TELEPHONE: 4 Chernyakhovskogo Street, Flat #126, Moscow, 125319. 151–6643; 334–5979 (home).

Nazarbayev, Nursultan Abishevich

POSITION: Kazakhstan Republic President; Commander in Chief of the Kazakhstan Armed Forces

BIRTHPLACE/DATE: Chemolgan village, Kaskelen district, Alma-Ata region, July 6, 1940

NATIONALITY: Kazakh

EDUCATION: Studied at the Karaganda Polytechnical Institute.

CAREER: From 1965, worked at the Karaganda Metallurgical Plant. From 1969, Party Functionary. From 1979, Secretary of the Kazakhstan Communist Party. From 1981 to 1986, member of the Central Auditing Commission. From 1984, Chairman of the Kazakh Council of Ministers. From 1986 to 1991, member of the Central Committee. From 1989 to 1991, First Secretary of the Kazakhstan Communist Party. From February 1990, Deputy of the USSR Supreme Soviet of the Tenth and Eleventh Convocations. From 1989 to 1992, USSR People's Deputy. From 1962 to 1991, member of the Communist Party.

MAJOR WORKS: *Nursultan Nazarbaev: Without Left- or Right-Wingers.*

HONORS/AWARDS: Order of the Red Banner of Labor; Order of the Badge of Honor.

FAMILY: Married with three daughters and a grandson.
ADDRESS/TELEPHONE: 4 Ploshchad Respubliki, Alma-Ata, 480091. 63–4664 (press service).

Nechayev, Andrey Alekseyevich
POSITION: President of the State Financial Corporation
BIRTHPLACE/DATE: Moscow, February 2, 1953
NATIONALITY: Russian
EDUCATION: Doctor of Economics.
CAREER: From 1979 to 1990, held positions at the USSR Academy of Sciences. From 1990 to 1991, Deputy Director of Scientific Work at the Institute of Economic Policy. From November 1991, Russian Federation First Deputy Minister of Economy and Finances. From July 1992, Deputy Chairman of the Government's Currency and Economic Commission. From 1984 to 1991, member of the Communist Party.
FAMILY: Married with a daughter.
ADDRESS/TELEPHONE: 6 Okhotny Ryad Street, Moscow, 103009. 292–7482 (office).

Nefedov, Oleg Matveyevich
POSITION: Vice President of the Russian Academy of Sciences; Vice President of the World Federation of Scientists; Academician of the Russian Academy of Sciences
BIRTHPLACE/DATE: Dmitrov, Moscow region, November 25, 1931
NATIONALITY: Russian
EDUCATION: From 1954 to 1956, postgraduate student. Doctor of Chemistry; Professor.
CAREER: From 1957 to 1988, worked at the N.D. Zelinski Institute of Organic Chemistry of the USSR Academy of Sciences. From 1988, Vice President of the USSR Academy of Sciences. From December 1991, Vice President of the Russian Academy of Sciences. From 1988 to 1991, Academician-Secretary of the USSR Academy of Sciences' General and Technical Chemistry Division. From December 1991, Laboratory Head at the Zelinski Institute of Organic Chemistry. From 1989 to 1992, USSR People's Deputy. From 1962 to 1991, member of the Communist Party. From 1990 to 1991, member of the Central Committee.
MAJOR WORKS: Research on the structure and reaction of carbons, uncombined radicals, ions, and small cycles. Author and co-author of 300 scientific works and more than 100 inventions.
HONORS/AWARDS: Order of the October Revolution; Order of the Red Banner of Labor; USSR State Prize.
FAMILY: Married with two children.
ADDRESS/TELEPHONE: 32-A Leninsky Prospekt, Moscow, 117334. 938–1372 (office).

Nenashev, Mikhail Fydorovich
POSITION: Board Chairman of the Kniga (Book)-Business Joint-Stock Association; member of the International Council of Bibliophiles; Vice President of the Chteniye (Reading) Society; Deputy of the Russian Federation Supreme Soviet of the Tenth and Eleventh Convocations
BIRTHPLACE/DATE: Borodinovka village, Varnensk district, Chelyabinsk region, November 10, 1929
NATIONALITY: Russian
EDUCATION: Doctor of History; Professor.
CAREER: From 1956, Lecturer, Department Head at the Magnitogorsk G.I. Nosov Institute of Ore Mining and Metallurgy. From 1963 to 1967, Secretary of the Magnitogorsk City Communist Party. From 1967 to 1968, Department Head of the Chelyabinsk Regional Communist Party. From 1968 to 1978, Secretary of the Chelyabinsk Regional Communist Party; Deputy Head of the Central Committee's Propaganda Department. From 1978 to 1986, Editor in Chief of *Sovietskaya Rossia* (*Soviet Russia*) newspaper. From 1986 to 1989, Chairman of the USSR Goskomizdat (State Committee for Publishing). From 1989 to 1990, Chairman of the USSR State Committee for Television and Radio. From November 1990, Chairman of the USSR State Press Committee. From 1991 to November 1991, USSR Minister of Information and Press. From 1952 to 1991, member of the Communist Party. From 1989 to 1991, member of the Central Committee.
MAJOR WORKS: Scientific works and booklets.
HONORS/AWARDS: Three Orders of the Red Banner of Labor; two Orders of the Badge of Honor; Order of the People's Friendship; Academician S.P. Korolev Medal.
FAMILY: Married with two children.
ADDRESS/TELEPHONE: 22 Tverskaya-Yamskaya Street, Moscow, 125047. 251–1931 (office).

Nesterenko, Yevgeni Yevgenyevich

POSITION: Opera Soloist (bass) of the Bolshoi Theater

BIRTHPLACE/DATE: Moscow, January 8, 1938

CAREER: From 1963, Soloist of the Leningrad Maly Opera and Ballet Theater. From 1967, Soloist of the Leningrad Opera and Ballet Theater. From 1971, Soloist of the Bolshoi Theater. From 1967 to 1972, Professor at the Leningrad Conservatory. From 1972 to 1974, Moscow Gnesiny State Musical Pedagogical Institute. From 1975, Head of the Solo Singing Department of the Moscow Conservatory. From 1989 to 1992, USSR People's Deputy. USSR People's Artist.

MAJOR WORKS: More than fifty leading parts, including Mephistopheles; Boris Godunov; Prince Igor; Konchak; Dosifei; Ruslan; Susanin; Grigory (*Quiet Don*); Zvambai (*Theft of the Moon* by Taktakishvili). Performs operas in their original languages.

HONORS/AWARDS: Hero of Socialist Labor; Prize of Lenin.

FAMILY: Married with a child.

ADDRESS/TELEPHONE: The Bolshoi Theater, 8/2 Okhotny Ryad Street, Moscow. 242–4789 (home).

Neverov, Valery Ivanovich

POSITION: Director-General of the GERMES (Hermes) Scientific-Technological Center in Tyumen; President of the GERMES Joint-Stock Company and Scientific-Technological Center (STC) in Kaliningrad; Chairman of the Board of Directors of the GERMES Tyumen-Moscow Exchange in Moscow; Chairman of the Board of Directors of the GERMES Trading House

BIRTHPLACE/DATE: Golyshmanovo, Tyumen region, 1952

EDUCATION: Graduated from Urals State University and from postgraduate studies at the Moscow Mining Institute. Doctor of Physics and Mathematics.

CAREER: Taught at Udmurtian and Tyumen Universities. In 1986, developed scientific projects for metalworking and oil-extracting. In 1988, left post as the Head of the Molecular Physics Department for postgraduate studies. In August 1990, registered the STC GERMES Company. In 1991, Co-Founder of the Tyumen Commodity and Stock Exchange (TCSE). Founded additional exchanges from Siberia to the Baltics. President of the Tyumen-Moscow GERMES Exchange. Opened the Tyumen International Scientific and Technological Center; organized numerous GERMES branches in Kuzbass, Krasnodar region, Kaliningrad and Rostov regions, and the Ukraine. In 1991, founded the Tyumen Trading House and the Moscow GERMES Joint-Stock Bank.

HONORS/AWARDS: Order of the Eagle, First Class (1992).

FAMILY: Divorced with a daughter.

ADDRESS/TELEPHONE: 2/1 Kalanchevskaya Street, Moscow, 107174. 291–8070; 291–7343; 261–1590; 308–9667 (office); Fax: 291–2255.

Nikitin, Andrey Vladimirovich

POSITION: Director-General of the Banso Legal Association

BIRTHPLACE/DATE: Vladivostok, 1955

CAREER: From 1979 to 1983, Engineer at the Central Institute of the Aircraft Engine Plant. From 1983 to 1984, Engineer-Economist at Tekhenergo (Technical Energy). From 1984 to 1987, Stoker at the Sokolniki Sanitarium. From 1988 to 1990, Head of various commercial enterprises.

FAMILY: Single.

ADDRESS/TELEPHONE: 21 Novozavodskaya Street, Moscow, 121309. 148–0806; 145–7829 (office).

Nikodim (Rusnak Nikodim Stepanovich)

POSITION: Metropolitan of Kharkov and Bogodukhovsk

BIRTHPLACE/DATE: Davidkovtsy village, Kitsmansky district, Ghernovtsy region, April 5, 1921

NATIONALITY: Ukrainian

CAREER: In 1945, took monastic vows. From 1950 to 1955, Abbot at the Saint-Ioann-Divine Kreshchatic Monastery. From 1958 to 1961, member of the Russian Ecclesiastical Mission in Jerusalem, Israel. From 1961 to 1964, Bishop of Kostroma and Galich. From 1964 to 1970, Administrator of the Parishes of the Russian Orthodox Church in South America (Buenos Aires). From 1970 to 1984, Archbishop of the Kharkov Diocese. From 1984 to 1989, Metropolitan of Lvov and Ternopol.

HONORS/AWARDS: Order of the Red Banner of Labor.

ADDRESS/TELEPHONE: 8 Universitetskaya Street, Kharkov, Ukraine, 310166. 201–2840 (Moscow).

Nikolayenko, Valery Dmitryevich

POSITION: Russian Federation Ambassador to Greece; Ambassador Extraordinary and Plenipotentiary

BIRTHPLACE/DATE: Moscow, July 4, 1941

NATIONALITY: Ukrainian

EDUCATION: Doctor of History.

CAREER: From 1962 to 1963, Interpreter for the USSR Trade Delegation to Cuba. From 1964 to 1966, Aide, Attaché at the USSR Embassy in Cuba. From 1966 to 1969, Attaché, Third Secretary of the Latin American Countries Department of the USSR Foreign Ministry. From 1969 to 1972, Second Secretary at the USSR Embassy in Mexico. From 1974 to 1975, First Secretary of the Latin American Countries Department of the USSR Foreign Ministry. From 1975 to 1979, First Secretary at the USSR Embassy in the United States. From 1979 to 1980, Counsellor, Section Head of the Latin American Countries Department of the USSR Foreign Ministry. From 1980 to 1987, Section Head, Deputy Head of the First Latin American Department of the USSR Foreign Ministry. From 1987 to 1988, Ambassador to Colombia. From 1988 to 1990, Ambassador to Nicaragua. From 1990 to 1991, Directorate Head of the USSR Foreign Ministry. From 1991 to 1992, USSR Deputy Foreign Minister.

FAMILY: Married with a daughter.

ADDRESS/TELEPHONE: Palaio Psychico, 28 Nikiforou Litra, Athens, Greece. 647–1395; 672–5235; 672–6130.

Nikolayev, Mikhail Yefimovich

POSITION: President of the Sakha (Yakutia) Republic

BIRTHPLACE/DATE: Oktem village, Ordjonikidze district, Yakut Republic, 1937

NATIONALITY: Yakut

CAREER: From 1961 to 1971, Chief Veterinary of the Zhigachinsk District. From 1971 to 1973, Party Functionary. From 1973, First Secretary of the Verkhneviluysk District Communist Party. From 1975, Deputy Chairman of the Yakut Republic Council of Ministers. From 1985 to 1989, Secretary of the Yakut Region Communist Party. From 1989 to 1990, Chairman of the Yakut Republic Supreme Soviet Presidium. From 1990 to 1991, Chairman of the Yakut Republic Supreme Soviet. From December 1991, President of Yakutia Republic; Chairman of the Yakut Republic Government. From 1990, Russian Federation People's Deputy. Elected Yakut Republic People's Deputy. From 1963 to 1991, member of the Communist Party.

HONORS/AWARDS: Honored Yakut Republic Worker of National Economy.

Nikolsky, Boris Vasilyevich

POSITION: First Deputy Premier of the Moscow Government

BIRTHPLACE/DATE: Moscow, May 1, 1937

CAREER: From 1959 to 1968, worked at the Experimental Design Mechanical Engineering Works of the All-Union Institute of Agricultural Mechanization. From 1968 to 1976, Party and Soviet Functionary in the Zhdanovsky District of Moscow. From 1976 to 1981, Deputy Chairman of the Moscow City Executive Committee. From 1981 to 1989, Party Functionary. From 1989 to 1990, First Deputy Chairman of the Moscow City Executive Committee Planning Commission. From 1990 to 1991, First Deputy Chairman of the Moscow Construction Committee. From 1991 to 1992, Deputy Premier of the Moscow Government; Head of the City Infrastructure Complex; Deputy of the USSR Supreme Soviet of the Eleventh Convocation; Deputy of the Russian Federation Supreme Soviet of the Tenth Convocation. From 1989 to January 1992, USSR People's Deputy. From 1963 to 1991, member of the Communist Party. From 1986 to 1990, Central Committee Alternate Member.

HONORS/AWARDS: Two Orders of the Red Banner of Labor; Order of the Badge of Honor; Order of the People's Friendship; medals.

FAMILY: Married with two children.

ADDRESS/TELEPHONE: 13 Tverskaya, Moscow, 103032. 229–2424 (office).

Nishanov, Rafik Nishanovich

POSITION: Vice President of the Novy Svet–500 (New World–500) Foundation; Chairman of the Guardians Board of the Grazhdanin (Citizen) Association; Ambassador Extraordinary and Plenipotentiary

BIRTHPLACE/DATE: Gazalkend village, Tashkent region, 1926
NATIONALITY: Uzbek
EDUCATION: Doctor of History.
CAREER: From 1951 to 1962, Komsomol and Party Functionary. From 1962 to 1963, Chairman of the Tashkent City Executive Committee. From 1963 to 1970, Secretary of the Uzbekistan Central Committee. From 1970 to 1978, USSR Ambassador Extraordinary and Plenipotentiary to Ceylon and the Maltese Republic. From 1978 to 1985, USSR Ambassador to the Hashemite Kingdom of Jordan. From 1985 to 1986, Uzbek Republic Foreign Minister. From 1986 to 1988, Presidium Chairman of the Uzbek Republic Supreme Soviet; Deputy Chairman of the USSR Supreme Soviet. From 1989 to 1991, First Secretary of the Uzbekistan Central Committee; Chairman of the USSR Supreme Soviet Council of Nationalities. Elected USSR People's Deputy.
HONORS/AWARDS: Two Orders of the Badge of Honor; two Orders of the Red Banner of Labor.
FAMILY: Married with five children.
ADDRESS/TELEPHONE: 3–97 Granovskogo Street, Moscow. 202–3473 (home).

Nit, Igor Vasilyevich
POSITION: Head of the Russian Federation President's Council of Experts
BIRTHPLACE/DATE: Moscow, February 26, 1929
NATIONALITY: Russian
EDUCATION: Completed postgraduate studies at Moscow State University. Doctor of Economics; Professor.
CAREER: From 1943 to 1944, Driller at the Precision Mechanics Trust of the Sverdlov District of Moscow. From 1954 to 1957, Teacher; Head of the Moscow UKP. From 1957 to 1958, Teacher at Boarding School #22 of the Moscow City Department of Public Education. From 1958 to 1961, Junior Researcher, Assistant, Senior Lecturer, Assistant Professor of the Economics Department at Moscow State University. From 1990 to 1991, Head of the Russian Federation Supreme Soviet Council of Experts.
MAJOR WORKS: *Interpretation of Industrial Planning as a Multi-story System* (1966); *Economic and Mathematics Methods in a Real Economic Mechanism* (1980); *Conception of the Gradual Transition to a Market Economy* (1991).
HONORS/AWARDS: Veteran of Labor Medal.
FAMILY: Married with three daughters and a son.
ADDRESS/TELEPHONE: The Kremlin, Moscow. 206–0831 (office).

Niyazov, Saparmurad Atayevich
POSITION: President of Turkmenistan; Head of the Turkmenistan Cabinet of Ministers; Chairman of the Turkmenistan Democratic Party
BIRTHPLACE/DATE: Askhabad, February 19, 1940
NATIONALITY: Turkmen
CAREER: From 1970 to 1984, Party Functionary of the Turkmenistan Central Committee. In 1985, Chairman of the Turkmenistan Republic Council of Ministers. From December 1985, First Secretary of the Turkmenistan Central Committee. From January 1990, Chairman of the Turkmenistan Republic Supreme Soviet. From October 1990, President of Turkmenistan Republic. From 1989 to 1992, USSR People's Deputy. From 1962 to August 1991, member of the Communist Party.
HONORS/AWARDS: Hero of Turkmenistan; Order of the People's Friendship. First to acquire the title of Hadji and the right to wear the green turban.
FAMILY: Married with a daughter and a son.
ADDRESS/TELEPHONE: 24 Karl Marx Street, Askhabad, 744014. 25–4534 (office).

Norshtein, Yuri Borisovich
POSITION: Animated Cartoon Artist; Producer
BIRTHPLACE/DATE: Andreyevka village, Penza region, 1941
CAREER: From 1961 to 1973, Animated Cartoon Artist at Soyuzmultfilm (Animated Cartoons Union) Studios; from 1973 to 1986, Producer. From 1979 to 1991, Lecturer at the Higher Producers' Courses of the USSR Goskino (State Committee for Cinematography). Lectured at various international seminars. From 1989, Producer of the All-Union Center of Cinematography and Television for Children and Youth. From December 1991, Producer of the Center of Cinematography and Television. Member of the Russian Union of Film Makers.

MAJOR WORKS: Cartoons: *Fox and Rabbit* (1973); *Heron and Crane* (1974); *Hedgehog in the Fog* (1975); *Fairy Tale of Fairy Tales* (1979).
HONORS/AWARDS: Highest awards at various international festivals; Grand Prix and Film Criticism Prize at the International Festival of Short Films; Russian Federation Honored Art Worker.
FAMILY: Married with a daughter and a son.
ADDRESS/TELEPHONE: 4 Butlerova Street, Building 2, Flat #88, Moscow, 117485. 335–0821 (home); 159–4444; 150–4323 (office).

Nosov, Valery Borisovich
POSITION: Director-General of the Moskovsky Podshipnik (First State Bearing Plant) Joint-Stock Association
BIRTHPLACE/DATE: Moscow, 1941
NATIONALITY: Russian
CAREER: From 1965 to 1984, worked to First Deputy Director-General of the Likhachev Automobile Plant. From August to November 1991, member of the USSR Committee for the Efficient Management of the National Economy.
FAMILY: Married with two children.
ADDRESS/TELEPHONE: 13 Sharikopodshipnikovskaya Street, Moscow, 109088. 275–9698 (assistant); Fax: 274–1244.

Nosovets, Sergey Anatolyevich
POSITION: Member of the Russian Federation Supreme Soviet Committee for Mass Media
BIRTHPLACE/DATE: Mezhdurechensk, Kemerovo region, 1958.
CAREER: From 1984 to 1990, worked at the Omsk Television Studio. Deputy of the Omsk Regional Council. Russian Federation People's Deputy.
FAMILY: Married with two daughters.
ADDRESS/TELEPHONE: 2 Krasnopresnenskaya Naberezhnaya, Moscow (office); 8 Akademika Koroleva, Building 2, Flat #581, Moscow (home). 205–5876 (office); 216–7840 (home).

Novikov, Valery Lvovich
POSITION: Editor in Chief of *Delovye Svyazi* (*Business Connections*) magazine; Editor of the Moscow Offset Print Joint Venture
BIRTHPLACE/DATE: Kazan, 1941
CAREER: From 1960 to 1963, Pattern Maker at the Kazan Metallurgical Works. From 1963 to 1967, served in the Northern Fleet Navy. From 1967 to 1970, Editorial Staff Editor of USSR Radio. From 1970 to 1975, worked for the International Journalism Department at the Moscow State Institute of International Relations.
FAMILY: Married.
ADDRESS/TELEPHONE: 31 Kakhovka Street, Moscow, 113461. 331–8900 (office).

Novikov, Vladimir Ivanovich
POSITION: Head of the Zarubezhchermet (Foreign Ferrous Metals) International Economic Association of the Russian Federation Ministry of Industry
BIRTHPLACE/DATE: Vologda region, 1941
NATIONALITY: Russian
CAREER: From 1963 to 1964, Sanitary Engineering Foreman at the Tula Special Construction and Assembly Directorate (SMU). From 1964 to 1966, Senior Engineer of the Technical Department of SMU. In 1966, Head of the Cherepovetsk SMU. In 1979, Chief Engineer of the Domnaremont (Blast-Furnace Repair) Center. In 1988, Repair Head of Blast-Furnace #2 at the Dunai Metallurgical Group of Enterprises.
HONORS/AWARDS: USSR State Prize; Order of Lenin; Order of the Red Banner of Labor.
FAMILY: Married with a son.
ADDRESS/TELEPHONE: 14 Razina Street, Moscow. 298–4663; 298–4747 (office).

Novodvorskaya, Valerya Ilyinichna
POSITION: Politician; Leader of the Demokratichesky Soyuz (Democratic Union) Party; Political Analyst of *Khozyain* (*Owner*) newspaper
BIRTHPLACE/DATE: Baranovichi, Byelorussia, May 17, 1950
NATIONALITY: Russian
CAREER: From 1968 to 1969, Staff Member of the Moscow Institute of Foreign Languages. In 1969, arrested and imprisoned in a special jail in Kazan. From 1973 to 1975, Teacher at a children's sanitarium. From 1975 to 1990, Teacher at a medical institute. From August 1991, Teacher at a privately owned night school. From 1985 to 1991, under administrative arrest seventeen times.

Nysanbayev, Ratbek

POSITION: Chairman of the Ecclesiastical Directorate of Kazakhstan's Moslems; Mufti

BIRTHPLACE/DATE: Muratbayeva village, Kelessk district, Chimkent region, (Kazakhstan), November 7, 1940

NATIONALITY: Kazakh

CAREER: From 1975 to 1990, worked from Secretary to Representative of the Ecclesiastical Directorate of Kazakhstan's Moslems. From 1979, Representative of the Ecclesiastical Directorate of Kazakhstan's Moslems. Kazakhstan People's Deputy.

ADDRESS: 12 Dzharkentskaya Street, Alma-Ata.

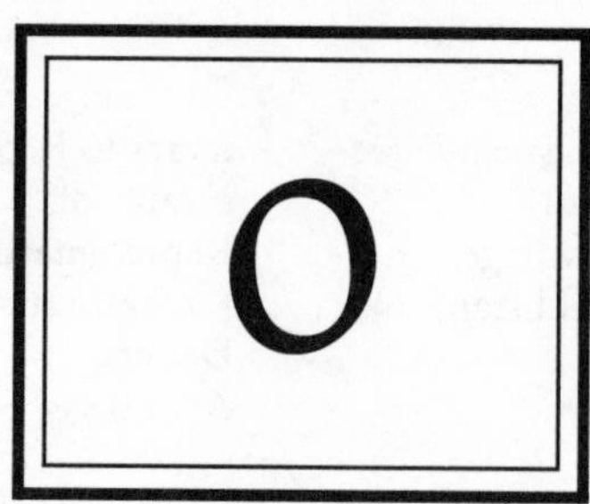

Obminsky, Ernest Yevgenyevich

POSITION: Former Russian Federation Deputy Foreign Minister; Ambassador Extraordinary and Plenipotentiary

BIRTHPLACE/DATE: Odessa, September 19, 1931

NATIONALITY: Russian

EDUCATION: Doctor of Economics; Professor.

CAREER: From 1962 to 1969, Senior Lecturer, Assistant Professor at the Moscow State Institute of International Relations of the USSR Foreign Ministry. From 1969 to 1973, Staff Member of the United Nations Committee for Trade and Development (UNCTAD) in Geneva. From 1975 to 1979, Pro-Rector of the Diplomatic Academy of the USSR Foreign Ministry. From 1979 to 1983, Counsellor at the USSR Embassy in Thailand. From 1983 to 1984, Department Head of the Institute of the World Economy and International Relations of the USSR Academy of Sciences in Moscow. From 1984 to 1986, Deputy Director of the Institute of the International Working Class Movement of the USSR Academy of Sciences in Moscow. From 1986 to 1989, Head of the International Economic Organizations Directorate (UMEO) of the USSR Foreign Ministry. From 1989 to 1990, Deputy USSR Foreign Minister; Head of UMEO. From 1990 to December 1991, Deputy USSR Foreign Minister. From December 1991, Russian Federation Foreign Minister.

FAMILY: Married.

ADDRESS/TELEPHONE: 32/34 Smolenskaya-Sennaya, Moscow, 121200. 244–1606.

Obraztsova, Yelena Vasilyevna

POSITION: Opera Singer (mezzo-soprano); Soloist of the Bolshoi Theater

BIRTHPLACE/DATE: Leningrad, July 7, 1937

CAREER: From 1976, Lecturer. From 1984, Professor at the Moscow Conservatory. From 1986, Producer. Performs abroad.

MAJOR WORKS: Marfa in *Khovanshchina*; Lyubasha in *The Tzar's Bride*; Countess, Marina Mnishek, Carmen, Eboli in *Don Carlos*; Amneris, Oberon in *Midsummer Night's Dream* by Britten; Frosya in *Semen Kotko*. Sings chamber vocal compositions by Russian, Soviet, and Western European composers. Produced *Werther* by Masne; sang the part of Charlotte. Opera films: *Carmen*; *Peasant's Honor*; *Masquerade-Ball* by Italian producer F. Dzefirelli; Soviet opera film *The Jolly Widow.*

HONORS/AWARDS: Russian Federation State Prize; Prize of Lenin; Russian Federation People's Artist; USSR People's Artist; Hero of Socialist Labor.

FAMILY: Married with a daughter.

ADDRESS/TELEPHONE: The Bolshoi Theater, 8/2 Teatralnaya Ploschad, Moscow. 292–0571 (office).

Obukhov, Aleksey Aleksandrovich

POSITION: Russian Federation Ambassador to the Kingdom of Denmark; Ambassador Extraordinary and Plenipotentiary

BIRTHPLACE/DATE: Moscow, November 12, 1937

NATIONALITY: Russian

EDUCATION: From 1961 to 1965, postgraduate student at the Moscow State Institute of International Relations of the USSR Foreign Ministry. Doctor of History.

CAREER: From 1961 to 1962, Secretary of the Komsomol Committee. From 1965 to 1966,

Attaché-Interpreter at the USSR Embassy in Thailand. From 1966 to 1968, Attaché, Third Secretary of the Department of South Asia of the USSR Foreign Ministry. From 1968 to 1969, Second Secretary of the Foreign Policy Coordinating Directorate of the USSR Foreign Ministry. From 1969 to 1973, First Secretary of the USSR Deputy Foreign Minister Secretariat. From 1973 to 1986, Counsellor, Section Head, Deputy Head of the U.S. Department of the USSR Foreign Ministry. From 1986 to 1989, Ambassador at Large. From 1989 to 1990, Head of the U.S. and Canada Directorate. From 1990 to 1991, Deputy USSR Foreign Minister. From December 1991 to May 1992, Russian Federation Deputy Foreign Minister.
HONORS/AWARDS: Two Orders of the Red Banner of Labor.
FAMILY: Married with two children.
ADDRESS/TELEPHONE: Russian Ambassador, Kristianiagade 5, 2100 Kobenhavn, Denmark. 42–5585; 42–5586; 38–2370.

Obukhov, Sergey Pavlovich
POSITION: Press Secretary of the Supreme Court
BIRTHPLACE/DATE: Lvov, 1958
NATIONALITY: Russian
EDUCATION: Doctor of Economics.
CAREER: From 1980 to 1981, Engineer at the Research Laboratories of Lvov Polytechnic. From 1981, Komsomol Functionary in the Lvov, Moscow, and Kostroma regions. From 1987 to 1990, worked at the International Department of the Komsomol Central Committee. From 1990, worked at the Supreme Soviet. From 1991, Deputy Head of the Russian Federation Supreme Soviet Press Center.
ADDRESS/TELEPHONE: 22 Ilyinka Street, Moscow. 206–6841 (office).

Ogorodnikov, Aleksandr Iolyevich
POSITION: Chairman of the Christian-Democratic Union of Russia; Publisher of *Herald of Christian Democracy* newspaper
BIRTHPLACE/DATE: Chistopol, May 26, 1950
CAREER: In 1973, joined the Orthodox Church. In 1974, founded the Christian Seminar on Problems of the Spiritual Revival of Russia. From 1974 to 1978, produced the samizdat (underground dissident literature) magazine, *Obschina* (*Community*). From 1976 to 1979, published articles and letters in defense of the Church. In 1978, refused to emigrate at the request of the KGB; arrested. From 1979 to 1985, transported to Leningrad; sentenced to seven years in reformatory camp and five years in exile for anti-Soviet agitation. In 1985, sentenced to an additional three years in camp. In 1987, as a result of the international campaign led by Margaret Thatcher and A.D. Sakharov, pardoned by USSR Supreme Soviet Decree. In 1987, Founder, Publisher, and Editor in Chief of the independent *Christian Public Bulletin* magazine.
FAMILY: Married with two children.
ADDRESS: 18 Prospekt Mira, Room 104, Moscow, 129010.

Oleynik, Boris Ilyich
POSITION: Ukrainian Poet; Secretary of the Writers Concord Board
BIRTHPLACE/DATE: Zachepilovka village, Poltava region, October 22, 1935
NATIONALITY: Ukrainian
CAREER: From 1958, Writer; Department Head of *Molod Ukrainy* (*Youth of Ukraine*) newspaper. From 1962, Executive Editor of *Zmina* (Ukraine Rising Generation) magazine; Deputy Executive Editor of *Dnipro* (*Dnieper*) magazine. From 1971 to 1974, Deputy Board Chairman of the Ukrainian Republic Writers' Union. From 1974 to 1976, Department Head of *Vitchyzna* (*Fatherland*) magazine. From 1976 to 1991, Board Secretary of the USSR Writers' Union; Board Secretary of the Ukrainian Republic Writers' Union. From 1989 to 1991, Deputy Chairman of the USSR Supreme Soviet Council of Nationalities. In 1991, Advisor to the USSR President; Board Chairman of the Ukrainian Culture Foundation. To 1991, Presidium Member of the Soviet Culture Foundation. USSR Supreme Soviet Member. Member of the Ukraine Central Committee. From 1989 to 1992, USSR People's Deputy. From 1961 to 1991, member of the Communist Party. From 1990 to 1991, member of the Central Committee.
MAJOR WORKS: Collections of poems and verses: *The Twentieth Wave; Choice; Circle.*
HONORS/AWARDS: Ukraine Republic State Ostrovski Prize; USSR State Prize; Order of the October Revolution; Order of the Red Banner of Labor.
FAMILY: Married.

ADDRESS/TELEPHONE: 2 Bankovaya Street, Kiev. 293–0171; 293–4573 (office).

Orlov, Victor Petrovich

POSITION: Chairman of the Russian Federation Government Committee on Geology and the Use of Mineral Resources

BIRTHPLACE/DATE: Chernogorsk, Khakass region, Krasnoyarsk, March 23, 1940

EDUCATION: Doctor of Economics; Doctor of Geology and Mineralogy.

CAREER: From 1968 to 1970, Geologist. From 1970 to 1975, Chief Geologist; Head of the Sheregeshevsk Geological Prospecting Party. From 1975 to 1978, worked in Iran. From 1978 to 1979, Chief Geologist of the Reconnaissance and Survey Group of the West Siberian Geological Directorate's Shalynsk Expedition. From 1979 to 1981, Senior Geologist; Deputy Head of the Geological Department of the Tsentrgeologiya (Central Geology) Industrial Geological Association. From 1981 to 1984, Deputy Head of the Geological Directorate of the Russian Federation Ministry of Geology. From 1986 to 1990, Director-General of Tsentrgeologiya. From August 1990 to November 1990, Deputy USSR Minister of Geology. From 1990 to 1991, First Deputy Chairman of the Russian Federation State Committee for Geology and the Use of Fuel and Energy, Mineral and Raw Materials Resources.

MAJOR WORKS: Thesis: "Scientific Bases for the Transition of the Geological Prospecting Industry to a Market Economy." Monograph: *Geological Prognostication* (1991).

FAMILY: Married with three daughters.

Orlov, Victor Vladimirovich

POSITION: Academician of the Academy of Natural Sciences; Deputy Director of the Research and Design Institute of Power Engineering

BIRTHPLACE/DATE: Moscow, 1930

NATIONALITY: Russian

EDUCATION: Doctor of Physics and Mathematics; Professor; Academician of the Russian Academy of Sciences.

CAREER: In 1965, Professor at the Moscow Institute of Engineering Physics (MIFI). From 1976 to 1988, Department Head of the Kurchatov Institute of Nuclear Energy. From 1988, Deputy Director of the Research and Design Institute of Power Engineering. From 1990 to 1991, President of the USSR Nuclear Society. From 1991, Full Member of the Russian Federation Academy of Natural Sciences.

HONORS/AWARDS: USSR State Prize; Prize of Lenin.

FAMILY: Married with two children.

ADDRESS/TELEPHONE: P.O. Box 788, Moscow, 101000. 264–2278 (office).

Osipov, Gennadi Vasilyevich

POSITION: Director of the Institute of Socio-Political Studies of the Russian Academy of Sciences; President of the Social Sciences Development Foundation; Full Member of the Russian Academy of Sciences; President of the All-Russia Society of Sociologists and Demographers

BIRTHPLACE/DATE: Ruzayevka, Mordovian Republic, 1929

NATIONALITY: Russian

EDUCATION: Doctor of Philosophy; Professor; Academician.

CAREER: From 1956 to 1958, Scientific Secretary; from 1958 to 1959, Deputy Director; from 1959 to 1962, Head of the Social Studies Department of the USSR Academy of Sciences' Institute of Philosophy. From 1962 to 1968, Deputy Director of the USSR Academy of Sciences' Institute of Social Studies. In 1966, Professor at the USSR Academy of Sciences' Institute of Philosophy. From 1989, President of the Social Sciences Development Foundation.

MAJOR WORKS: More than 20 monographs and 300 publications. *Theory and Practice of Social Studies in the USSR; Workbook of a Sociologist; Sociology Dimensions; Sociology and Socialism.*

FAMILY: Married with two children.

ADDRESS/TELEPHONE: 32-A Leninsky Prospekt, Moscow, 117334. 938–1910 (office).

Osipyan, Yuri Andreyevich

POSITION: Director of the Institute of Physics of Solids of the Russian Academy of Sciences; Presidium Member of the Russian Academy of Sciences

BIRTHPLACE/DATE: Moscow, February 15, 1931

NATIONALITY: Armenian

EDUCATION: Doctor of Physics and Mathematics; Professor.
CAREER: From 1962 to 1963, worked at the Institute of Crystallography. From 1963 to 1973, Deputy Director; from 1973, Director of the Institute of Physics of Solids of the USSR Academy of Sciences. From 1981, Academician of the USSR Academy of Sciences. From 1985, Editor in Chief of *Kvant* (*Quantum*) magazine. From 1988, Vice President of the USSR Academy of Sciences. From 1989, President of the International Union of Theoretical and Applied Physics. From 1990 to 1991, member of the USSR Presidential Council. From 1991, Advisor to the President of the USSR. From 1989 to 1992, USSR People's Deputy. From 1959, member of the Communist Party.
MAJOR WORKS: Physics of solids, primarily physics of dislocations. Discovered the so-called photoplastic effect in semiconductors.
HONORS/AWARDS: Hero of Socialist Labor (1986); Lebedev Gold Medal; Order of the Freedom and Unity Association for the Unity of Latin America.
FAMILY: Married with three children.
ADDRESS/TELEPHONE: 64-A Leninsky Prospekt, GSP-1 Moscow B-71, 117296. 132-7555; 930-3363 (office).

Osovtsov, Aleksandr Avraamovich
POSITION: Presidium Member of the Moscow Council; Chairman of the Permanent Commission on Social Policy; Moscow Council Deputy
BIRTHPLACE/DATE: Leningrad, 1957
EDUCATION: Doctor of Philosophy.
CAREER: From 1986 to 1990, worked at a publishing house.
FAMILY: Married with a son.
ADDRESS/TELEPHONE: 9-A Parkovaya Street, 3-3-5, Moscow, 105554. 367-0832 (home); 924-5352 (office).

Ostroumov, Georgy Sergeyevich
POSITION: Consultant to the President of the International Foundation for Socio-Economic and Political Studies (Gorbachev Foundation)
BIRTHPLACE/DATE: Moscow, November 8, 1932
NATIONALITY: Russian
EDUCATION: Doctor of Law.
CAREER: Worked at the Institute of Sinology of the USSR Academy of Sciences and at the Institute of State and Law of the USSR Academy of Sciences. From 1967, Editor-Consultant; from 1970, Deputy Executive Secretary of *Problemy Mira i Socializma* (*Problems of Peace and Socialism*) magazine. From 1972, Section Head at the Institute of the Socialist World Economy of the USSR Academy of Sciences. From 1973 to 1989, Consultant, Section Head, Deputy Department Head of the Central Committee. From 1989 to 1991, Assistant to the Secretary-General of the Central Committee. From September to December 1991, Head of the USSR President's Secretariat.
MAJOR WORKS: *Legal Deliberation of Reality* (1969).
HONORS/AWARDS: Order of the Badge of Honor.
FAMILY: Married.
ADDRESS/TELEPHONE: 49 Leningradsky Prospekt, Moscow, 125468. 943-9804 (office).

Ostrovenko, Yevgeni Dmitriyevich
POSITION: Russian Ambassador to Romania; Ambassador Extraordinary and Plenipotentiary
BIRTHPLACE/DATE: 1940
NATIONALITY: Russian
CAREER: From 1963 to 1968, worked at the USSR Embassy in Afghanistan. From 1970 to 1974, and from 1977 to 1985, Second, then First Secretary, Counsellor, Minister-Counsellor at the USSR Embassy in Iran. From 1985 to 1988, Expert; Deputy Head of the Middle East Department of the USSR Foreign Ministry. From 1989 to 1991, USSR Ambassador in Ghana. From 1991 to 1992, Head of the Middle East Countries Directorate. From 1992, Russian Ambassador to Afghanistan.

Ott, Urmas
POSITION: Commentator for Estonian Television; Host of the "Television Acquaintance" TV program
BIRTHPLACE/DATE: Otelya, Estonia, April 23, 1950
NATIONALITY: Estonian
CAREER: From 1977 to 1979, Freelance Employee of Estonian Radio. From 1979 to July 1991, Anchorman of Estonian TV.
FAMILY: Single.

Address/Telephone: Estonian Television, Tallinn, Estonia. 430–470 (office).

Ovchinnikov, Vladimir Alekseyevich

Position: Director-General of the Aleksandrovsky Radiozavod (Radio Plant) Joint-Stock Association
Birthplace/Date: Aleksandrov, 1938
Nationality: Russian
Career: From 1970 to 1978, Foreman; Deputy Director of the Semi-Conducting Devices Plants in Aleksandrov. From 1978 to 1989, Director of the Potentsial (Potential) Plant in Mariyskaya Republic. In 1991, Board Member of the Russian Federation Union of Industrialists. In 1991, Presidium Member of the Moscow Chamber of Commerce; Presidium Member of the Central Moscow Stock Exchange Council. From 1989, Director-General of the Aleksandrovsky Radiozavod Scientific and Industrial Association; member of the Supreme Soviet Committee for Industry. Russian Federation People's Deputy. Member of the Demokraticheskaya Rossiya (Democratic Russia) Movement.
Family: Married with two children.
Address/Telephone: 13 Lenina Street, Vladimir region, Aleksandrov. 274–0116 (office); 584–5840.

Ovinnikov, Richard Sergeyevich

Position: Former USSR Ambassador to Canada
Birthplace/Date: Voronezh, 1930
Nationality: Russian
Education: Studied at the Moscow State Institute of International Relations of the USSR Foreign Ministry. Doctor of History.
Career: From 1958 to 1960, Attaché of the International Organizations Department of the USSR Foreign Ministry. From 1960 to 1966, Interpreter, Attaché, Third Secretary, Second Secretary, First Secretary at the USSR Permanent Mission to the UN in New York. From 1966 to 1970, First Secretary, Counsellor of the International Organizations Department of the USSR Foreign Ministry. From 1970 to 1977, Senior Counsellor, Deputy Permanent USSR Representative to the UN in New York. From 1977 to 1980, Counsellor, Group Head to the USSR Foreign Minister. From 1980 to 1985, USSR Deputy Permanent Representative to the UN in New York. In 1985, Head of the Foreign Policy Planning Directorate of the USSR Foreign Ministry. From 1985 to 1990, Rector and Board Member of the Moscow State Institute of International Relations of the USSR Foreign Ministry. In 1990, Chief Counsellor of the International Organizations Directorate of the USSR Foreign Ministry. From 1990 to December 1991, USSR Ambassador to Canada. In December 1991, released from duties.
Family: Married.
Telephone: 244–3448 (Foreign Ministry).

Ozherelyev, Oleg Ivanovich

Position: Former Assistant to the USSR President for Economic Problems
Birthplace/Date: Lipetsk region, 1942
Education: Doctor of Economics; Professor.
Career: Dean of the Department of Economics at Leningrad State University. From 1977, Party Functionary at the Leningrad City Party Committee; worked at the Department of Science of the Central Committee; Deputy Head of the Humanities Department of the Central Committee.
Major Works: Scientific books; political economy textbook (co-authored with V.A. Medvedev and L.I. Abalkin).
Family: Married with a son.
Address/Telephone: 4 Staraya Square, Moscow, 103132. Fax: 206–2511.

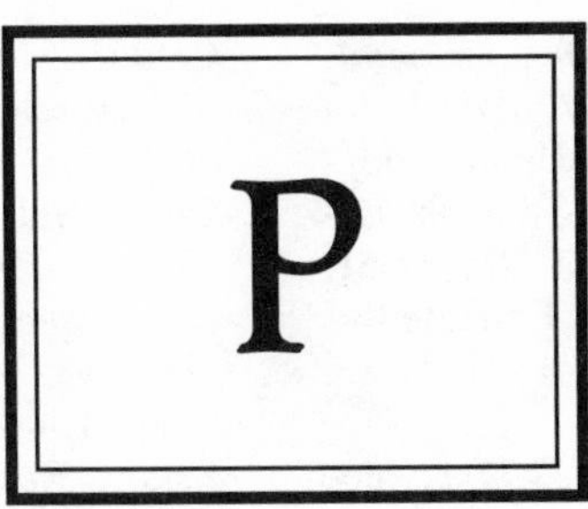

Pamfilova, Ella Aleksandrovna

POSITION: Russian Federation Minister of Social Protection of the Population
BIRTHPLACE/DATE: Uzbekistan, September 12, 1953
NATIONALITY: Russian
CAREER: From 1976 to 1989, Engineer, Forewoman, Chairman of the Trade Union Committee at the Central Mechanical-Repair Plant of the Mosenergo (Moscow Energy) Industrial Association. From 1990 to 1991, Chairwoman of the USSR Supreme Soviet Commission on Issues of Privileges. From November 1991, Russian Federation Minister of Social Protection of the Population. From July 1992, Official Representative of the Russian Federation President to a committee drafting a law to change state pensions. From 1989 to 1992, USSR People's Deputy. Elected USSR Supreme Soviet Deputy.
FAMILY: Married with a daughter.
ADDRESS/TELEPHONE: 4 Shabolovka Street, Moscow.

Panchenko, Aleksandr Mikhailovich

POSITION: Academician of the Russian Academy of Sciences; Head of the New Russian Literature Department at the Institute of Russian Literature (Pushkin House) of the Russian Academy of Sciences
BIRTHPLACE/DATE: Leningrad, 1937
NATIONALITY: Russian
EDUCATION: Doctor of Philosophy; Professor.
CAREER: From 1962 to 1989, worked at the Pushkin House. In 1983, Professor at the Herzen State Teachers' Training University.
MAJOR WORKS: More than 300 publications, including *Russian Poetic Culture of the 17th Century; Laughable World in Ancient Russia; Russian Culture On the Eve of Peter's Reforms.*
FAMILY: Married with three children.
ADDRESS/TELEPHONE: 4 Makarova Naberezhnaya, St. Petersburg, 199034. 218–0002; 218–0102 (office).

Panferov, Boris Victorovich

POSITION: Former Russian Federation Deputy Minister of Justice; State Minister of Justice, Second Class
BIRTHPLACE/DATE: Zheleznovodsk, 1946
CAREER: From 1971 to 1980, People's Judge of the Tushinsky District People's Court. From 1980 to 1990, Chairman of the Pervomaisky District People's Court. From July 1991, Russian Federation Deputy Minister of Justice. From 1980 to 1986, Russian Federation Supreme Soviet Deputy of the Pervomaisky District.
FAMILY: Married with three children.
ADDRESS/TELEPHONE: 4 Obukha Street, Moscow, 109803. 206–0081.

Pankin, Boris Dmitryevich

POSITION: Russian Federation Ambassador to Great Britain
BIRTHPLACE/DATE: Frunze (now Bishkek), October 20, 1931
NATIONALITY: Russian
EDUCATION: Studied at Moscow State University.
CAREER: From 1953 to 1973, Writer, Department Head, Editorial Board Member, Deputy

Editor in Chief, Editor in Chief of *Komsomolskaya Pravda* (*Komsomol Truth*) newspaper. From 1973 to 1982, Chairman of the All-Union Copyright Agency. From 1982 to 1990, USSR Ambassador to Sweden. From 1990 to 1991, USSR Ambassador to the Czech and Slovak Federate Republics. From August to November 1991, USSR Foreign Minister.
MAJOR WORKS: *At the Top of One's Voice* (co-authored with V. Chikin); *Where Khlestakovschina Leads*; *Strict Literature*; *Time and Word*; *Border-Lines and Books.*
HONORS/AWARDS: Two Orders of the Red Banner of Labor; Order of the People's Friendship; USSR State Prize; Journalists' Union Prize; medal.
FAMILY: Married with two children and a granddaughter.
ADDRESS/TELEPHONE: The Embassy of Russia in Great Britain, 13 Kensington Palace Garden, London W8. 229–3628; 229–3620; 229–3629.

Pankin, Vyatcheslav Vladimirovich
POSITION: President of the Moscow Central Stock Exchange
BIRTHPLACE/DATE: Tula region, 1958
CAREER: From 1977 to 1984, Economist at the Institute of Nuclear Engineering. From 1983 to 1985, Secretary of the Moscow City Komsomol Committee. From 1985 to 1990, Deputy Head of the Department of Organizational Problems of the Moscow City Executive Committee. From 1990 to 1991, Deputy Chairman of the Khoroshevsky District Council. From 1991 to 1992, Vice President; from 1992, President of the Moscow Central Stock Exchange. Khoroshevsky District Council Deputy; Deputy Chairman of the Board of Advisors of the Russian Foundation of Federal Property; Board Member of the Russian Federation Chamber of Commerce; Chairman of the Committee for Facilitating the Development of Exchange Structures.
FAMILY: Married with two children.
ADDRESS/TELEPHONE: 3/8 Birzhevaya Ploschad, Moscow. 921–2551; 202–8925; Fax: 921–4364.

Pankov, Anatoli Semyonovich
POSITION: Editor in Chief of the Moscow Council of People's Deputies' *Kuranty* (*Chiming Clock*) newspaper
BIRTHPLACE/DATE: Moscow, August 3, 1938
CAREER: From 1962 to 1966, Teacher at a secondary school. From 1966 to 1968, Correspondent for *Moskovsky Komsomolets* (*Moscow Komsomol Member*) newspaper. From 1968 to 1979, Journalist in Yakutia. From 1979 to 1984, Department Head of the Moscow Region *Leninskoye Znamya* (*Lenin's Banner*) newspaper. From 1984 to 1985, Correspondent for *Sovietskaya Rossiya* (*Soviet Russia*) newspaper. From 1985 to 1990, Deputy Department Head; Parliamentary Correspondent for *Trud* (*Labor*) newspaper. Moscow Council People's Deputy.
FAMILY: Married with a son.
ADDRESS/TELEPHONE: 12 Stankevicha Street, Moscow, 103009. 292–5515; 203–0610.

Pankratov, Valentin Andreyevich
POSITION: Director-General of the Russian Agency of Investments and Real Estate
BIRTHPLACE/DATE: Moscow, 1937
NATIONALITY: Russian
EDUCATION: Doctor of Technical Sciences.
CAREER: From 1959 to 1982, Chief Specialist of the Soyuz (Union) Association. From 1982 to 1992, Department Head at the Research Institute of Aircraft Materials. From 1992, Director-General of the Russian Agency of Investments and Real Estate.
MAJOR WORKS: More than 100 articles in scientific and popular scientific publications on aircraft technology and industry.
HONORS/AWARDS: USSR Council of Ministers Prize.
FAMILY: Married with two children.
ADDRESS/TELEPHONE: 4 Slavyanskaya Ploschad, Moscow, 103074. 220–9098; 928–6111 (office).

Pastchenko, Vladimir Lvovich
POSITION: Director of the Moscow Frezer Instrument Industrial Association
BIRTHPLACE/DATE: Moscow, 1937
NATIONALITY: Russian
CAREER: From 1956, worked at the Moscow Sergo Ordzhonikidze Instrument Plant; from 1974 to 1980, Deputy Director-General. From 1980 to 1984, Director of the Stankoagregat (Machine Assembly) Plant in Moscow.
FAMILY: Married with a daughter.

ADDRESS/TELEPHONE: 2/1 Pervaya Frezernaya Street, Moscow, 109202. 273–0601 (office).

Pastukhov, Boris Nikolayevich
POSITION: Russian Federation Deputy Foreign Minister; Ambassador Extraordinary and Plenipotentiary
BIRTHPLACE/DATE: Moscow, 1933
NATIONALITY: Russian
EDUCATION: Studied at the N.E. Bauman State Technical Institute.
CAREER: From 1958 to 1977, Komsomol Functionary. From 1977 to 1982, First Secretary of the Komsomol Central Committee. From 1982 to 1986, Chairman of the USSR State Committee for Publishing, Printing, and the Book Trade. From 1986 to 1989, USSR Ambassador to Denmark. From 1989 to 1992, USSR Ambassador to Afghanistan. Deputy of the USSR Supreme Soviet of the Seventh to Eleventh Convocations. From 1959 to 1991, member of the Communist Party.
HONORS/AWARDS: Order of Lenin (1981); three Orders of the Red Banner of Labor (1963, 1971, 1976); Order of the Red Star (1990).
FAMILY: Married.
ADDRESS/TELEPHONE: 32/34 Smolenskaya-Sennaya Ploschad, Moscow, 121200. 244–4246 (aide).

Patrikeyev, Valery Anisimovich
POSITION: Retired Colonel-General
BIRTHPLACE/DATE: Bogolyubovo village, Staro-Yuryevsh district, Tambov region, 1938
NATIONALITY: Russian
CAREER: From 1955, served in the Armed Forces: Division Commander, Corps Commander, Army Commander, Military District Commander. From 1989, Commander of the Trans-Caucasian Military District. From July 1992, received Plenary Powers of the Russian Government Representative.
FAMILY: Married with a son and a daughter.
TELEPHONE: 293–1806 (office).

Paulman, Valery Fyodorovich
POSITION: Economics Director of the RVC i Ko (RVC & Company) Joint-Stock Company (trading and mediation)
BIRTHPLACE/DATE: Yegoryevsk, Moscow region, 1937
NATIONALITY: Estonian
EDUCATION: Doctor of Economics.
CAREER: From 1960 to 1974, Economist, Senior Economist, Department Head, First Deputy Chairman of the Central Statistics Board of the Estonian Republic. From 1974 to 1983, Department Head, Directorate Head, Board Member, First Deputy Chairman of the Estonian Republic State Planning Committee. From 1983 to 1987, Head of the Economics Department of the Estonian Central Committee. From 1987 to 1988, Deputy Chairman of the Council of Ministers; Chairman of the Estonian Republic State Planning Committee. From 1988 to 1989, Chief Economist of the Estonian Central Statistics Board. From 1989 to 1991, Counsellor of Planning at the USSR Embassy in Cuba; Representative of the USSR State Planning Committee. From 1991 to December 1991, USSR Minister of Labor and Social Problems. Honored Economist of the Estonian Republic.
HONORS/AWARDS: Order of the Badge of Honor; Order of the People's Friendship.
FAMILY: Married with two children.
ADDRESS/TELEPHONE: 6 Pronksi Street, Flat #12, Tallinn. 438–912 (home).

Pavlovsky, Gleb Olegovich
POSITION: Board Chairman of the Informagentstvo Postfaktum (Postfactum Information Agency) Closed Joint-Stock Association; Executive Secretary of *Vek XX i Mir* (*20th Century and Peace*) magazine
BIRTHPLACE/DATE: Odessa, 1951
CAREER: From 1978 to 1980, Editorial Board Member of *Poiski* (*Searches*) magazine. From 1982 to 1985, in exile. In 1987, cooperated with *Vek XX i Mir* magazine. From 1988, Director of the Postfactum Agency.
FAMILY: Married with five children.
ADDRESS/TELEPHONE: 9 Maly Gnezdikovski Pereulok, Building 3–6, Moscow, 103009. 229–5297 (office); Fax: 229–0457.

Payula, Kuno
POSITION: Chairman of the Consistory of the Estonian Evangelical Lutheran Church; Archbishop
BIRTHPLACE/DATE: Kyaru village, Virumas region, Estonia, March 11, 1924

NATIONALITY: Estonian
CAREER: From 1949 to 1957, Priest of the Lutheran Parishes of Illuka and Nisaku (Estonia). From 1957 to 1987, Priest of the Yanovsky Lutheran Parish in Tallinn (Estonia).
FAMILY: Married with two children.
ADDRESS/TELEPHONE: 8 Kirchku Street, Tallinn. 451–682.

Pekarskaya, Tereza Kazimirovna
POSITION: Secretary of the Russian Federation Supreme Soviet Committee on Health Protection, Social Security, and Physical Education
BIRTHPLACE/DATE: Vitebsk, 1942
NATIONALITY: Polish
EDUCATION: From 1976 to 1979, postgraduate student in Kuibyshev.
CAREER: From 1959 to 1965, Military Unit Nurse in Seryshevo village, Amur region. From 1965 to 1970, Military Unit Nurse in Kuibyshev. From 1979 to 1976, worked at the Kuibyshev Medical Institute. From 1979 to 1980, Assistant at the Physiology Department in Kuibyshev. From 1980 to 1990, Doctor at the Children's Hospital in Kuibyshev. Member of the Council of the Republic; Secretary of the Left-Center Parliamentary Faction's Coalition to Support Democratic Reforms.
FAMILY: Married with two children.
ADDRESS/TELEPHONE: 2 Krasnopresnenskaya Naberezhnaya, Moscow, 103274. 205–5216 (office); 216–7818 (home).

Perelet, Renat Alekseyevich
POSITION: Leading Researcher of Ecology at the Institute of Systems Analysis of the Russian Academy of Sciences; Assistant Professor at Moscow State University
BIRTHPLACE/DATE: Kalinin, 1936
NATIONALITY: Russian
EDUCATION: Doctor of Economics.
CAREER: From 1958 to 1962, Engineer at the Radio Engineering Institute of the USSR Academy of Sciences. From 1962 to 1971, Expert of the International Organizations of the State Committee for Science and Technology. From 1972 to 1978, Staff Member of the Industrial Management Section of the United Nations Industrial Development Organization (UNIDO). From 1978 to 1985, member of the USSR Environmental Programs Commission to the United Nations (UNEP). From 1985 to 1987, Laboratory Head and Scientific Secretary of the Committee for Systems Analysis of the USSR Academy of Sciences. Consultant to UNEP, UNESCO, and the UN European Economic Commission; member of the Scientific Organizing Committee of the International Human Dimension Program; Board Member of the Russian Ecological Union; member of the International Federation for Peace and Concord; member of the Working Group on Risk Analyses of the President of the Russian Academy of Sciences; Committee Head of the Ecological Economy Center of the Committee on UNESCO's Human-Being and Biosphere Program; Consultant to the Russian Federation Supreme Soviet Ecology Commission.
MAJOR WORKS: About eighty publications on ecological problems.
FAMILY: Married with two children.
ADDRESS/TELEPHONE: 9 60-Letiya Oktyabrya Prospekt, Moscow, 117312. 135–4322 (office).

Peresypkin, Oleg Gerasimovich
POSITION: Rector of the Diplomatic Academy of the Russian Federation Foreign Ministry
BIRTHPLACE/DATE: Baku, August 12, 1935
NATIONALITY: Russian
EDUCATION: Doctor of History; Doctor of Philology; Professor.
CAREER: From 1959 to 1963, Interpreter, Attaché at the USSR Embassy in Yemen Arab Republic. From 1963 to 1965, Third Secretary of the Middle East Department of the USSR Foreign Ministry. From 1965 to 1969, worked at the USSR Embassy in Iraq Republic. From 1969 to 1971, First Secretary of the Middle East Department of the USSR Foreign Ministry. From 1971 to 1975, Counsellor at the USSR Embassy in the People's Democratic Republic of Yemen. From 1975 to 1980, Counsellor of the Middle East Department of the USSR Foreign Ministry. From 1980 to 1984, USSR Ambassador to Libya. From 1986 to December 1991, Rector of the Diplomatic Academy of the USSR Foreign Ministry.
HONORS/AWARDS: Order of the People's Friendship (1985).
FAMILY: Married with a daughter.
ADDRESS/TELEPHONE: The Diplomatic Academy of the Russian Federation Foreign Ministry,

53/2 Ostozhenka Street, Moscow, 119021. 245–3386 (office).

Perov, Aleksandr Leonidovich
POSITION: Former Editor in Chief of *Kommersant* (*Businessman*) daily newspaper
BIRTHPLACE/DATE: Moscow region, 1957
NATIONALITY: Russian
CAREER: From 1982, Correspondent for *Yunost* (*Youth*) magazine. From 1982 to 1984, Correspondent; from 1984 to 1987, Information Department Head of *Moskovsky Komsomolets* (*Moscow Komsomol Member*) newspaper. From 1987 to 1989, Freelance Journalist. From 1990 to 1991, Editor of the Business News Department of *Kommersant* newspaper; from 1991 to 1992, Deputy Editor in Chief.
FAMILY: Single.

Pershin, Aleksandr Maksimovich
POSITION: Director-General of the Interbuk Russian-Slovak Joint Venture
BIRTHPLACE/DATE: Prokhladny, Kabardin-Balkar Republic, 1940
CAREER: From 1963 to 1980, Attaché, First Secretary of the Department of Southeast Asia and the Fourth European Department. From 1980 to 1989, Head of the Directorate of International Relations Protocol of the USSR Goskomizdat (State Committee for Publishing).
FAMILY: Married.
ADDRESS/TELEPHONE: 1/4 Pervy Smolensky Pereulok, Moscow, 121099. 241–6399 (office).

Petrakov, Nikolay Yakovlevich
POSITION: Director of the Institute of Market Problems of the Russian Academy of Sciences (RAN); Academician of RAN; Board Member of the Russian Union of Industrialists and Entrepreneurs
BIRTHPLACE/DATE: Moscow, March 1, 1937
NATIONALITY: Russian
EDUCATION: Doctor of Economics; Professor.
CAREER: From 1959 to 1961, Junior Researcher at the Research Institute of Technical and Economic Studies of the USSR State Committee for Chemistry. From 1961 to 1965, Junior, Senior Researcher at the Economics Institute of the USSR State Planning Committee. From 1965 to 1990, Laboratory Head, Deputy Director of Scientific Work at the Central Economics and Mathematics Institute of the USSR Academy of Sciences. From 1990 to 1991, Assistant to the Secretary-General of the Central Committee; Assistant to the USSR President on Economic Problems. From 1991, Director of the Institute of Market Problems of RAN. From 1989 to 1991, USSR People's Deputy.
MAJOR WORKS: Papers on problems of price formation and methdology of optimization in a socialist economy.
HONORS/AWARDS: Order of the Badge of Honor; two medals.
FAMILY: Married with a daughter and a son.
ADDRESS/TELEPHONE: 32 Krasikova Street, Moscow, 117418. 129–1000 (office); 242–4447 (home).

Petrov, Rem Victorovich
POSITION: Vice President of the Russian Academy of Sciences; Editor in Chief of *Nauka v Rossii* (*Science in Russia*) magazine
BIRTHPLACE/DATE: Serafimovich, Volgograd region, March 22, 1930
NATIONALITY: Russian
EDUCATION: Doctor of Medicine; Professor; Academician.
CAREER: From 1953 to 1983, worked at the Institute of Biophysics of the USSR Ministry of Health. From 1978, Academician of the USSR Academy of Medical Sciences. From 1983 to 1988, Director of the Institute of Immunology of the USSR Ministry of Health. From 1983, Chairman of the Society of Immunologists. From 1984, Academician of the USSR Academy of Sciences (USSR AN). From 1988 to 1992, Vice President; Presidium Member of the USSR AN.
MAJOR WORKS: More than 300 scientific works; monograph *Immunology and Immunogenetics*; book: *Me, Or Not Me.*
HONORS/AWARDS: Hero of Socialist Labor; Order of the October Revolution; Mechnikov Gold Medal; Medal For Labor Valor.
FAMILY: Married with three children.
ADDRESS/TELEPHONE: 14 Leninsky Prospekt, Moscow. 954–3276 (aide).

Petrov, Yuri Vladimirovich

POSITION: Chairman of the State Investment Corporation
BIRTHPLACE/DATE: Nizhny Tagil, January 18, 1939
CAREER: From 1967 to 1972, Department Head of the Dzerzhinsky District, Nizhny Tagil City Communist Party. From 1972 to 1977, Second, First Secretary of the Nizhney Tagil City Communist Party. From 1977 to 1982, Secretary of the Sverdlovsk Regional Communist Party. From 1982 to 1985, Section Head, Deputy Head of the Department of Party Work Organization of the Central Committee. From 1985 to 1988, First Secretary of the Sverdlovsk Regional Communist Party. From 1988 to 1991, USSR Ambassador to Cuba. From 1991, Head of the Russian Federation President's Administration. Deputy of the USSR Supreme Soviet of the Eleventh Convocation; Deputy of the Russian Federation Supreme Soviet of the Ninth and Eleventh Convocations. From 1962 to 1991, member of the Communist Party.
HONORS/AWARDS: Two Orders of the Red Banner of Labor.
FAMILY: Married with a son.
ADDRESS/TELEPHONE: 22 Pilyushina Street, Moscow, 117390. 132–0074.

Petrovsky, Boris Vasilyevich

POSITION: Academician of the Russian Academy of Sciences
BIRTHPLACE/DATE: Yessentuki, June 27, 1908
EDUCATION: Doctor of Medicine; Professor.
CAREER: From 1941 to 1944, Leading Army Surgeon of the front line evacuation hospitals. From 1944 to 1945, Lecturer at the Military Medical Academy. From 1945 to 1948, Deputy Director of the Institute of Surgery of the USSR Academy of Medical Sciences (AMN). From 1948 to 1949, Professor at the Second Moscow Medical Institute. From 1949 to 1951, Professor at Budapest University. From 1951 to 1956, Professor at the Second Moscow Medical Institute. From 1956 to 1965, Department Head of the First Moscow Medical Institute. From 1957, Academician of the USSR AMN. From December 1991, Academician of the Russian AMN. From 1963 to 1965, Director of the All-Union Research Institute of Clinical and Experimental Surgery. From December 1991, Honorary Director of the Russian Scientific Surgery Center of RAN. From 1965 to 1980, USSR Minister of Health. From 1966, Academician of the USSR Academy of Sciences. From 1942 to 1991, member of the Communist Party. From 1966 to 1981, Alternate Member of the Central Committee. Honorary Member of the Academies of Sciences of Hungary, Poland, Bulgaria, Serbia; Honorary Member of the Royal Colleges of Great Britain and Scotland. Deputy of the USSR Supreme Soviet of the Sixth to Tenth Convocations.
MAJOR WORKS: On the surgical cure of gullet cancer; inborn and acquired heart diseases. First in the USSR to use prosthetic heart valve appliances. Developed and implemented methods of kidney transplantation and plastic for bronchial tubes and the trachea. More than 250 scientific works.
HONORS/AWARDS: Hero of Socialist Labor; four Orders of Lenin; Order of the October Revolution; Order of the Red Banner of Labor.
FAMILY: Married with a daughter.
ADDRESS/TELEPHONE: 2 Abrikosovski Pereulok, Moscow, 119874. 246–9265 (office).

Petrovsky, Vladimir Fyodorovich

POSITION: United Nations Under Secretary-General on Political Problems
BIRTHPLACE/DATE: Volgograd, April 29, 1933
NATIONALITY: Russian
EDUCATION: Doctor of History; Doctor of Jurisprudence.

Pilipenko, Yuri Vladimirovich

POSITION: Editor in Chief of *Sobesednik* (*Companion*) weekly newspaper for youth
BIRTHPLACE/DATE: Zabrody village, Kharkov region, March 25, 1954
CAREER: Worked from Correspondent to Deputy Editor in Chief of *Leninskaya Smena* (*Lenin's Successors*) newspaper for youth in Kharkov. From 1984 to 1989, worked at the Press Section of the Komsomol Central Committee.
HONORS/AWARDS: The S. Borvenko Prize of the Kharkov Journalists' Organization.
FAMILY: Married with a son.
ADDRESS/TELEPHONE: 73 Novoslobodskaya Street, Moscow, 101484. 285–7645 (office).

Pipko, Daniil Arkadyevich

POSITION: Editor in Chief of *Inzhenernaya Gazeta* (*Engineering Newspaper*)
BIRTHPLACE/DATE: Donetsk, 1935
NATIONALITY: Ukrainian
CAREER: From 1969 to 1989, worked at *Socialisticheskaya Industriya* (*Socialist Industry*) newspaper.

Pirumov, Vladimir Semyonovich

POSITION: Chairman of the Geopolitics and Security Section of the Russian Academy of Natural Sciences; Professor at the General Staff Academy
BIRTHPLACE/DATE: Kirovakan, 1926
NATIONALITY: Armenian
EDUCATION: From 1960, student, then advanced student at the Military Naval Academy. Doctor of Natural Sciences.
CAREER: From 1948 to 1960, served in the navy; Commander of a torpedo-boat destroyer. To 1974, Department Head at the Military Naval Academy. From 1974 to 1985, Directorate Head of the Navy General Headquarters. From 1985 to 1990, Department Head of the General Staff Academy. In 1990, Corresponding Member of the USSR (now Russian) Academy of Natural Sciences. In 1991, Academician of the Russian Academy of Natural Sciences.
MAJOR WORKS: More than 100 published works. *In the Naval Warfare* (1988).
HONORS/AWARDS: Russian Honored Worker of Science.
FAMILY: Married with two children.
ADDRESS/TELEPHONE: The General Staff Academy, 100 Vernadskogo Prospekt, Moscow. 438–9152 (office).

Pisemsky, Nikolay Georgyevich

POSITION: Board Chairman of the Konversbank Joint-Stock Conversion Bank
BIRTHPLACE/DATE: Moscow, 1948
NATIONALITY: Russian
CAREER: Chief Accountant at defense industry enterprises and organizations. To 1989, worked at the USSR Ministry of Nuclear Power Engineering and Industry.
FAMILY: Married with a son.
ADDRESS/TELEPHONE: 24/26 Bolshaya Ordynka, Moscow, 109017. 239–2620; Fax: 233–2540.

Pisigin, Valery Fridrikhovich

POSITION: President of the MKF Inter-Regional Cooperative Federation; Co-Chairman of the Bukharin Foundation; Editor in Chief of *Kontinent* (*Continent*) provincial weekly; member of the Presidential Consultative Council (PKS)
BIRTHPLACE/DATE: Chelyabinsk, 1957
NATIONALITY: Russian
CAREER: From 1975 to 1977, served in the Airborne Troops. From 1979 to 1988, Metalworker at the Kamsky Automobile Plant. In 1988, elected President of MKF. From February 1992, Presidium Member of the Russian League of Entrepreneurs and Cooperative Societies; Council of Founders Member of *Moskovskiye Novosti* (*Moscow News*) weekly.
MAJOR WORKS: Articles in central and provincial presses.
FAMILY: Married with a son.
ADDRESS/TELEPHONE: Naberezhnye Chelny, 26 Pushkinskaya Street, Flat #313, Tajikistan, 423818. 56–6631; 56–6540 (office); 54–0233 (home).

Pitirim (Nechayev Konstantin Vladimirovich)

POSITION: Metropolitan of Volokolamsk and Yuryevsk; Publishing Department Chairman of the Moscow Patriarchy
BIRTHPLACE/DATE: Michurinsk, Tambov region, January 13, 1926
NATIONALITY: Russian
EDUCATION: Doctor of Theology; Professor.
CAREER: From 1951 to 1962, Lecturer at the Moscow Ecclesiastical Academy. From 1963 to 1971, Bishop of Volokolamsk; Vicar of the Moscow Diocese. From 1971 to 1986, Archbishop of Volokolamsk. From 1963 to 1968, Executive Editor of *Zhurnal Moskovskoy Patriarkhii* (*Journal of Moscow Patriarchy*); Vice President of the International Foundation for Survival and the Development of Humanity; Board Member of the Russian (formerly Soviet) Culture Foundation; member of the Central Council of the Union of Soviet Societies for Friendship with Foreign Countries (SSOD). USSR People's Deputy.

HONORS/AWARDS: Order of the People's Friendship.
ADDRESS/TELEPHONE: 19/8 Chasovaya Street, Flat #66, Moscow. 246–9846; 246–9848; 246–2204.

Piyankov, Boris Yevgenyevich
POSITION: Head of the Military Experts Group; Deputy Commander in Chief of the CIS Armed Forces; Colonel-General
BIRTHPLACE/DATE: Sverdlovsk, 1935
NATIONALITY: Russian
CAREER: Served in the Trans-Caucasian Military District Army; Tank Platoon Commander; Company Commander in the Urals Military District. Served in the Strategic Missile Forces; Battalion Commander; Regiment Commander; Staff Head of the Tank Division; Trans-Caucasian Military District Division Commander. From 1991, Head of the USSR Civil Defense; Deputy USSR Defense Minister. From 1989 to 1992, USSR People's Deputy.
FAMILY: Married with a daughter and a son.
TELEPHONE: 293–1413 (office).

Pletchko, Vladimir Yakovlevich
POSITION: Russian Federation Ambassador to the Republic of Moldova; Ambassador Extraordinary and Plenipotentiary
BIRTHPLACE/DATE: 1934
NATIONALITY: Ukrainian
CAREER: From 1958 to 1960, Secretary of the USSR Consul-General in Bratislava. From 1960 to 1963, Attaché at the USSR Embassy in Czechoslovakia. From 1963 to 1965, Third Secretary of the Fourth European Department of the USSR Foregn Ministry. From 1965 to 1967, Third, Second Secretary of the USSR Foreign Minister's Secretariat. From 1967 to 1969, Second Secretary at the USSR Embassy in Great Britain. From 1969 to 1971, Second, First Secretary at the USSR Embassy in Czechoslovakia. From 1971 to 1973, Counsellor of the USSR Foreign Minister's Secretariat. From 1973 to 1979, Senior Counsellor of the Foreign Policy Planning Directorate of the USSR Foreign Ministry. From 1979 to 1980, USSR Consul-General in New York. From 1980 to 1985, Deputy Permanent Representative of the USSR to the UN in New York. From 1985 to 1987, Head of the Consulate Directorate of the USSR Foreign Ministry. From 1987 to 1991, USSR Ambassador to Malta. From 1991 to 1992, Department Head of the USSR (Russian Federation) Foreign Ministry.
HONORS/AWARDS: Order of the Badge of Honor.
ADDRESS/TELEPHONE: 32/34 Smolenskaya-Sennaya Ploschad, Moscow. 244–2061 (Moscow).

Pletnev, Mikhail Vasilyevich
POSITION: Chief Conductor and Art Director of the Russian National Symphony Orchestra
BIRTHPLACE/DATE: Arkhangelsk, 1957
CAREER: From 1981, Lecturer at the Moscow Conservatory. From 1990, Chief Conductor; Art Director; Soloist of the Russian National Symphony Orchestra. Performs abroad.
MAJOR WORKS: Musical compositions in various genres.
HONORS/AWARDS: Grand Prix at the Contest of Musical Youth (Paris, 1973); First Prize at the All-Union Contest of Pianists (1977) and at the Tchaikovsky International Contest; Russian Federation People's Artist.
FAMILY: Single.
ADDRESS/TELEPHONE: 33 Starokonyushenny Pereulok, Flat #16, Moscow, 121002. 241–4339 (home).

Pluchek, Valentin Nikolayevich
POSITION: Art Director of the Moscow Academic Satire Theater
BIRTHPLACE/DATE: Daugavpils, Dvinsk (now Latvia), 1909
CAREER: From 1929, worked at the Meyerhold Theater. In 1939, founded a theatrical studio in Moscow (with playwright A. Arbuzov); in 1940, staged *City at Daybreak* by A. Arbuzov. During the Great Patriotic War, Head of the Northern Fleet Theater. From 1950, Producer. From 1957, Art Director of the Moscow Satire Theater. For sixteen years, Head of the Producers Laboratory of the Russian Federation Metropolitan Drama Theater.
MAJOR WORKS: *Banya* (*Russian Baths*) (1953, 1967); *Klop* (*Bug*) by V.V. Mayakovsky (1955, 1974); *Misteriya-Buf* by V.V. Mayakovsky (1957); *Revizor* (*Auditor*) by Gogol (1972); *Tribunal* by V. Voinovich (1989).

HONORS/AWARDS: Order of Lenin; two Orders of The Great Patriotic War; Order of the Red Banner of Labor; Order of the Friendship of Peoples; USSR and Russian Federation People's Artist.
FAMILY: Married with a son.
ADDRESS/TELEPHONE: 2 Mayakovskogo Ploschad, Moscow, 103050. 299–9813; 299–9853 (office).

Pochinok, Aleksandr Petrovich
POSITION: Chairman of the Russian Federation Supreme Soviet Committee on Budget, Planning, Taxes, and Prices
BIRTHPLACE/DATE: Chelyabinsk, 1958
NATIONALITY: Russian
EDUCATION: From 1982 to 1985, postgraduate student at the USSR Academy of Sciences' Institute of Economics.
CAREER: From 1980 to 1982, Aide-Researcher, Junior Researcher at the Institute of Economics of the Urals branch of the USSR Academy of Sciences in Chelyabinsk. From 1986 to 1990, Junior Researcher, Researcher, Senior Researcher at the Institute of Economics of the Urals branch of the USSR Academy of Sciences. From 1990, Secretary, Deputy Chairman, Chairman of the Russian Federation Supreme Soviet Committee on Budget, Planning, Taxes, and Prices. Russian Federation People's Deputy.
FAMILY: Married with a daughter.
ADDRESS/TELEPHONE: 2 Krasnopresnenskaya Naberezhnaya, Room 2–23, Moscow, 103274. 205–4349 (office); Fax: 205–6414.

Podoprigora, Vladimir Nikolayevich
POSITION: Chairman of the Russian Federation Supreme Soviet Committee for Inter-Republican Relations, Regional Policy, and Cooperation Issues
BIRTHPLACE/DATE: Balkhash, Kazakh Republic, 1954
NATIONALITY: Russian
CAREER: From 1977, Engineer-Designer. From 1978, Production Engineer in Izhevsk. From 1979, Second Secretary of the Komsomol City Committee. From 1982, Instructor of the Industrial and Transport Department of the Komsomol City Committee. From 1984, Foreman of a shop. From 1985, Head of the Industrial and Transport Department of the City Communist Party. From 1989, First Deputy Chairman of the City Executive Committee. From 1990, Deputy Chairman of the Russian Federation Supreme Soviet Committee. Member of the Demokraticheskaya Rossiya (Democratic Russia) Party. Russian Federation People's Deputy.
FAMILY: Married with a daughter.
ADDRESS/TELEPHONE: 2 Krasnopresnenskaya Naberezhnaya, Moscow; 8 Akademika Koroleva Street, Building 2, Flat #450, Moscow. 205–6950; 205–9438; 286–2895.

Pogosyan, Stepan Karapetovich
POSITION: Former Politburo member; former First Secretary of the Armenian Central Committee
BIRTHPLACE/DATE: Agakchi village, Talin region, Armenian Republic, February 10, 1932
NATIONALITY: Armenian
CAREER: From 1955, Secretary of the Yerevan State University Komsomol Committee. From 1958, Deputy Department Head of the Armenian Komsomol Central Committee. From 1959 to 1962, Second, First Secretary of the Yerevan City Komsomol Committee. From 1962 to 1963, Secretary, First Secretary of the Armenian Komsomol Central Committee. From 1967, First Secretary of the Ararat District Armenian Communist Party. From 1970, Chairman of the Armenian Republic Council of Ministers State Committee. From 1978, Chairman of the Armenian Republic State Committee for Television and Radio. From 1988, Information Agency Director of the Armenian Republic Council of Ministers. From January 1990, Secretary of the Armenian Central Committee; First Secretary of the Yerevan City Committee of the Armenian Communist Party. From November 1990, First Secretary of the Armenian Central Committee. From 1990, member of the Politburo; member of the Central Committee.
HONORS/AWARDS: Order of the Red Banner of Labor; Order of the Badge of Honor; medals.
FAMILY: Widower.
ADDRESS/TELEPHONE: 19 Marshala Bagramyana Street, Yerevan, 375016. 52–0201 (office).

Polenov, Fyodor Dmitryevich
POSITION: Chairman of the Russian Federation Supreme Soviet Committee on Culture; Central Council Chairman of the All-Russia Society for the

Preservation of Historical and Cultural Monuments
BIRTHPLACE/DATE: Moscow, June 21, 1929
NATIONALITY: Russian
CAREER: From 1951, served in the navy. From 1962 to 1990, Director of the V.D. Polenov State Museum-Preserve in Zakoiski district, Moscow region. From 1990, Commission Chairman of the Russian Federation Supreme Soviet's Council of the Republic. From 1990, Russian Federation People's Deputy.
HONORS/AWARDS: Medal for Service in Battle; four other medals.
FAMILY: Married with two children.
ADDRESS/TELEPHONE: 2 Schuseva Street, Flat #39, Moscow.

Politkovsky, Aleksandr Vladimirovich
POSITION: Director-General of the Vzglyad (Glance) Joint-Stock Company
BIRTHPLACE/DATE: Moscow, 1953
NATIONALITY: Russian
CAREER: From 1979 to 1985, worked at the Sports Department of the State Committee for Television and Radio. From 1985 to 1991, worked at the Department for Youth. People's Deputy. Member of the Russian Federation Supreme Soviet Committee for Human Rights. Member of the Supreme Soviet Council of Nationalities.
FAMILY: Married with two children.
ADDRESS/TELEPHONE: 24 Herzena Street, Flat #2, Moscow, 103009. 290–3428.

Polosin, Vyacheslav Sergeyevich
POSITION: Presidium Member of the Russian Federation Supreme Soviet; Chairman of the Russian Federation Supreme Soviet Committee for Freedom of Conscience, Faith, Mercy, and Charity
BIRTHPLACE/DATE: Moscow, 1956
NATIONALITY: Russian
EDUCATION: From 1981 to 1983, student at the Theological Seminary in Zagorsk.
CAREER: From 1978 to 1979, worked at the USSR Goskino (State Cinematography Administration). From 1980 to 1981, Reciter in an Orthodox Temple. From 1983 to 1985, Priest in Dushanbe. From 1985 to 1988, Translator. From 1988 to 1991, Priest in Obninsk; elected Kaluga Region People's Deputy. Member of the Russian Christian-Democratic Movement. Russian Federation People's Deputy.
FAMILY: Married.
ADDRESS/TELEPHONE: 4 Ulitsa 1905 Goda Street, Flat #89, Moscow; 2 Krasnopresnenskaya Naberezhnaya, Moscow. 205–5305 (office).

Polozkov, Ivan Kuzmich
POSITION: Russian Federation People's Deputy; member of the Otchizna (Fatherland) Faction
BIRTHPLACE/DATE: Lestch-Plota village, Kursk region, February 16, 1935
NATIONALITY: Russian
EDUCATION: From 1959, student at the Higher Komsomol School of the Komsomol Central Committee. From 1978, student at the Academy of Social Sciences of the Central Committee.
CAREER: From 1954 to 1957, served in the army. From 1957, Collective Farm Worker in Kursk region; Chairman of the District Physical Education and Sports Committee. From 1959, Komsomol Functionary. From 1962, Communist Party Functionary. From 1969, Deputy Department Head of the Kursk Regional Party Committee. From 1975, Instructor of the Central Committee's Department of Party Work Organization. From 1978, worked at the Central Committee. From 1983, Secretary of the Krasnodar Region Party Committee. From 1984, Section Head of the Central Committee's Department of Party Work Organization. From 1985, First Secretary of the Krasnodar Region Party Committee. From 1990, Chairman of the Krasnodar Region Council of People's Deputies. From June 1990 to August 1991, First Secretary of the Russian Federation Central Committee. From July 1990 to 1991, member of the Politburo. From 1991, member of the Otchizna Faction. Deputy of the USSR Supreme Soviet of the Eleventh Convocation. From 1989 to 1990, USSR People's Deputy. From 1990, Russian Federation People's Deputy. From 1958 to 1991, member of the Communist Party.
HONORS/AWARDS: Order of the People's Friendship; Order of the Badge of Honor; medals.
FAMILY: Married with a daughter.
ADDRESS/TELEPHONE: 2 Molodogvardeyskaya, Flat #23, Moscow, 121467. 144–3684 (home).

Poltoranin, Mikhail Nikiforovich

POSITION: Head of the Federal Information Center of Russia
BIRTHPLACE/DATE: Leninogorsk, Eastern Kazakhstan, November 22, 1939
NATIONALITY: Russian
CAREER: Concrete worker at the Bratsk Hydro-Electric Power Station; served in the army; Correspondent for *Rudny Altai* (*Ore Altai*) and *Kazakhstanskaya Pravda* (*Kazakhstan Truth*) newspapers; Executive Secretary of *Kazakhstanskaya Pravda*. From 1975 to 1986, worked at *Pravda* (*Truth*) newspaper. From 1986 to 1987, Editor in Chief of *Moskovskaya Pravda* (*Moscow Truth*) newspaper. From 1988, Political Analyst of Novosti (News) Press Agency (APN). Board Secretary of the USSR Journalists' Union. From 1990, Russian Federation Minister of Press and Mass Media. Member of the USSR Supreme Soviet Committee for Problems of Glasnost and the Rights of Citizens. From February 1992, Deputy Chairman of the Russian Federation Government; Vice Premier. From 1989 to 1992, USSR People's Deputy.
FAMILY: Married with two sons.
ADDRESS/TELEPHONE: 5 Strastnoi Boulevard, Moscow, 101409. 205–5305 (office).

Ponomarev, Lev Aleksandrovich

POSITION: Chairman of the Subcommittee for Liaison with Public Organizations and Movements
BIRTHPLACE/DATE: Tomsk, September 2, 1941
NATIONALITY: Russian
EDUCATION: Doctor of Physics and Mathematics.
CAREER: From 1969 to 1990, Leading Researcher at the Institute of Theoretical and Experimental Physics. Initiator of the Memorial Society Foundation. Organizer of the Moscow Association of Voters and the Democratic Russia Movement. Empowered by A.D. Sakharov during the USSR People's Deputies elections; Co-Chairman of the Live Ring Movement. Member of the Russian Federation Supreme Soviet Glasnost Committee. From December 1990, Coordinating Council Co-Chairman of the Democratic Russia Movement. Russian Federation People's Deputy.
MAJOR WORKS: Scientific and socio-political publications for domestic and foreign mass media.
FAMILY: Married with four children.
ADDRESS/TELEPHONE: 2 Krasnopresnenskaya Naberezhnaya, Moscow. 205–5482 (office).

Popov, Gavril Kharitonovich

POSITION: Member of the Presidential Consultative Council; Chairman of the Russian Democratic Reforms Movement
BIRTHPLACE/DATE: Moscow, October 31, 1936
NATIONALITY: Greek
CAREER: From 1960, Secretary of Moscow State University's Komsomol Committee. From 1963 to 1988, worked at Moscow State University. From 1988 to 1990, Editor in Chief of *Voprosy Ekonomiki* (*Questions of Economics*) magazine. From 1989 to 1990, President of the Young Heads of Enterprises Association. From April 1990, Chairman of the Moscow City Council of People's Deputies. From June 1991 to 1992, Mayor of Moscow. From August 1991, member of the Political Council of the Russian Democratic Reforms Movement. From December 1991, Co-Chairman, and from February 1992, Chairman of the Russian Democratic Reforms Movement. From September 1991 to December 1991, member of the Political Consultative Council of the USSR President. From August 1991, Representative of the Russian Federation President in Moscow and Moscow region. From November 1991, President of the International American University. From 1989 to 1992, USSR People's Deputy. From 1959 to 1990, member of the Communist Party.
MAJOR WORKS: More than 100 scientific works. *Efficient Management; Luster and Poverty of the Administrative System.*
HONORS/AWARDS: M.V. Lomonosov Prize.
FAMILY: Married with two children.
ADDRESS/TELEPHONE: 36 Novy Arbat Street, Moscow, 121205. 414–8204 (office).

Popov, Oleg Georgyevich

POSITION: Head of the Moscow Government Glavsnab (Central Directorate of Supplies)
BIRTHPLACE/DATE: Moscow, 1938
NATIONALITY: Russian
CAREER: To 1991, Industrial Department Engineer of Moscow's Central Directorate of Construction Materials Industry. Department Head; Deputy Head of Moscow's Directorate of Building Materi-

als Industry; Head of Glavsnab. From 1991, Deputy Premier, Deputy Chairman, Chairman of the Moscow Committee of Industry and Material Resources.
FAMILY: Married with two children.
ADDRESS/TELEPHONE: 13 Tverskaya Street, Moscow. 271–0680 (receptionist); 272–0477 (aide).

Poptsov, Oleg Maksimovich
POSITION: President of the Russian Television and Radio Company
BIRTHPLACE/DATE: Leningrad, 1934
NATIONALITY: Russian
CAREER: First Secretary of the Leningrad Regional Komsomol Committee; worked for the Komsomol Central Committee. From 1968 to 1990, First Deputy Editor in Chief of *Moskovskiye Novosti* (*Moscow News*) newspaper; Editor in Chief of *Selskaya Molodezhr* (*Country Youth*) magazine. From 1990, Head of the Russian Television and Radio Company. Russian Federation People's Deputy. To 1991, member of the Communist Party.
MAJOR WORKS: Twelve books, including *Nominative Case*; *Orpheus Does Not Bring Happiness.*
HONORS/AWARDS: Lenin Komsomol Prize; Order of the Eagle, First Class.
FAMILY: Married with two daughters.
ADDRESS/TELEPHONE: 19/21 Pyataya Yamskogo Polya Street, Moscow, 125124. 214–4978 (office).

Posadskaya, Anastasia Ivanovna
POSITION: Head of the Gender Studies Center at the Institute of Socio-Economic Population Problems of the Russian Academy of Sciences
BIRTHPLACE/DATE: Moscow, 1958
NATIONALITY: Lithuanian
EDUCATION: Doctor of Economics.
CAREER: From 1985 to 1988, Lecturer. From 1988 to 1990, Junior Researcher, Researcher, Senior Researcher at the Gender Studies Center of the Institute of Socio-Economic Population Problems of the Russian Academy of Sciences.
FAMILY: Married with a child.
ADDRESS/TELEPHONE: 27 Krasikova Street, Moscow, 117218. 124–6185 (office); 449–1904 (home).

Potapenko, Sergey Mikhailovich
POSITION: Vice President of the Russian Union of Young Entrepreneurs
BIRTHPLACE/DATE: Novosibirsk region, 1956
NATIONALITY: Russian
CAREER: Engineer at the Gidrotyumenneftegaz (Tyumen Oil and Gas) Research Institute; Foreman and Brigade Leader at the Tyumen Region Pipeline Construction. To 1991, Secretary of Economics and Entrepreneurship at the Russian Federation Komsomol Central Committee. From 1990, Co-Chairman of the Russian Union of Young Entrepreneurs.
MAJOR WORKS: Publications on labor resources, general economics, and small business.
FAMILY: Married with a daughter.
ADDRESS/TELEPHONE: 4 Lutchnikov Pereulok, Moscow; 3/13 Moroseika Street, 102000. 206–8553 (office; fax at night).

Potapov, Aleksandr Serafimovich
POSITION: Editor in Chief of *Trud* (*Labor*) newspaper; Chairman of the Society for Friendship with Austria
BIRTHPLACE/DATE: Oktyabrskote village, Kharkov region, February 6, 1936
NATIONALITY: Russian
EDUCATION: From 1978 to 1981, postgraduate student in the Scientific Communism Division at the Central Committee's Academy of Social Sciences.
CAREER: From 1958 to 1960, Writer for *Leninskaya Smena* (*Lenin's Successors*) newspaper in Belgorod; from 1960 to 1964, Propaganda Department Head; from 1964 to 1966, Students Department Head. From 1966 to 1973, Cultural Department Head; Deputy Editor of *Belgorodskaya Pravda* (*Belgorod Truth*) regional newspaper. From 1973 to 1975, Propaganda and Agitation Department Head of the Byelorussian Regional Party Committee. From 1975 to 1978, Instructor of the Propaganda Department of the Central Committee. From 1981 to 1985, Instructor of the Propaganda Department of the Central Committee. From 1989 to 1992, USSR People's Deputy.
HONORS/AWARDS: Order of the Badge of Honor; Order of the Red Banner of Labor.
FAMILY: Married with a son.

ADDRESS/TELEPHONE: 4 Nastasyinski Pereulok, Moscow, 103792 GSP. 299–3906 (office).

Pozdnyak, Zenon Stanislavovich

POSITION: Chairman of the Byelorussian Popular Front
BIRTHPLACE/DATE: Vilensk territory, Western Byelorussia (now Lithuania), 1944
CAREER: From 1976, Senior Researcher at the Byelorussian Republic Institute of History. From October 1988, Leader of the Byelorussian Popular Front. Chairman of Parliamentary Opposition at the Byelorussian Republic Supreme Soviet. Byelorussian Republic People's Deputy.
FAMILY: Single.
ADDRESS/TELEPHONE: 41 Gerasimenko Street, Flat #185, Minsk. 29–6612; 32–5751; 39–5984 (deputy).

Pozner, Vladimir Vladimirovich

POSITION: Journalist; Co-host with Phil Donahue of a weekly TV program in the United States
BIRTHPLACE/DATE: Paris, 1934
CAREER: In 1959, invited to work with S.Y. Marshak as Literary Secretary. From 1961 to 1967, Senior Editor of the North American Periodicals Department; Department Head of Novosti (News) Press Agency (APN); Executive Secretary of *Soviet Life* (an APN publication). From 1967 to 1969, Executive Secretary of *Sputnik* (*Companion*) magazine. From 1969 to 1970, worked at the Central Department of Broadcasting for the United States and Great Britain. From 1970 to 1986, Commentator (for foreign countries) of the USSR State Committee for Television and Radio. From 1986 to April 1991, Political Analyst of Central Television and Radio.
FAMILY: Married with a son.
TELEPHONE: 201–7161 (home).

Prasolov, Oleg Fyodorovich

POSITION: Chairman of the Roskomagentstvo Russian Commercial Agency
BIRTHPLACE/DATE: Temashevsk, Krasnodar region, 1946
CAREER: From 1970 to 1980, Engineer of the All-Union Litsenztorg (Licensed Trade) Foreign Trade Association. From 1980 to 1983, member of the USSR Trade Delegation to Sweden. From 1983 to 1989, Director of the Litsenznauka (Licensed Science) Firm. From 1989 to 1990, Deputy Chairman of the Rosvneshtorg Foreign Trade Association.
FAMILY: Married with two children.
ADDRESS/TELEPHONE: 5 Yaroslavskoye Chaussée, Moscow, 129348. 182–2117; 182–3329 (office); Fax: 188–9674.

Pravotorov, Vladimir Fyodorovich

POSITION: Editor in Chief of *Nauka i Religiya* (*Science and Religion*) magazine
BIRTHPLACE/DATE: Rostov-on-Don, 1934
NATIONALITY: Russian
CAREER: Teacher at a secondary school; Worker at the Rostselmash (Rostov Agricultural Machinery) Plant; worked at the District and City Party Committee, and at the Central Committee's Propaganda Department.
MAJOR WORKS: Scientific works on theories of mass media and socio-economic relations.
FAMILY: Married with a daughter.
ADDRESS/TELEPHONE: 8 Tovarishcheski Pereulok, Moscow, 109004. 272–4986 (office); 272–2557.

Primakov, Yevgeni Maksimovich

POSITION: Director of the Foreign Intelligence Service of the Russian Federation; Academician of the Russian Academy of Sciences
BIRTHPLACE/DATE: Kiev, Ukraine, October 29, 1929
NATIONALITY: Russian
EDUCATION: Graduated in 1953 from the Moscow Institute of Oriental Studies; in 1956, from postgraduate study at Moscow State University. Doctor of Economics; Professor.
CAREER: From 1953 to 1956, Correspondent for the State Television and Radio Broadcasting Committee (Gosteleradio) of the USSR Council of Ministers. From 1956 to 1960, Editor, Editor in Chief of an Editorial Board of the Gosteleradio Main Administration for Radio Broadcasting. From 1960 to 1962, Deputy Editor in Chief of the Gosteleradio Main Editorial Board. From 1959, member of the Communist Party. From 1962 to 1970,

Analyst, Deputy Editor of the Asia and Africa Department, Middle East Correspondent for *Pravda* (*Truth*) newspaper. From 1970 to 1977, Deputy Director of the USSR Academy of Sciences' Institute of the World Economy and International Relations. From 1974 to 1979, Corresponding Member of the USSR Academy of Sciences. From 1977 to 1985, Director of the Institute of Oriental Studies of the USSR Academy of Sciences. From 1979, Academician of the USSR Academy of Sciences' Economics Department. From 1981 to 1985, Chairman of the All-Union Association of Orientalists. From 1983 to 1989, Board Member of the UN University. From 1985 to 1989, Director of the World Economy and International Relations Institute of the USSR Academy of Sciences. From 1988 to 1989, Academician-Secretary of the World Economy and International Relations Department of the USSR Academy of Sciences; Presidium Member of the USSR Academy of Sciences; Chairman of the Soviet National Committee for Asian-Pacific Economic Cooperation; Member of the Rome Club. From 1986 to 1989, Alternate Member of the Central Committee. From 1988, member of the Central Committee Commission for International Policy. From April 1989, member of the Central Committee. From June 1989 to September 1990, Chairman of the USSR Supreme Soviet Council of the Union. Delegate to the Twenty-Seventh Communist Party Congress and the Nineteenth All-Union Communist Party Conference. Attended the September 1989 Central Committee Plenum; elected Alternate Member of the Politburo. Former member of the USSR Presidential Council. In September 1991, appointed Chief of the First Main Directorate of the USSR KGB (now the Central Intelligence Service). Elected USSR People's Deputy. In 1991, member of the USSR Security Council.
MAJOR WORKS: *Countries of Arabia and Colonialism; Egypt: Time of President Nasser.*
HONORS/AWARDS: Order of the Red Banner of Labor; State Prize (1980); Order of the People's Friendship (1979); Order of the Badge of Honor; International Nasser Prize (1975); International Avicenna Prize (1983); USSR State Prize; medals.
FAMILY: Widower with a daughter.
ADDRESS/TELEPHONE: 11 Kolpachny Pereulok, Moscow, 101100. 923–6213 (press secretary).

Pristavkin, Anatoli Ignatyevich
POSITION: Writer; Secretary of the April Writers' Association
BIRTHPLACE/DATE: Lyubertsy, Moscow region, 1931
NATIONALITY: Russian
CAREER: From 1946 to 1952, worked at the Zhukovski Research Institute Airfield. From 1952 to 1954, served in the army. In the early 1960s, worked at the Bratsk Hydroelectric Power Station; Correspondent for *Po Sibiri* (*Around Siberia*) newspaper. From 1961 to 1991, member of the Confederation of Writers' Unions (formerly the USSR Writers' Union). From 1981, Lecturer at the Moscow Gorky Literary Institute. From 1989, Editor in Chief of the *April* Anthology and Co-Chairman of the April Writers' Association.
MAJOR WORKS: *Hard Childhood; Dove; Lyrical Book; Angara-River.* Story: "Golden Cloudlet Spent the Night" (1981).
HONORS/AWARDS: USSR State Prize.
FAMILY: Married with three children.
ADDRESS/TELEPHONE: 8 Usiyevicha Street, Flat #22, Moscow, 125319. 152–5503 (home).

Pritula, Yuri Nikolayevich
POSITION: Prefect of the Southwestern Region of Moscow City
BIRTHPLACE/DATE: Druzhinino station, Nizhny-Serginsk district, Sverdlovsk region, December 28, 1941
NATIONALITY: Ukrainian
CAREER: From 1958 to 1967, Metalworker, Shop Foreman of the Steam-Locomotive-Building Works. From 1967 to 1975, worked at the Ministry of Electrotechnical Industry. From 1975 to 1989, Deputy Director-General of the Moscow Electropromremont (Electrical Industry Repairs) Industrial Association. From 1989 to 1991, Executive Committee Chairman of the Zheleznodorozhny District Council of People's Deputies. From January 1992, member of the Moscow Government.
FAMILY: Married with two children.
ADDRESS/TELEPHONE: 28 Sevastopolski Prospekt, Building 4, Moscow, 113209. 128–2722 (office).

Prokhanov, Aleksandr Andreyevich
POSITION: Editor in Chief of *Den* (*Day*) newspaper
BIRTHPLACE/DATE: Tbilisi, 1938
CAREER: From 1960 to 1988, Novelist; Writer for *Pravda* (*Truth*) and *Literaturnaya Rossiya* (*Literary Russia*) newspapers. From 1989 to 1991, Editor in Chief of *Sovietskaya Literatura* (*Soviet literature*) magazine. Member of the Confederation of Writers' Unions; Secretary of the Confederation of Writers' Unions.
MAJOR WORKS: *Eternal City; Place of Action; Tree in the Center of Kabul; The Third Toast* (1991); *Angel Flew By* (1991).
HONORS/AWARDS: Order of the Red Banner of Labor; Order of the People's Friendship; Order of the Badge of Honor.
FAMILY: Married with three children.
ADDRESS/TELEPHONE: 30 Tsvetnoi Boulevard, Moscow, 103661. 200–3598 (office).

Prokhorov, Aleksandr Mikhailovich
POSITION: Academician of the Russian Academy of Sciences (RAN); Director of the Institute of General Physics of RAN
BIRTHPLACE/DATE: Australia, June 28, 1916
NATIONALITY: Russian
EDUCATION: Doctor of Physics and Mathematics; Professor.
CAREER: From 1941 to 1944, served in the army. From 1946, worked at the Physics Institute of the USSR Academy of Sciences (USSR AN); from 1954, Laboratory Head; from 1968, Deputy Director. From 1959, Professor at Moscow State University. From 1966, Academician of the USSR Academy of Sciences (USSR AN). From 1969, Editor in Chief of the *Big Soviet Encyclopaedia*. From 1971, Department Head of the Moscow Physics and Technical Institute. From 1973 to December 1991, Academician-Secretary of the General Physics and Astronomy Branch of the USSR AN. From 1982, Director of the Institute of General Physics of the USSR AN; President of the Joint Presidium of Russian Academies. From 1969 to 1991, member of the Communist Party.
MAJOR WORKS: Created with N.G. Basov the first quantum generator-maser. Works on paramagnetic masers, open resonators, nonline optics, and the interaction of powerful laser radiation with substances.
HONORS/AWARDS: Prize of Lenin (1959); Hero of Socialist Labor (1969, 1986); Nobel Prize with N.G. Basov and C. Townos (1964).
FAMILY: Married with a child.
ADDRESS/TELEPHONE: 14 Leninsky Prospekt, 38 Ulitsa Vavilova, GSP–1, Moscow, B–71, 117901. 135–2366 (office).

Prokhovnik, Aleksandr Borisovich
POSITION: Vice President of the Biznes (Business) Commercial Tourist Joint-Stock Company
BIRTHPLACE/DATE: Moscow, 1950
NATIONALITY: Russian
CAREER: From 1975 to 1979, Aide to the Sputnik Bureau of International Youth Tourism. In 1980, Protocol Department Head of the Olympics–80 Coordinating Committee. From 1980 to 1990, Deputy Foreign Relations Department Head of different branches of the Industrial Center for Computer Engineering and Information Science. From 1990 to 1991, Leading Specialist at Sputnik.
FAMILY: Married with two children.
ADDRESS/TELEPHONE: 71 Izmaylovskoye Chaussée, Moscow, 105613. 166–6755; 166–5219 (office).

Prokofyev, Yuri Anatolyevich
POSITION: Former First Secretary of the Moscow City Communist Party; former member of the Politburo
BIRTHPLACE/DATE: Muinake, Kara-Kalpak Republic, February 20, 1939
NATIONALITY: Russian
EDUCATION: Doctor of Economics.
CAREER: From 1968, Party Functionary in Moscow. From 1985, Department Head of the Moscow City Communist Party. From 1986, Secretary of the Moscow City Executive Committee. From 1988, Secretary, Second Secretary, and from 1989, First Secretary of the Moscow City Communist Party. From 1990, member of the Communist Party of the Central Committee and Politburo. From 1960 to 1991, member of the Communist Party.
HONORS/AWARDS: Government awards.
FAMILY: Married.

ADDRESS/TELEPHONE: 6 Staraya Ploschad, Moscow, 103070. 222–9311; 222–9525.

Proshechkin, Yevgeni Victorovich

POSITION: Chairman of the Moscow Anti-Fascist Center; Coordinating Committee Member of the Moscow and Republican Demokraticheskaya Rossiya (Democratic Russia) Movement
BIRTHPLACE/DATE: Riga, 1957
NATIONALITY: Russian
CAREER: From 1989 to 1990, Organizing Committee Member of the Democratic Russia Movement. In 1991, elected Deputy of Tushinsky District Council. In July 1991, elected Co-Chairman of the Democratic Russia Union.
FAMILY: Married with a daughter.
ADDRESS/TELEPHONE: 17 Ulitsa Geroyev Panfilovtsev Street, Building 4, Flat #62, Moscow, 123480. 496–3580 (home); 458–7461 (office).

Prostyakov, Igor Ignatyevich

POSITION: Former Business-Administrator of the USSR Council of Ministers
BIRTHPLACE/DATE: Krasnodar, 1941
NATIONALITY: Russian
EDUCATION: Doctor of Economics.
CAREER: From 1965, held various positions at the USSR State Planning Committee. From 1978 to 1982, Assistant to the Chairman of the USSR Council of Ministers. From 1982 to 1987, Administrative Directorate Head of the USSR Council of Ministers. From 1987, First Deputy Chairman of the USSR Council of Ministers' Committee for Social Development; Chairman of the Scientific Council. From 1991 to 1992, Business-Administrator of the USSR Council of Ministers, USSR Minister.

Prudnikov, Victor Alekseyevich

POSITION: Commander in Chief of the Air Defense Forces; Colonel-General of the Air Forces
BIRTHPLACE/DATE: Rostov-on-Don, February 4, 1939
NATIONALITY: Russian
CAREER: From 1956, served in the Armed Forces; Division Commander; Army Commander. From 1989, Commander of the Moscow Air Defense District. From September 1991, Commander in Chief of the Air Defense Forces, Deputy USSR Defense Minister. From March 1992, Commander of the Air Defense Forces of the Confederation of Independent States Unified Armed Forces. From August 1992, Commander in Chief of the Russian Federation Air Defense Forces. From 1960 to 1991, member of the Communist Party.
HONORS/AWARDS: Order of the Red Star; Order for Service to the Motherland in the USSR Armed Forces.
FAMILY: Married with two sons.
ADDRESS/TELEPHONE: Commander in Chief of the Air Defense Forces, Moscow, K–160, 103160. 525–8276 (Secretariat); 528–8213; 525–9050.

Pumpyansky, Aleksandr Borisovich

POSITION: Editor in Chief of *Novoye Vremya* (*New Time*) magazine
BIRTHPLACE/DATE: Moscow, December 18, 1940
CAREER: From 1962 to 1963, Writer for *Rovesnik* (*Contemporary*) magazine. From 1963 to 1978, Writer, Deputy Editor of the International Department, Executive Secretary of *Komsomolskaya Pravda* (*Komsomol Truth*) newspaper; from 1975 to 1976, New York Correspondent. From 1978 to 1986, Deputy Editor in Chief of *Moskovskiye Novosti* (*Moscow News*) newspaper; from 1986 to 1991, Deputy Editor in Chief. From 1991, member of the Council on Foreign Policy.
MAJOR WORKS: *Happening on Tuesdays; Incident in the Vicinity of Golgotha.* Documentary films: *Romance of the Century; Peace March.*
HONORS/AWARDS: Vorovski Prize; International Press Institute Prize; Inter-Press Service Prize.
FAMILY: Divorced with a daughter.
ADDRESS/TELEPHONE: *Novoye Vremya* Editorial Office, Pushkinskaya Ploschad, GSP Moscow K–6, 103782. 209–0128 (office).

Pushkarev, Victor Yakovlevich

POSITION: Editor in Chief of *Torgovaya Gazeta* (*Trade Newspaper*); member of the Confederation of Journalists' Unions
BIRTHPLACE/DATE: Serebryannye Prudy, Moscow region, March 21, 1924
NATIONALITY: Russian
CAREER: From 1947 to 1960, Writer, Editor, Deputy Editor in Chief of the regional paper in

Serebryannye Prudy. From 1960 to 1964, Correspondent, Department Head, Deputy Editor in Chief of the Moscow *Leninskoye Znamya* (*Lenin's Banner*). From 1964 to 1967, worked at the Central Committee's Propaganda Department. From 1967 to 1973, Deputy Editor in Chief of *Sovietskaya Rossiya* (*Soviet Russia*) newspaper.
HONORS/AWARDS: Order of the Red Banner of Labor; Order of the Patriotic War; Order of the People's Friendship; Order of the Badge of Honor; Russian Federation Honored Worker of Culture.
FAMILY: Married with two children and three grandchildren.
ADDRESS/TELEPHONE: 14 Razina Street, Moscow, 103687. 298–4451 (office).

Pyadyshev, Boris Dmitryevich

POSITION: Editor in Chief of *Mezhdunarodnaya Zhizn* (*International Affairs*) magazine; member of the Journalists' Union; Corresponding Member of the Russian Academy of Arts; Board Member of the Russian Federation Foreign Ministry; Ambassador Extraordinary and Plenipotentiary
BIRTHPLACE/DATE: Saratov, 1932
EDUCATION: Doctor of History.
CAREER: From 1956 to 1968, worked from Attaché to Deputy Head of the Press Department of the USSR Foreign Ministry. From 1968 to 1971, Counsellor at the USSR Embassy in London. From 1971 to 1974, Deputy Head of the Press Department of the USSR Foreign Ministry. In 1974, Consultant to the International Department of the Central Committee. From 1974 to 1975, Assistant to the USSR Council of Ministers Chairman on Foreign Policy Problems. From 1975 to 1983, Minister-Counsellor at the USSR Embassy in Bulgaria. From 1983 to 1986, Deputy Head of the U.S. Department of the USSR Foreign Ministry. From 1986 to 1988, First Deputy Head of the Information Directorate of the USSR Foreign Ministry.
MAJOR WORKS: More than twenty monographs on international relations and American studies. *Russia and the World: New Views on Russian Foreign Policy* (Carol Publishing, New York, 1991).
FAMILY: Married with two children.
ADDRESS/TELEPHONE: 14 Gorokhovski Pereulok, Moscow, 103064. 265–3781 (office).

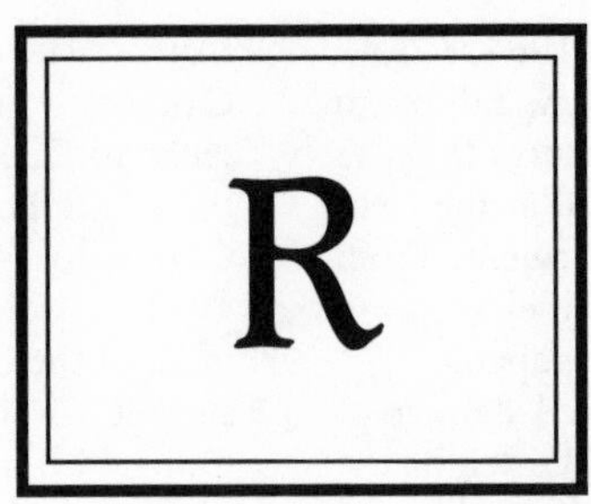

Radugin, Nikolay Petrovich
POSITION: Assistant to the Russian Federation Vice President
BIRTHPLACE/DATE: Martynovka village, Nikolayevsky district, Moscow region, 1930
EDUCATION: From 1968 to 1970, studied at the Higher Party School of the Central Committee. Doctor of Economics.
CAREER: From 1960 to 1962, Director of the Stenkino State Farm in Ryazan region. From 1962 to 1968, Head of the Regional Directorate of Agriculture and Melioration; Deputy Chairman of the Ryazan Regional Executive Committee. From 1970 to 1988, Head of the Agriculture and Melioration Department of the Russian Federation Supreme Soviet. From 1988 to 1992, Chief Specialist of the Russian Federation Supreme Soviet Committee on Agricultural Problems.
MAJOR WORKS: Scientific articles and books on agriculture. *The Village Will Be Revived by an Owner* (1992).
HONORS/AWARDS: Order of the Red Banner of Labor; Order of the Badge of Honor.
FAMILY: Married with a daughter and a son.
ADDRESS/TELEPHONE: 8 Bezbozhny Pereulok, Flat #64, Moscow, 129010. 224–0117 (office).

Radzinsky, Edvard Stanislavovich
POSITION: Playwright
BIRTHPLACE/DATE: Moscow, 1936
CAREER: From 1965, member of the USSR Writers' Union. From December 1991, member of the Russian Writers' Union and the Union of Film Makers.
MAJOR WORKS: Plays: *Conversations with Sokrat* (1975); *Lunin, or Death of Jacques* (1979); *Theater in Times of Neron and Seneka* (1982). Novels: *The Last of the House of Romanovs* (1990); *Our Decameron* (1990).
FAMILY: Divorced.
ADDRESS/TELEPHONE: 8 Usiyevicha Street, Flat #96, Moscow, 125319. 155–7531 (home).

Ragulin, Aleksandr Pavlovich
POSITION: Former Ice Hockey Champion
BIRTHPLACE/DATE: Moscow, 1941
NATIONALITY: Russian
CAREER: Played for the Soviet Army Hockey Club; many-time USSR Champion. In 1961, Bronze Prize winner of the World Championship. From 1963 to 1970 and in 1973, European Champion. In 1961, 1968, and 1972, Silver Prize winner of the European Championship. From 1963 to 1971, and in 1973, World Champion. From 1964 to 1968, and in 1972, Winter Olympic Ice Hockey Champion. In 1972, World Championship Silver Prize winner. Coached Ice Hockey Team of the Novosibirsk SK (Sports Club). USSR Honored Master of Sports (ice hockey).
FAMILY: Married.
TELEPHONE: 271–1531.

Rakhimbayev, Gairat Faizullayevich
POSITION: Russian Federation Trade Representative to Sweden
BIRTHPLACE/DATE: 1929
CAREER: From 1966 to 1970, Head of the Machines and Equipment Department of the USSR Trade Delegation to Sweden; Deputy Chairman, Chairman, Director-General of the Prommashim-

port (Industrial Machinery Import) Foreign Trade Association. From 1982 to 1986, USSR Trade Representative to Sweden. From 1986, USSR Deputy Foreign Trade Minister; USSR Deputy Minister of Foreign Economic Relations; Head of the USSR Ministry of Foreign Economic Relations (MVES) Central Directorate of Machine and Equipment Import and Export.
ADDRESS/TELEPHONE: 32/34 Smolenskaya-Sennaya Ploschad, Moscow, 121200. 244–2450; 244–2301 (MVES).

Rakitov, Anatoli Ilyich
POSITION: Head of the Analytical Information Center of the Russian Federation President; Director-General of the Institute of the Informatization of Society and the Development of Science
BIRTHPLACE/DATE: Moscow, 1928
EDUCATION: Doctor of Philosophy; Professor.

Rasputin, Valentin Grigoryevich
POSITION: Writer
BIRTHPLACE/DATE: Ust-Uda village, Irkutsk region (Siberia), 1937
NATIONALITY: Russian
EDUCATION: Graduated in 1959 from the History and Philology Department at Irkutsk State University.
CAREER: Member of the USSR Writers' Union; Board Secretary of the USSR and Russian Federation Writers' Unions. Initiator of movements to preserve Baikal Lake and increase the natural resources of Siberia, the Far East, and other regions. USSR People's Deputy; member of the USSR Supreme Soviet Committee for Ecology and the Rational Use of Natural Resources. In 1990, member of the USSR Presidential Council.
MAJOR WORKS: *Money for Maria* (1967); *Live and Remember* (1974); *Parting with Matera* (1976); *The Fire* (1985).
HONORS/AWARDS: USSR State Prize (1987); Hero of Socialist Labor.
FAMILY: Married with children.
ADDRESS/TELEPHONE: 67 Pyataya Ulitsa Armii Street, Flat #68, Irkutsk, 664000. 4–7100.

Raykin, Konstantin Arkadyevich
POSITION: Art Director and Producer of the A.I. Raykin Satirikon Theater
BIRTHPLACE/DATE: Leningrad, 1950
CAREER: From 1971 to 1983, Actor of the Moscow Sovremennik Theater. From 1983 to 1987, Actor of the State Theater of Miniatures. Russian Federation Honored Artist.
MAJOR WORKS: *What About Our Life; Maugli; Hercules and Aegean Stables.*
HONORS/AWARDS: Lenin Komsomol Prize.
FAMILY: Married with a daughter.
ADDRESS/TELEPHONE: 8 Sheremetyevskaya Street, Moscow. 218–1019 (secretary).

Razov, Sergey Sergeyevich
POSITION: Russian Ambassador to Mongolia; Ambassador Extraordinary and Plenipotentiary
BIRTHPLACE/DATE: 1953
NATIONALITY: Russian
EDUCATION: Doctor of Economics.
CAREER: From 1975 to 1979, USSR Trade Delegate to the People's Republic of China. From 1979 to 1990, worked at the International Department of the Central Committee. From 1990 to 1991, Head of the Socialist Countries of Asia Directorate of the USSR Foreign Ministry. From 1991 to 1992, Head of the Far East and Indo-China Directorate of the USSR Foreign Ministry.
FAMILY: Married.
ADDRESS/TELEPHONE: Ulan Bator Khot, Enkh Taivny Gudamzh "A6." 2–7506; 2–7071.

Repchenko, Nikolay Mikhailovich
POSITION: Board Chairman of the Rosbiznesbank Russian Commercial Bank
BIRTHPLACE/DATE: Boguchar, Voronezh region, 1948
NATIONALITY: Russian
CAREER: From 1977 to 1978, Inspector of the USSR Finance Ministry. From 1981 to 1985, Leading Financier, Senior Legal Advisor of the Stroimashzagranpostavka (Foreign Supply of Construction Equipment) All-Union Association. From 1985 to 1990, Leading Specialist, Chief Legal Advisor of the USSR Vneshekonombank (Foreign Economic Bank).
FAMILY: Married with a son.
ADDRESS/TELEPHONE: 9 Trekhprudny Pereulok, Moscow, 103001. 299–5771 (office).

Reshetov, Yuri Aleksandrovich

POSITION: Russian Member of the UN Committee for the Elimination of Racial Discrimination; Russian Federation Ambassador to Iceland; Ambassador Extraordinary and Plenipotentiary

BIRTHPLACE/DATE: Nizhny Novgorod, January 10, 1935

NATIONALITY: Russian

EDUCATION: From 1969 to 1971, student at the Higher Diplomatic School of the USSR Foreign Ministry. Doctor of Philosophy; Doctor of Law.

CAREER: From 1959 to 1963, Interpreter at the USSR Embassy in Iceland. From 1963 to 1964, Aide to the Department of Scandinavian Countries. From 1964, Senior Aide to the Department of Operative Information (OOI). From 1964 to 1966, Attaché at the USSR Embassy in Iceland. From 1966 to 1968, Attaché at the USSR Embassy in Denmark. From 1968 to 1969, Third Secretary of the OOI. From 1971 to 1972, Second Secretary of the Department of International Economic Organizations of the USSR Foreign Ministry. From 1972 to 1973, Second Secretary of the Legal and Treaties Department (DPO). From 1973 to 1975, First Secretary of DPO. From 1975 to 1980, Head of the Department to Prevent Discrimination and Protect Minorities of the Human Rights Department at the UN Secretariat in Geneva. From 1980 to 1986, Senior Researcher at the Institute of State and Law of the USSR Academy of Sciences. From 1986 to 1988, Expert, Deputy Head of the Directorate for Humanitarian and Cultural Relations. From February 1989 to 1992, Head of the Directorate of International Humanitarian Cooperation and Human Rights.

MAJOR WORKS: *International Order of Law, and Ways to Strengthen It; On International Legal Responsibility for the Violation of Human Rights.*

FAMILY: Married with a son.

ADDRESS/TELEPHONE: The Russian Embassy in Iceland, 33, Gardastrastraeti, Reykjavik, Iceland. 1–5156; 2–8564.

Resin, Vladimir Iosifovich

POSITION: First Deputy Premier of the Moscow Government

BIRTHPLACE/DATE: Minsk, February 21, 1936

CAREER: From 1958 to 1965, worked at organizations of the USSR Coal Industry and Minmontazhspetstroi (Special Construction). From 1965 to 1987, Trust Manager, First Deputy, Head of the Central Directorate of Glavmosinzhenerstroi (Moscow Directorate of Mechanical Engineering); Deputy Chairman of the Moscow City Executive Committee; Chairman of the Mosstroi (Moscow Construction) Committee. From 1991 to 1992, Deputy Premier of the Moscow Government; Head of the Moscow Construction-Investment Complex.

HONORS/AWARDS: Order of the Badge of Honor; Order of the People's Friendship; two Orders of the Red Banner of Labor; four medals.

FAMILY: Married with a daughter.

ADDRESS/TELEPHONE: 11 Novy Arbat Street, Building 11, Moscow, 121019. 202–0911 (office).

Revenko, Grigory Ivanovich

POSITION: Vice President of the International Foundation of Socio-Economic and Political Studies (Gorbachev Foundation)

BIRTHPLACE/DATE: Studenaya village, Peschansk district, Vinnitsy region, April 29, 1936

NATIONALITY: Ukrainian

CAREER: From 1958 to 1961, Engineer at the Odessa Refrigerating Mechanical Engineering Plant. From 1961, Second, First Secretary of the District Committee; Secretary, Second Secretary of the Odessa Regional Komsomol Committee. From 1968, Secretary of the Ukrainian Komsomol Central Committee. From 1972, Inspector of the Ukranian Central Committee; Secretary, Second Secretary of the Kiev Regional Party Committee. From 1980 to 1984, Ukraine Supreme Soviet Presidium Member; Chairman of the Ukranian Communist Party Auditing Commission. From 1984, Inspector of the Central Committee; Deputy Head of the the Central Committee's Department of Party Work Organization. From 1985, First Secretary of the Kiev Regional Party Committee. From 1990, member of the USSR Presidential Council; Advisor to the USSR President. In August 1991, Head of the USSR President's Staff. Member of the Central Committee's Foreign Policy Commission. Alternate Member of the Ukraine Politiburo; USSR People's Deputy. From 1989 to 1990, USSR Supreme Soviet Deputy. From 1962 to 1991, member of the Communist Party.

HONORS/AWARDS: Twelve orders and medals,

including Orders of Lenin; Order of the October Revolution; Order of the Red Banner of Labor; two Orders of the Badge of Honor.
FAMILY: Married with two daughters and a granddaughter.
ADDRESS/TELEPHONE: 49 Leningradsky Prospekt, Moscow, 125468. 943–9904 (office).

Rigert, David Adamovich
POSITION: Athlete; Weight Lifter
BIRTHPLACE/DATE: Kazakhstan, 1947
NATIONALITY: German
CAREER: In 1976, Olympic Champion. From 1971 to 1976, and from 1978 to 1980, World Champion. From 1971 to 1976, and from 1978 to 1980, European Champion. From 1987, Chairman of the Disk Cooperative Company.
HONORS/AWARDS: Established sixty-three World Records. USSR Honored Master of Sports.
FAMILY: Married with three children.
ADDRESS/TELEPHONE: 49 Frunze Street, Taganrog, 347900. 6–3234 (home).

Rodimtseva, Irina Aleksandrovna
POSITION: Director of the the Moscow Kremlin State Historic and Cultural Preserve; Vice President of the International Committee of Museums (IKOM)
BIRTHPLACE/DATE: Moscow, 1934
NATIONALITY: Russian
CAREER: From 1951 to 1979, Museum Guide. From 1979 to 1984, Head of the Museums Directorate of the Ministry of Culture. In 1985, Director of the Kremlin Museums; Vice President of the National IKOM Committee; Board Member of the Moscow Culture Foundation; Editorial Board Member of *Sovietsky Musey* (*Soviet Museum*) magazine; Russian Federation Honored Worker of Arts.
MAJOR WORKS: Popular scientific publications on the Moscow Kremlin and the art of Fabergé.
FAMILY: Married with a son.
ADDRESS/TELEPHONE: The Kremlin Museum-Preserve, Moscow, 103073. 202–3776 (office).

Rodionov, Yuri Nikolayevich
POSITION: Deputy Commander in Chief of the CIS Unified Armed Forces Personnel Department; Colonel-General
BIRTHPLACE/DATE: Taganrog, Rostov region, March 12, 1938
NATIONALITY: Russian
CAREER: Served in the Armed Forces. From 1967 to 1972, worked at the Research Institute of the USSR Ministry of Defense. From 1972 to 1976, Deputy Head, Department Head of the Computer Center of the USSR Ministry of Defense. From 1976 to 1991, occupied various positions at the Central Personnel Directorate of the USSR Ministry of Defense. From April 1991, Deputy Chairman, then Chairman of the Russian Federation State Defense and Security Committee. From September to December 1991, USSR Deputy Minister of Defense Personnel, Head of the Central Personnel Directorate of the USSR Ministry of Defense.
FAMILY: Married with two children.

Rodnina, Irina Konstantinovna
POSITION: Figure Skating Coach in the United States
BIRTHPLACE/DATE: Moscow, 1949
NATIONALITY: Russian
CAREER: In 1972, 1976, and 1980, Winter Olympic Winner (pair figure skating). World, European, and USSR Champion. USSR Honored Master of Sports (pair figure skating).
FAMILY: Married with a son.
ADDRESS/TELEPHONE: 8 Luzhnetskaya Naberezhnaya, Moscow. 201–1231 (Federation).

Rogachev, Igor Alekseyevich
POSITION: Russian Ambassador to China; Ambassador Extraordinary and Plenipotentiary
BIRTHPLACE/DATE: Moscow, March 1, 1932
NATIONALITY: Russian
EDUCATION: Studied at the Institute of Oriental Studies and at the Moscow State Institute of International Relations of the USSR Foreign Ministry. Doctor of History.
CAREER: From 1955 to 1956, Interpreter for the Amur Complex Expedition of the USSR Academy of Sciences. In 1956, Interpreter for the State Council of the People's Republic of China. From 1956 to 1958, Editorial Office Translator for the newspaper and magazine *Druzhba* (*Friendship*) in China. From 1958 to 1961, Interpreter, Attaché at the USSR Embassy in China. From 1961 to 1965,

Third Secretary, Second Secretary of the Far East Department of the USSR Foreign Ministry (MID). In 1965, First Secretary of the USSR Deputy Foreign Minister's Secretariat. From 1965 to 1969, First Secretary at the USSR Embassy in the United States. From 1969 to 1972, Counsellor at the USSR Embassy in China. From 1972 to 1975, Section Head, Deputy Head of the First Far East Department of the USSR MID. From 1975 to 1978, Senior Counsellor, Department Head of the Foreign Policy Planning Directorate of the USSR MID. From 1978 to 1983, Head of the South Asia Department of the USSR MID. From 1983 to 1986, Head of the First Far East Department; Board Member of the USSR MID. In 1986, Head of the Socialist Countries of Asia Directorate of the USSR MID. From 1986 to 1991, Deputy USSR Foreign Minister.
HONORS/AWARDS: Order of the Badge of Honor (1971); Order of the People's Friendship (1982); medals.
FAMILY: Married with a son.
ADDRESS/TELEPHONE: Duntchimennay Baytchuntze 4, Peking. 532–2051; 532–1291; 532–1381 (office); 244–2900.

Romanov, Mikhail Alekseyevich
POSITION: Russian Federation Ambassador to Kirgistan; Ambassador Extraordinary and Plenipotentiary
BIRTHPLACE/DATE: Moscow, January 25, 1936
NATIONALITY: Russian
EDUCATION: From 1976 to 1977, student of the advanced course for senior diplomats at the Diplomatic Academy of the USSR Foreign Ministry.
CAREER: From 1964 to 1971, worked at the USSR Embassy in Thailand and the USSR Foreign Ministry. From 1971 to 1976, Second Secretary at the USSR Embassy in Thailand. From 1977 to 1981, First Secretary, Counsellor of the Department of Southeastern Asia of the USSR Foreign Ministry. From 1981 to 1987, Counsellor at the USSR Embassy in the Kingdom of Nepal. From 1987 to 1992, Section Head, Department Head of the Directorate of South Asia of the USSR Foreign Ministry. From February 1992 to June 1992, Senior Counsellor of the Department of West and South Asia of the Russian Foreign Ministry.
FAMILY: Married with a daughter.
ADDRESS/TELEPHONE: The Embassy of Russia in Kirgistan, Bishkek. 244–1606 (Foreign Ministry).

Romanov, Victor Anatolyevich
POSITION: Board Chairman of the Development Twenty-First Century Commercial Bank
ADDRESS/TELEPHONE: 21 Tverskaya-Yamskaya, Moscow. 250–9641 (office).

Romanovsky, Sergey Kalistratovich
POSITION: Former USSR Ambassador to Spain; Ambassador Extraordinary and Plenipotentiary
BIRTHPLACE/DATE: Novoseltsy village, Rudnyansk district, Smolensk region, 1923
NATIONALITY: Russian
CAREER: From 1948 to 1950, Editor of *Komsomolskaya Pravda* (*Komsomol Truth*) newspaper. From 1950 to 1953, Secretary of the World Federation of Democratic Youth (Hungary). From 1953 to 1957, Chairman of the USSR Committee of Youth Organizations. From 1957 to 1959, Secretary of the Komsomol Central Committee. From 1959 to 1960, Deputy USSR Minister of Culture. From 1960 to 1962, Deputy Chairman of the State Committee for Cultural Relations with Foreign Countries of the USSR Council of Ministers. From 1962 to 1968, Chairman of the USSR Commission to UNESCO; Board Member of the USSR Foreign Ministry. From 1968 to 1975, USSR Ambassador to Norway. From 1975 to 1984, USSR Ambassador to Belgium. From 1984 to 1986, First Deputy Chairman of the All-Union Copyright Agency. From 1986 to December 1991, USSR Ambassador to Spain.
HONORS/AWARDS: Order of the Red Star (1942); Order of the Badge of Honor (1971); Order of the People's Friendship (1981); Order of the Patriotic War, First Class (1985); medals.
FAMILY: Married.

Romanyuk, Valery Yakovlevich
POSITION: Editor in Chief of *Biznes dlya Vsekh* (*Business for Everybody*) newspaper
BIRTHPLACE/DATE: Odessa region, 1940
EDUCATION: From 1971 to 1974, postgraduate student. Doctor of History.
CAREER: From 1965 to 1971, Correspondent for *Volzhskaya Kommuna* (*Volga Commune*) news-

paper in Kuibyshev. From 1974 to 1991, Economics Department Analyst of *Izvestia* (*News*) newspaper. Member of the Confederation of Journalists' Unions.
MAJOR WORKS: Books on the problems of perestroika and economic reform. *Red Hieroglyphs* (on reform in China); *Volzhskaya Kommuna* (*Volga Commune*).
HONORS/AWARDS: Order of the Badge of Honor; Order of the People's Friendship.
FAMILY: Married with two children.
ADDRESS/TELEPHONE: 26 Volgogradsky Prospekt, Moscow, 109316. 270–9064; 270–0930 (office).

Roshka, Yuri Ivanovich
POSITION: Executive Committee Chairman of the Moldovan Popular Front Council
BIRTHPLACE/DATE: Kishinev, 1963
CAREER: Worked at the Literary Department of Moldova State Television and Radio, and at the Literary Museum of the Moldova Writers' Union. Founder of the Democratic Movement to Support Perestroika (now the Popular Front).
FAMILY: Married with two children.
ADDRESS/TELEPHONE: 5 Nikolay Yorga Street, Kishinev, 277014. 22–5064; Telex: 234480 (Popular Front).

Rotgolts, Iosif Anatolyevich
POSITION: Board Chairman of Aktiv Commercial Bank
BIRTHPLACE/DATE: Moscow, 1940
CAREER: Economist, Deputy Manager of the District Office of the State Bank in Moscow. Head, Chief Economist of a large factory. Directorate Head of the Lyublinsky District Executive Committee in Moscow.
FAMILY: Married with a son.
ADDRESS/TELEPHONE: 3 Markhlevskogo Street, Flat #64, Moscow, 101000. 928–3540.

Rozov, Victor Sergeyevich
POSITION: Playwright
BIRTHPLACE/DATE: Yaroslavl, 1913
EDUCATION: Professor.
CAREER: From the late 1970s, Lecturer at the Gorky Literary Institute; Board Secretary of the USSR Writers' Union. From 1991, Secretary of the Russian Writers' Union; member of the Russian PEN Center.
MAJOR WORKS: *In Search of Joy* (1957); *Traditional Gathering* (1967); *The Nest of Wood-Grouse* (1978); *Wild Boar* (1985); *Journey to Different Ways* (1987).
HONORS/AWARDS: USSR State Prize (1967).
FAMILY: Married with two children and a granddaughter.
ADDRESS/TELEPHONE: 4 Chernyakhovskogo Street, Flat #75, Moscow, 125319. 151–6824 (home).

Ruban, Galina Alekseyevna
POSITION: Director-General of the Rosika Russian Information Commercial Agency
BIRTHPLACE/DATE: Cheboksary, Chuvashia, March 31, 1955
NATIONALITY: Chuvashian
CAREER: From 1982 to 1985, Journalist. From 1985 to 1988, Teacher. From 1988 to 1992, Journalist for *Molodoy Kommunist* (*Young Communist*) magazine; Editor in Chief of *Rosika* magazine.
FAMILY: Married.
ADDRESS/TELEPHONE: 6 Razina Street, Moscow. 298–0995; 451–8560.

Rubiks, Alfred Petrovich
POSITION: Former First Secretary of the Latvian Central Committee; under arrest and being investigated
BIRTHPLACE/DATE: Daugavpils (Latvia), 1935
NATIONALITY: Latvian
CAREER: Komsomol Functionary: Factory Komsomol Committee Secretary; Riga City Komsomol Committee Secretary; Deputy Department Head of the Latvian Central Committee; Local Minister of Industry; Chairman of the Riga City Executive Committee. From April 1990 to August 1991, First Secretary of the Latvian Central Committee. From 1990 to 1991, member of the Politburo. Elected USSR People's Deputy; member of the USSR Supreme Soviet Council of Nationalities; member of the USSR Supreme Soviet Committee for Issues of the Councils of People's Deputies and the Development of Self-Government.

FAMILY: Married with two sons and a granddaughter.
TELEPHONE: 32–6093; 32–3322.

Rubtsov, Aleksandr Ivanovich
POSITION: Director-General of the Ernst and Young Vneshkonsult (Foreign Consulting) Company; President of the Economics and Management Consultants Association
BIRTHPLACE/DATE: Moscow, 1958
NATIONALITY: Russian
CAREER: From 1984 to 1988, Director of the Vneshtekhnika (Foreign Technics) Firm. From 1988, Director-General of Vneshkonsult.
FAMILY: Married with a child.
ADDRESS/TELEPHONE: 20/12 Posokhinsky Pereulok, Moscow.

Rumyantsev, Aleksandr Konstantinovich
POSITION: Former Editor in Chief of *Face to Face* business magazine
BIRTHPLACE/DATE: Polotsk, Vitebsk region, March 17, 1950
CAREER: Worked in the Federal Republic of Germany, the United States, and the USSR; worked at State Television and Radio, and for the scientific and technical press.
FAMILY: Married with a son.

Rumyantsev, Oleg Germanovich
POSITION: Executive Secretary of the Constitutional Commission; member of the Russian Federation Supreme Soviet
BIRTHPLACE/DATE: Moscow, 1961
NATIONALITY: Russian
CAREER: In 1983, worked in Hungary. In 1987, Co-Chairman of the Demokraticheskaya Perestroika (Democratic Reconstruction) Independent Political Club. From 1990 to October 1992, Co-Chairman of the Social-Democratic Association; Deputy Chairman of the Russian Federation Social-Democratic Party. From June 1990, Executive Secretary of the Constitutional Commission. In 1992, Chairman of the Committee.
FAMILY: Single.
ADDRESS/TELEPHONE: 2 Krasnopresnenskaya Naberezhnaya, Moscow, 103274. 205–9076 (office).

Rusak, Nikolay Ivanovich
POSITION: Chairman of the Sports and Physical Education Committee of the USSR Council of Ministers
BIRTHPLACE/DATE: Prilepitsy village, Pleshenitsk district, Minsk region, 1934
NATIONALITY: Byelorussian
CAREER: From 1954 to 1957, Physical Education Teacher. From 1959 to 1961, Instructor of the Sports Department of the Komsomol Central Committee; Deputy Chairman of the Central Council of Burevestnik (Stormy Petrel) Voluntary Sports Society. From 1973 to 1983, Propaganda Department Instructor of the Central Committee; First Deputy Chairman of the USSR State Sports and Physical Education Committee. To February 1992, Chairman of the USSR State Sports and Physical Education Committee. From February 1992, Secretariat Head of the CIS Sports Council.
HONORS/AWARDS: Order of the Badge of Honor; Order of the People's Friendship.
FAMILY: Married with a daughter.
ADDRESS/TELEPHONE: 8 Luzhnetskaya Naberezhnaya, Moscow. 248–2466 (reception).

Rutskoy, Aleksandr Vladimirovich
POSITION: Former Russian Federation Vice President
BIRTHPLACE/DATE: Kursk, September 16, 1947
NATIONALITY: Russian
CAREER: From 1965, Pilot-Instructor at the Borisoglebsk Aviation School. From 1980 to 1985, Squadron Commander; Regiment Staff Head in the German Democratic Republic (GDR) with the Guard's Air Regiment of Fighter-Bombers. From 1985 to 1986, Detached Air Regiment Commander of an assault aircraft in Afghanistan. From 1986 to 1988, Deputy Commander of the Lipetsk Center for Aviation Personnel Training. From 1988, Deputy Commander of the Air Force in Afghanistan. Shot down and taken prisoner; exchanged for an intelligence agent; returned to the USSR. Graduated from the General Staff Academy of the USSR Armed Forces. Appointed Head of the Lipetsk Center for Aviation Personnel Training. From 1990 to June 1991, Chairman of the Russian Federation Supreme Soviet Committee for Disabled Veterans of War and Labor, and Social Protection of Servicemen and Their Families. From

June 1991, Russian Federation Vice President; Chairman of the Russian Democratic Party of Communists. Russian Federation People's Deputy. To 1991, member of the Communist Party. From 1990 to 1991, member of the Russian Federation Central Committee.
HONORS/AWARDS: Hero of the USSR; other government awards.
FAMILY: Married with two sons.

Rybakov, Anatoli Naumovich
POSITION: Writer
BIRTHPLACE/DATE: Chernigov, January 14, 1911
EDUCATION: Doctor of Philosophy (Tel Aviv University, Israel); Honorary Doctor of Philology (Tel Aviv University, 1991).
CAREER: To December 1991, President of the Russian International PEN Center (founded in 1989). Member of the USSR Writers' Union. From December 1991, member of the Confederation of Writers' Unions.
MAJOR WORKS: *Kortik (The Dagger)* (1948); film with the same title (1964). Films: *Bronze Bird* (1956); *Shot* (1975). Novels: *Drivers; Yekaterina Voronina* (1955); *Summer in Sosnyaki* (1964); *Heavy Sand* (1978); *Children of the Arbat* (1987); *1935 and Other Years* (1989); *Fear* (1990). Stories: "The Adventures of Krosh" (1960); "Vacations of Krosh" (1966); "The Unknown Soldier" (1971).
HONORS/AWARDS: USSR State Prize; Russian Federation Prize; Orders of the Patriotic War, First and Second Class; Order of the Red Banner of Labor.
FAMILY: Married with two children.
TELEPHONE: 593–0354; 291–9569 (PEN Center).

Rybin, Aleksandr Georgyevich
POSITION: Director of the Gorky Film Studio
BIRTHPLACE/DATE: Odessa, 1935
NATIONALITY: Russian
CAREER: From 1954 to 1958, Assistant Operator of the Studio of Popular Scientific Films. From 1958 to 1963, Operator of the Yalta Studios of Feature Films. From 1963 to 1987, Operator of the Gorky Film Studio. From 1961, member of the USSR Union of Film Makers. From 1991, member of the Confederation of Film Maker's Unions.
MAJOR WORKS: *Friends-Comrades* (1959); *Little Fugitive* (1966); *Pirates of the Twentieth Century* (1978); *To Stars Through the Thorns* (1982).
HONORS/AWARDS: State Prize.
FAMILY: Married with children.
ADDRESS/TELEPHONE: 8 Eisenstein Street, Moscow, 129226. 181–0183 (office).

Rybin, Vladimir Alekseyevich
POSITION: Director of the Russian State Military-Historical Archives
BIRTHPLACE/DATE: Moscow, 1950
NATIONALITY: Russian
CAREER: In 1973, Researcher of the Central State Archives of the USSR National Economy. From 1975 to 1981, Early Texts Specialist of the USSR Central Archives. From 1981 to 1986, Senior State Records Inspector of the USSR Central Archives. From 1986 to 1989, Deputy Director; from 1989, Director of the Central State Military-Historical Archives (CGVIA). Vice President of the Association of Military Historians and Russian Early Texts Specialists.
FAMILY: Married with four children.
ADDRESS/TELEPHONE: 3 Vtoraya Baumanskaya Street, Moscow, 107005. 261–8696 (office).

Rybkin, Ivan Petrovich
POSITION: Moscow Member of the Russian Federation Supreme Soviet Committee for Issues of the Councils of People's Deputies and the Development of Self-Government; Chairman of the Communists of Russia Faction
BIRTHPLACE/DATE: Semigorovka village, Ternovsky district, Voronezh region, 1946
NATIONALITY: Russian
EDUCATION: Doctor of Technical Sciences; Assistant Professor.
CAREER: Department Head of the Volgograd Agricultural Institute. From 1987 to 1990, First Secretary of the Sovietsky District Communist Party in Volgograd. From 1990 to 1991, Second Secretary of the Volgograd Regional Communist Party. From February to September 1991, Head of the Russian Federation Central Committee's Liaison Department for the Councils of People's Deputies. Coordinator of the Communists of Russia Faction. Russian People's Deputy. To August 1991, member of the Communist Party.

FAMILY: Married with two children.
ADDRESS/TELEPHONE: 2 Krasnopresnenskaya Naberezhnaya, Moscow, 103274. 205–3006 (office).

Ryzhkov, Nikolay Ivanovich
POSITION: Former USSR Prime Minister
BIRTHPLACE/DATE: Dyleyevka village, Dzerzhinsky district, Donetsk region, September 28, 1929
NATIONALITY: Russian
CAREER: From 1971, Director-General of the Uralmash Industrial Association. From 1975 to 1979, USSR First Deputy Minister for Heavy and Transport Mechanical Engineering Industry. From February 1979, First Deputy Chairman of the USSR State Planning Committee. From 1982 to 1985, Secretary, Head of the Diplomatic Department of the Central Committee. From September 1985 to 1991, Chairman of the USSR Council of Ministers. From March 1990, member of the USSR Presidential Council. From 1985 to 1990, member of the Politburo. In 1988, Head of the Politburo's Coordinating Commission to help the victims of the earthquake in Armenia. Candidate for the Russian Federation Presidency. Elected USSR Supreme Soviet Deputy of the Ninth to Eleventh Convocations. From 1989 to 1992, USSR People's Deputy. From 1956 to 1991, member of the Communist Party.
MAJOR WORKS: *Perestroika: Series of Betrayals.*
HONORS/AWARDS: Two USSR State Prizes; Order of Lenin; Order of the October Revolution, two Orders of the Red Banner of Labor; medals.
FAMILY: Married with a daughter.

Ryzhov, Yuri Alekseyevich
POSITION: Russian Federation Ambassador to France; member of the President's Consultative Council
BIRTHPLACE/DATE: Moscow, October 28, 1930
NATIONALITY: Russian
EDUCATION: Doctor of Technical Sciences; Academician of the Russian Academy of Sciences.

Rzayev, Valekh Sabir Ogly
POSITION: Consultant on Azerbaijanian Literature to the Confederation of Writers' Unions
BIRTHPLACE/DATE: Baku, 1960
NATIONALITY: Azerbaijanian
CAREER: Taught at the Children's Literary Studio. From 1983, Consultant on Azerbaijanian literature to the USSR Writers' Union.
FAMILY: Married with a son.
ADDRESS/TELEPHONE: 33–4–112 Isakovskogo Street, Moscow, 123631. 944–0583 (home).

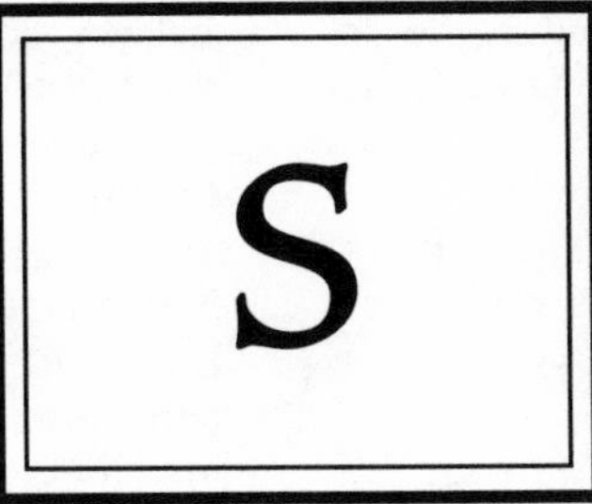

Sadovnichi, Victor Antonovich

POSITION: Rector of Moscow State University
BIRTHPLACE/DATE: Krasnopavlovka village, Kharkov region, 1939
NATIONALITY: Russian
EDUCATION: Graduated in 1963 from the Mechanics and Mathematics Department at Moscow State University. Doctor of Physics and Mathematics; Professor. Speaks English.
CAREER: To 1982, engaged in scientific work at Moscow State University. From 1982 to 1984, Head of the Mathematics Analysis Division of the Mechanics and Mathematics Department at Moscow State University. From 1984 to 1992, Vice Rector, First Vice Rector of Moscow State University, Deputy of Leninsky District Committee, Deputy of the Moscow Council of People's Deputies. Full Member of the Russian Academy of Technological Sciences; Standing Committee Member of the European Conference of Rectors. Academician of the Academy of Technology and Natural Sciences. Academician of the Academy of Arts.
MAJOR WORKS: Over eighty scientific papers, including seventeen textbooks, manuals, and monographs.
HONORS/AWARDS: State Prize; M. Lomonosov Prize (1973); two Orders of the Red Banner of Labor; Medal For Labor Valor.
FAMILY: Married with three children.
ADDRESS/TELEPHONE: Moscow State University, Leninsky Gory, Moscow, 119899. 939–2729 (reception).

Sadovsky, Vadim Nikolayevich

POSITION: Head of the Department of Philosophy and Social Problems at the Institute of Systems Analysis (BNIISI)
BIRTHPLACE/DATE: 1934, Orenburg
NATIONALITY: Russian
EDUCATION: Doctor of Philosophy; Professor.
CAREER: From 1958 to 1962, Junior Researcher at the Philosophy Institute. From 1962 to 1967, Consultant, Deputy Department Head of *Voprosy Filosofii* (*Questions of Philosophy*) magazine. From 1967 to 1978, Senior Researcher at the Institute of the History of Natural Sciences and Technology of the USSR Academy of Sciences, Assessor of the Logic, Methodology, and Philosophy Division of the International Union for the History of Philosophy and Science. From 1978, Department Head of the Institute of Systems Analyses (VNIISI). Editorial Board Member of *Synthesis* magazine and *Epistemology* magazine.
MAJOR WORKS: Author of over 200 publications; translator into Russian of works by K. Potter, J. Piaget, T. Kun, I. Lakatosh.
FAMILY: Married with a child.
ADDRESS/TELEPHONE: 9 60-Letiya Oktyabrya, Moscow, 117312. 135–4433 (office).

Safaryan, Igor Anatolyevich

POSITION: Director-General of the Brokinvest-service Company; Moscow Headquarters President of the International Brokers Guild
BIRTHPLACE/DATE: Moscow, 1954
EDUCATION: Graduated in 1977 from the Moscow Aviation Technology Institute. Speaks German.
CAREER: From 1971 to 1988, worked from Lab-

oratory Assistant to Laboratory Head in the defense industry. From 1988 to 1991, Commercial Director of the Scientific Youth Center.
FAMILY: Married with a son.
ADDRESS/TELEPHONE: 60 Herzen Street, Building 3, Moscow. 202–9112; 202–3793 (office).

Safonov, Ernst Ivanovich
POSITION: Editor in Chief of *Literaturnaya Rossiya* newspaper
BIRTHPLACE/DATE: Saray, Ryazan region, 1938
EDUCATION: Studied at the Ryazan Teachers' Training Institute. Graduated in 1962 from the Gorky Literary Institute in Moscow.
CAREER: From 1955 to 1957, Staff Member of the Saray district newspaper *Kolkhozny Put* (*The Collective Farm Way*). From 1957 to 1960, worked for the newspapers *Ryazansky Komsomolets* (*Ryazan Komsomol Member*), *Za Pedagogicheskiye Kadry* (*For Pedagogical Staff*). From 1960 to 1965, worked at *Izvestia* (*News*) and *Literaturnaya Gazeta* (*Literary Newspaper*) newspapers, *Ogonyek* (*Beacon*) and *Roman-Gazeta* (*Novel-Newspaper*) journals, and All-Union Radio. From 1966, engaged in professional literary activity. In 1969, evicted from Moscow for ideological unsteadiness (refused to vote for Solzhenitsyn's expulsion from the USSR Writers' Union). From 1983, Head of the Literary Art Seminar at the Higher Literary Courses of the Russian Writers' Union. Board Secretary of the Russian Writers' Union; member of the Russian Federation Supreme Soviet Literature and Art State Prize Commission; Board Member of the Culture Foundation; Presidium Member of the All-Russia Society of Book-Lovers; Board Member of the International Slavic Literature and Culture Foundation.
MAJOR WORKS: *Rain in a Cupped Hand* (1965); *Under High Skies* (1976); *People at Public Cost* (1981). *Don't Forget to Glance Back* (TV film). Translated over twenty books from the Tatar, Bashkir, and Buryat languages.
HONORS/AWARDS: Prizes of the Russian Writers' Union.
FAMILY: Married with two children.
ADDRESS/TELEPHONE: 30 Tsvetnoi Boulevard, Moscow, 103662. 200–4005; 200- 2324 (office).

Sagalayev, Eduard Mikhailovich
POSITION: Chairman of Channel 6, a private TV company
BIRTHPLACE/DATE: Samarkand, Uzbekistan, 1946
NATIONALITY: Russian
EDUCATION: Graduated from the Philology Department at Alisher Navoi State University in Samarkand; and from the Central Committee's Academy of Social Sciences.
CAREER: From 1967, Anchorman; from 1968 to 1969, Senior Editor of the Samarkand Radio Broadcasting Committee. From 1969 to 1972, worked for *Leninsky Put* (*Lenin's Way*) Samarkand region newspaper. From 1972 to 1973, Executive Editor of *Komsomolets Uzbekistana* (*Uzbekistan Komsomol Member*) newspaper. From 1973 to 1975, Functionary of the All-Union Komsomol Central Committee in Moscow. Member of the Communist Party. From 1975 to 1988, Deputy Chief Editor, Chief Editor of Central TV's Main Administration for Youth Programs. From 1988 to 1989, Editor in Chief of Central TV's Main Administration for Information Programs. From 1989 to 1991, Deputy Chairman of the USSR State Television and Radio Broadcasting Committee. From 1991, Chairman of the USSR Journalists' Union (From 1992, Confederation of Journalists' Unions). From August 1991, Deputy Chairman of the All-Union State Television and Radio Broadcasting Company. From January 1992 to June 1992, Director-General of Ostankino Television and Radio Broadcasting Company. From June 1992, Chairman of the Ostankino Council for Television Programs.
FAMILY: Married with two children.
ADDRESS/TELEPHONE: 12 Academician Korolev Street, Moscow, 127000. 217–9666 (office).

Sagdeyev, Roald Zinnurovich
POSITION: Chief Researcher at the Space Research Institute
BIRTHPLACE/DATE: Moscow, December 26, 1932
NATIONALITY: Tatar
EDUCATION: Graduated in 1955 from Moscow State University.
CAREER: From 1956 to 1961, worked at the Atomic Energy Institute. From 1961 to 1970, Lab-

oratory Head of the Nuclear Physics Institute of the Siberian branch of the USSR Academy of Sciences. From 1968, Academician of the USSR Academy of Sciences. From 1970 to 1973, Laboratory Head at the Institute of High Temperature Physics of the USSR Academy of Sciences. From 1973 to 1988, Director of the Space Research Institute. From 1986, Head of the Scientific and Methodological Center for Analytical Research. In October 1988 worked in the United States. From 1989 to 1991, USSR People's Deputy.
MAJOR WORKS: On plasma physics: Investigated oscillations and instability of plasma; discovered the so-called noncollision shock waves in plasma. Developed the theory of transfer processes in Tokamak installations.
HONORS/AWARDS: Hero of Socialist Labor (1986); Prize of Lenin (1984); Order of the October Revolution; Order of the Red Banner of Labor.
FAMILY: Married with two children.
ADDRESS/TELEPHONE: The Space Research Institute, 84/32 Profsoyuznaya Street, B–485, Moscow, GSP–7, 117810. 333–2588 (office).

Sakharov, Eduard Victorovich
POSITION: Former Director-General of the Pekin Hotel Complex
BIRTHPLACE/DATE: May 1, 1939
EDUCATION: Doctor of Technical Sciences; Assistant Professor.
CAREER: From 1957 to 1978, Worker, Engineer, Department Head, Chief Engineer. From 1978 to 1992, Director of a printing plant. From 1990 to 1991, Executive Committee Chairman. From March 1992, Director-General of the Pekin Hotel Complex.
MAJOR WORKS: Five published books; around sixty articles.
FAMILY: Married with a child.

Salnikov, Vladimir Valeryevich
POSITION: Athlete; Deputy Director-General of Olimp, a multi-purpose firm
BIRTHPLACE/DATE: Leningrad (now St. Petersburg), 1960
NATIONALITY: Russian
EDUCATION: Graduated in 1982 from the Lesgaft State Institute of Physical Education in St. Petersburg. Speaks English.
CAREER: In 1978 and 1982, World Champion Swimmer. Won three Gold Medals at the 1980 Summer Olympics. From February 1989 to March 1990, Coach of the USSR National Swimming Team.
HONORS/AWARDS: USSR Honored Master of Sports.
FAMILY: Married with a child.
ADDRESS/TELEPHONE: 5 Bolshoi Rzhevski Pereulok, Moscow, 121069. 286–8988 (office).

Saltykov, Boris Georgyevich
POSITION: Deputy Chairman of the Russian Federation Government; Russian Federation Minister of Science, Higher Education and Technological Policy; Russian Federation Government Plenipotentiary Representative at the United International Nuclear Research Institute
BIRTHPLACE/DATE: Moscow, 1940
NATIONALITY: Russian
EDUCATION: Graduated in 1964 from the Moscow Institute of Physics and Technology; in 1967, from postgraduate study. Doctor of Economics. Good command of English.
CAREER: From 1967 to 1986, Junior Researcher, Senior Researcher, Laboratory Head, Department Head at the USSR Academy of Sciences' Central Economics and Mathematics Institute. From 1986 to 1991, Department Head at the USSR Academy of Sciences' Institute of Economics and Forecasts of Scientific and Technological Progress. From 1991, Deputy Director of the USSR Academy of Sciences' Analytical Center.
FAMILY: Married with a child.
ADDRESS/TELEPHONE: 11 Tverskaya Street Moscow, 103905. 229–2501 (office).

Salye, Marina Yevgenievna
POSITION: Russian Federation People's Deputy; Leader of the Leningrad Popular Front; Co-Chairwoman of the Demokratischeskaya Rossiya (Democratic Russia) Movement
BIRTHPLACE/DATE: Leningrad, October 19, 1934
EDUCATION: Graduated in 1957 from the Geology Department at Leningrad State University. Doctor of Geology and Mineralogy.
CAREER: From 1957, worked at the Institute of Geology and Geochronology of the USSR Acad-

emy of Sciences. From August 1990, LenSoviet Food Commission Chairperson of the Leningrad Council of People's Deputies. Russian Federation People's Deputy. Deputy of the Leningrad Council of People's Deputies. In December 1989, Organizing Member of the Democratic Party of Russia. In May 1990, left the party due to disagreement with Nikolay Travkin, Party Chairman, on leadership methods. In October 1990, Organizing Committee Member of the Free Democratic Party of Russia. From 1992, Leader of the Russian Constituent Union.
FAMILY: Divorced.
ADDRESS/TELEPHONE: 55 Veteranov Prospekt, Flat #94, St. Petersburg. 152–9155.

Samarin, Aleksey Aleksandrovich
POSITION: Director-General of the Dina Joint-Stock Company
BIRTHPLACE/DATE: Moscow, 1963
NATIONALITY: Russian
EDUCATION: Graduated in 1986 from the Moscow Ordizhnovikidze Aviation Institute.
CAREER: From 1988, Chairman of a cooperative. From 1989, Board Chairman of a cooperative alliance.
FAMILY: Married with a son.
ADDRESS/TELEPHONE: 18 K. Tsarev Street, Moscow, 125080. 158–0185.

Samolets, Tatyana Victorovna
POSITION: Press Secretary to the Director of the Foreign Intelligence Service
BIRTHPLACE/DATE: Gorlovka, Donetsk region, 1947
EDUCATION: Graduated in 1972 from the Journalism Department at Moscow State University.
CAREER: From 1965, Staff Member of *Flag Rodiny* (*Flag of the Motherland*) newspaper in Sevastopol. From 1966 to 1967, Proofreader at a military unit in Sevastopol. From 1974 to November 1991, Editorial Assistant, Correspondent, then Assistant Editor of the Mailing and Public Relations Department.
FAMILY: Married with a son.
ADDRESS/TELEPHONE: 11 Kolpachny Pereulok, Moscow, 101000. 923–6213; 224–3020 (office).

Samsonov, Victor Nikolayevich
POSITION: General Staff Head of the Commonwealth of Independent States Armed Forces; First Deputy Commander in Chief of the Unified Forces of the Commonwealth
BIRTHPLACE/DATE: Dukhovnitsky district, Saratov region, November 10, 1941
NATIONALITY: Russian
CAREER: From 1964, Marine Company Commander of the Pacific Ocean Fleet Detached Regiment. From 1972, Staff Head, Motorized Infantry Regiment Commander, Tank Division Staff Head. From 1981, Motorized Infantry Division Commander, Army Staff Head, Army Commander, Staff Head of the Trans-Caucasian Military Dictrict. From 1990, Commander of the Leningradsky Military District. From December 1991, General Staff Head of the USSR Armed Forces, USSR First Deputy Defense Minister.
FAMILY: Married with two children.
ADDRESS/TELEPHONE: The CIS Armed Forces General Staff, K–160, Moscow, 130060. 293–2869 (office); 293–1413 (Defense Ministry).

Saprykin, Igor Aleksandrovich
POSITION: Russian Ambassador to the Byelorussian Republic; Ambassador Extraordinary and Plenipotentiary
BIRTHPLACE/DATE: Moscow, April 3, 1938
EDUCATION: Graduated in 1961 from the Moscow State Institute of International Relations. From 1988 to 1989, student of the advanced course for senior diplomats at the Diplomatic Academy of the USSR Foreign Ministry. Speaks English and French.
CAREER: In 1961, Reserve Member of the Second European Department of the USSR Foreign Ministry. From 1961 to 1962, Expert-Trainee at the USSR Embassy in Great Britain and Northern Ireland. From 1962 to 1963, Interpreter, and from 1963 to 1966, Attaché at the USSR Embassy in Great Britain and Northern Ireland. From 1966 to 1968, Third Secretary, and from 1968 to 1970, Second Secretary of the Directorate of Foreign Policy Planning of the USSR Foreign Ministry. From 1970 to 1971, Second Secretary, and from 1971 to 1973, First Secretary at the USSR Embassy in the Central African Republic. From 1973 to 1975, First Secretary of the Second European Depart-

ment of the USSR Foreign Ministry. From 1975 to 1979, Counsellor at the USSR Embassy in Australia. From 1979 to 1980, Counsellor of the Second European Department of the USSR Foreign Ministry. From 1980 to 1986, Section Head of the Second European Department of the USSR Foreign Ministry. From 1986 to 1987, Section Head of the Pacific Department of the USSR Foreign Ministry. From 1987 to 1988, Deputy Directorate Head of the Pacific and Southeast Asia Department of the USSR Foreign Ministry.
FAMILY: Married with three children.
ADDRESS/TELEPHONE: 32/34 Smolenskaya-Sennaya Square, Moscow. 244–4433 (office).

Saprykin, Pyotr Vasilyevich
POSITION: Minister of the Moscow City Government
BIRTHPLACE/DATE: Moscow, 1936
EDUCATION: Graduated in 1966 from the All-Union Correspondence Power Engineering Institute.
CAREER: From 1957 to 1981, Group Head of a military unit; held leading engineering and technological posts at the Kurchatov Institute of Nuclear Energy. From 1981 to 1988, First Deputy Chairman, Chairman of the Voroshilovsky District Executive Committee. From 1988 to 1990, First Deputy Chairman of the Planning Commission of the Moscow City Executive Committee. From 1990 to 1991, Acting Head of the Mossoviet Executive Committee's Main Administration for Planning, Registering, and Distributing Housing and Public Buildings, Deputy Chairman of the Mossoviet Executive Committee. From 1991 to 1992, Deputy Premier of Moscow City Government.
FAMILY: Married with two children.
ADDRESS/TELEPHONE: 14 Bolshaya Bronnaya Street, Moscow. 292–1560 (office).

Sariyev, Temir Argembayevich
POSITION: President of the Kirghiz Commodity and Raw Materials Exchange
BIRTHPLACE/DATE: Belogonnoye village, Kirghizia (Kirgistan), 1963
NATIONALITY: Kirghiz
CAREER: From 1981 to 1983, served in the army. From 1984 to 1987, Forwarder, Financial Department Economist, Senior Financial Department Economist of a fur factory. From 1987 to 1988, Organization of Work Instructor, Scientific and Technical Creativity Department Head for Youth and Working Youth, Director of the Youth Center, and Head of the Youth Association of the District Komsomol Committee. From 1989 to 1990, Instructor of the District Party Committee. From 1990 to 1991, Deputy Chairman of the Alomedinsky District Executive Committee. From January 1991 to August 1991, Director of the Kirghiz Commodity and Raw Materials Exchange. Participates in the Congress of the Private Entrepreneurs Movement.
FAMILY: Married with a daughter.
ADDRESS/TELEPHONE: 40 Belinskogo Street. 22–1375; 22–0458 (office); Fax: 22–2744.

Sats, Natalya Ilyinichna
POSITION: Director and Chief Producer of the Moscow State Academic Musical Theater for Children
BIRTHPLACE/DATE: Moscow, 1903
CAREER: In 1918, Co-Organizer of the first Mossoviet (Moscow Council) Children's Theater; at the age of 15, Art Director of the Theater. In 1936, the theater became the Central Children's Theater. In 1937, arrested and exiled for seventeen years for not informing against her husband. Released during World War II and worked at the Alma-Ata Opera and Ballet Theater. Co-Organizer of the Kazakhstan Children's and Youth Theater. From 1946, Head of the Moscow Central Children's Theater, then Head of the world's first Children's Musical Theater; from the mid–1980s, Director and Chief Producer. From 1978, Vice President of the Soviet ASSITEJ Center (International Association of Theaters for Children and Youth). From 1987 to 1991, Board Member of the Lenin Soviet Children's Foundation. From December 1991, Board Member of the Russian Children's Foundation.
MAJOR WORKS: Plays: *The Blue Bird*; *Madame Butterfly*; *The Magic Flute*; *King Lear*; *I'll Beg No Pardon*.
HONORS/AWARDS: USSR People's Artist; Prize of Lenin; Lenin Komsomol Prize; Order of the People's Friendship; Order of the October Revolution.

ADDRESS/TELEPHONE: 5 Vernadsky Prospekt, Moscow. 930–5946; 930–5243 (office).

Savchenko, Larisa Ivanovna

POSITION: Professional Tennis Player
BIRTHPLACE/DATE: Lvov, 1966
NATIONALITY: Ukrainian
CAREER: In 1989, French Open Champion (Women's Doubles). In 1991, Wimbledon Champion (Women' Doubles). From 1992, competes for Latvia.
HONORS/AWARDS: USSR Honored Master of Sports in Tennis.
FAMILY: Married.
ADDRESS/TELEPHONE: 67 Artema Street, Flat #79, Lvov. 65–2224; 65–2181 (Yurmala Federation).

Savisaar, Edgar Elmarovich

POSITION: Deputy Speaker of the Estonian Parliament
BIRTHPLACE/DATE: Estonia, 1950
NATIONALITY: Estonian
EDUCATION: Doctor of Philosophy; Assistant Professor.
CAREER: Former Chairman of the Estonian Republic Government, Prime Minister of Estonia. USSR People's Deputy. Former member of the USSR Supreme Soviet Committee for Issues of the Councils of People's Deputies and the Development of Self-Government. In January 1992, granted extraordinary powers by the Estonian Parliament to implement economic reforms; resigned on January 23, 1992. Former Head of the Estonian People's Front. Leader of the People's Centrist Party of Estonia.
FAMILY: Married with two children.
ADDRESS/TELEPHONE: 1 Lossi Plats, 200001, Tallinn. 60–6796 (reception).

Sayenko, Gennadi Vasilyevich

POSITION: Member of the Russian Federation Supreme Soviet Council of Nationalities' Commission for the Social and Economic Development of the Republics
BIRTHPLACE/DATE: Malaya Kuznetsovka village, Zernogradsky district, Rostov region, 1945
NATIONALITY: Russian
EDUCATION: Graduated in 1968 from the Azov and Black Sea Institute of Agricultural Mechanization and Electrification; in 1981, from the Central Committee's Higher Party School. Doctor of History. Speaks English.
CAREER: From 1968 to 1970 worked at a plant in Salsk, Rostov region. From 1970 to 1991, Communist Party and Komsomol Functionary; Second Secretary of the Kursk Regional Party Committee. From 1989, Russian Federation People's Deputy. From October 1991, member of the Socialist Workers' Party, Chairman of the Control Subcommission.
FAMILY: Married with three children.
ADDRESS/TELEPHONE: 2 Krasnopresnenskaya Naberezhnaya, Moscow. 205–4374 (office).

Saykin, Valery Timofeyevich

POSITION: Former First Deputy Chairman of the Committee of Machine-Building Industry of the USSR Council of Ministers
BIRTHPLACE/DATE: Moscow, 1937
NATIONALITY: Russian
EDUCATION: Graduated from the Higher Educational Institution.
CAREER: From 1956, Molder at the Moscow Likhachev Automobile Plant (ZIL). By age 18, two-time USSR Junior Wrestling Champion; Master of Sports. Worked at ZIL as Foreman, Engineer-Technologist, Deputy Chief Engineer of Metallurgical Production. First Deputy Director-General of the Industrial Association. From 1982, Chairman of the Moscow City Executive Committee of the Council of People's Deputies. From 1990, First Deputy Chairman of the Russian Federation Council of Ministers. From August 1990, First Deputy Chairman of the Committee of Machine-Building Industry of the USSR Council of Ministers.
HONORS/AWARDS: Order of Lenin; Order of the October Revolution; Order of the Red Banner of Labor; USSR State Prize; three medals.
FAMILY: Married with a son.
ADDRESS/TELEPHONE: 13 Tverskaya Street, Moscow, 103032.

Scherbakov, Vladimir Ivanovich

POSITION: President of the Interprivatizatsia International Foundation for the Promotion of Privatization and Foreign Investments

BIRTHPLACE/DATE: Sysoyevka village, Primorye region, 1949
NATIONALITY: Russian
EDUCATION: Graduated from Tolyatti Polytechnic. From 1971 to 1976, postgraduate student at the Higher Komsomol School of the Komsomol Central Committee. Doctor of Economics.
CAREER HISTORY: Engineer of a building administration; Controller of the Volga Automobile Plant. From 1971, Komsomol Functionary. From 1977, Deputy Chief, Chief of the Planning and Economics Department of the Volga Automobile Plant. From 1982, Deputy Director-General, Director for Economics and Planning of the Kama Heavy-Load Truck Production Association. From 1985, held senior posts at the USSR State Committee for Labor and Social Issues. In 1988, appointed First Deputy Head of the Economics Management Section of the Administrative Department of the USSR Council of Ministers. From 1989, Chairman of the USSR State Committee for Labor and Social Issues.
FAMILY: Married with a child.
ADDRESS/TELEPHONE: 3 Solyanka, Building 3, Moscow, 109028. 924–6061 (office).

Sedykh-Bondarenko, Yuri Petrovich
POSITION: Mossoviet (Moscow Council) Deputy Chairman
BIRTHPLACE/DATE: Labinsk, Krasanodar region, 1935
NATIONALITY: Russian
EDUCATION: Graduated in 1967 from the Higher School of the USSR Ministry of Internal Affairs; and in 1970, from the postgraduate program. Doctor of Law.
CAREER: From 1962 to 1987, worked at the Ministry of Internal Affairs. From 1976, held leading posts at the Academy of the USSR Ministry of Internal Affairs. From 1981 to 1983, served in Afghanistan. From 1988 to 1990, Deputy Director of the Russian Federation Republican Advanced Training Courses for Workers of Law-Enforcement Bodies. Moscow City and Timiryazev District Councils People's Deputy. Chairman of the Mossoviet Standing Commission for Legality, Law and Order, and the Defense of Human Rights.
FAMILY: Married with a daughter.
ADDRESS/TELEPHONE: 13 Tverskaya Street, Moscow, 103032. 200–5938 (office).

Seleznev, Gennadi Nikolayevich
POSITION: Editor in Chief of *Pravda* (*Truth*) newspaper
BIRTHPLACE/DATE: Serov, Sverdlovsk region, October 6, 1947
NATIONALITY: Russian
EDUCATION: From 1963 to 1965, student at the Leningrad Professional Technical School (PTU).
CAREER: From 1968 to 1970, served in the army. From 1968 to 1970, Secretary of the Komsomol Committee at the Leningrad PTU. From 1970 to 1971, Instructor, Department Head of the Vyborgsky District Komsomol Committee. From 1972 to 1975, Deputy Editor in Chief, and from 1975 to 1980, Editor in Chief of *Smena* (*Rising Generation*) newspaper in Leningrad. From 1980, First Deputy Head of the Propaganda Department of the Komsomol Central Committee. From 1980 to 1988, Editor in Chief of *Komsomolskaya Pravda* newspaper. From 1991 to November 1991, First Deputy Editor in Chief of *Pravda*. Former member of the Central Committee. Member of the Communist Party from 1970 to 1991.
HONORS/AWARDS: Order of the People's Friendship.
ADDRESS/TELEPHONE: 24 Pravdy Street, Moscow, 125867. 257–3502 (office).

Seleznev, Igor Sergeyevich
POSITION: Constructor-General of the Raduga (Rainbow) Design Bureau; Vice President of the Russian Union of Industrialists and Entrepreneurs
BIRTHPLACE/DATE: Buzuluk, Orenburg region, 1931
NATIONALITY: Russian
CAREER: Engineer-Constructor of the Raduga Machinery Plant in Dubna, Moscow region; from 1974, Chief Constructor of the Plant. Former Co-Chairman of the Scientific-Industrial Group of the USSR People's Deputies. From January 1992, Vice President of the Russian Union of Industrialists and Entrepreneurs. USSR People's Deputy.
HONORS/AWARDS: Hero of Socialist Labor; USSR State Prize.
FAMILY: Married with a child.
ADDRESS/TELEPHONE: 2 Zhukovskogo Street,

Dubna, Moscow Region, 141980. 926–2246 (office).

Seleznev, Sergey Pavlovich
POSITION: Commander of the Leningradsky Military District
BIRTHPLACE/DATE: Russkaya Ivanovka village, Belgorod-Dnestrovsky district, Odessa region, July 10, 1944
CAREER: From 1974 to 1978, Training Platoon Commander, Motorized Infantry Regiment Deputy Commander. From 1978 to 1985, Regiment Commander, Deputy Division Commander, Division Commander. From 1985, First Deputy Commander of the Army. From 1989, Army Commander. From 1991, Staff Head, First Deputy Commander of the Leningradsky Military District.
HONORS/AWARDS: Order of the Red Banner; Order of the Red Star; Order for Service to the Motherland in the USSR Armed Forces, Second and Third Class.
FAMILY: Married with a son and a daughter.
TELEPHONE: 293–2869; 293–1413 (office).

Semchenko, Oleg Ivanovich
POSITION: President of the Siberian Mercantile Exchange; Chairman of the Exchange Committee
BIRTHPLACE/DATE: Novosibirsk region, 1947
NATIONALITY: Russian
EDUCATION: Graduated in 1982 from the Novosibirsk Institute of Electrical Engineering.
CAREER: From 1983 to 1986, Deputy Director-General, and from 1986 to 1990, Director-General of the Komintern (Communist International) Production Association. From 1990 to 1991, Chairman of the Novosibirsk City Executive Committee. Novosibirsk City Council People's Deputy.
FAMILY: Married with three children.
ADDRESS/TELEPHONE: 25 Krasny Prospekt, Novosibirsk. 22–0861 (office).

Semenchenko, Valery Pavlovich
POSITION: Head of the Office of the Russian Federation President
BIRTHPLACE/DATE: Sofia, February 2, 1946
NATIONALITY: Russian
EDUCATION: Graduated in 1969 from the Azovo-Chernomyrsky Institute of Agricultural Mechanization.
CAREER: From 1969 to 1976, Engineer, Senior Engineer, Deputy Laboratory Head of the Institute of Agricultural Electrification. From 1976 to 1980, Instructor, Deputy Department Head of Volgogradsky District Communist Party in Moscow. From 1980 to 1988, Instructor, Section Head of the Moscow City Communist Party. From 1988 to 1990, Deputy Chairman, then Chairman, of the Volgogradsky District Executive Committee in Moscow. From 1990 to 1991, Correspondence Department Head, General Department Head of the Russian Federation Supreme Soviet Presidium. From 1991, Deputy Head of the Russian Federation President's Secretariat.
HONORS/AWARDS: Veteran of Labor Medal.
FAMILY: Married with a daughter and a granddaughter.
ADDRESS/TELEPHONE: The Presidential Office, The Kremlin, Moscow. 206–6765 (office).

Semenyaka, Lyudmila Ivanovna
POSITION: Ballet Soloist of the Bolshoi State Academic Theater
BIRTHPLACE/DATE: Leningrad, 1952
EDUCATION: Graduated in 1970 from the Leningrad (now St. Petersburg) Choreography School. Former student of Galina Ulanova.
CAREER: From 1970 to 1972, danced at the Kirov Opera and Ballet Theater in Leningrad. In 1972, Bolshoi Theater Troupe Member. Performs in the United States, France, and Japan. USSR People's Artist. Member of the Soviet Peace Committee. Member of the Academy of Arts.
MAJOR WORKS: Roles: Anastasia in *Ivan the Terrible*; Katerina in *The Stone Flower*; Rita in *The Golden Age*; Odetta-Odylia in *Swan Lake*; Masha in *The Nutcracker Suite*. Also performed leading parts in: *Spartacus*; *Raimonda*; *Sleeping Beauty*; *Giselle*; *Bayaderka*; *Romeo and Juliet*.
HONORS/AWARDS: USSR State Prize; Lenin Komsomol Prize; Anna Pavlova Prize of the Paris Dance Academy; Yelena Smirnova Medal (Buenos Aires, Argentina); First Prize and Gold Medal at the Tokyo International Ballet Contest.
FAMILY: Divorced with a son.
ADDRESS/TELEPHONE: 8/2 Okhotny Ryad, Moscow. 253–8742 (home).

Semin, Vyacheslav Nikolayevich
POSITION: Chairman of the Raznoimport (Various Import) All-Russia Foreign Economic Association
BIRTHPLACE/DATE: Moscow, 1935
NATIONALITY: Russian
EDUCATION: Graduated in 1959 from the Moscow Bauman State Technical Institute; in 1967, from the All-Union Academy of Foreign Trade.
CAREER: From 1967, worked at institutions of the USSR Ministry of Foreign Economic Relations. From 1971 to 1976, Office Director of Mashinoexport (Machinery Export). From 1976 to 1980, Department Head at the USSR Trade Mission in France. From 1980 to 1984, Deputy Director-General of Mashinoexport. From 1984 to 1987, USSR Deputy Trade Representative in Morocco. From 1987 to 1988, Director-General of the Tyazhmash (Heavy Industry) All-Union Association. From 1988, Acting Director-General of the Metallurgimport (Metal Import) Association.
FAMILY: Married with two sons and a daughter.
ADDRESS/TELEPHONE: 18/1 Ovchinnikovskaya Naberezhnaya, Moscow. 220–1849 (office).

Semizorova, Nina Lvovna
POSITION: Ballet Company Lead of the Bolshoi Theater
BIRTHPLACE/DATE: Krivoi Rog, 1956
EDUCATION: Graduated in 1975 from the Kiev Choreography School; in 1983, from the State Institute of Dramatic Art. Speaks French.
CAREER: From 1975, danced at the Shevchenko Theater. In 1978, joined the Bolshoi Company.
MAJOR WORKS: Roles: Frigia and Odetta-Odylia in *Swan Lake*; Lady Macbeth (by Molchanov, Choreographer: Vasilyev); Aurora in *The Sleeping Beauty.*
HONORS/AWARDS: Ukraine Honored Artist; Russian Federation People's Artist; First Prize at the Moscow International Contest of Ballet Dancers (1977); Lenin Komsomol Prize.
FAMILY: Married with a daughter.
ADDRESS/TELEPHONE: 9 Chistoprudny Boulevard, Flat #53, Moscow. 924–8436 (home).

Semyonov, Vladimir Gavrilovich
POSITION: Board Chairman of the Commercial Industrial and Construction Joint-Stock Bank
BIRTHPLACE/DATE: Krasnoyarsk, 1944
CAREER: From 1959 to 1963, worked at a plant in Leningrad. From 1963 to 1966, served in the army. From 1966 to 1969, Metalworker-Mechanic of the Elektropribor (Electrical Instrument) Central Research Institute. From 1969 to 1973, Engineer of the All-Union Research Institute. From 1973 to 1976, Assistant at the Division of Economics and Mining Industry Organization of the Institute of Mines. From 1976 to 1988, Party Functionary. From 1988 to 1990, Head of the Lenpromstroibank (Leningrad Industrial Construction Bank).
FAMILY: Married with a child.
ADDRESS/TELEPHONE: 38 Nevski Prospekt, St. Petersburg, 191011. 110–4703.

Senko, Fyodor Petrovich
POSITION: Former USSR Deputy Prime Minister
BIRTHPLACE/DATE: Kozlyakevichi village, Byelorussia, 1936
NATIONALITY: Byelorussian
EDUCATION: Doctor of Economics.
CAREER: Deputy Chairman, then Chairman of a collective farm; First Deputy Chairman of the Executive Committee of the Grodno Regional Council of People's Deputies. From 1976, Bylorussian Republic First Deputy Minister, then Minister of Agriculture. From 1985 to 1990, Deputy Head of the Department of Agriculture and Food Industry, Deputy Head of the Agrarian Department of the Central Committee. From 1990, Deputy Chairman of the Bylorussian Council of Ministers. From 1991, USSR Deputy Prime Minister.
ADDRESS: 3 Rybny Pereulok, Moscow.

Serapion, Fadeyev Nikolay Sergeyevich
POSITION: Metropolitan of Tula and Belevsk
BIRTHPLACE/DATE: Moscow, May 27, 1933
NATIONALITY: Russian
EDUCATION: From 1966 to 1969, postgraduate student at the MDA. Doctor of Theology.
CAREER: In 1957, took the monastic vows. From 1969 to 1971, aide to the Foreign Church Relations Department of the Moscow Patriarchy. In 1971, ordained Archimandrite. From 1971 to 1974, Representative of the Russian Orthodox Church at the Antiokhiysky Patriarchy in Syria.

From 1974 to 1979, Bishop of Irkutsk and Chita. In 1979, ordained Archbishop. From 1989 to 1987, Archbishop of Vladimir and Suzdal. In 1987, Archbishop of Kishinev and Moldavia (Moldova). In 1987 ordained Metropolitan. From 1987 to 1989, Metropolitan of Kishinev and Moldavia. From 1990, Metropolitan of Tula and Belevsk.
ADDRESS/TELEPHONE: 61 Zhukovsky Street, Tula. 230–2118; 230–2431; 235–0454.

Serebrennikov, Mark Parfentyevich
POSITION: Director-General of the Transnational Exchange
BIRTHPLACE/DATE: Moscow, 1939
EDUCATION: Graduated in 1961 from the Moscow Aviation Technology Institute; in 1970, from the All-Union Academy of Foreign Trade. Speaks English and French.
CAREER: From 1961 to 1967, Engineer, Senior Engineer, Head Engineer of the Moscow Saturn Aviation Enterprise. From 1971 to 1977, Staff Member of the Foreign Relations Board of the State Committee for Science and Technology. From 1977 to 1978, Scientific Consultant, Program Director of the UN abroad. From 1978 to 1988, First Deputy Director of an institute of the State Committee for Standards. From 1988 to 1992, Officer of the Council for Mutual Economic Assistance (CMEA).
FAMILY: Married with two children.
ADDRESS/TELEPHONE: 35 Myasnikovskaya Street, Moscow, 101001. 207–6881; 207–6867 (office).

Sergeyev, Aleksey Alekseyevich
POSITION: Coordinating Council Member of the Russian Patriotic Movements Association; Coordinating Council Member of the Rabochaya Rossiya (Working Russia) Movement; Organizing Committee Member of the Russian Communist Party; Leading Researcher at the Academy of Labor and Social Relations
BIRTHPLACE/DATE: Molchanovo village, Tomsk region, 1930
NATIONALITY: Russian
EDUCATION: Graduated in 1953 from the Law Department at Tomsk State University. Doctor of Economics; Professor.
CAREER: From 1953 to 1963, Lecturer at Tomsk University. From 1963 to 1969, Political Economy Department Head at the Krasnoyarsk Non-Ferrous Metals Institute. From 1969 to 1972, Political Economy Department Head at Tver University. From 1972 to 1978, Section Head at the Institute of Economics of the USSR Academy of Sciences. From 1978 to 1982, Working Group Leader for the Committee to Combat National Economic Crimes of the USSR Ministry of Internal Affairs. From 1982 to 1987, Section Head at the Institute of Economics of the USSR Academy of Sciences. From 1987, Political Economy Department Head at the Academy of Labor and Social Relations.
HONORS/AWARDS: Medal for Labor Valor; two Prizes for Science of the USSR Ministry of Higher Education; Honorary Medals of the Academy of the USSR Ministry of Internal Affairs.
FAMILY: Married with two children.
ADDRESS/TELEPHONE: 19 Filyovsky Boulevard, Flat #75, Moscow, 121601. 142–2739 (home).

Serkov, Igor Aleksandrovich
POSITION: Editor in Chief of *Nedelya* (*Week*) weekly newspaper
BIRTHPLACE/DATE: Tashkent, 1950
EDUCATION: Graduated in 1973 from Moscow State University. Speaks German.
CAREER: From 1973 to 1975, served in the army. From 1975 to 1978, Correspondent for *Selskaya Molodezh* (*Country Youth*) newspaper. From 1979 to 1985, Correspondent, Editor of *Smena* (*Rising Generation*) magazine. From 1985 to 1987, Deputy Chief Editor of *Nedelya*.
FAMILY: Married with a son.
ADDRESS/TELEPHONE: 5 Pushkinskaya Square, Moscow. 209–4311 (office).

Setunsky, Nikolay Konstantinovich
POSITION: Deputy Editor in Chief of ITAR-TASS Foreign News Agency
BIRTHPLACE/DATE: Moscow, 1934
EDUCATION: Graduated in 1971 from the Academy of Social Sciences of the Central Committee. Doctor of History.
CAREER: From 1971 to 1972, Editor, Head of the American Countries Department of TASS (Telegraph Agency of the Soviet Union). From 1972 to 1978, TASS Correspondent in the U.S. From 1982 to 1987, TASS U.S. Bureau Chief. From

1987 to February 1992, Editor in Chief of *Ekho Planety* (*Echo of the Planet*) magazine. From February 1992, Deputy Editor in Chief of ITAR-TASS.
MAJOR WORKS: Books on U.S. politics.
FAMILY: Married with four children.
ADDRESS/TELEPHONE: 10 Tverskoi Boulevard, Moscow. 202–4459 (office).

Shakhlin, Boris Anfijanovich
POSITION: Assistant Professor at the Kiev Institute of Physical Education
BIRTHPLACE/DATE: Ishim, Tumen region, 1932
NATIONALITY: Russian
CAREER: From 1956 to 1960, and in 1964, Olympic Champion in Gymnastics. Won seven Gold Medals. Sports Instructor of the Ukraine State Physical and Sports Committee; former Coach of the USSR Combined Competitive Gymnastics Team at the Interdepartmental Olympics Center of the Ukraine State Sports Committee. From 1980, Instructor at the Kiev Institute of Physical Education. Honored Master of Sports (gymnastics).
FAMILY: Married with a daughter.
ADDRESS/TELEPHONE: The Kiev Institute of Physical Culture, Kiev. 74–3064 (Kiev).

Shakhnazarov, George Khosroevich
POSITION: Director of the Global Programs Center of the International Foundation for Socio-Economic and Political Studies (Gorbachev Foundation)
BIRTHPLACE/DATE: Baku, Armenia, 1924
EDUCATION: Doctor of Law.
CAREER: Worked for Politicheskaya Literatura (Political Literature) Publishing House, *Politicheskoye Samoobrazovanie* (*Political Self-Education*) magazine, *Problemy Mira i Socializma* (*Problems of Peace and Socialism*) magazine, the Central Committee's Liaison Department for Communist and Workers' Parties of Socialist Countries. From 1989 to 1990, Aide to the Secretary-General of the Central Committee. From 1990 to December 1991, Aide to the USSR President; member of the USSR Supreme Soviet Committee for Legislation, Law and Order; President of the USSR Political Science Association; Corresponding Member of the USSR Academy of Sciences; from December 1991, Corresponding Member of the Russian Academy of Sciences. USSR People's Deputy. Member of the Communist Party to August 1991.
MAJOR WORKS: Author of many studies and articles on state legislature and politics; *Failure of the Future*; *The Coming World Order.*
HONORS/AWARDS: USSR State Prize.
FAMILY: Married with a son.
ADDRESS/TELEPHONE: 49 Leningradsky Prospekt, Moscow, 125468. 943–9943 (office).

Shaposhnikov, Yevgeni Ivanovich
POSITION: Commander in Chief of the CIS Armed Forces; Air Force Marshal
BIRTHPLACE/DATE: Bolshoi Log village, Aksay district, Rostov-on-Don region, 1942
NATIONALITY: Russian
EDUCATION: Graduated in 1963 from the Kharkov Higher Military-Aviation School; in 1969, from the Yuri Gagarin Air Force Academy; and in 1984, from the General Staff Academy.
CAREER: From 1971 to 1973, Jet-Fighters Regiment Deputy Commander of Political Education; from 1973 to 1979, Commander. From 1979 to 1984, Karpaty Military District Air Force Deputy Commander of Combat Training, Head of the Training and Higher Educational Establishments Department. From 1984 to 1985, Deputy Commander, Odessa Military District Air Force Military Council Member. From 1985 to 1987, Odessa Military District Air Force Commander. In 1987, Odessa Military District Deputy Commander in Chief of Aviation. From 1987 to 1990, Group Air Force Commander of USSR Troops in Germany, Group Deputy Commander in Chief of Aviation of USSR Troops in Germany, Air Force Army Commander, First Deputy Commander in Chief of the Air Force. From 1990 to 1991, USSR First Deputy Defense Minister; from August to December 1991, USSR Defense Minister.
FAMILY: Married with two daughters and a son.
ADDRESS/TELEPHONE: 41 Leningradsky Prospekt, Moscow. 293–3854 (office).

Shatalin, Stanislav Sergeyevich
POSITION: Academician-Secretary of the Department of Economics of the Russian Academy of

Sciences (RAN); President of the Reforma (Reform) Foundation.
BIRTHPLACE/DATE: Pushkin, Leningrad region, Russia, August 24, 1934
EDUCATION: Doctor
CAREER: From 1958 to 1965, worked at the Scientific Research Institute of Economics of the USSR State Planning Committee. From 1965 to 1976, worked at the Central Institute of Economics and Mathematics. From 1976 to 1986, worked at the All-Union Scientific Research Center of Systems Analysis of the USSR Academy of Sciences. From 1986 to 1991, Head of the Institute of National Economic Forecast of the USSR Academy of Sciences. From 1987, Academician of the USSR (now Russian) Academy of Sciences; Academician-Secretary of the Department of Economics of the USSR Academy of Sciences. In 1991, Head of the 500 Days Economic Reforms Program. From 1990 to 1991, member of the Presidential Council; member of the Foreign Policy Council. From 1963 to 1991, member of the Communist Party and the Central Committee.
MAJOR WORKS: On theory and methodology of systems analysis and its utilization in solving social economic and scientific problems.
HONORS/AWARDS: USSR State Prize; Order of the Badge of Honor.
FANILY: Married with two children.
ADDRESS/TELEPHONE: 32 Krasikov Street, B-418, Moscow, 117418. 129–0711 (office); 243-3597 (home).

Shatrov (Marshak), Mikhail Filippovoch
POSITION: Playwright
BIRTHPLACE/DATE: Moscow, 1932
CAREER: Wrote first play *Clean Hands* in 1955, which was staged at the Moscow Theater for Youth; wrote *Brest Peace Treaty* in 1962. Secretary of the Confederation of Writers' Unions. From 1986 to 1992, Board Secretary of the Theater Workers Union.
MAJOR WORKS: Historic plays: *The Day of Silence*; *In the Name of Revolution*; *July 6*; *Further . . . Further . . . Further . . .*; *Bolshevicks*; *Blue Horses on the Red Grass*; *We Will Win!*; *The Dictatorship of Conscience*. Historical novel: *February*.
HONORS/AWARDS: Order of the Red Banner; Order of the People's Friendship; USSR State Prize.
FAMILY: Married with a child.
ADDRESS/TELEPHONE: 2 Serafimovich Street, Flat #349, Moscow, 109072. 231–8464 (home).

Shayevich, Adolf Solomonovich
POSITION: Chief Rabbi of the Moscow Choral Synagogue
BIRTHPLACE/DATE: Khabarovsk, October 28, 1937
EDUCATION: Graduated in 1980 from the Higher Rabbinical School in Budapest, Hungary.
CAREER: From 1980 to 1984, Assistant Rabbi, then Chief Rabbi, of the Moscow Choral Synagogue. From 1991, Chairman of the All-Union Council of Jewish Religious Communities.
FAMILY: Married with two children.
ADDRESS/TELEPHONE: 8 Maly Komsomolsky Pereulok, Moscow. 924–2424.

Shchedrin, Rodion Konstantinovich
POSITION: Composer
BIRTHPLACE/DATE: Moscow, 1932
CAREER: From 1990, works for the German Steinway Company. From 1958, USSR People's Actor; member of the USSR Union of Composers. From 1992, member of the International Association of Composers Organizations (MAKO).
MAJOR WORKS: Operas: *Not Just Love* (1961); *Dead Souls* (1976). Ballets: *Hunchback Horse* (1960); *Carmen-Suite* (1967); *Anna Karenina* (1972).
HONORS/AWARDS: USSR State Prize; Prize of Lenin.
FAMILY: Married.
ADDRESS/TELEPHONE: 8/10 Nezdanova Street, Moscow, 103009. 229–5218.

Shchekochikin, Victor Vladimirovich
POSITION: President of the Inter-Republican Organization of the Russian Union of Property Owners; Chairman of the Moscow Union of Businessmen; President of the Zemlyane (Citizens of Earth) Private Family Association
CAREER: From 1985 to 1986, Chief Accountant of an association of gardeners. In 1986, opened a Moscow consultative bureau of financial legislature. In 1987, opened the Commerchesky (Com-

mercial) Accounting Family Cooperative. From 1988, President of the Zemliane Association; Manager of the Zemliane Bank. From 1990, President of the Inter-Republican Organization of the Russian Union of Property Owners; Chairman of the Moscow Union of Businessmen; member of the President's Business Council.
FAMILY: Married with four children.
ADDRESS/TELEPHONE: P.O. Box 550, Moscow, 119034. 281–8192 (office).

Shchekochikhin, Yuri Petrovich
POSITION: Correspondent for *Literaturnaya Gazeta* (*Literary Newspaper*)
BIRTHPLACE/DATE: Kirovobad, Azerbaijan, 1950
CAREER: From 1967, Correspondent for *Moskovsky Komsomolets* newspaper. From 1972, wrote for *Komsomolskaya Pravda* (*Komsomol Truth*) daily newspaper; wrote a column for children in *Aly Parus* (*The Red Sail*). From 1980, Correspondent and Editorial Board Member of *Literaturnaya Gazeta*. USSR People's Deputy.
MAJOR WORKS: On problems of youth.
HONORS/AWARDS: Moscow Journalists' Union Prize.
FAMILY: Married with two sons.
ADDRESS/TELEPHONE: 13 Kostyansky Pereulok, Moscow. 208–9140 (office).

Shcherbakov, Konstantin Aleksandrovich.
POSITION: Russian Federation First Deputy Minister of Culture
BIRTHPLACE/DATE: Moscow, 1938
EDUCATION: Doctor of Philosophy.
CAREER: From 1960 to 1963, worked from Reporter to Editor of the Literature and Art Department of *Moskovsky Komsomolets* daily newspaper. From 1963 to 1975, Head of the Literature and Art Department, Editor, Editorial Board Member, Correspondent for *Komsomolskaya Pravda* (*Komsomol Truth*) daily. From 1975 to 1982, Representative of the All-Union Copyright Agency in Poland. From 1972 to 1987, Editorial Board Member and Editor of the Culture Department of *Druzhba Narodov* (*People's Friendship*) magazine. From 1987, Editor in Chief of *Iskusstvo Kino* (*Art of Cinematography*) magazine. From 1992, Russian Federation Deputy Minister of Culture and Tourism.
MAJOR WORKS: *On the Way to Becoming Courageous*; *Hero, Time, Artist*; *To Check In Action*; *With the Wish of Truth*.
HONORS/AWARDS: USSR Journalists' Union Lunacharsky Prize (1969).
FAMILY: Married.
ADDRESS/TELEPHONE: 9 Usiyevich Street, Moscow, 125319; 7 Kitaisky Proyezd, Moscow, 103693. 151–0272 (office); 220–4562.

Shcherbakov, Vladimir Pavlovich
POSITION: Chairman of the United Confederation of Trade Unions
BIRTHPLACE/DATE: Moscow, March 21, 1941
NATIONALITY: Russian
EDUCATION: Doctor of Technology.
CAREER: From 1958, Electrician. From 1961 to 1986, worked at the Moscow Automatic Systems Plant from Mechanic to Director-General. From 1986, Chairman of the USSR Moscow Council of Trade Unions. From 1990, Chairman of the USSR United Confederation of Trade Unions (now the United Confederation of Trade Unions). Member of the Communist Party to 1991. USSR People's Deputy from 1989 to 1992.
HONORS/AWARDS: Order of Lenin; Order of the Red Banner of Labor.
FAMILY: Married with two children.
ADDRESS/TELEPHONE: 42 Leninsky Prospekt, Moscow, 117119. 938–8222 (office).

Sheinis, Victor Leonidovich
POSITION: Researcher General of the Institute of the World Economy and International Relations of the Russian Academy of Sciences (RAN); Deputy Executive Secretary of the Russian Federation Constitutional Council
BIRTHPLACE/DATE: Kiev, 1931
EDUCATION: From 1957 to 1958, postgraduate student at the Institute of Oriental Research of the USSR Academy of Sciences, and at Leningrad University. Doctor of Economics.
CAREER: From 1953 to 1956, History Teacher at Leningrad high schools. From 1958 to 1964, worked at the Leningrad Kirov Factory. To 1975, Assistant, Professor at Leningrad University. From 1975 to 1977, Senior Researcher at the Institute of

Social and Economic Problems of the USSR Academy of Sciences in Leningrad. State Advisor, Legislative Advisor to the Russian President; member of the Council of Nationalities; member of the Constitutional Committee; member of the Congress and Supreme Soviet Regulations Committee; Chairman of the Kazakh Rehabilitation Committee. From January 1992, Head of the Russian Federation State Department of Legislation. To April 1992, Head of the Russian State Black Sea Navy Committee; member of the Russian Federation State Committee's Military and Navy Department. Russian Federation People's Deputy. Member of the Communist Party to 1990.
FAMILY: Married.
ADDRESS: 8 Ilyinka Street, 20, Room 606, Moscow.

Shelov-Kovediaev, Fyodor Vadimovich
POSITION: Former Russian Federation Deputy Foreign Minister
NATIONALITY: Russian
EDUCATION: Doctor of History.
CAREER: From 1982 to 1990, worked at the Institute of History of the USSR Academy of Sciences. From 1990 to 1991, Chairman of the Russian Federation Supreme Soviet Subcommittee for Inter-Republican Relations. From 1991 to 1992, Russian Federation Deputy Foreign Minister; Exclusive Representative of the Russian President. Retired from October 1992.
TELEPHONE: 244–1606 (reception); 244–9225 (office).

Shenin, Oleg Semyonovich
POSITION: Former member of the Politburo; Secretary of the Central Committee
BIRTHPLACE/DATE: Volgograd region, July 27, 1937
NATIONALITY: Russian
CAREER: From 1955, worked at various construction organizations in Krasnoyarsk. From 1974, Party Official. From 1982, Secretary of the Krasnoyarsk Region Party Committee. From 1985, Secretary-General of the Khakass Region Party Committee. From 1987, Secretary-General of the Krasnoyarsk Region Party Committee. From April 1990, Chairman of the Krasnoyarsk Region Council of People's Deputies. From 1990, member of the Politburo and Secretary of the Central Committee. From December 1989 to June 1990, member of the Russian Central Committee; from 1990 to August 1991, member of the Russian Federation Central Committee; in August 1991, arrested on charges of participation in the attempted coup. USSR People's Deputy; member of the Communist Party from 1962; member of the Central Committee from 1990.
HONORS/AWARDS: Order of the October Revolution; Order of the Red Banner; two Orders of the Badge of Honor; Medal and Order of the Afghan Republic.
FAMILY: Married with two daughters, a son, and two grandchildren.
TELEPHONE: 229–4662 (Russian Federation Prosecutor's Office).

Sherbakov, Vladimir Ivanovich
POSITION: President of the Interprivatizatsia International Foundation for the Promotion of Business and Foreign Investments
BIRTHPLACE/DATE: Novaya Sisoyevka, Promorsk region, December 5, 1949
NATIONALITY: Russian
EDUCATION: From 1974 to 1976, postgraduate student at the Higher Komsomol School of the Central Committee. Doctor of Economics.
CAREER: From 1969 to 1970, Instructor of the Tolyatti Komsomol City Committee in Kuibyshev region. From 1970 to 1971, Engineer of the Department of Construction; Division Dispatcher at the Volga Auto Plant. From 1971, worked for the Komsomol. From 1977, Deputy Chief, then Chief of the Planning and Economic Department of the Volga Auto Plant. From 1982, Deputy Director-General, Planning and Economic Director of the Kamsk Industrial Association of Heavy Trucks. From 1985, Head of the Car and Metal Department, then Head of the Salary and Wages Department of the USSR State Committee of Labor and Society. In 1988, First Deputy Head of the Department of National Economic Development of the USSR Council of Ministers' Department of Internal Affairs. From 1989, Chairman of the USSR State Committee of Labor and Society. In 1991, USSR Deputy Prime Minister. From September 1991, President of Interprivatizatsia. Member of the Communist Party from 1970.

FAMILY: Married with a child.
ADDRESS/TELEPHONE: 3 Solanka Street, Str. 3, Moscow, 109028. 924–6061 (office).

Sherimkulov, Medetkan Sherimkulovich
POSITION: Chairman of the Kirghiz Republic Supreme Soviet
BIRTHPLACE/DATE: Chapayevo, Sokuluksk district, Kirghiz Republic, November 17, 1939
CAREER: From 1957, Carpenter at a Frunze (now Bishkek) factory; taught in the Scientific Communism Department at Kirghiz University. From 1971 to 1977, Instructor of the Department of Science and Schools of the Kirghiz Central Committee; from 1973 to 1976, Secretary of the State University Party Committee. From 1976 to 1980, Secretary of the Issyk-Kul Regional Party Committee, then Head of the Department of Political Education of the Kirghiz Central Committee. From 1985, Rector of the Kirghiz State Institute of Physical Education, Chairman of the Kirghiz Central Committee, Chairman of the Kirghiz Central Committee's Auditing Commission. From 1987 to 1990, Secretary of the Kirghiz Central Committee; member of the Kirghiz Politburo. In December 1990, Chairman of the Kirghiz Supreme Soviet. People's Deputy of Kirgistan. From 1962 to 1991, member of the Communist Party.
FAMILY: Married with two sons.
ADDRESS/TELEPHONE: The Kirghiz Republic Supreme Soviet, Bishkek, 720005. 22–5523 (office).

Shilov, Aleksandr Maksovich.
POSITION: Artist
BIRTHPLACE/DATE: Moscow, 1943
CAREER: Worked at the Timiryazev House of Young Pioneers Art Studio; Vice President of the Soviet-Malta Society; Presidium Member of the Russian Federation Cultural Foundation; Presidium Member of the Soviet-Japanese Society (now the Society of Friendship with Japan); USSR People's Artist.
MAJOR WORKS: Artist of portraits of priests (*Metropolitan Mephody*; *Metropolitan Philaret*; *Monk Zinovy*), scientists (*Academician Semyonov*; *Surgeon Fyodorov*), actors (*Actor Mark Zakharov*), children, women, and the collection of portraits *Returning Home*, dedicated to the soldiers who served in Afghanistan.
HONORS/AWARDS: Hero of Socialist Labor; Lenin Komsomol Prize.
FAMILY: Married with a daughter.
ADDRESS/TELEPHONE: 2/14 Nezdanove Street, Flat #35, Moscow. 229–5689 (home).

Shimko, Vladimir Ivanovich
POSITION: President of the Radiocomplex Corporation
BIRTHPLACE/DATE: Zelenodolsk, Tatar Republic, 1938
NATIONALITY: Russian
CAREER: From 1961 to 1963, Engineer-Constructor of a Kiev engineering organization. From 1963 to 1968, Chief Engineer, Laboratory Head, Division Head of the Micromechanisms Scientific Research Institute of the Ministry of Electronic Industry. From 1968 to 1987, Instructor, Division Head, Department Head of the Central Committee. From 1988 to 1989, Head of the Social and Economic Department of the Central Committee. From 1989 to 1991, USSR Minister of Radio Industry. From 1991, President of the Radiocomplex Corporation of Radio and Electronics. USSR Supreme Soviet Deputy. Member of the Communist Party from 1964 to 1991.
HONORS/AWARDS: Order of the October Revolution; Order of the Red Banner; Order of the Badge of Honor.
FAMILY: Married with a son and a daughter.
ADDRESS/TELEPHONE: 35 Miasnitskaya Street, Moscow, 101959. 207–6000 (office).

Shlyaga, Nikolay Ivanovich
POSITION: Former Head of the USSR Armed Forces Main Military and Political Directorate; Colonel-General
BIRTHPLACE/DATE: Peredreika, Petrikovsk district, Gomel region, 1935
CAREER: From 1955, served in the USSR Armed Forces; Military Division Political Department Head, Joined Military Forces Political Department Head, Deputy Head of the Main Political Directorate of the USSR Army and Navy. From 1990 to December 1991, Head of the Main Military and Political Department of the USSR Armed Forces; USSR Deputy Minister of Defense.
FAMILY: Married with two daughters.
TELEPHONE: 293–2869; 293–1413.

Shlyakhtin, Vladimir Ivanovich

POSITION: Russian Federation Deputy Minister of Defense

BIRTHPLACE/DATE: Dolopovka, Taganrog district, Rostov region, 1940

NATIONALITY: Russian

CAREER: Frontier Region Commander in Central Asia during the Afghan war; worked for the Interdepartmental Committee to Regulate the Russian State Borders. From June 1992, Russian Federation Deputy Minister of Defense. Lieutenant-General.

HONORS/AWARDS: Military Order of the Red Banner; Order of the Red Star; nineteen orders.

FAMILY: Married with two daughters.

ADDRESS/TELEPHONE: 2 Lubyanka Street, Moscow, 101000. 224–2137 (office).

Shorin, Vladimir Pavlovich

POSITION: Chairman of the Russian Federation Supreme Soviet Committee for Science and Education; Russian Federation People's Deputy

BIRTHPLACE/DATE: Nizhny Lomov, Penza region, July, 27, 1939

EDUCATION: From 1956 to 1963, student at the Kuibyshev Aviation Institute, then postgraduate student. Doctor of Technology; Professor.

CAREER: From 1963 to 1990, Engineer, Assistant, Senior Teacher, Assistant Professor, Department Head, Pro-Rector, Rector of the Kuibyshev Aviation Institute. From 1990, Chairman of the Russian Federation Supreme Soviet Committee for Science and Education; member of the Council of the Republic. Honored Scientist of the Russian Federation; member of the Russian Academy of Sciences. Russian Federation People's Deputy. Member of the Communist Party to 1991.

MAJOR WORKS: 230 scientific articles, more than sixty inventions, five research studies, and six scientific manuals.

FAMILY: Married with a daughter.

ADDRESS/TELEPHONE: 8 Academician Korolev Street, Building 2, Flat #560, Moscow, 129515. 205–4324 (office); 286–2680 (home).

Shostakowski, Viacheslaw Nikolayevich

POSITION: Director of the Social Studies Center of the International Foundation for Socio-Economic and Political Studies (Gorbachev Foundation)

BIRTHPLACE/DATE: Stemas, Alatir district, Chuvash Republic, October, 23, 1937

NATIONALITY: Ukrainian

EDUCATION: Doctor of Philosophy; Professor.

CAREER: From 1960 to 1962, Assistant to the Department of Pharmaceutical Chemistry at the Lvov Medical Institute. From 1962 to 1967, Instructor, Deputy Sector Head, Head of the Youth and Students Sector of the Komsomol Central Committee. From 1967 to 1971, Head of the Youth and Students Department of the Komsomol Central Committee. From 1973 to 1978, Scientific Secretary of the Central Committee's Academy of Social Sciences. From 1978 to 1986, Instructor of the Party Official Education Department of the Central Committee's Department of Party Activities. From 1986 to 1990, Rector of the Moscow Highest Party School; Director of the Perspectiva (Perspective) Independent Research Information Agency; Co-Creator of the Democratic Faction of the Communist Party; Co-Chairman of the Russian Federation Republican Party. From 1991 to 1992, Co-Chairman of the Democratic Reforms Movement. From 1992, Director of the Social Studies Center of the Gorbachev Foundation. Member of the Communist Party from 1961 to 1990.

MAJOR WORKS: More than 200 scientific articles.

HONORS/AWARDS: Order of the People's Friendship; Medal For Labor Valor; Medal For the Development of Tselina (Virgin Land); Veteran of Labor Medal.

FAMILY: Married with a son.

ADDRESS/TELEPHONE: 49 Leningradsky Prospekt, Moscow, 125468. 943–9895 (office).

Shoub, Yuli Germanovich.

POSITION: Editor in Chief of *Teatr* (*Theater*) magazine

BIRTHPLACE/DATE: Moscow, 1920

CAREER: From 1945 to 1964, member and Head of the Artistic Department of the All-Union Theatrical Society (VTO). From 1960 to 1964, Editor in Chief of the VTO Publishing Department. From 1965 to 1973, Deputy Editor in Chief of Iskusstvo (Arts) Publishing House. From 1973 to 1982, Dep-

uty Editor in Chief of *Teatr* (*Theater*) magazine; from 1982 to 1992, First Deputy Editor in Chief; from 1992, Editor in Chief. Honored Cultural Worker; member of the Union of Theater Workers; member of the Confederation of Journalists' Unions.
HONORS/AWARDS: Order of the Badge of Honor; Order For Labor Valor During World War II.
FAMILY: Married with two children and two granddaughters.
ADDRESS/TELEPHONE: 49 Herzen Street, Moscow, 121069. 291–5788 (office).

Shulyatyeva, Nadezhda Aleksandrovna
POSITION: President of the Russian Union of Small Enterprises; President of the Euroasian League of Small and Medium Enterprises of the National Committeee of the World Association of Small and Medium Enterprises
BIRTHPLACE/DATE: Turinsk, Sverdlovsk region, 1941
NATIONALITY: Russian
EDUCATION: Graduated in 1967 from the Moscow Aviation Technology Institute.
CAREER: From 1967 to 1972, worked at Yakovlev's Aircraft Design Office. From 1972 to 1985, worked at the Research Institute of Thermal Processes. From 1985 to 1989, worked at a District Committee, then at the Moscow City Executive Committee Department of Housing Construction Planning. Full Member of the Russian Academy of Economic Sciences and Entrepreneurship.
FAMILY: Married with two children.
ADDRESS/TELEPHONE: 13 Ilyinka Street, Moscow. 206–9419 (office); 202–9306 (home).

Shumeyko, Vladimir Filippovich
POSITION: First Deputy Chairman of the Government; Russian Federation First Deputy Prime Minister
BIRTHPLACE/DATE: Rostov-on-Don, February 18, 1945
NATIONALITY: Russian
EDUCATION: Doctor of Technology.
CAREER: From 1963 to 1970, Fitter, Design Engineer of Electronic and Measuring Devices in Krasnodar. From 1970 to 1985, Engineer, Senior Engineer, Chief Engineer, Laboratory Head, Department Head of the Krasnodar All-Union Research Institute of Electronic and Measuring Devices. From 1985 to 1990, General Designer, General Engineer, Director-General of the Krasnodar Industrial Complex of Electronic and Measuring Devices. From 1990 to 1992, Deputy Chairman of the Supreme Soviet Committee for Economic Reforms and Property. From 1991 to 1992, Deputy Chairman of the Russian Federation Supreme Soviet. From 1992, First Deputy Chairman of the Russian Federation Government; President of the Confederation of Unions of Businessmen. From 1990 to 1992, Russian People's Deputy.
FAMILY: Married with two daughters.

Shushkevich, Stanislav Stanislavovich
POSITION: Chairman of the Byelorussian Republic Supreme Soviet
BIRTHPLACE/DATE: Minsk, December 15, 1934
NATIONALITY: Byelorussian
EDUCATION: Doctor; Professor.
CAREER: From 1959, Junior Researcher at the Institute of Physics of the Byelorussian Republic Academy of Sciences. From 1960 to 1961, Senior Engineer of the Special Designing Bureau at the Minsk Radio Factory. From 1961 to 1967, Senior Engineer, Chief Engineer, Laboratory Sector Head at Lenin Byelorussian State University (BGU). From 1967 to 1969, Scientific Pro-Rector of the Minsk Institute of Radio and Technology. From 1969, Assistant Professor, Professor, Department Head of Nuclear Physics at BGU. From 1986, Scientific Pro-Rector of BGU. From 1990, First Deputy Chairman of the Byelorussian Republic Supreme Soviet. From 1991, Chairman of the Byelorussian Supreme Soviet; Corresponding Member of the Byelorussian Academy of Sciences. People's Deputy from 1989 to 1992. Member of the Communist Party to 1991.
HONORS/AWARDS: Byelorussian Supreme Soviet State Prize; USSR Council of Ministers awards.
FAMILY: Married with a daughter and a son.
ADDRESS/TELEPHONE: The House of Parliament, Minsk, 220010. 29–6008 (office).

Shustko, Lev Sergeyevich
POSITION: Commander of the North-Caucasus Military Region; Colonel-General

BIRTHPLACE/DATE: Mitichi, Moscow region, 1935
NATIONALITY: Russian
CAREER: From 1952, served in the USSR Military Forces: Division Commander, Army Commander, Military Region Deputy Commander. From 1986, Commander of the North-Caucasus Military Region. USSR People's Deputy.
FAMILY: Married with two daughters.
ADDRESS/TELEPHONE: The Officers Department of the North-Caucasus Military Region, Rostov-on-Don, 344026. 293–2938; 293–1413.

Sidorov, Yevgeni Yuryevich
POSITION: Russian Federation Minister of Culture and Tourism
BIRTHPLACE/DATE: Sverdlovsk (now Yekaterinburg), 1938
EDUCATION: Graduated in 1961 from the Law Department at Moscow State University. Completed postgraduate studies at the Central Committee's Academy of Social Sciences. Professor.
CAREER: From 1961, Head of the Literature and Art Department of *Moskovsky Komsomolets* (*Moscow Komsomol Member*) newspaper; worked at *Literaturnaya Gazeta (Literary Newspaper)* newspaper; Head of the Aesthetic Education and Criticism Department of *Yunost* (*Youth*) magazine. From 1971, member of the USSR Writers' Union (now Confederation of Writers' Unions). From 1978, Pro-Rector, and from 1987, Rector of the Moscow Literary Institute. Conducts seminars on literary criticism. From 1992, Russian Federation Minister of Culture.
MAJOR WORKS: *On the Stylistic Diversity of Soviet Prose*; *Time, Writer, Style*; *On the Way to Synthesis*.
HONORS/AWARDS: Order of the People's Friendship; Order of the Badge of Honor.
FAMILY: Married with a son.
ADDRESS/TELEPHONE: 7 Kitaisky Proyezd, Moscow, 103693. 925–1195 (office).

Sidorski, Philipp Philippovich
POSITION: Russian Federation Ambassador to Uzbekistan; Ambassador Extraordinary and Plenipotentiary
BIRTHPLACE/DATE: Moscow, August 21, 1937
NATIONALITY: Russian
CAREER: From 1966 to 1970, Interpreter, Attaché at the USSR Embassy in Afghanistan. From 1970 to 1972, Attaché, Third Secretary of the Middle East Department of the USSR Foreign Ministry. From 1972 to 1976, Third, Second Secretary at the USSR Embassy in Iran. From 1978 to 1979, First Secretary of the Middle East Department of the USSR Foreign Ministry. From 1979 to 1985, First Secretary, Counsellor at the USSR Embassy in Iran. From 1985 to 1988, Counsellor, Expert of the Middle East Department of the USSR Foreign Ministry. From 1988 to 1992, Minister-Counsellor at the USSR (now Russian Federation) Embassy in Afghanistan. From April 1992, Russian Federation Ambassador to the Republic of Uzbekistan.
HONORS/AWARDS: Order of the People's Friendship; Order of the Badge of Honor.
FAMILY: Married with two children.
TELEPHONE: 244–1606 (Foreign Ministry).

Silayev, Ivan Stepanovich
POSITION: Russian Federation Permanent Representative to the European Economic Community (Brussels, Belgium); Ambassador Extraordinary and Plenipotentiary
BIRTHPLACE/DATE: Bakhtyzino, Voznesensky district, Gorky region, October 21, 1930
NATIONALITY: Russian
EDUCATION: Graduated in 1954 from the Kazan Tupolev Aircraft Institute.
CAREER: From 1959, Foreman at the Gorky Aircraft Plant; from 1969, Chief Engineer; from 1971 to 1974, Director. From 1974 to 1977, USSR Deputy Minister, and from 1976 to 1980, USSR First Deputy Minister of Aviation. From 1980 to 1981, USSR Minister of the Machine and Tool Industry. From 1981 to 1985, USSR Minister of Aviation. From October 1985, Deputy Chairman of the USSR Council of Ministers; Board Head of the USSR Council of Ministers. From June 1990, Chairman of the Russian Federation Council of Ministers. From August 1991, Head of the USSR National Economy Committee. From October 1991, Chairman of the Inter-Republican Economic Committee.
HONORS/AWARDS: Hero of Socialist Labor (1975); Prize of Lenin (1972); Order of Lenin

(1975); Order of the October Revolution (1981); government awards.
FAMILY: Married.
ADDRESS/TELEPHONE: 2 Krasnopresnenskaya Naberezhnaya, Moscow, 103274. 244–3651.

Silkova, Nina Prokopyevna
POSITION: Former Secretary of the Russian Federation Central Committee; former member of the Politburo
BIRTHPLACE/DATE: Ilansky, Krasnoyarsk region, 1939
NATIONALITY: Russian
EDUCATION: Doctor of History.
CAREER: In 1957, Secondary School Young Pioneer Leader. From 1961 to 1968, Komsomol and Party Functionary: Department Head, Second Secretary, First Secretary of the Ilansky District Komsomol Committee, Head of the Political Education Room of the Ilansky Communist Party. From 1968 to 1977, Secretary of the Krasnoyarsk Region Komsomol Committee, Secretary of the Krasnoyarsk Central District Communist Party. From 1977 to 1987, Secretary of the Krasnoyarsk City Communist Party, Instructor, Head of the Propaganda and Agitation Department, Secretary of the Krasnoyarsk Region Communist Party. From 1987 to 1990, USSR Deputy Minister of Culture. From 1990 to 1991, Secretary of the Russian Federation Central Committee. Member of the Communist Party from 1962 to 1991.
HONORS/AWARDS: Government awards.
FAMILY: Married with a daughter.
ADDRESS/FAMILY: 4 Staraya Ploschad, Moscow, 103032. 206–5497.

Sillari, Ann-Arno Augustovich
POSITION: Former First Secretary of the Estonian Central Committee; former member of the Politburo
BIRTHPLACE/DATE: Tallinn, 1944
NATIONALITY: Estonian
CAREER: From 1967 to 1974, Assistant Foreman, Chief Foreman, Head of Production, Deputy Chief Engineer of the Keila Factory. From 1974, Department Head of the Leninsky District Party Committee in Tallinn, Instructor, Section Head, Inspector, Deputy Department Head of the Estonian Central Committee. From 1981, worked for the Central Committee. From 1984, First Secretary of the Estonian Tartu City Committee. From 1986, First Secretary of the Estonian Tallinn City Committee. From 1989, Secretary, and from 1990, First Secretary of the Estonian Central Committee.
FAMILY: Married with two children.
ADDRESS/TELEPHONE: 21-A Tina, Flat #10, Tallinn, 200100. 44–5118.

Simonenko, Valentin Konstantinovich
POSITION: First Vice Premier of Ukraine; Socio-Economic Advisor to the Ukrainian President
BIRTHPLACE/DATE: Odessa, 1940
CAREER: From 1962 to 1964, Foreman, Engineer, Department Head, Technical Department Head, Director of the Odessa Ferro-Concrete Structures Plant. From 1964 to 1968, First Secretary of the Primorsky District Party Committee in Odessa. From 1973 to 1982, Construction Department Head, Second Secretary of the Odessa City Party Committee. From 1983 to 1992, Chairman of the Odessa City Executive Committee. From February to March 1992, Ukraine Presidium Representative in Odessa region. From 1992, Ukrainian First Vice Premier. Ukraine People's Deputy.
HONORS/AWARDS: Two Orders of the Red Banner of Labor; Order of the People's Friendship; Ukraine Supreme Soviet Diploma; three medals.
FAMILY: Married with two children.
ADDRESS/TELEPHONE: 11 Bankovaya Street, Kiev, 252220. 291–5278 (office).

Simonyan, Nikita Pavlovich
POSITION: First Vice President of the Russian Football Union
BIRTHPLACE/DATE: Armavir, Krasnodar region, 1926
NATIONALITY: Armenian
EDUCATION: Graduated from the State Institute of Physical Education.
CAREER: Member of the 1956 Summer Olympic Champion Football Team. Coach of the Spartak, Ararat, and Chernomorets Football Clubs. From 1976 to 1979, Coach of the USSR National Football Team. From 1990 to 1991, First Vice President of the USSR Football Federation.
HONORS/AWARDS: Honored USSR Master of Sports; Order of the Red Banner of Labor; Order of the Badge of Honor; Veteran of Labor Medal.

FAMILY: Married with a daughter.
ADDRESS/TELEPHONE: 16 Stankevich Street, Flat #71, Moscow, 103009. 201–1622 (office); 229–3749 (home).

Sineva, Ulyana Fyodorovna
POSITION: Board Chairperson of the Bryansksotsbank (Bryansk Social Bank) Universal Commercial Bank
BIRTHPLACE/DATE: Pochep, Bryansk region, 1938
NATIONALITY: Russian
EDUCATION: Graduated in 1986 from the All-Union Extramural Financial and Economic Institute.
CAREER: From 1958 to 1970, Bank Economist. From 1970 to 1978, Senior Bank Economist. From 1978 to 1981, Bank Department Deputy Manager. From 1981 to 1987, Bank Department Manager. From 1987 to 1990, Bryansk Region Directorate Head of the Zhilsotsbank (Housing and Social Service Bank).
FAMILY: Married with two children.
ADDRESS/TELEPHONE: 34 Gorky Street, Bryansk, 241000. 4–2012 (office).

Sister, Vladimir Grigoryevich
POSITION: Prefect of the Moscow Northeastern Administrative District
BIRTHPLACE/DATE: Gorlovka, Donetsk region, January 10, 1945
NATIONALITY: Ukrainian
EDUCATION: From 1969, postgraduate student at the Moscow State Institute of Nitric Industry. Doctor of Technical Sciences.
CAREER: From 1962 to 1963, Laboratory Assistant at the Kemerovsky Complex. In 1968, Researcher at the Kiev Institute of Chloric Industry. To 1976, Senior Engineer at the Moscow State Institute of Nitric Industry. From 1976 to 1990, Senior Researcher, Section Head at the Research Institute of the Ministry of Chemical and Gas Engineering Industry. From 1990 to 1991, Chairman of the Kirovsky District Council. From July 1991, Prefect of the Moscow Northeast Administrative District. Kirovsky District Council Deputy.
FAMILY: Married with a daughter.
ADDRESS/TELEPHONE: 18 Prospekt Mira, Moscow, 129005. 281–4386 (office).

Sitaryan, Stepan Aramaisovich
POSITION: Director of the Institute of Foreign Economic Studies; Vice President of the Social and Economic Reforms Foundation
BIRTHPLACE/DATE: Alaverdy, Armenia, September 27, 1930
NATIONALITY: Armenian
EDUCATION: Graduated in 1953 from Moscow State University. From 1953 to 1957, postgraduate student at Moscow University. Doctor of Economics; Professor (1970).
CAREER: In 1957, Political Economy Lecturer at Moscow State University. From 1957 to 1959, Senior Economist, and from 1959 to 1966, Senior Research Analyst at the Research Institute of Finance of the USSR Ministry of Finance. Joined the Communist Party in 1960. From 1966 to 1970, Deputy Director, and from 1970 to 1974, Director of the Research Institute of Finance. From 1970 to 1985, Professor of the Department of Political Economy at Moscow State University. From 1974 to 1983, Deputy USSR Finance Minister. From 1983 to 1986, Deputy Chairman of the USSR State Planning Committee. From 1986 to 1989, First Deputy Chairman of the USSR State Planning Committee. From 1987, Academician of the Economics Department of the USSR Academy of Sciences. From 1989, Deputy Chairman of the USSR Council of Ministers, Chairman of the USSR State Foreign Economic Commission. From July 1991 to November 1991, Deputy Chairman of the Union-Republican Committee on Currency.
MAJOR WORKS: On national income and finances.
HONORS/AWARDS: Order of the Red Banner of Labor; Order of the Badge of Honor.
FAMILY: Married with two children.
ADDRESS/TELEPHONE: 5-A Varvarka Street, Moscow. 298–7763 (office); 245–4139 (home).

Skokov, Yuri Vladimorovich
POSITION: Secretary of the Russian Federation Security Council; Secretary of the Council of Heads of Member-States
BIRTHPLACE/DATE: 1938
NATIONALITY: Russian
EDUCATION: Graduated in 1961 from the Leningrad Electrotechnical Institute. Doctor of Sciences.

CAREER: Junior Researcher at the All-Union Research Institute of Power Supply Sources. Director-General of the Kvant (Quantum) Research and Production Association, Board Chairman of the Kvant Inter-Regional State Association. From September 1990, First Deputy Chairman of the Russian Council of Ministers. From July 1991 to May 1992, State Counsellor, Chairman of the Russian Federation Council of the Republic. Russian Federation People's Deputy. Member of the Russian Supreme Soviet Committee for Economic Reforms. From September 1991 to May 1992, Secretary of the Russian President's Commission for the Status, Structure, and Activities of the Russian Federation Security Council. From June 1992, Secretary of the Russian Federation Security Council. From July 1992, headed the adoption of the Russian Federation President's Decree to Implement the Decisions of the Russian Federation Security Council.
FAMILY: Married with a daughter.
ADDRESS/TELEPHONE: 2 Krasnopresnenskaya Naberezhnaya, Moscow, 103274. 205–5593 (office).

Skrinsky, Aleksandr Nikolayevich
POSITION: Academician-Secretary of the Nuclear Physics Department of the Russian Academy of Sciences; Director of the Institute of Nuclear Physics of the Russian Academy of Sciences' Siberian branch
BIRTHPLACE/DATE: Orenburg, January 15, 1936
NATIONALITY: Russian
EDUCATION: Graduated in 1959 from Moscow State University.
CAREER: From 1959, worked at the Nuclear Physics Institute of the USSR Academy of Sciences' Siberian branch. From 1967, Professor at Novosibirsk University. From 1970, Academician of the USSR Academy of Sciences. From 1978, Director of the Nuclear Physics Institute. From 1988, Academician-Secretary of the Nuclear Physics Department of the USSR Academy of Sciences.
MAJOR WORKS: On high-energy physics, acceleration of charged particles, and synchrotronic irradiation. Co-creator of the opposite beams method.
HONORS/AWARDS: Prize of Lenin (1967); Order of the Red Banner of Labor.
FAMILY: Married with two children.
ADDRESS/TELEPHONE: 32-A Leninsky Prospekt, Moscow, 117901. 938–6500; 938–5437 (office).

Sladkyavichus, Vincent
POSITION: Archbishop of Kaunas; Cardinal
BIRTHPLACE/DATE: Guronyu village, Kayshyadorsky district, Lithuania, August 29, 1920
NATIONALITY: Lithuanian
CAREER: From 1944 to 1982, Roman-Catholic Priest at various Catholic parishes in Lithuania. From 1982 to 1988, Apostolic Administrator of the Kayshyadorsky Diocese, Bishop. From 1988, Cardinal, Archbishop of Kaunas.
ADDRESS: 15 Gedrio Street, Kayshyadoris.

Sliva, Anatoli Yakovlevich
POSITION: Official Legal Representative of the Russian Federation President to the Russian Federation Supreme Soviet; Deputy Head of the Russian Federation State Judicial Department
BIRTHPLACE/DATE: Propoisk, Slavgorod, 1940
EDUCATION: Graduated in 1967 from the Law Department at Moscow State University. Doctor of Law. Speaks German.
CAREER: From 1971 to 1988, Lecturer, Senior Lecturer, Assistant Professor, Dean of the All-Union Law Institute Correspondence Courses. From 1988 and 1992, Senior Scientific Consultant, Deputy Department Head of the USSR Supreme Soviet Committee for Issues of the Councils of People's Deputies. From January 1992, Deputy Head of the Russian Federation State Law Department.
MAJOR WORKS: Publications on the activities of representative government bodies.
HONORS/AWARDS: Medal for Labor Valor; Medal for the Development of Virgin Lands.
FAMILY: Married with a daughter.
ADDRESS/TELEPHONE: 8/4 Ilyinka Street, Moscow. 206–2955 (office).

Smetanina, Raisa Petrovna
POSITION: Olympic Champion Skier
BIRTHPLACE/DATE: Mokhcha village, Izhevsk, Komi Republic, February 29, 1952
NATIONALITY: Russian.
CAREER: 1976 Olympic Champion (10-km; 4 x 5-km relay-race); Silver Medal (5-km). 1980 Olympic Champion (5-km; 4 x 5-km relay-race;

10-km; 20-km). 1984 Olympic Champion (10-km; 20-km). World Champion seven times; Silver Medal five times; Bronze Medal four times. USSR Champion twenty-one times; Silver Medal fourteen times; Bronze Medal fifteen times. 1992 Olympic Champion.
FAMILY: Single.
HONORS/AWARDS: Komi Republic Honored Worker of Sports; USSR Honoured Master of Sports.
ADDRESS: 42 Krasnykh Partizan Street, Flat #31, Syktyvkar, Komi Republic.

Smirnov, Andrey Sergeyevich
POSITION: Film Director; Playwright; Scriptwriter
BIRTHPLACE/DATE: Moscow, 1941
EDUCATION: Graduated in 1962 from the Film Directors' Department at the All-Union State Institute of Cinematography. Good command of English, French, and Italian.
CAREER: From 1962, Film Director of Mosfilm (Moscow Film) Studio. From 1988 to 1990, Acting First Secretary of the USSR Union of Film Makers. From 1987, Artistic Council Member of the Debyut (Debut) Studio. Member of the Confederation of Film Makers' Unions.
MAJOR WORKS: Directed *The Byelorussian Terminal* (1971); *The Fall* (1974); *I Did All I Could* (1986).
FAMILY: Married with four children.
ADDRESS/TELEPHONE: 8 Suvorovsky Boulevard, Flat #13, Moscow, 121019. 291–6526 (home).

Smirnov, Georgy Lukich
POSITION: Chief Researcher at the Russian Independent Institute of Social and National Problems
BIRTHPLACE/DATE: Antonov village, Volgograd region, November 14, 1922
NATIONALITY: Russian
EDUCATION: Graduated in 1952 from the History Department at the Stalingrad (now Volgograd) Teachers' Training College.
CAREER: Joined the Communist Party in 1943. From 1957, Functionary of the Central Committee. From 1962, worked at *Kommunist* magazine. From 1969 to 1983, Deputy Department Head of the Central Committee. From 1983 to 1985, Director of the Philosophy Institute of the USSR Academy of Sciences. From 1985 to 1987, worked at Central Committee institutions. From 1987, Director of the Theory and History of Socialism Institute of the Central Committee (formerly the Institute of Marxism and Leninism). From 1987, Academician of the USSR Academy of Sciences. From December 1991, Academician of the Russian Academy of Sciences.
MAJOR WORKS: On historical materialism and scientific communism.
HONORS/AWARDS: Order of the October Revolution; two Orders of the Red Banner of Labor.
FAMILY: Married with three children
ADDRESS/TELEPHONE: 4 Wilhelm Pieck Street, Moscow, 129256. 181–0112 (office).

Smirnov, Igor Nikolayevich
POSITION: President of the Pridnestrovsky Moldavian (Moldovan) Republic
BIRTHPLACE/DATE: Petropavlovsk-Kamchatski, 1941
CAREER: From 1959 to 1987, worked from Engineer to Director of the Elektromash (Electrical Machinery) Plant in Zaporozhye; Director of the Elektromash in Tiraspol. From August 1989, Chairman of the Tiraspol Unified Council of Working Collectives. From May 1990, Chairman of the Tiraspol City Council. From December 1991, President of the Pridnestrovsky Moldavian Republic. Moldovan People's Deputy from 1990 to 1992. Member of the Communist Party from 1963 to 1990.
FAMILY: Married with two sons.
ADDRESS/TELEPHONE: The President's Residence, Tiraspol, Moldova. 35–257.

Smirnov, Oleg Mikhailovich
POSITION: Chairman of the Promsyryoimport (Industrial Raw Materials Import) Foreign Trade Association
BIRTHPLACE/DATE: Moscow, 1936
NATIONALITY: Russian
EDUCATION: Graduated in 1959 from the Moscow Light Industry Technological Institute; in 1979, from the All-Union Foreign Trade Academy.
CAREER: From 1971 to 1974, worked at the USSR Trade Mission in Romania. From 1974 to 1975, Deputy Office Director of Promsyryoimport; from 1975 to 1982, Office Director. From

1982 to 1985, USSR Deputy Trade Representative in India. From 1985 to 1986, Acting Director-General of Promsyryoimport; from 1986 to 1988, Deputy Director-General.
HONORS/AWARDS: Medal for Labor Valor.
FAMILY: Married with three children and a grandson.
ADDRESS/TELEPHONE: 13 Novinsky Boulevard, Moscow. 203–4446 (office).

Smirnov, Vyacheslav Vladimirovich
POSITION: Deputy Chairman of Roskomagentstvo
BIRTHPLACE/DATE: Kalinin, Tver region, 1939
CAREER: From 1968 to 1970, worked at a plant; from 1968 to 1970, Plant Engineer. From 1970 to 1974, worked in foreign trade, from Senior Engineer to Deputy. From 1974 to 1978, Foreign Trade Company Representative in Damascus, Syria; from 1983 to 1986, Company Head in Cuba. From 1991, Deputy Chairman of Roskomagentstvo.
FAMILY: Married with a daughter.
ADDRESS/TELEPHONE: 5 Yaroslavskoye Chaussée, 15th Floor, Moscow, 129348. 182–2117; 182–3329 (office).

Smolensky, Aleksandr Pavlovich
POSITION: Board Chairman of the Stolichny (Metropolitan) Commercial Bank
BIRTHPLACE/DATE: Moscow, 1954
EDUCATION: Graduated from the Dzhambul Geological Technology Institute, majoring in Economics.
CAREER: Worked at construction sites. In November 1987, organized a construction co-operative.
FAMILY: Married with a son.
ADDRESS/TELEPHONE: 72 Pyatnitskaya Street, Moscow, 113095. 233–5892 (office).

Smolyakov, Leonid Yakovlevich
POSITION: Russian Federation Ambassador to Ukraine; Ambassador Extraordinary and Plenipotentiary.
BIRTHPLACE/DATE: Novosibirsk, 1942.
NATIONALITY: Russian
EDUCATION: From 1969 to 1971, postgraduate student at the All-Union Polytechnical Institute (by correspondence). Doctor of Philosophy; Professor.
CAREER: From 1965 to 1967, Engineer, Senior Engineer of the Kiev Promenergoproyekt (Industrial Energy Planning). From 1967 to 1969, Lecturer Group Head of the Kiev Regional Committee of the Ukranian Komsomol. From 1971 to 1987, Senior Lecturer, Assistant Professor, Professor at the Higher Party School of the Ukraine Central Committee. From 1987 to 1991, Professor at the Academy of Social Sciences of the Central Committee. In 1991, Chairman of the Committee for Science, Education and Personnel Policy at the Congress of Russian Business. From 1991 to 1992, Russian Federation Plenipotentiary Representative in Ukraine. From 1992, Russian Ambassador to Ukraine.
ADDRESS/TELEPHONE: 32/34 Smolenskaya-Sennaya Ploschad, Moscow, 121200. 244–1606 (Foreign Ministry).

Smyslov, Vasily Vasilyevich
POSITION: Chess Player
BIRTHPLACE/DATE: Moscow, 1921
NATIONALITY: Russian
EDUCATION: Graduated from the Leningrad Central Physical Education Institute in Moscow. Speaks English.
CAREER: World Title Champion at the 1953 and 1956 Match of Contenders; 1957 World Champion (versus Mikhail Botvinnik); Champion at the 1982 Inter-Zonal Tournament; World Title Champion at the 1983 Match of Contenders (versus Robert Huebner and Zoltan Ribli). Ten-time Champion of the World Chess Olympiads. Former Editor in Chief of *Shakhmatnaya Moskva* (*Moscow Chess*) magazine, Chairman of the USSR Chess Federation Council of Coaches.
HONORS/AWARDS: International Grand Master; USSR Honored Master of Sports; Order of Lenin; Order of the People's Friendship.
FAMILY: Married.
ADDRESS/TELEPHONE: Chess Federation, 14 Gogolevsky Boulevard, Moscow. 255–4060 (home).

Snegur, Mircha Ion
POSITION: President of Moldova (Moldavia) Republic
BIRTHPLACE/DATE: Trifaneshty village, 1940
NATIONALITY: Moldavian

EDUCATION: From 1968, postgraduate student at the Kishinev Agricultural Institute's Department of Field-Crop Cultivation. Doctor of Agricultural Sciences.
CAREER: From 1961, Senior Agroculturist, Chief Agroculturist, Chairman of the Put k Kommunizmu (Road to Communism) Collective Farm. To 1971, Director of the Kishinev Agricultural Institute's Experiment Station of Field-Crop Cultivation. From 1971 to 1978, Head of the Central Directorate of Farming and Progressive Technology in Field-Crop Cultivation, Head of the Central Directorate of Agricultural Science of the Moldavian Republic Ministry of Agriculture. From 1978 to 1981, Director of the Moldavian Research Institute of Field-Crop Cultivation and Director-General of the Selektsia (Selection) Industrial Association. From 1981, First Secretary of the Moldavian Yedinetsky District Committee. From 1985, Secretary of the Moldavian Central Committee. From 1989, Chairman of the Moldavian Republic Supreme Soviet. From 1990, Chairman of the Moldavian Republic Supreme Soviet. From 1990, President of the Moldovan Republic. Former member of the USSR President's Council of the Union. USSR People's Deputy; Deputy of Moldova.
HONORS/AWARDS: Order of the Badge of Honor; three medals.
FAMILY: Married with two children.
ADDRESS/TELEPHONE: 1 Mary Adunel Natsionale Square, Kishinev, 277073. 23–7122 (Secretariat).

Snychev, Ivan Matveyevich (Ioann)
POSITION: Metropolitan of Leningrad and Ladoga; Permanent Member of the Holy Synod of the Russian Orthodox Church
BIRTHPLACE/DATE: Mayachka village, Kakhovka district, Kherson region, Ukraine, October 9, 1927
NATIONALITY: Russian
EDUCATION: Graduated in 1955 from the Leningrad Ecclesiastical Academy.
CAREER: From 1956 to 1957, Lecturer at the Minsk Ecclesiastical Seminary. From 1957 to 1959, Priest of the Presentation at the Cheboksary Blessed Virgin Cathedral. From 1959 to 1960, Lecturer at the Saratov Ecclesiastical Seminary. From 1960 to 1965, Priest at the Kuibyshev Intercession Cathedral. From 1965 to 1990, Bishop, Administrator of the Kuibyshev Russian Orthodox Church Diocese.
ADDRESS/TELEPHONE: 51 Klyanovskaya Street, Kuibyshev. 235–0454; 230–2118; 230–2431 (Moscow).

Sobchak, Anatoli Aleksandroviich
POSITION: Mayor of St. Petersburg (formerly Leningrad); member of the Presidential Consultative Council
BIRTHPLACE/DATE: Chita, Russian Federation, 1937
NATIONALITY: Russian
EDUCATION: Graduated from the Law Department at Leningrad State University. Doctor of Law; Professor.
CAREER HISTORY: From 1960, Lawyer of the Bar, Head of the Legal Consulting Bureau, Bar Member in Stavropol region; Lecturer at a Special Police School of the USSR Ministry of Internal Affairs in Leningrad; Lecturer at the Technical Institute for the Pulp and Paper Industry in Leningrad; Economic Law Department Head of the Law Division at Leningrad State University. From 1988 to 1990, member of the Communist Party. In 1988, Director of the Legal Consultation Cooperative in Leningrad. From 1989, Deputy of the USSR Congress of People's Deputies; member of the USSR Supreme Soviet Council of the Union; Chairman of the USSR Supreme Soviet Subcommittee for Economic Legislation, Legality, and Law and Order. From 1989 to 1990, Chairman of the USSR Congress of People's Deputies Tbilisi Investigative Commission (for investigating the events of April 1989 in Tbilisi). From 1990, Chairman of the Leningrad Council of People's Deputies. From 1989, Chairman of the Consumer Societies Federation; member of the Bureau of Foreign Trade Associations; member of the Higher Consultative Coordinating Council of the Russian Supreme Soviet Chairman. From September 1991 to December 1991, member of the USSR President's Political Consultative Council. Professor at Portland University in the United States. From December 1991, Board Co-Chairman of the Democratic Reforms Movement.
MAJOR WORKS: Author of fifteen books and

140 publications, including *Tested by the Power* (published in France in 1991).
HONORS/AWARDS: Harriman Institute Prize (1992).
FAMILY: Married with two daughters.
ADDRESS/TELEPHONE: 6 Isakiyevskaya Square, St. Petersburg. 319–9865 (office).

Sobkov, Vasily Timofeyevich
POSITION: Commander of the Prikarpatsky Military District; Colonel-General.
BIRTHPLACE/DATE: Lisanovtsy village, Khmelnitsk region, 1944
NATIONALITY: Ukrainian
CAREER: Former Tank Platoon Commander and Tank Regiment Staff Head. From 1984 to 1987, Motorized Infantry Division Commander of the Trans-Caucasian Military District. From 1987 to 1989, Commander of the Turkestansky Military District, Western Forces Army Tank Commander. From June 1992, Central Staff Head of the Ukrainian Armed Forces, Ukrainian First Deputy Minister of Defense. From 1993, Commander of the Prikarpatsky Military District.
HONORS/AWARDS: Order of the Red Star; medals.
FAMILY: Married with two children.
ADDRESS/TELEPHONE: The Headquarters of the Prikarpatsky Military District, Lvov. 293–0319 (Ukraine Defense Ministry press service).

Sokolov, Aleksandr Sergeyevich
POSITION: Member of the Russian Federation Supreme Soviet Committee for Foreign Affairs and International Economic Relations
BIRTHPLACE/DATE: Kulakovo village, Moscow region, 1947
NATIONALITY: Russian
EDUCATION: Graduated from the Moscow Hydro-Amelioration Institute and from the Academy of Social Sciences of the Central Committee.
CAREER: Mechanical Engineer at the Tehlmann Collective Farm in Ramenskoye district, Moscow region. From 1972, Komsomol and Communist Party Functionary. From 1976, Deputy Chairman of the Ramenskoye City Executive Committee in Moscow region. From 1980, Director of the Podmoskovye Research and Production Enterprise. From 1985, First Secretary of the Ramenskoye City Communist Party. From 1989, Secretary of the Moscow Region Communist Party. From 1990, Secretary of the Russian Central Committee. Russian Federation People's Deputy. Coordinator of the Communists of Russia Faction.
FAMILY: Married with two children.
ADDRESS/TELEPHONE: 2 Krasnopresnenskaya Naberezhnaya, Moscow. 205–4262; 205–4323 (office).

Sokolov, Vadim Pavlovich
POSITION: Literary Critic; Secretary of the Russian Writers' Union
BIRTHPLACE/DATE: Grivno station, Moscow region, 1927
CAREER: From 1950 to 1956, Staff Member of *Literaturnaya Gazeta* newspaper. From 1956 to 1960, Staff Member of *Komsomolskaya Pravda* (*Komsomol Truth*) newspaper and *Moskva* magazine. From 1961 to 1964, Deputy Editor in Chief of Iskusstvo (Art) Publishing House. From 1965 to 1967, Editor in Chief of the Telefilm Creative Association. From 1968 to 1990, Editorial Board Member of the Ekran (Screen) Association at Central Television. Member of the USSR Writers' Union from 1960. From 1991, Secretary of the Russian Writers' Union. Member of the Confederation of Film Makers' Unions.
MAJOR WORKS: Numerous critical literary publications.
FAMILY: Married with two children and three grandchildren.
ADDRESS/FAMILY: 16 Bezbozhny Pereulok, Flat #17, Moscow, 129010. 280–6804 (home).

Sokolov, Vladimir Nikolayevich
POSITION: Editor in Chief of *Vek* (*Century*) newspaper
BIRTHPLACE/DATE: Tashkent, 1946
NATIONALITY: Russian
EDUCATION: Graduated in 1969 from the Tashkent Institute of Communications; in 1984, from the Gorky Literary Institute. Speaks German and Uzbek.
CAREER: From 1969 to 1983, worked from Engineer to Deparment Head at scientific research institutions of the Uzbek Academy of Sciences. From 1985 and 1987, Uzbekistan Correspondent for *Literaturnaya Gazeta*. From 1988 to 1991, Head of

the Economics Department, Editorial Board Member of *Literaturnaya Gazeta* (*Literary Newspaper*). From October to December 1991, Consultant to the USSR President's Cabinet. From January 1992, Founding and Organizing Committee Chairman of *Vek*. Member of the Confederation of Journalists' Unions.
MAJOR WORKS: Holds ten copyright invention certificates; articles in *Literaturnaya Gazeta*.
HONORS/AWARDS: Diploma and Medal of the UNESCO Man and Biosphere Committee; a number of literary prizes.
FAMILY: Married with three children.
ADDRESS/TELEPHONE: 13 Kostyansky Pereulok, Moscow. 208–8921 (office); 413–9045 (home).

Solomin, Yuri Mefodyevich
POSITION: Art Director of the Maly Theater
BIRTHPLACE/DATE: Chita, 1935
NATIONALITY: Russian
EDUCATION: Graduated in 1957 from the Shchepkin Drama School in Moscow.
CAREER: Worked at the Moscow Maly Theater. From 1982, Assistant Professor of the Professional Acting Department at the Shchepkin Drama School; from 1986, Professor. From 1990 to December 1991, Russian Federation Minister of Culture.
MAJOR WORKS: Leading roles include: Tsar Fyodor Ioanovich (by Aleksei Tolstoy); Goblin (by Anton Chekhov). Productions include: *Inspector-General* (by Nikolai Gogol). Starred in more than fifty TV and feature films, including: *The Red Tent*; *Darsu Urzala*; *Inspector of Criminal Investigation*. Films directed: *The Scandalous Affair in a Brick-Mill* (after the play by Joseph Priestly); *The Shore of His Life*.
HONORS/AWARDS: USSR People's Artist; Order of the People's Friendship; Veteran of Labor Medal; Russian Federation Vasilyev Brothers State Prize.
FAMILY: Married with a daughter.
ADDRESS/TELEPHONE: 1/6 Teatralnaya Ploshchad, Moscow, 103009. 925–9868 (office).

Solovyov, Sergey Aleksandroviich
POSITION: Film Director and Scriptwriter
BIRTHPLACE/DATE: Kem, Karelia, 1944
NATIONALITY: Russian
EDUCATION: Graduated in 1968 from the Moscow State Institute of Cinematography.
CAREER: From 1960 to 1962, worked at the Leningrad TV Studio. From 1969 to 1982, Film Director of Mosfilm Studio. From 1980, Lecturer at the State Institute of Cinematography and at the Higher Film Directors' Courses. From 1982, Art Director of the Debyut (Debut) Association. From 1990 to 1991, Board Member and Secretary of the USSR Union of Film Makers. From 1990, Chairman of the Moscow Union of Film Makers. From December 1990, Co-Chairman, Secretary of the Russian Union of Film Makers.
MAJOR WORKS: Productions: *Station Master* (1972); *100 Days After Childhood* (1974); *The White Night's Tunes* (a co-production with the Japanese Toho, 1976); *Rescuer*; *Direct Descendant*; *The Chosen Few* (USSR-Columbia, 1982); *Assa* (1988); *Red Rose Is an Emblem of Sorrow, White Rose Is an Emblem of Love* (1989); *A House Under a Star-Studded Sky* (1991).
HONORS/AWARDS: Russian Federation Honored Worker of Arts; Lenin Komsomol Prize; USSR State Prize.
FAMILY: Married with a son and a daughter.
ADDRESS/TELEPHONE: 8 Akademician Pilyugin Street, Building 1, Flat #330, Moscow, 117393. 132–3695.

Sorokin, Anatoli Dmitryevich
POSITION: Director-General of the First Exemplary Printing House
BIRTHPLACE/DATE: Moscow, 1943
NATIONALITY: Russian
EDUCATION: Graduated from the Moscow Institute of Printing.
CAREER: Worked as a Mechanic, Shop Superintendent at the First Exemplary Printing House. Representative of the All-Union Vneshtorgizdat (Foreign Trade Publishers) Association in the German Democratic Republic. Deputy Director-General of Vneshtorgizdat.
FAMILY: Married with a son and a daughter.
ADDRESS/TELEPHONE: 28 Valovaya Street, Moscow, 113054. 237–3612.

Sorokina, Maria Ivanovna
POSITION: Member of the Russian Federation Supreme Soviet Committee for Human Rights.

BIRTHPLACE/DATE: Berezovka village, Terbunsky district, Lipetsk region, 1946
NATIONALITY: Russian
EDUCATION: Graduated in 1968 from the Yelets State Teachers' Training Institute.
CAREER: From 1969 to 1970, Correspondent for a district newspaper. From 1970 to 1972, Correspondent for a Kursk youth newspaper. From 1972 to 1986, Department Head, Deputy Chief Editor of a Lipetsk regional youth newspaper. From 1986 to 1990, Correspondent for a Lipetsk regional newspaper. From 1990, People's Deputy.
FAMILY: Single.
ADDRESS/TELEPHONE: 8/2 Korolev Street, Flat #527, Moscow. 216–4071 (home); 72- 5726 (Lipetsk).

Sotkilava, Zurab Lavrentyevich
POSITION: Opera Soloist (lyric-dramatic tenor) of the Moscow Bolshoi Academic Theater
BIRTHPLACE/DATE: Sukhumi, 1937
EDUCATION: Graduated from the Tbilisi Polytechnic and from the Tbilisi Conservatory.
CAREER: From 1965, Soloist of the Georgian Opera and Ballet Theater. From 1966 to 1968, performed at La Scala Theater in Italy. Directed vocal classes at the Moscow Conservatory.
MAJOR WORKS: Roles: Othello; José; Arzakan (*Theft of the Moon* by Taktakishvili).
HONORS/AWARDS: First Prize and Grand Prix at the Vinias International Vocalists Contest (Barcelona, 1970); Second Prize at the Tchaikovsky International Contest (Moscow, 1970); State Prize of Georgia (1983); USSR People's Artist; Honorary Member of the Bologna Arts Academy (1980).
FAMILY: Married with two daughters.
ADDRESS/TELEPHONE: 8/2 Okhotny Ryad, Moscow. 244–0731 (home).

Sotnikov, Aleksandr Dmitryevich
POSITION: Board Chairman of the Yedinstvo (Unity) Joint-Stock Consumer Societies Bank (formerly the Centrosoyuz Bank)
BIRTHPLACE/DATE: Voronezh region, 1921
NATIONALITY: Russian
EDUCATION: Graduated from the Moscow Finance and Economics Institute.
CAREER: Worked in Tomsk as Economist, Department Head, Regional Office Head, State Bank Office Head, Chairman of the Tomsk Region Executive Committee, Credit Department Head of the USSR State Bank Board. From November 1988, Board Chairman of the Centrosoyuz (Central Union) Cooperative Bank.
MAJOR WORKS: Theoretical papers on monetary circulation and credit.
FAMILY: Married with two children and two grandchildren.
ADDRESS/TELEPHONE: 15 Bolshoi Cherkassky Pereulok, Moscow, 103626. 928–7621 (office).

Sotnikov, Fyodor Ivanovich
POSITION: Director of the Solnechnogorsk Polymer Plant
BIRTHPLACE/DATE: Prilepy village, Chernyansky district, Belgorod region, 1950
EDUCATION: Graduated from the Goryachkin Institute of Agriculture in Moscow. Speaks English.
CAREER: From 1965 to 1968, Tally Clerk of a tractor team. From 1971 to 1974, Passenger Car Column Head. From 1974 and 1979, Chief of Motor Vehicle Management. From 1981 to 1985, Chief of Motor Vehicle Management of the USSR Academy of Medical Sciences. District Council Deputy.
FAMILY: Married with two children.
ADDRESS/TELEPHONE: 5 Telnov Street, Solnechnogorsk. 539–3188 (office); 532–6089 (home).

Spitsyn, Vladimir Vladimirovich
POSITION: Director of the Moscow Zoo
BIRTHPLACE/DATE: Nizhny Novgorod, 1941
CAREER: From 1959 to 1974, Animal Technician, Deputy Director of the Leningrad Zoo. From 1974 to 1977, Deputy Director, and from 1977, Director of the Moscow Zoo. Member of the Russian Society of Ornithologists. From 1971 to 1991, Coordinating Council Chairman of the USSR Zoological Gardens. Member of the Group for Breeding Rare Animals of the International Union of Zoo Directors.
MAJOR WORKS: Over fifty publications on the protection of wild animals and the breeding of rare animals.
FAMILY: Married with a child.
ADDRESS/TELEPHONE: 1 Bolshaya Gruzinskaya Street, Moscow, 123242. 252–3580 (office).

Spivakov, Vladimir Teodorovich
POSITION: Art Director and Soloist of the Virtuosy Moskvy (Moscow Virtuosos) of the Moscow State Chamber Orchestra
BIRTHPLACE/DATE: Ufa, Bashkir, September 12, 1944
EDUCATION: Graduated from the Moscow Conservatory and its postgraduate program.
CAREER HISTORY: From 1967, Soloist of the Moscow State Philharmonic Society. Member of the Virtuosos of the Moscow Orchestra. From 1975, Lecturer at the Moscow Gnesiny Musical Pedagogical Institute. From 1979, Leading Conducter of the Virtuosos of the Moscow Orchestra. From 1988, Art Director of the Carmare International Music Festival in France. Performs in Spain.
HONORS/AWARDS: USSR State Prize (1989); international prizes.
FAMILY: Married with two children.
ADDRESS/TELEPHONE: The Moscow Orchestra, 3 Nemirovich-Danchenko Street, Moscow, 103808. 923–9732 (office).

Srybnykh, Vyacheslav Mikhailovich
POSITION: Editor in Chief of *Kazakhstanskaya Pravda* (*Kazakh Truth*) newspaper
BIRTHPLACE/DATE: Alma-Ata, 1950
NATIONALITY: Russian
CAREER: Correspondent for *Stepnoy Mayak* (*Lighthouse in the Field*) newspaper in Kokchetav, Deputy Editor in Chief of *Avtomobilist Kazakhstana* magazine, Instructor of the Kazakhstan Central Committee. From 1991, Editor in Chief of *Kazakhstanskaya Pravda*.
FAMILY: Married with a son.
ADDRESS/TELEPHONE: 39 Gogolya Street, Alma-Ata, 480044. 63–0398 (office).

Stankevich, Sergey Borisovich
POSITION: Advisor to the Russian Federation President
BIRTHPLACE/DATE: Moscow region, 1954
NATIONALITY: Ukrainian
EDUCATION: Graduated in 1977 from the History Department at the Lenin State Teachers' Training Institute in Moscow. Doctor of History, specializing in U.S. History.
CAREER: Senior Researcher at the Institute of World History of the USSR Academy of Sciences. Member of the Tbilisi Investigative Commission. USSR People's Deputy. Member of the USSR Supreme Soviet Legislation Committee. Member of the Inter-Regional Parliamentary Faction. From 1987 to 1990, member of the Communist Party. From April 1990 to July 1991, First Deputy Chairman of the Mossoviet (Moscow Council). Editor in Chief of *Vedomosti MosSovieta* (*News from Moscow Council*) magazine. Board Chairman of the Moscow Joint-Stock Commercial Bank. From August 1991 to February 1992, Russian Federation Public Relations State Counsellor. Council Member of the Socio-Political Research Foundation. From February 1992, Russian Federation State Counsellor for Political Issues.
MAJOR WORKS: More than thirty articles on U.S. political history.
HONORS/AWARDS: American Center of International Leadership Award.
FAMILY: Married with a daughter.
ADDRESS/TELEPHONE: The Kremlin, Moscow. 224–1524; 292–1647 (office).

Stankyavichus, Cheslovas
POSITION: Deputy Chairman of the Lithuanian Republic Supreme Soviet
BIRTHPLACE/DATE: Sheshtinai village, Vikavis region, 1937
NATIONALITY: Lithuanian
CAREER: Former Technician, Engineer, and from 1974, Chief Engineer of the Kaunass Institute of City Construction Projects. Member of the Sayudis Movement from its founding in 1988; former Chairman of the Sayudis Kaunass City Council. In February 1989, elected Lithuanian Republic People's Deputy; Deputy Chairman of the Lithuanian Supreme Soviet.
FAMILY: Married with two children and two grandchildren.
ADDRESS/TELEPHONE: The Lithuanian Republic Supreme Soviet, 53 Gyadiminasa Prospekt, Vilnius, 232008. 62–1654.

Starkov, Vladislav Andreyevich
POSITION: Editor in Chief of *Argumenty i Fakty* (*Arguments and Facts*) weekly
BIRTHPLACE/DATE: Tomsk, 1940
EDUCATION: Graduated in 1962 from the

Rostov-on-Don Civil Engineering Institute; in 1973, from the Journalism Department at Rostov University.
CAREER: From 1962 to 1973, Senior Engineer of the USSR Hydrometorological Center. From 1973 to 1977, Moscow Programs Correspondent for the USSR State Television and Radio Broadcasting Committee. From 1977 to 1979, Senior Scientific Editor of Znaniye (Knowledge) Publishers. From 1979 to 1980, Section Head of Mezhdunarodnye Otnosheniya (International Relations) Publishers. Russian Federation People's Deputy.
FAMILY: Married with a daughter.
ADDRESS/TELEPHONE: 42 Myasnitskaya Street, Moscow, 101000. 921–0234 (office).

Starovoitova, Galina Vasilyevna
POSITION: Former Counsellor to the Russian Federation President on Ethnic and International Relations Issues; Member of the Russian Federation Supreme Soviet Committee for Human Rights
BIRTHPLACE/DATE: Chelyabinsk, 1946
NATIONALITY: Russian
EDUCATION: Graduated in 1971 from the Psychology Department at Leningrad State University. From 1973 to 1976, postgraduate student at the USSR Academy of Sciences' Institute of Ethnography in Leningrad. Doctor of History. Speaks English.
CAREER: From 1968 to 1971, Engineer-Sociologist of the Krasnaya Zarya (Red Dawn) Scientific-Production Association in Leningrad. From 1972 to 1973, Senior Engineer-Sociologist of the Leningrad Central Research Institute of Ship-Building Technology. From 1977 to 1991, Researcher, then Senior Researcher at the USSR Academy of Sciences' Institute of Economics. From 1989 to 1991, USSR People's Deputy. From 1991 to 1992, International Relations Advisor to the Russian Federation President. Organizing Committee Member of the Liberal Union; member of the Democratic Russia Movement. Russian Federation People's Deputy.
FAMILY: Divorced with a son.
ADDRESS/TELEPHONE: 10 Ilyinka Street, Moscow. 206–5743; 206–4442 (office).

Stasyuk, Pyotr Nikitovich
POSITION: Director-General of the Belgosstrakh Byelorussian State Insurance Commercial Organization
BIRTHPLACE/DATE: Lyusha village, Kamenets district, Brest region, 1934
NATIONALITY: Byelorussian
CAREER: From 1960 to 1962, Senior Economist, and from 1962 to 1974, Head of the Agriculture Financing Department of the Brest Regional Financial Department. From 1974, Head of the Agriculture Financing Directorate of the Byelorussian Republic Ministry of Finance. In 1985, appointed Central Directorate Head of the Byelorussian Republic State Insurance (now the Belgosstrakh Organization).
ADDRESS/TELEPHONE: 10 Kollektornaya Street, Minsk, 220048. 20–6258; 20–6297 (office).

Stepankov, Valentin Georgyevich
POSITION: Russian Federation Prosecutor General
BIRTHPLACE/DATE: Urals, 1951
NATIONALITY: Russian
EDUCATION: Graduated from the Law Department at Perm State University.
CAREER: Served in the Armed Forces; Staff Member of a military unit newspaper. From 1975, worked at a district prosecutor's office, then at the Perm region Prosecutor's Office; Public Prosecutor of Gubakha; worked at the Perm Region Communist Party Administrative Department; Public Prosecutor of a regional center; worked at the USSR Prosecutor's Office in Moscow; Public Prosecutor of the Khabarovsk Region in the Soviet Far East. From 1991, Russian Federation Prosecutor General. Russian Federation People's Deputy. Member of the Russian Supreme Soviet.
FAMILY: Married with a child.
ADDRESS/TELEPHONE: 15-A Pushkinskaya Street, Moscow 103793. 229–4662.

Stepanov, Andrey Ivanovich
POSITION: Russian Federation Ambassador to Switzerland; Ambassador Extraordinary and Plenipotentiary
BIRTHPLACE/DATE: Kaluga, February 13, 1930
NATIONALITY: Russian
EDUCATION: Doctor of History; Assistant Professor.
CAREER: From 1956 to 1962, worked at the

USSR Foreign Ministry in the German Democratic Republic and in Moscow: Vice Consul; Second Secretary. From 1962 to 1972, Senior Lecturer, Assistant Professor at the Higher Diplomatic School of the USSR Foreign Ministry. From 1972 to 1978, Pro-Rector of the Diplomatic Academy of the USSR Foreign Ministry. From 1978 to 1982, Counsellor at the USSR Embassy in Austria. From 1982 to 1987, Senior, then Chief Counsellor of the Directorate of Estimates and Planning of the USSR Foreign Ministry. From 1987 to 1990, First Deputy Head of the Central Directorate of Personnel and Educational Institutions of the USSR Foreign Ministry, Directorate Head of Educational Institutions. From 1990 to 1992, Rector of the Moscow State Institute of International Relations of the USSR Foreign Ministry. From October 1992, Russian Federation Ambassador to Switzerland.
MAJOR WORKS: Over 200 scientific works and publications.
HONORS/AWARDS: USSR State Prize.
FAMILY: Married with two children.
ADDRESS/TELEPHONE: Botschaft der Russischen Federation Brunnadernrein, 37 3006, Berne, Switzerland. 44–0566.

Stepanov, Vladimir Aleksandrovich
POSITION: Board Chairman of the Russian National Bank
ADDRESS/TELEPHONE: 5/9 Taganskaya Street, Moscow, 109004. 180–5246; Fax: 189–1870.

Stepashin, Sergey Vadimovich
POSITION: Former Russian Deputy Minister of Security; Chairman of the Russian Federation Supreme Soviet Committee for Defense and Security
BIRTHPLACE/DATE: Port Arthur, 1932
CAREER: Russian People's Deputy; Chairman of the Committee on the Affairs of Invalids, War and Labor Veterans, and the Social Protection of Servicemen and their Families. Member of the State Committee for the Investigation of Security Bodies.

Stolyarov, Nikolay Sergeyevich
POSITION: Aide to the Commander in Chief of the CIS Joint Armed Forces
BIRTHPLACE/DATE: Gomel region, Byelorussia, 1947
NATIONALITY: Byelorussian
EDUCATION: Graduated from the Yeisk Higher Flying School; and from the Gagarin Aviation Academy. Doctor of Philosophy; Assistant Professor. Knowledge of German.
CAREER: Served in the Air Force; Philosophy Lecturer at the Gagarin Air Force Academy. From 1990, Chairman of the Central Control Commission of the Russian Communist Party. In 1991, Deputy Chairman of the State Security Service (KGB). From December 1991, Aide to the Defense Minister and Chairman of the Committee for Personnel Work.
FAMILY: Married with a son and a daughter.
ADDRESS/TELEPHONE: 8/4 Kuibyshev Street, Moscow, 103132. 206–3948 (office).

Strelkov, Aleksander Aleksandrovich
POSITION: Russian Federation Deputy Minister of Security; Major-General of the Internal Affairs Service
BIRTHPLACE/DATE: Arkhangelsk region, 1941
CAREER: From 1975 to 1978, Head of the Mekhrengsky Directorate of Forest Reformatory Institutions. From 1978 to 1980, Deputy Head of the Internal Affairs Directorate of the Arkhangelsk Regional Executive Committee. From 1980 to 1987, Deputy Head, Chief Engineer, First Deputy Head of the Central Directorate of Forest Reformatory Institutions of the USSR Ministry of Internal Affairs. From 1987 to 1992, Head of Forest Reformatory Institutions. From January 1992, Head of the Central Directorate of Forest Reformatory Institutions of the Russian Federation Ministry of Internal Affairs.
ADDRESS/TELEPHONE: 16 Zhitnaya Street, Moscow, 117049. 239–7500.

Stroyev, Andrey Alekseyevich
POSITION: Board Chairman and President of the Perestroika Joint Venture; Vice President of the Joint Ventures Association and of the Moscow Joint Ventures Association
BIRTHPLACE/DATE: Moscow, 1947
NATIONALITY: Russian
EDUCATION: Graduated in 1970 from the Kuibyshev Construction Engineering Institute in Moscow; in 1985, graduated from the USSR Council

of Ministers' Academy of National Economy. Doctor of Economics. Good command of English.
CAREER: From 1970 to 1976, Foreman, Superintendent at Moscow construction sites. From 1976 to 1980, Chief Engineer of the Moscow Construction Administration. From 1981 to 1983, Chief Engineer of the Stalmontazh (Steel Assembling) Trust in Moscow. From 1985 to 1987, First Deputy Head, and from 1987, Head of the Mosinzhstroi (Moscow Engineering and Construction) Association. From 1989, Board Chairman of the Sloboda Joint Venture.
FAMILY: Married with two sons.
ADDRESS/TELEPHONE: 15-B Malaya Bronnaya Street, Moscow. 202–1648; 202–5648; 299–7013.

Studennikov, Igor Ivanovich
POSITION: Russian Federation Ambassador to the Republic of Guinea; Envoy Extraordinary and Plenipotentiary, First Class
BIRTHPLACE/DATE: 1940
NATIONALITY: Russian
EDUCATION: Graduated in 1968 from the Moscow State Institute of International Relations.
CAREER: From 1968, worked at the Foreign Ministry. From 1968 to 1970, Aide, Interpreter at the USSR Embassy in the Democratic Republic of the Congo. From 1973 to 1979, Third, Second, First Secretary at the USSR Embassy in the Algerian People's Democratic Republic. From 1981 to 1982, Counsellor at the USSR Embassy in the Republic of Niger. From 1982 to 1987, Cultural Attaché at the USSR Embassy in Algeria. From 1990 to 1991, Deputy Head of the African Countries Directorate.
ADDRESS/TELEPHONE: Ambassade de la Russia en Republique de Guinee, Matam-Port, Km. 9, B.P. 329, Conakry, Republique de Guinee. 46–1459; 46–1460; 46–1461.

Subachev, Victor Grigoryevich
POSITION: Director-General of the Kirov Dynamo Production Association in Moscow
BIRTHPLACE/DATE: Denisovka, Kustanai region, Kazakhstan, 1932
NATIONALITY: Russian
EDUCATION: Graduated in 1955 from Urals Polytechnic.
CAREER: From 1955 to 1963, Industrial Engineer, Shop Superintendent at the Lysva Turbine-Building Works in Perm region. From 1966 to 1981, held various administrative posts at the Ministry of Power Industry. From 1981 to 1986, USSR Deputy Minister of Power Industry.
FAMILY: Married with a son.
ADDRESS/TELEPHONE: 4 Masterkov Street, Moscow, 109068. 275–1462 (office).

Sukharev, Aleksey Grigoryevich
POSITION: Director-General of the Infort Joint-Stock Company; Professor at Moscow State University
BIRTHPLACE/DATE: Grozny, 1946
EDUCATION: Graduated in 1968 from the Mechanics and Mathematics Department at Moscow University. Doctor of Physics and Mathematics; Professor. Speaks English.
CAREER: From 1968, Assistant, Senior Lecturer, Assistant Professor, Professor of the Physics and Mathematics Department at Moscow State University.
MAJOR WORKS: A number of books on mathematics.
FAMILY: Married with a son.
ADDRESS/TELEPHONE: The Research Center of the Infort Joint-Stock Company, Moscow State University, Moscow, 119899. 939–1784 (office).

Sukhoruchenkov, Sergey Nikolayevich
POSITION: Former Olympic Cycling Champion
BIRTHPLACE/DATE: Bryansk region, 1956
NATIONALITY: Russian
EDUCATION: Graduated from the Lesgaft State Institute of Physical Education in Leningrad.
CAREER: 1980 Olympic Cycling Champion. Winner of the 1979 and 1984 Peace Race, and the 1979 and 1980 French Tour de l'Avenir Race. From 1988, Professional Cyclist. From 1988 to 1990, member of the Alfa Lume (San Marino) Professional Team.
HONORS/AWARDS: Russian Federation Honored Master of Sports.
FAMILY: Married with four sons.
TELEPHONE: 312–1541 (St. Petersburg Sports Committee).

Sukhorukov, Vladimir Pavlovich
POSITION: Board Chairman of the Volgo-Kaspiysky Commercial Bank in Astrakhan
BIRTHPLACE/DATE: Astrakhan, 1949
NATIONALITY: Russian
EDUCATION: From 1964 to 1968, studied at the Astrakhan Technical School of Construction. Graduated in 1981 from the Volgograd Civil Construction Institute; in 1989, from a special Department at the Moscow Institute of Finance.
CAREER: From 1968 to 1970, served in the army. From 1970 to 1982, Superintendent, Chief Engineer, Construction Board Head. From 1982 to 1986, Chief Engineer of Astrakhanselstroi (Astrakhan Country Construction). From 1986 to 1990, Deputy Head of the Promstroibank (Industrial Construction Bank) Regional Board.
ADDRESS/TELEPHONE: 20 Lenin Street, Astrakhan. 2–1698 (office).

Sulakshin, Stepan Stepanovich
POSITION: Tomsk Region Spokesman for the Russian President
BIRTHPLACE/DATE: Tomsk, 1954
NATIONALITY: Russian
EDUCATION: Graduated from the Radio Physics Department at Tomsk State University. Doctor of Physics and Mathematics.
CAREER: To 1990, Laboratory Head at the Tomsk Institute of Nuclear Physics. From 1990, USSR People's Deputy; member of the USSR Supreme Soviet Commission for Economic Reforms. Co-Founder of the Democratic Platform of the Communist Party.
FAMILY: Married with two children.
ADDRESS/TELEPHONE: 43–7A Lenin Street, Tomsk, 634004.

Suleimanov, Olzhas Onarovich
POSITION: First Board Secretary of the Kazakh Republic Writers' Union
BIRTHPLACE/DATE: Alma-Ata, 1936
NATIONALITY: Kazakh
CAREER: From 1983, First Board Secretary of the Kazakh Writers' Union, Board Secretary of the USSR Writers' Union, Chairman of the Semipalatinsk-Nevada Public Movement to Ban Nuclear Tests. Member of the USSR Supreme Soviet Legislation Committee. Member of the International Lenin Prizes Committee. USSR People's Deputy.
MAJOR WORKS: Best known for the poem, "Land, Bow Before the Human-Being" (1961); selected poems, *Over White Rivers* (1970). Screenplays: *Land of Fathers* (1966); *Blue Route* (1968); several popular scientific films.
FAMILY: Married with two daughters.
ADDRESS/TELEPHONE: 105 Kommunisticheski Prospekt, Alma-Ata, 480091. 62–6295 (office).

Suntsov, Sergey Aleksandrovich
POSITION: Commentator for Ostankino ITA Novosti (News) Television and Radio Company
BIRTHPLACE/DATE: Moscow, 1956
NATIONALITY: Russian
CAREER: From 1978 to 1983, Correspondent for the Central Broadcasting for Foreign Countries Department of the USRR State Committee of Television and Radio. From 1983 to 1985, French Interpreter in Algeria. From 1985 to 1991, Special Correspondent for the Central Broadcasting for Foreign Countries Department of the State Committee of Television and Radio. From February 1991, Commentator for Ostankino.
FAMILY: Married with a son.
ADDRESS/TELEPHONE: 12 Koroleva Street, Moscow. 245–2683 (home).

Surkov, Mikhail Semenovich
POSITION: Former member of the Politburo; member of the USSR Supreme Soviet Committee for Defense and Security; Major-General
BIRTHPLACE/DATE: Chelyabinsk, 1945
NATIONALITY: Russian
CAREER: From 1965, Army Squad Commander, Deputy Company Commander, Assistant Political Department Head, Deputy Division Commander. From 1985, First Deputy Political Department Head of the Army. From 1988, member of the Military Council, Political Department Head of the Army Guard. From 1990, Executive Party Commission Secretary of the USSR Army and Navy Central Political Directorate. From March 1991, Secretary of the All-Army Party Committee. Member of the USSR Supreme Soviet Committee for Defense and Security. In April 1991, elected member of the Politburo. USSR People's Deputy. Central Committee member.

ADDRESS/TELEPHONE: The USSR Supreme Soviet, The Kremlin, Moscow.

Suzdaltsev, Yuri Anatolyevich

POSITION: Board Chairman of the Russian Fuel and Energy Exchange (RosTEB)
BIRTHPLACE/DATE: Irkutsk, 1944
EDUCATION: Graduated in 1969 from the Karaganda Polytechnical Institute. Speaks English.
CAREER: From 1969 to 1981, worked to Shift Head of the Nevinnomyssk State Regional Electric Power Station in Stavropol region. From 1981 to 1983, Shift Head of the Moscow Heat-and-Power Plant in Moscow. From 1983 to 1984, Department Head of the USSR State Supplies Committee. From 1984 to 1986, Section Head of the Berezovskaya State Regional Electric Power Station in Krasnoyarsk region. From 1986 to 1990, Department Head of the USSR Ministry of Power Industry. In 1990 and 1991, Main Administration Deputy Chief Engineer, Director of the Yuzhtekhenergo (Southern Technical Energy) Enterprise.
FAMILY: Married with a daughter.
ADDRESS/TELEPHONE: 7 Kitaisky Proyezd, Moscow, 103074. 220–5527; 220–4116 (office).

Syrovatko, Vitaly Grigoryevich

POSITION: Presidium Secretary of the Russian Federation Supreme Soviet
BIRTHPLACE/DATE: Kremenchug, Poltava region, 1940
NATIONALITY: Ukrainian
CAREER: Former Secretary of the Bryansk Regional Party Committee, Executive Committee Chairman of the Russian Federation Bryansk Region Council of People's Deputies. Chairman of the Russian Federation Supreme Soviet Commission of the National State System. Deputy Chairman of the Russian Federation Supreme Soviet Council of Nationalities. Russian Federation People's Deputy.
FAMILY: Married with two daughters and two granddaughters.
ADDRESS/TELEPHONE: 2 Krasnopresnenskaya Naberezhnaya, Moscow, 103274. 205–4428; 205–4517 (office).

Systsov, Apollon Sergeyevich

POSITION: Vice President of the Russian Union of Aircraft Industry Complexes, Enterprises, and Associations
BIRTHPLACE/DATE: 1929
NATIONALITY: Russian
EDUCATION: Graduated in 1962 from Tashkent Polytechnic, specializing in Aviation Mechanical Engineering.
CAREER: From 1948 to 1975, worked from Motorist to Chief Engineer of the Tashkent Industrial Aviation Association. From 1975 to 1981, Director-General of the Ulyanovsk Industrial Aviation Complex. From 1981 to 1985, USSR First Deputy Minister of Aviation Industry. From 1985 to 1991, USSR Minister of Aviation Industry. Academician of the Russian Academy of Technological Sciences.
HONORS/AWARDS: Order of Lenin; two Orders of the Red Banner of Labor.
FAMILY: Married with a son, a daughter, and four grandchildren.
ADDRESS/TELEPHONE: 16 Ulansky Pereulok, Moscow, GSP 101849. 207–0670 (office).

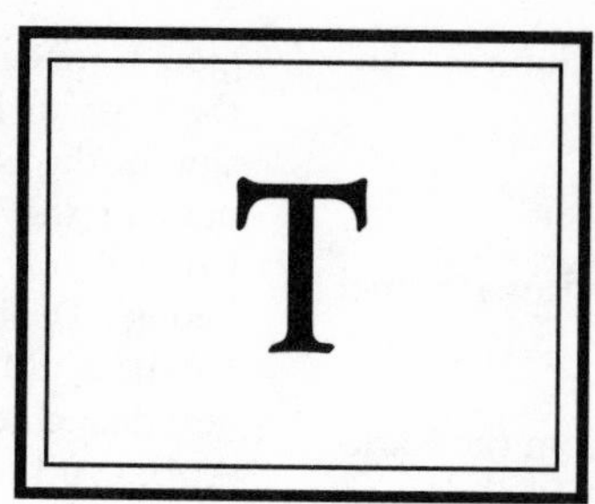

Tabakov, Oleg Pavlovich

POSITION: Art Director of the Moscow Tabakov Theater

BIRTHPLACE/DATE: Saratov, August 17, 1935

CAREER: From 1957 to 1970, Actor of the Sovremennik Theater. From 1970 to 1983, Director and Actor of the Sovremennik Theater. From 1983, Company Member of the Moscow Academic Art Theater (MKhAT). In 1974, Co-Founder of a studio at the MKhAT; in 1987, the studio became the Tabakov Theater. From 1974, Lecturer at the State Institute of Dramatic Art (GITIS). From 1974 to 1986, Board Secretary of the Russian Federation Union of Theater Workers; Presidium Member of the All-Union Workers of Aesthetic Education Association. People's Artist.

MAJOR WORKS: More than eighty parts in movies, including Sherbuk (*Unfinished Piece for Mechanical Piano*, 1974); Miss Andrew (*Mary Poppins, Good-Bye*, 1984); Oblomov (*Few Days from Oblomov's Life*, 1979); Nikolay Pavlovich (*Flights in Dreams and Waking Hours*, 1983); Iskremas (*Sparkle, Sparkle, My Star*).

HONORS/AWARDS: USSR State Prize; Order of the Red Banner of Labor; Order of the Badge of Honor.

FAMILY: Married with a daughter and a son.

ADDRESS/TELEPHONE: 1-A Chaplygina Street, Moscow, 103068. 924–6137 (theater); 924–7690 (home).

Tadzhuddinov, Talgat Safich

POSITION: Chairman of the Ecclesiastical Directorate of Moslems of European Regions of the CIS and Siberia; Mufti

BIRTHPLACE/DATE: Kazan, October 12, 1948

NATIONALITY: Tatar

EDUCATION: Graduated in 1978 from Cairo Al-Azkhar University in Egypt.

CAREER: From 1973, Second Imam-Khatib of the Cathedral Mosque of Kazan. From 1978, First Imam-Khatib of the Kazan Cathedral Mosque. Represented Soviet Moslems at UNESCO.

FAMILY: Married with five children.

ADDRESS/TELEPHONE: 50-A Tukayevskaya Street, Ufa.

Taranenko, Leonid Arkadyevich

POSITION: Weight Lifter

BIRTHPLACE/DATE: Talorita, Brest region, June 13, 1956

NATIONALITY: Byelorussian

CAREER: In 1980, Olympic Champion; World and European Champion. In 1991, European Champion. Established sixteen World and European Records. Physical Education Instructor at the Byelorussian VFSO (All Union Physical Education and Sports Society) Council of Trade Unions.

FAMILY: Married with two children.

ADDRESS/TELEPHONE: Minsk. 36–1354.

Tarasov, Anatoli Vladimirovich

POSITION: Instructor at the Institute of Physical Education; President of the Golden Puck Club

BIRTHPLACE/DATE: 1918, Moscow

NATIONALITY: Russian

EDUCATION: Doctor of Educational Sciences; Professor.

CAREER: Metalworker-Instrumentalist, Military Officer-Instructor of the Central Army Club

(TSSKA); Senior Coach of the TSSKA Ice Hockey Team; Senior Coach of the USSR National Ice Hockey Team.
FAMILY: Married with two daughters.

Tazabekov, Marat Kasymbekovich
POSITION: Board Chairman of the Universalnaya Birzha Kyrghyzstan (Universal Kirgistan Stock Exchange) Joint-Stock Company
BIRTHPLACE/DATE: Osh district, Kirghizia (Kirgistan), 1958
NATIONALITY: Kirghiz
CAREER: From 1981 to 1982, Faculty Member of the Economics Department at Moscow State University. From 1982 to 1984, Junior Researcher at the Institute of Economics of the Kirghiz Republic State Planning Committee. From 1984 to 1988, Economist, Senior Expert, Chief Specialist of the Services Department of the Kirghiz State Planning Committee. From 1988 to 1990, Head of the Foreign Economic Relations Department of the Kirghiz State Planning Committee. From 1990 to 1991, Board Chairman of Nogra Foreign Company, Ltd.
FAMILY: Married with two children.
ADDRESS/TELEPHONE: 96 Tchui Prospekt, Bishkek, 720000. 26–5322; Fax: 26–5305.

Tenyakov, Eduard Veniaminovich
POSITION: President of the Chelyabinsk Universal Exchange
BIRTHPLACE/DATE: Chelyabinsk, 1952
NATIONALITY: Russian
CAREER: From 1971 to 1976, Head of the Polyot (Flight) Industrial-Dispatching Exchange in Chelyabinsk. From 1976 to 1979, Mechanical Shop Head of the Polyot Industrial Association. From 1979 to 1982, Deputy Director-General of the Commercial Service. From 1982 to 1985, Director of the Chelyabinsk Floor Covering Plant. From 1985 to 1987, Chairman of the Construction-Repair Cooperative Society. From 1987 to 1990, Board Chairman of the Cooperative Bank. From 1990, President of the Moscow Central Stock Exchange.
MAJOR WORKS: *Best Possible Option.*
FAMILY: Married with a daughter.
ADDRESS/TELEPHONE: 35 Lenina Prospekt, Chelyabinsk. 36–0498; Fax 36–5765.

Terekhov, Vladislav Petrovich
POSITION: Russian Federation Ambassador to Germany; Ambassador Extraordinary and Plenipotentiary
BIRTHPLACE/DATE: Rostov-on-Don, November 5, 1933
NATIONALITY: Russian
CAREER: From 1957 to 1961, Senior Aide at the USSR Embassy in Australia. From 1961 to 1962, Senior Aide; from 1962 to 1963, Attaché; from 1963 to 1964, Third Secretary; from 1964, Second Secretary of the Third European Department of the USSR Foreign Ministry (MID). From 1964 to 1967, Third Secretary; from 1967 to 1969, Second Secretary; from 1969 to 1970, First Secretary at the USSR Embassy in the Federal Republic of Germany. From 1970 to 1973, First Secretary; from 1973 to 1976, Section Head; from 1976 to 1981, Deputy Head of the Third European Department of the USSR MID. From 1981 to 1986, Minister-Counsellor at the USSR Embassy in the Federal Republic of Germany. From 1986 to 1988, Head of the Directorate for Work with Soviet Embassies of the USSR MID. From 1988 to 1990, Board Member and Head of the Central Directorate of Personnel and Educational Institutions of the USSR MID. From 1990, USSR (now Russian Federation) Ambassador to Germany.
HONORS/AWARDS: Order of the Red Banner of Labor; Honorary Diploma of the Russian Federation Supreme Soviet Presidium; four medals.
FAMILY: Married with a son.
ADDRESS/TELEPHONE: Botschaft der UdSSR in der Bundesrepublic Deutschland, Waldstrasse 42, 5300 Bonn. 31–2085; 31–2087; 31–2074.

Tereshkova, Valentina Vladimirovna
POSITION: Deputy Chairman of the Russian Agency for International Cooperation and Development; former USSR Pilot-Cosmonaut
BIRTHPLACE/DATE: Maslennikovo, Yaroslavl region, March 6, 1937
NATIONALITY: Russian
EDUCATION: Studied at the School of Cosmonauts. Doctor of Technical Sciences.
CAREER: In June 1963, first woman in the world to fly into outer space aboard the spacecraft Vostok–6. From 1963 to 1968, Instructor-Cosmonaut at the Yuri Gagarin Center for Cosmonaut Train-

ing. From 1968 to 1987, Chairwoman of the Committee on Soviet Women. From 1974 to 1991, member of the USSR Supreme Soviet Committee for International Affairs. From November 1987, Chairwoman of the Presidium of the Union of Soviet Societies for Friendship and Cultural Relations with Foreign Countries; from 1992, Deputy Chairwoman of the Russian Agency for International Cooperation and Development. Colonel-Engineer. USSR Supreme Soviet Deputy of the Seventh to Eleventh Convocations. USSR Supreme Soviet Presidium Member. From 1989 to 1992, USSR People's Deputy. From 1962 to 1991, member of the Communist Party. From 1971 to 1990, member of the Central Committee.
HONORS/AWARDS: Hero of the USSR; two Orders of Lenin; Order of the Red Banner of Labor; Order of the October Revolution; Order of the People's Friendship.
FAMILY: Married with a daughter.
ADDRESS/TELEPHONE: 14 Vozdvizhenka Street, Moscow, 103885. 290–1245 (office).

Ter-Petrosyan, Levon Akopovich
POSITION: President of the Armenian Republic; member of the Armenian Writers' Union and the Association of Orientalists and French Asian Society
BIRTHPLACE/DATE: Aleppo, Syria, January 9, 1945
NATIONALITY: Armenian
CAREER: From 1972 to 1978, worked at the Institute of Literature of the Armenian Academy of Sciences. From 1978 to 1985, Scientific Secretary of the Mashtots Matendaran (Institute of Ancient Manuscripts). From 1985, Senior Researcher at the Matendaran. In May 1988, joined the Armenian Karabakh Movement. From December 1988 to May 1989, under arrest. From 1989, Board Chairman of the Armenian National Movement. From 1990 to 1991, Chairman of the Armenian Supreme Soviet. Armenian Republic Supreme Soviet Deputy.
MAJOR WORKS: Six monographs and more than seventy scientific works published in Armenian, Russian, and French devoted to Armenian-Assyrian cultural relations and the Armenian Kilikiyski state.
FAMILY: Married with a son.
ADDRESS/TELEPHONE: 19 Marshala Bagramyana Street, Yerevan, 375016. 52–0204 (office).

Tikhonov, Aleksandr Ivanovich
POSITION: Biathlon Athlete
BIRTHPLACE/DATE: Uisk village, Chelyabinsk region, 1947
NATIONALITY: Russian
CAREER: Serviceman. Member of the Dynamo Sports Society. In 1968, 1972, 1976, 1980, Winter Olympic Champion. In 1969, 1970, 1973, World Champion (20-km race). In 1975, Silver Medal winner. In 1976 and 1977, World Champion (10-km race). In 1979, Bronze Medal winner.
HONORS/AWARDS: USSR Honored Master of Sports (biathlon).
FAMILY: Married.
ADDRESS/TELEPHONE: Novosibirsk. 297–419.

Tikhonov, Victor Vasilyevich
POSITION: Senior Coach of the Central Army Hockey Club
BIRTHPLACE/DATE: Moscow, 1930
NATIONALITY: Russian
CAREER: Air Force Sports Instructor of the Moscow Military District; Sports Instructor of the Moscow City Council Dynamo Club; Hockey Coach at the Riga Dynamo Club. Senior Coach of the USSR National Ice Hockey Team; Senior Coach of the Central Army Hockey Club. In 1978, 1979, 1981 to 1983, 1986, 1989, 1990, World Champion. In 1978, 1979, 1981 to 1983, 1985 to 1987, 1989 to 1991, European Champion. In 1984 and 1988, Winter Olympic Ice Hockey Champion. From 1977, Senior Coach of the USSR (now CIS) Ice Hockey Team.
HONORS/AWARDS: Order of Lenin; Order of the October Revolution; Order of the People's Friendship; Order of the Red Banner of Labor; Medal For Labor Distinction. USSR Master of Sports (hockey); USSR Honored Coach.
FAMILY: Married with a son.
ADDRESS/TELEPHONE: 39 B. Gruzinskaya, Flat #49, Moscow, 123056. 213–6716 (office).

Tikhonov, Vladimir Aleksandrovich
POSITION: President of the Russian League of Entrepreneurs and Cooperative Societies; member of the Russian Federation Presidential Council;

Vice President of the Russian Union of Industrialists and Entrepreneurs
BIRTHPLACE/DATE: Verkhoturye, Sverdlovsk region, 1927
NATIONALITY: Russian
CAREER: From 1959 to 1976, engaged in scientific and pedagogical work at Urals State University; Director of the All-Union Research Institute of Agricultural Labor and Management. From 1976 to 1986, Head of the Agrarian Problems of Socialism Department at the Institute of Economics of the Academy of National Economy and the USSR Council of Ministers. Academician of the All-Union Lenin Academy of Agricultural Scinces (now the Academy of Agricultural Sciences). From 1989 to 1992, President of the USSR Union of United Cooperative Societies. USSR People's Deputy.
FAMILY: Married with a daughter.
ADDRESS/TELEPHONE: 14 Tokmakov Pereulok, Moscow, 107066. 261–1911 (office).

Timofeyev, Timur Timofeyevich
POSITION: Director of the Institute of Comparative Politics and Problems of the Workers' Movement (formerly the Institute of the International Workers' Movement); Director of the Interdepartmental Center for Comparative Socio-Political Studies
BIRTHPLACE/DATE: Ivanovo, November 30, 1928
NATIONALITY: Russian
CAREER: From 1950 to 1955, Program Author of the USSR State Television and Radio Committee's Foreign Broadcasting Service. From 1956 to 1966, Staff Member of the Institute of the World Economy and International Relations of the USSR Academy of Sciences. From 1966, Corresponding Member of the USSR Academy of Sciences. From 1991, Corresponding Member of the Russian Academy of Sciences.
MAJOR WORKS: Comparative socio-political studies in the field of labor relations.
HONORS/AWARDS: Order of the Red Banner of Labor; Order of the October Revolution; Order of Lenin; International Prize of the USSR Academy of Sciences.
FAMILY: Married with two children.
ADDRESS/TELEPHONE: 9-A Kolpachny Pereulok, Moscow, 101831. 227–3703 (office).

Tishkov, Valery Aleksandrovich
POSITION: Russian Federation Minister; Chairman of the State Committee for National Policy; Director of the Institute of Ethnology and Anthropology of the Russian Academy of Sciences (RAN); Russian Federation Government Representative for Problems in Ossetia
BIRTHPLACE/DATE: Nizhny Sergi village, Sverdlovsk region, November 5, 1941
EDUCATION: Studied at Moscow State University. Doctor of History; Professor.
CAREER: From 1969 to 1972, Assistant Professor, Dean of the History Department at the Magadan State Teachers' Training Institute. From 1972 to 1976, Researcher at the Institute of World History of the USSR Academy of Sciences (USSR AN). From 1976 to 1982, Scientific Secretary of the History Department of the USSR AN. From 1982 to 1992, Head of the American Section at the Institute of Ethnography of the USSR AN (now RAN). From 1988 to 1989, Deputy Director of the Institute of Ethnography.
MAJOR WORKS: *The Country of the Maple Leaf: Beginning of History; The Liberation Movement in Colonial Canada; History of Canada* (co-author); *History and Historians of the United States.* Monographs and scientific articles.
HONORS/AWARDS: Medal for Labor Valor.
FAMILY: Married with a son.
ADDRESS/TELEPHONE: The Institute of Ethnology and Anthropology of the Russian Academy of Sciences, 32-A Leninsky Prospekt, Moscow. 938–0712 (office).

Titkin, Aleksandr Alekseyevich
POSITION: President of the Tiross (Technology and Investments of Russia) Financial and Investment Company
BIRTHPLACE/DATE: Arsenyevo village, Tula region, September 12, 1948
NATIONALITY: Russian
CAREER: From 1972 to 1978, worked from Construction Worker to Chief Engineer of the Novgorod Complex Association. From 1978 to 1986, worked from Shop Head to Production Director of the Atommash (Atomic Machinery) Association.

From 1986 to 1991, worked from Director of the Bolokhovsky Machine-Building Plant to President of the Gefes Joint-Stock Company (Russia's first private machine-building enterprise) of the Tyazhprommash (Heavy Industry Machinery) Association in Tula. From 1991 to 1992, Russian Minister of Industry. Russian Federation People's Deputy.
FAMILY: Married with three children and a granddaughter.
ADDRESS/TELEPHONE: 26 Dimitrova Street, Building 3-A, Flat #210, Moscow. 252–1124.

Titov, Yuri Yevlampiyevich
POSITION: President of the International Federation of Gymnastics (FIG)
BIRTHPLACE/DATE: Omsk, 1935
NATIONALITY: Russian
EDUCATION: Doctor of Pedagogy.
CAREER: In 1956, Summer Olympic Gymnastics Champion. In 1962, Absolute World Gymnastics Champion. Gymnastics Instructor of the Central Council of the Burevestnik Sports Society; Sports Instructor for the Central Army Club in Kiev; Head of the Sports and Defense Department of the Komsomol Central Committee; Head of the Gymnastics Directorate of the USSR State Committee for Sports; Executive Secretary of the USSR National Olympic Committee; USSR National Team Coach in Gymnastics of the USSR State Committee for Sports.
HONORS/AWARDS: Order of Lenin; Order of the Red Banner of Labor; Order of the People's Friendship; USSR Honored Master of Sports (gymnastics); USSR Honored Coach.
FAMILY: Married with a son and a daughter.
ADDRESS/TELEPHONE: 8 Luzhnetskaya Naberezhnaya, 119871. 201–0777 (office).

Titova, Ludmila Yevgenyevna
POSITION: Skater; Deputy Director of the Metelitsa (Snowstorm) Expedition Club
BIRTHPLACE/DATE: 1946
NATIONALITY: Russian
CAREER: In 1968, Winter Olympic Silver Medal. In 1968 and 1970, World Skating Champion. In 1972, Winter Olympic Bronze Medal. To 1991, Deputy Chairman of the USSR National Olympics Committee.
FAMILY: Married.
ADDRESS/TELEPHONE: 42 Akademika Anokhina Street, Building 2, Moscow, 117602. 433–2620 (Federation).

Tolkachev, Oleg Mikhailovich
POSITION: Prefect of the Southern District of Moscow
BIRTHPLACE/DATE: Moscow, November 18, 1948
NATIONALITY: Russian
EDUCATION: Doctor of Physics and Mathematics.
CAREER: From 1972 to 1990, Engineer, Junior Researcher, Senior Researcher at the Institute of Physics of the USSR Academy of Sciences. From 1990 to 1991, Chairman of the Moskvoretsky District Executive Committee. From July 1991, Prefect of the Southern District of Moscow. From January 1992, member of the Moscow Government. From 1975 to 1991, member of the Communist Party.
FAMILY: Married with two children.
ADDRESS/TELEPHONE: 10 Avtozavodskaya Street, Moscow, 109280. 275–0636.

Tolmachev, Gennadi Ivanovich
POSITION: Editor in Chief of *Prostor* (*Space*) literary magazine
BIRTHPLACE/DATE: Alma-Ata, 1939
NATIONALITY: Russian
EDUCATION: Doctor of History.
CAREER: Writer for *Kazakhstanskaya Pravda* (*Kazakhstan Truth*) newspaper; Correspondent for *Komsomolskaya Pravda* (*Komsomol Truth*) newspaper; Staff Member of the Central Committee's Academy of Social Sciences; Editor in Chief of the Zhazushi Publishing House; Editor in Chief of *Ogni Alatau* newspaper; Deputy Editor in Chief of *Partiynaya Zhizn Kazakhstana* (*Party Life of Kazakhstan*) newspaper; Secretary of the Kazakhstan Writers' Union.
FAMILY: Married with a son.
ADDRESS/TELEPHONE: 105 Prospekt Ablai-Khana Street, Alma-Ata, 480091. 69–6319 (office); 62–3596 (home).

Tosunyan, Garegin Ashotovich

POSITION: Board Chairman of the Moscow Bank of Science and Technology Development (Tekhnobank)
BIRTHPLACE/DATE: Yerevan, 1955
NATIONALITY: Armenian
EDUCATION: Doctor of Physics and Mathematics.
CAREER: Researcher, Deputy Department Head of the All-Union Electrotechnical Institute; Chief Specialist of the Central Directorate for Science and Technology of the Moscow City Executive Committee. Head of the Scientific and Industrial Cooperation Department of the Moscow City Executive Committee.
MAJOR WORKS: Works on plasma physics, economics, and law.
FAMILY: Married with two children.
ADDRESS/TELEPHONE: 56 Bolshaya Gruzinskaya Street, Moscow, 123056. 254–4611.

Travkin, Nikolay Ilyich

POSITION: Chairman of the Democratic Party of Russia; Administrative Chief of the Moscow Region Shakhovsky District
BIRTHPLACE/DATE: Novo-Nikolayevka village, Shakhovsky district, Moscow region, March 19, 1946
NATIONALITY: Russian
EDUCATION: Graduated in 1987 from the Physics and Mathematics Department at the Kolomna Teachers' Training Institute. From 1988 to 1989, student at the Moscow Higher Party School. Speaks German.
CAREER: From 1969 to 1986, Team-Leader of Construction Workers. From 1986 to 1987, Manager of the Mosoblselstroi (Moscow Region Country Construction) Trust. From 1987 to 1988, Deputy Head of Glavmosoblstroi (Main Moscow Region Constructions). In March 1990, quit the Communist Party. From 1989 to May 1990, Chairman of the Russian Federation Supreme Soviet Subcommittee for Issues of the Councils of People's Deputies and the Development of Self-Government; Presidium Member of the Russian Federation Supreme Soviet. USSR People's Deputy. Russian Federation People's Deputy.
HONORS/AWARDS: Order of the Red Banner of Labor (1984); Order of Lenin; Sickle and Hammer Gold Medal; Hero of Socialist Labor (1985).
FAMILY: Married with two sons.
ADDRESS/TELEPHONE: 18 Poltavskaya Street, Moscow, 103287. 285–7856; 285–6191 (office).

Trebkov, Andrey Adamovich

POSITION: Chairman of the International Non-Governmental Union of Jurists Association
BIRTHPLACE/DATE: Tevriz village, Omsk region, 1937
NATIONALITY: Russian
CAREER: People's Judge; Chairman of the People's Court in Tyumen region. From 1976 to 1980, Secretary of the Tyumen City Party Committee. From 1980 to 1982, Propaganda Department Head of the Tyumen Regional Party Committee. From 1982 to 1988, Head of the Directorate of Legal Information and the Legal Education of the Population; Board Member of the USSR Ministry of Justice. From 1988 to 1989, Consultant to the State Law Department of the Central Committee. In 1989, Chairman of the USSR Union of Jurists.
FAMILY: Married with a daughter.
ADDRESS/TELEPHONE: 12 Twenty-Six Bakinskikh Komissarov Street, Building 6, Flat #27, Moscow. 433–7362 (home).

Tretyak, Ivan Moiseyevich

POSITION: Army General
BIRTHPLACE/DATE: Malaya Popovka village, Khorolski district, Poltava region, 1923
NATIONALITY: Ukrainian
CAREER: From 1939, served in the Armed Forces: Division Commander; Army Commander; Military District Commander; Commander in Chief of the Far East Forces; USSR Deputy Minister of Defense and Chief Inspector. From 1987 to August 1991, Commander in Chief of the Air Defense Forces; Deputy USSR Minister of Defense. USSR People's Deputy.
HONORS/AWARDS: Hero of the USSR; Hero of Socialist Labor.
FAMILY: Married with two sons.
TELEPHONE: 293–2869; 293–1413 (office).

Tretyak, Vladislav Aleksandrovich

POSITION: Sports Consultant to the International Youth Cooperation Foundation

BIRTHPLACE/DATE: Orudyevo village, Moscow region, 1952

NATIONALITY: Russian

CAREER: In 1963, Hockey Player of the Central Army Club (TSSKA) Groups for Youth and Children; played for the National Team. In 1970, 1973 to 1975, 1978, 1979, 1981 to 1983, World and European Champion. In 1971, World Champion. In 1972, 1976, 1984, Winter Olympic Champion. In 1980, Winter Olympic Silver Medal winner. In 1974, 1979, 1981 and 1983, World's Best Goalkeeper. In 1981, Canadian Cup winner. Sports Instructor of the Central Army Club; Officer of the USSR Defense Ministry Sports Club.

HONORS/AWARDS: Order of Lenin; Order of the People's Friendship; Order of the Badge of Honor; Order of the Red Banner of Labor; USSR Honored Master of Sports.

FAMILY: Married with a daughter and a son.

ADDRESS/TELEPHONE: 43/1 Profsoyuznaya Street, Flat #241, Moscow, 117420. 331–2061 (home).

Tretyakov, Vitaly Toviyevich

POSITION: Editor in Chief of *Nezavissimaya Gazeta (Independent Newspaper)*

BIRTHPLACE/DATE: Moscow, 1953

EDUCATION: Graduated in 1976 from the International Journalism Department at Moscow State University. Command of French.

CAREER: From 1976 to 1988, held positions from Trainee to Managing Editor of Novosti (News) Press Agency (APN). From 1988 to 1990, Analyst, Deputy Editor in Chief of *Moskovskiye Novosti* (*Moscow News*) weekly. Member of the Foreign Policy Council.

FAMILY: Married.

ADDRESS/TELEPHONE: 13 Myasnitskaya Street, Building 10, Moscow, 101000. 924–6961 (office).

Trubin, Nikolay Semyonovich

POSITION: Legal Department Head of the Rosagropromstroi Russian Agricultural Construction Joint-Stock Corporation

BIRTHPLACE/DATE: Burdygino village, Orenburg region, 1931

NATIONALITY: Russian

EDUCATION: Doctor of Law.

CAREER: From 1953 to 1960, Assistant Procurator at a reformatory camp; District Procurator of the Komi Republic. From 1960 to 1972, Investigator of the Public Prosecutor's District Office; District Procurator; Department Procurator of the Krasnodar Region Public Prosecutor's Office; Senior Aide to the Procurator; Investigation Department Head of the Public Prosecutor's Regional Office. From 1972 to 1978, Deputy Department Head, Deputy Directorate Head of the USSR Public Prosecutor's Office. From 1978 to 1990, Deputy Procurator, First Deputy Procurator, Russian Federation Procurator. From 1991 to January 1992, USSR Procurator-General. From 1992, Legal Department Head of Rosagropromstroi.

HONORS/AWARDS: Order of the Red Banner of Labor; Order of the Badge of Honor.

FAMILY: Married with a son.

ADDRESS/TELEPHONE: 16 Krasina Pereulok, Moscow. 254–3660 (office).

Tsaregorodtsev, Vladimir Ivanovich

POSITION: President of the Rossiya (Russian) Association of Joint-Stock Commercial Industrial and Construction Banks; Board Chairman of the Kreditprombank (Great Industrial Bank) Commercial Bank

BIRTHPLACE/DATE: Yaransk, Kirov region, 1938

NATIONALITY: Russian

CAREER: From 1959 to 1966, Credit Inspector; Head of the Kirov Region USSR Stroibank. From 1966 to 1974, Senior Credit Inspector; Head of the Ivanovo Region USSR Stroibank. From 1974 to 1980, Manager of the Ivanovo Region USSR Stroibank. From 1980 to 1987, Deputy Manager of the Russian Republic Stroibank. From 1987 to 1988, First Deputy Chairman of the Russian Republic USSR Promstroibank. From 1988 to 1990, Board Chairman of the Russian Republic USSR Promstroibank. Ivanovo City Council People's Deputy; Chairman of the Planning and Budget Commission.

HONORS/AWARDS: Diploma of the Russian Federation Supreme Soviet Presidium.

FAMILY: Married with a daughter.

ADDRESS/TELEPHONE: 84 Mira Prospekt, Moscow, 129868. 284–4365; 284–4395 (office).

Tsipko, Aleksandr Sergeyevich

POSITION: Head of the Political Studies Center at The International Foundation for Socio-Economic and Political Studies (The Gorbachev Foundation)

BIRTHPLACE/DATE: Odessa, 1941

NATIONALITY: Ukrainian

EDUCATION: From 1970 to 1972, postgraduate student at Moscow State University. Doctor of Philosophy.

CAREER: From 1965 to 1967, worked at *Komsomolskaya Pravda* (*Komsomol Truth*) newspaper. From 1967 to 1970, worked for the Komsomol Central Committee. From 1972 to 1986, Deputy Director of the Institute of the Socialist World Economy of the USSR Academy of Sciences. From 1986 to 1990, member of the Central Committee. From March 1990, Deputy Director of the Institute of International Economic and Political Studies of the Russian Academy of Sciences. To 1991, member of the Communist Party.

MAJOR WORKS: *Socialism: Life of the Society and of an Individual.*

FAMILY: Married with two children.

ADDRESS/TELEPHONE: 49 Leningradsky Prospekt, Moscow, 125468. 943–9437; 943–9546 (office).

Tsybukh, Valery Ivanovich

POSITION: Former USSR Supreme Soviet Presidium Member; Chairman of the USSR Supreme Soviet Committee on Youth Policy

BIRTHPLACE/DATE: Storozhinets, Chernovtsy region, Ukraine, 1951

NATIONALITY: Ukrainian

CAREER: From 1974 to 1977, First Secretary of the Zheleznodorozhny District Komsomol Committee. In 1977, Shop Head, Section Head of the Kiev Ministry of Civil Aviation Works. From 1978 to 1989, Second, First Secretary of the Ukrainian Komsomol Central Committee. From May 1989, People's Deputy; USSR Supreme Soviet Presidium Member; member of the Parliament Communist Group; member of the Group of Deputies-Physicians for Protecting People; member of the USSR Young People's Deputies.

FAMILY: Married with a daughter and a son.

Tuleyev, Aman-Geldy Moldagazyevich

POSITION: Chairman of the Kemerovo Regional Council of People's Deputies

BIRTHPLACE/DATE: Krasnovodsk, Turkmenia, 1944

NATIONALITY: Turkmen

CAREER: Worked from Assistant Station-Master to Head of the Kemerovo Railroad Directorate. From 1986 to 1988, Head of the Transportation and Communications Department of the Kemerovo Regional Party Committee. From May 1990 to August 1991, Executive Committee Chairman of the Kemerovo Regional Council of People's Deputies. In 1991, Russian Federation Presidential Candidate. Russian Federation People's Deputy.

FAMILY: Married with two children.

ADDRESS/TELEPHONE: 62 Sovietsky Prospekt, Kemerovo, 650099. 23–4142 (office).

Turanov, Sergey Anatolyevich

POSITION: President of the Agentstvo Ekonomicheskikh Novostei (Economic News Agency) Joint-Stock Company

BIRTHPLACE/DATE: Moscow, 1951

NATIONALITY: Russian

CAREER: Worked at the Institute of Metallurgy of the USSR Academy of Sciences and at the Ministry of Ferrous Metallurgy. From 1987, worked at the Economic Department of TASS (Telegraph Agency of the Soviet Union) News Agency.

FAMILY: Married with a daughter.

ADDRESS/TELEPHONE: 9 Ogareva Street, Building 7, Moscow, 103009. 229–4236; 229–9311.

Turbin, Vitaly Borisovich

POSITION: Russian Federation Deputy Minister of Internal Affairs; Lieutenant-General of the Internal Affairs Service

BIRTHPLACE/DATE: Kursk region, 1938

CAREER: From 1958, worked for the Internal Affairs Service. From 1961 to 1984, worked at the Belgorod Region Department of Internal Affairs. From 1984 to 1987, Department Head of GUBKhSS (Main Directorate of Social Services) of the USSR Ministry of Internal Affairs. From 1987 to 1991, Head of the Directorate of Internal Affairs of the Tambov Region Executive Committee. From September 1991 to January 1992, USSR Deputy Minister of Internal Affairs. From January

1992, Russian Federation Deputy Minister of Internal Affairs and the Central Directorate of Personnel, Medical Services, and Educational Facilities.
ADDRESS/TELEPHONE: 16 Zhitnaya Street, Moscow, 117049. 222–6066 (office).

Turisheva, Ludmila Ivanovna
POSITION: President of the Ukraine Federation of Gymnastics
BIRTHPLACE/DATE: Grozny, 1952
NATIONALITY: Russian
CAREER: In 1968, Summer Olympic Gold Medal winner. In 1972, winner of two Summer Olympic Gold Medals. In 1976, Summer Olympic Gold Medal winner. From 1976, Senior Gymnastics Coach of the Kiev Dynamo Club.
HONORS/AWARDS: Order of Lenin; Order of the People's Friendship; Order of the Badge of Honor; USSR Honored Master of Sports.
FAMILY: Married with a daughter.
ADDRESS/TELEPHONE: 8 Luzhnetskaya Naberezhnaya, Moscow, 119871. 220–0200 (Kiev).

Tutov, Nikolay Dmitryevich
POSITION: Chairman of the Orenburg Region Administration of the Russian Federation Government
BIRTHPLACE/DATE: Aktyubinsk region, 1961
NATIONALITY: Russian
CAREER: From 1985, Komsomol Committee Secretary of an Air Force Military Unit. In 1989, joined the Social-Democratic Association; from 1990 to 1991, Co-Chairman; helped establish the USSR Supreme Soviet Social-Democratic Faction. From April 1991, Board Member of the Social-Democratic Party of Russia (SDPR); from May 1991, Executive Secretary. USSR People's Deputy.
FAMILY: Married.
ADDRESS/TELEPHONE: 3 Chekhova Street, Moscow, 109044. 299–3914 (office); 415–5346 (home).

Tutov, Victor Trofimovich
POSITION: Board Chairman of the Visa Republican Universal Commercial Joint-Stock Bank
BIRTHPLACE/DATE: Kryukovo village, Moscow region, January 6, 1941
CAREER: From 1966 to 1974, Staff Member of the Material and Technical Supplies Directorate of the Moscow City USSR Gossnab (State Supplies). From 1974 to 1975, Deputy Department Head of the Economic Directorate of the USSR Gossnab. From 1975 to 1987, Assistant to the Chairman of the USSR Gossnab. From 1987 to 1989, Department Head of the USSR Gossnab. From 1989 to 1991, Head of the Secretariat of the First Deputy Chairman of the USSR Council of Ministers.
HONORS/AWARDS: Order of the Badge of Honor; two medals.
FAMILY: Married with two children.
ADDRESS/TELEPHONE: 3/2 Gogolevski Boulevard, Moscow, 121019. 291–9514.

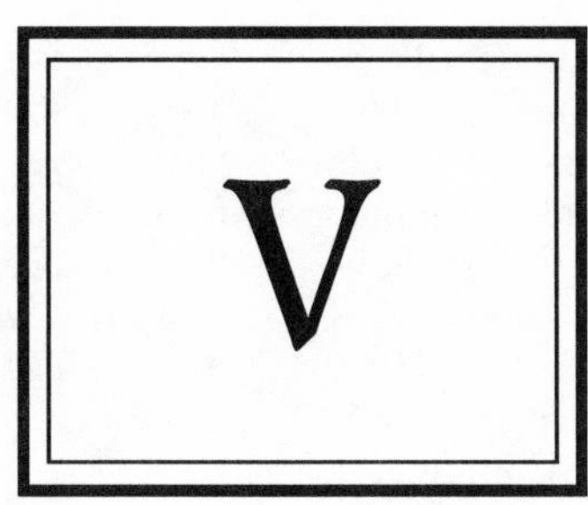

Vagnorius, Gediminas

POSITION: Lithuanian Prime Minister
BIRTHPLACE/DATE: Vilkaychay village, Plungessky district
NATIONALITY: Lett
EDUCATION: Doctor of Economics.
CAREER: Senior Researcher at the Institute of Economics of the Lithuanian Academy of Sciences. Participated in the preparation and implementation of economic reforms in Lithuania and the Baltic region. In February 1989, elected Deputy of the Lithuanian Supreme Soviet. Presidium Member of the Supreme Soviet.
FAMILY: Married with two children.
ADDRESS/TELEPHONE: 11 Giadimino Prospekt, Vilnus, 232039. 62–2101.

Vardanyan, Yurik Norainovich

POSITION: Weight Lifting Coach (in the United States)
BIRTHPLACE/DATE: Leninakan
NATIONALITY: Armenian
CAREER: 1980 Olympic Champion. World Champion six times, European Champion four times. Set thirty-seven World Records. Chairman of the Armenian Trade Union Council.
HONORS/AWARDS: USSR Honored Master of Sports.
FAMILY: Married with two children.
TELEPHONE: 201–0152 (Moscow).

Varennikov, Valentin Ivanovich

POSITION: Former Chief Commander of the Land Forces; former USSR Deputy Defense Minister
BIRTHPLACE/DATE: Krasnodar, December 15, 1923
NATIONALITY: Russian
CAREER: From 1941, served in the Armed Forces: Division Commander, Corps Commander, Army Commander, First Deputy Chief of the General Staff of the USSR Armed Forces. From 1989 to August 1991, Chief Commander of the Land Forces, Deputy Defense Minister; USSR Supreme Soviet Deputy; USSR People's Deputy. Member of the Communist Party to August 1991. In August 1991, arrested for participating in the attempted coup.
HONORS/AWARDS: Hero of the USSR; Order of Lenin; Order of the October Revolution; Order of the Red Banner; Order of the Patriotic War.
FAMILY: Married with two children.
TELEPHONE: 293–2869; 293–1413 (office).

Varov, Vladimir Konstantinovich

POSITION: Chairman of the Political Reforms Subcommittee of the Russian Federation Supreme Soviet Legislative Committee; Constitutional Commission Member
BIRTHPLACE/DATE: Perm, May 13, 1947
NATIONALITY: Russian
EDUCATION: Graduated from the Law Department at Perm University in 1974.
CAREER: From 1966 to 1968, served in the army. From 1974 to 1978, Investigator of the Procurator's Office in Pskov and Pskov region. From 1979 to 1982, Head of Legal Services at the Leningrad Lenelektronmash (Electronic Machinery Plant). From 1982 to 1989, Legal Inspector of the Le-

ningrad Regional Trade Union Committee. From 1990 to September 1990, Secretary-Chief Legal Inspector of the Yediniye (Independent Trade Unions) All-Russian Council of Trade Unions. From 1990, Chairman of the Political Reform Subcommittee of the Russian Federation Supreme Soviet Legislative Committee. Russian Federation People's Deputy. From 1970, participated in various non-government organizations; Coordinator of the Radical Democrats Faction; member of the Reform Coalition Committee.
MAJOR WORKS: Author of scientific and critical publications in the field of politics, philosophy, and law.
FAMILY: Married with two children.
TELEPHONE: 205–5962; 205–5936 (office).

Vasilyev, Dmitri Dmitryevich
POSITION: Chairman of the Pamyat (Memory) National Patriotic Front
BIRTHPLACE/DATE: Vyatka
NATIONALITY: Russian
CAREER: Worked as a Journalist, TV Producer, Scriptwriter, Photographer. Exhibited and published works. From 1983, Leader of the Pamyat National Patriotic Front. In 1985, stopped working as a Journalist following official persecution by authorities. Editor and Publisher of *Pamyat Almanac*. Chairman of an agricultural co-op.
MAJOR WORKS: Movie, *Where the Battlefield Is a Human Heart*, about talented Russians, never released. Collection of photos: *Field of Military Honor.*
FAMILY: Widower with a son, a daughter, and a grandson.
ADDRESS/TELEPHONE: 32 Volovaya Street, #4, Moscow, 113054. 237–3971 (office).

Vasilyev, Vladimir Victorovich
POSITION: Ballet Dancer
BIRTHPLACE/DATE: Moscow, 1940
CAREER: In 1959, debuted as Danila (*The Stone Flower*, Prokofev) at the Bolshoi Theater. From 1985, Head of the Choreography Department at the State Institute of Dramatic Art. Member of the Academy of Dramatic Art. Academician.
MAJOR WORKS: Performed in *Spartacus*; *Nutcracker*; *Macbeth*. Produced *Icarus*; *These Charming Sounds* (1978); *Macbeth*; *Don Quixote* (New York, 1980); *Anyuta* (1989).
HONORS/AWARDS: 1964 Nijinsky Prize (Paris Dance Academy); Grand Prize at the International Ballet Dancers Contest in Varna.
FAMILY: Married.
ADDRESS/TELEPHONE: 5/13 Smolenskaya Naberezhnaya, #62, Moscow, 121099. 244–0227.

Vasin, Vladimir Alekseyevich
POSITION: Vice President of the Russian Federation Olympics Committee
BIRTHPLACE/DATE: Moscow, 1947
NATIONALITY: Russian
EDUCATION: From 1973 to 1974, postgraduate student at Moscow State University.
CAREER: In 1972, Summer Olympic Diving Champion. From 1972 to 1973, Instructor of the Spartak Sports Club. From 1976 to 1986, Head of the Sports Department of the USSR Komsomol Central Committee. From 1986 to 1990, Propaganda Department Instructor of the Central Committee. From 1990 to 1991, Deputy Chairman of the USSR Sports Committee. From 1991 to March 1992, Chairman of the Russian Federation Olympics Committee.
HONORS/AWARDS: Honored Master of Sports; Order of the People's Friendship; two Orders of the Badge of Honor; Medal For Labor Valor.
FAMILY: Married with a son and a daughter.
ADDRESS/TELEPHONE: 26 Dimitrov Street, #37, Moscow. 267–7369 (office); 230–7717 (home).

Vasnetsov, Andrey Vladimirovich
POSITION: Artist (monumental art); Painter; Professor at the Moscow Institute of Printing; member of the Russian Academy of Arts
BIRTHPLACE/DATE: Moscow, February 24 (year unknown)
NATIONALITY: Russian
CAREER: During World War II, fought in combat. Painter for the Exhibition of Economic Achievements and for the Monumental Art and Decoration Works. From 1975, Lecturer at the Moscow Institute of Printing. From 1986, Professor, Department Head. From 1990, member of the Academy of Arts. From 1988 to 1989, Board Secretary of the Russian Federation Union of Artists. Member of the Council of Nationalities Commit-

tee for Preserving Languages, Culture, National and International Traditions, and Historical Heritage. From 1989 to 1992, USSR People's Deputy. Member of the Communist Party to August 1991.
MAJOR WORKS: Paintings: *Sergeants*; *Varshavyanka*; *Conversation*.
HONORS/AWARDS: Lenin Komsomol Prize; State Prize; USSR Council of Ministers Prize; USSR and Russian Federation People's Artist.
FAMILY: Married with a son.
ADDRESS/TELEPHONE: 2-A Pryashnikov Street, Moscow. 976–2475 (office); 290–3030 (home).

Vasyukov, Anatoli Ivanovich
POSITION: Board Chairman of the St. Petersburg Astrobank Commercial Bank
BIRTHPLACE/DATE: Leningrad, 1951
NATIONALITY: Russian
CAREER: From 1975 to 1982, Engineer at building industry enterprises in Leningrad region. From 1982 to 1985, Frunze Department Manager of the Leningrad Region USSR Building Bank; from 1985 to 1989, Dzerzhinsky Department Manager. From 1989, Board Chairman of the Leningrad Astrobank. From 1990, Vice President of the Soyuz Business Service Association. Member of the Stockholders Committee of the International Institute for Teaching and Developing Bank and Stock Business.
FAMILY: Married with two children.
ADDRESS/TELEPHONE: 5 Dostoevski Street, St. Petersburg. 311–3600 (office).

Vazgen I (Paldjan Vazgen Abramovich)
POSITION: Chief Catholic Patriarch of All-Armenias
BIRTHPLACE/DATE: Bucharest, September 20, 1908
NATIONALITY: Armenian
CAREER: From 1936 to 1943, Teacher at the Armenian School in Bucharest. From 1943 to 1955, Head of the Romanian Eparchy of the Armenian Church.
ADDRESS/TELEPHONE: Monastery, Echmiadzin, Armenia. 27–1240 (Yerevan).

Vedernikov, Aleksandr Fillippovich
POSITION: Opera Singer (bass) of the Bolshoi Theater
BIRTHPLACE/DATE: Mokino village, Kirov region, 1927
CAREER: From 1958, Soloist of the Bolshoi Theater. Gives concerts. Tours abroad.
MAJOR WORKS: Parts include: Susanin; Melnik; Boris Godunov; Kochak; Philipp II (*Don Carlos*); Don Basilio; "Petersburg Songs" by Sviridov.
HONORS/AWARDS: First Prize of the International Vocalists Contest (Berlin, 1956); USSR State Prize.
FAMILY: Married with three children.
ADDRESS/TELEPHONE: 8/10 Nezdanova Street, #21, Moscow. 229–7625 (home).

Vedernikov, Gennadi Georgyevich
POSITION: Former USSR Ambassador to Denmark; Ambassador Extraordinary and Plenipotentiary
BIRTHPLACE/DATE: Aldan, Yakutia, 1937
NATIONALITY: Russian
CAREER: From 1960 to 1970, Foreman, Shop Head of the Chelyabinsk Metallurgical Plant. From 1970 to 1973, Second Secretary of the Chelyabinsk District Communist Party. From 1973 to 1978, Deputy Chief Engineer, Chief Engineer of the Chelyabinsk Metallurgical Plant. From 1978 to 1983, Second Secretary, First Secretary of the Chelyabinsk Communist Party. From 1983 to 1984, Inspector of the Central Committee. From 1984 to 1986, First Secretary of the Chelyabinsk Region Communist Party. From 1986 to 1991, Deputy Chairman of the USSR Council of Ministers. From 1989 to 1991, USSR Ambassador to Denmark. From 1992, Russian Federation Ambassador to Denmark.
HONORS/AWARDS: Medal For Labor Valor; Order of the Badge of Honor; Order of Lenin.
FAMILY: Married

Vekilova, Irada Agadzavadovna
POSITION: Director of Assa-Irda Azerbaijan International Agency
BIRTHPLACE/DATE: Ashkhabad, August 20, 1935
NATIONALITY: Azerbaijanian
CAREER: From 1957 to 1963, Department Head, Deputy Editor in Chief, Editor in Chief of *Molodez Azerbaijana* (*Youth of Azerbaijan*) news-

paper. From 1963 to 1990, Department Head of *Vyshka* (*Tower*) newspaper.
FAMILY: Married with two children.
ADDRESS/TELEPHONE: 22 Mir-Dzalala Street, #9, Baku, 310258. 95–8537 (office).

Velichko, Victor Ivanovich
POSITION: Chairman of the Tekhnoexport (Export of Technology) Russian International Economic Association
BIRTHPLACE/DATE: Moscow, 1940
NATIONALITY: Russian
EDUCATION: Graduated from the Moscow Aviation Institute in 1963.
CAREER: From 1963 to 1967, Engineer of the Iskra Moscow Machine-Building Plant. From 1967 to 1974, Expert, Senior Expert, Chief Engineer. From 1974 to 1977, Engineer at the USSR Embassy in Syria. From 1977 to 1983, Senior Expert, Chief Engineer, Office Director of Tekhnoexport. From 1983 to 1986, Deputy Economic Counsellor at the USSR Embassy in Hanoi (Socialist Republic of Vietnam); from 1986 to 1988, Economic Counsellor. From 1988 to 1990, USSR Trade Representative to the Socialist Republic of Vietnam.
HONORS/AWARDS: Medal For Labor Valor; Order of the People's Friendship.
FAMILY: Married with two children.
ADDRESS/TELEPHONE: 18/1 Ovchinnikovsky Naberezhnaya, Moscow. 220–1782 (office).

Velichko, Vladimir Makarovich
POSITION: Former USSR First Deputy Prime Minister
BIRTHPLACE/DATE: 1937
CAREER: Worked from Assistant Foreman to Director of the Leningrad Mashinist (Engineer) Plant. From 1975, First Deputy Minister. From 1987, Minister of Heavy Energy and Transport Enginering. From 1989, Minister of Power Industry. From 1990, Minister of Heavy Industry. From 1991 to November 28, 1991, USSR First Deputy Prime Minister.
ADDRESS/TELEPHONE: 3 Rybny Pereulok, Moscow. 206–7929 (office).

Velikhov, Yevgeni Pavlovich
POSITION: Vice President of the Russian Academy of Sciences; President of the Kurchatov Institute
BIRTHPLACE/DATE: Moscow, February 2, 1935
NATIONALITY: Russian
EDUCATION: Doctor of Physics and Mathematics; Professor.
CAREER: From 1955, worked at the Institute of Nuclear Energy; from 1962, Department Head. From 1968, Professor at Moscow University. From 1974, Academician of the USSR Academy of Sciences. From 1977, Vice President of the USSR Academy of Sciences. From 1989 to 1990, member of the USSR Supreme Soviet.
MAJOR WORKS: In the field of plasma physics and magnetic hydrodynamics; co-author of the monograph, *Space Weapons: Security Dilemma.*
HONORS/AWARDS: Hero of Socialist Labor; Lenin and State Prizes; Order of Lenin; Order of the Red Banner of Labor.
FAMILY: Married with three children.
ADDRESS/TELEPHONE: 14 Leninsky Prospekt, Moscow, B–71, 117901. 237–4532 (office); 196–9241 (Institute).

Veprev, Arkady Filimonovich
POSITION: Former Head of the Krasnoyarsk Region Administration
BIRTHPLACE/DATE: Varenitsy village, Kirov region
NATIONALITY: Russian
CAREER: From 1957 to 1959, Chief Agronomist. From 1959 to 1991, Director of the Nazarovsky State Farm in Krasnoyarsk region. USSR People's Deputy. From May 1991, member of the USSR Supreme Soviet. Chairman of the Committee of Agricultural and Food Policy. Member of the Ecological Deputy Group. Member of the Siberia and Far East Deputy Group. From January 1992, Head of the Krasnoyarsk Region Administration. Member of the Communist Party to 1991.
HONORS/AWARDS: Hero of Socialist Labor; two Orders of Lenin.
FAMILY: Married with a son and a daughter.
ADDRESS/TELEPHONE: 110 Mir Prospekt, Krasnoyarsk, 660009. 22–4207 (office).

Vilchek, Mikhail Ivanovich

POSITION: Deputy Chairman of the Russian Federation Supreme Soviet Committee for Science and National Education

BIRTHPLACE/DATE: Kuibyshev (Samara), 1942

NATIONALITY: Russian

EDUCATION: Graduated from postgraduate studies at the Kuibyshev Aviation Institute. Doctor of Technical Science.

CAREER: From 1960 to 1961, Metalworker at the Kuibyshev Progress Plant. From 1961 to 1967, worked at the Kuibyshev Aviation Institute. From 1967 to 1990, Engineer, Researcher-Engineer, Junior Researcher, Assistant, Senior Researcher, Docent of the Kuibyshev Aviation Institute. Russian Republic People's Deputy. From 1990, member of the Supreme Soviet Committee for Science and National Education; in 1991, elected Vice Chairman. Member of the Svobodnaya Rossiya (Free Russia) and the Koalitsya Reform (Reform Coalition) Factions. Member of the Communist Party to August 1991.

FAMILY: Married with a son.

ADDRESS/TELEPHONE: 2 Krasnopresnenskaya Naberezhnaya, Moscow, 103224. 205–4314.

Vinogradov, Andrey Georgyevich

POSITION: Former President of the Commercial Information Company of the Russian Information Agency

BIRTHPLACE: Ashkhabad, 1955

NATIONALITY: Russian

CAREER: From 1979 to 1991, worked from Junior Editor to Editor in Chief of Novosti (News) Press Agency. From August 1991 to January 1992, Director-General of Novosti Information Agency.

FAMILY: Married with a son.

TELEPHONE: 245–1860.

Vinogradov, Vasily Valentinovich

POSITION: Head of the Russian Federation Foreign Ministry Consulate Service; Counsellor, First Grade

BIRTHPLACE/DATE: Port-Arthur, People's Republic of China

NATIONALITY: Russian

EDUCATION: Graduated from the Moscow State Institute of International Relations in 1971.

CAREER: From 1971 to 1974, Aide to the Consulate Department of the USSR Foreign Ministry; from 1974 to 1977, Attaché; from 1977 to 1978, Third Secretary. From 1978 to 1979, Assistant Department Head. In 1978 to 1980, Third Secretary at the USSR Consulate-General in New York. From 1980 to 1981, Third Secretary at the USSR Embassy in the United States; from 1981 to 1984, Second Secretary. From 1984 to 1986, First Secretary of the Consulate Department of the USSR Foreign Ministry. From 1986, Head of the USSR Temporary Consulate Office in Vancouver, Canada. From 1986 to 1987, First Secretary of the Consulate Department of the USSR Foreign Ministry. From 1987, Counsellor; from 1987 to 1990, Department Head; from 1990 to 1991, Deputy Head of the Consulate Department; from 1991 to 1992, Head of the Russian Federation Foreign Ministry Consulate Department.

FAMILY: Married with a son.

TELEPHONE: 200–3245 (office).

Vinogradov, Vladimir Victorovich

POSITION: Board Chairman of the Moscow Innovation Commercial Bank (Incombank); Board Member of the Russian Union of Industrialists and Entrepreneurs

BIRTHPLACE/DATE: Ufa (Bashkiria), 1955

NATIONALITY: Russian

EDUCATION: Graduated from the Moscow Aviation Institute, majoring in Mechanical Engineering. Took the postgraduate course of the Moscow Production Association at the Research Institute for Mechanical Engineering Technology.

CAREER: From 1983 to 1985, Secretary of the Komsomol Committee at the Special Designers Office of the USSR Ministry of Power Industry. From 1988, Senior Economist of Promstroibank (Industrial Construction Bank). From October 1988, Board Chairman of the Moscow Innovation Commercial Bank. From 1990 to 1992, member of the USSR President's Entrepreneurship Council.

FAMILY: Married with two children.

ADDRESS/TELEPHONE: 14 Nametkin Street, Building 1, Moscow, 117420. 332–0678 (office).

Vinogradova, Irina Victorovna

POSITION: Secretary of the Russian Federation Supreme Soviet Committee for Science and Na-

tional Education; member of the Council of the Republic
BIRTHPLACE/DATE: Krasnoyarsky region, 1941
NATIONALITY: Russian
CAREER: Worked as a Komsomol Leader, Schoolteacher, Head of Extracurricular Programs, School Principal. From 1990, People's Deputy. Coordinator of the Svobodnaya Rossiya (Free Russia) Faction. Member of the Svobodnaya Rossiya Party.
FAMILY: Single.
ADDRESS/TELEPHONE: 2 Krasnopresnenskaya Naberezhnaya, 5–63, Moscow, 103274. 205–4358 (office).

Vishnevsky, Yuri Aleksandrovich
POSITION: Director-General of the Kognito Firm
BIRTHPLACE/DATE: Tashkent, 1958
EDUCATION: From 1986 to 1987, postgraduate student at Moscow State University.
CAREER: From 1986 to 1988, Junior, then Senior Researcher of the Economics Department at Moscow State University. From 1989 to 1990, Cooperative Chairman. From 1990 to 1991, Director of the Moscow branch of the X Company.
FAMILY: Married with two children.
ADDRESS/TELEPHONE: 11 Panferov Street, Moscow, 117261. 134–6548 (office).

Vitebsky, Vitaly Yakovlevich
POSITION: Deputy Chairman of the Russian Federation Supreme Soviet Committee for Industry and Energy; member of the Constitutional Commission
BIRTHPLACE: Kurgan, 1941
CAREER: From 1963 to 1965, Assistant; to 1970, Researcher at the Mountain Industry Institute. From 1970 to 1990, Metalworker, Engineer, Laboratory Head of the Kurganpribor (Kurgan Instrument) Industrial Complex. From 1972, Chief Designer; from 1974 to 1975, Deputy Chief Engineer. Member of the Svobodnaya Rossiya (Free Russia) Faction. Russian Federation People's Deputy. Member of the Communist Party to August 1991.
FAMILY: Married with a son and a daughter.
ADDRESS/TELEPHONE: 8 Academician Korolev Street, #477, Moscow, 129515. 205–5620 (office); 216–4155 (home).

Vladimir (Sabodan, Victor Markianovich)
POSITION: Metropolitan of Kiev and All Ukraine; Permanent Member of the Holy Synod of the Russian Orthodox Church; Administrator of the Moscow Patriarchy
BIRTHPLACE/DATE: Markovtsy village, Khmelnitsk region, November 23, 1935
NATIONALITY: Ukrainian
EDUCATION: Doctor of Theology.
CAREER: From 1962 to 1966, Lecturer, Rector of the Odessa Ecclesiastical Seminary. From 1966 to 1968, Representative of the Russian Orthodox Church to the International Council of Churches in Geneva. From 1969 to 1973, Bishop of Chernigov and Nezinsky. From 1973 to 1982, Rector of the Moscow Ecclesiastical Academy, Archbishop. From 1986, Administrator of the Moscow Patriarchy.
HONORS/AWARDS: Order of the People's Friendship.
ADDRESS/TELEPHONE: 55 Mendeleev Street, Kiev. 235–0454; 230–2118; 230–2431.

Vladimirov, Boris Grigoryevich
POSITION: Former Editor in Chief of *Ekonomika i Zhizn* (*Economics and Life)* newspaper; Advisor to the President of the Russian Industrialists and Entrepreneurs Union
BIRTHPLACE/DATE: Moscow, 1934
NATIONALITY: Russian
EDUCATION: Degree in Technical Science.
CAREER: Worked for an industrial enterprise and the Central Committee. Former Journalist. From 1982 to 1984, Aide and Consultant to the Secretary-General of the Communist Party. Member of the Central Auditing Commission. From 1988, member of the Central Committee's Commission for Socio-Economic Policy. To August 1991, member of the Communist Party. In August 1991, dismissed from position.
FAMILY: Married with two children.
ADDRESS/TELEPHONE: 10/4 Staraya Square, Moscow.

Vladimirov, Vasily Sergeyevich
POSITION: Director of the Steklov Mathematics Institute of the Russian Academy of Sciences
BIRTHPLACE/DATE: Leningrad region, January 9, 1923

NATIONALITY: Russian
CAREER: From 1948, worked at the Steklov Mathematics Institute; from 1989, Director. In 1991, Academician of the Russian Academy of Sciences.
MAJOR WORKS: In the field of calculative mathematics, physics, and quantum theory.
HONORS/AWARDS: USSR State Prize (1953, 1987); Hero of Socialist Labor; Order of the Red Banner of Labor.
FAMILY: Married with two children.
ADDRESS/TELEPHONE: 42 Vavilov Street, B–333, Moscow, 117966. 135–2291 (office); 124–7864 (home).

Vladislayev, Aleksandr Pavlovich
POSITION: First Vice President of the Russian Union of Industrialists and Entrepreneurs; Co-Chairman of the Democratic Reforms Movement; member of the Grazhdansky Soyuz (Civic Accord) Political Consultative Council
BIRTHPLACE/DATE: Moscow, May 21, 1936
NATIONALITY: Russian
EDUCATION: Lecturer and Administrator at the Gubkin Oil and Gas Institute in Moscow. Department Head, Vice Rector. Komsomol Functionary for three years: First Secretary of the Oktyabrsky District Komsomol Committee, Department Head of the USSR Youth Organizations Committee. From 1974 to 1986, Deputy Chairman of the Znaniye (Knowlege) All-Union Society. From 1986, First Board Secretary of the USSR Association of Researchers and Engineers. From 1980 to 1988, Vice President of the International Council for Adult Education. From 1985, member of the UNESCO Board of Directors. From 1988, member of the UN Consultative Committee for Science and Technology. Former USSR People's Deputy. Member of the USSR Supreme Soviet for Science, National Education and Culture. Member of the USSR Supreme Soviet Commission for Foreign Affairs. Political Council Member of the Democratic Reforms Movement. In 1991, Vice President of the USSR Scientific-Industrial Union. From November 1991 to December 1991, USSR First Deputy Foreign Minister. From 1992, member of the Russian President's Entrepreneurship Council. From 1961 to 1991, member of the Communist Party.
HONORS/AWARDS: Order of the Red Banner of Labor; Order of the Badge of Honor.
FAMILY: Married with a son.
ADDRESS/TELEPHONE: 10/4 Staraya Square, Moscow, 103007. 206–7017 (office).

Vlasov, Albert Ivanovich
POSITION: Former Chairman of Novosti Information Agency
BIRTHPLACE/DATE: Myatlevo village, Kaluga region, 1930
NATIONALITY: Russian
EDUCATION: Doctor of History; Professor.
CAREER: Former TASS (Telegraph Agency of the Soviet Union) Correspondent in China and Burma; First Deputy Chairman of Novosti Press Agency. From 1976, held diplomatic positions, worked as a Party Functionary. From 1988, Chairman of Novosti Press Agency. From July 1990 to August 1991, Chairman of Novosti Information Agency.
FAMILY: Married with a daughter.

Vlasov, Aleksey Feliksovich
POSITION: Executive Manager of the Rossiyskaya Tovarno-Syryevaya Birzha (Russian Mercantile Exchange) Joint-Stock Company
BIRTHPLACE/DATE: Tver, October 20,1954
NATIONALITY: Russian
CAREER: From 1977 to 1980, Electrician, Programmer for the Serp i Molot (Sickle and Hammer) Plant. From 1981 to 1990, Junior Researcher, Researcher, Senior Researcher in different research institutes. From 1990 to 1992, Co-Chairman of the Russian Mercantile Exchange. Member of the Economic Freedom Party.
MAJOR WORKS: More than fifteen publications.
FAMILY: Married with two children.
ADDRESS/TELEPHONE: 30 Frunzenskaya Naberezhnaya, Moscow; 26 Maysnitskaya Street, Moscow, 119146. 201–0490 (office).

Vokov, Yuri Vasilyevich
POSITION: President of the Russian Business Agency
BIRTHPLACE/DATE: Moscow, 1948
NATIONALITY: Russian
EDUCATION: Doctor of Technical Sciences.
CAREER: From 1964 to 1967, Metalworker, Assembler, Quality Department Controller of the

Moscow Mechanical Plant. From 1967 to 1975, Designer, Senior Engineer of the Rosproyect (Russian Project) Institute. From 1979 to 1980, worked at the Moscow Institute of Railway Engineers. From 1980 to 1984, Deputy Department Head of the USSR Ministry of Higher and Special Secondary Education. From 1984 to 1988, First Deputy Personnel Head of the USSR Ministry of Public Utilities. From 1988 to 1990, Vice Rector of the Moscow Technological Institute.
FAMILY: Married with two children.
ADDRESS/TELEPHONE: 8 Yaroslavskaya Street, Moscow, 129243. 217–6049; 217–6044 (office).

Volchek, Galina Borisovna
POSITION: Art Director of the Sovremennik Theater
BIRTHPLACE/DATE: Moscow, 1933
CAREER: From 1956, worked at the Sovremennik Theater: Co-Founder; from 1961, Producer; from 1972, Chief Producer.
MAJOR WORKS: Productions: *Three Sisters*, by A. Chekhov; *Sharp Route*, by Y. Ginzburg; *Two on the Swing*, by W. Gibson; *Common Story* by Goncharov. Roles include: Miss Amelia (1967); Martha (*Who's Afraid of Virginia Woolf?*, 1985). In 1988, staged *Echelon*, by M. Roshchin in the United States.
HONORS/AWARDS: USSR People's Artist.
FAMILY: Divorced with a son.
ADDRESS/TELEPHONE: 19-A Chistoprudny Boulevard, Moscow, 101000. 921–06053 (office); 328–8708.

Volin, Vladimir Pavlovich
POSITION: Editor in Chief of *Megapolis-Express* newspaper
BIRTHPLACE/DATE: Neya, Kostroma region
NATIONALITY: Russian
CAREER: Correspondent in Kirov. Agriculture Department Head of a local district newspaper. Department Head of a district newspaper in Lubertsy, Moscow region. Chief Editor of a city broadcasting unit in Lubertsy. Deputy Department Editor of *Trud* (*Labor*) daily. Department Head, Deputy Editor in Chief of the USSR State Television and Radio Broadcasting Committee in Moscow. Editor of *Moscow News* weekly.
FAMILY: Married with a son.
ADDRESS/TELEPHONE: 16 Maly Lubyanka Street, Moscow, 101000. 925–1473.

Volkogonov, Dmitri Antonovich
POSITION: Defense Advisor to the Russian Federation President; Russian Federation People's Deputy; member of the Presidential Consultative Council; Colonel-General
BIRTHPLACE/DATE: Chita region, 1928
NATIONALITY: Russian
EDUCATION: Graduated from the Orel Tank School and from the Lenin Military-Political Academy. Doctor of Philosophy; Professor.
CAREER: From 1964 to 1970, Lecturer at the Lenin Military-Political Academy. From 1970, Deputy Head of the Chief Political Administration of the USSR Army and Navy. Former Director of the Military History Institute of the USSR Defense Ministry. From 1990, Russian Federation People's Deputy, Russian Federation Supreme Soviet Member. From July 1990 to August 1990, Vice Chairman of the Russian Federation Supreme Soviet Council of Nationalities; relieved of duties at own request. From February 1991, Security and Defense Advisor to the Russian Federation Supreme Soviet Chairman; from July 1991, Russian Federation State Counsellor for Defense. Former member of the Supreme Consultative Council of the Russian Federation Supreme Soviet Chairman. Coordinator of the Left-Center Parliamentary Faction. Council Member of the Socio-Political Studies Foundation.
MAJOR WORKS: Author of numerous books published in the USSR and in fifteen countries. Best known for *Triumph and Tragedy*, about Stalin.
FAMILY: Married with two daughters.
ADDRESS/TELEPHONE: 2 Krasnopresnenskaya Naberezhnaya, Moscow, 103274. 205–5252 (office); 290–2564 (home).

Volmer, Yuri Mikhailovich
POSITION: Former USSR Fleet Minister
BIRTHPLACE/DATE: Krasitskoye village, Khabarovsky region, 1933
NATIONALITY: Russian
EDUCATION: From 1978 to 1980, postgraduate student at the Academy of National Economy of the USSR Council of Ministers.

CAREER: Captain's Assistant, Tanker Captain, Personnel Official. From 1975 to 1978, Head of the Primorsk Ship Company. From 1980, Head of the Far East Ship Company. From 1986 to November 1991, USSR Fleet Minister.
FAMILY: Married with a son and a granddaughter.
ADDRESS: 1/4 Rozdestvenka Street, Moscow, 103759.

Volobuyev, Pavel Vasilyevich
POSITION: Chief Researcher at the Russian History Institute of the Russian Academy of Sciences; Chairman of the Scientific Council on Historical Issues of the Russian Revolution
BIRTHPLACE/DATE: Yevgenovka village, Kustanay region, 1923
NATIONALITY: Russian
EDUCATION: Doctor of History; Professor.
CAREER: From 1953 to 1955, Lecturer of the History Department at Moscow State University, Instructor of the Central Committee's Science and Culture Department. From 1974 to 1990, Senior Researcher at the Institute of History, Natural Science and Technology of the USSR Academy of Sciences. Editorial Board Member of *Voprosy Istorii* (*Questions of History*), *Rodina* (*Motherland*), and *Svobodnaya Mysl* (*Free Thought*) magazines. Academician.
MAJOR WORKS: More than 150 publications; three monographs, including: *Economic Policy of Provisional Government*; *Proletariat of Bourgeois Russia.*
FAMILY: Married with two children.
ADDRESS/TELEPHONE: 19 D. Ulyanov Street, Moscow; 109/1 Leninsky Prospekt, #116, Moscow, 117221. 126–9480; 126–9449 (Secretariat).

Volodchenko, Gannadi Anatolyevich
POSITION: Employee of the Moscow Business Cooperation Center
BIRTHPLACE/DATE: Leningrad, 1950
NATIONALITY: Russian
CAREER: From 1976 to 1979, worked in trade organizations. From 1979 to 1990, Party Functionary for the development of international economic relations. Consultant to the Russian Federation Supreme Soviet Committee of Anti-Monopoly Policy and Support of New Economic Structures (provides consulting support for joint ventures, assistance to foreign companies in search of potential partners, and advice on tax and bookkeeping).
FAMILY: Married with two children.
TELEPHONE: 271–5151 (office).

Vologzhin, Valentin Mikhailovich
POSITION: Former Presidium Member of the USSR Supreme Soviet; former Chairman of the USSR Supreme Soviet Committee for Economic Reforms
BIRTHPLACE/DATE: Kezma, Krasnoyarsk region, 1937
NATIONALITY: Russian
CAREER: From 1959 to 1973, Designer, Technologist, Foreman, Deputy Head, Chief Engineer, Head of the Planning and Economic Department at the Krasnoyarsk Machine-Building Plant. From 1973 to 1980, Deputy Chief Technologist of the Lvov Bus Plant. From 1980 to 1989, Chief Engineer, Director-General of the Konveyer (Assembly Line) Industrial Complex. From May 1989, USSR People's Deputy; Presidium Member of the USSR Supreme Soviet; Chairman of the USSR Supreme Soviet Committee for Economic Reforms. Former member of Soyuz (Union) and Communist Deputy Groups. President of the Small Enterprise Development and Support Faction. Academician of the Engineering Academy.
FAMILY: Married with a child.
ADDRESS/TELEPHONE: 27 Kalinin Prospekt, Moscow. 203–6456 (office).

Volovets, Sergey Aleksandrovich
POSITION: Deputy Editor in Chief of *Rodina* (*Motherland*) magazine
BIRTHPLACE/DATE: Moscow, 1938
CAREER: From 1961 to 1986, Correspondent, Chief Editor, Deputy Editor in Chief of APN (Novosti Press and News Agency). From 1986 to 1987, International Department Head of *Sovietskaya Rossiya* (*Soviet Russia*) newspaper. From 1987 to 1988, International Department Head of *Rodina* (*Motherland*). From 1988 to 1991, International Department Head, Deputy Editor in Chief of *Moscow News*. From 1991, Editor in Chief of *TV Review.*
MAJOR WORKS: Articles.

Honors/Awards: Order of the Badge of Honor.
Family: Married with three children.
Address/Telephone: 19 Novy Arbat, Moscow. 202–5663 (office).

Volsky, Arkady Ivanovich
Position: President of the Russian Union of Industrialists and Entrepreneurs; Chairman of the International Congress of Industrialists and Entrepreneurs
Birthplace/Date: Dobrushe, Gomel region, 1932
Nationality: Russian
Education: Graduated from the Moscow Institute of Steel and Alloys.
Career: For 15 years, Engineer at the Likhachev Motor Plant in Moscow. From 1969 and 1989, Staff Member of the Central Committee; First Deputy Head of the Central Committee's Mechanical Engineering Department. From July 1988, Central Committee Representative in the Nagorno-Karabakh Autonomous Region in the Caucasus. From January 1989 to November 1989, Chairman of the Committee for Special Control of the Nagorno-Karabakh Region. From 1984 to 1992, USSR People's Deputy. From 1989 to 1992, member of the USSR Supreme Soviet Defense and State Security Committee. From 1986 to 1990, member of the Central Committee. From 1990, President of the USSR Scientific-Industrial Union. From August 1991, Deputy Head of the Committee for Rapid Control of the National Economy. From September 1991 to December 1991, member of the USSR President's Political Consultative Council. From December 1991, Board Co-Chairman of the Democratic Reforms Movement.
Honors/Awards: USSR State Prize.
Family: Married with a son and a daughter.
Address/Telephone: 10/4 Staraya Ploshchad, Moscow, 103007. 206–7016 (office).

Volsky, Victor Vatslavovich
Position: Director of the Latin America Institute of the Russian Academy of Sciences; member of the Russian Academy of Sciences
Birthplace/Date: Zlynka village, Bryansk region, August 10, 1921
Education: From 1945, student, then postgraduate student at the Moscow Institute of Intentional Relations.
Career: From 1941 to 1945, fought in combat. To 1952, Docent of the Moscow Institute of Intentional Relations. From 1958 to 1959, Senior Researcher at the Institute of the World Economy and International Relations of the USSR Academy of Sciences. From 1959 to 1966, Department Head of Moscow State University. Member of the USSR (now Russian) Academy of Sciences.
Major Works: Publications in the field of international and Latin American economies.
Honors/Awards: Hero of the USSR; Order of the Red Star; Order of the Red Banner; Order of Lenin; USSR State Prize.
Family: Widower with a daughter.
Address/Telephone: 21 Bolshaya Ordynka, Moscow, 113035. 231–5323 (office).

Vorobyev, Andrey Ivanovich
Position: Director of the Hematology Scientific Center of the Russian Federation Health Ministry
Birthplace/Date: Moscow, 1928
Nationality: Russian
Education: Doctor of Medicine; Professor.
Career: From 1953 to 1956, Doctor at a district hospital in Volokolamsk. From 1956 to 1966, Intern, Assistant, Docent of the Therapy Department. From 1966 to 1971, Department Head of the Institute of Geophysics. From 1971 to 1974, Therapy Department Head. From 1974 to 1987, Hematology Department Head. From 1987 to 1988, Director of the Hematology and Blood Transfusion Central Research Institute. From 1988 to 1991, Director of the Hematology Scientific Center of the Russian Federation Health Ministry. USSR People's Deputy. Member of the Deputy Group for Protecting National Health. From November 1991 to October 1992, Russian Federation Health Minister. Academician of the Russian Academy of Sciences.
Honors/Awards: USSR State Prize.
Family: Married with two children.
Address/Telephone: 14-A Novozyukinsky Prospekt, Moscow, 125167. 212–2123.

Voronin, Vladimir Vasilyevich
Position: Chairman of the Central Block of Political Parties and Movements; Executive

Committee Chairman of the Sakharov Democratic Union
BIRTHPLACE/DATE: Valilyeva Gora village, Tver region, 1937
NATIONALITY: Russian
CAREER: From 1965 to 1967, Engineer of the Novosibirsk Aviation Plant. From 1967 to 1968, Technological Department Head of the Inter-Regional Design Bureau; Schoolteacher. From 1971 to 1976, Lecturer, Coach of the Mining Industry Institute. In 1976, arrested; on May 26, 1977, sentenced to five years in prison; in 1979, released on parole. From 1980 to 1983, Chairman of the Municipal Sports Committee in Skhodniay. In 1983, resigned due to health. From 1989, member of the Kirov Region Veteran Council in Moscow. Elected Acting Moscow Chairman of the Bibirev Regional Council for Issues of the Development of Self-Government. From 1990, Leader of the Central Block of Political Parties and Movements. In 1990, Initiator and Organizer of the Sakharov Democratic Union; from April 1990, Chairman of the Executive Committee. Founder and Editor in Chief of *Tsentr* (*Center*) newspaper and *Country's Open World* magazine. From 1991, President of the Parliamentary and People's Initiatives International Fund; Chairman of the International Congress of Centrists.
MAJOR WORKS: *To Shoot Twice*.
FAMILY: Married with a son.
ADDRESS/TELEPHONE: 26 Petrovka, Suite 317, Moscow, 101409. 407–0587 (home); 932–0265; 932–6843 (office).

Voronov, Yuri Aleksandrovich
POSITION: Vice Rector of Peasant Academic University in Luga; Vice President of the Petrovsky Academy; Professor at Havana University
BIRTHPLACE/DATE: Leningrad, 1927
EDUCATION: From 1954 to 1957, postgraduate student at Leningrad State University. Doctor of Biology.
CAREER: From 1958 to 1961, Physics and Biophysics Department Assistant; Head of the Leningrad Veterinary Institute. From 1961 to 1982, Researcher at the Ukhtomsky Institute of Leningrad State University. From 1982 to 1991, Chief Researcher at the Mathematics Calculation Institute of Leningrad State University. Academician of the Russian National Academy.
MAJOR WORKS: Author of more than sixty-two publications.
FAMILY: Married with three children.
ADDRESS/TELEPHONE: 2 Fontanka Street, #340, St. Petersburg. 315–4448.

Vorontsov, Nikolay Nikolayevich
POSITION: Chief Researcher at the Koltsov Biology Development Institute; Vice President of the Russian Academy of Natural Sciences; member of the Russian Federation Supreme Soviet Committee for Ecology and the Rational Use of Natural Resources
BIRTHPLACE/DATE: Moscow, 1934
NATIONALITY: Russian
EDUCATION: Doctor of Biology; Professor.
CAREER: Worked at the Zoology Institute in Leningrad. Taught at the Moscow State Pirogov Second Medical Institute. From 1964, Scientific Secretary of the Presidium of the Siberian branch of the USSR Academy of Sciences and Lecturer at Novosibirsk State University. From 1971 to 1977, worked at the Biology and Soil Institute of the Far East Scientific Center of the USSR Academy of Sciences; Presidium Member. Lectured at Far East State University. From 1977 to 1989, worked at the Kolpov Biology Development Institute; taught at the Moscow Region Teachers' Training Institute. From 1989 to 1991, Chairman of the USSR State Committee for Nature Protection. From 1991, USSR Minister of Environment Protection and the Rational Use of Natural Resources. From 1992, Vice President of the Russian Federation Academy of Natural Sciences; Chief Researcher at the Biology Development Institute of the Russian Academy of Natural Sciences; Russian Federation People's Deputy. In May 1992, elected member of the Swedish Royal Academy of Sciences. Member of the Demokraticheskaya Rossiya (Democratic Russia) and Koalitsiya (Reform Coalition) Factions.
MAJOR WORKS: More than 400 scientific works. Head of forty-one scientific expeditions.
HONORS/AWARDS: USSR State Prize.
FAMILY: Married with two daughters.
ADDRESS/TELEPHONE: 26 Vavilov Street, Moscow, 117334. 135–7583 (office).

Vorontsov, Valery Aleksandrovich

POSITION: Deputy Chairman of the Coordinating Committee for the Affairs of Invalids of the Russian Federation President; member of the Supreme Soviet Committee for Health Protection, Social Services, Sports, and Ecology
BIRTHPLACE/DATE: Perm, 1938
NATIONALITY: Russian
CAREER: From 1965 to 1970, Senior Researcher. From 1971 to 1990, Department Head. From 1990 to 1991, Advisor to the Russian Republic Prime Minister. Member of the Left-Center and Grazhdanskoye Obshchestvo (Civic Society) Factions; Russian Federation People's Deputy.
FAMILY: Married with two children.
ADDRESS/TELEPHONE: 4 Sokolnicheskaya Square, #164, Moscow, 107113. 268–2625 (home); 206–4153 (office); 298–7440 (office).

Vorontsov, Yuli Mikhailovich

POSITION: State Counsellor to the Russian President for Foreign Policy Issues; Russian Federation Permanent Representative to the UN
BIRTHPLACE/DATE: Leningrad, October 7, 1929
NATIONALITY: Russian
EDUCATION: Graduated in 1952 from the Moscow State Institute of International Relations.
CAREER: From 1952 to 1954, Aide, Senior Aide, Attaché of the Second European Department (Australia, Canada, Ireland, Malta, New Zealand, United Kingdom) of the USSR Foreign Ministry. From 1954 to 1955, Attaché; from 1955 to 1958, Third Secretary at the USSR Permanent Mission to the UN. From 1958 to 1963, Second Secretary, First Secretary, Counsellor of the Department for International Organizations of the USSR Foreign Ministry. From 1963 to 1965, Counsellor at the USSR Permanent Mission to the UN. From 1965 to 1966, Deputy Head of the International Organizations Department of the USSR Foreign Ministry. From 1966 to 1977, Counsellor, Minister-Counsellor and Chargé d'Affaires Ad Interim at the USSR Embassy in the United States. In 1977, Deputy Head of the Directorate for Foreign Policy Planning of the USSR Foreign Ministry. From 1977 to 1983, USSR Ambassador to India. From 1983 to 1986, USSR Ambassador to France. From 1986 to 1988, USSR First Deputy Foreign Minister. From 1988 to 1989, USSR First Deputy Foreign Minister, USSR Ambassador to Afghanistan. From 1989 to 1990, USSR First Deputy Foreign Minister. From 1990, USSR Permanent Representative to the UN.
HONORS/AWARDS: Order of Lenin; Order of the Red Banner of Labor; Order of the Badge of Honor.
FAMILY: Married with a daughter.
ADDRESS/TELEPHONE: The Permanent Mission of the Russian Federation to the UN, 136 East 67th Street, New York, NY 10021. 861–4900.

Vyalyas, Vaino Iosipovich

POSITION: Former Chairman of the Estonian Communist Party
BIRTHPLACE/DATE: Khiyiumaa Island
NATIONALITY: Estonian
CAREER: Worked as a Komsomol Activist. From 1952, Secretary of the Tartu Region Komsomol Committee. From 1953, First Secretary of the Tartu City Komsomol Committee. From 1955 to 1961, Head of the Estonian Komsomol. In 1961, First Secretary of the Tallin City Communist Party. From 1971, Secretary of the Estonian Central Committee. From 1980, USSR Ambassador to Venezuela, then Nicaragua. In 1988, elected member of the Estonian Delegation to the Nineteenth All-Union Party Conference. Elected First Secretary of the Estonian Central Committee. In 1990, Chairman of the Estonian Communist Party. Former USSR and Estonian People's Deputy.
FAMILY: Married with two children.
ADDRESS/TELEPHONE: 9 Estonia Boulevard, Tallin, 200001. 44–5258.

Vyzutovich, Valery Victorovich

POSITION: Correspondent for *Izvestia* daily; Host of the "Political Kitchen" TV program
BIRTHPLACE/DATE: Pavlodar, 1951
CAREER: From 1974 to 1980, Correspondent for *Komsomolskaya Pravda* (*Komsomol Truth*) daily. From 1980 to 1988, Correspondent for *Literaturnaya Gazeta* (*Literary Newspaper*). From 1988 to 1989, Editor of *Ogonyek* (*Beacon*) weekly.
MAJOR WORKS: "Reserve Player"; "Making a Decision."
FAMILY: Married with a son.
ADDRESS/TELEPHONE: 5 Pushkinskaya Square, Moscow, 129075. 209–5181 (office).

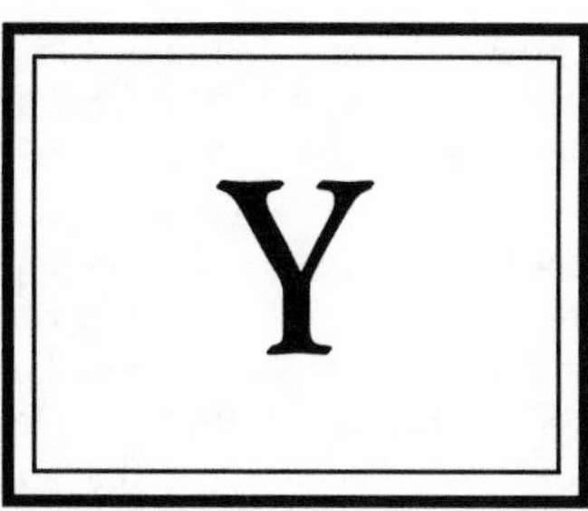

Yadov, Vladimir Aleksandrovich

POSITION: Director of the Institute of Sociology of the Russian Academy of Sciences; Professor

BIRTHPLACE/DATE: Leningrad, 1929

NATIONALITY: Russian

EDUCATION: From 1954 to 1956, postgraduate student at Leningrad State University (LGU). Defended dissertations in 1959 and 1968.

CAREER: From 1952 to 1954, Secondary School Teacher. From 1956 to 1959, Secretary of the District Komsomol Committee. From 1959 to 1968, Professor and Head of the Sociological Laboratory of the Philosophy Department at LGU. From 1968 to 1975, Leningrad Department Head of the Institute of Sociological Research of the USSR Academy of Sciences. From 1975 to 1983, Department Head of the Institute of Social and Economic Problems of the USSR Academy of Sciences. From 1984 to 1987, Senior Researcher at the Institute of the History of Natural Sciences and Technology. From 1971, Professor at LGU. From 1987, Director of the Institute of Sociology of the Russian Academy of Sciences. From 1988, Professor at Moscow State University. Member of the International Sociological Association. Member of the European Association of Experimental Social Psychology. Co-President of the Russian Society of Sociology. Editor of *Sociology: Methodology, Methods, Mathematical Models* magazine.

MAJOR WORKS: *A Person and His Work* (co-author, 1971); *Self-regulation and Prognosis of Social Behavior* (co-author, 1979); *Sociological Research: Methodology, Program, Methods*; *The Sociology of Perestroika* (1990).

FAMILY: Married with a child.

ADDRESS/TELEPHONE: 24/35 Krzhizhanovskogo Street, Building 5, Moscow, 112259. 128–9109 (office).

Yakimov, Boris Alekseevich.

POSITION: Chairman of Sudimport (Ship Import) Foreign Trade Association

BIRTHPLACE/DATE: Moscow, 1936

CAREER: From 1962 to 1967, Senior Engineer of the Aviaexport Trade Association of the USSR Ministry of Foreign Trade. From 1967 to 1970, Representative of Aviaexport in Indonesia. From 1970 to 1974, Deputy Director, then Director of Aviaexport. From 1974 to 1979, USSR Trade Representative in Bulgaria. From 1979 to 1982, Deputy Chairman of the Sudimport All-Union Trade Association. From 1982 to 1988, USSR Trade Representative in Cuba.

HONORS/AWARDS: Medal For Heroic Labor on the One Hundredth Anniversary of Lenin's Birthday.

FAMILY: Married with a daughter.

ADDRESS/TELEPHONE: 10 Uspenski Pereulok, Moscow, 103006. 299–6849 (office).

Yakovlev, Aleksandr Maximovich

POSITION: Department Head of the Institute of State and Law of the Russian Academy of Sciences

BIRTHPLACE/DATE: Leningrad, 1927

NATIONALITY: Russian

EDUCATION: Doctor of Law.

CAREER: From 1952 to 1957, Editor of the Gosyurizdat State Legal Publishing House. From 1957 to 1960, Researcher at the Main Department of the USSR Ministry of Foreign Affairs. From

1960 to 1968, Senior Researcher at the All-Union Research Institute of Law. From 1968 to 1975, Deputy Director of the Institute of Soviet Law of the USSR Ministry of Justice. From 1975, Head of the Criminal Law, Justice and Criminology Division of the Institute of State and Law of the USSR (now Russian) Academy of Sciences. Member of the Legislative Committee of the USSR Supreme Soviet. From 1991, Honored Doctor of Law of the University of Alberta (Canada). USSR People's Deputy.
MAJOR WORKS: *To Live as A Criminal* (1967); *Struggle with Dangerous Criminals* (1964).
HONORS/AWARDS: USSR State Prize (1984).
FAMILY: Married.
ADDRESS/TELEPHONE: The Institute of State and Law, 10 Znamenka Street, Moscow. 291–3476 (office).

Yakovlev, Aleksandr Nikolayevich
POSITION: Vice President of the International Foundation for Socio-Economic and Political Studies (Gorbachev Foundation); Chairman of the Moscow General Assembly
BIRTHPLACE/DATE: Korolyovo village, Yaroslavl region, December 2, 1923
NATIONALITY: Russian
EDUCATION: Graduated in 1946 from the Ushinsky State Teachers' Training Institute in Yaroslavl; in 1960, from the Central Committee's Academy of Social Sciences. From 1957 to 1958, studied at Columbia University (United States). Doctor of History (1967); Professor (1969). Corresponding Member of the Russian Academy of Sciences.
CAREER: From 1941 to 1943, served in the army. Joined the Communist Party in 1944. Took part in World War II: Platoon Commander of the Sixth Detached Marine Brigade at the Volkhov front; gravely wounded, transferred to the reserve. From 1946, held Communist Party posts: Instructor, Deputy Head, Department Head of the Yaroslavl Region Communist Party. From 1953, worked at the Central Committee: Instructor, Section Head, First Deputy to the Propaganda Department Head. From 1973 to 1983, USSR Ambassador Extraordinary and Plenipotentiary to Canada. From 1983, Director of the World Economy and International Relations Institute of the USSR Academy of Sciences. From July 1985, Head of the Central Committee's Propaganda Department and from March 1986, Secretary of the Central Committee. At the September 1988 Central Committee Plenum, appointed Chairman of the Central Committee Foreign Policy Commission. From 1971 to 1976, member of the Central Committee Auditing Commission. From 1986, member of the Central Committee. Delegate to the Twenty-third, Twenty-fourth, and Twenty-seventh Communist Party Congresses and the Nineteenth All-Union Communist Party Conference. In January 1987, elected Alternate, and in June 1987, Full Member of the Politburo. From March 1990 to January 1991, member of the USSR Presidential Council. Academician of the USSR Academy of Sciences. USSR People's Deputy. In July 1991, resigned as Senior Advisor to the USSR President to become Chairman of the Moscow General Assembly. From September to December 1991, Presidential Advisor and member of the Political Presidential Council of the USSR President. From December 1991, Board Co-Chairman of the CIS International Democratic Reforms Movement.
MAJOR WORKS: In the field of history, theory of international relations, and U.S. foreign policy.
HONORS/AWARDS: Order of the October Revolution; Order of the Patriotic War, First Class; three Orders of the Red Banner of Labor; Orders of the People's Friendship; Order of the Red Star; medals.
FAMILY: Married with two children.
ADDRESS/TELEPHONE: 49 Leningradsky Prospekt, Moscow, 125468. 943–9436 (office).

Yakunin, Gleb Pavlovich
POSITION: Co-Chairman of the Council of Representatives of the Democratic Russia Movement
BIRTHPLACE/DATE: Moscow, 1934
NATIONALITY: Russian
EDUCATION: Graduated in 1958 from the Irkutsk Agricultural Institute.
CAREER: From 1963, Priest of the Russian Orthodox Church. In 1965, forbidden by the Patriarch to perform religious rites because of his pronouncements in defense of believers' human rights. In the 1970s, campaigned for human rights. In 1976, Co-Sponsor of the Christian Committee to Defend Believers' Human Rights in the USSR. In 1979, arrested. In 1980, sentenced by the Moscow

City Court to six years of imprisonment and five years of exile, according to Article 70 of the Russian Criminal Code. In 1987, granted amnesty, and restored to the priesthood. In 1990, elected Russian People's Deputy and member of the Russian Federation Supreme Soviet. In October 1991, rehabilitated by the Russian Supreme Soviet. Deputy Chairman of the Russian Federation Supreme Soviet Committee for the Freedom of Conscience. From 1990, Co-Chairman of the Coordinating Council of the Democratic Russia Movement.
FAMILY: Married with three children.
ADDRESS/TELEPHONE: 2 Krasnopresnenskaya Naberezhnaya, Moscow. 205–9151 (office).

Yakunin, Viktor Konstantinovich
POSITION: Board Chairman of the Commercial Bank of Wholesale Trade Development (Toko-Bank)
BIRTHPLACE/DATE: Krasnokamsk, Perm region, 1957
NATIONALITY: Russian
EDUCATION: From 1979 to 1981, attended special course at the Moscow Institute of Finance.
CAREER: In 1970, Economist of the Yakut USSR State Bank (Gosbank). From 1970 to 1971, Credit Representative of the Credit Department of the Mednogorsk USSR Gosbank (Orenburg region). From 1971 to 1974, Manager of the Belyayev USSR Gosbank (Orenburg region). From 1974 to 1979, Deputy Manager of the Kalinin USSR Gosbank (Kalinin City). From 1981 to 1987, Deputy Chief of the Industry Credits Department of the Moscow USSR Gosbank. From 1987 to 1989, Head of the Metal Industry Credits Department of the USSR Promstroibank (Industrial Construction Bank). From 1989 to 1990, Deputy Chief of the Economics Department of the USSR Gossnab (State Directorate of Supplies).
FAMILY: Married with three children.
ADDRESS/TELEPHONE: 5 Orlikov Street, Moscow, 107801. 204–8984 (secretary); 204–0666 (advisor).

Yakutin, Yuri Vasilevich
POSITION: Editor in Chief of *Ekonomika i Zhizn* (*Economy and Life*) weekly newspaper
BIRTHPLACE/DATE: Orekhovo-Zuevo, Moscow region, June 4, 1955
EDUCATION: From 1977 to 1987, student, then postgraduate student and researcher in the Economics Department at Moscow State University. Doctor of Economics.
CAREER: From 1987 to 1991, Deputy Editor, Deputy Editor in Chief, First Deputy Editor in Chief of *Economy and Life*. Board Member of the Russian Union of Industrialists and Entrepeneurs. Board Member of the International Union of Leaseholders and Entrepeneurs. Advisor to the Highest Econonic Committee of the Russian Supreme Soviet. Advisor to the Chairman of the Russian Federation Supreme Soviet.
MAJOR WORKS: Numerous articles and works on the problems of market development.
FAMILY: Married with a son and a daughter.
ADDRESS/TELEPHONE: 4 Udaltsov Street, Flat #35, Moscow (home); 14 Bumazhny Proyezd, GSP, Moscow, 101452 (office). 250–5793 (office).

Yankovski, Oleg Ivanovich
POSITION: Actor of the Moscow Lenin Komsomol Theater
BIRTHPLACE/DATE: Dzezkazgan, Karaganda region, February 23, 1944
CAREER: From 1967 to 1973, Actor of the Saratov Theater. From 1973, Actor of the Moscow Lenin Komsomol Theater. Member of the Union of Film Actors.
MAJOR WORKS: Played leading parts in *My Gentle and Tender Friend* (Kamishev, 1978); *That Same Munchausen* (Munchausen, 1979); *I Am Dreaming All Day Long* (Sergei, 1983); *The Kiss* (based on stories by Chekhov, 1985); *Kreutzer Sonata* (Pozdnishev, 1986); *Nostalgia* (A. Tarkovsky, 1988); *To Kill the Dragon* (M. Zakharov).
HONORS/AWARDS: Russian Federation State Prize.
FAMILY: Married with a son.
ADDRESS/TELEPHONE: 6 Chekhov Street, Moscow. 242–3285 (home); 299–9668 (theater).

Yanovski, Rudolf Grigoryevich
POSITION: Senior Researcher at the Institute of Social and Political Research of the Russian Academy of Sciences
BIRTHPLACE/DATE: Suzdal, Vladimir region, June 16, 1929
NATIONALITY: Russian

CAREER: From 1954 to 1955, taught at the Technical College in Voznesenskaya village, Kuban. From 1955 to 1961, Komsomol Leader. From 1961 to 1965, Professor at Novosibirsk State University. From 1965 to 1976, Party Leader of the Novosibirsk District Party Committee. From 1976 to 1978, Department Head of the Novosibirsk Region Party Committee. From 1978 to 1983, Deputy Head of the Central Committee's Science Department. From 1987, Corresponding Member of the USSR (now Russian) Academy of Sciences. From November 1991, Senior Researcher at the Institute of Social and Political Research of the Russian Academy of Sciences. Member of the Communist Party to 1991.
HONORS/AWARDS: Order of the Red Banner; Order of the October Revolution; Order of the Badge of Honor; Vavilov Prize.
FAMILY: Married with a daughter.
ADDRESS/TELEPHONE: 32-A Leninsky Prospekt, Moscow, 117334. 202–6950.

Yaremenko, Yuri Vasilyevich
POSITION: Director of the Institute of National Economy of the Russian Academy of Sciences; Professor
BIRTHPLACE/DATE: Chita, August 8, 1935
NATIONALITY: Russian
EDUCATION: Doctor of Economics.
CAREER: From 1960 to 1973, Junior, Senior Researcher, Acting Division Head of the Research Institute of the USSR Gosplan (State Planning Administration). From 1973 to 1986, Laboratory Head, Deputy Director of the Central Institute of Economics and Mathematics of the USSR Academy of Sciences. From 1986 to 1988, Deputy Director, Acting Director of the Institute of Economics and Forecasts of Technical Progress of the USSR Academy of Sciences. From 1988, Director of the Institute of National Economic Forecast of the USSR (now Russian) Academy of Sciences. From 1987, Corresponding Member of the USSR Academy of Sciences. From 1990 to 1991, Advisor to the USSR President. From 1976 to 1991, Member of the Communist Party and the Central Committee.
HONORS/AWARDS: Order of the Badge of Honor; Medal for Labor Valor.
FAMILY: Married with three children.
ADDRESS/TELEPHONE: 32 Krasikov Street, Suite 1409, B–418, Moscow, 117418. 129–3944 (office); 434–8005 (home).

Yarin, Venyamin Aleksandrovich
POSITION: Former People's Deputy; member of the USSR Supreme Soviet Committee on Women, Family and Demography
BIRTHPLACE/DATE: Krasnoufimsk, Sverdlov region, 1940
NATIONALITY: Russian
CAREER: From 1958 to 1989, Senior Regulatory Board Operator of Mill 650 at the Nizhny Tagil Metallurgical Plant in Sverdlov region. Member of the Constructive Cooperation Deputy Group. Member of the Worker's Deputies Group. Member of the Otechestvo (Fatherland) Deputy Group. Member of the Communist Group. Former member of the Presidential Council.
FAMILY: Married with two children.

Yastrzhembski, Sergey Vladimirovich
POSITION: Ambassador to Slovakia; Former Director of the Department of Information and Press of the Russian Foreign Ministry (MID)
BIRTHPLACE/DATE: Moscow, December 4, 1953
NATIONALITY: Russian
EDUCATION: Doctor of History.
CAREER: Junior Researcher at the Academy of Social Sciences of the Central Committee. Editor, Deputy Executive Secretary of *Problems of Peace and Socialism* magazine (Czechoslovakia). From 1989 to 1990, Senior Representative of the Central Committee's International Division. From 1990 to 1991, Deputy Editor in Chief of *Megapolis* international magazine. From 1991 to 1992, Editor in Chief of *VIP* magazine. From November to December 1991, Deputy Director-General of the Foundation for Social and Political Research. From 1992 to 1993, Director of the Information and Press Department of the Russian Foreign Ministry.
MAJOR WORKS: Many books and articles on Portuguese history and the problems of international social democracy.
FAMILY: Married with two sons.
ADDRESS/TELEPHONE: 32/34 Smolenskaya-Sennaya Street, G–200, Moscow, 121200. 444–4119.

Yavlinsky, Grigory Alekseevich

POSITION: Board Chairman of the Epicenter Economic and Political Research Center
BIRTHPLACE/DATE: Lvov, April 10, 1952
NATIONALITY: Russian
EDUCATION: Doctor of Economics.
CAREER: From 1976 to 1980, worked at the All-Union Institute of Carbon Industry. From 1981 to 1984, worked at the Research Institute of the Goscomitet State Committee for Labor and Society. From 1984 to 1989, Deputy Department Head of the State Committee for Labor and Society. From 1989 to 1990, Department Head of the Commission for Economic Reforms of the USSR Council of Ministers. In 1990, Russian Federation Deputy Prime Minister; Chairman of the Russian Federation State Commission for Economic Reforms. Resigned when the Five Hundred Days Plan for economic reform was not adopted by the USSR Supreme Soviet. From 1990 to 1991, Deputy Economic Reforms Chairman of the Russian Federation Council of Ministers. From October to December 1991, member of the USSR President's Political Consultative Council. From September to December 1991, USSR First Deputy Chairman of the Committee for the Operational Administration of the National Economy.
MAJOR WORKS: Scientific articles on problems of labor and wages.
FAMILY: Married with two children.
ADDRESS/TELEPHONE: 54 Novy Arbat, Moscow; P.O. Box 696, Moscow, 101000. 290–7878 (reception); 205–5707 (office).

Yefimov, Nikolay Ivanovich

POSITION: Editorial Staff Member of *Modus Vivendi International*
BIRTHPLACE/DATE: Moscow, 1932
CAREER: From 1956 to 1957, Department Editor of Sovinformburo (Soviet Information Service) in Great Britain; from 1957 to 1961, Editor of Sovinformburo in England. From 1961 to 1963, Chief Secretary of the APN's (Novosti Press Agency) Western and Northern Europe Editorial Staff of *Soviet Weekly* and *Soviet News* newspapers for England and Norway; from 1963 to 1965, Chief Editor of APN's England and Northern Europe Publications. From 1966 to 1971, Embassy Counsellor, APN Chief in England. From 1971 to 1972, Chief Editor of *Sputnik* magazine. From 1972 to 1976, Chief Department Editor of APN; from 1976 to 1980, Deputy Board Chairman of APN, Director of the APN Publishing House; from 1980 to 1983, Deputy Board Chairman of APN, Chief Editor of *Moscow News*. From 1983 to 1988, Editorial Staff Member, First Deputy Editor in Chief of *Izvestia* (News) daily. From 1988 to 1989, Deputy Head of the Central Committee's Ideology Department. From 1989 to 1990, Chairman of the USSR State Press Committee. From 1990 to 1991, Editor in Chief of *Izvestia*; resigned in September 1991.
FAMILY: Married with a daughter
TELEPHONE: 299–4425.

Yefimov, Vitaly Borisovich

POSITION: Russian Federation Minister of Transport
BIRTHPLACE/DATE: Moscow region, 1940
EDUCATION: Graduated in 1964 from the Gorky Agriculture Institute. Doctor of Technology. Speaks German.
CAREER: From 1964 to 1968, Engineer of the Gorky Agriculture Institute. From 1968 to 1973, Chief Engineer of a truck fleet in Gorky. From 1973 to 1976, Chief Engineer of the Gorky Freight Transport Production Association. From 1976 to 1983, Chief Engineer of the Volgo-Vyatka Transportation Directorate in Gorky. From 1983 to 1986, Head of the Gorky Region Freight Road Transport Association. From 1986 to 1990, Russian Federation Deputy Minister of Road Transport.
FAMILY: Married with a child.
ADDRESS/TELEPHONE: 10 Sadovaya-Samotechnaya Street, Moscow, 101433. 200–0803; 200–0095 (office).

Yefimov, Yevgeni Borisovich

POSITION: Editor in Chief of *Gorizont* (*Horizon*) magazine
BIRTHPLACE/DATE: Semipalatinsk, 1954
EDUCATION: Graduated in 1978 from the History Department at the Lenin Teachers' Training Institute in Moscow.
CAREER: From 1979, Editor of Kniga Publishers. From 1984, Editor of Moskovsky Rabochy Publishers.

MAJOR WORKS: Papers on socio-economic problems.
FAMILY: Married with a son.
ADDRESS/TELEPHONE: 8 Chistoprudny Boulevard, Moscow, 101854. 924–1454 (office).

Yefremov, Oleg Nikolayevich
POSITION: Art Director of the Moscow Academic Art Theater
BIRTHPLACE/DATE: Moscow, 1927
EDUCATION: Graduated in 1949 from the Moscow Art Theater Studio.
CAREER: In 1949, performed at the Central Children's Theater Company in Rozov's play, *Her Friends* (1949), and produced *Dimka-the-Invisible* (1955). In 1957, Founder and Head of the Young Actors' Studio, which became the Sovremennik (Contemporary) Theater-Studio in 1958. From 1958 to 1970, Head of the Sovremennik Theater, one of the most popular companies of the time. From 1970, Head Art Director of the Moscow Art Theater. From 1955, Film Actor (sixty parts). USSR People's Deputy. First Secretary of the Russian Federation Union of Theater Workers. From 1992, Vice President of the International Confederation of Theater Workers' Unions.
MAJOR WORKS: Productions: *They Will Live Forever* (1957) and *Looking for Joy* by Victor Rozov; *Five Evenings* by Alexander Volodin; *The Fourth* by Konstantin Simonov (played in all productions); *The Steelmakers* by Gennadi Bokarev (1972); *The Party Committee Meeting* by Aleksandr Gelman; *And Thus We'll Win* by Mikhail Shatrov (State Prize, 1983); *Ivanov* (1976), *Uncle Vanya* (1985), *The Seagull* (1980), and *The Cherry Orchard* (1989) by Anton Chekhov; *Pearl Zinaida* and *The Deer and Shalashovka* by Aleksandr Solzhenitsyn (1991); and others.
HONORS/AWARDS: Hero of Socialist Labor; State Prize (1983).
FAMILY: Divorced with a son and a daughter.
ADDRESS/TELEPHONE: 3 Proyezd Khudozhestvennogo Teatra, Moscow. 229–3312; 229–0351 (office).

Yegorov, Sergey Yefimovich
POSITION: President of the Russian Commercial Banks Association; Vice President of the Russian Union of Industrialists and Entrepreneurs
BIRTHPLACE/DATE: Orenburg region, 1928
NATIONALITY: Russian
EDUCATION: Graduated in 1950 from the Saratov Institute of Economics; and from the Leningrad Academy of Finance.
CAREER: Staff Member of the Altai Region State Bank; Deputy Administration Head of the USSR State Bank Central Office. For ten years, Functionary of the Central Committee. From 1973 to 1988, Board Chairman of the Russian Federation State Bank. From 1989, Director-General of the Moscow Union of Banks. Former member of the USSR President's Entrepreneurship Council.
FAMILY: Married with two children.
ADDRESS/TELEPHONE: 4/2 Pushkinskaya Street, Moscow. 292–0244 (office).

Yegorov, Valery Aleksandrovich
POSITION: Chairman of the All-Russia Tyazhpromexport (Heavy Industry Export) Association
BIRTHPLACE/DATE: 1937
NATIONALITY: Russian
EDUCATION: Graduated in 1960 from the Moscow Engineering and Economics Institute; in 1970, from the All-Union Academy of Foreign Trade.
CAREER: From 1971 to 1973, Senior Engineer, Chief Engineer, Deputy Administration Head of Tyazhpromexport. From 1973 and 1974, Deputy Chief Engineer for Plant Construction in Turkey. From 1974 to 1975, Deputy Counsellor for Economic Issues at the USSR Embassy in Turkey. Subsequently, Administration Head, Deputy Chairman of Tyazhpromexport.
HONORS/AWARDS: Medal For Labor Valor; Veteran of Labor Medal; USSR Supreme Soviet Honorary Certificate.
FAMILY: Married with a son.
ADDRESS/TELEPHONE: 18/1 Ovchinnikovskaya Naberezhnaya, Moscow. 220–1610 (office).

Yekimov, Vyacheslav Vladimirovich
POSITION: Professional Cyclist
BIRTHPLACE/DATE: Vyborg, February 4, 1966
NATIONALITY: Russian
CAREER: 1986 World Champion; 1987 World Champion (team races); 1988 Olympic Champion (team races); 1989 Silver Medal; 1990 World Champion (professional). From 1990, member of the Panasonic Team (Holland).

HONORS/AWARDS: Honored Master of Sports; Winner of a stage of the Tour de France.
FAMILY: Married.
ADDRESS/TELEPHONE: 9 Deputatskaya Street, St. Petersburg. 201–1741 (office); 201–0436 (Moscow Federation).

Yeliseyev, Anatoli Aleksandrovich
POSITION: Chairman of the All-Russia Selkhozpromexport (Agricultural Industry Export) Foreign Trade Association
BIRTHPLACE/DATE: Moscow, 1934
NATIONALITY: Russian
EDUCATION: Graduated in 1957 from the Moscow Technological Fisheries Institute; in 1966, from the All-Union Academy of Foreign Trade.
CAREER: From 1957 to 1963, Design Engineer of the All-Union Research and Development Institute of Food Industry Engineering. From 1966 to 1967, Senior Engineer, and from 1967 to 1970, Staff Expert to the Counsellor of Economics at the USSR Embassy in Sudan. From 1970 to 1971, Expert, Senior Expert, and from 1971 to 1973, Acting Chief Engineer, Chief Engineer of the Department for Construction of Agricultural Produce Processing and Storage Facilities of Selkhozpromexport. From 1973 to 1978, Staff Expert to the Counsellor of the USSR Embassy in Hungary. In 1978, Chief Engineer of the Department for Construction of Agricultural Produce Processing and Storage Facilities of Selkhozpromexport. From 1978 and 1980, Director of the Department for the Construction of Food, Microbiological, and Timber Industry Enterprises of Selkhozpromexport. From 1980 to 1988, Deputy Counsellor, Counsellor of Economics at the USSR Embassy in Hungary. From 1988 to 1989, Deputy Chairman of Selkhozpromexport.
HONORS/AWARDS: Medal For Labor Valor; Order of the Badge of Honor.
FAMILY: Married with two children.
ADDRESS/TELEPHONE: 18/1 Ovchinnikovskaya Naberezhnaya, Moscow. 220–1692 (office).

Yelizarov, Nikolay Mikhailovich
POSITION: Russian Federation Ambassador to the Republic of Venezuela and the Dominican Republic; Ambassador Extraordinary and Plenipotentiary
BIRTHPLACE/DATE: 1937
NATIONALITY: Russian
EDUCATION: Graduated in 1966 from the Saratov Polytechnical Institute; in 1974, from the Higher Diplomatic School of the USSR Foreign Ministry.
CAREER: From 1974, involved in diplomatic work. From 1974 to 1979, First Secretary, Counsellor at the USSR Embassy in Argentina. From 1979 to 1982, Sector Head of the Department of Latin American Countries. From 1982 to 1989, Minister-Counsellor at the USSR Embassy in Colombia. From 1989 to 1992, Deputy Head, First Deputy Head of the Main Directorate of Personnel and Educational Establishments of the USSR Foreign Ministry.
ADDRESS/TELEPHONE: Embajada de la Rôssia en Venezuela, Quinta "Soyuz" calle Las Lomas, Las Mercedes, Caracas, Venezuela. 752–2264; 752–5312.

Yeltsin, Boris Nikolayevich
POSITION: Russian Federation President; Supreme Commander of the Russian Federation Armed Forces
BIRTHPLACE/DATE: Butka, Sverdlovsk region, February 1, 1931
NATIONALITY: Russian
EDUCATION: Graduated in 1955 from Urals Polytechnic in Sverdlovsk (now Yekaterinburg) with a degree in Civil Engineering.
CAREER: From 1955 to 1957, Foreman of the Nizhny Isetsk Construction Administration in Sverdlovsk region. From 1957 to 1963, Construction Supervisor, Chief Construction Supervisor, Chief Engineer, Head of the Construction Administration of the Yuzhgorstroi Trust in Sverdlovsk region. From 1963 to 1965, Chief Engineer of the Sverdlovsk Housing Construction Complex. From 1965 to 1968, Head of the Sverdlovsk Housing Construction Complex. Joined the Communist Party in 1961 and quit in 1990. From 1968 to 1975, Head of the Construction Department of the Sverdlovsk Regional Party Committee; from 1975 to 1976, Secretary of Industry. From 1976 to 1985, worked at the Sverdlovsk Regional Committee. From 1976 to 1985, First Secretary of the Sverdlovsk Regional Committee, member of the Military Council of the Urals Military District. From

1978 to 1989, USSR Supreme Soviet Deputy (Council of the Union). From 1979 to 1984, member of the Commission for Transport and Communications. From 1981 to 1990, member of the Central Committee. During 1984 and 1985, Presidium Member of the USSR Supreme Soviet. From April to December 1985, Head of the Construction Department of the Central Committee. From July to December 1985, Central Committee Secretary of Construction. In December 1985, elected First Secretary of the Moscow City Communist Party. Relieved of his post in November 1987. From 1985 to 1987, member of the Military Council of the Moscow Military District. From 1986 to 1988, Alternate Member of the Politburo. From 1986 to 1988, Presidium Member of the USSR Supreme Soviet. From 1987 to 1989, First Deputy Chairman of the USSR State Construction Committee (Gosstroi), member of the USSR Council of Ministers. USSR People's Deputy. From 1989 to December 1990, member of the USSR Supreme Soviet Council of Nationalities. In 1989, Presidium Member of the USSR Supreme Soviet. From June 1989 to June 1990, Chairman of the USSR Supreme Soviet Committee for Construction and Architecture. In March 1990, elected Russian Federation People's Deputy, Chairman of the Russian Federation Supreme Soviet. On June 12, 1991, elected President of the Russian Federation. Chairman of the Russian Federation Constitutional Commission. Chairman of the Extraordinary Committee on Food Supplies. Chairman of the Supreme Board of Advisors. From November 1991 to June 1992, Head of the Russian Government. From March 1992, President of the Presidential Consultative Council. From May 7, 1992, Supreme Commander of the Russian Federation Armed Forces.
HONORS/AWARDS: Order of Lenin (1981); two Orders of the Red Banner of Labor; Order of the Badge of Honor; Capri–90 International Literary Prize; medals.
FAMILY: Married with two daughters.
ADDRESS/TELEPHONE: The Kremlin, Moscow. 206–3513; 205–4601.

Yemelyanov, Mikhail Pavlovich
POSITION: Ambassador to Ecuador; Counsellor Extraordinary and Plenipotentiary, First Grade
BIRTHPLACE/DATE: Stary Oskol, Belgorod region
NATIONALITY: Russian
EDUCATION: Graduated from the All-Union Institute of Civil Engineering in 1957. From 1969 to 1972, postgraduate student at the All-Union Diplomatic School of the USSR Foreign Ministry.
CAREER: From 1957 to 1958, Senior Foreman, Chief Engineer of Construction in Belgorod. From 1958 to 1961, Instructor, Department Head of the City Party Committee. From 1966 to 1969, Deputy Chairman of the Executive Committee of the Regional Council. In 1972, First Secretary of the Middle East Department. From 1972 to 1976, Counsellor at the USSR Embassy in Yemen. From 1977 to 1979, Counsellor of the Latin America Department; from 1979 to 1980, Sector Head. From 1980 to 1983, Sector Head of the First Latin America Department. From 1983 to 1988, Minister-Counsellor at the USSR Embassy in Bolivia. From 1988 to 1989, Expert of the Second Latin America Department. From 1988 to 1992, Vice Rector of the Diplomatic Academy Personnel.
FAMILY: Married with a daughter.
TELEPHONE: 244–3263.

Yenirshelov, Vladimir Petrovich
POSITION: Editor in Chief of *Nashe Naslediye* (*Our Heritage*) magazine
BIRTHPLACE/DATE: Moscow, 1940
EDUCATION: Graduated in 1968 from the Gorky Literary Institute. Doctor of Philology.
CAREER: From 1974 to 1987, Senior Editor, Literature Department Head, Editorial Board Member of *Ogonyek* (*Beacon*) magazine. Former Deputy Chairman of the Soviet Culture Foundation. Former member of the USSR Writers' Union.
FAMILY: Married.
ADDRESS/TELEPHONE: 4 First Neapolimovsky Pereulok, Moscow. 244–0106 (office).

Yeregin, Yuri Anatolyevich
POSITION: Russian Federation President's Representative in Chukotka Autonomous District
BIRTHPLACE/DATE: Sukhoi Log, Sverdlovsk region, November 28, 1953
EDUCATION: From 1970 to 1974, student at a river shipping school in Vologda Region. Graduated in 1986 from the Novosibirsk Institute of Water Transport.

CAREER: From 1974 to 1977, served in the navy. From 1978 and 1985, Skipper-Mechanic of the Madina Ship in Anadyr. From 1985 and 1989, Communist Party Secretary of Anadyr Seaport. From 1990 to 1991, Director of the Tseolir Association. In 1991, Mayor of Anadyr. Anadyr City Council People's Deputy.
FAMILY: Married with three children.
ADDRESS/TELEPHONE: 33 Otke Street, Flat #22, Anadyr, 686710. 4–6197 (office); 4–0820 (home).

Yeremin, Alvin Yevstafyevich
POSITION: Chairman of the Russian Federation Supreme Soviet Committee for Industry and Power Engineering
BIRTHPLACE/DATE: Kunikovo village, Kostroma region, 1932
EDUCATION: Graduated in 1967 from the Moscow Technological Institute. From 1971 to 1973, student at the Higher Party School.
CAREER: From 1948 to 1951, Turner at the Rabochy Metallist (Metalworker) Plant. From 1951 to 1955, served in the army. From 1965 to 1960, Turner, Engineer, Secretary of the Communist Party at a textile engineering factory. From 1960 to 1967, Instructor, Head of the Industrial-Transport Department of the Kostroma City Communist Party. From 1967 to 1971, Deputy Chairman of the Kostroma City Executive Committee. From 1973 to 1980, Head of the Industrial-Transport Department of the Kostroma Regional Committee. From 1980 to 1984, Deputy Chairman, First Deputy Chairman of the Regional Executive Committee. From 1984 to 1986, Second Secretary of the Kostroma Regional Committee. From 1986 to 1991, Chairman of the Kostroma Regional Executive Committee. Russian Federation People's Deputy. Member of the Council of the Republic. Member of the Industrial Union Faction. Kostroma Regional Council People's Deputy.
FAMILY: Married with two children.
ADDRESS/TELEPHONE: 2 Krasnopresnenskaya Naberezhnaya, Moscow, 103274. 205–5398 (office).

Yeremin, Yuri Ivanovich
POSITION: Art Director of the Pushkin Drama Theater in Moscow
BIRTHPLACE/DATE: Kolomna, 1944
NATIONALITY: Russian
EDUCATION: Graduated from the Actors Department at the Anatoli Lunacharski State Institute of Theatrical Art. Professor.
CAREER: From 1970 to 1973, Actor of the Moscow Young Spectators Theater. From 1973 to 1974, Producer; from 1974 to 1978, Chief Producer of the Lenin Komsomol Young Spectators Theater in Rostov-on-Don. From 1978 to 1981, Head of the Rostov Maxim Gorky Drama Theater. From 1981 to 1987, Head of the USSR Central Army Theater. From 1987, Art Director of the Moscow Pushkin Drama Theater. Professor at the Lunacharsky Institute of Dramatic Art. From 1986, Secretary of the USSR Union of Theater Workers. From 1989, Course Head of the Moscow Art Theater College-Studio. From 1991, Secretary of the Russian Union of Theater Workers. From 1991, Vice President of the International Association of Theater Producers' Unions. Russian Federation People's Deputy.
MAJOR WORKS: Productions: *We, the Undersigned*, by Aleksandr Gelman; *The Optimistic Tragedy*, by Vsevolod Vishnevsky; *The Soldiers*; *The Roads to Borodukhino*; *The Article*; *Ward No. 6*, by Anton Chekhov; *The Dregs*, by Glovatsky, *The Possessed*, by Fyodor Dostoevski.
HONORS/AWARDS: Russian Federation People's Artist; Order of Literature and Art of France.
FAMILY: Married with two children.
ADDRESS/TELEPHONE: 23 Tverskoi Boulevard, Moscow. 203–4214.

Yerin, Victor Fyodorovich
POSITION: Russian Federation Minister of Internal Affairs; Lieutenant-General
BIRTHPLACE/DATE: Kazan, January 17, 1944
CAREER: From 1964, Operational Agent at the Tatar Ministry of Internal Affairs. From 1980 to 1983, Head of the Tatar Homicide Department. From 1983 to 1988, Chief of the Service for Combatting Economic Crime of the USSR Ministry of Internal Affairs. From 1988 to 1990, Armenian First Deputy Minister of Internal Affairs. From 1990 to 1991, Russian Republic Deputy Minister of Internal Affairs. From September to December 1991, USSR First Deputy Minister of Internal Affairs. From December 1991 to January 1992, Rus-

sian Federation First Deputy Minister of Security and Internal Affairs.
FAMILY: Married with two children.
ADDRESS/TELEPHONE: 16 Zhitnaya Street, Moscow, 117049. 239–6532 (office).

Yevenko, Leonid Ivanovich
POSITION: Rector of the Higher School of International Business at the Academy of National Economy of the Russian Federation Government
BIRTHPLACE/DATE: Moscow, 1941
NATIONALITY: Russian
EDUCATION: Graduated in 1963 from the Plekhanov Institute of National Economy in Moscow. Doctor of Economics. Speaks English.
CAREER: From 1964 to 1968, Teacher, Assistant Professor at the Plekhanov Institute of National Economy. From 1983, Professor and Management Expert. From 1985, Editorial Board Member of *USA: EPI (Ecology, Politics, Ideology)* magazine. In 1987, Lecturer at Hokkaido University in Japan. From 1988, Board Member of the Free Economic Society of Russia. In 1989, Lecturer at San Francisco State University (United States). From 1968 to 1990, Staff Member, Department Head at the Institute of the U.S. and Canada. From 1990, Director-General of the Amscort Soviet-American Joint Venture.
MAJOR WORKS: *Organization of State Programs* (1981); *Organizational Structures in U.S. Industrial Corporations* (1983).
FAMILY: Married with two children.
ADDRESS/TELEPHONE: 82 Vernadsky Prospekt, Moscow, 117571. 434–1146.

Yevtushenko, Yevgeni Aleksandrovich
POSITION: Poet; Co-Chairman of the April Writers' Association
BIRTHPLACE/DATE: Zima village, Irkutsk region, 1933
NATIONALITY: Russian
EDUCATION: From 1951 to 1954, studied at the Gorky Literary Institute.
CAREER: First publications appeared in 1949. From 1952, member of the USSR Writers' Union. In 1963, published "Autobiography" in the French weekly *Express*, which stirred sharp criticism at the Fourth Plenary Meeting of the USSR Writers' Union Board in March 1963. In 1984, elected Chairman of the Council for Georgian Literature of the USSR Writers' Union; in 1986, Board Secretary. Former USSR People's Deputy.
MAJOR WORKS: Author of numerous world-renowned poems.
HONORS/AWARDS: USSR State Prize (1984); SIMBA Academy International Literary Prize (1984); Golden Lion International Prize (Venice).
FAMILY: Married with two children.
ADDRESS/TELEPHONE: 2/1 Kutuzovsky Prospekt, Flat #101, Moscow. 593–1798; 243–3769; 288–7303.

Yudaltsov, Arkady Petrovich
POSITION: Editor in Chief of *Literaturnaya Gazeta (Literary Newspaper)*
BIRTHPLACE/DATE: Vologda, 1936
CAREER: From 1961 to 1968, Engineer at CAGI in Zhukovski, Moscow region. From 1968 to 1974, Editor in Chief of *Moskovsky Komsomolets (Moscow Komsomol Member)* newspaper. From 1974 to 1991, Deputy Editor in Chief of *Literaturnaya Gazeta.*
MAJOR WORKS: Books on ecology, ethics, journalistic skills, and science.
FAMILY: Married with a son.
ADDRESS/TELEPHONE: 13 Kostyanski Pereulok, Moscow, 103654. 200–2865 (office).

Yulyanov, Boris Vasilyevich
POSITION: Prefect of the Eastern District of Moscow
BIRTHPLACE/DATE: Solnechnogorsk, Moscow region, 1941
EDUCATION: From 1959 to 1962, student at the Technical Secondary School.
CAREER: From 1958 to 1959, Electrician in Solnechnogorsk. In 1962, Electrician at the Radio Valves Plant. From 1962 to 1965, served in the army. From 1965 to 1989, Technician, Engineer, Senior Engineer, Section Head, Deputy Secretary, Party Committee Secretary of the Research Institute for Long-Distance Radio Communications. From 1989 to 1991, Chairman of the Auditing Commission of the Kuibyshev District Party Committee; Chairman of the Executive Committee of the Kuibyshev District Council. From 1991 to 1992, Deputy Prefect of the Northeastern District of Moscow.

FAMILY: Married with two children.
ADDRESS/TELEPHONE: 9 Preobrazhenskaya Ploschad, Moscow, 107076. 161–9887; 161–1203 (reception).

Yurzinov, Vladimir Vladimirovich

POSITION: Senior Coach of the Moscow Dynamo Ice Hockey Team; Coach of the CIS National Ice Hockey Team
BIRTHPLACE/DATE: Moscow, 1940
NATIONALITY: Russian
EDUCATION: Graduated in 1961 from the State Institute of Physical Education; and in 1964, from Moscow State University.
CAREER: In 1963 and 1969, World and European Ice Hockey Champion. Sports Instructor of the Dynamo Moscow City Council. From 1974 to 1979, Ice Hockey Team Senior Coach of the Moscow Dynamo Sports Club. From 1979 to 1989, Senior Coach of the Riga Dynamo Ice Hockey Team. Seven-time World Ice Hockey Champion; three-time Olympic Champion.
HONORS/AWARDS: USSR Honored Master of Sports; USSR Honored Coach; Latvian Republic Honored Coach; Order of the Red Banner of Labor; two Orders of the Badge of Honor.
FAMILY: Married with a son and a daughter.
ADDRESS/TELEPHONE: The Dynamo Club, 36 Leningradsky Prospekt, Moscow. 212–8111 (office); 571–6537 (home).

Yuvarov, Arnold Vitalyevich

POSITION: President of the Public Relations Agency Consortium
BIRTHPLACE/DATE: Moscow, 1967
CAREER: From 1990 to 1991, Engineer of the Vostokintorg Foreign Trade Association; Commercial Director of the Kiss Company. From 1991 to 1992, Public Relations Director of the Alisa Exchange.
FAMILY: Married with a son.
ADDRESS/TELEPHONE: 27/3 Pervy Kolobovski Pereulok, Moscow, 103051. 923–4046; Fax: 921–4958.

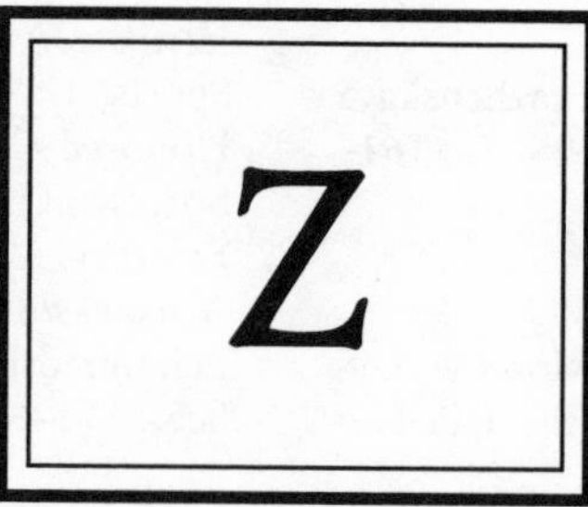

Zabelin, Ilya Ilyich

POSITION: Director-General of the Ekran Joint-Stock Company
BIRTHPLACE/DATE: Smolensk region, 1932
CAREER: From 1969 to 1989, worked in the Warranty Department of a Television Plant.
FAMILY: Married with a child.
ADDRESS/TELEPHONE: 15 Sredny Pereulok, St. Petersburg, 199053. 218–5560.

Zadonsky, Georgy Ivanovich

POSITION: Member of the Council of the Republic Committee on Budget, Planning, Taxes, and Prices of the Russian Federation Supreme Soviet
BIRTHPLACE/DATE: Gomel, Byelorussia, 1940
NATIONALITY: Ukrainian
EDUCATION: Graduated in 1965 from the Bauman State Technical Institute in Moscow. From 1967 to 1970, postgraduate student in the Theoretical Physics Department at the Krupskaya Teachers' Training Institute. Speaks English.
CAREER: From 1964 to 1967, Engineer-Experimenter at the Institute of Engines. From 1970 to 1977, Senior Researcher at the All-Union Research Institute. From 1977 to 1990, Senior Researcher at the Institute of Biophysics of the USSR Health Ministry. Russian Federation People's Deputy. Coordinator of the Radical Democrats Faction; member of the Democratic Russia Movement. Member of the Commission for Regulation Observance of the Sixth Congress of Russian Federation People's Deputies.
FAMILY: Married with two daughters and a grandchild.
ADDRESS/TELEPHONE: 2 Krasnopresnenskaya Naberezhnaya, Second Floor, Room #13, Moscow. 205–4819 (office).

Zadornov, Mikhail Nikolayevich

POSITION: Art Director of the Theater of Miniatures; Writer-Satirist
BIRTHPLACE/DATE: Yurmala, 1948
CAREER: In 1976, Senior Engineer; Actor and Producer of the Rossiya amateur student theater at the Moscow Aviation Institute. In 1977, published first story in *Teatr* (*Theater*) magazine. From 1984 to 1985, Head of the Satire Department of *Yunost* (*Youth*) magazine; performed. In 1991, organized a theater and became its Art Director. From May 1990, member of the Russian Federation Writers' Union.
MAJOR WORKS: Short stories, parodies, and shows. *Mystery of the Blue Planet*; *Length of Line Is 15,000 Meters.*
FAMILY: Married with a child.
ADDRESS/TELEPHONE: 4-A Dubosekovskaya, Moscow, 125080. 928–5081.

Zagladin, Nikita Vadimovich

POSITION: Editor in Chief of *Kentavr* (*Centaurus*) magazine
BIRTHPLACE/DATE: Moscow, December 5, 1951
NATIONALITY: Russian
EDUCATION: Graduated from the Moscow State Institute of International Relations in 1975. Doctor of History (1985); Professor.
CAREER: From 1978, worked at the Central Committee's Academy of Social Sciences; Lecturer on International Communist Party Activities and International Policy. From 1984, Deputy Head of

the Science Department. From 1991, Editor in Chief of *Kentavr* independent political magazine; Deputy Director of the Center for Strategic Studies. From January to March 1992, taught at Yale University in the United States.
MAJOR WORKS: *History of Successes and Failures of Soviet Diplomacy* (1990).
FAMILY: Married with two children.
ADDRESS/TELEPHONE: 15 Pelshe Street, Flat #104, Moscow, 116702. 437–1689 (home).

Zagladin, Vadim Valentinovich
POSITION: Counsellor to the President of The International Foundation for Socio-Economic and Political Studies (Gorbachev Foundation)
BIRTHPLACE/DATE: Moscow, June 23, 1927
NATIONALITY: Russian
EDUCATION: Graduated in 1949 from the World History Department (History and Diplomacy) of the Moscow State Institute of International Relations. Completed postgraduate studies in 1952. Doctor of History (1953); Doctor of Philosophy; Professor (1973).
CAREER: From 1952, Assistant, Lecturer, Senior Lecturer at the Moscow State Institute of International Relations. From 1954, Senior Editor, Consultant-Analyst, Managing Editor of *Novoye Vremya* (*New Time*) magazine. From 1960 to 1964, Deputy Managing Editor; Department Head of the Prague-based *World Marxist Review* journal. From 1964 to 1967, Consultant, Head of the Consulting Group of the Central Committee's International Department. From 1967, Deputy; from 1975 to 1988, First Deputy Head of the Central Committee's International Department. From 1988, Advisor to the Chairman of the USSR Supreme Soviet Presidium. From March 1990, Aide to the USSR President. From 1989, Chairman of the USSR Committee for Security and Cooperation in Europe.
HONORS/AWARDS: Two Orders of Lenin (1977, 1982); Order of the Red Banner of Labor (1987).
FAMILY: Married with two children.
ADDRESS/TELEPHONE: 49 Leningradsky Prospekt, Moscow, 125468. 241–8733 (home); 943–9976 (office).

Zaikin, Aleksandr Aleksandrovich
POSITION: Board Chairman of the Russian Solidarnost (Solidarity) Bank of Trade Union Solidarity and Social Investments
BIRTHPLACE/DATE: Moscow region, 1949
EDUCATION: Graduated in 1970 from the Moscow Institute of Finance. Speaks German.
CAREER: From 1970 to 1971, Bank Employee. From 1971 to 1972, Komsomol Functionary. From 1972 to 1975, worked at the USSR Ministry of Finance. From 1975 to 1985, Financial Board Head of the Moscow Region Trade Union Center. From 1985 to 1989, Head of the Auditing Service of the All-Union Central Council of Trade Unions. From 1990 to 1991, Financial Management Head of the Russian Center of Independent Trade Unions.
FAMILY: Married with two children.
ADDRESS/TELEPHONE: 42 Leninsky Prospekt, Building 5, Moscow. 930–8651; 938–8171 (office).

Zaitsev, Aleksandr Gennadyevich
POSITION: Senior Figure Skating Coach of the Dynamo Sports Club
BIRTHPLACE/DATE: Moscow, 1952
NATIONALITY: Russian
CAREER: In 1976 and 1980, Olympic Champion; European and World Champion.
HONORS/AWARDS: USSR Honored Master of Sports.
FAMILY: Married with a son.
ADDRESS/TELEPHONE: 8 Luzhnetskaya Naberezhnaya, Moscow. 201–1231 (Federation).

Zaitsev, Anatoli Safronovich
POSITION: Ambassador to the Congo; Ambassador Extraordinary and Plenipotentiary
BIRTHPLACE/DATE: Borisov, Minsk region
NATIONALITY: Byelorussian
EDUCATION: Graduated from the Institute of Oriental Languages in 1960. From 1987 to 1989, postgraduate student at the Diplomatic Academy of the USSR Foreign Ministry.
CAREER: From 1960 to 1961, Translator at the Central Komsomol School of the Komsomol Central Committee. From 1961 to 1962, Translator for the Fleet Ministry's Expert Group in the Democratic Republic of Vietnam. From 1962 to 1964, Senior Translator for the Economic Counsellor at the USSR Embassy in Vietnam. From 1964 to 1966, Junior Researcher at the Institute of Asian

People of the USSR Academy of Sciences. From 1966 to 1967, Attaché at the USSR Embassy in Vietnam. From 1967 to 1969, Third Secretary, and from 1969 to 1970, Second Secretary of the Southeastern Asia Department. From 1970 to 1971, Second Secretary of the International Economic Relations Department. From 1971 to 1975, First Secretary at the USSR Permanent Mission to the UN and Other International Organizations in Geneva. From 1975 to 1977, Counsellor, and from 1977 to 1979, Expert of the Second European Department. From 1979 to 1982, Foreign Minister's Aide, Senior Counsellor. From 1983 to 1987, Department Head of the Southeastern Asia Department.
FAMILY: Married with a daughter.
TELEPHONE: 244–2471.

Zaitsev, Igor Andreyevich
POSITION: Designer
BIRTHPLACE/DATE: Dneprodzerzhinsk, 1939
NATIONALITY: Russian
CAREER: From 1962 to 1967, Engineer-Designer at the Lenin Komsomol Automobile Plant. From 1967 to 1971, Chief Designer at the Research Institute of Aviation Technology. From 1971 to 1987, Head of the Designer Bureau; Chief Designer. From 1978 to 1990, Board Secretary of the USSR Designers' Union. From 1990 to 1991, Board Chairman of the USSR Designers' Union. From January 1992, Board Chairman of the International Association of Designers' Unions.
FAMILY: Married with two children and a grandson.
ADDRESS/TELEPHONE: 1/2 Arbartskaya Ploschad, Moscow, 121019. 202–4648.

Zaitsev, Vyacheslav Mikhailovich
POSITION: Director-General of the Moscow House of Fashion; Fashion Designer
BIRTHPLACE/DATE: Ivanovo, 1938
CAREER: Designer at a sewing factory; Fashion Designer; Chief Fashion Designer at the All-Union House of Fashion; from October 1988, Director.
HONORS/AWARDS: Order of the Badge of Honor; Medal For Labor Valor; Gold and Silver Medals of the USSR Exhibition of National Economic Achievements; Russian Federation Honored Artist; Honorable Citizen.
FAMILY: Divorced with a son.
ADDRESS/TELEPHONE: 21 Mir Prospekt, Moscow, 129110. 971–1122 (office).

Zaitsev, Yuri Vladimirovich
POSITION: Permanent Representative of International Organizations in Vienna; Ambassador Extraordinary and Plenipotentiary
BIRTHPLACE/DATE: Moscow, August 2, 1933
NATIONALITY: Russian
EDUCATION: Graduated from the Moscow Civil Engineering Institute. Doctor of Technical Sciences; Professor.
CAREER: In 1958, Acting Senior Researcher at the Central Institute of Scientific Information for Construction and Architecture. From 1959 to 1964, Researcher, then Senior Researcher at the Research Institute of Concrete of the Academy of Construction and Architecture. From 1964 to 1990, Docent, Department Head, Dean, Rector of the All-Union Correspondence Polytechnical Institute of the USSR Committee for National Education. From 1990 to 1992, Chairman of the Russian President's Committee for Citizenship Issues; member of the Russian Federation Supreme Soviet. Russian People's Deputy.
MAJOR WORKS: Eighteen monographs and books; more than 200 articles in scientific journals.
FAMILY: Married with two children.
TELEPHONE: 244–4211.

Zakharov, Mark Anatolyevich
POSITION: Art Director of the Moscow Lenkom Theater (formerly the Lenin Komsomol Theater); member of the Presidential Consultative Council; member of the Consultative Council of the Russian Federation Minister of Culture and Tourism
BIRTHPLACE/DATE: Moscow, 1933
NATIONALITY: Russian
EDUCATION: Graduated in 1955 from the Anatoli Lunacharsky State Institute of Dramatic Art. Professor.
CAREER: From 1965 to 1973, Producer of the Moscow Satire Theater. From 1973, Art Director of the Moscow Lenkom Theater. USSR People's Deputy; member of the USSR Supreme Soviet Committee for Sciences, Public Education, Culture, and Upbringing. To 1991, Board Secretary of

the USSR Union of Theater Workers. From December 1991, President of the Theater Producers' Association.
MAJOR WORKS: *Wake Up and Sing*; *Mother Courage*; *Strange Person*; *Dictatorship of Conscience* (USSR State Prize, 1987); *Till Eulenspiegel*; *Junona and Avos*; *Sage*; *Funeral Prayer*. Films produced: *That Same Munchausen* (Best Director Prize at the Zlata Praha Seventeenth International Festival of TV Films); *An Ordinary Miracle*; *Count Caliostro*; *To Kill the Dragon*.
HONORS/AWARDS: USSR People's Artist; USSR State Prize; Order of the People's Friendship.
FAMILY: Married with a daughter.
ADDRESS/TELEPHONE: 6 Chekhov Street, Moscow. 299–1261 (office).

Zalygin, Sergey Pavlovich
POSITION: Editor in Chief of *Novy Mir* (*New World*) magazine; Writer
BIRTHPLACE/DATE: Durasovka village, Bashkiria, 1913
EDUCATION: Degree in Technical Sciences.
CAREER: In 1932, Agronomist. From 1939, Engineer in Omsk. From 1942 to 1945, Senior Technician of the Weather Report Service. In 1945, Assistant at the Omsk Agricultural Institute. From 1946 to 1955, Department Head of the Omsk Agricultural Institute. From 1955 to 1967, worked at the Novosibirsk Agricultural Institute of the Siberian branch of the USSR Academy of Sciences. From 1991, member of the USSR Writers' Union. From December 1991, member of the Russian Writers' Union; Chairman of the Ecology and the World Association; USSR People's Deputy.
MAJOR WORKS: Novels: *South American Variant*; *After the Storm*; *On the Irtysh*. Essay: "My Poet." Author of 200 books, including books on ecology, translated into thirty languages.
HONORS/AWARDS: USSR State Prize; Hero of Socialist Labor.
FAMILY: Married with a daughter.
ADDRESS/TELEPHONE: 1/2 Maly Putnikovsky Pereulok, Moscow, 103806. 209–5702 (office).

Zamyatin, Leonid Mitrofanovich
POSITION: Former Diplomat and Party Leader
BIRTHPLACE/DATE: Nizhny Devitsk, Voronezh region, 1922
NATIONALITY: Russian
CAREER: From 1946 to 1948, Attaché of the Third European Department. From 1948 to 1949, Second Secretary of the USSR Deputy Foreign Minister's Secretariat. From 1949 to 1950, Second Secretary of the USSR Foreign Minister's Secretariat; from 1950 to 1952, First Secretary. From 1952 to 1953, Assistant Department Head of the Third European Department. From 1953 to 1954, First Secretary at the USSR Mission to the UN in New York. From 1954 to 1957, Political Counsellor at the USSR Mission to the UN in New York. In 1957, USSR Deputy Permanent Representative to the International Agency of Nuclear Energy in Vienna. From 1957 to 1959, USSR Deputy Permanent Representative to the Executive Council of the International Nuclear Energy Agency in Vienna; from 1959 to 1960, USSR Permanent Representative. From 1960 to 1962, Deputy Department Head of the Department of American Countries of the USSR Foreign Ministry. From 1962 to 1970, Press Department Head and Collegium Member of the USSR Foreign Ministry. From 1972 to 1978, Director-General of TASS (Telegraph Agency of the Soviet Union) of the USSR Council of Ministers. From 1978 to 1986, Department Head of the Central Committee. From 1986 to November 1991, USSR Ambassador to the United Kingdom of Great Britain and Northern Ireland; Ambassador Extraordinary and Plenipotentiary.
HONORS/AWARDS: Order of Lenin; Order of the Red Banner of Labor; Order of the October Revolution; Order of the People's Friendship.
FAMILY: Married.

Zarechkin, Yuri Vladimirovich
POSITION: Editor in Chief of *24* newspaper
BIRTHPLACE/DATE: Ufa, 1941
NATIONALITY: Russian
EDUCATION: Degree in Philosophy.
CAREER: From 1966 to 1972, Newspaper Editor in Bashkiria. From 1973 to 1980, Correspondent, Department Editor, Editor in Chief of *Molodoy Kommunist* (*Young Communist*) magazine. From 1981 to 1991, Editor of the Political Problems Department; Editorial Board Member of *Literaturnaya Gazeta* (*Literary Newspaper*).
MAJOR WORKS: Author of articles on management, democracy, political structure, and politics.

Family: Married with a son.
Address/Telephone: 10/12 Tverskoi Boulevard, Moscow, 103004. 296–3609; 292–3091 (office).

Zaslavskaya, Tatyana Ivanovna

Position: President of the Russian Poll Center; Academician of the Russian Academy of Sciences
Birthplace/Date: Kiev, September 9, 1927
Nationality: Russian
Education: Completed postgraduate studies at the Institute of Economics of the USSR Academy of Sciences. Doctor of Economics.
Career: From 1950 to 1963, Junior, then Senior Researcher at the Institute of Economics of the USSR Academy of Sciences. From 1963 to 1966, Senior Researcher at the Novosibirsk Institute of Economics and Industrial Production Management. From 1966 to 1967, Senior Researcher. From 1967 to 1987, Social Problems Department Head. From January 1988, Director of the All-Union Poll Center. From 1968, Corresponding Member of the USSR Academy of Sciences. From 1981, member of the USSR (now Russian) Academy of Sciences. From 1986 to 1991, President of the Soviet Sociology Association. From 1991, Honorary President.
Major Works: In the field of sociology, social and economic problems, labor resources, and the migration of rural populations. Co-author of textbook, *Political Economy.*
Honors/Awards: Order of the October Revolution; Order of the Red Banner; Order of the People's Friendship; Karpinsky Prize.
Family: Divorced with two daughters.
Address/Telephone: 17 Nikolskaya Street, Moscow. 921–8079; 928–2112 (office).

Zaslavsky, Ilya Iosifovich

Position: Plenipotentiary Representative of the Mayor of Moscow; President of the Miloserdiye i Kultura (Charity and Culture) Association
Birthplace/Date: Moscow, 1960
Education: Graduated from the Moscow Textile Institute and its postgraduate program. Doctor of Technology. Good command of English and French.
Career: In 1989, elected USSR People's Deputy. From November 1990 to July 1991, Chairman of the Oktyabrsky District Council of People's Deputies in Moscow. Presidium Member of the Gryadushcheye (Future) Foundation. Organizing Committee Co-Chairman of the Democratic Russia Movement in Moscow; Chairman of Democratic Russia's International Relations Committee. UN Expert on the affairs of invalids.
Family: Married with a daughter.
Address/Telephone: 9 Krymsky Val Street, Moscow. 238–2317 (assistant).

Zelenov, Victor Matveyevich

Position: Ambassador to Guinea-Bissau; Ambassador Extraordinary and Plenipotentiary
Birthplace/Date: Nesteary village, Gorky region, December 1, 1937
Nationality: Russian
Education: Studied at the State Institute of Ship Engineering. From 1973 to 1976, student at the Diplomatic Academy of the USSR Foreign Ministry. Doctor of Economics.
Career: From 1961 to 1966, Foreman, Department Head, Shop Head at the Kuibyshev Ship Repair Plant; from 1966 to 1970, Director. From 1970 to 1972, Second Secretary of the Samara District Communist Party in Kuibyshev. From 1972 to 1973, Department Head of the Kuibyshev Region Communist Party. From 1976 to 1977, First Secretary of the International Economic Relations Department of the USSR Foreign Ministry. From 1977 to 1978, First Secretary at the USSR Embassy in India. From 1978 to 1983, Counsellor at the USSR Embassy in Pakistan. From 1983 to 1984, Counsellor, Expert of the Personnel Department. From 1984 to 1986, Consul-General in Karachi. From 1986 to 1987, Expert of the General Secretariat of the USSR Foreign Ministry. From 1987 to 1988, Department Head of the USSR Foreign Ministry. From 1988 to 1991, Head of the Consulate Department.
Honors/Awards: Order of the People's Friendship; Order of the Badge of Honor.
Family: Married with a son.
Telephone: 244–2471.

Zemskov, Mikhail Aleksandrovich

Position: Editor in Chief of *Patriot* newspaper
Birthplace/Date: Kazan, 1948

EDUCATION: From 1977 to 1980, studied at the Military Academy.
CAREER: From 1974 to 1977, Correspondent for *Za Rodinu* (*For the Motherland*) magazine. From 1980 to 1983, Correspondent for *Armia* (*Army*) magazine. From 1983 to 1989, Aide to the USSR Defense Ministry.
HONORS/AWARDS: Order For Service to the Motherland.
FAMILY: Married with two children.
ADDRESS/TELEPHONE: 26 Petrovka, Moscow K–51, 101406. 200–3890 (office).

Zemsky, Vladimir Vasilyevich
POSITION: Ambassador to Georgia; Ambassador Extraordinary and Plenipotentiary
BIRTHPLACE/DATE: Moscow, 1939
NATIONALITY: Russian
EDUCATION: Graduated from the Moscow State Institute of International Relations in 1967.
CAREER: From 1967 to 1968, Aide, then Senior Aide of the Latin America Department of the USSR Foreign Ministry. From 1968 to 1970, Aide, Aide-Trainee at the USSR Embassy in Cuba. From 1970 to 1972, Attaché. From 1972 to 1974, Third Secretary of the Latin America Department. From 1974 to 1977, Second Secretary at the USSR Embassy in Portugal. From 1979 to 1983, First Secretary of the First European Department. From 1983 to 1985, Counsellor. From 1985 to 1986, Counsellor at the USSR Embassy in Spain. From 1986 to 1990, Minister-Counsellor at the USSR Embassy in Portugal. From 1990 to 1991, Minister-Counsellor at the USSR Embassy in Angola. From 1991 to 1992, Expert of the Board of Union Republics. From 1992, First Deputy Head of the CIS (Commonwealth of Independent States) Department.
FAMILY: Married with two children.
TELEPHONE: 244–1492.

Zenkov, Boris Gennadyevich
POSITION: Ambassador to Cyprus; Counsellor Extraordinary and Plenipotentiary, Second Grade
BIRTHPLACE/DATE: Semipalatinsk, May 25, 1946
NATIONALITY: Russian
EDUCATION: Graduated from the Moscow State Institute of International Relations. From 1987 to 1988, student of the advanced course for senior diplomats at the Diplomatic Academy.
CAREER: From 1970 to 1972, Trainee at the USSR Embassy in Greece. From 1972 to 1974, Attaché. From 1974 to 1976, Third Secretary. From 1976 to 1977, Third Secretary of the Fifth European Department. From 1977 to 1981, Second Secretary at the USSR Embassy in Cyprus. From 1981 to 1985, First Secretary of the Fifth European Department. In 1985, Counsellor. From 1985 to 1987, USSR Foreign Minister Deputy Aide. From 1988 to 1990, Consul-General in Casablanca.
FAMILY: Married with two children.
TELEPHONE: 244–2281.

Zhabotinsky, Leonid Ivanovich
POSITION: Pro-Rector of the Moscow Institute of Commerce
BIRTHPLACE/DATE: Zaporozhye, 1938
NATIONALITY: Ukrainian
EDUCATION: Graduated in 1965 from the Kharkov Teachers' Training Institute.
CAREER: In 1964 and 1968, Summer Olympic Weight Lifting Champion; four-time World Champion. Set nineteen World Records.
HONORS/AWARDS: USSR Honored Master of Sports.
FAMILY: Married with two children.
ADDRESS/TELEPHONE: 36 Smolnaya Street, Moscow. 458–4651 (office); 458–7367 (home).

Zhalinsky, Vitaly Alfredovich
POSITION: Director-General of the Interkross Joint Venture
BIRTHPLACE/DATE: Rostov-on-Don, January 24, 1956
EDUCATION: Graduated in 1978 from the Law Department at Moscow State University.
CAREER: From 1978 to 1988, held different posts in law-enforcement bodies of the Ministry of Internal Affairs and in the Russian Federation Ministry of Justice. From 1988, worked for the Agroplast Firm.
FAMILY: Married with a daughter.
ADDRESS/TELEPHONE: 21 Bolshoi Sukharevsky Pereulok, Building 1, Moscow. 208–5957 (office).

Zharikhin, Vladimir Leonidovich
POSITION: Head of the Public Relations Department of the Board of the Svobodnaya Rossiya (Free Russia) People's Party (SRPP); Organizing Committee Member of the Democratic Russia Movement
BIRTHPLACE/DATE: Kronshtadt, Leningrad region, 1948
EDUCATION: Graduated in 1972 from the Mendeleyev Institute of Chemical Technology. Speaks English.
CAREER: From 1972 to 1988, Researcher of nuclear technology at the All-Union Non-Organic Materials Research Institute. From 1988 to 1990, Deputy Secretary of the Communist Party; member of the Democratic Platform of the Communist Party; Candidate for Russian Federation People's Deputy from the Democratic Russia Electoral Association. From 1990, Secretary of the Communist Party; Co-Chairman of the Moscow Conference of Secretaries of Grassroots Party Organizations; Coordinator of the Democratic Movement of Communists; Bakatin's Agent at the Russian Presidential Elections.
FAMILY: Married with a daughter.
ADDRESS/TELEPHONE: 9-A Bolshaya Cherkizovskaya Street, Flat #15, Moscow. 168–6974 (home); 297–9131 (office).

Zhebrovsky, Stanislav Mikhailovich
POSITION: Member of the Supreme Soviet; Deputy Chairman of the Liberal-Democratic Party
BIRTHPLACE/DATE: Kansk, Krasnodar region, 1942
NATIONALITY: Russian
EDUCATION: Graduated in 1965 from the Physics Department at Moscow State University; in 1975, from the postgraduate program. Speaks French and English.
CAREER: Physics Lecturer at the African Center of Oil and Textile Industry in Algeria. From 1976 to 1982, Science Editor at Soviet Encyclopedia Publishers. From 1982 to 1992, Deputy Head of the Physics and Astronomy Publications Department of Mir (World) Publishers. From 1991, Liberal-Democratic Party Supreme Council Member.
FAMILY: Married with a daughter.
ADDRESS/TELEPHONE: 3 Rybnikov Pereulok, Third Floor, Moscow. 923–6370 (office).

Zhelamsky, Andrey Nikolayevich
POSITION: Board Chairman of Toribank Joint-Stock Bank
BIRTHPLACE/DATE: Moscow, 1965
NATIONALITY: Russian
EDUCATION: Graduated in 1989 from the State Academy of Finance. Speaks English.
CAREER: From 1989 to 1991, Incombank Chief Economist. From 1991, Chief Economist of Delovaya Rossiya (Business Russia) Joint-Stock Bank.
FAMILY: Single.
ADDRESS/TELEPHONE: 29 Kalanchevskaya Street, Moscow, 107078. 264–3098 (office).

Zheleznovsky, Andrey Nikolayevich
POSITION: Speed Skating Champion; Officer of the Central Army Sports Club
BIRTHPLACE/DATE: Orsha, 1963
CAREER: USSR Champion. In 1985, World Champion (500-meter race). In 1986, World Champion (1000-meter race). In 1988, Bronze Medal winner at the Winter Olympics. In 1989, Officer of the Central Army Sports Club. In 1990, World Champion (500- and 1000-meter races). In 1991, World Champion (1000-meter race).
FAMILY: Married with two children.
TELEPHONE: 201–0322 (Moscow Federation).

Zhirinovsky, Vladimir Volfovich
POSITION: Chairman of the Liberal-Democratic Party
BIRTHPLACE/DATE: Alma-Ata, 1946
NATIONALITY: Russian
EDUCATION: Graduated in 1970 from the Institute of Asian and African Countries at Moscow State University. Command of English, French, German, and Turkish.
CAREER: Head of the Law Service at Mir (World) Publishers. In 1967, entered politics. In December 1989, participated in the Founding Congress of the Liberal-Democratic Party; wrote the Party's Program and Charter. In 1991, ran for the Russian Presidency.
FAMILY: Married with a son.

ADDRESS/TELEPHONE: 3 Rybnikov Pereulok, Third Floor, Moscow. 923–6370 (office).

Zhukov, Aleksey Dmitryevich

POSITION: Board Head and Chief Secretary of the UNESCO Commission of the International Humanitarian and Cultural Cooperation Department of the USSR Foreign Ministry; Counsellor Extraordinary and Plenipotentiary, First Grade
BIRTHPLACE/DATE: Moscow, March 2, 1944
NATIONALITY: Russian
EDUCATION: Graduated from the Moscow State Institute of International Relations in 1966.
CAREER: From 1966 to 1967, Trainee at the International Economic Organizations Department of the USSR Foreign Ministry. From 1967 to 1968, Aide. From 1968 to 1969, Senior Aide. From 1970 to 1971, Third Secretary. From 1971 to 1973, Third Secretary at the USSR Embassy in Ceylon. From 1973 to 1974, Second Secretary at the USSR Embassy in Sri Lanka. From 1974 to 1975, Second Secretary of the International Economic Organizations Department. From 1975 to 1978, First Secretary. From 1978 to 1981, Deputy Secretary of the USSR Foreign Ministry Party Committee. From 1981 to 1984, Deputy Head of the International Economic Organizations Department. From 1984 to 1989, USSR Deputy Permanent Representative to the UN and Other International Organizations in Geneva. From 1989 to 1990, Deputy Chief Secretary of the USSR UNESCO Commission Secretariat. From 1990 to 1992, Chief Secretary.
HONORS/AWARDS: Order of the Badge of Honor.
FAMILY: Married with two children.
TELEPHONE: 290–0853.

Zhurakovsky, Vasily Maksimilianovich

POSITION: Russian Federation Deputy Minister of Science, Higher Education, and Technical Policy; Deputy Chairman of the Committee for Higher Education
BIRTHPLACE/DATE: Rostov-on-Don, 1940
EDUCATION: Graduated in 1962 from the Rostov Institute of Agricultural Engineering. Doctor of Technological Sciences; Professor. Speaks German and English.
CAREER: To 1982, Department Head at the Rostov Institute of Agricultural Engineering. From 1982 to 1990, Rector of the Rostov Higher Educational Establishment at the Rosselmash (Russian Agricultural Machinery) Plant. From 1990 to 1992, Deputy Chairman of the Russian Federation State Committee for Science and Higher Education.
MAJOR WORKS: Creator of more than 100 scientific inventions and scientific articles on the creation and use of wear-proof materials in mechanical engineering.
FAMILY: Married with a daughter.
ADDRESS/TELEPHONE: 51 Lyusinovskaya Street, Moscow, 113833. 237–5834 (office).

Zhuravlev, Mikhail Ivanovich

POSITION: President of the Moscow Commercial Construction Joint-Stock Bank (Mosstroibank)
BIRTHPLACE/DATE: Solikamsk, Perm region, 1934
EDUCATION: Graduated in 1959 from the Sverdlovsk Institute of National Economy. Speaks English and German.
CAREER: From 1959 to 1969, worked at the Perm City USSR Prombank (Industrial Bank). From 1969 to 1975, Head of the Perm City USSR Prombank. From 1975 and 1979, Deputy Manager of the Moscow City USSR Stroibank. From 1979 to 1989, Manager of the Moscow Region USSR Stroibank. From 1989 to 1992, Board Chairman of Mosstroibank.
FAMILY: Married with two children.
ADDRESS/TELEPHONE: 21/18 Chekhov Street, Moscow, 101443. 209–3992 (office); Fax: 299–0527.

Zhurkin, Vitaly Vladimirovich

POSITION: Director of the Institute of Europe of the Russian Academy of Sciences
BIRTHPLACE/DATE: Moscow, 1928
NATIONALITY: Russian
EDUCATION: Academician; Doctor of History; Professor.
CAREER: From 1951 to 1964, worked for the USSR State Television and Radio Broadcasting Committee; worked at *Pravda* (*Truth*) daily. From 1965 to 1968, worked at the USSR Foreign Ministry. From 1968 to 1987, worked to Deputy Director of the Institute of the U.S. and Canada. From

1987, Presidium Member of the Russian Academy of Sciences; Academician-Secretary of the International Economy and International Relations Department; member of the European Academy of Science and Art (Paris); member of SEPRE (Stokholm); Vice President of the Association of Social Sciences; Vice President of the Committee for European Security and Cooperation; Board Chairman of the Russian European Studies Association.
MAJOR WORKS: *International Conflicts* (1972); *USSR-USA: 1980* (1982); *European Dimension of Soviet Foreign Policy* (1989); *Construction of Big Europe* (1990); *Pan-European Architecture*.
HONORS/AWARDS: Order of the Red Banner of Labor; Order of the Badge of Honor; Order of the People's Friendship; USSR State Prize.
FAMILY: Married with a son.
ADDRESS/TELEPHONE: 18/3 Marx Prospekt, Moscow, 103873. 230–0070 (home); 203–7343 (office).

Zhvanetsky, Mikhail Mikhailovich
POSITION: Art Director of the Moscow Theater of Miniatures; Writer-Satirist; member of the Consultative Council of the Russian Federation Minister of Culture and Tourism; President of the World Club of Odessites (Citizens of Odessa)
BIRTHPLACE/DATE: Odessa, 1934
EDUCATION: Graduated in 1956 from the Odessa Institute of Merchant Marine Engineering.
CAREER: From 1956 to 1960, Mechanic at Odessa Port. From 1960 to 1964, Design Engineer at a designer's office in Odessa. From 1964 to 1970, Literature Section Head of the Leningrad State Theater of Miniatures headed by Arkady Raikin. From 1978, member of the USSR Writers' Union.
MAJOR WORKS: *Meetings in the Streets* (1980); *A Year for Two* (1989).
FAMILY: Divorced.
ADDRESS/TELEPHONE: 16-B Tverskaya-Yamskaya Street, Flat #7, Moscow. 250–3893; 251–5083.

Zimyatov, Nikolay Semenovich
POSITION: Coach of the Men's National Ski Team
BIRTHPLACE/DATE: Rumyantsevo village, Moscow region
NATIONALITY: Russian
CAREER: In 1978, Silver Medal winner (30-km race). In 1980, Olympic Champion (30- and 50-km races). In 1984, World Champion (30-km race). USSR National Team Coach (Central Army Sports Club).
HONORS/AWARDS: USSR Honored Master of Sports; Order of the Red Banner of Labor; Order of the People's Friendship.
FAMILY: Married with two children.
ADDRESS/TELEPHONE: 39 Leningradsky Prospekt, Moscow, 123458. 498–4355.

Zorin, Valentin Sergeyevich
POSITION: Political Analyst for Ostankino TV and Radio Broadcasting Company; Leading Researcher at the Institute of the U.S. and Canada of the Russian Academy of Sciences
BIRTHPLACE/DATE: Moscow, 1926
EDUCATION: Doctor of History; Professor.
CAREER: From 1948 to 1960, worked for USSR State TV and Radio Broadcasting. From 1960 to 1962, Deputy Editor in Chief of *Mirovaya Ekonomika i Mezhdunarodnye Otnosheniya* (*World Economy and International Relations*) magazine. From 1963 to November 1991, Political Analyst for USSR State TV and Radio Broadcasting. In November 1991, Political Analyst for Ostankino.
MAJOR WORKS: Twelve monographs on U.S. domestic and foreign policy.
HONORS/AWARDS: USSR State Prize; Russian Federation State Prize; Vorovsky Prize; Order of the October Revolution.
FAMILY: Married with a daughter.
ADDRESS/TELEPHONE: 25 Pyatnitskaya Street, Moscow, 113324. 233–6245.

Zotov, Aleksandr Ivanovich
POSITION: Ambassador to Syria; Ambassador Extraordinary and Plenipotentiary
BIRTHPLACE/DATE: Moscow, June 20, 1941
NATIONALITY: Russian
EDUCATION: Graduated from the Moscow State Institute of International Relations in 1964. Studied at Baghdad University in Iran.
CAREER: From 1964 to 1966, Trainee at the USSR Embassy in Iraq. From 1966 to 1967, Translator. From 1967 to 1968, Attaché. From 1968 to

1969, Attaché of the Middle East Department of the USSR Foreign Ministry. From 1969 to 1970, Third Secretary. From 1970 to 1971, Third Secretary at the USSR Embassy in Libya. From 1971 to 1975, Second Secretary. From 1975 to 1977, First Secretary of the Middle East Department. From 1977 to 1980, First Secretary at the USSR Embassy in the United States. From 1980 to 1985, Deputy Head of the Middle East Department. From 1986, Deputy Department Head of the Board of Middle East and South African Countries. From 1988 to 1989, Consultant to the Central Committee's International Department. From 1988 to 1989, Acting Ambassador at Large; Ambassador at Large for the Group of Ambassadors at Large of the USSR Foreign Ministry.
FAMILY: Married with two children.
TELEPHONE: 244–4013.

Zotov, Sergey Sergeyevich
POSITION: Ambassador at Large; Head of the Russian Delegation at the Latvian Negotiations; Ambassador Extraordinary and Plenipotentiary
BIRTHPLACE/DATE: Tashkent, June 26 (year unknown)
NATIONALITY: Russian
EDUCATION: Graduated from the Moscow State Institute of International Relations in 1966. Doctor of Economics.
CAREER: From 1966 to 1967, Aide at the Foreign Trade Ministry. From 1967 to 1970, Secretary of a *Humanité* Moscow Correspondent. From 1970 to 1973, Third Secretary of the First European Department of the USSR Foreign Ministry; from 1973 to 1976, Second Secretary. From 1976 to 1978, Second Secretary at the USSR Embassy in France; from 1978 to 1983, First Secretary; from 1983 to 1984, Attaché, Counsellor. From 1984 to 1986, Expert of the Foreign Policy Planning Department of the USSR Foreign Ministry. From 1986 to 1987, Senior Counsellor. From 1987 to 1990, Deputy Department Head of the European Security and Cooperation Department of the USSR Foreign Ministry. From 1990 to 1992, First Deputy Head.
HONORS/AWARDS: Medal For Labor Valor.
FAMILY: Married with a daughter.
TELEPHONE: 241–5354.

Zotov, Vladimir Borisovich
POSITION: Prefect of the Southeastern District of Moscow
BIRTHPLACE/DATE: Novo-Mikhailovskoye, Krasnodarsk region, October 26, 1946
NATIONALITY: Russian
EDUCATION: Studied at the Rostov Automobile School.
CAREER: From 1965 to 1968, served in the army. From 1968 to 1969, Engineer in Rostov-on-Don. From 1969 to 1973, Transport Test Center Head. From 1973 to 1976, Engineer of the Meliovodstroi (Melioration Water Construction) Trust. From 1976 to 1980, Shop Head of the Elektroapparat Plant. From 1980 to 1983, Head of the Rostov-on-Don Passenger Bus Company. From 1983 to 1990, Department Head; Technical Board Head of Mosgortrans (Moscow Municipal Transport). From 1990 to 1991, Chairman of the Leningrad District Council.
FAMILY: Married with a son.
ADDRESS/TELEPHONE: 10 Aviamotornaya, Moscow, 111024. 362–4288; 361–3260.

Zrelov, Petr Semenovich
POSITION: Director-General of the Dialogue Russian-American Joint Venture
BIRTHPLACE/DATE: Riga, 1947
NATIONALITY: Russian
EDUCATION: Doctor of Technical Sciences.
CAREER: In 1970, Engineer at a design bureau in Moscow; Head of the Programming Department of Stroibank (Construction Bank); Laboratory Head at a research institute; Chief Technologist; Deputy Director for economic issues of KAMAZ (Kamsky Automobile Plant). From 1987, Director-General of Dialogue; Vice President of the Russian Federation Association of Joint Ventures; Board Member of the Exporters' Association.
FAMILY: Married with two children.
ADDRESS/TELEPHONE: 13 Spartakovskaya Street, Moscow, 107066. 261–4417; 261–4407 (office).

Zvereva, Natalya Maratovna
POSITION: Professional Tennis Player
BIRTHPLACE/DATE: Minsk, 1971
NATIONALITY: Russian
CAREER: Wimbledon Champion; French and

Australian Open (pairs and doubles) Champion. In 1988, Finalist at the French Open.
HONORS/AWARDS: USSR Honored Master of Sports.
FAMILY: Single.
ADDRESS/TELEPHONE: 23 Chervyakov Street, #15, Minsk. 37–7890 (home).

Zyuganov, Gennadi Andreyevich
POSITION: Coordinating Council Chairman of the Popular Patriotic Forces
BIRTHPLACE/DATE: Mymrino village, Orlov region, 1944
NATIONALITY: Russian
EDUCATION: Doctor of Philosophy.
CAREER: In 1961, School Principal in Orlov region; served in the army. From 1976, Trade Union, Komsomol, and Party Functionary; Lecturer at the Orlov Teacher's Training Institute; First Secretary of the District Komsomol Committee, the City Komsomol Committee, and the Region Komsomol Committee. From 1974, Secretary, then Second Secretary of the Orlov Region Communist Party; Propaganda Department Head. From 1983, Instructor, Propaganda Department Head of the Central Committee. From 1989, Deputy Head of the Ideology Department of the Central Committee; member of the Politburo; Secretary of the Russian Federation Central Committee.
FAMILY: Married with two children.

Zyukin, Vladimir Mikhailovich
POSITION: President of the International Cooperation Foundation
BIRTHPLACE/DATE: Bereznyaki, Perm region, May 11, 1954
NATIONALITY: Russian
CAREER: From 1978, Komsomol Functionary in Khabarovsk region. From 1986 to 1987, First Secretary of the Khabarovsk Region Komsomol Committee. In 1987, worked for the Komsomol Central Committee. In 1989, Secretary of the Komsomol Central Committee. From April 1990 to 1991, First Secretary of the Komsomol Central Committee. From October 1991, President of the International Cooperation Foundation. To August 1991, member of the Communist Party.
HONORS/AWARDS: Medal for BAM (Baikal-Amur Highway) Construction; Medal for Labor Valor.
FAMILY: Married with a daughter.
ADDRESS/TELEPHONE: 15 Kosygin Street, Moscow. 939–8587 (office).

Appendix A

Listing by Profession or Occupation

Academician
Akayev, Askar
Basov, Nikolay Gennadyevich
Bekhtereva, Natalya Petrovna
Bogomolov, Oleg Timofeyevich
Borkovsky, Gennadi Alekseyevich
Chazov, Yevgeni Ivanovich
Chelyshev, Yevgeni Petrovich
Goldansky, Vitaly Iosifovich
Ilyichev, Victor Ivanovich
Kon, Igor Semyonovich
Kotelnikov, Vladimir Aleksandrovich
Kovalchenko, Ivan Dmitryevich
Likhachev, Dmitri Sergeyevich
Lopukhin, Yuri Mikhailovich
Makarov, Igor Mikhailovich
Maksimova, Yekaterina Sergeyevna
Nefedov, Oleg Matveyevich
Orlov, Victor Vladimirovich
Panchenko, Aleksandr Mikhailovich
Petrakov, Nikolay Yakovlevich
Petrovsky, Boris Vasilyevich
Primakov, Yevgeni Maksimovich
Prokhorov, Aleksandr Mikhailovich
Shatalin, Stanislav Sergeyevich
Skrinsky, Aleksandr Nikolayevich
Zaslavskaya, Tatyana Ivanovna

Actor
Basilashvili, Oleg Valeryanovich
Bykov, Rolan Anatolyevich
Filatov, Leonid Alekseyevich
Mikhalkov, Nikita Sergeyevich
Yankovski, Oleg Ivanovich

Actress
Miroshnichenko, Irina Petrovna

Architect
Kasim-Zade, Elbay Enver Ogly

Art Director
Goncharov, Andrey Aleksandrovich
Gordeyev, Vyacheslav Mikhailovich
Grigorovich, Yuri Nikolayevich
Lavrov, Kirill Yuryevich
Lyubimov, Yuri Petrovich
Molchanov, Vladimir Kirillovich
Pletnev, Mikhail Vasilyevich
Pluchek, Valentin Nikolayevich
Raykin, Konstantin Arkadyevich
Solomin, Yuri Mefodyevich
Spivakov, Vladimir Teodorovich
Tabakov, Oleg Pavlovich
Volchek, Galina Borisovna
Yefremov, Oleg Nikolayevich
Yeremin, Yuri Ivanovich
Zadornov, Mikhail Nikolayevich
Zakharov, Mark Anatolyevich
Zhvanetsky, Mikhail Mikhailovich

Artist
Norshtein, Yuri Borisovich
Shilov, Aleksandr Maksovich
Vasnetsov, Andrey Vladimirovich

Artistic Director
Khazanov, Gennadi Victorovich

Athlete
Gorokhova, Galina Yevgenyevna
Mamatov, Victor Fyodorovich
Rigert, David Adamovich
Salnikov, Vladimir Valeryevich
Tikhonov, Aleksandr Ivanovich
see also Olympics; Sports

Ballet
Grigorovich, Yuri Nikolayevich
Maksimova, Yekaterina Sergeyevna
Semenyaka, Lyudmila Ivanovna
Simizorova, Nina Lvovna
Vasilyev, Vladimir Victorovich

Chess
Averbakh, Yuri Lvovich
Botvinnik, Mikhail Moiseyevich
Chiburdanidze, Maya Grigoryevna
Gaprindashvili, Nonna Terentyevna
Gik, Yevgeni Yakovlevich
Karpov, Anatoli Yevgenyevich
Smyslov, Vasily Vasilyevich

Coach
Andrianov, Nikolay Yefimovich
Arkayev, Leonid Yakovlevich
Beskov, Konstantin Ivanovich
Bilozerchev, Dmitri Vladimirovich
Blokhin, Oleg Vladimirovich
Bondarchuk, Anatoli Pavlovich
Byshovets, Anatoli Fyodorovich
Davydov, Vitaly Semyoenovich
Gurzinov, Vladimir Vladimirovich
Kapitonov, Victor Arsenyevich
Kashirin, Yuri Alekseyevich
Kulakova, Galina Alekseyevna
Rodnina, Irina Konstantinovna
Tikhonov, Victor Vasilyevich
Vardanyan, Yurik Norainovich
Yurzinov, Vladimir
Vladimirovich
Zaitsev, Aleksandr Gennadyevich
Zimyatov, Nikolay Semenovich

Commentator (TV/radio)
Suntsov, Sergey Aleksandrovich

Composer
Khrennikov, Tikhon Nikolayevich
Shchedrin, Rodion Konstantinovich

Correspondent
Akhundova, Elmira Guseinovna
Grachev, Andrey Serafimovich
Granik, Irina Vadimovna
Vyzutovich, Valery Victorovich

Counsellor
to President of The International Foundation for Socio-Economic and Political Studies (Gorbachev Foundation)
Zagladin, Vadim Valentinovich

Presidium
Basov, Nikolay Gennadyevich

to Russian Federation President
Burkov, Valery Anatolyevich
Granberg, Aleksandr Grigoryevich
to Russian Federal Supreme Soviet Chairman
Chilingarov, Artur Nikolayevich
Counsellor, First Class
Berdennikov, Grigory Vitalyevich
Counsellor, First Grade
Babynin, Igor Vladimirovich
Bulay, Igor Borisovich
Gorelik, Aleksandr Semyonovich
Vinogradov, Vasily Valentinovich
Counsellor Extraordinary and Plenipotentiary
Bocharnikov, Mikhail Nikolayevich
Counsellor Extraordinary and Plenipotentiary, First Grade
Balabanov, Yuri Sevostyanovich
Biryulev, Sergey Vasilyevich
Borshchevsky, Eduard Iosifovich
Dmitryev, Andrey Victorovch
Counsellor Extraordinary and Plenipotentiary, Second Grade
Beli, Mikhail Mikhailovich

Designer
Zaitsev, Igor Andreyevich
Diplomat
Karpov, Victor Pavlovich
Zamyatin, Leonid Mitrofanovich (former)
Director (theater)
Khomsky, Pavel Osipovich
Sats, Natalya Ilyinichna
see also Film Director

Economist
Gritsenko, Nikolay Nikolayevich
Editor
Abakumov, Igor Borisovich
Burlakova, Yelena Borisovna
Editor in Chief
Abramov, Sergey Aleksandrovich
Ananyev, Anatoli Andreyevich
Andreyeva, Iren Aleksandrovna
Arifdzhanov, Rustam Mustafayevich
Atamalyev, Farkhd Mutalib Ogly
Averbakh, Yuri Lvovich
Avraamov, Dmitri Sergeyevich
Baklanov, Grigory Yakovlevich
Baklanov, Mikhail Grigoryevich (former)
Batarchuk, Boris Aleksandrovich
Belyanchikova, Yuliya Vasilyevna
Belyayev, Albert Andreyevich
Belyayev, Anatoli Aleksandrovich
Bikkenin, Nail Baryevich
Biryukov, Vadim Osipovich
Borisenkov, Yevgeni Panteleymonovich
Borovik, Artyom Genrikhovich
Bystrov, Yevgeni Ivanovich
Chervyakov, Aleksander Alekseyevich
Chikin, Valentin Vasilyevich
Chupakhin, Vladimir Leonidovich
Dementyev, Andrey Dmitryevich
Diligensky, German Germanovich
Dodolev, Yevgeni Yuryevich
Dolmatov, Vladimir Petrovich
Drozdov, Aleksandr Alekseyevich
Dushenkin, Vladimir Nikolayevich
Dzhaganova, Altynshash Kairdzhanovna
Finko, Oleg Aleksandrovich
Fomenko, Aleksander Vladimirovich
Fronin, Vladislav Aleksandrovich
Golembiovsky, Igor Nestorovich
Golenkolsky, Tankred Grigoryevich
Gorlov, Aleksandr Georgyevich
Grigoryanets, Sergey Ivanovich
Gusev, Pavel Nikolayevich
Gushin, Lev Nikitovich
Iskenderov, Akhmed Akhmedovich
Izyumov, Yuri Petrovich
Kainarskaya, Irina Yakovlevna
Kalinina, Lidiya Georgyevna
Kapitsa, Mikhail Stepanovich
Karpinsky, Len Vyacheslavovich
Khalitov, Akhmet Kharisovich
Kirpichnikov, Yuri Aleksandrovich
Korepanov, Sergey Ivanovich
Korzun, Sergey Lvovich
Krupin, Vladimir Nikolayevich
Krylov, Vasily Ivanovich
Kucher, Valery Nikolayevich
Kudryavtsev, Valery Georgyevich
Kunyayev, Stanislav Yuryevich
Kupriyanova, Anastasiya Victorovna
Lagovsky, Igor Konstantinovich
Lakshin, Vladimir Yakovlevich
Leonov, Yuri Yuryevich
Lisin, Aleksandr Ivanovich
Litvinchuk, Victor Ivanovich
Logunov, Valentin Andreyevich
Loskutov, Andrey Iosifovich
Lukasik, Yulian Stanislavovich
Malgin, Andrey Victorovich
Malinov, Aleksandr Vasilyevich
Maslennikov, Arkady Afrikanovich
Mikhalchuk, Oleg Nikolayevich
Mishcharin, Aleksandr Nikolayevich
Morozov, Sergey Nikolayevich
Muladzhanov, Shud Saidovich
Musaelyan, Gennadi Samvelovich
Novikov, Valery Lvovich
Pankov, Anatoli Semyonovich
Perov, Aleksandr Leonidovich (former)
Petrov, Rem Victorovich
Pilipenko, Yuri Vladimirovich
Pipko, Daniil Arkadyevich
Pisigin, Valery Fridrikhovich
Potapov, Aleksandr Serafimovich
Pravotorov, Vladimir Fyodorovich
Prokhanov, Aleksandr Andreyevich
Pumpyansky, Aleksandr Borisovich
Pushkarev, Victor Yakovlevich
Pyadyshev, Boris Dmitryevich
Romanyuk, Valery Yakovlevich
Safonov, Ernst Ivanovich
Seleznev, Gennadi Nikolayevich
Serkov, Igor Aleksandrovich
Shoub, Yuli Germanovich
Sokolov, Vladimir Nikolayevich
Srybnykh, Vyacheslav Mikhailovich
Starkov, Vladislav Andreyevich
Tolmachev, Gennadi Ivanovich
Tretyakov, Vitaly Toviyevich
Vladimirov, Boris Grigoryevich (former)
Volin, Vladimir Pavlovich
Yakutin, Yuri Vasilevich
Yefimov, Yevgeni Borisovich
Yenirshelov, Vladimir Petrovich
Yudaltsov, Arkady Petrovich
Zagladin, Nikita Vadimovich
Zalygin, Sergey Pavlovich
Zarechkin, Yuri Vladimirovich
Zemskov, Mikhail Aleksandrovich
Editor in Chief, Deputy
Gik, Yevgeni Yakovlevich
Setunsky, Nikolay Konstantinovich
Volovets, Sergey Aleksandrovich
Editor-Publisher
Anpilov, Victor Ivanovich
Editorial Staff

Yefimov, Nikolay Ivanovich

Engineer

Bondarev, Grigory Semyonovich

Fashion Designer

Zaitsev, Vyacheslav Mikhailovich

Film Director

Abdrashitov, Vadim Yusupovich
Adamovich, Aleksandr Mikhailovich (Ales Adamovich)
Bykov, Rolan Anatolyevich
Klimov, Yelem Germanovich
Rybin, Aleksandr Georgyevich
Smirnov, Andrey Sergeyevich
Solovyov, Sergey Aleksandrovich

Film Producer

Govorukhin, Stanislav Sergeyevich
Mikhalkov, Nikita Sergeyevich

Gymnastics

Andrianov, Nikolay Yefimovich
Arkayev, Leonid Yakovlevich
Latynina, Larisa Semyonovna
Titov, Yuri Yevlampiyevich
Turisheva, Ludmila Ivanovna

Journalist

Brumel, Valery Nikolayevich
Karyakin, Yuri Fyodorovich
Pozner, Vladimir Vladimirovich

Lawyer

Lushchikov, Sergey Gennadyevich

Literary Critic

Sokolov, Vadim Pavlovich

Military

Arkhipov, Vladimir Mikhailovich
Bizhan, Ivan Vasilyevich
Burlakov, Matvey Prokopyevich
Chechevatov, Victor Stepanovich
Chernavin, VladimirNikolayevich
Fuzhenko, Ivan Vasilyevich
Grachev, Pavel Sergeyevich
Gromov, Boris Vsevolodovich
Gromov, Feliks Nikolayevich
Ignatenko, Aleksandr Stepanovich
Ivanov, Vitaly Pavlovich
Kalinin, Nikolay Vasilyevich
Khvatov, Gennadi Aleksandrovich
Kobets, Konstantin Ivanovich
Kolesnikov, Mikhail Petrovich
Kondratyev, Georgy Grigoryevich
Kuzmin, Fyodor Mikhailovich
Lebed, Aleksandr Ivanovich
Lobov, Vladimir Nikolayevich
Lopatin, Mikhail Alekseyevich
Makashov, Albert Mikhailovich
Maksimov, Yuri Pavlovich
Mironov, Valery Ivanovich
Mironov, Vyacheslav Petrovich
Patrikeyev, Valery Anisimovich (retired)
Piyankov, Boris Yevgenyevich
Prudnikov, Victor Alekseyevich
Rodionov, Yuri Nikolayevich
Samsonov, Victor Nikolayevich
Seleznev, Sergey Pavlovich
Shaposhnikov, Yevgeni Ivanovich
Shlyaga, Nikolay Ivanovich
Shustko, Lev Sergeyevich
Sobkov, Vasily Timofeyevich
Stolyarov, Nikolay Sergeyevich
Surkov, Mikhail Semenovich
Tretyak, Ivan Moiseyevich
Varennikov, Valentin Ivanovich

Music, Musicians

Eisen, Artur Arturovich
Pletnev, Mikhail Vasilyevich
see also Opera Singer

Olympics

Borzov, Valery Filippovich
Klimova, Marina Vladimirovna
Kulakova, Galina Alekseyevna
Medved, Aleksandr Vasilyevich
Tikhonov, Aleksandr Ivanovich

Opera Singer

Arkhipova, Irina Konstantinovna
Kasrashvili, Makvala Filimonovna
Khvorostovsky, Dmitri Aleksandrovich
Nesterenko, Yevgeni Yevgenyevich
Obraztsova, Yelena Vasilyevna
Sotkilava, Zurab Lavrentyevich
Vedernikov, Aleksandr Fillippovich

Painter

Vasnetsov, Andrey Vladimirovich

Party Leader

Zamyatin, Leonid Mitrofanovich (former)

Pianist

Kisin, Yevgeni Vladimirovich
Krainev, Vladimir Vsevolodovich

Pilot-Cosmonaut

Tereshkova, Valentina Vladimirovna (former)

Playwright

Radzinsky, Edvard Stanislavovich
Rozov, Victor Sergeyevich
Shatrov (Marshak), Mikhail Filippovoch
Smirnov, Andrey Sergeyevich

Poet

Kugultinov, David Nikitovich
Oleynik, Boris Ilyich
Yevtushenko, Yevgeni Aleksandrovich

Political Analyst

Borovik, Genrikh Avyezerovich
Kondrashov, Stanislav Nikolayevich
Kravchenko, Leonid Petrovich
Latsis, Otto Rudolfovich
Novodvorskaya, Valerya Ilyinichna
Zorin, Valentin Sergeyevich

Political Director

Malashenko, Igor Yevgenyevich

Political Leader

Kashin, Vladimir Ivanovich

Politician

Gamsakhurdia, Zviad Konstantinovich
Grachev, Andrey Serafimovich
Karasev, Valentin Ivanovich
Maslyukov, Yuri Dmitryevich
Novodvorskaya, Valerya Ilyinichna

Prisoner

Lukyanov, Lanatoli Ivanovich

Producer

Filatov, Leonid Alekseyevich
Kozak, Roman Yefimovich
Mitta, Aleksandr Naumovich
Norshtein, Yuri Borisovich
Raykin, Konstantin Arkadyevich
Sats, Natalya Ilyinichna
see also Film Producer

Professor

Arnoldov, Arnold Isayevich
Basov, Nikolay Gennadyevich
Bondarchuk, Anatoli Pavlovich
Bondarev, Grigory Semyonovich
Klyuyev, Vladimir Vladimirovich
Yadov, Vladimir Aleksandrovich

Publicist

Burlatsky, Fyodor Mikhailovich
Govorukhin, Stanislav Sergeyovich
Grachev, Andrey Serafimovich
Granin, Daniil Aleksandrovich

Scriptwriter

Smirnov, Andrey Sergeyevich

Scriptwriter (*cont'd*)
Solovyov, Sergey Aleksandrovich
Sexologist
Kon, Igor Semyonovich
Sports
Kashirin, Yuri Alekseyevich
Kolesov, Anatoli Ivanovich
Kopylov, Sergey Vladimirovich
Lagutin, Boris Nikolayevich
Medved, Aleksandr Vasilyevich
Savchenko, Larisa Ivanovna
Simonyan, Nikita Pavlovich
Smetanina, Raisa Petrovna
Taranenko, Leonid Arkadyevich
Titov, Yuri Yevlampiyevich
CYCLING
Kapitonov, Victor Arsenyevich
Kopylov, Sergey Vladimirovich
Sukhoruchenkov, Sergey Nikolayevich
Yekimov, Vyacheslav Vladimirovich
FOOTBALL
Blokhin, Oleg Vladimirovich
Dasayev, Rinat Faizrakhmovich
HOCKEY
Tikhanov, Victor Vasilyevich
ICE HOCKEY
Ragulin, Aleksandr Pavlovich
Yurzinov, Vladimir Vladimirovich
SKATING
Bestemyanova, Natalya Filimonovna
Bukin, Andrey Anatolyevich
Gorshkov, Aleksandr Georgyevich
Gulyayev, Nikolay Alekseyevich
Klimova, Marina Vladimorovna
Rodnina, Irina Konstaninovna
Titova, Ludmila Yevgenyevna
Zaitsev, Aleksandr Gennadyevich
Zheleznovsky, Andrey Nikolayevich
SKIING
Kulakova, Galina Alekseyevna
Smetanina, Raisa Petrovna
Zimyatov, Nikolay Semenovich
TENNIS
Chesnokov, Andrey Eduardovich
Savchenko, Larisa Ivanovna
Zvereva, Natalya Maratovna
TRACK AND FIELD
Averina (Barabash), Tatyana Borisovna
Bondarchuk, Anatoli Pavlovich
WEIGHT LIFTING
Rigert, David Adamovich
Taranenko, Leonid Arkadyevich
Vardanyan, Yurik Norainovich
see also Gymnastics; Olympics
Sports Consultant
Tretyak, Vladislav Aleksandrovich
State Counsellor
Vorontsov, Yuli Mikhailovich
Theater
Borisov, Oleg (Albert) Ivanovich
Goncharov, Andrey Aleksandrovich
Khomsky, Pavel Osipovich
Sats, Natalya Ilinichna
Writer
Adamovich Aleksandr Mikhailovich (Ales Adamovich)
Arkanov, Arkady Mikhailovich
Bondarev, Yuri Vasilyevich
Brumel, Valery Nikolayevich
Chernichenko, Yuri Dmitryevich
Gamsakhurdia, Zviad Konstantinovich
Granin, Daniil Aleksandrovich
Iskander, Fazil Abdulovich
Korotich, Vitaly Alekseyevich
Likhanov, Albert Anatolyevich
Nagibin, Yuri Markovich
Pristavkin, Anatoli Ignatyevich
Rasputin, Valentin Grigoryevich
Rybakov, Anatoli Naumovich
Zalygin, Sergey Pavlovich
Writer-Satirist
Zadornov, Mikhail Nikolayevich
Zhvanetsky, Mikhail Mikhailovich

Appendix B

Listing by Organization or Government Affiliation

Note: For ambassadors, ministers, and other government officials, see also "Russian Federation."

A.I. Raykin Satirikon Theater
Raykin, Konstantin Arkadyevich
Academy of Arts
Maksimova, Yekaterina Sergeyevna
Academy of Labor and Social Relations
Gritsenko, Nikolay Nikolayevich
Sergeyev, Aleksey Alekseyevich
Academy of Medical Sciences
Borodin, Yuri Ivanovich
Academy of National Economy
Aganbegyan, Abel Gezevich
Academy of National Economy of the Russian Federation Government
HIGHER SCHOOL OF INTERNATIONAL BUSINESS
Yevenko, Leonid Ivanovich
Academy of Natural Sciences
Orlov, Victor Vladimirovich
Academy of Pedagogical Sciences
Likhanov, Albert Anatolyevich
Academy of Urban Environment
Glazychev, Vyacheslav Leonidovich
Aeroflot Bank
Karavdin, Victor Semyonovich
Agentstvo Economicheskikh Novostei (Economic News Agency) Joint-Stock Company
Turanov, Sergey Anatolyevich
Agrika (Agricultural) Commercial Bank
Bashayev, Ibragim Yakubovich
Air Defense Forces
Prudnikov, Victor Alekseyevich
Air Forces
Prudnikov, Victor Alekseyevich
Aircraft Builders' Society
Batkov, Aleksandr Mikhailovich
Aktiv Commercial Bank
Rotgolts, Iosif Anatolyevich
Aleksandrovsky Radiozavod (Radio Plant) Joint-Stock Association
Ovchinnikov, Vladimir Alekseyevich
All-Armenias, Chief Catholic Patriarch
Vazgen I (Paldjan Vazgen Abramovich)
All-Russia Exchange Bank
Maslennikov, Arkady Afrikanovich
All-Russia Foreign Trade Tekhnopromexport (Technical and Industrial Equipment Export) Association
Bokov, Stanislav Nikolayevich
All-Russia Grazhdanskoye Soglasiye (Civic Accord) Movement
Lipitsky, Vasily Semyonovich
All-Russia Real Estate Exchange
Avdeyev, Vadim Borisovich
All-Russia Research Institute of Film Making
Adamovich, Aleksandr Mikhailovich (Ales Adamovich)
All-Russia Selkhozpromexport (Agricultural Industry Export) Foreign Trade Association
Yeliseyev, Anatoli Aleksandrovich
All-Russia Society for the Preservation of Historical and Cultural Monuments Central Council
Polenov, Fyodor Dmitryevich
PROPAGANDA AND SOCIAL INITIATIVES CENTER
Kokunko, Georgy Valentinovich
All-Russia Society of Sociologists and Demographers
Osipov, Gennadi Vasilyevich
All-Russia Tekhnopromimport (Technical and Industrial Equipment Import) Foreign Trade Association
Boyko, Vitaly Ivanovich
All-Russia Tyazhpromexport (Heavy Industry Export) Association
Yegorov, Valery Aleksandrovich
All-Russian Fund for Progress, Human Rights, and Charity
Gdlyan, Telman Khorenovich
All-Union Bolshevik Party
Andreyeva, Nina Aleksandrovna
All-Union Civic Accord Public Organization
POLITICAL COUNCIL
Gusenov, Georgy Georgyevich
All-Union Health Improvement and Sports Foundation
Lagutin, Boris Nikolayevich
All-Union State Television and Radio Company
Kravchenko, Leonid Petrovich
Ambassador at Large
Andropov, Igor Yurevich
Bondarenko, Aleksandr Pavlovich
Bykov, Dmitri Vasilyevich
Dubinin, Yuri Vladimirovich
Kireyev, Genrikh Vasilyevich
Komplektov, Victor Georgyevich
Kovalev, Feliks Nikolayevich
Zotov, Sergey Sergeyevich

Ambassador Extraordinary and Plenipotentiary
Andropov, Igor Yuryevich
Astakhov, Yevgeni Mikhailovich
Avdeyev, Aleksandr Alekseyevich
Belonogov, AleksandrMikhailovich
Bondarenko, Aleksandr Pavlovich
Bovin, Aleksandr Yevgenyevich
Burlay, Yan Anastasyevich
Bykov, Dmitri Vasilyevich
Churkin, Vitaly Ivanovich
Derkovsky, Oleg Mikhailovich
Deryabin, Yuri Stepanovich
Dolgov, Vyacheslav Ivanovich
Drukov, Anatoli Matveyevich
Dubinin, Yuri Vladimirovich
Gerasimov, Gennadi Ivanovich
Glukhov, Aleksey Iliych
Grinevsky, Oleg Alekseyevich
Gromov, Vasily Petrovich
Gudev, Vladimir Victorovich
Gusarov, Yevgeni Petrovich
Ilyichev, Gennadi Victorovich
Ivanov, Igor Sergeyevich
Kalinin, Arnold Ivanovich
Kapralov, Yuri Semyonovich
Karlov, Yuri Yevgenyevich
Karpov, Victor Pavlovich
Kireyev, Genrikh Vasilyevich
Komplektov, Victor Georgyevich
Kovalev, Feliks Nikolayevich
Kvitsinsky, Yuli Aleksandrovich
Luchinsky, Pyotr Kirillovich
Nishanov, Rafik Nishanovich
Ostrovenko, Yevgeni Dmitriyevich
Zaitsev, Anatoli Safronovich
Zaitsev, Yuri Vladimirovich
Zelenov, Victor Matveyevich
Zemsky, Vladimir Vasilyevich
Zotov, Aleksandr Ivanovich
Zotov, Sergey Sevgeyevich
FIRST GRADE
Kadakin, Aleksander Mikhailovich
Ambassador to Angola
Kapralov, Yuri Semyonovich
Ambassador to Austria
Dolgov, Vyacheslav Ivanovich
Ambassador to Bolivia
Kiselev, Vladimir Ivanovich
Ambassador to Chad
Gumenyuk, Gennadi Vladimirovich
Ambassador to Chile
Gromov, Vasily Petrovich
Ambassador to Costa Rica
Kalmyk, Valerya Nikolayevna
Ambassador to Cuba
Kalinin, Arnold Ivanovich
Ambassador to Cyprus
Zenkov, Boris Gennadyevich
Ambassador to Ecuador
Yemelyanov, Mikhail Pavlovich
Ambassador to Finland
Deryabin, Yuri Stepanovich
Ambassador to Georgia
Zemsky, Vladimir Vasilyevich
Ambassador to Guinea-Bissau
Zelenov, Victor Matveyevich
Ambassador to India
Drukov, Anatoli Matveyevich
Ambassador to Iran
Gudev, Vladimir Victorovich
Ambassador to Lebanon
Ilyichev, Gennadi Victorovich
Ambassador to Luxembourg
Aitmatov, Chingiz Torekulovich
Ambassador to Nepal
Kadakin, Aleksander Mikhailovich
Ambassador to Seychelles
Kiselev, Sergey Borisovich
Ambassador to Slovakia
Yastrzhembski, Sergey Vladimirovich
Ambassador to Spain
Ivanov, Igor Sergeyevich
Ambassador to Sweden
Grinevsky, Oleg Alekseyevich
Ambassador to Syria
Zotov, Aleksandr Ivanovich
Ambassador to the Congo
Zaitsev, Anatoli Safronovich
Ambassador to the Republic of South Afrida
Gusarov, Yevgeni Petrovich
Ambassador to the United Arab Emirates
Derkovsky, Oleg Mikhailovich
Ambassador to Turkey
Akhmedov, Khan
Ambassador to Yemen Republic
Ivashchenko, Igor Georgyevich
Ambassador to Zaire
Ionaytis, Vladislav Vladislavovich
American-Russian Business Council
BOARD OF DIRECTORS
Makharadze, Vakhtank Vakhtangovich
Analytical Center for Presidential Social Programs
Malyshev, Nikolay Grigoryevich
Analitik (Analyst) Joint-Stock Company
Berezkin, Andrey Vladimirovich
Anti-Monopoly Exchanges Conference
Morozov, Yuri Vanentinovich
April Writers' Association
Chernichenko, Yuri Dmitryevich
Pristavkin, Anatoli Ignatyevich
Yevtushenko, Yevgeni Aleksandrovich
Archbishop of Kaunas
Sladkyavichus, Vincent
Archbishop of Novozybkov, Moscow and All Russia
Antonov, Guryan Vasilyevich (Gennadi)
Argumenty i Fakty (Arguments and Facts) weekly
Starkov, Vladislav Andreyevich
Armed Forces Academy
Kalinin, Nikolay Vasilyevich
Armenian Central Committee
Pogosyan, Stepan Karapetovich (former member)
Armenian Republic
DEFENSE MINISTER
Manukyan, Vazgen Mikaelovich
PRESIDENT
Ter-Petrosyan, Levon Akopovich
Armenian Writers' Union
Ter-Petrosyan, Levon Akopovich
Artel Joint-Stock Company
Lerner, Edvin Yuryevich
Asia and Africa Today magazine
Kapitsa, Mikhail Stepanovich
Asmoral Football Team
Beskov, Konstantin Ivanovich
Assa-Irda Azerbaijan International Agency
Vekilova, Irada Agadzavadovna
Association of Credit and Financial Enterprises (MENATEP)
Khodorkovsky, Mikhail Borisovich
Association of Orientalists and French Asian Society

Ter-Petrosyan, Levon Akopovich
Atlas of Hydrometerological Data of the World's Continents
Borisenkov, Yevgeni Panteleymonovich
Atomenergoexport (Nuclear Energy Export) Foreign Trade Association
Kozlov, Victor Vasilyevich
Aviabank
Frantskevich, Mikhail Ivanovich
Avtopromimport (Importer of Automobile Industry Products) Foreign Economic Association
Dorofeyev, Vitaly Vadimovich
AvtoVAZ (Volga Automobile Plant) Production Association
Kadannikov, Vladimir Vasilyevich
Azerbaijan First Deputy Plenipotentiary Representative to Moscow
Guseinov, Rafael Gzhagidovich
Azerbaijan Plenipotentiary Mission in Moscow
Gadziev, Fuad Nazim Ogly
Azerbaijan Republic
Gasanov, Gasan Aziz Ogly
Azerbaijan Supreme Soviet
Aliyev, Geydar Aliyevich
Kafarova, Elmira Mikhail Kyzy
Azerbaijan Writers' Union
Akhundova, Elmira Guseinovna
Aziatskaya Birzha Joint-Stock Company
Firsov, Andrey Petrovich

Baku, Chief Architect of
Kasim-Zade, Elbay Enver Ogly
Banso Legal Association
Nikitin, Andrey Vladimirovich
"Before and After Midnight" (TV program)
Molchanov, Vladimir Kirillovich
BelavtoMAZ (Byelorussian Automobile Complex) Industrial Association
Lavrinovich, Mikhail Fyodorovich
Belgosstrakh Byelorussian State Insurance Commercial Organization
Stasyuk, Pyotr Nikitovich
Beloretsk Metallurgical Complex
Kulesha, Vadim Anatolyevich
Bezopasnost (Security) Research and Industrial Center
Gunayev, Benjamin Avtolumovich
Birzhevye Vedomosti (Stock Exchange News) newspaper
Maslennikov, Arkady Afrikanovich
Biznes (Business) Commercial Tourist Joint-Stock Company
Prokhovnik, Aleksandr Borisovich
Biznes dlya Vsekh (Business for Everybody) newspaper
Romanyuk, Valery Yakovlevich
Bolshoi Academic Theater
Kasrashvili, Makvala Filimonovna
Bolshoi State Academic Theater
Lazerev, Aleksandr Nikolayevich
Maksimova, Yekaterina Sergeyevna
Semenyaka, Lyudmila Ivanovna
Bolshoi Theater
Arkhipova, Irina Konstantinovna
Eisen, Artur Arturovich
Nesterenko, Yevgeni Yevgenyevich
Obraztsova, Yelena Vasilyevna
Semizorova, Nina Lvovna
Vedernikov, Aleksandr Fillippovich
STATE ACADEMIC BALLET
Grigorovich, Yuri Nikolayevich
Brain Center
Bekhtereva, Natalya Petrovna
Brokinvestservice Company
Safaryan, Igor Anatolyevich
Bryansksotsbank (Bryansk Social Bank) Universal Commercial Bank
Sineva, Ulyana Fyodorovna
Bubka Sports Club
Bubka, Sergey Nazarovich
Bukharin Foundation
Pisigin, Valery Fridrikhovich
Burdenko Institute of Neurosurgery
Konovalov, Aleksandr Nikolayevich
Business and Banks newspaper
Korepanov, Sergey Ivanovich
Business Commercial Tourism Company
Krasikov, Aleksandr Aleksandrovich
Business Week
Krylov, Vasily Ivanovich
Butek and Rusbaltvest Joint-Stock Companies
Bocharov, Mikhail Aleksandrovich
Byelorussia, Trade Minister of
Baidak, Valentin Ivanovich
Byelorussia (Belorus), Defense Minister of
Kozlovsky, Pavel Pavlovich
Byelorussia Federation of Free- Style Wrestling
Medved, Aleksandr Vasilyevich
Byelorussia International Olympics Committee
Medved, Aleksandr Vasilyevich
Byelorussian (Belorus) Council of Ministers
Kebich, Vyacheslav Frantsevich
Byelorussian Popular Front
Pozdnyak, Zenon Stanislavovich
Byelorussian Republic Supreme Soviet
Shushkevich, Stanislav Stanislavovich
Byelorussian Supreme Soviet
Dementey, Nikolay Ivanovich
Byelorussian Union of Entrepreneurs
Maslakov, Arkady Dmitryevich
Bytbank Commercial Bank of Consumer Services Development
Dudenkov, Ivan Grigoryevich

Cardiology Research Center
Chazov, Yevgeni Ivanovich
Catholic Patriarch of All-Georgia
Ilya II (Shiolashvili, Irakly Georgyevich)
Caucasus Stock Exchange
Kadagishvili, Amiran
Center for Political Analysis
Bessmertnykh, Aleksandr Aleksandrovich
Center for the Economics of Legal Protection Association
Lerner, Edvin Yuryevich
Central Administrative District
Muzykantsky, Aleksandr Ilyich
Central Army Sports Club
Zheleznovsky, Andrey Nikolayevich

Central Asia Moslems (SADUM)
Ecclesiastical Directorate
Mukhammad, Sodyk Muhammad Yusuf
Central Block of Political Parties and Movements
Voronin, Vladimir Vasilyevich
Central Bank of Russia
Gerashchenko, Victor Vladimirovich
Central Committee
Ivashko, Vladimir Antonovich
Shenin, Oleg Semyonovich
Central Forestry Institute (CRFI)
Department of Nature Preserves and Rare Animals at Glavokhota's (Main Hunting Administration)
Dezhkin, Vadim Vasilyevich
Central Lenin Museum
Melnichenko, Vladimir Yefimovich
Centrocredit Furniture Industry Crediting and Development Commercial Bank
Gerasimov, Vladimir Nikolayevich
Chamber of Commerce
Malkevich, Vladislav Leonidovich
Channel 6 (TV company)
Sagalayev, Eduard Mikhailovich
Chechen Armed Forces
Dudayev, Dzhokhar Museyevich
Chechen Cabinet of Ministers
Dudayev, Dzhokhar Museyevich
Chechen-Ingush Republic
Gazabayev, Chahit
Chechen Republic
Dudayev, Dzhokhar Museyevich
Chechen (formerly Chechen-Ingush) University
Chakhkiyev, Bashir Akhmedovich
Chelovek i Stikhiya (Man and the Elements) collection
Borisenkov, Yevgeni Panteleymonovich
Chelyabinsk Investment and Mercantile Exchange
Freidkin, Lev Grigoryevich
Chelyabinsk Universal Exchange
Tenyakov, Eduard Veniaminovich
Chemical Industry Commercial Bank (Khimbank)
Mazayev, Ivan Sergeyevich
Chemical Physics
Burlakova, Yelena Borisovna
Chess Federation
Averbakh, Yri Lvovich
Christian-Democratic Union of Russia
Ogorodnikov, Aleksandr Iolyevich
Christian Evangelist Integrated Union
Bilas, Bronislav Ivanovich
Chteniye (Reading) Society
Nenashev, Mikhail Fydorovich
CIS Armed Forces
Piyankov, Boris Yevgenyevich
Shaposhnikov, Yevgeni Ivanovich
CIS Joint Armed Forces
Stolyarov, Nikolay Sergeyevich
CIS Commander in Chief of the Navy
Chernavin, Vladimir Nikolayevich
CIS National Figure Skating Team
Gorshkov, Aleksandr Georgyevich
CIS National Gymnastics Team
Andrianov, Nikolay Yefimovich
Arkayev, Leonid Yakovlevich
CIS National Ice Hockey Team
Yurizinov, Vladimir Vladimirovich
CIS Seventh-Day Adventists Church Council
Kulakov, Mikhail Petrovich
CIS Sports Council Secretariat
Kolesov, Anatoli Ivanovich
CIS Track and Field National Hammer-Throwing Team
Bondarchuk, Anatoli Pavlovich
CIS Unified Armed Forces
Personnel Department
Rodionov, Yuri Nikolayevich
CIS (formerly USSR) National Football Team
Byshovets, Anatoli Fyodorovich
Combined Hockey Team of the Commonwealth of Independent States
Gurzinov, Vladimir Vladimirovich
Commercial Bank of Wholesale Trade Development (Toko-Bank)
Yakunin, Viktor Konstantinovich
Commercial Industrial and Construction Joint-Stock Bank
Semyonov, Vladimir Gavrilovich
Committee for Construction, Architecture, and Municipal Housing Economy
Bulygin, Victor Vasilyevich
Committee for Health Protection
Denisenko, Bella Anatolyevna
Committee for Higher Education
Zhurakovsky, Vasily Maksimilianovich
Committee for Inter-Republican Relations, Regional Policies, and Cooperation Issues
Granberg, Aleksandr Grigoryevich
Commonwealth of Independent States Armed Forces
Samsonov, Victor Nikolayevich
Commonwealth of Independent States Joint Armed Forces
Fuzhenko, Ivan Vasilyevich
Commonwealth of Independent States (CIS) Unified Armed Forces
Strategic Forces
Maksimov, Yuri Pavlovich
Communists of Russia Faction
Rybkin, Ivan Petrovich
Confederation of Film Makers' Unions
Khudonazarov, Dovlatnazar
Confederation of Journalists' Unions
Maslennikov, Arkady Afrikanovich
Muladzhanov, Shud Saidovich
Pushkarev, Victor Yakovlevich
Confederation of Trade Unions
Bashtankyuk, Gennadi Sergeyevich
Confederation of Writers' Unions
Bondarev, Yuri Vasilyevich
Chernichenko, Yuri Dmitryevich
Kugultinov, David Nikitovich
Rzayev, Valekh Sabir Ogly
Constitutional Commission
Varov, Vladimir Konstantinovich
Vitebsky, Vitaly Yakovlevich
Constitutional Committee
Badmayev, Sanal Alekseyevich
Constitutional Democrats Party
Astafyev, Mikhail Georyevich

Cooperative Society
Morozov, Yuri Valentinovich
Council for International Cooperation in the Exploration and Use of Outer Space (Intercosmos)
Kotelnikov, Vladimir Aleksandrovich
Council of Heads of Member-States
Skokov, Yuri Vladimorovich
Council of Nationalities
Andronov, Iona Ionovich
Badmayev, Sanal Alekseyevich
Basin, Yefim Vladimirovich
Council of the Republic
Vinogradova, Irina Victorovna
Counsellor, First Grade
Kislyak, Sergey Ivanovich
Counsellor Extraordinary and Plenipotentiary
Karisin, Grigory Borisovich
First Grade
Ionaytis, Vladislav Vladislavovich
Ivashchenko, Igor Georgyevich
Kalmyk, Valerya Nikolayevna
Kiselev, Vladimir Ivanovich
Yemelyanov, Mikhail Pavlovich
Zhukov, Aleksey Dmitryevich
Second Grade
Gumenyuk, Gennadi Vladimirovich
Kenyaykin, Valery Fyodorovich
Kiselev, Sergey Borisovich
Zenkov, Boris Gennadyevich
Counsellor for Mutual Relations with International Financial Organizations
Zagalovsky, Konstantin Grigoryevich
Counsellor to Russian Federation Vice-President for Foreign Affairs
Andronov, Iona Ionovich
Counsellor to the Russian Federation President
Starovoitova, Galina Vasilyevna (former)
Credo-Bank
Agapov, Yuri Vasilyevich

Daily Glasnost newspaper
Grigoryanets, Sergey Ivanovich
Delovye Lyudi (Business People) magazine
Biryukov, Vadim Osipovich
Delovoy Mir (Business World)
Akhundova, Elmira Guseinovna
Delovye Svyazi (Business Connections) magazine
Novikov, Valery Lvovich
Demidov Foundation
Mesyats, Gennadi Andreyevich
Democratic Congress Consultative Council
Kharichev, Igor Aleksandrovich
Democratic Movement of Russia
Lipitsky, Vasily Semyonovich
Democratic Party of Russia
Travkin, Nikolay Ilyich
Democratic Party of the Smena-Novaya Politika (Rising Generation—New Politics) Faction
Muravyev, Igor Vladislavovich
Demoractic Reforms Movement
Vladislayev, Aleksandr Pavlovich
Democratic Russia Movement
Denisenko, Bella Anatolyevna
Kharichev, Igor Aleksandrovich
Zharikhin, Vladimir Leonidovich
Council of Representatives
Yakunin, Gleb Pavlovich
Demokratichesky Soyuz (Democratic-Union) Party
Novodvorskaya, Valerya Ilyinichna
Democraticheskaya Rossiya (Democratic Russia) Movement
Ignatyev, Kirill Borisovich
Demokraticheskaya Rossiya (Democratic Russia) Movement
Mashkov, Vitaly Vladimirovich
Murashev, Arkady Nikolayevich
Muzykantsky, Aleksandr Ilyich
Salye, Marina Yevgenievna
Den (Day) newspaper
Prokhanov, Aleksandr Andreyevich
Department of International Organizations and Global Problems, Board of Analysis and Prognosis
Agayev, Tofik Ogly
Department of Regional Cooperation and Economic Problems
Biryulev, Sergey Vasilyevich
Borshchevsky, Eduard Iosifovich
Department of West and South Asia
Alekseyev, Aleksandr Yuryevich
Deputy Minister of Culture
Miroshnichenko, Irina Petrovna
Deputy Minister of Justice
Gudushkin, Stanislav Markovich
Design for All
Andreyeva, Iren Aleksandrovna
Designers' Union
Andreyeva, Iren Aleksandrovna
Detektiv i Politika (Detective and Politics) magazine
Borovik, Artyom Genrikhovich
Development Twenty-First Century Commercial Bank
Romanov, Victor Anatolyevich
Dialogue Russian-American Joint Venture
Zrelov, Petr Semenovich
Dina Joint-Stock Company
Samarin, Aleksey Aleksandrovich
Domostroi (Housebuilder) weekly
Kalinina, Lidiya Georgyevna
Donskaya Birzha Joint-Stock Company (Don Stock-Exchange)
Belushkin, Valery Aleksandrovich
Dynamo Sports Club
Zaitsev, Aleksandr Gennadyevich

Ecclesiastical Directorate of Kazakhstan's Moslems
Nysanbayev, Ratbek
Ecclesiastical Directorate of Moslems of European Regions of the CIS and Siberia
Tadzhuddinov, Talgat Safich
Economic Freedom Party
Fyodorov, Svyatoslav Nikolayevich
Ekho Moskvy (Moscow Echo) Radio Station
Korzun, Sergey Lvovich
Ekonomicheskiye Nauki (Economic Sciences) magazine
Manukovsky, Andrey Borisovich
Ekonomicheskaya Svoboda (Economic Freedom) Party
Borovoy, Konstantin Natanovich
Ekonomika i Zhizn (Economics and Life) newspaper
Vladimirov, Boris Grigoyyevich
Ekonomika i Zhizn (Economy and Life) weekly newspaper
Yakutin, Yuri Vasilevich
Ekran Joint-Stock Company
Zabelin, Ilya Ilyich

Elephant Broker Company
Artamonov, Vyacheslav Yuryevich
Envoy Extraordinary and Plenipotentiary, First Class
Lavrov, Sergey Victorovich
Epicenter Economic and Political Research Center
Yavlinsky, Grigory Alekseevich
Estonian Central Committee
Sillari, Ann-Arno Augustovich
Estonian Communist Party
Vyalyas, Vaino Iosipovich
Estonian Evangelical Lutheran Church, Consistory
Payula, Kuno
Estonian Parliament
Savisaar, Edgar Elmarovich
Estonian Television
Ott, Urmas
European Foundation for Management Development (Brussels)
Manukovsky, Andrey Borisovich
Evangelical Christian-Baptist Union
Komendant, Grigory Ivanovich
Evangelical Lutheran Church of Lithuania, Consistory
Kalvanas, Ionas
Exchange Committee
Semchenko, Oleg Ivanovich
Exchange Congress
Aleinikov, Boris Nikolayevich
Exportkhleb (Bread Export) Foreign Economic Joint-Stock Company
Klimov, Oleg Aleksandrovich

Far East Military District
Chechevatov, Victor Stepanovich
Federal Information Center of Russia
Poltoranin, Mikhail Nikiforovich
Figure Skating Federation
Gorshkov, Aleksandr Georgyevich
Film and TV Center for Children and Youth
Bykov, Rolan Anatolyevich
Finance Minister (former)
Fyodorov, Boris Grigoryevich
First Deputy Chairman of the Government
Shumeyko, Vladimir Filippovich
First Exemplary Printing House
Sorokin, Anatoli Dmitryevich
Foreign Intelligence Service
Semolets, Tatyana Victorovna
Foreign Ministry
DEPARTMENT OF CENTRAL AND SOUTH AMERICA
Burlay, Yan Anastasyevich
DEPARTMENT OF INTERNATIONAL ORGANIZATIONS
Gorelik, Aleksandr Semyonovich
Foreign Policy Association
Bessmertnykh, Aleksandr Aleksandrovich
Kvitsinsky, Yuli Aleksandrovich
Fourteenth Army in Transdnyestria (Dniester River Region)
Lebed, Aleksandr Ivanovich
Free Labor Party
Eksler, Aleksey Andreyevich
Friendship Fund Between the Peoples of Central Asia and Kazakhstan
Karimov, Islam Abguganievich
Frunze Military Academy
Kuzmin, Fyodor Mikhailovich
Fund for the Social and Economic Rehabilitation of Invalids
Godunov, Andrey Vladimirovich

General Staff Academy
Pirumov, Vladimir Semyonovich
General Trade Union Confederation
Kuzmenok, Vladimir Vladimirovich
Georgia, President of
Gamsakhurdia, Zviad Konstantinovich (former)
Georgian National Olympics Committee
Gaprindashvili, Nonna Terentyevna
Geoservice
Gabrielyants, Grigory Arkadyevich
German Lutheran Church
Kalnins, Kharalds
GERMES (Joint-Stock Company and Scientific-Technological Center (STC))
Neverov, Valery Ivanovich
GERMES Trading House
Neverov, Valery Ivanovich
GERMES Tyuman-Moscow Exchange in Moscow
Neverov, Valery Ivanovich
GERMES (Hermes) Scientific- Technological Center in Tyuman
Neverov, Valery Ivanovich
Glasnost Commission of the Sverdlovsk Region Council
Mishustina, Larisa Pavlovna
Glasnost (Free Speech) newspaper
Izyumov, Yuri Petrovich
Glasnost Public Foundation
Grigoryanets, Sergey Ivanovich
Glavokhota Hunting Preserves Administration
Gabuzov, Oleg Semyonovich
Global Problems of Survival Research Center
Burlak, Vadim Nikolayevich
Golden Puck Club
Tarasov, Anatoli Vladimirovich
Gorizont (Horizon) magazine
Yefimov, Yevgeni Borisovich
Gorky Film Studio
Rybin, Aleksandr Georgyevich
Grazhdansky Soyuz (Civic Accord) Political Consultative Council
Vladislayev, Aleksandr Pavlovich
Group for Negotiations with the Big Seven
Morozov, Aleksey Mikhailovich
Guardians Board of the Grazhdanin (Citizen) Association
Nishanov, Rafik Nishanovich

Havana University
Voronov, Yuri Aleksandrovich
Herald of Christian Democracy newspaper
Ogorodnikov, Aleksandr Iolyevich
Higher Ecological Council of Russia
Khozin, Grigory Sergeyevich
Holy Patriarch of Moscow and All-Russia
Aleksei II (Aleksei Mikhailovich Ridiger)
House of Brokers
Lapshin, Mikhail Ivanovich

Igor Bobrin Theater of Skating Arts
Bestemyanova, Natalya Filimonovna
Bukin, Andrey Anatolyevich
IMA-Press Agency
Ilyin-Adaev, Kirill Olegovich
IMA-Press News Agency

Loskutov, Andrey Iosifovich
Industrial Union Faction
Ivanilov, Yuri Pavlovich
Informagentstvo Postfactum (Postfactum Information Agency) Closed Joint-Stock Association
Pavlovsky, Gleb Olegovich
Information Research Center
Babynin, Igor Vladimirovich
Infort Joint-Stock Company
Sukharev, Aleksey Grigoryevich
Ingushia State Radio and Television
Chakhkiyev, Bashir Akhmedovich
Inostrannaya Literatura (Foreign Literature) magazine
Lakshin, Vladimir Yakovlevich
Institute for Economic Problems of the Transitional Period
Mau, Vladimir Aleksandrovich
Institute for Socio-Political Studies
ANALYTICAL CENTER
Lipitsky, Vasily Semyonovich
Institute of Chemical Physics
Goldansky, Vitaly Iosofovich
Institute of Comparative Politics and Problems of the Workers' Movement
Timofeyev, Timur Timofeyevich
Institute of Foreign Economic Studies
Sitaryan, Stepan Aramaisovich
Institute of Geology, Mineralogy, and Geochemistry
Laverov, Nikolay Pavlovich
Institute of Physical Education
Tarasov, Anatoli Vladimirovich
Institute of Systems Analysis (BNIISI)
DEPARTMENT OF PHILOSOPHY AND SOCIAL PROBLEMS
Sadovsky, Vadim Nikolayevich
Institute of the Informatization of Society and the Development of Science
Rakitov, Anatoli Ilyich
Inter-Bank Financial Firm
Mironov, Vladimir Nikolayevich
Interbuk Russian-Slovak Joint Venture
Pershin, Aleksandr Maksimovich
Interdepartmental Center for Comparative Socio-Political Studies
Timofeyev, Timur Timofeyevich
Interfax Agency
Grishenko, Boris Sergeevich
POLITICAL INFORMATION DEPARTMENT
Abdullin, Renat Raisovich
Interfax Joint-Stock Company
Martynov, Andrey Vladimirovich
Interferma and Alfakor Enterprises
Makharadze, Vakhtang Vakhtangovich
Interkross Joint Venture
Zhalinsky, Vitaly Alfredovich
Internal Affairs Service
Streklov, Aleksander Aleksandrovich
Turbin, Vitaly Borisovich
International Academy of Environmental Reconstruction
Arbatov, Aleksandr Arkadyevich
International Association for Dialogue and Cooperation with the Countries of Asia and the Pacific
Dzasokhov, Aleksandr Sergeyevich
International Association of Children's Foundations
Likhanov, Albert Anatolyevich
International Association of Composers' Organizations
Khrennikov, Tikhon Nikolayevich
International Association of Enterpreneurs of Eastern Europe and Asia
Baskin, Ilya Mikhailovich
International Brokers Guild
Safaryan, Igor Anatolyevich
International Commission for Dynamical Meteorology
Borisenkov, Yevgeni Panteleymonovich
International Committee of Museums (IKOM)
Rodimtseva, Irina Aleksandrovna
International Committee of Youth Organizations
Kovylov, Aleksey Ivanovich
International Confederation of Theater Unions
Lavrov, Kirill Yuryevich
International Congress of Industrialists and Entrepreneurs
Volsky, Arkady Ivanovich
International Cooperation Foundation
Zyukin, Vladimir Mikhailovich
International Council of Bibliophiles
Nenashev, Mikhail Fydorovich
International Culture Association
Gubenko, Nikolay Nikolayevich
International Detective and Political Novel Association, Moscow Headquarters
Borovik, Artyom Genrikhovich
International Federation of Gymnastics (FIG)
Titov, Yuri Yevlampiyevich
International Foundation for Socio-Economic and Political Studies (The Gorbachev Foundation)
Brutents, Karen Nersesovich
Chernyayev, Anatoli Sergeyevich
Gorbachev, Mikhail Sergeyevich
Ostroumov, Georgy Sergeyevich
Revenko, Grigory Ivanovich
Shostakowski, Viacheslaw Nikolayevich
Yakovlev, Aleksandr Nikolayevich
Zagladin, Vadim Valentinovich
GROUP OF ADVISORS, CONSULTANTS, AND AIDES
Gusenkov, Vitaly Semyonovich
POLITICAL STUDIES CENTER
Tsipko, Aleksandr Sergeyevich
International Leaseholders' and Entrepreneurs' Union
Bunich, Pavel Grigoryevich
International Non-Governmental Union of Jurists Association
Trebkov, Andrey Adamovich
International Peace Fund Association
Karpov, Anatoli Yevgenyevich
International Scientific and Technical Cooperation
Kislyak, Sergey Ivanovich
International Theater Institute
RUSSIAN CENTER
Khazanov, Valery Gershevich
International Youth Cooperation Foundation
Tretyak, Vladislav Aleksandrovich
Interprivatizatsia International Foundation for the Promotion of Privatization and Foreign Investments
Scherbakov, Vladimir Ivanovich

Interprivatizatsia International Foundation for the Promotion of Business and Foreign Investments
Sherbakov, Vladimir Ivanovich
Inter-Republican Security Council
Bakatin, Vadim Victorovich
Intertelecom (International Telecommunications) (Joint-Stock Society)
Kudryavtsev, Gennadi Georgyevich
Inzhenernaya Gazeta (Engineering Newspaper)
Pipko, Daniil Arkadyevich
Ioffe Institute of Physics and Technology
Alferov, Zhores Ivanovich
ITAR-TASS (Information Agency)
Ignatenko, Vitaly Nikitovich
ITAR-TASS Foreign News Agency
Setunsky, Nikolay Konstantinovich
ITEX Joint-Stock Company
Grigoryev, Ivan Glebovich
"Itogi" ("Results") political program
Kiselev, Yevgeni Aleksayevich
Izvestia daily
Vyzutovich, Valery Victorovich
Isvestia (News) daily
Golembiovsky, Igor Nestorovich
Kondrashov, Stanislav Nikolayevich
Latsis, Otto Rudolfovich

Joint Ventures Association
Stroyev, Andrey Alekseyevich
Journalists' Union
Pyadyshev, Boris Dmitryevich

Kalibr Instrument Factory
Nadvikov, Aleksey Matveyevich
KAMAZ Joint-Stock Company
Bekh, Nikoley Ivanovich
Kazakh
FINANCE MINISTER
Derbisov, Erkeshbay Zaylaubayevich
KGB
Dagayev, Leonid Sergeyevich
LABOR MINISTER
Beisenov, Saiat Dusenbayevich
STATE TAX INSPECTION
Derbisov, Erkeshbay Zaylaubayevich
Kazakh Republic Writers' Union
Suleimanov, Olzhas Onarovich
Kazakh State Counsellor
Karamanov, Uzakbay Karamanovich
Kazakhstan Aelderi magazine
Dzhaganova, Altynshash Kairdzhanovna
Kazakhstan Armed Forces
Nazarbayev, Nursultan Abishevich
Kazakhstan Republic President
Nazarbayev, Nursultan Abishevich
Kazakhstanskaya Pravda (Kazakh Truth) newspaper
Srybnykh, Vyacheslav Mikhailovich
Kemerovo Regional Council of People's Deputies
Tuleyev, Aman-Geldy Moldagazyevich
Kentavr (Centaurus) magazine
Zagladin, Nikita Vadimovich
Kharkov Regional Democratic Revival of Ukraine Movement
Gubin, Dmitri Markovich
Kharkov Region New United Ukraine Organization
Gubin, Dmitri Markovich
Khozyain (Owner) newspaper
Novodvorskaya, Valerya Ilynichna
Kiev Military District
Chechevatov, Victor Stepanovich
Kiev State Institute of Physical Education
DEPARTMENT OF TRACK AND FIELD
Bondarchuk, Anatoli Pavlovich
Kirghiz Academy of Sciences
Akayev, Askar
Khirghiz Commodity and Raw Materials Exchange
Sariyev, Temir Argembayevich
Kirghiz Republic Supreme Soviet
Sherimkulov, Medetkan Sherimkulovich
Kirgistan (formerly Kirghizia) Republic
FIRST VICE PREMIER
Kuznetsov, German Serapionovich
PRESIDENT
Akayev, Askar
Kirov Dynamo Production Association in Moscow
Subachev, Victor Grigoryevich
Kniga (Book)-Business Joint-Stock Association
Nenashev, Mikhail Fydorovich
Kognito Firm
Vishnevsky, Yuri Aleksandrovich
Koltsov Biology Development Institute
Vorontsov, Nikolay Nikolayevich
Kommersant (Businessman) daily newspaper
Perov, Aleksandr Leonidovich
Komsomolskaya Pravda (Komsomol-Truth) newspaper
Fronin, Vladislav Aleksandrovich
Konsolidatsiya All-Union Confederation of Trade Unions
Lerner, Edvin Yuryevich
Konstantin Stanislavsky Drama Theater in Moscow
Kozak, Roman Yefimovich
Kontinent (Continent) provincial weekly
Pisigin, Valery Fridrikhovich
Konversbank Joint-Stock Conversion Bank
Pisemsky, Nikolay Georgyevich
Korgan Center
Anchevsky, Igor Georgyevich
Krainsk (Ukranian Republican Party)
Lukyanenko, Levko Grigoryevich
Krasnaya Zvezda (Red Star) newspaper
Chupakhin, Vladimir Leonidovich
Krasnoyarsk Region Administration
Veprev, Arkady Filimonovich
Kreditprombank (Great Industrial Bank) Commercial Bank
Tsaregorodtsev, Vladimir Ivanovich
Krestyanka (Country Woman) magazine
Kupriyanova, Anastasiya Victorovna
Krestyanskaya Tsentralnaya Birzha

(Farmers' Central Exchange) Joint-Stock Company
Baklanov, Anatoli Semyonovich
Krestyanskiye Vedomosti (Farmers' News)
Abakumov, Igor Borisovich
Kriogenika Concern
Kurtashin, Vladimir Yegorovich
Kultura (Culture) newspaper
Belyayev, Albert Andreyevich
Kuranty (Chiming Clock) newspaper
Pankov, Anatoli Semyonovich
Kurchatov Institute
Velikhov, Yevgeni Pavlovich
Kuznetsov Naval Academy
Ivanov, Vitaly Pavlovich

Land Forces, Commander of
Varennikov, Valentin Ivanovich
Latvian Central Committee
Rubiks, Alfred Petrovich
Latvian Council of Ministers
Godmanis, Ivars Teodorovich
Latvian Democratic Labor Party
Kezbers, Ivars Yanovich
Latvian Government Security Council
Gorbunov, Anatoli Valeryanovich
Latvian Supreme Soviet
Gorbunov, Anatoli Valeryanovich
Lebedev Physics Institute
QUANTUM RADIO-PHYSICS DEPARTMENT
Basov, Nikolay Gennadyevich
Left-Center Faction
Ivanov, Sergey Nikolayevich
Mashkov, Vitaly Vladimirovich
Mishustina, Larisa Pavlovna
Left-Center Parliamentary Faction
Basin, Yefim Vladimirovich
Lenexpo Foreign Economic Exhibition Association
Alekseyev, Sergey Pavlovich
Leningrad District Communist Party
Gidaspov, Boris Veniaminovich
Leningrad Gorky Academic Drama Theater
Lavrov, Kirill Yuryevich
Leningrad Popular Front
Salye, Marina Yevgenievna
Leningradsky Military District
Seleznev, Sergey Pavlovich
Lenregionbank
Kovalev, Yuri Nikolayevich
Liberal-Democratic Party
Zhebrovsky, Stanislav Mikhailovich
Zhirinovsky, Vladimir Volfovich
CENTRAL COMMITTEE
Khalitov, Akhmet Kharisovich
Liberal magazine
Khalitov, Akhmet Kharisovich
Literaturnaya Gazeta (Literary Newspaper)
Akhundova, Elmira Guseinovna
Yudaltsov, Arkady Petrovich
Literaturnaya Rossiya newspaper
Safonov, Ernst Ivanovich
Lithuanian Central Committee
Burokiavicius, Mikolas Martinovich
Lithuanian Prime Minister
Vagnorius, Gediminas
Lithuanian Republic Supreme Soviet
Stankyavichus, Cheslovas
Lithuanian Seim (Parliament)
Landsbergis, Vitautas

M Studio (International Programs and Video-Exchange) of Ostankino Television
Lyubimov, Aleksandr Mikhailovich
Maly Theater
Solomin, Yuri Mefodyevich
Marketing and Foreign Trade Center
Bobrik, Vladimir Ilyich
Mayakovsky Theater in Moscow
Goncharov, Andrey Aleksandrovich
Medasko Medical Insurance Company
Leleko, Valery Vladimirovich
Megapolis-Continent newspaper
Lukasik, Yulian Stanislavovich
Megapolis-Express newspaper
Volin, Vladimir Pavlovich
Megapolis international magazine
Bystrov, Yevgeni Ivanovich
Megapolis-Metro newspaper
Arifdzhanov, Rustam Mustafayevich
MENATEP Commercial Innovation Bank
Lebedev, Platon Leonidovich
Men's National Ski Team
Zimyatov, Nikolay Semenovich
Metelitsa (Snowstorm) Expedition Club
Titova, Ludmila Yevgenyevna
Metropolitan of Kharkov and Bogodukhovsk
Nikodim (Rusnak Nikodim Stepanovich)
Metropolitan of Kiev and All Ukraine
Vladimir (Sabodan, Victor Markianovich)
Metropolitan of Krutitsi and Kolomna
Guvenaly, Projarkov Vladimir Kirillovich
Metropolitan of Leningrad and Ladoga
Snychev, Ivan Matveyevich (Ioann)
Metropolitan of Minsk and Slutsk
Filaret (Vakhromeyev Kirill Varfolomeyevich)
Metropolitan of Odessa and Kherson
Agafangel (Savvin Aleksey Mikhailovich)
Metropolitan of St. Petersburg and Ladoga
Ioann Snychev, Ivan Matveyevich
Metropolitan of Smolensk and Kalingrad
Kirill (Gundyayev, Vladimir Mikhailovich)
Metropolitan of Stavropol and Baku
Dokukin, Aleksandr Nikolayevich (Gedeon)
Metropolitan of Tula and Belev
Fadayev, Nikolay Sergeyevich (Serapion)
Metropolitan of Tula and Belevsk
Serapion, Fadayev Nikolay Sergeyevich
Metropolitan of Volokolamsk and Yuryevsk
Pitirim (Nechayev Konstantin Vladimirovich)
Metropolitan of Voronezh and Lipetsk
Mefody (Nemtsov, Nikolay Fyodorovich)
Mezhdunarodnaya Zhizn (International Affairs) magazine
Pyadyshev, Boris Dmitryevich

Mikrokhirurgiya Glaza (Eye Microsurgery Institute) Scientific and Technological Complex
Fyodorov, Svyatoslav Nikolayevich
Military Experts Group
Piyankov, Boris Yevgenyevich
Militia
Kalinin, Yuri Ivanovich
Kulikov, Aleksandr Nikolayevich
Miloserdiye i Kultura (Charity and Culture) Association
Zaslavsky, Ilya Iosifovich
Ministry of Foreign Affairs
DEPARTMENT OF ASIA AND THE PACIFIC
Beli, Mikhail Mikhailovich
Minsk State Enterprises Association
Lavrinovich, Mikhail Fyodorovich
Minsk Union of Small Enterprises and Entrepreneurs
Maslakov, Arkady Dmitryevich
Minsk Watch Factory
Abramchik, Vladimir Vasilyevich
MFK Inter-Regional Cooperative Federation
Pisigin, Valery Fridrikhovich
Modus Vivendi International
Yefimov, Nikolay Ivanovich
Moldava (Moldavia) Republic
Snegur, Mircha Ion
Moldava Republic Parliament
Luchinsky, Pyotr Kirillovich
Moldavian Republic Prime Minister
Muravsky, Valery Tudor
Moldavian Republic Supreme Soviet
Moshanu, Aleksandr Konstantinovich
Moldovan Popular Front Council
Roshka, Yuri Ivanovich
Molniya (Lightning) newspaper
Anpilov, Victor Ivanovich
Molodaya Rossiya (Young Russia) Union
Glinsky (Vasilyev), Dmitri Yuryevich
"Moment of Truth" TV show
Karaulov, Andrey Victorovich
Mono Variety Show Company
Khazanov, Gennadi Victorovich
Montazhspetsstroi (Specialized Construction) Joint-Stock Corporation
Mikhalchenko, Aleksandr Ivanovich
Morbank Merchant Marine Joint-Stock Bank
Kapinos, Vladimir Aleksandrovich
Moscow
EASTERN DISTRICT PREFECT
Yulyanov, Boris Vasilyevich
NORTHEASTERN ADMINISTRATIVE DISTRICT
Sister, Vladimir Grigoryevich
NORTHERN PREFECTURE
Demin, Mikhail Timofeyevich
SOUTHEASTERN DISTRICT PREFECT
Zotov, Vladimir Borisovich
SOUTHERN DISTRICT
Tolkachev, Oleg Mikhailovich
Moscow, Mayor of
Luzhkov, Yuri Mikhailovich
FIRST DEPUTY TO
Burlayev, Konstantin Eduardovich
PLENIPOTENTIARY REPRESENTATIVE
Zaslavsky, Ilya Iosifovich
Moscow Academic Art Theater
Yefremov, Oleg Nikolayevich
Moscow Academic Satire Theater
Pluchek, Valentin Nikolayevich
Moscow and Republican Demokraticheskaya Rossiya (Democratic Russia) Movement
Proshechkin, Yevgeni Victorovich
Moscow Anti-Fascist Center
Krazman, Denis Leonidovich
Proshechkin, Yevgeni Victorovich
Moscow Architectural Institute
Kudryavtsev, Aleksandr Petrovich
Moscow Bank of Science and Technology Development (Tekhnobank)
Tosunyan, Garegin Ashotovich
Moscow Banking Union's Auditing Commission
Chudnovsky, Grigory Aleksandrovich
Moscow Bolshoi Academic Theater
Sotkilava, Zurab Lavrentyevich
Moscow Brokers Guild
Lapshin, Mikhail Ivanovich
Moscow Business Cooperation Center
Volodchenko, Gannadi Anatolyevich
Moscow Central Stock Exchange
Pankin, Vyatcheslav Vladimirovich
Moscow Choral Synagogue
Shayevich, Adolf Solomonovich
Moscow City, Southwestern Region
PREFECT
Pritula, Yuri Nikolayevich
Moscow City Communist Party
Profofyev, Yuri Anatolyevich
Moscow City Council of People's Deputies
Gonchar, Nikolay Nikolayevich
Moscow City Department of Engineering Provision
Matrosov, Aleksandr Sergeyevich
Moscow City Government
Saprykin, Pyotr Vasilyevich
Moscow City Union of State Scientific-Industrial Enterprises
Mikhailov, Nikolay Vasilyevich
Moscow Commercial Bank for Social Development (Glavmosstroibank)
Dronov, Vitaly Yakovlevich
Moscow Commercial Construction Joint-Stock Bank (Mosstroibank)
Zhuralev, Mikhail Ivanovich
Moscow Conservatory
Krainev, Vladimir Vsevolodovich
Moscow Cossacks Society
Kokunko, Georgy Valentinovich
Moscow Council
Malgin, Andrey Victorovich
Osovtsov, Aleksandr Avraamovich
Moscow Council Deputy
Osovtsov, Aleksandr Avraamovich
Moscow Council of People's Deputies
Pankov, Anatoli Semyonovich
Moscow Democratic Russia Movement
COMMISSION ON PROBLEMS OF LIAISON WITH SERVICEMEN AND LAW-ENFORCEMENT BODIES
Krazman, Denis Leonidovich
Moscow Dynamo Hockey Team
Davydov, Vitaly Semyoenovich
Gurzinov, Vladimir Vladimirovich
Yurzinov, Vladimir Vladimirovich

Moscow Ecclesiastical Academy
Aleksei II (Aleksei Mikhailovich Ridiger)
Moscow Frezer Instrument Industrial Association
Pastchenko, Vladimir Lvovich
Moscow General Assembly
Yakovlev, Aleksandr Nikolayevich
Moscow Government
Andreyev, Yuri Emanuilovich (former)
Braginsky, Aleksandr Pavlovich
Gusev, Pavel Nikolayevich
Korobchenko, Victor Alekseyevich
Korostelev, Yuri Victorovich
Matrosov, Aleksandr Sergeyevich
Muzykantsky, Aleksandr Ilyich
Nikolsky, Boris Vasilyevich
Resin, Vladimir Iosifovich
Economic Reforms Department
Buravlev, Konstantin Eduardovich
Moscow Government Glavsnag (Central Directorate of Supplies)
Popov, Oleg Georgyevich
Moscow House of Fashion
Zaitsev, Vyacheslav Mikhailovich
Moscow Innovation Commercial Bank (Incombank)
Vinogradov, Vladimir Victorovich
Moscow Innovation Joint-Stock Bank
Grebnev, Aleksandr Danilovich
Moscow Institute of Chemical Industry
Mazayev, Ivan Sergeyevich
Moscow Institute of Commerce
Zhabotinsky, Leonid Ivanovich
Moscow Institute of Engineering and Physics
Basov, Nikolay Gennadyevich
Belyaev, Vladimir Nikitovich
Moscow Institue of Printing
Vasnetsov, Andrey Vladimirovich
Moscow Investment Fund Joint-Stock Company
Mityayev, Ivan Ivanovich
Moscow Izdat-Bank Commercial Publishing Bank
Kulikov, Valeryan Nikolayevich
Moscow Joint Ventures Association
Stroyev, Andrey Alekseyevich
Moscow Kremlin State Historic and Cultural Preserve
Rodimtseva, Irina Aleksandrovna
Moscow Lenin Komsomol Theater
Yankovski, Oleg Ivanovich
Moscow Lenkom Theater
Zakharov, Mark Anatolyevich
Moscow magazine
Musaelyan, Gennadi Samvelovich
Moscow Main Internal Affairs Directorate (City Police)
Murashev, Arkady Nikolayevich
Moscow Mayor's Administration
Bakirov, Ernest Aleksandrovich
Moscow N.E. Bauman Technical University
Bondarev, Grigory Semyonovich
Moscow News
Grachev, Andrey Serafimovich
Moscow News weekly
Karpinsky, Len Vyacheslavovich
Moscow Offset Print Joint Venture
Novikov, Valery Lvovich
Moscow Patriarchy
Pitirim (Nechayev Konstantin Vladimirovich)
Vladimir (Sabodan, Victor Markianovich)
Foreign Relations Department
Kirill (Gundyayev, Vladimir Mikhailovich)
Moscow Pushkin Theater
Miroshnichenko, Irina Petrovna
Moscow Region Shakhovsky District
Travkin, Nikolay Ilyich
Moscow Russian Ballet State Theater
Gordeyev, Vyacheslav Mikhailovich
Moscow Spectr (Spectrum) Research Industrial Association
Klyuyev, Vladimir Vladimirovich
Moscow State Academic Theater for Children
Sats, Natalya Ilyinichna
Moscow State Chamber Orchestra
Virtuosy Moskvy (Moscow Virtuosos)
Spivakov, Vladimir Teodorovich
Moscow State Institute of Culture
Department of Theory and the History of Culture
Arnoldov, Arnold Isayevich
Moscow State Institute of International Relations
International Business School
Manukovsky, Andrey Borisovich
State Law Department
Ilyinsky, Igor Pavlovich
Moscow State University
Averina (Barabash), Tatyana Borisovna
Perelet, Renat Alekseyevich
Sadovnichi, Victor Antonovich
Sukharev, Aleksey Grigoryevich
Geography Department, Political Geography Laboratory
Berezkin, Andrey Vladimirovich
Moscow Tabakov Theater
Tabakov, Oleg Pavlovich
Moscow Taganka Theater of Drama and Comedy
Lyubimov, Yuri Petrovich
Moscow Theater of Miniatures
Zhvanetsky, Mikhail Mikhailovich
Moscow Trade and Industry Department
Gorodinsky, Mikhail Lvovich
Moscow Union of Businessmen
Shchekochikin, Victor Vladimirovich
Moscow Vice Mayor, Advisor to
Katushev, Konstantin Fyodorovich
Moscow Zoo
Spitsyn, Vladimir Vladimirovich
Mosfilm Studio
Mitta, Aleksandr Naumovich
Moskovskaya Pravda (Moscow Truth) newspaper
Muladzhanov, Shud Saidovich
Moskovskaya Pravda Joint-Stock Company
Muladzhanov, Shud Saidovich
Moskovsky Komsomolets (Moscow Komsomol Member) newspaper
Gusev, Pavel Nikolayevich
Moskovsky Podshipnik (First State Bearing Plant) Joint-Stock Association
Nosov, Valery Borisovich
Moskva (Moscow) magazine
Krupin, Vladimir Nikolayevich
Mossoviet (Moscow Council)
Lipitsky, Vasily Semyonovich
Deputy Chairman

Mossoviet (*cont'd*)
Sedykh-Bondarenko, Yuri Petrovich
Mossoviet Theater
Khomsky, Pavel Osipovich
Mufti
Gazabayev, Chahit
Nysanbayev, Ratbek
Tadzhuddinov, Talgat Safich

Nakhichevan Republic Medjalis (Parliament)
Aliyev, Geydar Aliyevich
Narodnaya Gazeta (People's Newspaper)
Mikhalchuk, Oleg Nikolayevich
Nash Sovremennik (Our Contemporary) magazine
Kunyayev, Stanislav Yuryevich
Nashe Naslediye (Our Heritage) magazine
Yenirshelov, Vladimir Petrovich
National Christian-Democratic Front of Moldavia
Druk, Mircha George
National Salvation Front
Alksnis, Victor Imantovich
National Ski-Racing Team
Kulakova, Galina Alekseyevna
Nauka i Biznes (Science and Business) weekly
Malinov, Aleksandr Vasilyevich
Nauka i Religiya (Science and Religion) magazine
Pravotorov, Vladimir Fyodorovich
Nauka i Zhizn (Science and Life) magazine
Lagovsky, Igor Konstantinovich
Nauka v Rossii (Science in Russia) magazine
Petrov, Rem Victorovich
Navy
Ivanov, Vitaly Pavlovich
Nedelya (Week) newspaper
Serkov, Igor Aleksandrovich
Neva-Credit-Bank
Griko, Nikolay Petrovich
Nezavissimaya Gazeta (Independent Newspaper)
Tretyakov, Vitaly Toviyevich
Nizhny-Volzhskaya Mercantile and Raw Material Exchange Joint-Stock Company
Grigoryev, Ivan Glebovich
North-Caucasus Military Region
Shustko, Lev Sergeyevich
North Ossetian People's Deputy
Kozayev, Valery Kuzmich
North Ossetian Prosecutor, First Deputy
Kozayev, Valery Kuzmich
North Ossetian Supreme Soviet
Galazov, Akhsarbek Khadzimurzayevich
Novaya Rossiya (New Russia) magazine
Mishcharin, Aleksandr Nikolayevich
Novaya Rossiya (New Russia) Party
Glinsky (Vasilyev), Dmitri Yuryevich
Novgorod Region Council of People's Deputies
Grazhdankin, Nikolay Ivanovich
Novosti Information Agency
Vlasov, Albert Ivanovich
Novoye Vremya (New Time) magazine
Pumpyansky, Aleksandr Borisovich
Novy Mir (New World) magazine
Zalygin, Sergey Pavlovich
Novy Svet–500 (New World–500) Foundation
Nishanov, Rafik Nishanovich
Novy Vzglyad Joint-Stock Company
Dodolev, Yevgeni Yuryevich
Novy Vzglyad (New Outlook) newspaper
Dodolev, Yevgeni Yuryevich

***Ogonyet* (*Beacon*) weekly**
Gushin, Lev Nikitovich
***Oktyabr* (*October*) magazine**
Ananyev, Anatoli Andreyevich
Old Orthodox Archdiocese
Antonov, Guryan Vasilyevich (Gennadi)
Oleg Borisov Private Theatrical Company
Borisov, Oleg (Albert) Ivanovich
Olimp (firm)
Salnikov, Vladimir Valyerevich
Olympics
Kashirin, Yuri Alekseyevich
Salnikov, Vladimir Valeryevich
Smetanina, Raisa Petrovna
Sukhoruchenko, Sergey Nikolayevich
Titov, Yuri Yevlampiyevich
Titova, Ludmila Yevgenyevna
Turisheva, Ludmila Ivanovna
Vardanyan, Yurik Norainovich
Vasin, Vladimir Alekseyevich
Yekimov, Vyacheslav Vladimirovich
Yurizinov, Vladimir Vladimirovich
Zaitsev, Aleksandr GennadyevichZimyatov, Nikolay Semenovich
Olympikos Football Club (Greece)
Blokhin, Oleg Vladimirovich
Omega Company
Melnikov, Igor Ivanovich
Optimum Commercial Bank
Chudnovsky, Grigory Aleksandrovich
Orbita Commercial Bank
Klimov, Fyodor Matveyevich
***Oriental Express* magazine**
Atamalyev, Farkhd Mutalib Ogly
Orlan Universal Stock Center
Berketov, Saparbek Sultanovich
Ostankino ITA Novosti (News) Television and Radio Company
Suntsov, Sergey Aleksandrovich
Ostankino State Television and Radio Company
Fesunenko, Igor Sergeyevich
Ostankino Television and Radio Company
Malashenko, Igor Yevgenyevich
Ostankino TV and Radio Broadcasting Company
Borovik, Genrikh Avyezerovich
Ignatyev, Kirill Borisovich
Zorin, Valentin Sergeyevich
TELEVISION NEWS AGENCY
Medvedev, Sergey Konstantinovich
Otchizna (Fatherland) Faction

Polozkov, Ivan Kuzmich
Pacific Oceanology Institute
Ilyichev, Victor Ivanovich
Pal Inform Business News Agency
Granik, Irina Vadimovna
Pamyat (Memory) National Patriotic Front
Vasilyev, Dmitri Dmitryevich

Parfumflakon (Perfume Bottle) Joint-Stock Company
Gasinsky, Grigory Yakovlevich
Parliamentary Reform Coalition
Bondarev, Grigory Semyonovich
Patriarch's Exarch of Byelorussia
Filaret (Vakhromeyev Kirill Varfolomeyevich)
***Patriot* newspaper**
Zemskov, Mikhail Aleksandrovich
Peace and Accord World Federation
Borovik, Genrikh Avyezerovich
Peasant Academic University in Luga
Voronov, Yuri Aleksandrovich
Peasants' Party of Russia
Chernichenko, Yuri Dmitryevich
Pekin Hotel Complex
Sakharov, Eduard Victorovich
Penza Mercantile Exchange
Aleinikov, Boris Nikolayevich
People's Deputy
Yarin, Venyamin Aleksandrovich (former)
People's Party of Russia
Gdlyan, Telman Khorenovich
Perestroika Joint Venture
Stroyev, Andrey Alekseyevich
Permanent Commission on Social Policy
Osovtsov, Aleksandr Avraamovich
Permanent Representative of International Organizations in Vienna
Zaitsev, Yuri Vladimirovich
PetroSoviet (St. Petersburg Council)
Boltyansky, Andrey Vladimirovich
Petrovod International Joint-Venture, Ltd.
Godunov, Andrey Vladimirovich
Petrovskaya Academy of Arts and Sciences
Borisenkov, Yevgeni Panteleymonovich
Petrovsky Academy
Voronov, Yuri Aleksandrovich
Petrovsky Commercial Bank
Golovin, Yuri Victorovich
PI-fond (Investment and Progress)
Bossert, Victor Davidovich
***Poisk* (*Search*) newspaper**
Gik, Yevgeni Yakovlevich
Politburo
Aliyev, Geydar Aliyevich
Ivashko, Vladimir Antonovich
Kashin, Vladimir Ivanovich
Ligachev, Yegor Kuzmich
Pogosyan, Stepan Karapetovich
Prokofyev, Yuri Anatolyevich
Shenin, Oleg Semyonovich
Silkova, Nina Prokopyevna
Sillari, Ann-Arno Augustovich
Surkov, Mikhail Semenovich
"Political Kitchen" TV program
Vyzutovich, Valery Victorovich
***Politika* (*Politics*) newspaper**
Fomenko, Aleksander Vladimirovich
Popular Patriotic Forces
Zyuganov, Gennadi Andreyevich
Power and Mechanical Engineering Joint-Stock Bank (St. Petersburg)
Bykov, Andrey Valeryanovich
***Provda* (*Truth*) newspaper**
Seleznev, Gennadi Nikolayevich
Presidential Consultative Council (PKS)
Pisigin, Valery Fridrikhovich
Popov, Gavril Kharitonovich
Sobchak, Anatoli Aleksandroviich
Volkogonov, Dmitri Antonovich
Zakharov, Mark Anatolyevich
President's Consultative State Council
Burbulis, Gennadi Eduardovich
President's Consultative Council
Ryzhov, Yuri Alekseyevich
President's Political Consultative Council
Bogomolov, Oleg Timofeyevich
Bunich, Pavel Grigoryevich
Pridnestrovsky Moldavian (Moldovan) Republic
Smirnov, Igor Nikolayevich
Pridnestrovye (Dniester River) Region Peace Negotiations
Komplektov, Victor Georgyevich
Prikavpatsky Military District
Sobkov, Vasily Timofeyevich
Prio-Vneshtorgbank (Foreign Trade Bank)
Mazayev, Vladimir Aleksandrovich
Privatbank in Grozny
Magomadov, Vakha Denisovich
Prodintorg Foreign Trade Association
Krivenko, Aleksandr Konstantinovich
Progress Independent TV
Molchanov, Vladimir Kirillovich
***Prolog* (*Prologue*) newspaper**
Batarchuk, Boris Aleksandrovich
Prometey International Charity Association
Gunayev, Banjamin Avtolumovich
Prominter Firm (International Industry)
Lukinsky, Vladimir Ivanovich
Promstroibank Joint-Stock Industrial Construction Bank
Dubenitsky, Yakov Nikolayevich
Promsyryoimport (Industrial Raw Materials Import) Foreign Trade Association
Smirnov, Oleg Mikhailovich
***Proster* (*Space*) literary magazine**
Tolmachev, Gennadi Ivanovich
Public Relations Agency Consortium
Krivonogov, Sergey Olegovich
Yuvarov, Arnold Vitalyevich
Public Relations Joint-Stock Company
Ganin, Vladimir Aleksandrovich
Pushkin Drama Theater in Moscow
Yeremin, Yuri Ivanovich

Quant International Joint Venture
Begalov, Yuli Vladimirovich

Rabochaya Rossiya (Working Russia) Movement
Sergeyev, Aleksey Alekseyevich
***Rabochy* (*Worker*) newspaper**
Leonov, Yuri Yuryevich
Radical Democrats Faction
Denisenko, Bella Anatolyevna
***Radiobiology* magazine**
Burlakova, Yelena Borisovna
Radiocomplex Corporation
Shimko, Vladimir Ivanovich
Raduga (Rainbow) Design Bureau
Seleznev, Igor Sergeyevich
Raznoimport (Various Import)
All-Russia Foreign Economic Association
Semin, Vyacheslav Nikolayevich
Reform Coalition
Ivanilov, Yuri Pavlovich

Reforma (Reform) Foundation
Shatalin, Stanislav Sergeyevich
Republican and Social-Democratic Parliamentary Faction
Bondarev, Grigory Semyonovich
Republican Humanitarian Party
Bokan, Yuri Ivanovich
Bolgarin, Gennadi Romanovich
Republican Party
Bondarev, Grigory Semyonovich
Research and Design Institute of Power Engineering
Orlov, Victor Vladimirovich
Research Institute of Economics, Planning, and Management of the Aviation Industry
Isayev, Aleksandr Sergeyevich
Revival of Russia
SOCIAL DEVELOPMENT FOUNDATION, CULTURE AND ART ASSOCIATION
Askerov, Eldar Aga-Yusuf Ogly
***Rodina* (*Motherland*) magazine**
Volovets, Sergey Aleksandrovich
Rosagropromstroi Russian Agricultural Construction Joint-Stock Corporation
Trubin, Nikolay Semyonovich
Rosbiznesbank Russian Commercial Bank
Repchenko, Nikolay Mikhailovich
Rosbumaga Exchange
Kudinov, Oleg Petrovich
Rosbumaga (Russian Paper) Investment Company
Kudinov, Oleg Petrovich
Roscomagentstvo Russian Commercial Agency
Lukinsky, Vladimir Ivanovich
Rosika Russian Information Commercial Agency
Ruban, Galina Alekseyevna
Rosinterbank (Russian International Bank)
Belousenko, Grigory Fyodorovich
Roskomagentstvo
Khaliulin, Vakhit Khadiyevich
Smirnov, Vyacheslav Vladimirovich
Roskomagentstvo Russian Commercial Agency
Prasolov, Oleg Fyodorovich
***Rossiya* (*Russia*)**
Drozdov, Aleksandr Alekseyevich
Rossiya Parliamentary Faction
Baburin, Sergey Nikolayevich
Rossiya (Russian) Association of Joint-Stock Commercial Industrial and Construction Bank
Tsaregorodtsev, Vladimir Ivanovich
***Rossiyskaya Gazeta* (*Russian Newspaper*)**
Logunov, Valentin Andreyevich
Rossiyskaya Tovarno-Syryevaya Birzha (Russian Mercantile Exchange) Joint Stock Company
Vlasov, Aleksey Feliksovich
***Rossiyskiye Vesti* (*Russian News*) newspaper**
Kucher, Valery Nikolayevich
Rostov-on-Don Institute of Railway Engineers, Economic Theory Division
Bratishchev, Igor Mikhailovich
Rus Professional Cycling Team
Kapitonov, Victor Arsenyevich
Russia-India Society
Chelyshev, Yevgeni Petrovich
Russian Academy of Arts
Pyadyshev, Boris Dmitryevich
Vasnetsov, Andrey Vladimirovich
Russian Academy of Medical Sciences
Chazov, Yevgeni Ivanovich
Doletsky, Stanislav Yakovlevich
Russian Academy of Natural Sciences
GEOPOLITICS AND SECURITY SECTION
Pirumov, Vladimir Semyonovich
Russian Academy of Pedagogical Sciences
Kon, Igor Semyonovich
Russian Academy of Sciences
Aganbegyan, Abel Gezevich
Basov, Nikolay Gennadyevich
Bakhtereva, Natalya Petrovna
Borkovsky, Gennadi Alekseyevich
Bunich, Pavel Grigoryevich
Chazov, Yevgeni Ivanovich
Chelyshev, Yevgeni Petrovich
Frolov, Konstantin Vasilyevich
Gidaspov, Boris Vaniaminovich
Goldansky, Vitaly Iosifovich
Gromyko, Anatoli Andreyevich
Ilyichev, Victor Ivanovich
Karyakin, Yuri Fyodorovich
Kasyanenko, Vasily Ignatyevich
Koptyug, Valentin Afanasyevich
Kotelnikov, Vladimir Aleksandrovich
Laverov, Nikolay Pavlovich
Likhachev, Dmitri Sergeyevich
Logunov, Anatoli Alekseyevich
Lopukhin, Yuri Mikhailovich
Makarov, Igor Mikhailovich
Malei, Mikhail Dmitryevich
Malyshev, Nikolay Grigoryevich
Mesyats, Gennadi Andreyevich
Nefedov, Oleg Matveyevich
Panchenko, Aleksandr Mikhailovich
Petrov, Rem Victorovich
Petrovsky, Boris Vasilyevich
Primakov, Yevgeni Maksimovich
Shatalin, Stanislav Sergeyevich
Velikhov, Yevgeni Pavlovich
Vorontsov, Nikolay Nikolayevich
Zaslavskaya, Tatyana Ivanovna
CLINICAL AND EXPERIMENTAL LYMPHOLOGY RESEARCH INSTITUTE
Borodin, Yuri Ivanovich
COMMISSION FOR THE STUDY OF PRODUCTION FORCES AND NATURAL RESOURCES
Arbatov, Aleksandr Arkadyevich
COMMISSION ON PRODUCTION FORCES AND NATURAL RESOURCES
Lemeshev, Mikhail Yakovlevich
COMPUTER CENTER
Moiseyev, Nikita Nikolayevich
COMPUTING MATHEMATICS INSTITUTE
Marchuk, Guri Ivanovich
GORKY INSTITUTE OF WORLD LITERATURE, ANCIENT LITERATURE DEPARTMENT
Averintsev, Sergey Sergeyevich
HISTORY DEPARTMENT
Kovalchenko, Ivan Dmitryevich
INSTITUTE OF ECONOMY
Abalkin, Leonid Ivanovich
INSTITUTE OF ETHNOLOGY AND ANTHROPOLOGY
Kon, Igor Semyonovich
Tishkov, Valery Aleksandrovich
INSTITUTE OF EUROPE
Zhurkin, Vitaly Vladimirovich
INSTITUTE OF EUROPEAN STUDIES

Karaganov, Sergey Aleksandrovich
INSTITUTE OF GENERAL PHYSICS
Prokhorov, Aleksandr Mikhailovich
INSTITUTE OF MARKET PROBLEMS
Petrakov, Nikolay Yakovlevich
INSTITUTE OF NATIONAL ECONOMY
Yaremenko, Yuri Vasilyevich
INSTITUTE OF ORIENTAL STUDIES
Kapitsa, Mikhail Stepanovich
INSTITUTE OF PEACE
Kislov, Aleksandr Konstantinovich
INSTITUTE OF PHILOSOPHY, PROBLEM GROUP FOR THE THEORY OF CULTURE
Arnoldov, Arnold Isayevich
INSTITUTE OF PHYSICS OF SOLIDS
Osipyan, Yuri Andreyevich
INSTITUTE OF RUSSIAN LITERATURE (PUSHKIN HOUSE), NEW RUSSIAN LITERATURE DEPARTMENT
Panchenko, Aleksandr Mikhailovich
INSTITUTE OF SOCIAL AND POLITICAL RESEARCH
Yanovski, Rudolf Grigoryevich
INSTITUTE OF SOCIO-ECONOMIC POPULATION PROBLEMS, GENDER STUDIES CENTER
Posadskaya, Anastasia Ivanovna
INSTITUTE OF SOCIOLOGY
Yadov, Vladimir Aleksandrovich
INSTITUTE OF SOCIO-POLITICAL STUDIES
Osipov, Gennadi Vasilyevich
INSTITUTE OF STATE AND LAW
Yakovlev, Aleksandr Maximovich
INSTITUTE OF SYSTEMS ANALYSIS
Leksin, Vladimir Nikolayevich
Perelet, Renat Alekseyevich
INSTITUTE OF THE U.S. AND CANADA
Arbatov, Georgy Arkadyevich
Burlatsky, Fyodor Mikhailovich
Zorin, Valentin Sergeyevich
INSTITUTE OF WORLD ECONOMIC AND POLITICAL RESEARCH
Bobomolov, Oleg Timofeyevich
INSTITUTE OF THE WORLD ECONOMY AND INTERNATIONAL RELATIONS
Kislov, Aleksandr Konstantinovich
Sheinis, Victor Leonidovich
INTERNATIONAL FORESTRY INSTITUTE
Isayev, Aleksandr Sergeyevich
LATIN AMERICA INSTITUTE
Volsky, Victor Vatslavovich
LITERATURE AND LANGUAGE DIVISION
Chelyshev, Yevgeni Petrovich
NUCLEAR PHYSICS DEPARTMENT
Skrinsky, Aleksandr Nikolayevich
RUSSIAN HISTORY INSTITUTE
Danilov, Victor Petrovich
Volobuyev, Pavel Vasilyevich
ST. PETERSBURG RESEARCH CENTER
Alferov, Zhores Ivanovich
SIBERIAN BRANCH
Koptyug, Valentin Afanasyevich
SIBERIAN BRANCH, INSTITUTE OF NUCLEAR PHYSICS
Skrinsky, Aleksandr Nikolayevich
STEKLOV MATHEMATICS INSTITUTE
Vladimirov, Vasily Sergeyevich
SYSTEMS ANALYSIS INSTITUTE
Gvishiani, Dzherman Mikhailovich

Russian Afro-Asian Solidarity and Cooperation Society
Dzasokhov, Aleksandr Sergeyevich
Kudryavtsev, Vladimir Nikolayevich

Russian Agency for International Cooperation and Development
Tereshkova, Valentina Vladimirovna

Russian Agency of Investments and Real Estate
Pankratov, Valentin Andreyevich

Russian Ambassador Extraordinary and Plenipotentiary
Rogachev, Igor Alekseyevich
Saprykin, Igor Aleksandrovich

Russian Ambassador to Argentina
Bulay, Igor Borisovich

Russian Ambassador to China
Rogachev, Igor Alekseyevich

Russian Ambassador to Israel
Bovin, Aleksandr Yevgenyevich

Russian Ambassador to Mongolia
Razov, Sergey Sergeyevich

Russian Ambassador to Portugal
Gerasimov, General Ivanovich (former)

Russian Ambassador to Romania
Ostrovenko, Yevgeni Dmitriyevich

Russian Ambassador to Thailand
Bostorin, Oleg Vladimirovich

Russian Ambassador to the Byelorussian Republic
Saprykin, Igor Aleksandrovich

Russian Ambassador to Zambia
Bocharnikov, Mikhail Nikolayevich

Russian Association of Business Schools
Manukovsky, Andrey Borisovich

Russian Bank Association
Bykov, Andrey Valeryanovich

Russian Business Agency
Vokov, Yuri Vasilyevich

Russian Center of Artists
Gubenko, Nikolay Nikolayevich

Russian Children's Foundation
Likhanov, Albert Anatolyevich
Mefody (Nemtsov, Nikolay Fyodorovich)

Russian-Christian-Democratic Movement Political Council
Aksyuchits, Victor Vladimirovich

Russian Commercial Banks Association
Yegorov, Sergey Yefimovich

Russian Commodities Exchange
AGRARIAN BRANCH
Lapshin, Mikhail Ivanovich

Russian Communist Party
Sergeyev, Aleksey Alekseyevich

Russian Communists Group
Bratishchev, Igor Mikhailovich

Russian Constitutional Court
Lubenchenko, Konstantin Dmitryevich

Russian Corporation of Defense Industry Joint-Stock Company
Belousov, Boris Mikhailovich

Russian Council
Gerasimov, Valery Ivanovich

Russian Delegation at the Latvian Negotiations
Zotov, Sergey Sergeyevich

Russian Democratic Reforms Movement
Popov, Gavril Kharitonovich

Russian Deputy Corps Academy
Ignatyev, Kirill Borisovich
Russian Deputy Minister of Security
Stepashin, Sergey Vadimovich (former)
Russian Federation Ambassador Extraordinary and Plenipotentiary
Adamishin, Anatoli Leonidovich
Afanasyevsky, Nikolay Nikolayevich
Aitmatov, Chingiz Torekulovich
Akhmedov, Khan
Aksenenok, Aleksandr Georgyevich
Bogdanov, Feliks Petrovich
Isakov, Victor Fyodorovich
Kashlev, Yuri Borisovich
Kerestedzhiyants, Leonid Vladimirovich
Kolokolov, Boris Leonidovich
Kovalev, Anatoli Gavrilovich
Kozyrev, Andrey Vladimirovich
Kozyrev, Nikolay Ivanovich
Krasavin, Igor Nikolayevich
Lomeiko, Vladimir Borisovich
Nikolayenko, Valery Dmitryevich
Obminsky, Ernest Yevgenyevich
Obukhov, Aleksey Aleksandrovich
Pastukhov, Boris Nikolayevich
Pletchko, Vladimir Yakovlevich
Pyadyshev, Boris Dmitryevich
Razov, Sergey Sergeyevich
Reshetov, Yuri Aleksandrovich
Romanov, Mikhail Alekseyevich
Sidorski, Philipp Philippovich
Silayev, Ivan Stepanovich
Smolyakov, Leonid Yakovlevich
Stepanov, Andrey Ivanovich
Terekhov, Vladislav Petrovich
Yelizarov, Nikolay Mikhailovich
AMBASSADOR TO ALGERIA
Aksenenok, Aleksandr Georgyevich
AMBASSADOR TO BELGIUM
Afanasyevsky, Nikolay Nikolayevich
AMBASSADOR TO BULGARIA
Avdeyev, Aleksandr Alekseyevich
AMBASSADOR TO CANADA
Belonogov, Aleksandr Mikhailovich
AMBASSADOR TO CROATIA
Kerestedzhiyants, Leonid Vladimirovich
AMBASSADOR TO DJIBOUTI
Abdullayev, Pulat Khabibovich
AMBASSADOR TO FRANCE
Ryzhov, Yuri Alekseyevich
AMBASSADOR TO GERMANY
Terekhov, Vladislav Petrovich
AMBASSADOR TO GREAT BRITAIN
Pankin, Boris Dmitryevich
AMBASSADOR TO GREECE
Nikolayenko, Valery Dmitryevich
AMBASSADOR TO HUNGARY
Aboimov, Ivan Pavlovich
AMBASSADOR TO ICELAND
Krasavin, Igor Nikolayevich
Reshetov, Yuri Aleksandrovich
AMBASSADOR TO IRELAND
Kozyrev, Nikolay Ivanovich
AMBASSADOR TO INDIA
Isakov, Victor Fyodorovich
AMBASSADOR TO JAPAN
Chizhov, Lyudvig Aleksandrovich
AMBASSADOR TO KIRGISTAN
Romanov, Mikhail Alekseyevich
AMBASSADOR TO NICARAGUA
Astakhov, Yevgeni Mikhailovich
AMBASSADOR TO POLAND
Kashlev, Yuri Borisovich
AMBASSADOR TO ROMANIA
Bogdanov, Feliks Petrovich
AMBASSADOR TO SWITZERLAND
Stepanov, Andrey Ivanovich
AMBASSADOR TO THE CENTRAL AFRICAN REPUBLIC
Balabanov, Yuri Sevostyanovich
AMBASSADOR TO THE KINGDOM OF DENMARK
Obukhov, Aleksey Aleksandrovich
AMBASSADOR TO THE REPUBLIC OF GUINEA
Studennikov, Igor Ivanovich
AMBASSADOR TO THE REPUBLIC OF MOLDAVA
Pletchko, Vladimir Yakovlevich
AMBASSADOR TO THE REPUBLIC OF VENEZUELA AND THE DOMINICAN REPUBLIC
Yelizarov, Nikolay Mikhailovich
AMBASSADOR TO THE UNITED STATES
Lukin, Vladimir Petrovich
AMBASSADOR TO UKRAINE
Smolyakov, Leonid Yekovlevich
AMBASSADOR TO UZBEKISTAN
Sidorski, Philipp Philippovich
CHIEF STATE INSPECTOR
Boldyrev, Yuri Yuryevich
COMMISSION FOR EXPORTS CONTROL
Khizha, Georgy Stepanovich
COMMITTEE FOR ISSUES OF THE COUNCILS OF PEOPLE'S DEPUTIES AND THE DEVELOPMENT OF SELF-GOVERNMENT
Blokhin, Aleksandr Victorovich
COUNCIL OF MINISTERS
Chernomyrdin, Victor Stepanovich
Fyodorov, Boris Grigoryevich
COUNSELLOR EXTRAORDINARY AND PLENIPOTENTIARY, FIRST GRADE
Abdullayev, Pulat Khabibovich
DEPUTY DEFENSE MINISTER
Gromov, Boris Vsevolodovich
Kondratyev, Georgy Grigoryevich
Mironov, Valery Ivanovich
Shlyakhtin, Vladimir Ivanovich
DEPUTY FOREIGN MINISTER
Chaplin, Boris Nikolayevich
Churkin, Vitaly Ivanovich
Kolokolov, Boris Leonidovich
Kovalev, Anatoli Gavrilovich (former)
Kunadze, Georgy Fridrikhovich
Lavrov, Sergey Victorovich
Mamedov, Georgy Enverovich
Obminsky, Ernest Yevgenyevich (former)
Pastukhov, Boris Nikolayevich
Shelov-Kovediaev, Fyodor Vadimovich
DEPUTY MINISTER OF EDUCATION
Badmayev, Sanal Alekseyevich
DEPUTY MINISTER OF FOREIGN AFFAIRS
Berdennikov, Grigory Vitalyevich
DEPUTY MINISTER OF INTERNAL AFFAIRS
Kozevnikov, Igor Nikolayevich
Kulikov, Aleksandr Nikolayevich
Mishenkov, Pyotr Grigoryevich
Turbin, Vitaly Borisovich
DEPUTY MINISTER OF JUSTICE
Muranov, Anatoli Ivanovich

Panferov, Boris Victorovich (former)
DEPUTY MINISTER OF SCIENCE, HIGHER EDUCATION, AND TECHNICAL POLICY
Zhurakovsky, Vasily Maksimilianovich
DEPUTY MINISTER OF SECURITY
Strelkov, Aleksander Aleksandrovich
ENVOY EXTRAORDINARY AND PLENIPOTENTIARY, FIRST CLASS
Mamedov, Georgy Enverovich
Studennikov, Igor Ivanovich
FIRST DEPUTY FOREIGN MINISTER
Adamishin, Anatoli Leonidovich
FIRST-DEPUTY MINISTER OF HEALTH
Densenko, Bella Anatolyevna
FIRST DEPUTY MINISTER OF INTERNAL AFFAIRS
Abramov, Yevgeni Aleksandrovich
Dunayev, Andrey Fyodorovich
FIRST DEPUTY MINISTER OF NUCLEAR ENERGY
Konovalov, Vitaly Fyodorovich
FIRST DEPUTY MINISTER OF SCIENCE, HIGHER EDUCATION AND TECHNICAL POLICY
Fonotov, Andrey Georgyevich
FIRST DEPUTY PRIME MINISTER
Shumeyko, Vladimir Filippovich
FOREIGN INTELLIGENCE SERVICE
Primakov, Yevgeni Maksimovich
FOREIGN MINISTER
Kozyrev, Andrey Vladimirovich
FOREIGN MINISTRY
Pyadyshev, Boris Dmitryevich
FOREIGN MINISTRY, DIPLOMATIC ACADEMY
Peresypkin, Oleg Gerasimovich
FOREIGN MINISTRY CONSULATE SERVICE
Vinogradov, Vasily Valentinovich
HIGHER ECONOMIC COUNCIL
Ispravnikov, Vladimir Olegovich
KHIZH GOVERNMENT SECRETARIAT OF THE DEPUTY CHAIRMAN
Bindar, Leonid Iosifovich
LIEUTENANT-GENERAL OF THE MILITIA (POLICE)
Abramov, Yevgeni Aleksandrovich
MINISTER
Borzov, Valery Filippovich
Chubais, Anatoli Borisovich
Tishkov, Valery Aleksandrovich
MINISTER OF AGRICULTURE
Khlystun, Victor Nikolayevich
MINISTER OF COMMUNICATIONS
Bulgak, Vladimir Borisovich
MINISTER OF CULTURE AND TOURISM
Sidorov, Yevgeni Yuryevich
MINISTER OF CULTURE AND TOURISM, CONSULTATIVE COUNCIL
Karyakin, Yuri Fyodorovich
Klimov, Yelem Germanovich
Lavrov, Kirill Yuryevich
Zakharov, Mark Anatolyevich
Zhvanetsky, Mikhail Mikhailovich
MINISTER OF DEFENSE
Grachev, Pavel Sergeyevich
MINISTER OF ECOLOGY AND NATURAL RESOURCES
Danilov-Danilyants, Victor Ivanovich
MINISTER OF EDUCATION
Dneprov, Eduard Dmitryevich (former)
MINISTER OF FINANCE
Barchuk, Vasily Vasilyevich
MINISTER OF FOREIGN ECONOMIC RELATIONS
Aven, Pyotr Olegovich
MINISTER OF INTERNAL AFFAIRS
Yerin, Victor Fyodorovich
MINISTER OF JUSTICE
Fyodorov, Nikolay Vasilyevich
MINISTER OF LABOR
Melikyan, Gennadi Georgyevich
MINISTER OF NUCLEAR ENERGY
Mikhailov, Victor Nikitovich
MINISTER OF RAILWAYS
Fadeyev, Gennadi Matveyevich
MINISTER OF SCIENCE, HIGHER EDUCATION AND TECHNOLOGICAL POLICY
Saltykov, Boris Georgyevich
MINISTER OF SECURITY
Barannikov, Victor Pavlovich
MINISTER OF SOCIAL PROTECTION OF THE POPULATION
Pamfilova, Ella Aleksandrovna
MINISTER OF TRADE AND RESOURCES
Anisimov, Stanilsav Vasilyevich (former)
MINISTER OF TRANSPORT
Yefimov, Vitaly Borisovich
MINISTRY OF CULTURE
Goncharov, Andrey Aleksandrovich
MINISTRY OF CULTURE AND TOURISM, CONSULTATIVE COUNCIL
Likhachev, Dmitri Sergeyevich
MINISTRY OF HEALTH, HEMATOLOGY SCIENTIFIC CENTER
Vorobyev, Andrey Ivanovich
MINISTRY OF HEALTH, PHYSICAL AND CHEMICAL MEDICINE RESEARCH INSTITUTE
Lopukhin, Yuri Mikhailovich
MINISTRY OF INDUSTRY ZARUBEZHCHERMET (FOREIGN FERROUS METALS) INTERNATIONAL ECONOMIC ASSOCIATION
Novikov, Vladimir Ivanovich
MINISTRY OF INDUSTRY, RUSSIAN AUTOMOBILE INDUSTRY DEPARTMENT
Karachurin, Rif Allayarovich
MINISTRY OF INTERNAL AFFAIRS, CORRECTION INSTITUTE
Kalinin, Yuri Ivanovich
MINISTRY OF NUCLEAR ENERGY, INSTITUTE OF HIGH ENERGY PHYSICS
Logunov, Anatoli Alekseyevich
MINISTRY OF TRADE AND MATERIAL RESOURCES, COMMITTEE FOR GRAIN PRODUCTS
Cheshisky, Leonid Stepanovich
NAVY FLEET
Gromov, Feliks Nikolayevich
OLYMPICS COMMITTEE
Vasin, Vladimir Alekseyevich
PERMANENT REPRESENTATIVE TO THE EUROPEAN ECONOMIC COMMUNITY
Silayev, Ivan Stepanovich
PERMANENT REPRESENTATIVE TO THE UN
Vorontsov, Yuli Mikhailovich
PERMANENT REPRESENTATIVE TO THE UNITED NATIONS AND OTHER INTERNATIONAL ORGANIZATIONS IN GENEVA

Permanent Representative to the United Nations (*cont'd*)
Makeyev, Yevgeni Nikolayevich
Permanent Representative to UNESCO
Lomeiko, Vladimir Borisovich
Representative of the Western Military Troops
Burlakov, Matvey Prokopyevich
Secretary of State to the President
Burbulis, Gennadi Eduardovich
Security Council
Skokov, Yuri Vladimorovich
Security Minister
Ivanenko, Victor Valentinovich
Security Minister, Russian Public Relations Center
Chernenko, Andrey Grigoryevich
State Committee for Cooperation with the Member-States of the Commonwealth
Mashits, Vladimir Mikhailovich
State Committee for Economic Cooperation with CIS Member States
Kirichenko, Vadim Nikitovich
State Committee for Managing State Property
Chubais, Anatoli Borisovich
State Committee for Standards (Gosstandart)
Bezverkhy, Sergey Fyodorovich
State Counsellor for Defense
Kobets, Konstantin Ivanovich
State Judicial Department
Sliva, Anatoli Yakovlevich
Supreme Economic Council
Leksin, Vladimir Nikolayevich
Trade Representative in China
Kachanov, Aleksandr Ivanovich
Trade Representative to Portugal
Kisin, Victor Ivanovich
Trade Representative to Sweden
Rakhimbayev, Gairat Faizullayevich
Union of Architects
Gnedovsky, Yuri Pertovich

Russian Federation Armed Forces
Kobets, Konstantin Ivanovich
Kolesnikov, Mikhail Petrovich
M ironov, Vyacheslav Petrovich
Yeltsin, Boris Nikolayevich

Russian Federation Central Committee
Milnikov, Aleksandr Grigoryevich
Silkova, Nina Prokopyevna

Russian Federation Chairman of the Government
Staff Advisor to
Lopukhin, Vladimir Mikhailovich

Russian Federation Constitutional Council
Sheinis, Victor Leonidovich

Russian Federation Government
Chubais, Anatoli Borisovich
Khizha, Georgy Stepanovich
Academy of National Economy
Leksin, Vladimir Nikolayevich
Yevenko, Leonid Ivanovich
Committee on Geology and the Use of Mineral Resources
Orlov, Victor Petrovich
Deputy Chairman
Saltykov, Boris Georgyevich
Economic Counsellor
Kagalovsky, Konstantin Grigoryevich
Monetary-Economic Commission
Aven, Pyotr Olegovich
Orenburg Region Administration
Tutov, Nikolay Dmitryevich
Plenipotentiary Representative at the United International Nuclear Research Institute
Saltykov, Boris Georgyevich
Representative for Problems in Ossetia
Tishkov, Valery Aleksandrovich

Russian Federation People's Artist
Mikhalkov, Nikita Sergeyevich

Russian Federation People's Deputy
Afanasyev, Yuri Nikolayevich
Baburin, Sergey Nikolayevich
Basilashvili, Oleg Valeryanovich
Basin, Yefim Vladimirovich
Boltyansky, Andrey Vladimirovich
Bondarev, Grigory Semyonovich
Chelnokov, Mikhail Borisovich
Chikin, Valentin Vasilyevich
Dzasokhov, Aleksandr Sergeyevich
Ivanilov, Yuri Pavlovich
Karachurin, Rif Allayarovich
Kokshirov, Boris Nikolayevich
Kulesha, Vadim Anatolyevich
Kuznetsov, Anatoli Mikhailovich
Lakhova, Yetaterina Filippovna
Lapshin, Mikhail Ivanovich
Muravyev, Igor Vladislavovich
Polozkov, Ivan Kuzmich
Salye, Marina Yevgenievna
Shorin, Vladimir Pavlovich
Volkogonov, Dmitri Antonovich

Russian Federation Politburo
Melnikov, Aleksandr Grigoryevich

Russian Federation President
Yeltsin, Boris Nikolayevich
Advisor to
Malei, Mikhail Dmitryevich
Malysher, Nikolay Grigoryevich
Stankevich, Sergey Borisovich
Volkogonov, Dmitri Antonovich
Analytical Center of Socio-Economic Policy
Filippov, Pyotr Sergeyevich
Analytical Information Center
Rakitov, Anatoli Ilyich
Coordinating Committee for the Affairs of Invalids
Burkov, Valery Anatolyevich
Vorontsov, Valery Aleksandrovich
Council of Experts
Furmanov, Boris Aleksandrovich
Kharlanov, Iven Ivenovich
Krivov, Victor Dmitryevich
Nit, Igor Vasilyevich
Counsellor to
Burkov, Valery Anatolyevich
Granberg, Aleksandr Grigoryevich
Starovoitova, Galina Vasilyevna (former)
Head of the Office of
Semenchenko, Valery Pavlovich
Official Legal Representative of, to Russian Federation Supreme Soviet
Sliva, Anatoli Yakovlevich
Press Secretary of

Kostikov, Vyacheslav Vasilyevich
Press Service
Krasikov, Anatoli Andreyevich
Representative
Cheshinsky, Leonid Stepanovich
Representative in Chukotka Autonomous District
Yeregin, Yuri Anatolyevich
Staff
Filatov, Sergey Aleksandrovich
Sverdlovsk Region Representative
Mashkov, Vitaly Vladimirovich
Russian Federation Presidential Council
Tikhonov, Vladimir Aleksandrovich
Russian Federation Procurator's Office
Research Institute for Strengthening Law and Legal Regulations
Karpets, Igor Ivanovich
Russian Federation Prosecutor General
Stepankov, Valentin Georgyevich
Russian Federation Supreme Soviet
Bulygin, Victor Vasilyevich
Dzasokhov, Aleksandr Sergeyevich
Commission for Foreign Affairs and International Economic Relations
Andronov, Iona Ionovich
Committee for Construction, Architecture, and Public Utilities
Basin, Yefim Vladimirovich
Committee for Defense and Security
Ivanov, Sergey Nikolayevich
Stepashin, Sergey Vadimovich
Committee for Ecology and the Rational Consuming of Natural Resources
Goryacheva, Svetlana Petrovna
Committee for Ecology and the Rational Use of Natural Resources
Vorontsov, Nikolay Nikolayevich
Committee for Economic Reforms
Ivanilov, Yuri Pavlovich
Committee for Foreign Affairs and International Economic Relations
Ambartsumov, Yevgeni Arshakovich
Bondarev, Grigory Semyonovich
Karachurin, Rif Allayarovich
Sokolov, Aleksandr Sergeyevich
Committee for Freedom of Conscience, Faith, Mercy and Charity
Astafyev, Mikhail Georgyevich
Polosin, Vyacheslav Sergeyevich
Committee for Freedom of Conscience, Faith, Mercy, and Charity, Subcommittee for Liaison with Foreign and Religious Organizations
Aksyuchits, Victor Vladimirovich
Committee for Health Care, Social Services and Physical Education
Gerasimov, Valery Ivanovich
Committee for Human Rights
Sorokina, Maria Ivanovna
Starovoitova, Galina Vasilyevna
Committee for Industry, Power Engineering, and Power Conversion
Mashkov, Vitaly Vladimirovich
Committee for Industry and Energy
Vitebsky, Vitaly Yakovlevich
Committee for Industry and Power Engineering
Isakov, Vladimir Borisovich
Kokshirov, Boris Nikolayevich
Yeremin, Alvin Yevstafyevich
Committee for Inter-Republican Relations
Lysov, Pavel Aleksandrovich
Committee for Inter-Republican Relations, Regional Policies, and Cooperation Issues
Dmitryev, Mikhail Yegorovich
Committee for Inter-Republican Relations, Regional Policy, and Cooperation Issues
Podoprigora, Vladimir Nikolayevich
Committee for Inter-Republican Relations and Regional Policies
Bratishchev, Igor Mikhailovich
Committee for Issues of the Councils of People's Deputies and the Development of Self-Government
Balala, Victor Alekseyevich
Muravyev, Igor Vladislavovich
Rybkin, Ivan Petrovich
Committee for Legality, Law and Order, and Combatting Crime
Aslakhanov, Aslanbek Akhmedovich
Kucherenko, Igor Mikhailovich
Committee for Mass Media
Mishustina, Larisa Pavlovna
Nosovets, Sergey Anatolyevich
Committee for Science and Education
Chelnokov, Mikhail Borisovich
Shorin, Vladimir Pavlovich
Committee for Science and National Education
Vilchek, Mikhail Ivanovich
Vinogradova, Irina Victorovna
Committee for the Management of State Property
Ivanilov, Yuri Pavlovich
Committee on Budget, Planning, Taxes, and Prices
Pochinok, Aleksandr Petrovich
Committee on Culture
Polenov, Fyodor Dmitryevich
Committee on Health Protection, Social Security, and Physical Education
Pekarskaya, Tereza Kazimorovna
Council of Nationalities
Abdulatipov, Ramazan Gadzhimuradovich
Council of Nationalities' Commission for the Social and Economic Development of the Republics
Sayenko, Gennadi Vasilyevich
Council of the Republic Committee on Budget, Planning, Taxes, and Prices
Zadonsky, Georgy Ivanovich
Counsellor to Chairman
Chilingarov, Artur Nikolayevich
Legislative Committee
Mityukov, Mikhail Alekseyevich

LEGISLATIVE COMMITTEE, POLITICAL REFORMS SUBCOMMITTEE
Varov, Vladimir Konstantinovich
OFFICIAL LEGAL REPRESENTATIVE OF THE RUSSIAN FEDERATION PRESIDENT TO
Sliva, Anatoli Yakovlevich
PRESIDIUM EXPERT
Berezkin, Andrey Vladimirovich
RODINA (MOTHERLAND) JOURNAL
Dolmatov, Vladimir Petrovich
SOCIO-ECONOMIC DEVELOPMENT DEPARTMENT
Isayev, Boris Mikhailovich
SUBCOMMITTEE FOR INDUSTRY AND ENERGY
Bespalov, Vladimir Vasilyevich
Russian Federation Supreme Soviet of the Tenth and Eleventh Convocations
Nenashev, Mikhail Fydorovich
Russian Federation Supreme Soviet Presidium
Syrovatko, Vitaly Grigoryevich
SUPREME ECONOMIC COUNCIL
Arbatov, Aleksandr Arkadyevich
Russian Federation Vice President
Rutskoy, Aleksandr Vladimirovich (former)
ADVISOR TO
Fyodorov, Andrey Vladimirovich
ASSISTANT TO
Radugin, Nikolay Petrovich
Russian Fizkultura i Sport (Physical Education and Sports) Charity Foundation
Latynina, Larisa Semyonovna
Russian Football Union
Simonyan, Nikita Pavlovich
Russian Foreign Ministry
Kenyaykin, Valery Fyodorovich
CENTRAL AND SOUTH AMERICA DEPARTMENT
Dmitryev, Andrey Victorovch
DEPARTMENT OF AFRICA AND THE MIDDLE EAST
Karasin, Grigory Borisovich
DEPARTMENT OF INFORMATION AND THE PRESS
Yastrzhembski, Sergey Vladimirovich (former)
EUROPEAN DEPARTMENT
Glukhov, Aleksey Iliych
Russian Fuel and Energy Exchange (ROSTEB)
Suzdaltsev, Yuri Anatolyevich
Russian Fund for International Humanitarian Aid and Cooperation
Chilingarov, Artur Nikolayevich
Russian Government Commission for Social Development of the Countryside
Khlystun, Victor Nikolayevich
Russian Government Council for Emergencies, Analyses, and Governmental Decisions
Moiseyev, Nikita Nikolayevich
Russian Government Trade Representative in Austria
Filshin, Gennadi Innokentyevich
Russian Government's Academy of National Economy
Bunich, Pavel Grigoryevich
Russian Independent Institute of Social and National Problems
Smirnov, Georgy Lukich
Russian Industrialists and Entrepreneurs Union
Vladimirov, Boris Grigoryevich
Russian Information Company
Vinogradov, Andrey Georgyevich
Russian Information Resources Exchange
Belov, Sergei Fadeyevich
Russian Intellectual Property Agency (RAIS)
Cherkizov, Andrey Aleksandrovich
Russian International Culture Foundation
Likhachev, Dmitri Sergeyevich
Russian IPP (International Organization for the Protection of Industrial Property) Group
Gorodinsky, Mikhail Lvovich
Russian League of Entrepreneurs and Cooperative Societies
Kivelidi, Ivan Kharlampyevich
Tikhonov, Vladimir Aleksandrovich
Russian Liberal Party
Krivonosov, Konstantin Andreyevich
Russian Management Academy
Gritsenko, Nikolay Nikolayevich
Russian Mercantile Exchange (RME)
Borovoy, Konstantin Natanovich
Russian Nashi (Our) Liberation
Alksnis, Victor Imantovich
Russian National Bank
Stepanov, Vladimir Aleksandrovich
Russian National Committee for Pacific Economic Cooperation
Granberg, Aleksandr Grigoryevich
Russian National Symphony Orchestra
Pletnev, Mikhail Vasilyevich
Russian Navy
Kasatonov, Igor Vladimirovich
Russian Novosti Information Agency
Litvinchuk, Victor Ivanovich
Russian Orthodox Church
HOLY SYNOD
Filaret (Vakhromeyev Kirill Varfolomeyevich)
Guvenaly, Pojarkov Vladimir Kirillovich
Ioann Snychev, Ivan Matveyevich
Kirill (Gundyayev, Vladimir Mikhailovich)
Snychev, Ivan Matveyevich (Ioann)
Vladimir (Sabodan, Victor Markianovich)
Russian Orthodox Staroobryadchesky (Old Belief) Church
Alimpy (Aleksandr Kapitonovich Gusev)
Russian Ostankino TV and Radio Broadcasting Company
Kiselev, Yevgeni Alekseyevich
Russian Patriotic Movements Association
Sergeyev, Aleksey Alekseyevich
Russian Peasant Farm and Agricultural Cooperatives Association
Bashmachnikov, Vladimir Fyodorovich
Russian People's Deputies Agrarian Faction
Lapshin, Mikhail Ivanovich
Russian People's Front
Aksyuchits, Victor Vladimirovich
Astafyev, Mikhail Georgyevich
Russian People's Union
Baburin, Sergey Nikolayevich

Russian Poll Center
Zaslavskaya, Tatyana Ivanovna
Russian President
State Counsellor to Vorontsov, Yuli Mikhailovich
Tomsk Region Spokesman for
Sulakshin, Stepan Stepanovich
Russian President's Administration
Control Department Head
Boldyrev, Yuri Yuryevich
Russian President's Group of Experts
Delyagin, Mikhail Gennadyevich
Russian President's Political Consultative Council
Arbatov, Georgy Arkadyevich
Russian President's Representative in Novgorod region
Kuznetsov, Anatoli Mikhailovich
Russian Press House
Musaelyan, Gennadi Samvelovich
Russian Representative to the Vatican
Karlov, Yuri Yevgenyevich
Russian Solidarnost (Solidarity) Bank of Trade Union Solidarity and Social Investments
Zaikin, Aleksandr Aleksandrovich
Russian State Herzen Teachers' Training Institute
Borkovsky, Gennadi Alekseyevich
Russian State Humanities University
Afanasyev, Yuri Nikolayevich
Russian State Library of Foreign Literature
Ivanov, Vyacheslav Vsevolodovich
Russian State Military-Historical Archives
Rybun, Vladimir Alekseyevich
Russian State TV and Radio Broadcasting Company
Lysenko, Anatoli Grigoryevich
Russian Supreme Soviet
Baburin, Sergey Nikolayevich
Ispravnikov, Vladimir Olegovich
Committee for Mass Media and Relations with Public Organizations
Lysenko, Vladimir Nikolayevich
Parliamentary Center
Lubenchenko, Konstantin Dmitryevich
Scientific Council
Bunich, Pavel Grigoryevich
Russian Television and Radio Company
Poptsov, Oleg Maksimovich
Russian Trade Representative in Italy
Burmistrov, Vladimir Nikolayevich
Russian Union of Aircraft Industry Complexes, Enterprises, and Associates
Systsov, Apollon Sergeyevich
Russian Union of Athletes
Gorokhova, Galina Yevgenyevna
Russian Union of Industrialists and Entrepreneurs
Balanovskaya, Nadezhda Avgustovna
Bekh, Nikolay Ivanovich
Borovoy, Konstantin Natanovich
Bunich, Pavel Grigoryevich
Kisin, Victor Ivanovich
Petrakov, Nikolay Yakovlevich
Seleznev, Igor Sergeyevich
Vinogradov, Vladimir Victorovich
Vladislayev, Aleksandr Pavlovich
Volsky, Arkady Ivanovich
Yegorov, Sergey Yefimovich
Russian Union of Property Owners
Inter-Republican Organization
Shchekochikin, Victor Vladimirovich
Russian Union of Proprietors
Auditing Commission
Morozov, Yuri Valentinovich
Russian Union of Small Enterprises
Shulyatyeva, Nadezhda Aleksandrovna
Russian Union of Woman
Fedulova, Alevtina Vasilyevna
Russian Union of Work Collectives
Lashch, Vera Grigoryevna
Russian Union of Young Entrepreneurs
Potapenko, Sergey Mikhailovich
Russian Vice President
Advisor to
Mikhalkov, Nikita Sergeyevich
Russian Writers' Union
Krupin, Vladimir Nikolayevich
Sokolov, Vadim Pavlovich
Executive Committee
Dementyev, Andrey Dmitryevich
Russia's Choice Party
Gaidar, Yegor Timurovich
RVC i Ko (RVC & Company) Joint-Stock Company
Paulman, Valery Fyodorovich

Sagan Ltd.
Anchevsky, Igor Georgyevich
Salanf Firm
Ivanov, Aleksandr Nikolayevich
St. Petersburg, Mayor of
Sobchak, Anatoli Aleksandroviich
St. Petersburg All-Russia State TV and Radio Broadcasting Company
Kurkova, Bella Alekseyevna
St. Petersburg Astrobank Commercial Bank
Vasyukov, Anatoli Ivanovich
Saint Petersburg Bank Joint-Stock Company
Lvov, Yuri Ivanovich
St. Petersburg Innovation Bank
Agayan, Aleksandr Aleksandrovich
St. Petersburg State University
Klyuchnikov, Igor Konstantinovich
St. Petersburg Stock Exchange
Klyuchnikov, Igor Konstantinovich
St. Petersburg Timber Industry Bank
Dzhikovich, Vladimir Veliykovich
Sakha (Yakutia) Republic
Nikolayev, Mikhail Yefimovich
Sakharov Democratic Union
Voronin, Vladimir Vasilyevich
Scientific Council for Ecological and Political Education Development
Moiseyev, Nikita Nikolayevich
Scientific Council on Historical Issues of the Russian Revolution
Volobuyev, Pavel Vasilyevich
Scientific-Research Developments and Rossyuz Aviaprom (Aviation Industry) Programs Center
Batkov, Aleksandr Mikhailovich
Scientific Research Testing Center for Radiation Safety of Space Objects

Scientific Research Testing Center (*cont'd*)
Kovalev, Yevgeni Yevgenyevich
Second Watch-Making Factory Production Association
Korolev, Vladimir Mikhailovich
Secretariat of the Vice Premier
Morozov, Aleksey Mikhailovich
***Semya* (*Family*) newspaper**
Abramov, Sergey Aleksandrovich
Serp i Molot (Sickle and Hammer) Metallurgical Plant
Izvekov, Nikolay Yakovlevich
Seventh-Day Adventists Church General Confederation
EUROPEAN-ASIAN DEPARTMENT
Kulakov, Mikhail Petrovich
***Shakhmatny Vestnik* (*Chess Herald*) weekly**
Averbakh, Yuri Lvovich
Siberian Commercial Bank (Sibbank) in Krasnoyarsk
Filippov, Andrey Nikolayevich
Siberian Mercantile Exchange
Semchenko, Oleg Ivanovich
Sign K-CP Publishing House
Grigoryanets, Sergey Ivanovich
Smena-Novaya Politika (Rising Generation-New Politics) Faction
Lysov, Pavel Aleksandrovich
***Sobesednik* (*Companion*) weekly newspaper**
Pilipenko, Yuri Vladimirovich
Social and Economic Reforms Foundation
Sitaryan, Stepan Aramaisovich
Social Ecology of Man Via Mass Creativity Public Organization (Dark-Blue Movement)
Bokan, Yuri Ivanovich
Bolgarin, Gennadi Romanovich
Society for Friendship Between the People of Russia and Finland
Maslennikov, Arkady Afrikanovich
Society for Friendship with Austria
Potapov, Aleksandr Serafimovich
Sodruzhestvo (Commonwealth) Trading House
Khshtoyan, Vilen Vartanovich
Sokolniki Railway-Carriage Repair Works (SVARZ)
Bragin, Nikolay Yevgenyevich
Solnechnogorsk Polymer Plant
Sotnikov, Fyodor Ivanovich
***Sovershenno Sekretno* (*Top Secret*) newspaper**
Borovik, Artyom Genrikhovich
"Sovershenno Sekretno" (Top Secret) TV Program
Borovik, Artyom Genrikhovich
Soviet Pacific Fleet
Khvatov, Gennadi Aleksandrovich
***Sovietskaya Rossia* (*Soviet Russia*) newspaper**
Chikin, Valentin Vasilyevich
***Sovietsky Sport* (*Soviet Sport*) newspaper; *Sovietsky Sport + 8* weekly**
Kudryavtsev, Valery Georgyevich
Sovintersport (International Sports Council) All-Russian Foreign Trade Organization
Galayev, Victor Ilyich
Sovremennik Theater
Volchek, Galina Borisovna
Soyuz (Union) Deputy Group
Alksnis, Victor Imantovich
Soyuzforinvest Joint-Venture
Khabitsov, Boris Batrbekovich
Soyuzneft-Export (Oil Export) Association
Arutyunyan, Vladimir Arutyunovich
Soyuztranzit (Union Transit) Firm
Melnik, Sergey Grigoryevich
Soyuzvneshtrans (International Transportation) Concern
Aliseichik, Valery Ivanovich
Soyuzpatent (Patent Experts Organization)
Gorodinsky, Mikhail Lvovich
Space Research Institute
Sagdeyev, Roald Zinnurovich
Spanish Seville Football Club
Dasayev, Rinat Faizrakhmovich
Special Plenipotentiary Representative of Russia to the United States
Kolosovsky, Andrey Igorevich
***Sputnik* (*Companion*) magazine**
Baklanov, Mikhail Grigoryevich
Litvinchuk, Victor Ivanovich
Staroobryadchesky Metropolitan of Moscow and All-Russia
Alimpy (Aleksandr Kapitonovich Gusev)
State Advisor of Justice, Second Class
Gudushkin, Stanislav Markovich
State Committee for Anti-Monopoly Policy
RIGHT TO EXERCISE EXCHANGE OPERATIONS, LICENSING COMMISSION
Morozov, Yuri Valentinovich
State Committee for National Policy
Tishkov, Valery Aleksandrovich
State Financial Corporation
Nechayev, Andrey Alekseyevich
State Institute of Dramatic Art (GITIS)
Maksimova, Yekaterina Sergeyevna
State Investment Corporation
Petrov, Yuri Vladimirovich
State Minister of Justice, Second Class
Panferov, Boris Victorovich
State Research Institute of Mechanical Engineering Science
Frolov, Konstantin Vasilyevich
State Security Committee (KGB)
Kryuchkov, Vladimir Aleksandrovich
Stolichny (Metropolitan) Commercial Bank
Smolensky, Aleksandr Pavlovich
***Stolitsa* (*Capital City*) magazine**
Malgin, Andrey Victorovich
Stroimaterialy (Construction Materials) Scientific and Industrial Association
Maslakov, Arkady Dmitryevich
Subcommittee for Liaison with Public Organizations and Movements
Ponomarev, Lev Aleksandrovich
Sudimport (Ship Import) Foreign Trade Association
Yakimov, Boris Alekseevich
Sudprom Russian Shipbuilding Corporation
Koksanov, Igor Vladimirovich
Supreme Court
PRESS SECRETARY
Obukhov, Sergey Pavlovich
Supreme Economic Council
Blokhin, Yuri Vitalyevich
Supreme Soviet
Zhebrovsky, Stanislav Mikhailovich
COMMITTEE FOR HEALTH PROTEC-

TION, SOCIAL SERVICES, SPORTS, AND ECOLOGY
Vorontsov, Valery Aleksandrovich
COMMITTEE FOR NATIONAL EDUCATION
Badmayev, Sanal Alekseyevich
COMMITTEE FOR WOMEN'S RIGHTS
Dzhaganova, Altynshash Kairdzhanovna
Supreme Soviet Council
Khalitov, Akhmet Kharisovich
***Svobodnaya Mysl* (*Free Thought*) magazine**
Bikkenin, Nail Baryevich
Svobodnaya Rossiya (Free Russia) People's Party (SRPP)
Fedosov, Pyotr Anatolyevich
Lipitsky, Vasily Semyonovich
Mironov, Vladimir Nikolayevich
BOARD, PUBLIC RELATIONS DEPARTMENT
Zharikhin, Vladimir Leonidovich
***Svobodny Mir* (*Free World*) newspaper**
Chervyakov, Aleksander Alekseyevich
Tajik Communist Party
Makhkamov, Kakhar

Tajik Supreme Soviet Council
Makhkamov, Kakhar
***Teatr* (*Theater*) magazine**
Shoub, Yuli Germanovich
Tekhnoexport (Export of Technology) Russian International Economic Association
Velichko, Victor Ivanovich
Tekhnokhimbank (Technology and Chemistry) Joint-Stock Bank
Dmitryev, Dmitri Ivanovich
Tekhnomashimport (Technical Equipment Import) Foreign Trade Complex
Grib, Victor Ivanovich
"Television Acquaintance" (TV program)
Ott, Urmas
Theater of Miniatures
Zadornov, Mikhail Nikolayevich
Tiross (Technology and Investments of Russia) Financial and Investment Company
Titkin, Aleksandr Alekseyevich
Tomsk Region Spokesman for the Russian President
Sulakshin, Stepan Stepanovich
TOO Ekorad Advertising Firm
Malinov, Aleksandr Vasilyevich
***Torgovaya Gazeta* (*Trade Newspaper*)**
Pushkarev, Victor Yakovlevich
Toribank Joint-Stock Bank
Zhelamsky, Andrey Nikolayevich
Trade Minister of Byelorussia
Baidak, Valentin Ivanovich
Transnational Exchange
Lapshin, Mikhail Ivanovich
Serebrennikov, Mark Parfentyevich
Transstroi (Transport Construction) State Corporation
Brezhnev, Vladimir Arkadyevich
***Trud* (*Labor*) newspaper**
Potapov, Aleksandr Serafimovich
Trudovaya Rossiya (Working Russia) Movement
Anpilov, Victor Ivanovich
Tryokhgornaya Manufaktura Integrated Cotton Mill (Moscow)
Balanovskaya, Nadezhda Avgustovna
Tula Higher Athletic Mastership School
Kopylov, Sergey Vladimirovich
Turkistan Military District Commander
Kondratyev, Georgy Grigoryevich
Turkmenistan
PRESIDENT OF
Niyazov, Saparmurad Atayevich
Turkmenistan Democratic Party
Niyazov, Saparmurad Atayevich
Turkmenistan Government
DEPUTY HEAD (FORMER)
Akhmedov, Khan
TV-Progress Independent Agency
Kainarskaya, Irina Yakovlevna
Tver Progressprombank (Industrial Progress) Joint-Stock Bank
Dudenkov, Anatoli Petrovich
Tveruniversalbank (Universal Bank of Tver)
Kozyreva, Aleksandra Mikhailovna
***24* newspaper**
Zarechkin, Yuri Vladimirovich
Udmurtian State Sports Committee
Kulakova, Galina Alekseyevna
Ukraine
DEPUTY DEFENSE MINISTER
Bizhan, Ivan Vasilyevich
Ighatenko, Aleksandr Stepanovich (former)
FIRST VICE PREMIER
Simonenko, Valentin Konstantinovich
PRESIDENT
Kravchuk, Leonid Makarovich
PRESIDENT, SOCIO-ECONOMIC ADVISOR TO
Simonenko, Valentin Konstantinovich
Ukraine Air Forces, Air Defense Commander
Lopatin, Mikhail Alekseyevich
Ukraine Cooperative Alliance
Lerner, Edvin Yuryevich
Ukraine Federation of Gymnastics
Turisheva, Ludmila Ivanovna
Ukraine State Council
Fokin, Vitold Pavlovich
Ukraine Supreme Soviet
Lukyanenko, Levko Grigoryevich
Ukrainian Defense Ministry
Ignatenko, Aleksandr Stepanovich
Ukrainian National Olympics Committee
Borzov, Valery Filippovich
Ukrainian Poet and Scriptwriter Organization
Drach, Ivan Fyodorovich
Ukrainian Writers' Union
Drach, Ivan Fyodorovich
UN Committee for the Elimination of Racial Discrimination
Reshetov, Yuri Aleksandrovich
UN Economic and Social Commission for Asia and the Pacific
Bostorin, Oleg Vladimirovich
Unified Forces of the Commonwealth
Samsonov, Victor Nikolayevich
Union of Russian Cossack Troops
Kokunko, Georgy Valentinovich
United Confederation of Trade Unions
Shcherbakov, Vladimir Pavlovich
United Editorial Board (*Militsia* magazine and *Shchit i Mech* newspaper)

Luntovsky, Georgy Ivanovich

Vostokintorg (Eastern International Trade) Foreign Trade Association

Kukhtenkov, Aleksey Semyonovich

Vostokstroi (Construction in the Eastern USSR) Commercial Bank

Chernikov, Nikolay Vikulovich

Vox Populi Poll Service

Grushin, Boris Andreyevich

Voyenkov Main Geophysical Observatory

Borisenkov, Yevgeni Panteleymonovich

Vybor-89 (Choice-89) Diversified Production Firm

Lerner, Edvin Yuryevich

Vympel (Pennant) Inter-Governmental Joint-Stock Corporation

Mikhailov, Nikolay Vasilyevich

Vzglyad (Glance) Joint-Stock Company

Politkovsky, Aleksandr Vladimirovich

***Vzglyad i Drugiye* (*Glance and Others*) newspaper**

Korotich, Vitaly Alekseyevich

Vzglyad iz Podpollya (Glance from the Underground) Joint-Stock Company

Lyubimov, Aleksandr Mikhailovich

Waterproof Fabrics Industrial Complex

Kokshirov, Boris Nikolayevich

Western Prefecture of Moscow

Bryachikhin, Aleksey Mikheyevich

Working Communist Party of Russia

CENTRAL COMMITTEE

Makashov, Albert Mikhailovich

World and Nature Public Center

Burlak, Vadim Nikolayevich

World Association of Small and Medium Enterprises

EUROASIAN LEAGUE OF SMALL AND MEDIUM ENTERPRISES

Shulyatyeva, Nadezhda Aleksandrovna

World Club of Odessites (Citizens of Odessa)

Zhvanetsky, Mikhail Mikhailovich

***World Economy and International Relations* magazine**

Diligensky, German Germanovich

World Federation of Scientists

Nefedov, Oleg Matveyevich

Writers Concord Board

Oleynik, Boris Ilyich

Writers' Union

Arkanov, Arkady Mikhailovich

Yedinstvo (Unity) Joint-Stock Consumer Societies Bank

Sotnikov, Aleksandr Dmitryevich

***Yevreyskaya Gazeta* (*Jewish Newspaper*)**

Golenkolsky, Tankred Grigoryevich

***Yunost* (*Youth*) magazine**

Dementyev, Andrey Dmitryevich

***Yuridicheskaya Gazeta* (*Legal Newspaper*)**

Finko, Oleg Aleksandrovich

Kravchenko, Leonid Petrovich

Yuzhnaya Universalnaya Birzha (Southern Universal Stock Exchange) Joint-Stock Company

Kozemyakin, Nikolay Aleksandrovich

***Za Rubezhom* (*Abroad*) newspaper**

Morozov, Sergey Nikolayevich

Zashchita (Protection) United Trade Unions of Independent Workers

Leonov, Yuri Yuryevich

Zashchitnik Otechestva (Defender of the Fatherland) Inter-Republican Foundation for Humanitarian Assistance to Servicemen

Lobov, Vladimir Nikolayevich

***Zdorovye* (*Health*) magazine**

Belyanchikova, Yuliya Vasilyevna

Zelenograd Prefecture of Moscow

Ishchuk, Aleksey Alekseyevich

Zemlyane (Citizens of Earth) Private Family Association

Shchekochikin, Victor Vladimirovich

***Zhurnalist* (*Journalist*) magazine**

Avraamov, Dmitri Sergeyevich

***Znamya* (*Banner*) magazine**

Baklanov, Grigory Yakovlevich

Appendix C

Listing of Recipients of Honors or Awards

Abdrashitov, Vadim Yusupovich
Aboimov, Ivan Pavlovich
Adamishin, Anatoli Leonidovich
Adamovich, Aleksandr Mikhailovich (Ales Adamovich)
Agafangel (Savvin Aleksey Mikhailovich)
Aganbegyan, Abel Gezevich
Aitmatov, Chingiz Torekulovich
Akayev, Askar
Akhmedov, Khan
Aleksei II (Aleksei Mikhailovich Ridiger)
Alferov, Zhores Ivanovich
Aliseichik, Valery Ivanovich
Aliyev, Geydar Aliyevich
Ananyev, Anatoli Andreyevich
Andreyev, Yuri Emanuilovich
Andrianov, Nikolay Yefimovich
Arbatov, Georgy Arkadyevich
Andropov, Igor Yurevich
Arkayev, Leonid Yakovlevich
Arkhipova, Irina Konstantinovna
Arnoldov, Arnold Isayevich
Averbakh, Yuri Lvovich
Averina (Barabash), Tatyana Borisovna
Averintsev, Sergey Sergeyevich

Bakatin, Vadim Victorovich
Baklanov, Grigory Yakolevich
Baklanov, Oleg Dmitrievich
Balabanov, Yuri Sevostyanovich
Basilashvili, Oleg Valeryanovich
Basin, Yefim Vladimirovich
Basov, Nikolay Gennadyevich
Batarchuk, Boris Aleksandrovich
Batkov, Aleksandr Mikhailovich
Bekh, Nikolay Ivanovich
Bekhtereva, Natalya Petrovna
Belonogov, Aleksandr Mikhailovich
Belousov, Boris Mikhailovich
Belyaev, Vladimir Nikitovich
Belyanchikova, Yuliya Vasilyevna
Beskov, Konstantin Ivanovich
Bestemyanova, Natalya Filimonovna
Bilozerchev, Dmitri Vladimirovich
Bindar, Leonid Iosifovich
Biryulev, Sergey Vasilyevich
Bizhan, Ivan Vasilyevich
Blokhin, Oleg Vladimirovich
Bocharnikov, Mikhail Nikolayevich
Bogomolov, Oleg Timofeyevich
Bokov, Stanislav Nikolayevich
Bondarenko, Aleksandr Pavlovich
Bondarev, Yuri Vasilyevich
Borisenkov, Yevgeni Panteleymonovich
Borisov, Oleg (Albert) Ivanovich
Borovik, Artyom Genrikhovich
Borovik, Genrikh Avyezerovich
Borshchevsky, Eduard Iosifovich
Borzov, Valery Filippovich
Bostorin, Oleg Vladimirovich
Botvinnik, Mikhail Moiseyevich
Bovin, Aleksandr Yevgenyevich
Brumel, Valery Nilolayevich
Bubka, Sergey Nazarovich
Bukin, Andrey Anatolyevich
Bunich, Pavel Grigoryevich
Burkov, Valery Anatolyevich
Burlakova, Yelena Borisovna
Burlatsky, Fyodor Mikhailovich
Bykov, Dmitri Vasilyevich
Bykov, Rolan Anatolyevich

Chaplin, Boris Nikolayevich
Chazov, Yevgeni Ivanovich
Chelyshev, Yevgeni Petrovich
Chernavin, Vladimir Nikolayevich
Chernichenko, Yuri Dmitryevich
Chernikov, Nikolay Vikulovich
Chernomyrdin, Victor Stepanovich
Chesnokov, Andrey Eduardovich
Chilingarov, Artur Nikolayevich
Chizhov, Lyudvig Aleksandrovich
Chupakhin, Vladimir Leonidovich

Dasayev, Rinat Faizrakhmovich
Davydov, Vitaly Semyoenovich
Delyagin, Mikhail Gennadyevich
Dementyev, Andrey Dmitryevich
Diligensky, German Germanovich
Dodolev, Yevgeni Yuryevich
Doletsky, Stanislav Yakovlevich
Dolgov, Vyacheslav Ivanovich
Dorofeyev, Vitaly Vadimovich
Drach, Ivan Fyodorovich
Dubinin, Yuri Vladimirovich
Dushenkin, Vladimir Nikolayevich
Dzasokhov, Aleksandr Sergeyevich

Eisen, Artur Arturovich

Filaret (Vakhromeyev Kirill Varfolomeyevich)
Filatov, Leonid Alekseyevich
Filatov, Sergey Aleksandrovich
Fokin, Vitold Pavlovich
Frolov, Konstantin Vasilyevich
Furmanov, Boris Aleksandrovich
Fyodorov, Andrey Vladimirovich
Fyodorov, Svyatoslav Nikolayevich

Gabrielyants, Grigory Arkadyevich
Galayev, Victor Ilyich
Gaprindashvili, Nonna Terentyevna
Gavrilov, Igor Trofimovich
Gerashchenko, Victor Vladimirovich
Gerasimov, Gennadi Ivanovich
Gidaspov, Boris Veniaminovich
Glukhov, Aleksey Iliych
Gnedovsky, Yuri Pertovich
Goldansky, Vitaly Iosifovich
Gonchar, Nikolay Nikolayevich
Goncharov, Andrey Aleksandrovich

Gorbachev, Mikhail Sergeyevich
Gordeyev, Vyacheslav Mikhailovich
Gorodinsky, Mikhail Lvovich
Gorokhova, Galina Yevgenyevna
Gorshkov, Aleksandr Georgyevich
Grachev, Pavel Sergeyevich
Granin, Daniil Aleksandrovich
Grigorovich, Yuri Nikolayevich
Grigoryanets, Sergey Ivanovich
Grinevsky, Oleg Alekseyevich
Grishenko, Boris Sergeevich
Gromov, Boris Vsevolodovich
Gromov, Feliks Nikolayevich
Gromyko, Anatoli Andreyevich
Gubenko, Nikolay Nikolayevich
Gulyayev, Nikolay Alekseyevich
Gurzinov, Vladimir Vladimirovich
Gusenov, Georgy Georgyevich
Guvenaly, Pojarkov Vladimir Kirillovich

Ignatenko, Vitaly Nikitovich
Ilyinsky, Igor Pavlovich
Isayev, Aleksandr Sergeyevich
Iskander, Fazil Abdulovich
Iskenderov, Akhmed Akhemdovich
Ivanov, Igor Sergeyevich
Ivanov, Vyacheslav Vsevolodovich
Izyumov, Yuri Petrovich

Kalinin, Arnold Ivanovich
Kalmyk, Valerya Nikolayevna
Kapitonov, Victor Arsenyevich
Kapitsa, Mikhail Stepanovich
Karimov, Islam Abguganievich
Karlov, Yuri Yevgenyevich
Karpet, Igor Ivanovich
Karpov, Anatoli Yevgenyevich
Kasatonov, Igor Vladimirovich
Kashirin, Yuri Alekseyevich
Kashlev, Yuri Borisovich
Kasrashvili, Makvala Filimonovna
Katushev, Konstantin Fyodorovich
Khizha, Georgy Stepanovich
Khomsky, Pavel Osipovich
Khrennikov, Tikhon Nikolayevich
Khshtoyan, Vilen Vartanovich
Khudonazarov, Dovlatnazar
Khvorostovsky, Dmitri Aleksandrovich
Kireyev, Genrikh Vasilyevich
Kisin, Yevgeni Vladimirovich
Kislyak, Sergey Ivanovich
Klimov, Yelem Germanovich
Klimova, Marina Vladimirovna
Klyuyev, Vladimir Vladimirovich
Kobets, Konstantin Ivanovich
Koksanov, Igor Vladimirovich
Kolesov, Anatoli Ivanovich
Komplektov, Victor Georgyevich
Kon, Igor Semyonovich
Kondratyev, Georgy Grigoryevich
Koptyug, Valentin Afanasyevich
Kopylov, Sergey Vladimirovich
Korepanov, Sergey Ivanovich
Korobchenko, Victor Alekseyevich
Korostelev, Yuri Victorovich
Korotich, Vitaly Alekseyevich
Kotelnikov, Vladimir Aleksandrovich
Kovalchenko, Ivan Dmitryevich
Kovalev, Anatoli Gavrilovich
Kovalev, Feliks Nikolayevich
Kovalev, Yevgeni Yevgenyevich
Kovylov, Aleksey Ivanovich
Kozlov, Victor Vasilyevich
Krainev, Vladimir Vsevolodovich
Krasikov, Aleksandr Aleksandrovich
Krasikov, Anatoli Andreyevich
Kravchenko, Leonid Petrovich
Kryuchkov, Vladimir Aleksandrovich
Kudryavtsev, Aleksandr Petrovich
Kudryavtsev, Gennadi Georgyevich
Kudryavtsev, Vladimir Nikolayevich
Kugultinov, David Nikitovich
Kulakova, Galina Alekseyevna
Kulikov, Valeryan Nikolayevich
Kurkova, Bella Alekseyevna
Kurtashin, Vladimir Yegorovich
Kvitsinsky, Yuli Aleksandrovich

Lagovsky, Igor Konstantinovich
Lagutin, Boris Nikolayevich
Latynina, Larisa Semyonovna
Laverov, Nikolay Pavlovich
Lavrinovich, Mikhail Fyodorovich
Lavrov, Kirill Yuryevich
Lazarev, Aleksandr Nikolayevich
Lemeshev, Mikhail Yakovlevich
Ligachev, Yegor Kuzmich
Likhachev, Dmitri Sergeyevich
Likhanov, Albert Anatolyevich
Lisin, Aleksandr Ivanovich
Lobov, Vladimir Nikolayevich
Logunov, Anatoli Alekseyevich
Lomeiko, Vladmir Borisovich
Lopatin, Mikhail Alekseyevich
Lopukhin, Yuri Mikhailovich
Luchinsky, Pyotr Kirillovich
Lukyanenko, Levko Grigoryevich
Lukyanov, Anatoli Ivanovich
Luzhkov, Yuri Mikhailovich
Lyubimov, Yuri Petrovich

Makarov, Igor Mikhailovich
Makashov, Albert Mikhailovich
Makeyev, Yevgeni Nikolayevich
Maksimov, Yuri Pavlovich
Maksimova, Yekaterina Sergeyevna
Malashenko, Igor Yevgenyevich
Malei, Mikhail Dmitryevich
Malkevich, Vladislav Leonidovich
Mamatov, Victor Fyodorovich
Marchuk, Guri Ivanovich
Maslakov, Arkady Dmitryevich
Maslennikov, Arkady Afrikanovich
Maslyukov, Yuri Dmitryevich
Matrosov, Aleksandr Sergeyevich
Melnikov, Aleksandr Grigoryevich
Mesyats, Gennadi Andreyevich
Mikhailov, Nikolay Vasilyevich
Mikhailov, Victor Nikitovich
Mikhalkov, Nikita Sergeyevich
Miroshnichenko, Irina Petrovna
Mirsaidov, Shukurulla Rakhmatovich
Mishcharin, Aleksandr Nikolayevich
Mitta, Aleksandr Naumovich
Moiseyev, Nikita Nikolayevich
Molchanov, Vladimir Kirillovich
Musaelyan, Gennadi Samvelovich

Nagibin, Yuri Markovich
Nazarbayev, Nursultan Abishevich
Nefedov, Oleg Matveyevich
Nanashev, Mikhail Fydorovich
Nesterenko, Yevgeni Yevgenyevich
Neverov, Valery Ivanovich
Nikodim (Rusnak Nikodim Stepanovich)
Nikolayev, Mikhail Yefimovich
Nikolsky, Boris Vasilyevich
Nishanov, Rafik Nishanovich
Nit, Igor Vasilyevich
Niyazov, Saparmurad Atayevich
Norshtein, Yuri Borisovich
Novikov, Vladimir Ivanovich

Obraztsova, Yelena Vasilyevna
Obukhov, Aleksey Aleksandrovich
Oleynik, Boris Ilyich

Orlov, Victor Vladimirovich
Osipyan, Yuri Andreyevich
Ostroumov, Georgy Sergeyevich

Pankin, Boris Dmitryevich
Pankratov, Valentin Andreyevich
Pastukhov, Boris Nikolayevich
Paulman, Valery Fyodorovich
Peresypkin, Oleg Gerasimovich
Petrakov, Nikolay Yakovlevich
Petrov, Rem Victorovich
Petrov, Yuri Vladimirovich
Petrovsky, Boris Vasilyevich
Pilipenko, Yuri Vladimirovich
Pirumov, Vladimir Semyonovich
Pitirim (Nechayev Konstantin Vladimirovich)
Pletchko, Vladimir Yakovlevich
Pletnev, Mikhail Vasilyevich
Pluchek, Valentin Nikolayevich
Pogosyan, Stepan Karapetovich
Polenov, Fyodor Dmitryevich
Polozkov, Ivan Kuzmich
Popov, Gavril Kharitonovich
Poptsov, Oleg Maksimovich
Potapov, Aleksandr Serafimovich
Primakov, Yevgeni Maksimovich
Pristavkin, Anatoli Ignatyevich
Prokhanov, Aleksandr Andreyevich
Prokhorov, Aleksandr Mikhailovich
Prokofyev, Yuri Anatolyevich
Prudnikov, Victor Alekseyevich
Pumpyansky, Aleksandr Borisovich

Radugin, Nikolay Petrovich
Rasputin, Valentin Grigoryevich
Raykin, Konstantin Arkadyevich
Resin, Vladimir Iosifovich
Revenko, Grigory Ivanovich
Rigert, David Adamovich
Rogachev, Igor Alekseyevich
Romanovsky, Sergey Kalistratovich
Romanyuk, Valery Yakovlevich
Rozov, Victor Sergeyevich
Rusak, Nikolay Ivanovich
Rutskoy, Aleksandr Vladimirovich
Rybakov, Anatoli Naumovich
Rybin, Aleksandr Georgyevich
Ryzhkov, Nikolay Ivanovich

Sadovnichi, Victor Antonovich
Safonov, Ernst Ivanovich
Sagdeyev, Roald Zinnurovich
Salnikov, Vladimir Valeryevich
Sats, Natalya Ilyinichna
Savchenko, Larisa Ivanovna
Saykin, Valery Timofeyevich
Seleznev, Gennadi Nikolayevich
Seleznev, Igor Sergeyevich
Seleznev, Sergey Pavlovich
Semenchenko, Valery Pavlovich
Semenyaka, Lyudmila Ivanovna
Semizorova, Nina Lvovna
Sergeyev, Aleksey Alekseyevich
Shakhnazarov, George Khosroevich
Shatalin, Stanislav Sergeyevich
Shatrov (Marshak), Mikhail Filippovoch
Shchedrin, Rodion Konstantinovich
Shchekochikhin, Yuri Petrovich
Shcherbakov, Konstantin Aleksandrovich
Shcherbakov, Vladimir Pavlovich
Shenin, Oleg Semyonovich
Shilov, Aleksandr Maksovich
Shimko, Vladimir Ivanovich
Shlyakhtin, Vladimir Ivanovich
Shostakowski, Viacheslaw Nikolayevich
Shoub, Yuli Germanovich
Shushkevich, Stanislav Stanislavovich
Sidorov, Yevgeni Yuryevich
Sidorski, Philipp Philippovich
Silayev, Ivan Stepanovich
Silkova, Nina Prokopyevna
Simonenko, Valentin Konstantinovich
Simonyan, Nikita Pavlovich
Sister, Vladimir Grigoryevich
Skrinsky, Aleksandr Nikolayevich
Sliva, Anatoli Yakovlevich
Smetanina, Raisa Petrovna
Smirnov, Georgy Lukich
Smirnov, Oleg Mikhailovich
Smyslov, Vasily Vasilyevich
Snegu, Mircha Ion
Sobchak, Anatoli Aleksandroviich
Sobkov, Vasily Timofeyevich
Sokolov, Vladimir Nikolayevich
Solomin, Yuri Mefodyevich
Solovyov, Sergey Aleksandroviich
Sotkilava, Zurab Lavrentyevich
Spivakov, Vladimir Teodorovich
Stankevich, Sergey Borisovich
Stepanov, Andrey Ivanovich
Sukhoruchenkov, Sergey Nikolayevich
Systsov, Apollon Sergeyevich

Tabakov, Oleg Pavlovich
Terekhov, Vladislav Petrovich
Tereshkova, Valentina Vladimirovna
Tikhonov, Aleksandr Ivanovich
Tikhonov, Victor Vasilyevich
Timofeyev, Timur Timofeyevich
Tishkov, Valery Aleksandrovich
Titov, Yuri Yevlampiyevich
Travkin, Nikolay Ilyich
Tretyak, Ivan Moiseyevich
Tretyak, Vladislav Aleksandrovich
Trubin, Nikolay Semyonovich
Tsaregorodtsev, Vladimir Ivanovich
Turisheva, Ludmila Ivanovna
Tutov, Victor Trofimovich

Vardanyan, Yurik Norainovich
Varennikov, Valentin Ivanovich
Vasilyev, Vladimir Victorovich
Vasin, Vladimir Alekseyevich
Vasnetsov, Andrey Vladimirovich
Vedernikov, Aleksandr Fillippovich
Vedernikov, Gennadi Georgyevich
Velichko, Victor Ivanovich
Velikhov, Yevgeni Pavlovich
Vladimir (Sabodan, Victor Markianovich)
Vladimirov, Vasily Sergeyevich
Vladislayev, Aleksandr Pavlovich
Volchek, Galina Borisovna
Volovets, Sergey Aleksandrovich
Volsky, Arkady Ivanovich
Volsky, Victor Vatslavovich
Vorobyev, Andrey Ivanovich
Vorontsov, Nikolay Nikolayevich
Vorontsov, Yuli Mikhailovich

Yakimov, Boris Alekseevich
Yakovlev, Aleksandr Maximovich
Yakovlev, Aleksandr Nikolayevich
Yankovski, Oleg Ivanovich
Yanovski, Rudolf Grigoryevich
Yaremenko, Yuri Vasilyevich
Yefremov, Oleg Nikolayevich
Yegorov, Valery Aleksandrovich
Yekimov, Vyacheslav Vladimirovich
Yeliseyev, Anatoli Aleksandrovich
Yeltsin, Boris Nikolayevich
Yeprev, Arkady Filimonovich
Yeremin, Yuri Ivanovich
Yevtushenko, Yevgeni Aleksandrovich
Yurzinov, Vladimir Vladimirovich

Zagladin, Vadim Valentinovich
Zaitsev, Aleksandr Gennadyevich
Zaitsev, Vyacheslav Mikhailovich
Zakharov, Mark Anatolyevich
Zalygin, Sergey Pavlovich
Zamyatin, Leonid Mitrofanovich
Zaslavskaya, Tatyana Ivanovna
Zelenov, Victor Matveyevich
Zemskov, Mikhail Aleksandrovich
Zhabotsinky, Leonid Ivanovich
Zhukov, Aleksey Dmitryevich
Zhurkin, Vitaly Vladimirovich
Zimyatov, Nikolay Semenovich
Zorin, Valentin Sergeyevich
Zotov, Sergey Sergeyevich
Zvereva, Natalya Maratovna
Zyukin, Vladimir Mikhailovich

Index of Works